The cover of *Marketing: Creating Value for Customers, Second Edition,* shows a picture of the terrace at the University of Wisconsin, Madison. The terrace looks out over Lake Mendota and is graced by the sight of over 500 bright orange, yellow, and green sunburst chairs.

The sunburst chair is a familiar image for most students and graduates — seeing one makes memories of sky blue water, sailboats, live music, and good friends come to life. For more than 60 years, these vibrantly colored iron chairs have added value to the terrace.

The sunburst chair demonstrates that marketers can create something their customers truly value. The chair has an image, character, and quality that make it unique and irreplaceable. This was our goal with *Marketing: Creating Value for Customers, Second Edition*. Its unique qualities are certain to create value for your marketing education.

Cover Photo by Marcia Friedman.
Chair Photo by Treva Breuch.

Marketing
Creating Value for Customers

THE IRWIN SERIES IN MARKETING

Alreck & Settle
THE SURVEY RESEARCH HANDBOOK, 2/E

Arens
CONTEMPORARY ADVERTISING, 6/E

Belch & Belch
INTRODUCTION TO ADVERTISING AND PROMOTION: AN INTEGRATED MARKETING COMMUNICATIONS APPROACH, 3/E

Bearden, Ingram & LaForge
MARKETING: PRINCIPLES & PERSPECTIVES, 1/E

Bernhardt & Kinnear
CASES IN MARKETING MANAGEMENT, 7/E

Berkowitz, Kerin, Hartley & Rudelius
MARKETING, 5/E

Boyd, Walker & Larreche
MARKETING MANAGEMENT: A STRATEGIC APPROACH WITH A GLOBAL ORIENTATION, 2/E

Cateora
INTERNATIONAL MARKETING, 9/E

Churchill, Ford & Walker
SALES FORCE MANAGEMENT, 5/E

Cole & Mishler
CONSUMER AND BUSINESS CREDIT MANAGEMENT, 10/E

Cravens
STRATEGIC MARKETING, 5/E

Cravens
STRATEGIC MARKETING MANAGEMENT CASES, 5/E

Crawford
NEW PRODUCTS MANAGEMENT, 5/E

Dillon, Madden & Firtle
ESSENTIALS OF MARKETING RESEARCH, 2/E

Dillon, Madden & Firtle
MARKETING RESEARCH IN A MARKETING ENVIRONMENT, 3/E

Faria, Nulsen & Roussos
COMPETE, 4/E

Futrell
ABC'S OF RELATIONSHIP SELLING, 5/E

Futrell
FUNDAMENTALS OF SELLING, 5/E

Gretz, Drozdeck & Weisenhutter
PROFESSIONAL SELLING: A CONSULTATIVE APPROACH, 1/E

Hawkins, Best & Convey
CONSUMER BEHAVIOR, 6/E

Hayes, Jenster & Aaby
BUSINESS TO BUSINESS MARKETING, 1/E

Johansson
GLOBAL MARKETING, 1/E

Lambert & Stock
STRATEGIC LOGISTICS MANAGEMENT, 3/E

Lehmann & Winer
ANALYSIS FOR MARKETING PLANNING, 4/E

Lehmann & Winer
PRODUCT MANAGEMENT, 2/E

Levy & Weitz
RETAILING MANAGEMENT, 2/E

Levy & Weitz
ESSENTIALS OF RETAILING, 1/E

Mason, Mayer & Ezell
RETAILING, 5/E

Mason & Perreault
THE MARKETING GAME!, 2/E

Meloan & Graham
INTERNATIONAL AND GLOBAL MARKETING CONCEPTS AND CASES, 1/E

Patton
SALES FORCE: A SALES MANAGEMENT SIMULATION GAME, 1/E

Pelton, Strutton & Lumpkin
MARKETING CHANNELS: A RELATIONSHIP MANAGEMENT APPROACH, 1/E

Perreault & McCarthy
BASIC MARKETING: A GLOBAL MANAGERIAL APPROACH, 12/E

Perreault & McCarthy
ESSENTIALS OF MARKETING: A GLOBAL MANAGERIAL APPROACH, 7/E

Peter & Donnelly
A PREFACE TO MARKETING MANAGEMENT, 7/E

Peter & Donnelly
MARKETING MANAGEMENT: KNOWLEDGE AND SKILLS, 4/E

Peter & Olson
CONSUMER BEHAVIOR AND MARKETING STRATEGY, 4/E

Peter & Olson
UNDERSTANDING CONSUMER BEHAVIOR, 1/E

Quelch
CASES IN PRODUCT MANAGEMENT, 1/E

Quelch, Dolan & Kosnik
MARKETING MANAGEMENT: TEXT & CASES, 1/E

Quelch & Farris
CASES IN ADVERTISING AND PROMOTION MANAGEMENT, 4/E

Quelch, Kashani & Vandermerwe
EUROPEAN CASES IN MARKETING MANAGEMENT, 1/E

Rangan
BUSINESS MARKETING STRATEGY: CASES, CONCEPTS & APPLICATIONS, 1/E

Rangan, Shapiro & Moriarty
BUSINESS MARKETING STRATEGY: CONCEPTS & APPLICATIONS, 1/E

Smith & Quelch
ETHICS IN MARKETING, 1/E

Stanton, Buskirk & Spiro
MANAGEMENT OF A SALES FORCE, 9/E

Thompson & Stappenbeck
THE MARKETING STRATEGY GAME, 1/E

Walker, Boyd & Larreche
MARKETING STRATEGY: PLANNING AND IMPLEMENTATION, 2/E

Weitz, Castleberry & Tanner
SELLING: BUILDING PARTNERSHIPS, 2/E

SECOND EDITION
Marketing
Creating Value for Customers

Gilbert A. Churchill, Jr.
Arthur C. Nielsen, Jr., Chair of Marketing Research / University of Wisconsin

J. Paul Peter
James R. McManus-Bascom Professor in Marketing / University of Wisconsin

Irwin
McGraw-Hill

Boston, Massachusetts Burr Ridge, Illinois Dubuque, Iowa Madison, Wisconsin New York, New York San Francisco, California St. Louis, Missouri

To our wives, Helen and Rose, and our children
for creating so much value in our lives.

McGraw-Hill
A Division of the McGraw-Hill Companies

 **Irwin McGraw-Hill**

MARKETING: CREATING VALUE FOR CUSTOMERS

1 2 3 4 5 6 7 8 9 0 VH/VH 9 1 0 9 8 7

ISBN 0-256-22877-9

Editorial director: *Michael W. Junior*
Executive editor: *Craig S. Beytien*
Sponsoring editor: *Patrice Schmitt*
Developmental editor: *Karen Hill/Elm Street Publishing Services, Inc.*
Marketing manager: *Colleen J. Suljic*
Senior project supervisor: *Mary Conzachi*
Senior production supervisor: *Laurie Sander*
Art director: *Keith McPherson*
Designers: Maureen McCutcheon/Keith J. McPherson
Photo research coordinator: *Keri Johnson/Elm Street Publishing Services, Inc.*
Compositor: *Shepard Poorman Communications*
Typeface: *10.5/12 Times Roman*
Printer: *Von Hoffmann Press, Inc.*

Library of Congress Cataloging-in-Publication Data

Churchill, Gilbert A.
    Marketing : creating value for customers / Gilbert A. Churchill.
  Jr., J. Paul Peter. — 2nd ed.
      p.   cm. — (The Irwin series in marketing)
    Includes bibliographical references and index.
    ISBN 0-256-22877-9
    1. Marketing.   I. Peter, J. Paul.   II. Title.   III. Series.
HF5415.C5275   1998
  658.8—dc21   97-13807

tp://www.mhcollege.com

Gilbert A. Churchill, Jr.,

received his DBA from Indiana University in 1966 and joined the University of Wisconsin faculty in 1966. Professor Churchill was named Distinguished Marketing Educator by the American Marketing Association in 1986—only the second individual so honored. The lifetime achievement award recognizes and honors a living marketing educator for distinguished service and outstanding contributions in the field of marketing education. Professor Churchill was also awarded the Academy of Marketing Science's lifetime achievement award in 1993 for his significant scholarly contributions. In 1996, he received a Paul D. Converse Award, which is given to the most influential marketing scholars, as judged by a national jury drawn from universities, business, and government. Also in 1996, the Marketing Research Group of the American Marketing Association established the Gilbert A. Churchill, Jr., lifetime achievement award, which is to be given each year to a person judged to have made significant lifetime contributions to marketing research.

Professor Churchill is a past recipient of the William O'Dell Award for the outstanding article appearing in the *Journal of Marketing Research* during the year. He has also been a finalist for the award five other times. He was named Marketer of the Year by the South Central Wisconsin Chapter of the American Marketing Association in 1981. He is a member of the American Marketing Association and has served as vice president of publications, on its board of directors, and on the association's Advisory Committee to the Bureau of the Census. In addition, he has served as consultant to a number of companies, including Oscar Mayer, Western Publishing Company, and Parker Pen.

Professor Churchill's articles have appeared in such publications as the *Journal of Marketing Research*, the *Journal of Marketing*, the *Journal of Consumer Research*, the *Journal of Retailing*, the *Journal of Business Research*, *Decision Sciences*, *Technometrics*, and *Organizational Behavior and Human Performance*, among others. He is the sole author of two books, *Marketing Research: Methodological Foundations*, Sixth Edition (Forth Worth, TX: Dryden, 1995); and *Basic Marketing Research*, Third Edition (Fort Worth, TX: Dryden, 1996). He is also the co-author of *Sales Force Management: Planning, Implementation, and Control*, Fifth Edition (Burr Ridge, IL: Irwin, 1997), and *Sales Force Performance* (Lexington, MA: Lexington Books, 1984), in addition to *Marketing: Creating Value for Customers*, Second Edition (Burr Ridge, IL: Irwin/McGraw-Hill, 1998). He is a former editor of the *Journal of Marketing Research* and has served on the editorial boards of the *Journal of Marketing Research*, the *Journal of Marketing*, the *Journal of Business Research*, the *Journal of Health Care Marketing* and the *Asian Journal of Marketing*. Professor Churchill is a past recipient of the Lawrence J. Larson Excellence in Teaching Award.

J. Paul Peter

is James R. McManus-Bascom Professor in Marketing at the University of Wisconsin—Madison. He has taught a variety of courses and has won teaching awards including Outstanding Marketing Professor and the John R. Larson Award. He has won the prestigious William O'Dell Award from the *Journal of Marketing Research* and was a finalist for the award on two other occasions.

Professor Peter's research has appeared in publications such as the *Journal of Marketing*, the *Journal of Marketing Research*, the *Journal of Consumer Research*, the *Journal of Retailing*, and the *Academy of Management Journal*, among others. He has also authored or coauthored a number of books, including *A Preface to Marketing Management*, Seventh Edition (Burr Ridge, IL: Irwin), *Marketing Management: Knowledge and Skills*, Fifth Edition (Burr Ridge, IL: Irwin), *Consumer Behavior and Marketing Strategy*, Fourth Edition (Burr Ridge, IL: Irwin), *Strategic Management: Concepts and Applications*, Third Edition (Burr Ridge, IL: Austen Press/Irwin), and *Marketing: Creating Value for Customers*, Second Edition (Burr Ridge, IL: Irwin/McGraw-Hill, 1998), among others.

Professor Peter has served as Editor of the American Marketing Association Professional Publications and as Editor of *JMR*'s Measurement Section. He has served on the review boards of the *Journal of Marketing*, the *Journal of Marketing Research*, the *Journal of Consumer Research*, and the *Journal of Business Research*. He has been a consultant for several corporations as well as the Federal Trade Commission.

A Marketing Text for Future Marketers

Future marketing managers will need a sound grounding in marketing principles and an understanding of the fast-paced, business world in which they will be working. This edition of *Marketing: Creating Value for Customers* involved a major revision to better capture the dynamic changes occurring in marketing and in the world. The text maintains its emphases on delivering a clear, concise explanation of the basic principles of marketing and the impact of globalization, diversity, ethics, and small businesses on marketing. However, a major change involves the complete development and integration of the idea of creating value for customers as the prime goal of marketing.

Successful marketers create and deliver superior value to their customers. By value, we mean the difference between customer perceptions of the benefits and costs of exchanges. By superior value, we mean that customers perceive the relative benefits to costs for purchasing and using a product or service to be greater than that of competitive offerings. We develop what we call value-driven marketing in Chapter 1 and integrate the value theme throughout the book. This theme helps students to better understand marketing principles and how elements of the marketing mix are used to create superior value for customers and achieve organizational objectives.

Organization of the Book

Based on extensive marketing research and our own judgment, four major changes were made in the organization of the book. First, the chapter on social and ethical issues was removed and information contained in it was integrated throughout the text. This change was made to highlight ethical issues in marketing as they pertain to specific marketing topics rather than offer a more general discussion of them. It was also made because the separate chapter on ethics led some students to believe that ethical problems are unique to marketing rather than concerns for all functions in an organization.

Second, the chapter on implementing and controlling marketing activities was moved to the end of the text. This change was made to give students a more sound grounding in marketing principles before discussing how marketing strategies should be implemented and controlled. In addition, moving this chapter helps classes to more quickly get to critical marketing principles involving customers and the marketing mix.

Third, the chapter on managing existing products was moved to precede the chapter on new products. While in some ways it seems that new product issues should be discussed first, students seem to understand this material better if they first have a grounding in existing product management issues.

Fourth, a new chapter on retailing was added to the text. While retailing was covered in part of a chapter in the first edition, the increasing power of retailers in marketing channels and the dynamic changes taking place in the field clearly indicated that a separate chapter was needed on this important topic.

New for the Second Edition

Reviewers overwhelmingly favored the idea that creating value was an excellent theme for our book. However, their opinions of the first edition, with which we agree, were that we had not fully explained and integrated this idea in the text. While student feedback was overwhelmingly positive, they too wanted to learn more about value creation. A major goal of this revision was to carefully delineate our concept of value and integrate it fully throughout the book. We worked diligently to do so and hope the book now creates superior value for both instructors and students. These and other changes to specific chapters, include:

Chapter 1. Marketing: Creating Value for Customers
Other than the introductory definitions and concepts, this is an entirely new chapter! It delineates value-driven marketing and explains how marketers can create value for customers.

Chapter 2. Environmental Analysis

This chapter involved a major revision which integrated some materials from Chapter 3 in the previous edition. It contains a new section on the natural environment and expanded discussions of the technological environment and the impact of environmental factors on marketing practices.

Chapter 3. Global Marketing Challenges

Changes in this chapter include an updated discussion of global trade agreements, expanded discussion on ways to enter foreign markets, and increased emphasis on the advantages and disadvantages of marketing globally.

Chapter 4. Marketing Planning and Organization Strategy

This chapter was completely revised to better explain the relationships between organizational and marketing strategies. The process of developing a marketing plan is also discussed to help students understand marketing tasks in an organization. A sample marketing plan is included at the end of the text.

Chapter 5. Marketing Research: Information and Technology

Changes in this chapter include increased emphasis on new methods of marketing research, the impact of the information technology revolution, and the strengths and weaknesses of single source data. The chapter was also reorganized to allow decision support systems to be discussed earlier.

Chapter 6. Consumer Behavior

This chapter has been reorganized around the consumer buying process and the social, marketing, and situational influences that affect it. It contains an expanded discussion of routine, limited, and extensive decision-making processes.

Chapter 7. Organizational Buyer Behavior

Changes in this chapter include a new section on the differentiating characteristics of organizational markets and increased emphasis on the role of strategic alliances in organizational buying.

Chapter 8. Market Segmentation

Changes in this chapter include a more complete treatment of ways to segment consumer and organizational markets and increased emphasis on the relationship between segmentation and positioning.

Chapter 9. Managing Existing Products

This chapter was restructured to improve the flow of the material and provide a better overview of product management issues. It includes an expanded discussion of branding and brand equity and a new discussion of the management of product lines and product mixes.

Chapter 10. Managing New Products

This chapter was restructured and rewritten to focus more specifically on new product issues. It contains an expanded discussion of the importance of new products in marketing today and a new section on selecting new product characteristics.

Chapter 11. Marketing Services

This chapter has increased emphasis on how services create value for customers, the impact of new technologies on service delivery, and how the differences between products and services affect marketing strategy.

Chapter 12. Fundamentals of Pricing

This chapter has been restructured to more clearly illustrate basic price setting approaches including cost, competition, and customer value.

Chapter 13. Pricing Goods and Services

This chapter contains a clearer discussion of pricing objectives and their impact on pricing strategy. It also includes new material on the role of price in determining relative value positions in a market.

Chapter 14. Managing Distribution Channels

This chapter includes a revamped discussion of basic channel options, including vertical marketing systems, and increased emphasis on how channels create customer value. It also includes expanded discussions of factors to evaluate in channel selection and channel options for serving global markets.

Chapter 15. Wholesaling and Physical Distribution

This chapter contains a more complete discussion of wholesaling and physical distribution issues. It has an expanded discussion of types of wholesalers and a new section on how wholesaling and physical distribution create customer value.

Chapter 16. Retailing

This new chapter overviews the key issues in retailing. It includes discussion of the changing environment of retailing and direct marketing.

Chapter 17. Managing Marketing Communications

This chapter includes expanded discussion of the functions of marketing communication and greater emphasis on integrated marketing communication.

Chapter 18. Advertising, Sales Promotion, and Publicity

This chapter includes an expanded discussion of sales promotion and new organizing frameworks for developing and managing advertising decisions.

Chapter 19. Personal Selling and Sales Management

This chapter includes greater emphasis on relationship selling and increased emphasis on performance criteria used to evaluate salespeople.

Chapter 20. Implementing and Controlling Marketing Activities

This is a completely revised chapter that emphasizes effective ways to implement and control marketing activities. It includes expanded discussions of sales, profitability, and customer satisfaction analyses and how they are used to control marketing strategies.

Pedagogy in the Book

The first edition of our text included a variety of pedagogical elements to enhance student interest and the learning experience. These included learning objectives; chapter-opening vignettes; boxed items titled "Marketing Movers & Shakers," "You Decide," and "Put It into Practice"; figures and tables; chapter summaries; key terms and glossary; review and discussion questions; chapter projects; chapter cases; and appendices. All of these features have been maintained, but enhanced in the following ways.

Learning Objectives. Each chapter's learning objectives are revised to reflect updates in chapter content.

Chapter-Opening Vignettes. All of the vignettes are new to this edition, providing enhanced currency and relevancy.

Boxed Items—All are new to this edition, and most include the "Explore More . . ." caption encouraging the students to learn more by accessing various sites on the World Wide Web.

> "Marketing Movers & Shakers" tells the story of an actual marketer. These boxes cover a diverse group of people working in both large and small organizations.
>
> "You Decide" discusses a current marketing issue and invites students to exercise their critical thinking skills by answering questions about the issue. Many of these issues have ethical implications.
>
> "Put It into Practice" provides applications for the students to try out marketing principles discussed in the chapter.

Figures and Tables. Many of the figures and tables are revised or new to this edition.

Chapter Summaries. Each chapter's summary is revised to reflect updates in chapter content.

Key Terms and Glossary. Definitions are revised and updated consistent with updates in chapter content, and a number of new terms have been added.

Review and Discussion Questions. Many of these are new and reflect updates in chapter content.

Chapter Projects. All of the projects are new for this edition.
Chapter Cases. All of the cases are new for this edition.
Appendices. Three appendices are included, on developing marketing plans, marketing arithmetic, and marketing careers. All are revised and updated.

Supplemental Resources

A number of supplements are available to enhance the value for you in using *Marketing: Creating Value for Customers,* Second Edition. We have been involved, as contributors and supervisors, in the production of all of the supplements that now accompany our text. Each of the supplements has been designed to offer benefits to both experienced and inexperienced instructors of marketing. A great amount of time and effort has gone into ensuring that the second edition supplement package is of the highest quality possible.

Instructor Resource Manual   The Instructor Resource Manual enables new instructors to teach the course with confidence, and experienced instructors to have access to a variety of new resources to complement lectures. The IRM includes standard and supplemental lecture notes, experiential exercises, discussion questions/answers, implications of the chapter project plus suggestions for additional projects, summaries of the boxed items ("Put It into Practice," "You Decide," "Marketing Movers & Shakers") and of the chapter case, plus an additional mini-case for each chapter. There is also a section recommending appropriate outside resources such as videos and guest-speakers—all tied in to giving your students a clearer understanding of marketing.

Testing System   Our test bank has been completely re-developed and then reviewed to provide an accurate and exhaustive source of test items for a wide variety of examination styles. It contains more than 3500 questions, categorized by topic and level of learning (definitional, conceptual or application), and many of the answers also include rationales. Our goal is to focus on ensuring that your students understand the application of marketing concepts. We have nearly 200 questions in each chapter (true/false, multiple choice, short answer and essay). For complete flexibility, both TELETEST, our unique phone-in test generation service, and COMPUTEST, our computerized test generator, are available to you in several formats!

Transparency Acetates   A set of 200 four-color overhead transparency acetates is available to adopters. There are nearly 100 advertisements, and 100 figures/tables to enhance your lecture visually. Each of the transparency acetates from outside of the text have accompanying lecture notes to enable you to integrate the materials.

Electronic Slides   This software includes the PowerPoint* viewer and 200 new slides to accompany this edition—including all of the figures and tables that are on the acetates, plus 100 more items from both in and outside of the text. Those instructors who have PowerPoint* can customize and add to this valuable presentation tool.

Videos   The new video package will give you the variety of current topics your students will want to see, and the tools needed to generate the thoughtful classroom discussions you value. A unique series of 20 videos, one for each chapter, covers a wide range of contemporary subjects—from the Internet and technology to clothing and sporting goods. Also accompanying each video are creative teaching suggestions promoting analytical thinking about the issues being addressed. *Alligator Records, Lands' End* and *Peapod* are just a few of the exciting video cases that are available with the Second Edition.

Presentation CD ROM   You can create your visual presentation and customize your lecture notes with this easy to use all-in-one, multimedia tool. The CD ROM contains the Instructor's Manual, the Test Bank, the PowerPoint Slides, the advertisements, Video clips, and more. Great for enhancing class presentations, this CD ROM enables the instructor to instantly demonstrate concepts with video clips or the electronic slides or even the World Wide Web.

Electronic Study Guide   The Electronic Study Guide allows your students to explore their knowledge of marketing terms and apply concepts in a fun and interactive format. You will find our Study Guide on our Homepage (see more below). We will also package a disk version of it with *Marketing: Creating Value for Customers,* **Second Edition,** upon request.

Homepage   The Homepage is intended to continually add value to your class every semester with the most current information available. You will find current events organized by topic, chapter quizzes, a Career Profile for each unit, a Customer Discussion Forum, Teaching Tips, Internet Application Questions with links to other Homepages and more! We invite you to explore the Churchill & Peter Homepage at www.mhhe.com/marketing/value.

Multi-Media Resource Guide   This inclusive media guide will show you how to best coordinate the media supplements (Video, PowerPoint, CD-ROM, Homepage) to enhance your own style of teaching! It includes suggestions for customizing your presentations both with what is available to you from the publisher, and with what is available to you from outside sources, such as the World Wide Web.

Virtual Marketing Careers CD ROM   More than just a careers application, this exciting and unique CD ROM allows your students to simulate the world of marketing and gives them the opportunity to apply the concepts they are learning in class. As your students work through the different business situations, they will strengthen their critical thinking, decision making, and communication skills. They will learn how to use the Internet to solve real business problems and they will learn the importance of building relationships in the business world. Marketing Interactive is organized around four careers: Brand Manager, Marketing Research Manager, Advertising Manager, and Sales Manager, and each is referenced in the text to encourage students to explore the subject further.

Acknowledgments

Many people contributed to this book. Certainly, the many scholars who developed the academic field of marketing deserve recognition for their efforts, insights, concepts and research. In addition, the many marketing practitioners who applied marketing principles to create both superior value for customers and examples of sound marketing practices for this book deserve our thanks. In this regard, a special thanks goes to Bob Drane from Oscar Mayer Foods Corporation for his insights into customer value.

Our product development team at Irwin, particularly Rob Zwettler, Patrice Schmitt, and Coleen Suljic, provided us with excellent marketing research, product development assistance, and marketing information. We also appreciate the fine work of Karen Schenkenfelder and Linda Buchanan who helped make the book come alive with creative examples and thoughtful pedagogy. Both Karen and Linda contributed invaluable assistance. Karen Hill of the Elm Street Publishing group did an excellent job of coordinating the team's efforts and keeping things on track. Janet Christopher's timely and efficient preparation of the manuscript is also greatly appreciated.

We extend our gratitude to the team of supplement and ancillary authors, beginning with S.J. Garner, Eastern Kentucky University, who led the Testing System team, including Kim Donahue, Indiana University—Indianapolis, and Rosemary Ramsey, Eastern Kentucky University; John Ronchetto, University of San Diego, who compiled the extensive Instructor's Manual; Tom Ainscough, University of Massachusetts, Dartmouth for developing the Media Resource Guide and coordinating the Power-Point and Acetate development; David Bloomberg and Mandep Singh, both of Western Illinois University, for creating the Electronic Study Guide and designing the Homepage.

A number of marketing academics played key roles in the book's development and we are grateful for their contributions. We wish to thank the following people who participated in focus group sessions designed to determine first, the level of satisfaction with books currently on the market, and second, how to enhance this book and its supplement package to bring about the greatest value for our adopters.

Hugh Daubek
Purdue University, Calumet
Kim Donahue
Indiana University, Indianapolis
Mike Drafke
College of DuPage
Jill King
South Suburban College
Lee Meadow
Northern Illinois University
Bob O'Keefe
DePaul University
Rodger Singley
Illinois State University
Bill Becker
Oregon State University

Kerry Curtis
Golden Gate University
Tom DeCarlo
Iowa State University
Barnett Greenberg
Florida International University
Russell Laczniak
Iowa State University
Ray Rody
Loyola Marymount University
John Ronchetto
University of San Diego
Brian van der Westhuizen
California State University, Northridge
David Wheeler
Suffolk University

Next, we would like to thank the group of professors who took the time to discuss many of the issues specific to the revision during phone interviews and meetings.

John Barnes
University of Texas, El Paso
Scott Greene
California State University, Fullerton
Laurence Jacobs
University of Hawaii
Bill Browne
Oregon State University

Brian van der Westhuizen
California State University, Northridge
Robert Roe
University of Wyoming
Sandra Gooding
Loyola College

In addition, we would like to thank the reviewers who were vital to the changes that were made for the second edition. You will see many of their recommended enhancements throughout this revision, and this book is certainly better because of them.

Sammy Amin
Frostburg State University
Phil Berger
Weber State University
William G. Browne
Oregon State University
Paul Chao
University of Northern Iowa
Catherine Cole
University of Iowa
Suresh Divakar
State University of New York at Buffalo

Michael Drafke
College of DuPage
A. J. Garner
Eastern Kentucky University
Lola Lackey
Hawaii Pacific University
Stephen LeMay
Mississippi State University
Robert D. O'Keefe
DePaul University
Peggy Osborne
Morehead State University

K. H. Padmanabhan
The University of Michigan—Dearborn
Richard E. Pesta
Frostburg State University
Allen Schaefer
Southwest Missouri State University
Murphy A. Sewall
University of Connecticut
James V. Spiers
Arizona State University

Mark Spriggs
University of Oregon
Timothy W. Sweeney
Bucknell University
David Wheeler
Suffolk University
Jerry W. Wilson
Georgia Southern University

And to those who specifically spent time reviewing the supplements:

Karen Bowman, *Morgan State University*
Gary Melberg, *University of Illinois at Chicago*
Joseph McAloon, *Fitchburg State University*
William Sannwald, *San Diego State University*
Sandra Gooding, *Loyola College of Maryland*

James Spiers, *Arizona State University*
Thomas E. DeCarlo, *Iowa State University*
Deborah Laverie, *Texas Tech University*
Brian van der Westhuizen, *California State University—Northridge*

Finally, we wish again to extend our thanks to the following people who participated in the development of the first edition of *Marketing: Creating Value for Customers*. Their contribution continues to shine through in the revision.

Roger Abshire, Sam Houston State University
Frank Acito, Indiana University
Tom Ainscough, University of Massachusetts, Dartmouth
Pamela Alreck, Salisbury State College
Rick Ambrose, College of San Mateo
Sammy Amin, Frostburg State
Herbert Amster, Elizabeth Seton School—Iona College
Fred Anderson, Indiana University of Pennsylvania
Larry Anderson, Long Island University
Linda Anglin, Mankato State University
Shelda Aultman, Caldwell Community College
Phillip Balsmeier, Nicholls State University
Gilbert Barcus, North Brunswick, New Jersey
John Barnes, The University of Texas at El Paso
Lysbeth Barnett, Ashland Community College
John Bass, Commonwealth College
Richard Becherer, Wayne State University
Bill Becker, Oregon State University
Karen Berger, Pace University
Phil Berger, Weber State University
Jennifer Berry, Parks Junior College
Roger Blackwell, Ohio State University
Angela Bloomfield, Montgomery, Alabama
Joe Boelter, BASF Corporation
Robert Boewadt, Georgia College at Milledgeville
John Boos, Ohio Wesleyan University
George Boulware, David Lipscomb College

Karen Bowman, Morgan State University
Duane Brickner, South Mountain Community College
Burton Brodo, Wharton School
Kent Brooks, Wayland Baptist University
Barbara Brown, San Jose State University
William Browne, Oregon State University
Robert Buckley, North Adams State College
Tom Burns, Long Lake, Minnesota
Jim Butts, American University
Charles Caravello, Tidewater Community College
Bill Carens, Geneseo, New York
Paul Chao, University of Northern Iowa
Gerri Chaplin, Joliet Junior College
Don Chatman, University of Wisconsin—Stout
Reid Christopherson, Saint Ambrose University
Maurice Claybaugh, University of Montevallo
Catherine Cole, University of Iowa
Kevin Coulson, University of Nebraska
Robert Cox, Salt Lake City Community College
Roger Crowe, Pellissippi State Technical College
James Crowell, University of Colorado—Denver
Richard Cummings, College of Lake County
Kerry Curtis, Golden Gate University
Nancy D'Albergana, University of Northern Colorado
Hugh Daubek, Purdue University, Calumet
Pierre David, Baldwin Wallace College
Brian Davis, Weber State University

Tom DeCarlo, Iowa State University

T. Dieck, Thomas Nelson Community College

Suresh Divakar, SUNY—Buffalo

Kim Donahue, Indiana University—Indianapolis

Michael Drafke, College of DuPage

Ronald Drozdenko, West Connecticut State University

Gary Ernst, Naperville, Illinois

William Ewald, Concordia University

Roland Eyears, Central Ohio Technical College

Barry Farber, University of Maine—Augusta

John Felt, Northern Virginia Community College

Edward Felton, Samford University

Jerry Field, Northeastern Illinois University

Charles Ford, Arkansas State University

Ann Fox, Erie Community College

Karen Fritz, Pellissippi State Technical College

S. J. Garner, Eastern Kentucky University

Herbert Gedicks, Liberty University

Mary Gerlow, Ohio State University

John Geubtner, Tacoma Community College

Michael Geurts, Brigham Young University

William Gittler, Fort Washington, Pennsylvania

John Godfrey, Springfield Technical Community College

Larry Goldstein, Iona College

David Good, Central Missouri State University

Sandra Gooding, Loyola College

John Grant, Southern Illinois University

Kent Granzin, University of Utah

Barnett Greenberg, Florida International University

Scott Greene, California State University, Fullerton

Barbara Gulley, Royal Oak, Michigan

B. Hamm, Oklahoma City University

Ed Hand, Lamar University

Judy Hanson, Las Positas College

Mary Harms, Iowa State University

John Havenek, JJH International

Douglas Hawes, University of Wyoming

Susan Heckler, University of Arizona

Kenneth Heischmidt, Southeast Missouri State University

Lewis Hershey, Northeast Missouri State University

Robert Hilton, University of the Ozarks

Alfred Holden, Fordham University

Sandra Hortman, Columbus College

Ronald Hoverstad, University of the Pacific

Jane Hudson, Muscatine Community College

Robert Ironside, North Lake College

Irving Jacobs, SUNY—Fredonia

Laurence Jacobs, University of Hawaii

Deb Jansky, Milwaukee Area Technical College

Gregory Johnson, City University

James Johnson, Saint Cloud State University

Ann Jones, Lamar University

Annamma Joy, Concordia University

Jackie Kacen, University of Illinois

Ira Kalb, University of Southern California

Sue Keaveney, University of Colorado—Denver

George Kelley, Erie Community College

J. Steven Kelly, DePaul University

Philip Kelman, Fashion Institute of Technology

A. B. King, Towson State University

Jill King, South Suburban College

Charles King, University of Illinois, Chicago

Wayne Kirklin, Heidelberg College

Pat Kishel, Cypress College

Greg Kitzmiller, Indiana University

Arno Kleimenhagen, University of Wisconsin—Whitewater

Arthur Knaus, Hartwick College

Quentin Korte, Our Lady of the Lake University

Julie Kothapa, Kennesaw, Georgia

Karl Kotteman, University of Missouri—St. Louis

Peter Kraus, Clark College

Lola Lackey, Hawaii Pacific University

Russell Laczniak, Iowa State University

Rosemary Lagace, University of South Florida

Fred Langrehr, Valparaiso University

Geoffrey Lantos, Stonehill College

Candace Larson, Rolfe, Iowa

John Lavin, Waukesha County Technical College

William Leahy, St. Joseph's University

Stephen LeMay, Mississippi State University

Dean Lewis, Sam Houston State University

G. Lincoln, Westchester Community College

Donald Lindgren, San Diego State University

Michael Littman, College of Buffalo

Annie Liu, Transylvania University

Doug Livermore, Morningside College

Alicia Lupinacci, Arlington, Texas

Richard Lutz, University of Florida

Rick Lytle, Abilene Christian University

Richard Marsh, Greenville Technical College

Pat Marzofka, Loras College

John McDowell, Davenport College

C. McElroy, Bucks County Community College

Lydia McKinley-Floyd, Clark Atlanta University

Joanne McManamy, Middlesex Community College

Ed McQuarrie, Santa Clara University

H. Lee Meadow, Eastern Illinois University

Gary Melberg, University of Illinois, Chicago

Michael Metzger, Tiffin University

William Meyer, Trinity College

Rebecca Mihelcic, Howard Community College

Edward Miller, Englishtown, New Jersey

James Miller, Lynn University

Lee Miller, Indiana Business College

Deborah Mitchell, Temple University

Iris Mohr-Jackson, Saint John's University

Robert Moore, University of Colorado—Denver

Wayne Moorhead, Brown Mackie College

Robert Morgan, Southeast Community College

Tom Moritz, Hardin Simmons University

Bill Moser, Ball State University

Reza Motameni, California State University—Fresno

John Mow, Bethel College

Robbie Mullins, Oklahoma Baptist University

Gurramkonda Naidu, University of Wisconsin—Whitewater

Sethuramon Narayandas, Purdue University

Don Norman, Pleasanton, California

Brad O'Hara, Southeast Louisiana State University

Eva O'Keefe, Massachusetts College of Pharmacy and Allied Health Sciences

Robert O'Keefe, DePaul University

Lawrence O'Neal, Stephen F. Austin State University

Peggy Osbourne, Morehead State University

K. H. Padmanbhan, University of Michigan, Dearborn

Al Page, University of Illinois—Chicago

Richard Pesta, Frostburg State

Phillip Peters, Keene State College

Doug Peterson, Southeast Community College—Lincoln

Tim Phillips, College at Cortland

Charles Pinzon, University of Kansas

Eric Pratt, New Mexico State University

Shane Premeaux, McNeese State University

Hank Prudent, Golden Gate University

Rosemary Ramsey, Eastern Kentucky University

Allan Reddy, Valdosta State College

Delores Reha, Fullerton College

Lynne Richardson, University of Alabama

Ray Rody, Loyola Marymount University

Robert Roe, University of Wyoming

Donald Rogers, Rollins College

Marilyn Romine, Northeast Missouri State University

John Ronchetto, University of San Diego

Leon Rosenfeld, Little Silver, New Jersey

Daniel Rountree, Midwestern State University

Carol Rowey, Community College of Rhode Island

Juanita Roxas, California State Polytechnic University

Ben Rudolf, Grand Valley State University

William Sannwald, San Diego State University

Allen Schaefer, SW Missouri State University

Regina Schlee, Seattle Pacific University

Darrell Scott, Idaho State University

James Sears, Rutgers University—Newark Campus

Harold Sekiguchi, University of Nevada

Murphy Sewall, University of Connecticut

Henry Shaw, Saint Thomas Aquinas College

Leonard Sheffield, Tri-State University

Sara Shryock, Biola University

Rodger Singley, Illinois State University

Leo Sloan, Daniel Webster College

Madeline Slutsky, Ray College of Design

Lois Smith, University of Wisconsin—Whitewater

James Spiers, Arizona State University

Richard Spiller, California State University—Long Beach

Mark Spriggs, University of Oregon

David Starr, Shoreline Community College

Sherri Stevens, University of Utah

Jeffrey Stoltman, Wayne State University

Charles Strang, Western New Mexico University

Harry Strickland, La Roche College

Gail Strickler, Michigan Christian College

Lynn Suksdorf, Salt Lake City Community College

R. Sukumar, University of Houston

Rawlie Sullivan, University of Saint Thomas

Tim Sweeney, Bucknell University

Albert Taylor, Austin Peay State University

Janice Taylor, Miami University

Ira Teich, Yeshiva University

Paul Thistlethwaite, Western Illinois University

B. Thornton, Darton College

Anthony Tiberini, Delaware Tech & Community College

Frank Titlow, Saint Petersburg Junior College

Nancy Torrence, Liberty University

Donna Treadwell, Johnson County Community College

Brian van derWesthuizen, California State—Northridge

John Vann, Ball State University

Scott Vitell, University of Mississippi

Ronald Volpe, Capital University

Randall Voorn, Trinity Christian College
Gary Walk, Lima Technical College
Kelly Wason, Texas Tech University
Paul Wellen, Roosevelt University
Jerry Wheat, Indiana University Southeast
David Wheeler, Suffolk University
Charles White, Edison Community College
Roland Whitehall, Volunteer State
  Community College
Patti Wilbur, Northwestern Oklahoma State
  University
Esther Williams, Western Iowa Tech
  Community College
Terrence Williamson, University of South
  Dakota
Tim Wilson, Clarion State College

Jerry Wilson, Georgia State University
Leon Winer, Pace University
Stephen Winter, Orange County Community
  College
Linda Withrow, Saint Ambrose University
Gene Wunder, Columbus College
Clyde Wynn, Bellevue College
Laurie Yale, Fort Lewis College
Donna Yancey, University of Northern
  Alabama
Jere Yates, Pepperdine University
G. Bernard Yevin, Lindenwood College
Mark Young, Winona State University
Murray Young, University of Denver
Sherilyn Zeigler, University of Hawaii—
  Manoa

Lastly, we would like to thank our teachers, students, and colleagues for their contribution to our understanding of marketing. While all of these people deserve credit for the book's strengths, we accept full responsibility for any errors or omissions. Please provide us with any comments or criticisms of the text so that we can improve its value in the future.

Gilbert A. Churchill, Jr.
J. Paul Peter
Madison, Wisconsin
July 1997

Brief Contents

PART 1 DEVELOPING MARKETING PLANS AND STRATEGIES

1 Marketing: Creating Value for Customers 4
2 Environmental Analysis 26
3 Global Marketing Challenges 54
4 Marketing Planning and Organization Strategy 82

PART 2 UNDERSTANDING CUSTOMERS AND MARKETS

5 Marketing Research: Information and Technology 110
6 Consumer Behavior 140
7 Organizational Buying Behavior 168
8 Market Segmentation 198

PART 3 MANAGING AND DEVELOPING PRODUCTS AND SERVICES

9 Managing Existing Products 228
10 Developing New Products 256
11 Marketing Services 284

PART 4 PRICING PRINCIPLES AND STRATEGIES

12 Fundamentals of Pricing 308
13 Pricing Goods and Services 332

PART 5 PLACEMENT: DISTRIBUTING GOODS AND SERVICES

14 Managing Distribution Channels 364
15 Wholesaling and Physical Distribution 390
16 Retailing 412

PART 6 PROMOTION: INTEGRATED MARKETING COMMUNICATIONS

17 Managing Marketing Communications 442
18 Advertising, Sales Promotion, and Publicity 468
19 Personal Selling and Sales Management 500

PART 7 EVALUATING MARKETING EFFECTIVENESS

20 Implementing and Controlling Marketing Activities 532

Appendix A Developing a Marketing Plan 558
Appendix B Career Opportunities in Marketing 568
Appendix C Mathematics Used in Marketing 576

Notes 587
Photo Credits 604
Glossary 606
Indexes 615

Contents

PART 1   DEVELOPING MARKETING PLANS AND STRATEGIES

Chapter 1   MARKETING: CREATING VALUE FOR CUSTOMERS   4

What Is Marketing?   6
Types of Marketing   7
Levels of Marketing Analysis   8
What Are the Traditional Orientations to Marketing?   8
Marketing Movers & Shakers: Jerry Stakhouse/Philadelphia 76ers   9
Production Orientation   9
Sales Orientation   10
Put It into Practice: Record How Nonprofit Organizations Try to
Create Value   11
Marketing Orientation   11
What Is Value-Driven Marketing?   12
Principles of Value-Driven Marketing   12
Value-Driven Marketing View of Customers   15
You Decide: Marketing Conflicts among Chinese Stakeholders   17
What Is Marketing Management?   21
Developing Marketing Plans and Strategies   21
Understanding Customers and Markets   22
Developing Marketing Mixes   22
Implementing and Controlling Marketing Activities   23
Summary   23

Chapter 2   ENVIRONMENTAL ANALYSIS   26

Scanning and Analyzing the Environment   28
Content of Environmental Scanning   29
Scope of Environmental Scanning   29
The Economic Environment   30
Business Cycles and Spending Patterns   30
Consumer Income   31
The Political and Legal Environment   33
Laws Affecting Marketing   33
Regulation of Marketing   35
Marketing Movers & Shakers: Robert Johnson/Black Entertainment
Television   40
Influences on Laws and Regulations   36
You Decide: The Bootlegging of American Products Overseas   37
Court Actions   37
Political and Legal Factors in the Global Environment   37
The Social Environment   38
Demographic Trends   38
Put It into Practice: Use Your Consumer Rights   36
Social Responsibility and Ethics   40
The Natural Environment   44
Availability of Resources   44
Responsibility to the Natural Environment   44
The Technological Environment   46
Information Technology   46
Technological Factors in the Global Environment   48
Technology and Value   48
The Competitive Environment   48
Types of Competition   48
Competitive Forces   49
Competition in the Global Environment   51
Summary   51

Chapter 3   GLOBAL MARKETING CHALLENGES 54

The Changing Global Environment 56
North America 57
The European Community 59
Japan 60
Other Nations 60
Environmental Scanning and Analysis of Foreign Markets 63
Economic Environment 63
Political and Legal Environment 67
Social Environment 70
You Decide: Whose Chicken Is Better? 74
Natural Environment 74
Technological Environment 74
Put It into Practice: How Many Foreign Products Do You Own or Use? 75
Competitive Environment 75
Marketing Movers & Shakers: Thomas Eck/Upton Tea Company 76
Modes of Entry into Global Markets 76
Exporting 76
Licensing 77
Joint Ventures 78
Direct Ownership 78
Summary 79

**Chapter 4   MARKETING PLANNING AND
               ORGANIZATION STRATEGY 82**

Strategic Planning in the Organization 84
Organizational Mission 85
Marketing Movers & Shakers: Guy Kawasaki/Apple Computer 86
Organizational Objectives 87
Organizational Strategies 87
Organizational Portfolio Plan 91
Business Portfolio Analysis 92
Boston Consulting Group's Growth/Share Matrix 92
General Electric's Industry Attractiveness/Business Strength Matrix 93
Marketing and Other Functional Areas in the Strategic
  Planning Process 94
Traditional Role of Marketing in the Planning Process 95
Cross-Functional Teams 96
Managing the Marketing Effort 97
Developing a Marketing Plan 98
Put It into Practice: Create Your Own Marketing Plan 101
Demand Estimation 101
Estimating Demand 101
You Decide: Is Predicting and Fulfilling Demand the Best Value for
  Customers? 102
Forecasting Sales 102
Evaluating the Forecast 104
Summary 105

PART 2   UNDERSTANDING CUSTOMERS AND MARKETS

**Chapter 5   MARKETING RESEARCH: INFORMATION
               AND TECHNOLOGY 110**

Information for Effective Marketing 112
Information versus Data 112
Marketing Information Systems 114
Sources of Information 115
Primary and Secondary Data 117

The Marketing Research Process   120
   Formulate the Problem   121
   Plan a Research Design   121
   Collect Data   124
Marketing Movers & Shakers: Martin McKendry and Charlie Bass/
  SoloPrint   127
   Analyze and Interpret Data   127
   Prepare the Research Report   129
Applications of New Technology   129
   Geographical Information Systems   129
   Virtual Reality   130
   The Internet   131
Ethical Considerations   131
Put It into Practice: Surf the 'Net   132
You Decide: How Much Information Should Marketers Have about
  Consumers?   133
   Deceit and Fraud in Marketing Research   134
   Invasion of Privacy   134
Global Marketing Research   135
Summary   136

Chapter 6   CONSUMER BEHAVIOR   140

The Consumer Buying Process   142
   Need Recognition   142
   Information Search   144
   Alternative Evaluation   145
   Purchase Decision   146
   Postpurchase Evaluation   146
Types of Consumer Decision Making   147
   Routine Decision Making   148
   Limited Decision Making   148
   Extensive Decision Making   149
Social Influences   149
   Culture   150
   Subcultures   151
   Social Class   154
   Reference Groups   155
   Family   157
Put It into Practice: Who Makes the Buying Decisions in Your
  Family?   158
Marketing Influences   159
   Product   159
   Pricing   160
   Placement (Channels of Distribution)   160
You Decide: Should Computers Be Cheaper?   161
   Promotion (Marketing Communications)   161
Situational Influences   161
   Physical Surroundings   162
Marketing Movers & Shakers: Mike Bartusick/Park Bench Cafe   163
   Social Surroundings   163
   Time   163
   Task   164
   Momentary Conditions   164
Summary   165

Chapter 7   ORGANIZATIONAL BUYING BEHAVIOR   168

Organizational Markets   170
   Characteristics of Organizational Markets   170
   Categories of Organizational Buyers   171
   Business Classifications   175
   International Exchanges   176

Major Forces in Organizational Markets   177
   Demand   177
   Competition   177
Marketing Movers & Shakers: Al Misale/Office Club   178
   Technology   179
You Decide: Could Russia Become the New Computing Capital of the
  World?   180
The Organizational Buying Process   182
   Types of Purchases   182
   Buying Criteria   184
   Characteristics of Organizational Buying   187
   The Nature of Organizational Exchanges   189
Interactions with Organizational Buyers   189
   Buyer–Seller Interactions   190
   The Buying Center   192
Put It into Practice: Who Is Involved in the Buying Center in Your
  Organization?   194
Summary   195

Chapter   8   MARKET SEGMENTATION   198

The Need for Market Segmentation   200
   What Is Market Segmentation?   201
   General Approaches to Serving Markets   201
Put It into Practice: Find Your Own Niche   202
Approaches to Segmenting Consumer Markets   204
Marketing Movers & Shakers: The Beretta Family/Beretta   204
   Demographic Segmentation   205
You Decide: What's the Market for Used Stuff?   207
   Geographic Segmentation   210
   Psychographic Segmentation   210
   Segmentation Based on Thoughts and Feelings   211
   Segmentation Based on Purchase Behavior   213
   Multiple Bases for Segmentation   214
Approaches to Segmenting Organizational Markets   215
   Geographic Segmentation   215
   Segmentation Based on Customer Type   215
   Segmentation Based on Organizational Buyer Behavior   217
The Market Segmentation Process   217
   Analyze Customer–Product Relationships   218
   Investigate Segmentation Bases   218
   Develop Product Positioning   219
   Select Segmentation Strategy   221
   Global Implications   222
Summary   224

**PART 3   MANAGING AND DEVELOPING GOODS
AND SERVICES**

Chapter   9   MANAGING EXISTING PRODUCTS   228

Product Classifications   230
   Consumer and Industrial Products   230
   Durables and Nondurables   234
The Product Life Cycle   234
   Introduction   235
   Growth   236
   Maturity   236
   Decline   236
   Evaluation of the Product Life Cycle   237
   Product Adoption and Diffusion   239
Branding and Brand Equity   239

Put It into Practice: Do You Know What Kind of Buyers You Know?   241
   Benefits of Branding   241
You Decide: Does Sub-Zero Create Superior Value?   242
   Types of Brands   242
   Selecting a Brand   244
   Protecting Trademarks   245
   Developing and Managing Brand Equity   246
Product Mixes and Product Lines   248
   Managing Product Mixes and Lines   249
Marketing Movers & Shakers: Harvey McLeod & Chris Freeman/Devil Sticks   251

Summary   253

Chapter 10   DEVELOPING NEW PRODUCTS   256

Types of New Products   258
The New Product Development Process   260
   Idea Generation   260
Put It into Practice: Generate Your Own Ideas for a New Product   261
   Idea Screening   262
   Business Analysis   263
   Product Development   264
   Test Marketing   265
   Commercialization   267
Selecting New Product Characteristics   268
   Quality Level   268
   Product Features   269
   Product Design   270
   Product Safety   271
Packaging and Labeling New Products   272
   Packaging   272
   Labeling   274
   Global Implications   274
You Decide: Do Eco-Labels Really Create Value for Consumers?   275
Reducing New Product Failures   276
   Why New Products Fail   276
   Organizing for Success   277
   Shortening Development Time   278
Marketing Movers & Shakers: Bill Gates & Doug Rowan/Corbis Corp.   279

Summary   281

Chapter 11   MARKETING SERVICES   284

The Service Economy   286
   Reasons for Growth   286
The Nature of Services Marketing   288
   Characteristics of Services   288
You Decide: Can Amtrak Deliver High-Speed Service?   292
   Classification of Services   293
   The Marketing Environment for Services   294
The Marketing Mix for Services   295
   Developing Services   295
Put It into Practice: Evaluate the Alternatives for a Service   296
   Pricing Services   297
   Distributing Services   298
   Promoting Services   299
Nonbusiness Services Marketing   300
   Nonprofit Organizations   300
Marketing Movers & Shakers: Paul Martin Du Bois & Francis Moore Lapp/ American News Service   301
   Government Agencies   302
   Political Groups   303
Summary   303

| PART 4 | PRICING PRINCIPLES AND STRATEGIES |

Chapter 12   FUNDAMENTALS OF PRICING   308

Economics of Pricing   310
  Demand Curves   310
Put It into Practice: Consider Psychological Factors in Pricing as a Consumer   313
  Marginal Analysis   315
Approaches to Pricing   317
  Pricing Based on Cost   317
  Pricing Based on Competition   320
  Pricing Based on Customer Value   322
Marketing Movers & Shakers: The New Bike Manufacturers   323
Legal and Ethical Issues in Pricing   325
  Government Regulation of Pricing   325
You Decide: Are Women Being Taken to the Cleaners?   327
  Ethics of Pricing   327
Summary   328

Chapter 13   PRICING GOODS AND SERVICES   332

Pricing Objectives   334
  Segmentation and Positioning Objectives   335
  Sales and Profit Objectives   335
  Competitive Objectives   336
  Survival Objectives   336
You Decide: Is Fingerhut's Pricing Strategy Socially Responsible?   337
  Social Responsibility Objectives   337
Pricing Strategies   337
  The Pricing Process   338
  Pricing New Products   340
  Pricing Existing Products   341
  Pricing Product Lines   343
Adjusting Prices   343
  Discounting   344
Marketing Movers & Shakers: Bill Dinardo/Tech-Ceram Corp.   348
  Psychological Pricing   350
  Geographic Pricing   352
Put It into Practice: Evaluate Your Own Response to Psychological Pricing   354
  Strategies for Global Marketers   354
Evaluation and Control of Pricing   356
  Competitor Responses   356
  Customer Responses   357
  Controlling the Price Level   358
Summary   359

| PART 5 | PLACEMENT: DISTRIBUTING GOODS AND SERVICES |

Chapter 14   MANAGING DISTRIBUTION CHANNELS   364

Introduction to Channels   366
  Distribution Functions   366
  Intermediaries and Costs   368
Channel Options   369
  Channels for Consumer Goods   369
Put It into Practice: Find Out How Products Get onto a Store's Shelf   370
  Channels for Organizational Goods   370
  Channels for Services   372

Multiple Distribution Channels *372*

Reverse Channels *373*

Vertical Marketing Systems **374**

Administered VMS *374*

Corporate VMS *374*

Contractual VMS *375*

Managing Channels of Distribution **376**

Selecting Channels *376*

Marketing Movers & Shakers: Michael P. Krasny/CDW Computer Centers Inc. 378

Managing Channel Relationships *381*

You Decide: When a Change in Channels Creates Conflict 383

Managing Global Channels *384*

Regulating Channels **385**

Legal Issues *385*

Political Issues *386*

Ethical Issues *387*

Summary **387**

Chapter 15   WHOLESALING AND PHYSICAL DISTRIBUTION   390

The Role of Wholesaling in Distribution **392**

Major Types of Wholesalers **393**

Merchant Wholesalers *394*

Marketing Movers & Shakers: Nanci Mackenzie/U.S. Gas Transportation 395

Agents and Brokers *396*

Marketing Strategies for Wholesalers **397**

Strategies to Attract Producers *397*

Strategies to Attract Retailers *398*

Trends in Wholesaling **398**

Put It into Practice: Help a Wholesaler Survive 399

Physical Distribution **399**

The Physical Distribution Process *399*

You Decide: Can Truckers and Wholesalers Establish a Better Relationship? 401

Managing Physical Distribution *406*

Trends in Physical Distribution *407*

Summary **410**

Chapter 16   RETAILING   412

The Role of Retailing in Distribution **414**

Major Types of Retailers **415**

Store Retailing *416*

Nonstore Retailing *418*

Marketing Strategy Decisions for Retailers **422**

Product Decisions *422*

Pricing Decisions *424*

Placement Decisions *425*

Put It into Practice: How Convenient Is Your Local Mall? 427

Promotion Decisions *427*

Store Image and Atmospherics *428*

You Decide: Does Wal-Mart Need a New Face? 429

Marketing Movers & Shakers: John L. Morris/Bass Pro Shops 430

Changing Environment of Retailing **430**

Changes in Types of Retailers *431*

Technological Changes in Retailing *432*

Global Scope of Retailing *435*

Legal and Ethical Issues in Retailing **436**

Summary **437**

PART 6　PROMOTION: INTEGRATED MARKETING COMMUNICATIONS

Chapter 17　MANAGING MARKETING COMMUNICATIONS　442

Goals of Marketing Communications　444
　Create Awareness　445
　Build Positive Images　445
　Identify Prospects　445
Put It into Practice: Observe How a Product's Image Is Created　446
　Build Channel Relationships　447
　Retain Customers　447
Understanding Marketing Communications　447
　The Communication Process　447
　The AIDA Model　448
　Communication with a Target Market　449
Elements of the Communications Mix　449
Marketing Movers & Shakers: Jason and Matthew Olim/CDnow　450
　Advertising　450
　Personal Selling　451
　Sales Promotion　451
　Publicity　452
　Integrated Marketing Communications　452
Managing Communications Strategy　454
　Setting Communications Objectives　454
　Selecting the Communications Mix　455
　Setting Communications Budgeting　457
　Implementing and Controlling the Communications Strategy　459
　Implications for Global Marketers　461
Legal and Ethical Issues in Marketing Communications　462
You Decide: How Do You Communicate in the New 'Net Culture?　463
　Regulation of Communications　463
　Socially Responsible Communications　465
Summary　465

Chapter 18　ADVERTISING, SALES PROMOTION, AND PUBLICITY　468

Advertising　470
　Types of Advertising　470
Developing and Managing Advertising Campaigns　472
Marketing Movers & Shakers: Michael Bronner/Bronner Slosberg Humphrey Inc.　473
　Review Advertising Goals and Budgets　474
Put It into Practice: How Many Slogans Do You Remember?　476
　Create Messages　476
　Select Media　477
　Pretest Ads　482
　Evaluate Advertising Effectiveness　483
　Adjust Advertising as Needed　485
　Legal and Ethical Issues in Advertising　485
Sales Promotion　486
　Consumer Promotions　487
　Trade Promotions　491
　Legal and Ethical Issues in Sales Promotion　492
Publicity　492
　Types of Publicity　492
　Managing Negative Publicity　494
　Ethical Issues in Publicity　494
You Decide: Was the Russian Election as American as Apple Pie?　495
Summary　496

Chapter 19 PERSONAL SELLING AND
SALES MANAGEMENT 500

The Nature of Personal Selling 502
The Role of Personal Selling 503
Activities of Salespeople 503
Relationship Selling 507
Marketing Movers & Shakers: Stuart Levine/Dale Carnegie &
Associates 508
Steps in the Selling Process 508
Prospect for Customers 509
Put It into Practice: Indentify Your Own Personal Selling Experience 510
Prepare for Sales Calls 510
Approach Qualified Prospects 511
Make Sales Presentations 511
Handle Objections 513
Close Sales 514
Build Long-Term Relationships 514
Sales Management 515
Organizing Sales Forces 515
Recruiting Salespeople 516
Training and Supervising Salespeople 518
Motivating and Compensating Salespeople 519
You Decide: What's the Best Way to Motivate Sales Support Staff? 522
Evaluating and Controlling Salespeople 522
Ethical Issues in Personal Selling 524
Manipulation of Prospects 525
Bribery 525
Accuracy of Reports 526
Summary 526

PART 7 EVALUATING MARKETING EFFECTIVENESS

Chapter 20 IMPLEMENTING AND CONTROLLING
MARKETING ACTIVITIES 532

Organizing Marketing Activities 534
Organizing Marketing within a Company 534
Organizing Marketing across Companies 535
Implementing Marketing Plans and Strategies 537
Staffing Marketing Positions 537
Coordinating Marketing Activities 538
Communicating Ideas and Information 540
Marketing Movers & Shakers: Small Business Counselors 541
Motivating Employees 542
Controlling Marketing Plans and Strategies 543
You Decide: Can Business Control the Direction of Technology? 544
The Control Process 544
Sales Analysis 546
Profitability Analysis 549
Put It into Practice: Give Feedback as a Customer 550
Customer Satisfaction Analysis 550
The Marketing Audit 552
Summary 554

Appendix A: Creating a Marketing Plan 558
Appendix B: Career Opportunities in Marketing 568
Appendix C: Mathematics Used in Marketing 576
Notes 587
Photo Credits 604
Glossary 606
Indexes 615

DEVELOPING MARKETING PLANS AND STRATEGIES

ONE

I've been in this business for 33 years, and it seems that every decade, we get reminded what this business is all about—providing better value to consumers.

John Pepper, *CEO, Procter & Gamble*

CHAPTER 1

Marketing: Creating Value for Customers

CHAPTER 2

Environmental Analysis

CHAPTER 3

Global Marketing Challenges

CHAPTER 4

Marketing Planning and Organization Strategy

Explore the Career Profiles on the Churchill and Peter Homepage at www.irwin.com/marketing/value

Chapter One

Marketing: Creating Value for Customers

CHAPTER OUTLINE
What Is Marketing?
  Types of Marketing
  Levels of Marketing Analysis
What Are the Traditional Orientations to Marketing?
  Production Orientation
  Sales Orientation
  Marketing Orientation
What Is Value-Driven Marketing?
  Principles of Value-Driven Marketing
  Value-Driven Marketing View of Customers
What Is Marketing Management?
  Developing Marketing Plans and Strategies
  Understanding Customers and Markets
  Developing Marketing Mixes
  Implementing and Controlling Marketing Activities
Summary

LEARNING OBJECTIVES
After completing this chapter, you should be able to:
1. Define marketing and know its major types.
2. Distinguish the levels of marketing analysis.
3. Identify three traditional orientations to marketing.
4. Discuss value-driven marketing and its principles.
5. Explain the types of customer benefits and costs.
6. Describe the marketing management process.
7. List the elements of a marketing mix.

Black Diamond Equipment Ltd.

While Pete Metcalf was hanging off a rope on Mount Hunter in Alaska, he learned a few lessons he hadn't expected. "To this day I believe that Alpinists, like entrepreneurs, are not risk takers," he writes. "You train and plan and prepare for your activity and deal with contingencies when they arise." Metcalf and his climbing friends had planned their climb of the difficult peak carefully; they were experienced and knowledgeable. But when bad weather and extreme cold held them on the mountain longer than they had anticipated and their food ran out, they had to come up with a new strategy to get themselves out of trouble.

Metcalf likens the predicament, and his climbing team's ultimate success on the mountain, to building his company, Black Diamond Equipment Ltd., based in Salt Lake City, Utah. "You can't know what a climb like that will be without actually doing it . . . If you decide there are no alternatives and you absolutely commit yourself to something, it is amazing how you . . . can convince yourself and others that you can do anything," he writes. "Those lessons served me extremely well during the five years of climbing the mountain that is Black Diamond, now a 200-employee company with more than $20 million in revenues."

The new Black Diamond emerged from the failure of the original climbing equipment company founded by renowned climber Yvon Chouinard. Perhaps Metcalf's most important job as head of the new company was to create value for his partners, his employees, resellers, his customers (retailers, outfitters, and the like), and consumers (who buy and use climbing equipment). He had to get them to believe in the quality of the company's products. "We had to assure loyal customers and partners that the new company would be as strong as the old one and that the new products would be comparable with the old ones. We had to build a new brand."

Perhaps the most obvious value of a climbing product is that it can save a climber's life, and Black Diamond emphasizes safety in all its products. In describing its ropes, the catalog notes, "At first glance, it might seem that the number of UIAA/CEN falls [a safety rating] a rope holds determines its value. The truth is more complex." The catalog goes on to explain that, for many climbers, the rope's value lies in how well it can withstand abrasion over rock edges.

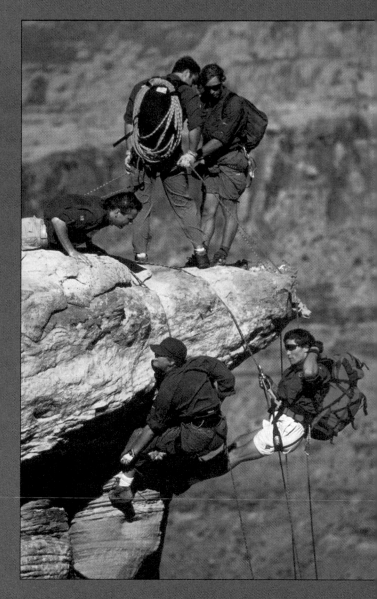

As a marketer and climber, Metcalf knows that the trust people place in his climbing products is also an important part of their value. Trust and confidence influence climbers to buy Black Diamond equipment and use it on dangerous climbs. He writes, "Perhaps the most crucial [lesson] is that just as with climbing, when you're running a business you develop a sense of purpose that propels you forward." Or upward.

As you begin this course in marketing, think about the ways in which goods and services you have purchased and used created value for you. Then think about ways in which you, as a marketer, could create value for other people. Who knows: The products you market may even save someone from a fall off a mountain!

Sources: Peter Metcalf, "Lessons Learned," *Inc.*, April 1995, pp. 35–36; *Black Diamond Equipment* Catalog, Spring 1996, pp. 50–51.

Explore more by searching "Climbing Equipment" on the Web.

At Sears, creating value for customers begins with learning what they want. To do this, Sears communicates with millions of customers to learn their opinions about new products (such as the oscillating spindle sander shown here) as well as to evaluate advertising and other marketing ideas. In the words of a Sears annual report, "value" means having "the right merchandise that our customers want, at the right price"—essential components of customer value.

Chapter Overview

Organizations like Black Diamond Equipment succeed because they offer value to customers, in this case, superior quality climbing equipment at an acceptable price. Other organizations offer superior value by providing better services, creating meaningful brands, pricing lower than competitors, or other ways.

This chapter provides an overview of marketing and value-driven marketing. It explains what marketing is, what it is used for, and at what levels marketing analysis can be employed. Then it explains three traditional marketing orientations and details our value-driven approach. Finally, it overviews marketing management and the tasks involved in doing it.

What Is Marketing?

You click on the TV and a commercial for Tide laundry detergent balloons on the screen, followed by one encouraging you to use a designated driver when you are out drinking. You stroll down a supermarket aisle and snap a 50 cent coupon for Seven Seas salad dressing out of a dispenser. At the end of the aisle, you try a sample of fat-free Lays potato chips. Back home, you answer a phone call asking you to participate in a survey about your radio-listening habits. At school, you visit the placement office to check out career opportunities and learn how to contact prospective employers. At your part-time job, you keep track of office supplies and order more when needed, and a friend asks you for advice on how to market a new software program.

All of these situations involve marketing. According to the American Marketing Association, **marketing** is "the process of planning and executing the conception, pricing, promotion, and distribution of ideas, goods and services to create exchanges that satisfy individual and organizational goals."[1] The essence of marketing is the

marketing
The process of planning and executing the conception, pricing, promotion, and distribution of ideas, goods and services to create exchanges that satisfy individual and organizational goals.

Many people want to relax and do the things they enjoy. In this advertisement, the California Division of Tourism appeals to people who want information about California vacations. The slogan "Do Your Own Thing" implies that in exchange for spending vacation dollars in California, tourists will receive a wide variety of recreational opportunities. The Internet site (http://gocalif.ca.gov) allows browsers to explore vacation options from family fun to nature outings. Thus, the exchanges involve consumers giving money and California organizations giving fun activities.

DO YOUR OWN THING.

Up here, you'll wear out tires long before you run out of views. Down there, a nice, plump Kokanee Salmon is probably waiting. And he might be real hungry. It's up to you. Whatever kind of vacation you're looking for, you'll find it in California. We'll prove it. With free insider vacation tips by fax or mail on Recreation of all kinds, Nature Outings, Romantic Getaways, and Family Fun. Just call us. In California, do your own thing isn't just a philosophy. It's a promise.

NATURE

exchange
A voluntary transaction between an organization and a customer designed to benefit both of them.

organizational buyers
People who purchase goods and services for businesses, government agencies, and other institutions.

consumers
People who purchase goods and services for their own use or for gifts to others.

needs
The goods or services consumers or organizational buyers require in order to survive.

wants
Specific goods and services that satisfy needs and additional goods and services that go beyond survival.

development of **exchanges** in which organizations and customers voluntarily engage in transactions that are designed to benefit both of them. For example, customers receive benefits from purchasing Healthy Choice Praline and Caramel ice cream and ConAgra, the company that sells Healthy Choice, receives benefits by getting money for it.

There are two types of customers that engage in business exchanges. First there are **organizational buyers,** who purchase goods and services for businesses, government agencies, and other institutions, such as hospitals and schools. Organizational buyers purchase goods and services to run their own companies (office supplies, machinery, computer networks, etc.) or to sell them to other organizations or consumers. Second, there are **consumers,** who buy goods and services for their own use or for gifts to others. Consumers include both individuals and households that make purchases to satisfy their needs and wants, solve their problems, or improve their lives.

Consumer or organizational buyer **needs** are the things required for them to survive. For example, consumers need food and shelter to survive while organizations may need computers to survive. **Wants** include specific goods and services to satisfy needs, as well as additional goods and services that go beyond survival. For example, while consumers need food, the specific type of food may be a want, such as a Big Mac. Consumers don't need a watch to survive, but a Timex Ironman is a product 500,000 consumers a year purchase and apparently want.

Types of Marketing

Marketing is used for developing both for-profit and nonprofit exchanges. Most of the types of marketing listed in Table 1.1 can be done for either purpose. For-profit exchanges are the goal of businesses that seek to generate revenues over and above

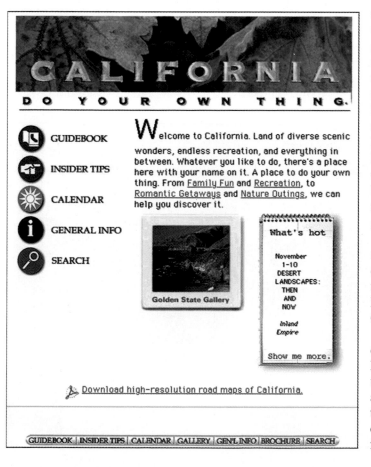

their costs. For example, clothing stores typically sell products for at least twice what they paid for them. The additional money covers their costs and gives them a profit. A nonprofit organization, on the other hand, may sell products at a profit, then use the profits to cover the organization's costs. For example, the Girl Scouts sell cookies each year to help cover the cost of operating the organization. In addition, persons can be marketed for profit (see Marketing Movers and Shakers: Jerry Stackhouse/ Philadelphia 76ers) or nonprofit, such as political candidates seeking donations or votes. Places can be marketed for profit, such as Disneyworld, or nonprofit, such as national parks promoted by a government tourist agency.

Nonprofit organizations also seek other goals, such as blood donations, votes for political candidates, reduced smoking, recycled packaging, or volunteer time for needy children or the elderly (see Put It into Practice, page 11: Record How Nonprofit Organizations Try to Create Value).

In general, for-profit marketing is a more fully developed body of knowledge than nonprofit marketing. However, for-profit marketing strategies usually are applicable to nonprofit organizations and can help them achieve their objectives. While the major focus of this book is for-profit, business-oriented marketing, it can also be used as a guide for nonprofit marketing strategies.

Type	Description	Example
Product	Marketing designed to create exchange for tangible products	Strategies to sell Gateway computers
Service	Marketing designed to create exchanges for intangible products	Strategies by Hertz to rent cars to travelers
Person	Marketing designed to create favorable actions toward persons	Strategies to get votes for Bill Clinton
Place	Marketing designed to attract people to places	Strategies to get people to vacation in Puerto Rico
Cause	Marketing designed to create support for ideas or issues or to get people to change socially undesirable behaviors	Strategies to get people to stop using illicit drugs
Organization	Marketing designed to attract donors, members, participants, or volunteers	Strategies to increase membership in the National Rifle Association

Levels of Marketing Analysis

macromarketing
The study of marketing processes, activities, institutions, and results at a societal level.

micromarketing
The study of marketing processes and activities at organizational, product, or brand levels.

Although the heart of marketing is developing strategies for domestic and global businesses, analysts also use marketing to describe and evaluate economic activities at other levels. Table 1.2 on page 10 lists a number of levels at which marketing analyses are useful. In general, issues and analyses at the global and national levels are called **macromarketing,** while those below the global and national level are called **micromarketing.** The major focus of this text is on micromarketing although macromarketing issues, such as social responsibility and ethics, are integrated throughout the book.

What Are the Traditional Orientations to Marketing?

Marketing can be oriented in several ways in organizations. The traditional ways include production, sales, and marketing orientations, all of which are summarized in Table 1.3 on page 10. In addition, Table 1.3 includes an overview of a value orientation, which is the approach we advocate and discuss in the next section.

The National Wildlife Federation, a 60-year-old organization whose mission is "to educate, inspire and assist individuals and organizations of diverse cultures to conserve wildlife" uses organization marketing to attract donors. The ad for the federation's Land Gifts program was printed in National Wildlife *magazine, another marketing tool for the organization.*

Your gift of real estate to the National Wildlife Federation will help us work on behalf of wildlife and the environment while freeing you from ownership problems. You'll enjoy tax savings and other benefits as well.

Homeowners can even make a Land Gift and retain the right to continue living on the property.

For more information about our Land Gifts program, just send in the attached reply card in this magazine. Or call Mike Green, Land Gifts Director, at 1-800-332-4949, extension 4020.

We'll send you information—without obligation—right away.

Jerry Stackhouse/ Philadelphia 76ers

The idea that individual athletes are vital to the marketing strategy of a team or a sport is as American as . . . basketball. Jerry Stackhouse, one of the latest in a line of young men whose role in marketing is probably more important than how well he can bounce a ball, illustrates this phenomenon well. Stackhouse, a talented ballplayer at the University of North Carolina, was signed by the Philadelphia 76ers for about $2 million a year. Far more complex—and ultimately more lucrative—was the deal he made with Advantage International, a sports-marketing firm.

Advantage set out to create value for Stackhouse with a strategy that included slogans capitalizing on the catchy sound of his name; polishing Stackhouse's image as a classy role model; and promoting Stackhouse as the best player on the 76ers team. The agency lined up an incredible array of commercial endorsements, ranging from Fila shoes to Mountain Dew softdrinks. The Fila deal alone is worth $15 million. Stackhouse may not have needed these opportunities on top of his player's salary, but he certainly wanted them.

Now came Stackhouse's part in the marketing strategy: to create value for customers, for the team, and the companies he represented. Advantage had this covered too, all in a proposal to companies stamped with the slogan "The Power to Move You."

"It conveys a double message," says Stackhouse's agent, Tom George. "The power to excite you with his play on the court, and also the power to move your company and your company's products." George continues, "More people will see Jerry in a shoe commercial than will ever see him bounce a basketball. And that notoriety means more business. . . . It helps drive other deals."

During his rookie year, Stackhouse's image was carefully cultivated. Fila sent him to give speeches at boys' and girls' clubs and introduce his academic and athletic excellence program for schoolchildren. This program was called Stack's Starts. "If we're serving Jerry up as an endorser," says a Fila spokesman, "we need to serve him up as a good citizen and a role model." Stackhouse's good image was designed to translate to a good image for Fila, and ultimately more sales of Fila products.

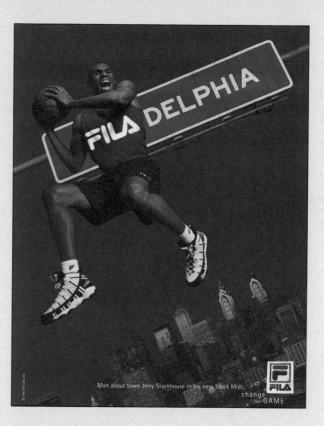

Man about town Jerry Stackhouse in his new Stack Mids.

FILA
change the GAME

Does the promotion of Stackhouse create value for fans and the general public? Supporters will say yes, if it increases their enjoyment of the game and influences the lives of youngsters in need in a positive way. Critics may counter that this kind of marketing doesn't benefit fans by, say, reducing the cost of tickets; they may also contend that the exchange of such huge sums of money for activities that are not directly related to Stackhouse's ability to play basketball may make the general public cynical toward him and the companies he represents. Either way, Jerry Stackhouse is a marketing force to be reckoned with—both on and off the court.

Source: Roger Thurow, "The 76ers Are Lowly, But Jerry Stackhouse Scores Big in Marketing," *The Wall Street Journal,* February 9, 1996, pp. A1, A6. Reprinted by permission of *The Wall Street Journal,* © 1996 Dow Jones & Company, Inc. All Rights Reserved Worldwide.

Explore more at www.nba.com/sixers/index/html

Production Orientation

production orientation
A business philosophy that emphasizes the manufacture and delivery of products.

Production orientation is focused on products and how to make them efficiently. It is assumed that if products are better, customers will buy them. Marketing's role in a production orientation is primarily delivering products to locations where they can be purchased.

Although a production orientation is much maligned by many marketers, there are situations where it is appropriate. For example, in rapidly changing high-tech markets there often is not enough time to do marketing research to ask customers what they want. Rather, the focus is on making products superior to those of competitors, and then informing customers about the benefits of buying them. Many successful products come about as the result of research and development activities that do not reflect direct inputs from customers. Similarly, for products such as cures for cancer or

TABLE 1.2
Levels of Marketing Analysis

Levels	Examples of Marketing Issues
Global	What are worldwide sales of automobiles?
	How do automobile exhausts affect global warming?
	Should consumers be encouraged to use less dangerous modes of transportation?
National	What are total automobile sales in the United States?
	How can smog be reduced in major U.S. cities?
	Should U.S. cities offer special lanes to passenger cars with multiple occupants on heavily traveled roads?
Organizational	What are the total sales of General Motors vehicles domestically and globally?
	How can GM reduce emissions and improve mileage for its vehicles?
	Should GM be banned from selling vehicles that get poor mileage?
Products	What are the sales of GM's truck line domestically and globally?
	How can GM sell more sport utility vehicles?
	Should GM be allowed to have gas tanks positioned outside of truck frames?
Brands	What are the sales of Saturn cars domestically and globally?
	How can GM sell more Saturns?
	Should Saturns be required to have stronger bumpers to reduce injuries in crashes?

TABLE 1.3
A Comparison of
Four Orientations

Orientation	Focus	Description
Production	Products	Produce goods and services, inform customers about them, let customers come to you.
Sales	Sales	Produce goods and services, go to customers, and get them to buy.
Marketing	Customers	Find out what customers need and want, produce goods and services they say they need and want, offer them to customers.
Value	Customer value	Understand customers, competitors and environments; create value for customers; consider other stakeholders.

AIDS there is no need to do marketing research to see if customers want or need such products.

Finally, when demand for products and services is far greater than supply, a production orientation may be appropriate. For example, while Harley-Davidson does do considerable marketing research, a major goal of the company is creating production facilities to better meet overwhelming demand. Also, when Laurie Baron founded Baron Messenger Service in Miami, Florida, the economy was booming and there was no other messenger service in the area. She concentrated on making deliveries efficiently. She informed customers about her service by having her husband, Larry Schwartz, drop off her business card when he made sales calls for Minolta copiers, his employer.[2]

Sales Orientation

sales orientation
A business philosophy that focuses marketing activities on selling available products.

A **sales orientation** involves focusing marketing activities on making sales for available products. It is used in some cases when supply of products and service facilities is greater than demand. An old story goes that a customer came into a general store and found that all of the shelves were filled with boxes of salt. He commented to the proprietor that the store must sell a lot of salt. The proprietor replied that the store didn't sell much, but the salt salesman did. The salt salesman clearly used a sales approach to marketing that was inappropriate.

Put It into Practice

Record How Nonprofit Organizations Try to Create Value

Nonprofit organizations, which include everything from the American Civil Liberties Union (ACLU) to the Sierra Club to Save the Children, and special interest groups engage in marketing, as do commercial enterprises. Nonprofit marketing can include persons, places, causes, or organizations when their goals are not to earn revenues greater than costs. In election years, we see political commercials that are examples of person marketing. Advertisements for places try to attract tourists to locations such as Canada, Mexico, or the Caribbean. Cause marketing is evident in public service advertisements, and even as part of political campaigns. Requests for donations or membership drives from organizations such as the Sierra Club, Childreach, and United Way frequently appear in the mail. They all attempt to create value for us in some way.

Record 10 examples of nonprofit marketing, such as mail you receive or TV commercials you see from nonprofit organizations asking for donations or membership. In what ways do these organizations try to create value in exchange for your donation, membership, or volunteer service? Have any of these attempts been successful with you? Have you donated or joined? Which are least successful, and why?

There are times when a sales orientation is appropriate, however. For example, stores sometimes have an excess supply of outdated merchandise. In order to sell it, they lower the price to create demand. A doctor may try to sell her patients on the idea of exercising regularly and eating more nutritious foods in order to be more healthy. The patients may not want to do so or need to do so to survive. However, the doctor may believe that it would be good for them and try to convince them to do so.

When Baron Messenger Service expanded to the point that it contracted with 20 independent drivers, it needed to increase demand to cover its costs. Larry Schwartz quit his job with Minolta and focused his efforts on selling customers delivery services.[3]

Marketing Orientation

marketing orientation
A business philosophy that focuses on understanding customer needs and wants and building products and services to satisfy them.

Although there are situations when production and sales approaches are appropriate, the chances of long-term success are increased with a **marketing orientation** in most cases. This approach depends on understanding customer needs and wants and building products and services to satisfy them. In this way, marketers can build loyalty and compete effectively with other marketers.

As Baron Messenger Service prospered, competitors entered the market. Baron responded by finding ways to better meet customer needs and wants. It became a technology innovator and increased the speed and reliability of its service. It used a computer system so that the dispatcher could communicate directly with drivers who carried pagers. By knowing traffic patterns and drivers' locations, dispatchers could speed up pickups and deliveries. Baron's reputation for speed and reliability made it a favorite for companies like AT&T and Kodak, which need to deliver critical parts.[4]

In sum, a marketing orientation emphasizes the importance of developing and marketing products and services based on what customers need and want. A concise

marketing concept
View that an organization should seek to meet its customers' needs and wants as it strives to achieve its own goals.

statement of this view is called the **marketing concept.** It argues that organizations should satisfy customer needs and wants as a means to achieve their own objectives, such as profits.

Limitations to a Marketing Orientation   While a marketing orientation is valuable, it does have limitations. First, as noted, it is not appropriate in some situations. Second, by focusing only on customers, it may encourage organizations to give insufficient attention to other important groups, such as employees and suppliers. Moreover, it ignores the ability of competitors to satisfy needs and wants more efficiently and effectively than the organization, thus causing it to fail. Finally, it gives little direction to organizations as to how to satisfy customers, how to compete with other companies, and how to perform marketing activities to be consistent with it. An extension of a marketing orientation that attempts to overcome these problems is value-driven marketing.

What Is Value-Driven Marketing?   **Value-driven marketing** is an orientation for achieving objectives by developing superior value for customers. It is an extension of the marketing orientation that is based on several principles and assumptions about customers.

value-driven marketing
A business philosophy that focuses on developing and delivering superior value to customers as a way to achieve objectives.

Principles of Value-Driven Marketing

Principles are fundamental, comprehensive rules for action. There are six principles of value-driven marketing which together form the core of the approach.

Customer Principle: Focus Marketing Activities on Creating and Delivering Customer Value   Value-driven marketing is customer-focused. This means marketers should recognize that exchanges with customers are the lifeblood of organizations. Companies should understand their customers, what they think, what they feel, and how they purchase and use products and services. However, value-driven marketing focuses not only on customers but, more specifically, on ways to create value for them. Marketers can achieve their own objectives by delivering superior customer value.

In many cases, marketers build long-term relationships with their customers. Of course, the revenue and potential profits from building long-term relationships must offset the increased costs. There are at least two types of relationships marketers can have with customers. In **direct relationships,** marketers know customers' names and other information, such as addresses, phone numbers, and preferences. They can communicate directly with customers by mail, phone, e-mail, fax, or in person. This is feasible when products or services are purchased frequently (industrial supplies, dry cleaning), have high unit prices (new buildings, automobiles), or have high profit margins (machinery, jewelry). Direct relationships allow companies to know and serve customers better, create better value for them, and increase profits.

direct relationships
Relationships in which marketers know their customers by name and can communicate directly with them.

Direct relationships are unusual for inexpensive products, even frequently purchased ones, since the costs are often too high. However, some marketers of inexpensive packaged goods do have computer files of individual customers. If costs of direct relationships are too high, marketers can still have **indirect relationships** with customers. In these relationships, products and brands have meaning to customers for an extended period, even a lifetime, but marketers may not know who their customers are by name. For example, Coke, Tide, and Oscar-Mayer are brands many customers know, trust, and have purchased for years, but these companies may not know individual purchasers by name.

indirect relationships
Relationships in which marketers do not know individual customers by name but marketers' products have meaning to customers.

Competitor Principle: Offer Customers Superior Value to Competitive Alternatives   Value-driven marketing recognizes that competitive strategies have

Marketers for CS First Boston identify businesses' needs for advisory services funds and seek to translate those needs into a desire for top-of-the-line investment banking services. In this ad, CS First Boston refers to a variety of transactions for which it has won industry praise. The different flavors of the ice cream symbolize that the company offers a variety of innovative products to suit individual customers.

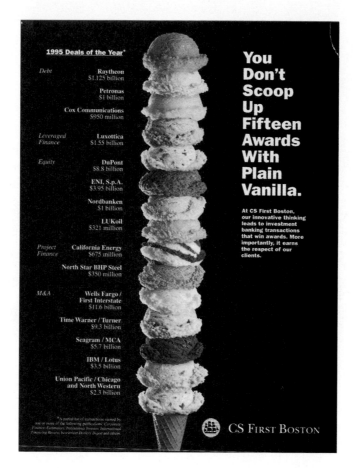

important influences on customers. For many products and services, customers could be well satisfied with a number of competitive alternatives. Thus, marketers should consider not only the value their products and services offer to customers, but also whether they offer value superior to competitive products and services. If not, and no strategy is available to do so, then a marketer may have a difficult time surviving in the long run. For example, companies like Apple Computer and Kmart may offer good value to customers, but their competitors, like IBM and Wal-Mart, may offer superior value. One possible strategy to increase value is to partner with competitors and create joint ventures, such as the one between Apple and IBM.

Proactive Principle: Change Environments to Improve the Chances for Success When Appropriate

Value-driven marketers do not just sit back and wait for changes in markets and environments and then react to them. While reacting to environments is usually sound strategy, marketers also should be proactive and change markets and environments to improve their competitive positions.[5]

Value-driven marketing does *not* argue that marketers should "manipulate" customers to achieve their own goals. It does *not* advocate doing illegal activities, unethical activities, or activities that are not socially responsible. It does *not* condone the activities of marketers who violate their responsibilities.

However, value-driven marketing does recognize that society gives organizations and marketers the right and responsibility to survive and succeed by changing environmental relationships. Organizations cannot serve customers and create value for them if they do not survive. Thus, organizations can and should influence shareholders and owners to invest money in them; banks to lend them money; suppliers to give them higher quality components or lower prices; resellers to do a good job for them; government agencies to regulate them fairly and approve their products, such as getting the FDA to approve the sale of new, safe, life-saving drugs; special interest

Cross-functional teams bring marketers together with employees from other business functions such as operations, finance, and research and development. The broad expertise of such a team can help an organization create value for its customers. In this advertisement, the Lever Brothers Company, which markets a wide range of products such as margarines, soaps and detergents, and health and beauty aids, tells grocery retailers that its cross-functional team can help them find solutions to a number of retailing challenges—and make them winners.

groups to support them; employees to work hard by giving them better benefits or higher pay; customers to buy their products by offering them superior value; competitors to change their strategies or work together on joint ventures; or local communities to support them with land, labor, and capital.

In sum, value-driven marketing recognizes that organizations are and should be both reactive and proactive in their marketing activities. Marketers clearly try to influence customers to buy their new or existing products and services, to switch to their brands from competitive ones, to watch their commercials, to go to their stores, to donate money for causes, to use their credit cards, and to be loyal customers. Doing so ethically and in ways that create superior customer value makes marketing a positive force in society.

Cross-Functional Principle: Use Cross-Functional Teams When They Improve Efficiency and Effectiveness of Marketing Activities

Marketing is not the only function in an organization and it is not everything an organization does. For example, while marketing and marketing research often have important roles to play in new product development, other functions including research and development, engineering, finance, and production also have key roles to play. Table 1.4 lists common sources of conflict between marketing and other functional areas.

Value-driven marketing recognizes the need for marketing personnel to interact with other functional personnel on a continuous basis. Many organizations use cross-functional teams and committees to accomplish planning, implementation, and control tasks. Value-driven marketing recognizes that having functions perform their own tasks independently often leads to more costly and less successful marketing strategies.

Continuous Improvement Principle: Continuously Improve Marketing Planning, Implementation, and Control

Value-driven marketing recognizes

T A B L E 1.4
Potential Sources of Conflict between Marketing and Other Functional Areas

Functions	What They May Want to Deliver	What Marketers May Want Them to Deliver
Research & Development	Basic research projects	Products that deliver customer value
	Product features	Customer benefits
	Few projects	Many new products
Production/ Operations	Long production runs	Short production runs
	Standardized products	Customized products
	No model changes	Frequent model changes
	Long lead times	Short lead times
	Standard orders	Custom orders
	No new products	Many new products
Finance	Rigid budgets	Flexible budgets
	Budgets based on return on investment	Budgets based on need to increase sales
	Low sales commissions	High sales commissions
Accounting	Standardized billing	Customized billing
	Strict payment terms	Flexible payment terms
	Strict credit standards	Flexible credit standards
Human Resources	Trainable employees	Skilled employees
	Low salaries	High salaries

the need for organizations to work continuously to improve their operations, processes, strategies, and products and services. While controlling marketing activities with periodic reviews and audits is valuable, it is also useful for all marketing and other personnel to be searching constantly for better ways to deliver value to customers.

Stakeholder Principle: Consider the Impact of Marketing Activities on Other Stakeholders   While value-driven marketing is customer-focused, it does not ignore the important obligations and relationships with other stakeholders in an organization. **Stakeholders** of organizations are individuals and groups who have a stake in the consequences of marketing decisions and can influence them. Stakeholders include customers as well as competitors who should be treated fairly. They also include owners, suppliers, lenders, government agencies, special interest groups, employees, local communities, and society at large, as shown in Figure 1.1.

There are inherent problems with focusing only on customers and ignoring other stakeholders. For example, customers may want beryllium-copper golf clubs, but working with this material can cause fatal illness for employees. Customers may want extremely low prices, but offering them can lead to losses for owners and lenders. Customers may want complete product lines and immediate delivery of all products, but this may not be economically feasible for suppliers and resellers. Value-driven marketing recognizes the need to consider all stakeholders when designing and implementing marketing strategies (see You Decide: Marketing Conflicts among Chinese Stakeholders on page 17).

stakeholders
Individuals and groups who are influenced and can influence marketing decisions.

Value-Driven Marketing View of Customers

Value-driven marketing is based on a simple view of why customers buy products and services. As shown in Figure 1.2, **customer value** is the difference between customer perceptions of benefits from purchasing and using products and services, and customer perceptions of the costs they incur to exchange for them. Value-driven marketing assumes that customers who are willing and able to make exchanges will do so when (1) the benefits of exchanges exceed the costs of exchanges and (2) the products or services offer superior value compared to alternatives.

customer value
The difference between customer perceptions of the benefits and costs of purchasing and using products and services.

F I G U R E 1.1
*Stakeholders in Marketing
Activities*

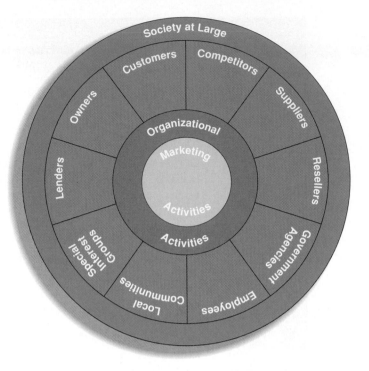

F I G U R E 1.1
*Stakeholders in Marketing
Activities*

The alternatives may be products or services currently or previously used. Customers may perceive that purchasing a product may solve a problem or improve their situation. For example, Duracell informed customers that its new batteries offered superior value to its older ones when it ran a series of ads claiming that the new batteries were the longest lasting it had ever made. Thus, Duracell was encouraging customers to perceive greater benefits in its new batteries and buy them.

The alternatives may also be competitive products and services. For example, Hardee's sought to influence customer value perceptions when it advertised that its burgers were bigger than McDonald's. Finally, the alternatives may be different ways for customers to handle their problems. For example, customers can buy lawncare services, or rent or buy equipment and do their own lawncare.

Value-driven marketing does *not* view customers as machines that finely calculate the sum of all benefits and subtract the sum of all costs of an exchange. The value equation is simply a useful representation of the idea that benefits have positive effects and costs have negative effects on value. Value-driven marketing does suggest that customers often consider various benefits and costs in making purchase decisions, likely in a loosely structured way. In some cases, such as purchases by organizational buyers or important purchases by consumers, customers may carefully evaluate a number of benefits and costs in their decisions.

In many cases, customers base their purchases on satisfaction with previously purchased products and services and do little or no assessment of the value of alternatives. This is why it is often difficult and expensive for marketers to attract new customers, and why current customers are so important to keep. In other cases, customers likely base their purchase decisions on broad generalizations such as "Campbell's Soup is a good buy" or "Wal-Mart sells good products and has low prices."

F I G U R E 1.2
The Value Equation

You Decide

Marketing Conflicts among Chinese Stakeholders

Founded by a former rickshaw operator, the China Motor Bus company wielded its power as the only bus service on Hong Kong island. Owned and run by a single family, the Ngans, the company enjoyed profits without competition, and never considered offering any kind of increased value to customers. After all, its buses did get customers from one place to another. As the buses began to break down with age, however, they traveled more slowly uphill than the average person could walk. Without air conditioning, they were stifling in the heat.

Passengers began to complain, insisting on better conditions, and the Hong Kong government stepped in. In one year, the government awarded 26 of the island's 100 routes to a new company, called CityBus. The new company immediately offered greater value to customers in the form of new, freshly painted, air conditioned buses. The government's action and the competition generated by CityBus did not drive China Motor Bus to improve its buses or its service, however. Instead, when the government pressured the company during franchise renewal negotiations, China Motor Bus threatened to stop its bus service altogether. While this might seem to be a solution to problems with China Motor Bus, the shutdown would have closed areas of Hong Kong that are completely dependent on the company's bus service. To add insult to injury, neither the government nor CityBus could have come up with additional buses or places to park them since all the bus depots belong to the Ngan family.

In the end, the Hong Kong government renewed China Motor Bus's franchise contract but gave 14 more routes to CityBus. China Motor Bus claimed that its profits were down, but it did order some new buses. What stakeholders are involved in China Motor Bus? How should the problem be resolved to serve all stakeholders? Can you think of an instance in which government pressure on a company or industry created greater value for customers in the United States?

Source: "Why the Buses Don't Run on Time," *The Economist*, March 9, 1996, p. 66. Copyright 1996 The Economist Newspaper Group, Inc. Reprinted with permission. Further reproduction prohibited.

Explore more at www.great-China.net/cmb

Value-driven marketing assumes that customers vary in their perceptions of value: Different customers can assess the same product in different ways. Some customers view a Saturn automobile as a good value because it provides reliable transportation at a relatively low cost while others view a Mercedes S320 as providing good value because it is a high-status car that lasts a long time. Thus, value-driven marketing stresses the importance of understanding customers well.

Finally, value-driven marketing assumes that customers' assessments of value can change over time and in different situations. Customers may think Reebok basketball shoes are a good value and buy them, but they may view Nike shoes as a better value the next time they purchase. In fact, one of the major challenges of marketing is to get customers to switch from competitive brands. Similarly, the value of products and services changes in different situations. A fast-food restaurant might be considered a good value alternative when looking for a quick lunch, but Olive Garden may be considered a good value for a leisurely dinner.

As shown in Figure 1.3, there are four common types of benefits customers can receive from purchasing and using products and services. There are also four types of costs they could try to reduce.

Types of Benefits The benefits customers can receive from purchasing products and services include:

functional benefits
The tangible benefits received from goods and services.

1. **Functional benefits** These are the tangible benefits of obtaining goods and services. Wearing Mephisto shoes protects feet on long walks and provides comfort to the hiker. Eating a taco provides energy and satisfies hunger. Healthcare services can cure illnesses and make the body feel better. Functional benefits are often promoted by marketers. Organizational buyers cite functional benefits as their key concern, and customers rent products, such as cars and garden tools, primarily for their functional benefits.

social benefits
The positive responses customers get from others for purchasing and using particular products and services.

2. **Social benefits** These are the positive responses customers get from others for purchasing and using particular products and services. Friends may enjoy the music played at a party and compliment the owner's good taste in CDs. Customers may also seek social benefits when they buy high-status brands like Lexus automobiles or Ralph Lauren shirts. Organizational buyers may get social benefits from the compliments they get from their bosses for buying exceptional products.

F I G U R E 1.3 *Creating Value for Customers*

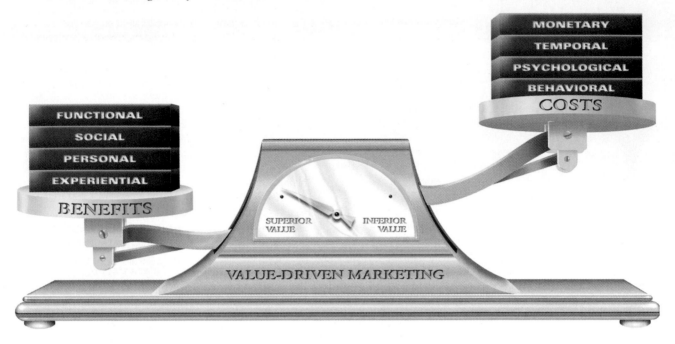

personal benefits
The good feelings that customers get from purchasing, owning, and using products, or receiving services.

experiential benefits
The sensory enjoyment customers get from products and services.

3. **Personal benefits** These are the good feelings that customers get from purchasing, owning, and using products or receiving services. Stamp collectors enjoy owning rare stamps even though they will never be used to mail letters. Environmentalists may get satisfaction from using a bicycle for transportation because they feel good about not polluting the environment with automobile exhaust fumes. Organizational buyers may get personal benefits from making purchases by feeling good about doing their job well.

4. **Experiential benefits** These reflect the sensory enjoyment customers get from products and services. Customers may enjoy playing a golf course or getting a massage. Products such as motorcycles and power boats offer experiential benefits in the adrenaline rush received from driving them. Tasty food, pleasant smelling perfume, comfortable clothes, beautiful works of art, and exciting music can all offer these experiential benefits.[6]

Many products have the potential to provide all four types of benefits. For example, toothpaste offers the functional benefit of getting teeth clean, the social benefit of having an attractive smile, the personal benefit of being assured of oral health, and the experiential benefit of a fresh, minty taste in the mouth. Toothpaste marketers have emphasized all of these benefits in different advertising campaigns.

Value-driven marketers can increase customer benefits to create superior value. For example, Zane's Cycles became the largest independent bicycle dealer serving the New Haven, Connecticut, area by focusing on offering superior benefits to customers. Although big retail chains were crushing other independent dealers, Zane's offered a superior lifetime guarantee on parts and labor purchased there. Chris Zane, the owner of the store, maintained that the lifetime purchases by customers far exceeded the costs to replace some parts. Zane's also offered an in-store coffee bar and a play area to keep children entertained while their parents shopped or waited for repairs. As a result of Zane's value-driven orientation, sales grew 25 percent per year.[7]

Types of Costs   As shown in Figure 1.3, there are also at least four categories of costs that can influence customer assessments of value.

1. **Monetary costs** These refer to the amount of money customers must pay to receive products and services. They include the price of the product or service, shipping and installation charges, charges for repairs, and interest charges for credit purchases. Monetary costs also include the risks of financial loss from product failure or poor performance. Organizational buyers often consider monetary costs as a primary decision criteria.

In some cases, however, higher monetary costs actually *increase* the value of products and services. This happens when paying high prices gives the customer social and experiential benefits. Similarly, some customers view high-priced products as having higher quality. By purchasing the most expensive products, they reduce their shopping costs.

2. **Temporal costs** Time is valuable to most people. Time spent purchasing products and, if necessary, getting them altered or repaired could be used for more pleasant or profitable activities. Waiting in a long line to check out at Office Depot may be considered a waste of time or waiting for pizza delivery can be unpleasant if customers are hungry. For organizational buyers, time spent evaluating alternative products and waiting for their delivery can be a significant cost if it reduces productivity or efficiency of the company.

Time spent shopping and purchasing or waiting for an order to be delivered is not always a cost, however. Some customers in some situations like spending time shopping and enjoy the anticipation of waiting for a special product to be delivered.

3. **Psychological costs** These are the mental energy and stress involved in making important purchases and accepting the risks of products and services not performing as expected. Purchasing complex or expensive products can involve investigating and evaluating lots of information and worrying about making the right choices. Waiting for a bus or cab to go shopping can be frustrating too. For some customers these efforts are psychologically draining, although for others making purchase decisions is exhilarating. Car dealers that offer "no haggle" sales appeal to customers who want to lower their psychological costs. Organizational buyers can be under great pressure to buy the right products at the right prices.

4. **Behavioral costs** Buying products and services usually requires some level of physical behavior. Activity costs are increased if customers have to travel long distances to go to malls, park in remote spots and walk long distances, hunt through many aisles looking for products, and stand for long periods waiting to check out. Organizational buyers who have to travel around the world to inspect various factories and products may exert considerable energy just getting to and from airplane gates. Of course, physical energy used in shopping is not always a cost since some customers enjoy walking in malls and stores and do so to get exercise.

Time, psychological, and activity costs can be considered collectively as **shopping costs** or **transactions costs.**

Marketers can increase customer value by working on one, the other, or both sides of the value equation. Since there are a variety of different benefits and costs, there are many combinations of strategies for creating superior customer value. For example, functional benefits can be improved over existing products or competitive products by offering superior quality, additional features, or more convenient packaging. Social benefits can be increased by creating positive images for products. Personal benefits can be increased by emphasizing the enjoyment others get from products and implying that customers who purchase will also get these good feelings. Experiential benefits can be increased by improving the sensory experiences involved in using products and receiving services.

Marketers can also improve value by lowering costs. Monetary costs can be lowered by reducing prices, lowering interest rates on credit purchases, or offering free

monetary costs
The amount of money customers pay to receive products and services.

temporal costs
The time spent purchasing products and services.

psychological costs
The mental energy and stress involved in making purchases and accepting product risks.

behavioral costs
The physical energy customers expend to buy products and services.

transaction (shopping) costs
The combination of temporal, psychological, and behavior costs.

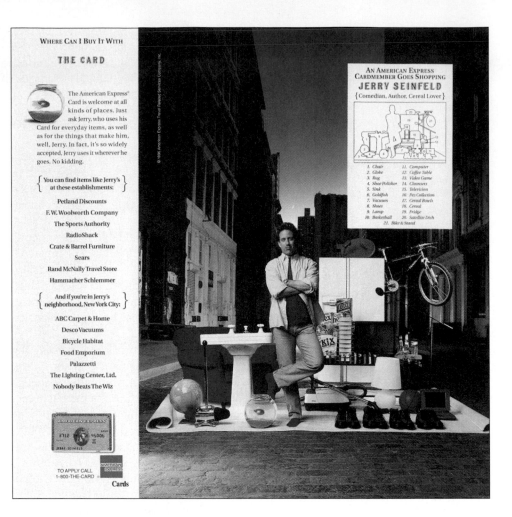

delivery or installation. Cereal companies lowered their prices to increase customer value relative to previous prices and alternative breakfast foods. Shopping costs can be lowered by making products and services easier to buy. This can be achieved by, for example, marketing in catalogs and on the Internet; reducing the number of different brands and sizes available, such as Procter & Gamble did; locating stores conveniently; accepting credit cards; having ample checkout facilities; and making products and services widely available.

As shown in Figure 1.4, providing superior customer value can lead to customer satisfaction and even delighted customers. This can lead to customer loyalty, which is desirable since keeping current customers is much more efficient than attracting new ones. Finally, customer loyalty leads to profitable, long-term relationships between customers and marketers. In sum, value-driven marketing is designed to offer better direction for organizations to achieve their objectives.

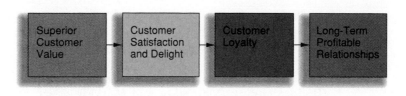

FIGURE 1.4
The Consequences of
Superior Customer Value

What Is Marketing Management?

Although other types of marketing are discussed, the major focus of this text is on for-profit, business marketing at the micromarketing level. As such, its major focus is on **marketing management** that involves what companies do and should do to deliver customer value and achieve objectives. In general, these tasks include (1) developing marketing plans and strategies and (2) executing marketing activities to implement and control them. Figure 1.5 offers an overview of the marketing management process and lists the chapters of this text devoted to discussion of them.

marketing management
The process of setting marketing goals for an organization and planning, implementing, and controlling strategies to meet them.

Developing Marketing Plans and Strategies

Marketing plans are documents created by organizations to record the results and conclusions of environmental analyses and to detail marketing strategies and their intended results. The marketing strategy portion of plans includes statements of marketing objectives, analyses of customers and markets, and suggested marketing mixes to achieve objectives. Marketing mixes are combinations of strategic tools used to create value for customers and achieve organizational goals. Marketing plans should also include budgets, forecasted sales and profits, and any other objectives that can be used to evaluate success or failure.

marketing plan
A document created by an organization to record the results and conclusions of environmental analysis and to detail the planned marketing strategy and its intended results.

FIGURE 1.5
An Overview of Marketing
Management

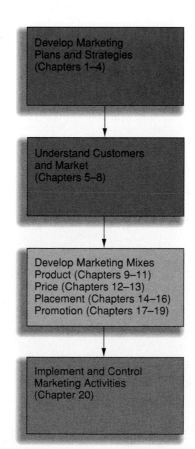

Part 1 of this text discusses value-driven marketing and approaches to analyzing environments and global opportunities. Marketing planning and its role in organizational strategy is also overviewed.

Understanding Customers and Markets

Value-driven marketing stresses the importance of understanding customers and markets. In order to do so, marketers need to research customers, divide them into segments, and select groups of them to serve. The groups selected are called target markets.

Part 2 of the text describes the tools and techniques of marketing research and offers discussions of consumer and organizational buyer behavior. It concludes with a discussion of ways to segment markets to deliver customer value.

Developing Marketing Mixes

As noted, a **marketing mix** is a combination of strategic tools used to create value for customers and achieve organizational objectives. There are four primary tools or elements in a marketing mix: product, price, placement, and promotion. As shown in Figure 1.6, these elements are sometimes called the "four P's"; a consistent mix of these elements has been found to be most effective. Their importance is evidenced by the fact that over half the book (Parts 3–6) is devoted to them.

The **product** element is concerned with what marketers offer to customers. This part of the book is divided into three areas: the management of existing products, the management of new products, and the management of services.

The **price** element concerns the amount of money or other resources marketers ask for their offerings. This part of the book discusses pricing fundamentals and management of pricing.

The **placement,** or channels of distribution, element concerns how products and services are delivered to markets to make them available for exchanges. This part of the book discusses managing channels of distribution, wholesaling and physical distribution, and retailing.

marketing mix
The strategic tools a firm uses to create value for customers and achieve organizational objectives.

product
Something offered by marketers to customers for exchange.

price
The amount of money or other resources required to exchange for products and services.

placement
The channels of distribution used to get products and services to market.

FIGURE 1.6
The Four P's

promotion
The personal and impersonal means used to inform, persuade, and remind customers about products and services.

The **promotion,** or communications, element concerns how marketers inform, persuade, and remind customers about products and services. This part of the book discusses integrated marketing communication, advertising, sales promotion, and publicity. It also provides an overview of personal selling and sales management.

Implementing and Controlling Marketing Activities

Marketing plans must be implemented in order to be effective and must be evaluated to see how well they work. While value-driven marketing stresses continuous improvement, it also recognizes the need to periodically review the overall success of plans and strategies.

Part 7 of this book discusses ways to evaluate the effectiveness of marketing activities. This is done by executing strategies, comparing their results with objectives and forecasts, and making changes to improve them.

Summary

Marketing is the process of planning and executing the conception, pricing, promotion, and distribution of ideas, goods, and services to create exchanges that satisfy individual and organizational goals. There are several types of both for-profit and nonprofit marketing. These include product, service, person, place, cause, and organization marketing. Marketing analysis can be done fruitfully at the global, national, organizational, product, and brand levels.

Traditional orientations to marketing include production, sales, and marketing. Production orientation focuses on producing goods and services efficiently, informing customers about them, and waiting for them to buy. Sales orientation focuses on producing goods and services and getting customers to buy them. Marketing orientation focuses on finding out what customers need and want, producing goods and services they say they need and want, and offering them to customers.

Value-driven marketing focuses on understanding customers and environments, creating superior value for customers, and building long-term relationships when appropriate. Value-driven marketing is based on six principles that encourage marketers to (1) focus on creating and delivering customer value; (2) offer customers greater value than competitors do; (3) change environments to improve the chances of success when appropriate; (4) use cross-functional teams when they improve the efficiency and effectiveness of marketing activities; (5) continuously improve marketing planning, implementation, and control; and (6) consider the impact of marketing activities on other stakeholders.

Customer value is the difference between customer perceptions of the benefits and costs of purchasing and using products and services. Typical customer benefits include functional, social, personal, and experiential. Typical customer costs include monetary, temporal, psychological, and behavioral.

Marketing management is what companies do and should do to deliver customer value and achieve objectives. It includes developing marketing plans and strategies, understanding customers and markets, developing marketing mixes, and implementing and controlling marketing activities.

Key Terms and Concepts

marketing (p. 6)
exchange (p. 7)
organizational buyers (p. 7)
consumers (p. 7)
needs (p. 7)
wants (p. 7)
macromarketing (p. 8)
micromarketing (p. 8)
production orientation (p. 9)
sales orientation (p. 10)
marketing orientation (p. 11)

marketing concept (p. 12)
value-driven marketing (p. 12)
direct relationships (p. 12)
indirect relationships (p. 12)
stakeholders (p. 15)
customer value (p. 15)
functional benefits (p. 17)
social benefits (p. 17)
personal benefits (p. 18)
experiential benefits (p. 18)
monetary costs (p. 19)

temporal costs (p. 19)
psychological costs (p. 19)
behavioral costs (p. 19)
transaction (shopping) costs (p. 19)
marketing management (p. 21)
marketing plan (p. 21)
marketing mix (p. 22)
product (p. 22)
price (p. 22)
placement (p. 22)
promotion (p. 23)

Review and Discussion Questions

1. Review the AMA definition of marketing and explain what it means in your own words.
2. Describe the six types of marketing and offer an example of each.

3. Explain the three traditional orientations to marketing and offer an example of a company using each one.
4. How could an in-line skates shop create superior value for its customers relative to other shops?

5. What are the six principles of value-driven marketing?
6. Name and describe the four types of benefits customers may seek in purchasing products and services. Offer examples of these benefits for various products and services.
7. Name and describe the four types of costs customers may seek to decrease in purchasing products and services. How could these costs be decreased in purchasing a home computer?
8. How could a marketer of high-quality stationery create superior value for customers?
9. Offer two examples of purchase situations in which you considered several types of benefits and costs in making your selections.
10. Briefly describe the four elements of a marketing mix.

Chapter Project

To get yourself thinking like a value-driven marketer, first start thinking about what you value. On your next visit to the supermarket, observe attempts how the store attempts to create value for you, and write them down. These attempts might include posting greeters at the door, installing electronic directories to help you locate products, offering custom bakery services, informing you of price reductions, and the like. As you write these down, make note of your response to them: Do you think they add value to this store or not? Write down which tactics create customer value for you and make written recommendations for further ways that the supermarket could provide value to you as a repeat customer.

Chapter Case   Creating Value at the Mall

Across the nation, malls have been in a slump, somehow unable to attract new business—stores willing to lease space—or the consumers they need in order to survive and profit. A mall that faced this problem was the Methuen Mall in Massachusetts, where department stores stood empty and the smaller shops could barely hang on. So the mall's owner, Metlife, decided to take a different approach to offer value to retailers and consumers. Metlife leased 150,000 square feet of space to Marvin Getman, president of an organization that creates trade shows and promotions. Getman's space was named the Valley Expo Center at the Methuen Mall.

The Expo Center planned to host events such as a boat show, a home show, an RV show, a bridal show, a craft fair, and even an indoor bazaar. Instead of traveling to major cities for these events, residents in surrounding communities would be able to get to the mall easily, enjoy free parking, have easy access to the mall food court, and relax. All of these factors would create value for consumers, and the increased foot traffic throughout the mall would create value for the mall's stores by drawing in potential shoppers.

This type of attention to what shoppers want and what retailers need has caught on at other malls as well. Some have attracted tenants that include libraries, banks, medical centers, museums, and child care centers. Mall organizers have even established programs such as daily walking clubs for senior citizens who like to get their exercise in a safe, controlled environment and who enjoy socializing with other walkers. The fact that these malls are taking on characteristics of the once-forgotten downtown is no accident: Mall developers realize that many shoppers miss the convenience and social aspect of shopping in their own downtowns. "The real winner in these types of situations is the consumer," says Mark Schoifet, spokesman for the New York-based International Council of Shopping Centers. Retailers and mall developers win, too. By taking the value approach to marketing the mall, they create exchanges that translate to profits.

Questions

1. Do you think that installing an expo center would add value in every mall? Why or why not?
2. In addition to the types of events mentioned above, what others can you think of that might add value to the mall?
3. Do you shop at a mall? Why or why not? Do the stores offer merchandise or services that you want or need? Are the temporal costs too high (that is, do you have to drive too far)? Do you get any kind of personal or experiential benefits from shopping at the mall?

Source: Tina Cassidy, "Troubled Mall Turns to Event-Type Tenant," *The Boston Globe*, p. 65. Reprinted courtesy of *The Boston Globe*.

Explore more by searching "Malls, Value" on the Web.

Environmental Analysis

CHAPTER OUTLINE

Scanning and Analyzing the Environment
  Contents of Environmental Scanning
  Scope of Environmental Scanning
The Economic Environment
  Business Cycles and Spending Patterns
  Consumer Income
The Political and Legal Environment
  Laws Affecting Marketing
  Regulation of Marketing
  Influences on Laws and Regulations
  Court Actions
  Political and Legal Factors in the Global Environment
The Social Environment
  Demographic Trends
  Social Responsibility and Ethics
The Natural Environment
  Availability of Resources
  Responsibility to the Natural Environment
The Technological Environment
  Information Technology
  Technological Factors in the Global Environment
  Technology and Value
The Competitive Environment
  Types of Competition
  Competitive Forces
  Competition in the Global Environment
Summary

LEARNING OBJECTIVES

After completing this chapter, you should be able to:

1. Explain how marketers scan and analyze the environment.
2. Describe the economic environment in terms of business cycles, spending patterns, and consumer income.
3. Describe the political and legal environment, including laws and regulations affecting marketing.
4. Summarize major demographic trends of interest to marketers.
5. Discuss the effect of cultural values on marketing.
6. Identify and evaluate ethical and social responsibility issues in marketing.
7. Define the natural environment and identify ways marketers can address concern for that environment.
8. Assess how technology affects marketing.
9. Identify competitive dimensions and their significance to marketers.

Home Health Care: M.J. Nursing Registry and Tender Care Doula Service

In different parts of the country, two women saw an opportunity: ways to provide health care to people in their own homes, for less than the cost of a hospital stay. In California, Mary Jane Stumpf founded M.J. Nursing Registry because, she says, "The more we learn about home care, the better we realize it is for patients and their families." In Ohio, Chris Morley founded Tender Care Doula Service, a service that provides postpartum care at home for new mothers. With more hospitals and insurance companies mandating early discharge of mothers and infants, Morley saw a chance to fill a health care gap. Morley can offer 20 hours of personalized home care to a new mother (four hours a day for five days) for a fraction of the cost of just one day in the hospital. That's value—not only for the patient, but also for the insurance companies that choose to use it. Morley hopes that in the near future her type of care will "become the norm in the insurance industry."

Stumpf and Morley have built their businesses on the changing market for health care. Just a decade ago, total sales in home health care were less than $10 billion; experts predict that by the turn of the century, sales will top $60 billion. Greater availability of home health services, improved technology, low cost, and in many cases, better care have all been factors in the industry's growth. Also, health care is a hot political topic—everyone agrees the system is ailing, but no one can agree on how to heal it.

In the meantime, entrepreneurs like Stumpf and Morley have taken all these factors—which comprise the environment—into account as they have developed services designed to provide the best value for their customers. "We have to care more about the patients than we do the money," notes Stumpf.

Kaye Daniels, president of Hospital Home Health Care Agency and chair of the National Association for Home Care, advises marketers interested in entering this business to stay current with regard to all the external forces that may affect the way they provide service: "Set up your business with the community in mind, and change your services as cycles in the community or industry demand." As you read this chapter, think about how environmental factors influence marketing plans, strategies, and activities.

Source: Gayle Sato Stodder, "What's Hot," *Entrepreneur*, February 1996, pp. 102, 106–107.

Explore more at www.nahc.org

Chapter Overview

External factors such as those encountered by M.J. Nursing Registry and Tender Care Doula Service are important to all kinds of organizations. Together they constitute the external environment of marketing: the economic, political and legal, social, natural, technological, and competitive factors that affect an organization's global and domestic marketing efforts.

This chapter discusses several dimensions of the external environment. In the economic environment, business conditions influence patterns of spending and production as well as the amount of money consumers have to spend. In the political and legal environment, laws, regulations, and consumer pressures influence the activities of marketers. The social environment includes the characteristics of people in markets such as their values and beliefs, including their expectations for ethical and socially responsible behavior. The natural environment includes the resources needed by and affected by organizations. The technological environment comprises the knowledge and tools available for executing organizational and marketing activities. Finally, the competitive environment consists of other organizations that can satisfy market demand. This chapter identifies the types of information marketers need to analyze about each of these dimensions.

Scanning and Analyzing the Environment

environmental scanning
The practice of tracking external changes that can affect markets, including demand for goods and services.

In an interview with *Newsweek*, Tom Magliozzi, cohost of National Public Radio's *Car Talk*, said about General Motors, "They can make a [good] car if they want to. It's just they don't know what . . . to make. . . . They have lost sight of who Americans are." His cohost and brother, Ray Magliozzi, continued, "They think all Americans live in Michigan. The hierarchy of GM is mostly men." Tom chimed in, "There just aren't that many people who want or can afford a Cadillac. So what are they wasting their time for, making a wonderful Cadillac? Make a wonderful Cavalier."[1]

Tom and Ray's strong indictment suggested that GM's managers were unaware of what customers want. In the Magliozzi brothers' minds, GM had failed in its efforts to understand customers and how they change. To do so, GM and other companies need to do environmental scanning. **Environmental scanning** is the practice of keeping track of environmental changes that can affect an organization and its markets. These changes occur in all of the dimensions of the external environment—economic, political and legal, social, natural, technological, and competitive, as shown in Figure 2.1.

Marketers should scan all dimensions of the external environment. The resulting information can help them identify opportunities to serve their markets better by creating superior value. Scanning also can help identify threats to an organization's ability to maintain an advantage and survive and prosper. The external environment not only affects what organizations can or should do, it also affects the behavior of consumers and organizational buyers. The external environment influences how these buyers assess the value of exchanges.

In the dynamic telecommunications industry, environmental scanning is essential to survival. Southern New England Telephone Company (SNET), based in Connecticut, obtains daily reports from an organization that reads every newspaper and watches every TV commercial in the state, hunting for evidence that a competitor has launched a new service. Every morning Ron Serrano, senior vice president of SNET, combines this information with fresh statistics on market share and reports from employees. SNET's objective is to counter any inroad by a competitor within 24 hours, with the ultimate goal of making SNET the supplier of every Connecticut household's communication and entertainment needs—not just phone calls, but TV, videogames, cellular phones, Internet services, movie rentals, and anything else that might travel on phone lines.[2]

FIGURE 2.1
*Dimensions of the
Marketing Environment*

TABLE 2.1
Some Questions in an
Environmental Scan by a Chain
of Quick-Printing Shops

Environments	Sample Questions
Economic	What stage of the business cycle are we in? What industries with major printing needs are doing well in the current economic climate?
Political and legal	What zoning laws affect our ability to open shops in areas of potentially high growth? Are our advertising claims legal and ethical?
Social	As the population of our community ages, will the demand for resume-printing services decline? If so, what needs will replace it? How can we foster good community relations?
Natural	What are the costs and benefits of selling environmentally friendly products such as recycled paper and double-sided copies?
Technological	What technological developments are likely to affect printing and desktop publishing?
Competitive	What other businesses offer printing services within a five-mile radius? What is their rate schedule? Which potential customers handle their own printing needs?

Contents of Environmental Scanning

Environmental scanning involves searching for changes that lead to opportunities or threats to an organization. It answers questions such as, How often does the average American family eat out? What laws are likely to affect the organization's choice of packaging? Is the demand for office space likely to increase? Are competitors planning to introduce a fax machine with more features or superior quality? Table 2.1 lists some of the questions that could be part of environmental scanning for a chain of quick-printing shops.

Scope of Environmental Scanning

Few if any organizations can afford to limit their view of the environment to the country in which they are based. Many organizations based in the United States have customers in at least a few other countries. In fact, about 70 percent of U.S. economic growth in recent years has come from exports.[3] Even organizations that market only in the United States are likely to have foreign competitors. Modern marketers need to take a global view of the external environment.

Marketers also have to broaden their scope beyond the slower-growing economies of the United States, Germany, and Japan. The fastest economic growth is occurring in parts of Asia. Economic prospects are expanding in Latin America, too. Moreover, the world is becoming more uniformly developed, creating a global economy characterized by greater diversity and faster change than in the United States.[4] Marketers cannot afford to overlook China. They must ask, as did one recent commentator, "What will happen when a fifth of mankind, already the biggest producers of large numbers of industrial and food products, really starts industrializing and exporting? When they start affording the big consumer and infrastructure goods like cars and telecom systems?"[5] Marketers who don't ask these questions may find they are cut off from an enormous share of the market and are unaware of some of their newest and biggest future competitors.

The Economic Environment

The U.S. economy has "matured." The rapid growth that followed World War II is not expected to return anytime soon. In a slow-growth economy, marketers may need to know their customers better in order to create value. In general, the **economic environment** for marketing comprises the overall economy, including business cycles and spending patterns, as well as consumer income issues.

economic environment
The overall economy, including business cycles, consumer income, and spending patterns.

Business Cycles and Spending Patterns

Learning about the economic environment helps marketers determine whether customers will be willing and able to spend money on products and services. Spending patterns are linked to the **business cycle,** or the pattern in the level of business activity that moves from prosperity to recession to recovery. Figure 2.2 shows the basic pattern of a business cycle. In general, the business cycles of the industrialized nations tend to parallel one another. However, major political upheavals can have sweeping effects on the economies of developing countries and their business cycles.

business cycle
The pattern of the level of business activity; moves from prosperity to recession to recovery.

Prosperity   During times of *prosperity,* production and employment are high. Many consumers demand more goods and services, and they spend freely not only on basics but on luxuries such as vacations, designer clothing, and entertainment. In addition, they may upgrade big-ticket items such as houses and cars. Many consumers in prosperous times want the "best" of everything and are willing to pay for it, so marketers introduce new luxury versions of products.

    Inflation—a rise in the overall price level—can occur at any stage in the business cycle, but it is typically most pronounced during periods of prosperity. During inflation, rising prices reduce the quantity of goods and services that can be purchased

inflation
A rise in the overall price level.

FIGURE 2.2
Basic Pattern of a Business Cycle

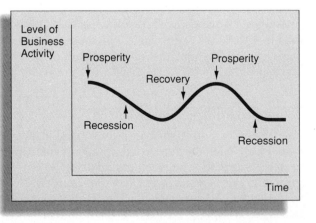

with each dollar. This is a problem for customers if their incomes do not keep pace with the rate of inflation.

Recession   During a *recession*, consumers fold their wallets and snap their purses closed; production decreases and unemployment generally rises. Decreased consumer demand leads organizational buyers to reduce their spending as well. Both types of buyers may stick to purchasing basics and look for the best deal.

Marketers of private-label (store brand) and generic goods may find they have an edge in creating value by offering good quality at less than brand-name prices. Some companies even offer "price rollbacks"—price decreases that echo previous, lower prices for individual products—or they advertise that they haven't raised a price in a certain number of years. In such ways, resourceful and creative marketers can prosper during a recession.

Recovery   While the economy is in the *recovery* stage, progressing from recession to prosperity, the level of production and employment increases. Consumers and organizational buyers may have more money to spend, but may still be reluctant to increase their purchases. They may recall the recent recession and be wary of another slump. Many consumers try harder to save money and buy few items on credit. As the economy becomes stronger, buyers begin to relax and spend more freely and prosperity can return.

Consumer Income

Although business cycles reflect the overall health of the economy, the income of individual households influences whether or not consumers buy products. Marketers are interested in three measures of consumer income: gross income, disposable income, and discretionary income.

gross income
The total amount of money earned in one year by an individual or household.

Gross Income   The total amount of money earned in one year by an individual or household is that person's or household's **gross income.** Figure 2.3 shows the median gross income for American households over several decades. "Current dollars" means the actual dollars the average household earned each year; as the figure shows, this measure of income has risen steadily. In contrast, "1993 dollars" measures the actual purchasing power of the average household; it is income adjusted for inflation. This measure has remained rather flat over the period shown. In other words, although American households are taking home more dollars now than in 1970, their purchasing power has not grown.

FIGURE 2.3
Trends in Median Household Income in the United States

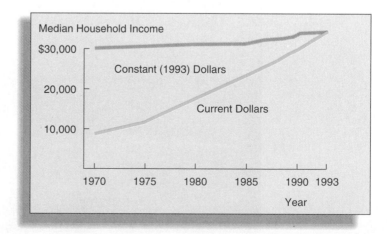

Source: U.S. Department of Commerce, *Statistical Abstract of the United States,* 115th ed. (Washington, D.C.: U.S. Government Printing Office, 1995), p. 469.

Besides showing trends over time, measures of gross income help marketers divide the market into various income groups. Marketers may be interested in targeting consumers at certain income levels.

Disposable Income   As every taxpayer knows, gross income overstates our purchasing power. Before we spend, the government taxes our income. **Disposable income** is the money an individual or household has left after paying taxes. This is the money consumers can save or spend on rent or a mortgage, groceries, clothing, and any other essentials or luxuries. Tax rates directly affect disposable income: Lower taxes mean more disposable income.

When some expenses rise or fall, people shift the way they spend their remaining disposable income. For example, as energy prices rise, people must spend more of their disposable income on gasoline, heating fuel, electricity, and so forth. This leaves less income for other purchases. Consumers may try to reduce the effect of higher energy prices by purchasing automobiles that get good gas mileage and other more energy-efficient products, from lower-wattage light bulbs to double-pane windows.

Discretionary Income   The money consumers have left to spend after paying taxes and living expenses is called **discretionary income.** While almost two-thirds of all households in the United States have some discretionary income, those making $50,000 a year or less average less than $10,000.[6] In general, discretionary income pays for vacations, hobbies, entertainment, designer clothing, jewelry, television and music, home decorations and furnishings, gifts, and the like—the extras that can make life more fun.

disposable income
The money an individual or household has left after paying taxes.

discretionary income
The money an individual or household has left after paying taxes and living expenses.

In the United States, many consumers consider a car to be a basic living expense. However, a top-of-the-line car like the 250-horsepower Oldsmobile Aurora shown in this advertisement could be a luxury for many consumers. So, General Motors is targeting this message to consumers who have the discretionary income to enjoy a car with a fine sound system—and the theater.

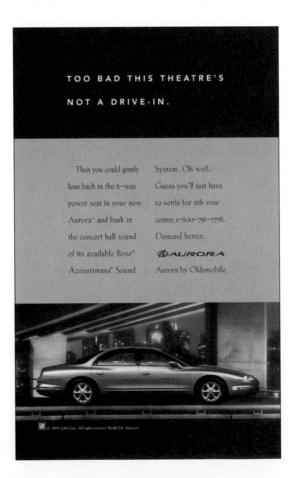

TOO BAD THIS THEATRE'S NOT A DRIVE-IN.

Then you could gently lean back in the 8-way power seat in your new Aurora® and bask in the concert hall sound of its available Bose® Acoustimass® Sound System. Oh well. Guess you'll just have to settle for 8th row center, 1-800-718-7778. Demand better.

AURORA
Aurora by Oldsmobile.

The distinction between disposable and discretionary income is somewhat arbitrary because what one person views as a necessity may be a luxury to another. In the 1970s, when only 6 percent of urban Chinese households owned a washing machine, that appliance probably was viewed as a luxury. Today, the number has risen to well over 80 percent, so most urban Chinese probably now think of a washer as a necessity.[7]

The Political and Legal Environment

political–legal environment
The laws, regulations, and political pressures affecting marketers.

An organization doesn't function strictly by its own set of rules. It has to serve its customers and listen to federal, state, and local governments, as well as special interest groups; together, these comprise the **political–legal environment.** This environment influences marketing strategies through laws, regulations, and political pressures.

Laws and regulations cover many marketing activities, including product testing, packaging, pricing, advertising, and sales to minors. Laws and regulations can limit marketing activities or be a source of opportunity for organizations that provide goods and services. Abiding by laws not only helps organizations avoid fines and lawsuits, but promotes confidence among customers as well. Marketers must be familiar with the foreign, state, and local laws and regulations in areas where they seek to do business.

Laws Affecting Marketing

Although the U.S. government exerts less control over business activities than do some other nations, it does set limits in many areas. Its first major effort to regulate business occurred in the late nineteenth and early twentieth centuries. These laws were designed to prevent industry power from being concentrated among a handful of giant firms and included the Sherman Antitrust Act (1890), the Clayton Act (1914), and the Federal Trade Commission Act (1914). During the Great Depression, Congress focused on protecting independent merchants from overwhelming competition by large chain stores. It did so by passing the Robinson-Patman Act (1936) and the Miller-Tydings Resale Price Maintenance Act (1937). Beginning in the 1950s, Congress placed more emphasis on laws designed to protect consumers. These laws included the National Traffic and Safety Act (1958), the Fair Packaging and Labeling Act (1967), and the Consumer Product Safety Act (1972). Table 2.2 lists these and other federal laws that govern marketing.

The idea that consumers would benefit from industry deregulation became popular in the late 1970s and early 1980s. To lift regulations on specific industries, Congress passed laws such as the Airline Deregulation Act of 1978 and the Depository Institutions Deregulation and Monetary Control Act of 1980. Deregulation has reshaped the external environment for telecommunications repeatedly. In Connecticut, Southern New England Telephone once had an edge over AT&T because SNET was allowed to offer both local and long-distance phone service, but AT&T had to stay out of the business of providing local phone service. Now AT&T, with its massive resources, may compete with SNET to provide all types of telephone service. Furthermore, cable TV operators have begun preparing to offer phone service as well as television programming on their own cables and fiber optic lines.[8] Such changes are the reasons SNET does environmental scanning to adjust its marketing strategy.

Besides federal laws, marketers must be up-to-date on relevant state and local laws. For example, Maine has banned the sale of individual juice boxes. A Minneapolis ordinance requires that all packaging be biodegradable or returnable. Consumers can buy fireworks in New Hampshire, but only if they live elsewhere; they cannot buy fireworks to use in New Hampshire.

T A B L E 2.2
Some Major Federal Laws
Affecting Marketing

Laws That Seek to Promote Fair Competition

Sherman Antitrust Act (1890)	Prohibits monopolies and unreasonable restraint of trade
Clayton Act (1914)	Prohibits actions that substantially limit competition, including exclusive dealing and the tying of a sale to the buyer's promise to buy only from that seller
Federal Trade Commission Act (1914)	Prohibits unfair competition and deceptive trade practices in interstate commerce
Wheeler-Lea Amendment (1938)	Prohibits unfair and deceptive practices, whether or not they damage competitors

Laws That Limit Product Strategy

Pure Food and Drug Act (1906)	Controls the quality and labeling of food and drugs in interstate commerce
Child Protection Act (1966)	Prohibits sale of hazardous toys
Fair Packaging and Labeling Act (1967)	Requires that labels on consumer products identify the product, the supplier's name and address, and (where relevant) the serving size
Consumer Product Safety Act (1972)	Created the Consumer Product Safety Commission to set safety standards for many consumer goods
Magnuson-Moss Warranty/ FTC Improvement Act (1975)	Authorizes the Federal Trade Commission to make rules for consumer warranties and class-action lawsuits
Nutrition Labeling and Education Act (1990)	Requires that the labels on most food products provide detailed nutrition information.

Laws That Limit Pricing Strategy

Robinson-Patman Act (1936)	Prohibits price discrimination under various circumstances
Miller-Tydings Resale Price Maintenance Act (1937)	Exempts interstate fair-trade (price fixing) agreements from complying with antitrust requirements
Automobile Information Disclosure Act (1958)	Requires manufacturers to post suggested retail prices on cars
Consumer Goods Pricing Act (1975)	Prohibits certain pricing agreements between retailers and manufacturers

Laws That Limit Placement Strategy

Flammable Fabrics Act (1953)	Prohibits shipment in the United States of any clothing or material that can easily ignite
Fair Credit Reporting Act (1970)	Requires that a consumers' credit reports contain only accurate, relevant, and recent information
Motor Carrier Act and Staggers Rail Act (1980)	Permits trucking and rail firms to negotiate rates and services

Laws That Limit Promotion Strategy

Federal Cigarette Labeling and Advertising Act (1967)	Requires cigarette ads and packages to carry a health warning
Truth in Lending Act (1968)	Requires that lenders state the true cost of a loan, including statement of the annual percentage rate in advertisements
Public Health Cigarette Smoking Act (1971)	Prohibits broadcast advertisements of tobacco products
Children's Television Act (1990)	Limits the amount of advertising that may be shown during children's television programs.

Voters also can pass laws affecting marketers. In state and local elections, voters can decide such issues as when and where liquor may be sold, whether stores may stay open on holidays or Sundays, whether special taxes should be levied on cigarettes and gasoline, and where billboards may be placed.

Regulation of Marketing

regulations
Rules written by government agencies that have the force of law.

When legislatures pass a law, they may set up an agency to enforce that law. The agency then writes **regulations,** which are rules that have the force of law. Thus, even though regulations are prepared by the executive rather than the legislative branch of government, marketers are legally bound to abide by them. Regulations can apply to advertising, manufacturing, distribution, pricing, sales, and other areas of business.

Federal, State, and Local Regulations   At the federal level, many agencies regulate business. For example, the Federal Trade Commission (FTC) seeks to prevent "unfair methods of competition" and "unfair or deceptive acts or practices," and the Food and Drug Administration (FDA) regulates the distribution and sale of foods and medicines to ensure that they are safe and marketed honestly.

Regulation is also conducted at the state and local levels. For instance, zoning laws limit the locations where stores may be built. Sometimes federal and state regulations conflict. For example, the Massachusetts Department of Environmental Protection's definition of wetlands differs from federal guidelines, making it difficult to determine whether a piece of property may be developed commercially.

Many organizations complain that extensive regulation is burdensome. Before the FDA allowed Quaker Oats to print a claim on its oatmeal packages that the product could reduce heart disease when consumed as part of a low-fat diet, the agency required over two decades of research, including three dozen studies on humans.

Furthermore, this decision was the first time the FDA had allowed a health claim on a food product.[9] Is such a process worthwhile even when a company gains the desired FDA approval? Perhaps not, since competitors can use the health claim if they market the product, whether or not they contributed to the research.

Television is an industry where the results of self-regulation and legislation are criticized. Children in the United States spend more of their time staring at a TV screen than attending school, so the industry has a powerful capacity to teach, inform, inspire, and entertain them. The Children's TV Act of 1990 was passed to control and improve TV programming for children. Yet, in many instances industry members have only followed the letter of the law and provided the minimum educational programming needed to renew licenses. Recently, in an attempt to further regulate the industry, a law was passed that requires stations to provide educational programming for three hours per week.

Self-Regulation   In many industries, companies have recognized that they have more control over their operations if they regulate themselves so voters and legislators do not step in and set limits. To regulate themselves, organizations use industry groups to set and enforce standards for ethical behavior and for dealing with customers. The Better Business Bureau and the American Medical Association, for example, lack legal authority but are nonetheless powerful regulators.

An organization or industry may work alone or in conjunction with other groups to establish self-regulations and promote a positive, responsible image. Anheuser-Busch, which markets Budweiser beer, works with the National Commission Against Drunk Driving to sponsor ads that promote responsible drinking.

Some people charge that self-regulation is like asking the fox to guard the chicken coop, and certainly abuses do occur. However, self-regulation by those who know the industry intimately can be both efficient and effective. An industry that monitors itself closely can promote quality in its products, processes, and people.

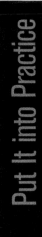

Use Your Consumer Rights

Take yourself on a shopping trip (although you don't have to buy anything). Before you go, choose an item for which you want to shop—it could be a computer, a can of paint, a box of laundry detergent, a CD player, or anything else. As you shop for the item, note the following: Are there enough items from which to choose to suit your wants? Are there instructions or specifications available for you to read, or is there a knowledgeable salesperson nearby to answer questions about the product? Is there a phone number for complaints printed on the package, or will the store or salesperson accept and handle complaints? Can you be assured that the product is safe when used properly?

Answering these questions as you shop not only helps you become a better consumer, it also will help you become a better marketer. If you think in terms of fulfilling consumers' wants and needs as a marketer, then you will be thinking in terms of creating value.

Influences on Laws and Regulations

Legislators and regulators who develop laws and regulations are also influenced by external forces. For example, public pressure encouraged legislators to trim defense spending, which in turn forced defense contractors to adjust their marketing mixes to appeal more to buyers in the private sector. Primary sources of influence in the political/legal sphere include lobbyists and consumer interest groups.

Lobbyists   Because laws and regulations can be far reaching, individuals and organizations often try to influence government officials. Yet it's not practical to call officials every time an important bill comes up for a vote. Rather, organizations use lobbyists to represent their views. Lobbyists represent big corporations, industry trade groups, and public-interest organizations of all kinds, from the American Medical Association, which represents physicians, to the American Association of Retired Persons, which was formed to represent people age 50 and older.

consumerism
A social force intended to protect consumers by exerting legal, moral, and economic pressures on the business community.

Consumer Interest Groups   Consumers and consumer interest groups are important forces in the political–legal environment. **Consumerism** encompasses a range of activities—including legal, moral, and economic pressures on businesses—intended to protect consumers. Consumerism took a solid hold in the American consciousness during the 1960s. In 1962, President John F. Kennedy spelled out four consumer rights:

1. *The right to choose freely*—Consumers should have the freedom to choose from among a variety of goods and services.

2. *The right to be informed*—Consumers should be informed about products so that they can be responsible buyers.

3. *The right to be heard*—Consumers should have the opportunity to express their complaints to sellers and government regulatory agencies.

4. *The right to be safe*—Consumers should be confident that goods and services they purchase are not harmful with normal use. Products should be designed so that they can easily be used safely.

Consumers often consider these rights to be a minimal standard of acceptable marketing activities (see "Put It Into Practice: Use Your Consumer Rights").

Perhaps no single person has done more to influence marketing by crusading for consumer rights than Ralph Nader. The founder or supporter of more than 30 separate consumer interest groups, Nader actively campaigned for legislation regulating auto and highway safety, insurance rates, water safety, pension rights, responsible

The Bootlegging of American Products Overseas

Knockoffs—facsimiles (reasonable or otherwise) of products, from clothes to toys to cheeseburgers—have probably been around for as long as there have been products. Thus, there are trademark, copyright, and patent laws protecting creators and inventors of products. These protections are part of the marketer's legal environment; they also may be part of the political and economic environment.

Many travelers can attest to seeing knockoffs of prestigious or popular products around the world. In Bangkok and Nairobi, street vendors offer fake Gucci handbags and Lacoste polo shirts; on a New York street, anyone can buy a knockoff Rolex watch for 10 or 20 dollars; in Belize, patrons can enjoy an evening at the Hard Rock Cafe, if they don't mind the cafe's inauthenticity.

The Chinese and Indian governments take knockoffs a step further: Both have state-run bootleg industries—music production in China and generic drugs in India. Needless to say, none of the original creators, inventors, or producers of these products (protected by law in their own countries) has received any royalty or other fee for the fakes.

Until recently, a major exception has been Mexico. In its desire to win the North American Free Trade Agreement, the Mexican government has instituted tough laws prohibiting bootlegging and has conducted much-publicized raids of suspicious groups or locations. But the severe recession in Mexico has resulted in an increase in the number of products—and previously legitimate companies—that have become part of the Mexican black market. Officials have seized everything from counterfeit computer software to video tapes of movies such as "Batman Forever" and "Apollo 13." Now some of the companies that stand to lose revenues to the fakes—Disney, Louis Vuitton, and others—have launched an effort called "Operation Amigo," in which their own detectives search around Mexico for culprits. Do you think this type of sleuthing by companies is a necessary part of marketing, or do you think that marketers should simply take knockoffs into consideration as part of their environmental scanning? Why or why not? Do you think that copyright, patent, and trademark laws should hold up from one country to another? Why or why not?

Source: "False Friends," *The Economist,* January 13, 1996, p. 66.

Explore more by searching "Knockoffs" on the Web.

genetics, and occupational safety. Some of his better-known organizations include the Public Safety Research Institute, Center for Auto Safety, Public Interest Research Groups, Public Citizen, Inc., and Citizens Television System, Inc.[10] Although Nader is popular among the general public, he has not escaped controversy since lawyers who earn considerable income from personal injury lawsuits are among his strongest supporters. Still, Nader has raised the consciousness of consumers and marketers in the United States.

Consumerism dovetails nicely with a commitment to creating value for customers. Value creation requires marketers to communicate truthfully and offer products that are safe, nutritious, nonpolluting, and otherwise beneficial. Marketers with a value orientation listen carefully to customers so they can anticipate and meet wants and needs.

Court Actions

Not only do the legislative and executive branches of government affect marketing. So does the judicial branch. Its impact occurs through the interpretation judges have for laws and regulations. For example, the U.S. Supreme Court upheld a federal law forbidding ads for lotteries in states that ban them.[11] If the court had instead affirmed the lower-court ruling against this law, lottery officials would have had more freedom in advertising.

Political and Legal Factors in the Global Environment

Global marketers are affected by agreements between countries and by the laws in countries in which they operate (see "You Decide: The Bootlegging of American Products Overseas"). Some of the more vital political and legal factors in the global environment are international trade agreements. For example, the North American Free Trade Agreement (NAFTA) is designed to drop trade barriers among Canada, the United States, and Mexico through means such as the elimination of tariffs. Similarly, the European Union (EU) is designed to reduce trade barriers among member nations.

In some cases, foreign markets may be attractive because they have less restrictive laws and regulations. For example, although the U.S. government strictly limits health claims marketers can make about foods, other countries allow and even encourage such claims. The Japanese government encourages development of foods said to deliver special health benefits, and it has devised a symbol for labeling these as Foods for Special Health Use. These so-called functional foods include bottled enriched "vita drinks" and a chewing gum that contains compounds thought to prevent cavities.[12]

The Social Environment

social environment
The people in a society and their values, beliefs, and behaviors.

The **social environment** of marketing is made up of the people in a society and their values, beliefs, and behaviors. Marketers describe this environment in terms of who the people are (their ages, incomes, hometowns, and so forth) and the characteristics of their culture. Changes in the social environment, whether subtle or dramatic, can present marketers with new opportunities and challenges.

Demographic Trends

demographics
The study of the chracteristics of a human population.

To describe the social environment, marketers begin with basic demographic data. **Demographics** is the study of the characteristics of a human population. These characteristics include age, birth rate, death rate, marital status, education, religious affiliation, ethnic background, immigration, geographical distribution, and so forth. Typically, marketers combine data on several demographic characteristics. Thus, it isn't enough to know only how many people moved to San Diego in a given year. Rather, marketers can better identify and serve target markets if they know how many of those people are retired, are single parents, or are able to afford restaurant meals.

Marketers use demographic data from a number of sources. Government agencies, including the U.S. Bureau of the Census, the National Center for Health Statistics, the Bureau of Labor Statistics, and the Social Security Administration, are major suppliers of data on the U.S. population. Private organizations such as the Roper Organization and the Gallup Poll provide valuable demographic statistics as well. Publications such as *American Demographics* also offer useful demographic information. A large organization may employ its own demographers to help analyze its markets.

Marketers use demographics to analyze markets, learn about customers, and create value for them. Pinpointing changes or trends in a population is vital to marketing strategy.

Diversity in the United States   The population of the United States has never been uniform. Even before the first Europeans arrived, the land was populated by many tribes and nations. Today, however, the diversity of the population is greater than ever (see "Marketing Movers & Shakers: Robert Johnson/Black Entertainment Television"). Immigrants speaking different languages and bringing different values continue to arrive in the United States.

Geographic location, age, race, sex, and levels of income and education are just a few of the ways in which people differ. For example, between 1990 and 2000, the number of African-American households in the United States was expected to grow five times faster than the number of white Anglo households, and the number of Hispanic households was expected to grow even faster.[13] Thus, marketers who think only in terms of white households could miss out on these growth markets.

The changing composition of the American family also interests marketers. During the 1950s, 70 percent of American families consisted of a stay-at-home mother, a working father, and one or two children. By the middle 1990s, less than 20 percent of American households fit this mold.[14] Today's families include blended families (the merging of two families through a second marriage or relationship), single-parent families, adoptive or foster parent families, and gay families. Even the composition of single-parent families is changing; although most children of divorce live with their mothers, men are being awarded custody more often. Moreover, although 60 percent

Robert Johnson/ Black Entertainment Television

Smart marketers recognize the changing face of the United States: Diversity among consumers is one of the most important things for a marketer to consider when scanning the environment. Over a decade ago, Robert Johnson, founder and head of Black Entertainment Television (BET), realized that the infant cable industry did not have the type of diverse programming it needed to enter urban markets. He decided to offer it to them. Lack of existing competition made his entry into the market relatively easy.

Since its inception, BET has had great success. It was the second African-American-controlled company ever to go public on the stock market, and its market value is over $500 million. Johnson has been able to sink some of BET's profits into new ventures: a jazz cable channel, a venture with Microsoft, magazines including a new weekend entertainment guide, and a pay-per-view service. Johnson's new goal is the silver screen. He has already produced a "small," critically acclaimed film called "Once Upon a Time . . . When We Were Colored"; now he wants to go after the huge, African-American moviegoing public in a big way. (African Americans comprise 25 percent of all movie audiences.) Johnson also wants to build the first black-controlled movie studio.

However, there are some obstacles to Johnson's entry into the movie market. First, he is a Hollywood outsider, which does not deter him. Second, big-name stars like Denzel Washington and Whoopi Goldberg have declined to be involved with Johnson's company, partly because they fear productions will be low budget and partly because Johnson hasn't been

able to tell them exactly which projects he plans to pursue. And BET hasn't built its success—or its reputation—on original dramatic programming; instead, it has relied on music videos, infomercials, and the like.

Perhaps a situation like this requires a little give and take. Johnson could loosen his purse strings a bit to attract the stars; the stars, in turn, could lend their talent, names, and reputations to an enterprise (for a bit less money) that, if it succeeds, could create value not only for consumers but also for shareholders. How about Hollywood itself? Movie moguls would do well to scan their environments. Competition in the form of BET, like diversity itself, is here to stay.

Source: Johnnie L. Roberts, "Trials of a Black Mogul," *Newsweek,* April 1, 1996, pp. 71-72. Caroline Waxler, "Bob Johnson's Brainchild," *Forbes* April 22, 1996, pp. 98–100; Rich Brown and Don West, "Bob Johnson on the Information Revolution: All Ahead Slow," *Broadcasting and Cable,* July 3, 1995, pp. 16–19.

Explore more at www.betnetworks.com

of single fathers are divorced, 25 percent have never been married, creating still another category of single-parent family.[15]

Another important shift has occurred in the age distribution of the U.S. population. The baby boom generation, people born between 1946 and 1964, is so large that roughly half the population was under 28 in 1970, and almost half are expected to be 40 or older in the year 2010.[16] As this group ages, the demand for various products, such as houses, child care, and mutual funds, changes. In addition, many marketers have focused on the younger generation—sometimes called baby busters or Generation X—because the typical member of this age group has not yet sacrificed discretionary income to house payments and the expenses of raising children.

As illustrated in Figure 2.4, the geographical distribution of the U.S. population is shifing as well. During the 1980s, the population grew fastest in the western and southwestern states, with the southeastern states close behind. In contrast, the population of a few states actually fell. Some marketers use these data to engage in *regional marketing,* which focuses on the specific tastes, needs, and interests of residents of a particular area. Regional marketing can target a broad region such as Thailand or the southern United States, or it can be more focused—say, to encompass only residents of Minneapolis or even of particular neighborhoods.

Demographics help identify patterns of diversity so that marketers can target their goods and services appropriately. Marketers also need to appreciate diversity issues in order to work effectively with their customers. Especially in the case of companies that market services, a diverse customer base may want to receive services from people they identify as being like themselves. MacTemps, which provides temporary

F I G U R E   2.4 *Population Changes: 1990–2010*

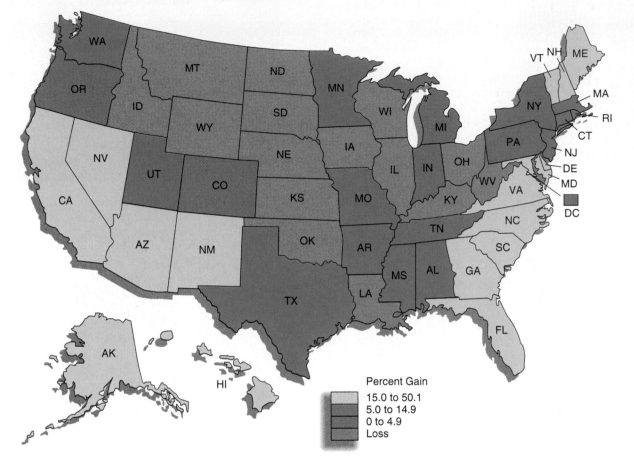

Source: U.S. Bureau of the Census, Current Population Reports, Series P–25, No. 1053, *Projections of the Population of States by Age, Sex, and Race: 1990 to 2010* (Washington, D.C.: U.S. Government Printing Office, 1990), p. 13.

workers, has two Miami clients that work with it only because it has an assignment manager who is fluent in Spanish.[17]

Global Trends   The demographic characteristics of foreign countries are important to global marketers. For instance, the population size of the Pacific Rim—Asia and Australia—makes it an attractive market for many U.S. firms. Nearly 2 billion people live in Asia, and although many live in poverty, it is estimated that by the year 2000 more than 110 million (excluding those in Japan) will have household incomes of more than $10,000.[18] This income is low compared to many industrialized countries, yet in some Asian countries, such as Nepal, average annual household income is less than $200.[19]

Social Responsibility and Ethics

While the social environment influences the success of marketing strategies, strategies can also have an impact on the social environment. For example, marketers who encouraged consumers to buy personal computers and modems for home use helped create a social environment in which people consider it normal to carry on electronic "conversations" with individuals they cannot see and have never met in person. Some people obtain information and meet people they might not have had access to in more traditional ways. On the downside, children may be able to participate in conversations that are inappropriate for them, and people of all ages risk being tricked by con artists taking advantage of their anonymity.

Do marketers who sell computers and software have obligations to protect the people who buy and use their products? Is an organization obligated to behave only in

This ad is one of a series in which State Farm Insurance enhances community relations by announcing a winner of its Good Neighbor Award. In this case, language arts teacher Linda Fisk of West Palm Beach, Florida, won an award for her innovative use of video equipment to build students' skills and enthusiasm. State Farm also gave $5,000 in Mrs. Fisk's name to her school, U. B. Kinsey/Palmview Elementary School. Through this socially responsible marketing, State Farm benefits the community and communicates its own commitment to the communities it serves.

ways that support the values of the cultures it interacts with? These questions raise issues of social responsibility and ethics.

Social Responsibility   Many economists maintain that the primary responsibility of a business is to earn profits for its owners. Value-driven marketing adds that a business should do this by creating value for customers and interacting appropriately with other stakeholders. **Social responsibility** is the term used to describe an organization's obligations to society.

social responsibility
Concern for the social consequences of a person's or institution's acts as they may affect the interests of others.

One marketer who acts in a socially responsible manner is Joseph Crilley, owner of Crilley's Circle Tavern in Bringantine, New Jersey. Crilley wanted to give his customers an alternative to driving after they drank at his bar, so he bought and fixed up an old bus to provide free shuttle service. The bus is available to pick up customers if they wish and to take them where they want to go after they leave Circle Tavern. This protects not only the customers, but also others who are on the road when they could be driving. An additional benefit is that the bus, which bears the tavern's name, generates plenty of publicity when it is parked outside or cruising the streets. It even gets used in the daytime, occasionally shuttling schoolchildren and senior citizens to activities around town.[20]

Social responsibility is in the organization's best interests in the long run. Potential customers will be more likely to buy from an organization if it looks after their welfare. Potential customers who have trouble choosing from among competing products may well buy from the company they most respect. Ben & Jerry's assumes a link between social responsibility and business performance when it defines its "marketing emphasis" as "a companywide focus on community involvement and its status as a socially responsible business."[21]

Social responsibility can involve ceasing negative activity or taking positive action, such as consumer education, partnerships with community service agencies, or funding for special projects. Positive actions not only benefit the community, they also can enhance community relations and reinforce a positive image. The organization's efforts are most likely to lead to good community relations when they are related to its strengths and involve the community in some way. The Home Depot chain of home improvement stores, based in Atlanta, focuses its corporate giving on community programs to build and renovate low-cost housing. Besides contributing money, the company encourages its employees to volunteer their time to these projects.[22]

cause-related marketing
Marketing designed to promote a cause or an issue.

Some organizations undertake **cause-related marketing,** in the communities they serve. For example, charitable donations can be tied directly to the sales of specific products. Cause-related marketing is popular among marketers because it sets up a win-win situation. Products are promoted, and sales often increase. In addition, customers receive value, members of the community benefit from the donations, and community relations are enhanced.

Being a responsible member of the community can be more complex for organizations that operate in more than one country. Organizations need to know what global communities expect or want and must find ways to offer value to them.

The increasing global presence of U.S. companies has led them to make charitable contributions in other countries. For example, Alcoa worked with local officials in southern Brazil to build a sewage plant, and IBM donated computer expertise and equipment to the National Parks Foundation of Costa Rica to develop strategies to preserve rain forests.[23]

ethics
The moral principles and values that govern the way an individual or group conducts its activities.

marketing ethics
The principles, values, and standards of conduct considered appropriate for marketers.

Ethical Issues in Marketing   The acceptance of social responsibility is based in part on the view that it is in the organization's best interests, but the issue is also an ethical one. **Ethics** are the moral principles and values that govern the way an individual or group conducts its activities. **Marketing ethics** are the principles, values, and standards of conduct considered appropriate for marketers.

Marketers and other business people often struggle to find solutions to ethical problems. One reason is that ethical standards vary from one person to another and from one culture to another. Operating in a global marketplace thus makes ethical issues even more complicated. Also, available courses of action often contain activities that can hurt some stakeholders and help others. Even when people agree on what is the most ethical course of action, that alternative may be unduly costly—especially to the owner of a start-up company with little cash or to an employee trying to hold onto a job.

Public perception of business people is sometimes negative. Marketers reinforce this view whenever they bend the rules, favoring quick sales over long-term relationships. By obeying the law marketers can avoid actions that have legal penalties, but this may not be sufficient to avoid unethical actions. Conversely, actions that some marketers might consider ethical, such as arranging with competitors to avoid a major price increase, might violate the law. As a practical matter, however, most ethical behavior is legal.

Ethical principles are important for marketers from both a moral and a business standpoint. Pinchas Fleischman makes this point in telling about a sales call he made early in his career. He was demonstrating a garbage-packer truck to a prospective customer, a refuse contractor. The contractor asked several questions to which Fleischman did not know the answer; despite his growing conviction that he was losing the sale, Fleischman simply replied that he did not know but would call and get an answer. As he prepared to leave, the contractor stopped him, saying, "Your competition didn't know the answers to my questions either, but they tried to bluff their way through. You were honest. After you call me with the answers to my questions, order me this exact model you demonstrated."[24]

Ethical issues arise throughout the marketing process, from research to control of marketing strategies. With regard to marketing research, organizations particularly need to avoid deception. Unethical tactics include disguising sales attempts as surveys and failing to protect the privacy of people in a study. Ethical issues can also arise with regard to all elements of the marketing mix: the product itself, its price, its placement, and its promotion.

Product Issues   An important ethical issue related to products is their quality. A common complaint about product quality is planned obsolescence. Obsolescence refers to products wearing out or becoming obsolete. Planned obsolescence means the producer built the products not to last, at least not as long as buyers would like to use them. Computers are a notable example of products that become obsolete quickly because more powerful models become available. To satisfy customers, should marketers offer computers that wear out in the short time it takes to become technologically obsolete, thereby holding down the cost so customers can afford to replace them? Should computer companies make longer-lasting products and provide ways to continually upgrade them? These are just two alternatives marketers consider in trying to create value and avoid criticism of planned obsolescence.

Another product-related issue is whether to market products that pose a danger. Of course, there are dangerous or risky ways to use almost any product—after all, eating too many vegetables can give you a stomachache. But some products may pose risks even when used as intended. In one scare, a book titled *Our Stolen Future* claimed that a variety of chemicals used in applications from electrical transformers to plastics to fungicides mimic hormones, interfere with hormonal functions, and may cause problems in reproduction and brain development.[25] How can marketers weigh the benefits of such products against their potential costs? What if buyers want the products in spite of the damage they might do?

Packaging decisions, too, have ethical implications. In a highly competitive market, it may be tempting to offer packages that seem to contain more than those of competitors, even when they really don't. Large packages take up more shelf space, so they may get more attention and look as if they offer more of the products. The label on the package also may be deceptive. Printing pictures of fruit along with the words "All natural" on a label does not turn sugar water inside a carton into fruit juice. Is it ethical to associate such a product with fruit?

price fixing
Reaching an agreement with competitors about what price to charge.

Pricing Issues   In many instances, pricing is regulated by law. For example, **price fixing,** or reaching an agreement with competitors about what price to charge, is illegal. Some states require retailers to display their return policies, including whether they offer cash refunds or store credit.

Placement Issues   The relationship between a manufacturer and its resellers is vital, and high standards of ethical conduct are important. The way companies in a marketing channel exercise control over one another can have ethical implications. For example, is it ethical for a supermarket to demand payment for shelf space from a supplier? Is it ethical for a brand name manufacturer to require a retailer to carry the firm's entire product line in order to get access to the particular item it wants?

Promotion Issues   The ethics of promotion strategy are often tied to the ethics of product strategy, particularly in the case of false or exaggerated claims about a product. Other unethical practices include bribes and kickbacks given by salespeople and "bait and switch" advertising. This last practice involves advertising that a product is for sale at a low price, then claiming that it is unavailable and offering a higher-priced item in its place when customers seek to buy it.

Advertising aimed at children—particularly television commercials—has been under intense scrutiny during the last two decades. Believing that children are highly influenced by advertising, the children's advocacy group Action for Children's Television has argued for laws reducing advertising time during children's television programs and has fought programs that are clearly tied to commercial products. In general, unethical marketing messages may result in one-time sales, but they are less likely to build long-term relationships.

People who don't buy a product should benefit from it too.

Let's make things better

PHILIPS

The Natural Environment

From a marketer's perspective, the **natural environment** involves the natural resources available to or affected by the organization.

Air, water, minerals, plants, and animals all may be part of an organization's natural environment. The organization may use some of these resources to produce its goods or services. Its ability to provide goods and services may be influenced by the weather, as well. Moreover, the organization's activities may affect the natural environment by depleting or replenishing resources and by adding to or cleaning up pollution.

natural environment
The natural resources available to or affected by the organization.

Availability of Resources

To market newspapers, publishers have traditionally relied on paper and ink; to market cheeseburgers requires beef, cheese, and buns. Both products require natural resources to produce them. The availability of a product at the price the organization charges may be related to the availability of certain resources. Resources may be in short supply because demand for products exceeds the capacity to produce them. The organization may experience a shortage because the supply of a natural resource is running out, or it is difficult to obtain the resource because of an embargo, a war, or political or economic sanctions.

When supply of resources is limited, marketers may respond in a variety of ways. They may develop a marketing mix for selling less of the product but at a higher price. In some cases, marketers even engage in **demarketing,** an effort to reduce demand for a product. A common use of demarketing is the effort by many electric utilities to provide their customers with tips on how to save energy: insulate their home, use fans instead of air conditioners, install more efficient lighting. Not only do these demarketing efforts help reduce demand, they also may enhance the utility's public image as an organization concerned about the natural environment.

In some cases, the organization's marketing and other activities can influence the long-run availability of resources. For example, a logging organization can plant new trees and a catalog company can select recycled paper. An organization may save on expenses as well as fuel consumption by arranging for its sales force to sell over the phone rather than in person.

demarketing
A marketing strategy used to decrease the consumption of a product.

Responsibility to the Natural Environment

Marketers have found environmental consciousness is often both necessary and profitable. At many organizations, these efforts include **green marketing,** or marketing efforts designed to meet customers' desire to protect the environment.

Green marketing can benefit an organization in various ways. First, it appeals to the values of many people. Some people feel better buying a detergent or air condi-

green marketing
Marketing efforts designed to minimize negative effects on the physical environment or to improve its quality.

Many organizations that practice green marketing use recycled materials in their products. Ford Motor Company's Sheldon Road plant in Plymouth, Michigan, was the first automotive plant to use 25 percent post-consumer materials in all of its plastic products. The Sheldon Road employees shown here are posing with recycled bottle caps, plastic strapping, and cotton bale wrap that are recycled into material used to make about 65 different parts.

tioner that is environmentally friendly. Organizational customers may "buy green" for other reasons as well. One reason is to save money otherwise spent to dispose of waste, mail catalogs or brochures to uninterested people, and ship bulky packages. Another motivation is the need to comply with environmental laws.

Organizations that practice green marketing try to ensure that their products are helpful to the environment or at least cause little or no harm. They may make recyclable goods or use recycled materials in products. Carmakers increasingly are doing both. Ford Motor Company claimed that over three-quarters of its Taurus and Sable cars were made of readily recyclable components. In addition, the protective seat covers used at Taurus assembly plants are made of 40 percent recycled plastic; when the cars arrive at dealerships, the seat covers are shipped back to the factories for reuse. Volvo's Dutch-built S40 sedan is 90 percent recyclable and designed for easy dismantling and sorting.[26]

Green marketers also seek to package goods in ways that have less impact on the environment, using recycled packaging or simply less packaging. The choice is not always simple, however. Containers made of recycled plastic are more likely to break, so manufacturers have to use more of the material, making the containers heavier and requiring more energy to transport them.[27]

A product friendly to the environment does not necessarily command a higher price. According to one study, 93 percent of adults said a product's environmental impact was important to them in making purchase decisions, but two-thirds said environmentally friendly products should not cost more.[28]

Green marketing seeks to ship goods with a minimal amount of energy and to reuse packing materials. Furniture maker Herman Miller used a waste prevention team to evaluate its shipping practices. The team determined that 80 percent of the products could be shipped in movers' blankets rather than complete cardboard and plastic packaging.[29]

Many consumers are concerned about the amount of paper devoted to mailing catalogs and advertisements. Thus, green marketers look for ways to limit their mailings without sacrificing sales. Hanna Andersson, a mail-order supplier of cotton children's clothing, offered a gift certificate to customers who reported that they received duplicate catalogs. Patagonia limits the number of catalog mailings per year.

Given the demand for "green" products, it is tempting to position products as beneficial to the environment. However, exaggerated or vague claims can mislead customers. Moreover, such behavior may violate laws and regulations, including guidelines developed by the Federal Trade Commission for green marketing.[30] Keeping claims modest not only avoids disappointing customers, it also is less likely to attract one-upsmanship from competitors.

The Technological Environment

Scientific knowledge, research, inventions and innovations that result in new or improved goods and services all make up the **technological environment** of marketing. Technological developments provide important opportunities to improve customer value.

technological environment
Scientific knowledge, innovations, and inventions that result from research.

When organizations fail to keep up with technological change, technology becomes a threat. IBM's dominance of the market for large mainframe computers did not spare the company from posting a huge loss when customers found they could get all the computing power they needed from personal computers.[31] To succeed in this volatile industry, computer makers innovate continually.

Keeping up with technological developments is especially important for marketers who serve business customers. Organizational buyers may rely on technological innovations for their very survival in competitive markets.

Information Technology

In recent years, many of the most dramatic technological advances have involved the exchange of information. Some people say that we live in an information age. A variety of computer, telecommunications, and other firms are constructing a kind of information superhighway. "Traveling" this superhighway with computers, telephone hookups, satellite transmissions, and cellular devices, consumers and organizations can send and receive text, pictures, video, data, and sounds.

Internet
A linked, global network of computers at government agencies, universities, businesses, and Internet access providers.

The Internet   Just a few years ago, the future of the information superhighway was thought to be interactive television, but consumers have since decided they can get more for their money from a computer. Many of them are using their modems to dial up the **Internet**—an extensive global network of computers at government agencies, universities, businesses, and Internet access providers, all linked by telephone lines. The Internet was once limited to academicians and government employees sharing technological information, but it has grown explosively in terms of the number of users and the kinds of information available; the Internet now links more than 50 million people from 150 countries.[32] Its popularity is due in part to the fact that access requires only a personal computer with the right software and modem plus a service provider, a commercial on-line service such as America Online, CompuServe, Microsoft Network, or Prodigy, or a direct provider such as Netcom.

World Wide Web
A system that allows users to receive text, graphics, video, and sound by clicking on particular words and images.

Many Internet users browse the **World Wide Web,** a hypertext system that allows users to receive text, graphics, video, and sound. "Hypertext" means a method for displaying text and graphics that permits users to click on particular words and images, thereby jumping to related documents or images. The Web's hypertext links may send users from the documents of one organization to those of another—perhaps originating across the world. In a period of less than two years, the number of Web sites rose from less than 1,300 to over 15,000, and it continues to increase at the rate of over 200 a week.[33] In fact, the growth rate of this technology has exceeded that of any other communications medium or consumer electronics technology, including the personal computer.[34]

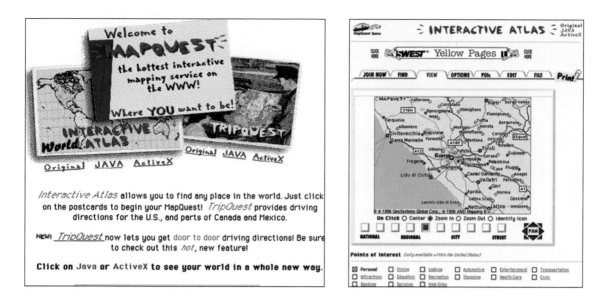

MapQuest *is an example of a World Wide Web home page. The site, created by GeoSystems Global Corporation and provided free to the user, prints out requested detailed maps of the entire United States and major foreign regions and cities (such as Rome, Italy) after clicking on the Interactive World Atlas icon. It also provides travel instructions between over 150,000 U.S. cities by clicking on the TripQuest icon. Companies pay GeoSystems to list their business locations within the interactive database, which in return provides them with marketing exposure on the World Wide Web.*

The Internet is potentially useful throughout the marketing process. It provides access to a wealth of demographic data and other information about the external environment. Web sites also are a means to communicate with existing and potential customers. Organizations can make available information about themselves and their products, cultivate long-term business relationships, and offer products for sale. Procter & Gamble uses the Internet to add value to its exchanges by offering information about appropriate product usage. For example, consumers can get fast answers when they ask the Tide Stain Detective how to attack troublesome stains.[35] Hammacher Schlemmer, Lands' End, and Tower Records are three of the many organizations that offer full-color catalogs on the World Wide Web. A Boston Girl Scout council sold cookies over the Internet; it received payment by credit card and had the cookies delivered by UPS.[36] In addition, marketers can receive direct feedback about their products, their promotions, and other activities on the Internet. Marketers also can use the Internet to build links with their markets and members of their distribution channels at low cost.

Benefits and Challenges   Information technology is especially beneficial for marketers whose products and services are based on information. These include investments, distribution services, and research services. Information technology can enhance these product offerings or make them more readily accessible. An organization selling information in the form of, say, advice or computer software can transfer it directly to customers over the Internet. Producers of goods also rely on information technology to help them tailor their products to individual customers.

When marketers rely heavily on customer information, products tend to have shorter life cycles, reflecting feedback from customers that leads to changes.[37] Such marketers must have flexible processes for product development, distribution, and promotion. In addition, the global nature of modern information technology raises communication challenges. As Internet use grows in non-English-speaking parts of the world, marketers have to identify ways to send and receive messages in more than one language. IBM is a leader in meeting this challenge. The IBM Web site allows users to get information about IBM and its products in any country in a number of languages.[38]

Finally, maintaining privacy can be difficult when disseminating information electronically. Many consumers are wary about giving out their credit card number on the Internet for fear that the numbers will be stolen by computer thieves. Furthermore, messages meant to be private may be intercepted or misrouted. *Inc.* magazine's Vladimir Edelman once received a misrouted message about developments in the European market from an IBM manager; Edelman observed that the message could have wound up just about anywhere in the world—and not necessarily on the computer of someone who would take the ethical approach of informing the message's sender (as he did).[39]

Technological Factors in the Global Environment

Thanks to advances in information technology, marketers are linked more closely than ever to their suppliers and customers throughout the world. Such changes are timely for U.S. marketers, who increasingly depend on foreign customers for sales increases.

The level of technology available in foreign countries affects marketers. For example, communicating with customers on the Internet requires an adequate base of customers with the necessary hardware, software, and knowledge to go on-line. So far the per-capita stock of Internet host computers is highest in Finland, followed by the United States and Australia. Most of the host computers are in North America and Western Europe.[40]

Technology and Value

Organizations can use technology to create value for their customers. Pitney Bowes used technology to develop a high-tech postage meter called the Paragon that helped to transform the company "from a stodgy office equipment supplier into a technologically sophisticated manufacturer with its sights set on growth."[41] The Paragon automatically seals letters, weighs them, prints the appropriate amount of postage on the corner, and shoots them out at the astonishing rate of 240 letters per minute, saving the average mail room as much as three worker-hours each day.

The Competitive Environment

competitive environment
All the organizations that could potentially create value for the organization's customers.

competitive advantage
An ability to outperform competitors in providing something that the market values.

It is rare for an organization to be the sole supplier of a particular product or service. Rather, marketers must find out what their competitors are doing and predict what they might do in the future. These activities concern the **competitive environment,** that is, all the organizations that could potentially create value for the organization's customers. The ultimate objective of analyzing the competitive environment is to help the organization develop a **competitive advantage**—an ability to outperform competitors in providing something that the market values. Organizations do this by delivering greater value, either by lowering the costs of purchasing and use or by offering greater benefits.[42] For example, Procter & Gamble's Head & Shoulders became the best-selling shampoo in China, despite much higher prices, because it offered something desired in that market: a control for dandruff.[43]

In scanning the competitive environment, marketers must remember to consider existing or potential competition from foreign as well as local organizations. Bank of America was able to maintain a strong position by recognizing that its major competitors were not other U.S. banks, but bigger and stronger banks based in Japan and Europe.

Types of Competition

The nature of the competitive environment depends in part on the type of competition. Economists describe four main types of competition: pure competition, monopolistic competition, oligopoly, and monopoly.

pure competition
A type of competition that occurs when there are many sellers of identical products and each seller has a relatively small market share.

monopolistic competition
A type of competition that occurs when there are many sellers of similar, but somewhat differentiated products, and each seller has a relatively small market share.

oligopoly
A type of competition that occurs when a few sellers of very similar products control most of the market.

monopoly
A situation in which only a single organization sells a product in a market area.

Pure competition occurs when similar products are offered, buyers and sellers are familiar with the products, and both buyers and sellers can easily enter the market. Examples include the markets for farm goods and forestry products. In this form of competition, marketers compete mainly on the basis of price.

Monopolistic competition occurs when there are many sellers of similar, but somewhat differentiated products or services, and each seller has a relatively small market share. For example, banks compete with other banks, credit unions, and savings and loan institutions to provide financial services to individuals and businesses. Monopolistic competition is the most common form of competition in the U.S. economy, and it forces marketers to find ways to distinguish their products. Banks use their locations, personnel, interest rates, and other features to differentiate themselves from their competitors.

Oligopoly occurs when products are similar and a few sellers control most of the market. Examples are air travel and long-distance telephone service. These are industries with high start-up costs, which is a major reason for the small number of competitors.

In some cases, a single company maintains a **monopoly** on a product—it is the only organization selling it in a given area. A monopoly organization has great control over the prices it charges. Monopolies, though, are rare in the U.S. economy. Electric utilities once held monopolies in the regions they served, but a federal law now permits independent power producers to send electricity over the big utilities' transmission lines. This allows the often cheaper independents to break the monopolies. Some products enjoy temporary monopolies (as in the case of a drug with patent protection) or manage to grab most of the market share and hold on to it, as has Gatorade, which recently held 90 percent of the market for sports drinks.[44]

In a market with few competitors, developing a competitive advantage may seem simpler, but marketers in such an environment still must be on guard. For one thing, changing conditions may encourage new competitors to enter the market. Also, if organizations with huge market shares become complacent, other companies may be able to offer customers superior value. This happened to European aircraft maker Airbus. Enjoying government aid and the biggest share of the market for commercial aircraft, Airbus let its production efficiency slide while Boeing Company was making gains. Boeing's lower costs enabled it to reap big profits on its 747s, and it used the earnings to offer attractive package deals on several models of aircraft causing Airbus's market share to slip.[45]

In the air cargo industry, many companies compete to provide air cargo services to businesses. To distinguish itself in this environment of monopolistic competition, Team Air Express advertises that tough competition has motivated it to continuously improve. Team positions itself as offering "a domestic system of 52 dedicated offices, a worldwide network of international partners, and the determination to be simply the best."

Competitive Forces

Given that most organizations have competitors, marketers should consider how these competitors can affect the industry and the organization. For example, perhaps a new company will begin marketing a competing product, as in the case of a new maker of IBM-compatible personal computers. Perhaps an organization will begin marketing new goods or services that take away sales from an existing product, as CD players drove down sales of tape decks. One way to evaluate the competitive forces affecting

FIGURE 2.5

Types of Competitive Forces

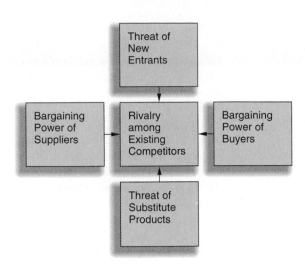

Source: Adapted with permission from Michael F. Porter, "Industry Structure and Competitive Strategy: Keys to Productivity," *Financial Analysts Journal,* July–August 1980. Copyright 1980, The Financial Analysts Federation, Charlottesville, VA. All rights reserved.

organizations is to categorize them into five types: rivalry among existing competitors, threat of new entrants, threat of substitute products, bargaining power of suppliers, and bargaining power of buyers.[46] These are illustrated in Figure 2.5.

Rivalry among Existing Competitors

To develop successful marketing strategies, marketers need to be aware of existing competitors. Who are the major competitors? What are their annual sales? How much of the market do they control? What are their strengths and weaknesses? What are their marketing strategies? With answers to such questions, marketers may draw customers away from competitors by offering superior value to them.

Threat of New Entrants

There usually is a possibility that new competitors will enter a market. In some cases, governments actually encourage new entrants. In Hong Kong, frustration with poor bus service by China Motor Bus (CMB) led the government to end CMB's monopoly status by awarding some of its routes to CityBus.[47] Aside from poor performance, the threat of new entrants is especially great when an earlier company's success signals a demand for particular products.

Some markets are easier to enter than others. Barriers to entry might include a need for heavy financial investment or years of experience to reduce the cost of production. For instance, the start-up cost for a new automobile manufacturer would be a lot higher than that for a restaurant. Industries with low entry barriers are more likely to have new entrants.

Threat of Substitute Products

Marketers in an industry are competing with others who offer substitute products. For instance, supermarkets in New England worry that the success of the Boston Markets chain of carry-out restaurants will lure away customers with the promise of convenient meals.[48] Video conferencing is a substitute for air travel for face-to-face business meetings.

The availability of substitutes helps cap the prices of some products. A price that is too high compared to the substitute may lead to lost sales. Thus, if a business finds that buying accounting software and hiring a part-time bookkeeper is cheaper than paying fees to an accounting firm, the accounting firm could lose sales to the software maker.

Bargaining Power of Suppliers Suppliers are a key competitive force because they can determine the price or quality of parts or raw materials. When a few suppliers control a large share of the market, as in an oligopoly, buyers may have to accept a price increase or a lower level of quality. However, increasingly manufacturers look for suppliers willing to work closely with them to help them deliver value.

Bargaining Power of Buyers Buyers can force prices down, bargain for higher quality or more services, and set competitors against each other. Whereas a small buyer may have to live with a price increase from a supplier, a large buyer may have the clout to demand a lower price, as Wal-Mart did when Rubbermaid tried to increase the prices of its plastic kitchen products. Buyers also can purchase a firm that supplies them or purchase another firm within the supplier's industry.

Competition in the Global Environment

Many U.S. companies have entered the global market. Foreign markets are especially appealing when growth is expected to be faster there than at home. Soft-drink marketers see growth potential in Chinese consumption patterns: on average, a Chinese person drinks 15 colas a year compared to the average American, who manages to down 800 colas annually.[49]

Just as U.S. firms are entering foreign markets aggressively, foreign companies are providing stiff competition in the United States. For example, given the relatively small size of most European countries, organizations based there must serve global markets in order to achieve sales growth.[50]

Summary

To recognize and respond to opportunities and threats an organization faces, marketers scan the external environment. Environmental scanning includes reviewing the economic, political and legal, social, natural, technological, and competitive dimensions of the environment.

The economic environment includes the patterns of business activity, consumer income, and spending patterns. Business activity follows a cycle of prosperity, recession, and recovery. Consumer income may be measured as gross income (a household's total annual income), disposable income (money left over after taxes), and discretionary income (gross income minus taxes and normal living expenses).

The political and legal environment includes federal, state, and local laws and regulations relevant to marketing activities, as well as political pressure. Lobbyists and consumer interest groups influence which laws are passed. In addition, many court decisions interpreting these laws and regulations affect marketers. At the global level, marketers should be familiar with any international agreements that affect their activities, as well as the relevant laws of countries in which they operate.

The social environment describes the people in society and their values, beliefs, and behaviors. Demographics include data on population characteristics such as age, race, sex, geographic distribution, education, income, and marital status. The values, beliefs, and behaviors of people in the United States are diverse. Marketers operating in foreign countries must also take into account differences among values, beliefs, and behaviors.

The natural environment consists of the natural resources available to or affected by the organization. Some resources may be depleted; the organization must make decisions about how to conserve such resources or even use demarketing to limit demand for products that include them. Marketing practices that demonstrate care for the natural environment may enhance the organization's standing in the eyes of customers, regulators, and the general public. Such marketing, called green marketing, may include environmentally friendly strategies for each element of the marketing mix.

The technological environment comprises scientific knowledge, research, inventions, and innovations that result in new or improved goods or services. Technological developments can bring opportunities to organizations to create value for customers and threats to organizations that are unprepared for change. Of particular importance to marketers today is the Internet, a global computer network that provides a variety of opportunities for marketers to communicate with customers and other stakeholders. On the Internet, the World Wide Web can send a combination of text, images, video, and sound. Web sites are fast becoming a means for organizations to educate computer users about themselves and their products.

The competitive environment consists of all the organizations that could potentially create value for a particular market. Competition in various industries takes the form of pure competition, monopolistic competition, oligopoly, or monopoly. Marketers need to anticipate competition from existing competitors, new entrants, substitute products, suppliers, and buyers on a global basis.

Key Terms and Concepts

environmental scanning (p. 28)
economic environment (p. 30)
business cycle (p. 30)
inflation (p. 30)
gross income (p. 31)
disposable income (p. 32)
discretionary income (p. 32)
political–legal environment (p. 33)
regulations (p. 35)
consumerism (p. 36)

social environment (p. 38)
demographics (p. 38)
social responsibility (p. 41)
cause-related marketing (p. 42)
ethics (p. 42)
marketing ethics (p. 42)
price fixing (p. 43)
natural environment (p. 44)
demarketing (p. 44)
green marketing (p. 44)

technological environment (p. 46)
Internet (p. 46)
World Wide Web (p. 46)
competitive environment (p. 48)
competitive advantage (p. 48)
pure competition (p. 49)
monopolistic competition (p. 49)
oligopoly (p. 49)
monopoly (p. 49)

Review and Discussion Questions

1. Name and briefly define the six dimensions of the marketing environment.
2. What steps might the owner of a clothing store take to prosper during a recessionary economy?
3. Imagine that you want to open an Italian restaurant that will sell a variety of pasta dishes, bottled water, beer, and wine. With what laws and regulations would you expect to have to comply?
4. Do you think self-regulation by the medical profession is effective? Why or why not?
5. If you were a marketer with a travel agency that focused on international adventure travel, what demographic trends would you research before introducing new trips or tours?
6. Why is an awareness of diversity among markets and marketers important?
7. Based on what you can learn or deduce about the demographics and values of your class members, do you think your class would be a good target market for top-of-the-line CD players? for life insurance? Explain.
8. How might the producer of a movie based on a story of child abuse engage in cause-related marketing?

9. Describe the difference between ethical and legal behavior.
10. Despite great health risk, thousands of people buy and smoke cigarettes every year. Do you think it is ethical to market tobacco products? Why or why not?
11. Why is advertising aimed at children considered an ethical issue?
12. In what ways might a company that sells cosmetics via catalog and personal sales, such as Avon, conserve natural resources?
13. Name three steps that a manufacturer of ice cream could take to practice green marketing.
14. Technological advances in electronic information and medicine have evoked many new questions of ethics in marketing. In what other areas might technological developments give rise to new ethical questions?
15. In what ways could the installation of technology that allows videoconferencing in a medical group's office create value for patients?
16. Name and define the four types of competition. Which do you think would be faced by a company that markets accounting services to small businesses? Explain.

Chapter Project Social Responsibility in Marketing

Many marketers now take the view that their organizations are accountable to society as a whole—adhering to high standards in the economic, legal and ethical, social, natural, technological, and competitive environments in a way that gives something back to society.

For your chapter project, put yourself in the marketer's seat. Choose a large industry that interests you (such as tobacco, auto, toys, fast-food, telecommunications, etc.). Imag-

ine that you are a marketer at a company within this industry. Plan how you would go about scanning one aspect of the environment for your company—economic, political/legal, social, natural, technological, or competitive. Then determine how you would use that information to launch some related, socially responsible marketing action. Describe both steps in writing.

Chapter Case Quikava

Starbucks, Seattle's Best Coffee, even Dunkin' Donuts have been battling it out for customers in recent years as the popularity of coffee, especially gourmet coffee, has made a comeback. Now Chock Full o' Nuts has jumped back into the java wars with a new subsidiary, Quikava. Quikava shops are drive-through coffee shops "catering to people in a rush,"

according to Gerry Pelissier, cofounder and vice president of Quikava.

Chock Full o' Nuts closed its original chain of shops during the 1980s, when consumer spending patterns and certain demographic trends translated to slow sales. But various aspects of the environment have changed—and the new Quikava chain is intended to respond to those changes, bringing value to consumers by offering them what they want. "Our concept speaks to what people want in the computer age," says Pelissier. "People are looking for quick service and convenience." Thus, Quikava shops are located on heavily traveled roads in densely populated areas. The company also hopes to open shops in or adjacent to gas stations. Quikava shops offer not only specialty coffees, but also bagels, scones, and "roll-up" sandwiches that are easy to eat on the run.

Quikava engages in regional marketing in places like Boston, where it faces plenty of competition. Experts say that higher education levels and sophisticated tastes make Boston a good place to market specialty products such as gourmet coffee. "There are big time coffee drinkers in Boston," says Jim Clarke, vice president of marketing for competitor Seattle's Best Coffee. "From a socioeconomic standpoint, Boston is a good, vital place. The weather helps, too. It's a good place to enjoy coffee." Thus, not only does the economic environment and social environment play a part in the regional marketing, but so does the natural environment.

Quikava's competitors have taken different approaches to reaching consumers. Starbucks focuses on offering premium-priced, premium-flavored coffees to those who consider themselves connoisseurs of the drink. Dunkin' Donuts has added new flavors of specialty coffees so that customers will buy both products—doughnuts and coffee—at their shops. Quikava plans to saturate the market quickly by selling franchises.

The Specialty Coffee Association estimates a 7 to 10 percent growth in the coffee market over the next few years. Quikava marketers can probably keep pace by continually scanning their environment. As expressed by Steven Buckley, vice president of Chock Full o' Nuts Restaurant Group: "We're going back to our heritage. The stakes are high and the competition is there, but we are [expanding] in a way that is unique and addresses a specific niche."

Questions

1. What environmental factors might Quikava have to take into account if the company decided to conduct regional marketing in Florida?

2. How might Quikava engage in green marketing?

3. As the competition intensifies, what steps might Quikava take to create greater value for its customers?

Source: Kathy McCabe, "The Newest Mug in Town," *The Boston Globe*, March 13, 1996, pp. 45, 48. Reprinted courtesy of *The Boston Globe*.

Explore more at www.franchise-update.com/quikava.htm

chapter Three

Global Marketing Challenges

CHAPTER OUTLINE

The Changing Global Environment
  North America
  The European Community
  Japan
  Other Nations
Environmental Scanning and Analysis of Foreign Markets
  Economic Environment
  Political and Legal Environment
  Social Environment
  Natural Environment
  Technological Environment
  Competitive Environment
Modes of Entry into Global Markets
  Exporting
  Licensing
  Joint Ventures
  Direct Ownership
Summary

LEARNING OBJECTIVES

After completing this chapter, you should be able to:

1. Identify important characteristics of the major trading partners of the United States.

2. Define basic measures of a nation's economic condition.

3. Discuss the political and legal considerations that marketers weigh when deciding whether to enter foreign markets.

4. Describe the impact of cultural characteristics on the success of a marketing effort.

5. Identify major demographic and lifestyle trends of interest to marketers serving foreign markets.

6. Discuss global issues concerning the natural environment.

7. Summarize the issues marketers consider when scanning the technological environment on a global scale.

8. Contrast the basic modes of entry into foreign markets.

Creating Customer Value

TLI International Corp.

As political boundaries have become blurry or have disappeared entirely, the world has become a series of larger markets. But this world is complicated; differences in culture, language, economics, laws, natural resources, and the like can make the global marketplace seem like a maze. A husband-and-wife team based in Chicago recognized this a number of years ago and decided to start a firm devoted to helping companies conduct their business overseas. "I thought foreign firms needed help setting up offices and doing business in this country," recalls TLI's president, Lyric Hughes, of their initial efforts. Later Hughes and her husband, James Liebling, discovered that most of their repeat business actually came from American companies that wanted to establish themselves abroad. However, foreign companies also hire TLI to help them with issues outside the United States.

TLI (originally called Trans-Lingual Communications Inc., until Hughes and Liebling learned that Japanese clients could not pronounce the name) strives to create value for its customers in every conceivable way. Nalco Chemical hired TLI to train its employees in language, culture, and other differences they may encounter while working overseas. TLI and China's *People's Daily,* the world's largest newspaper, formed an alliance to help American firms conduct marketing activities through the newspaper's bureaus. Consequently, TLI now has an office in Beijing. TLI also produces videos and print materials, provides a language service for translations, and offers just about any kind of consulting expertise a customer may want.

It takes a certain amount of understanding to offer so much value to so many different kinds of customers. Hughes and Liebling understand global challenges very well. Hughes speaks six languages fluently, and has lived in several different countries. Liebling has a master's degree in international relations. "A lot of companies think the Asian market is one homogeneous sector. It's not," says Hughes. "There are huge differences between doing business in Japan and China. Japan has a higher standard of living, spends more on consumer goods and advertising, and its advertising field is cluttered. China has a lower standard of living, lower expectations about consumer goods, its advertising field is less cluttered and costs are cheaper, though that's changing." As you read this chapter, think about how important it is to consider factors such as economics, political climate, culture and language, lifestyle, and ethics when marketing in the global arena.

Source: Barbara B. Buchholz, "Zapping Away Culture Shock," *Crain's Small Business,* February 1995, p. 26.

Explore more at www.tliinter.com//TLIhome.htm

Chapter Four

Marketing Planning and Organization Strategy

CHAPTER OUTLINE

Strategic Planning in the Organization
  Organizational Mission
  Organizational Objectives
  Organizational Strategies
  Organizational Portfolio Plan
Business Portfolio Analysis
  Boston Consulting Group's Growth/Share Matrix
  General Electric's Industry Attractiveness/Business Strength Matrix
Marketing and Other Functional Areas in the Strategic Planning Process
  Traditional Role of Marketing in the Planning Process
  Cross-Functional Teams
Managing the Marketing Effort
  Marketing Management Functions
  Developing a Marketing Plan
Demand Estimation
  Estimating Demand
  Forecasting Sales
  Evaluating the Forecast
Summary

LEARNING OBJECTIVES

After completing this chapter, you should be able to:

1. Describe the process of strategic planning.
2. Summarize the principles of business portfolio analysis.
3. Discuss the role of marketing in strategic planning as it is carried out traditionally and with cross-functional teams.
4. Identify the tasks of marketing management.
5. Describe how marketers develop and evaluate marketing plans.
6. Explain how forecasting supports the process of creating a marketing plan.
7. Describe major types of forecasting.

Booklet Binding Inc.

Tom Patrevito and John Z. Kosowski started their business, Illinois-based Booklet Binding, 20 years ago with $20,000 in capital and a lot of good ideas. "We were businessmen in an industry made up of craftsmen," recalls Kosowski. They bought the most up-to-date binding machinery and offered service that their old-line competitors never even thought about. "They were very forward-looking," says William Mead, a former Booklet Binding salesperson. "They sold quality, they sold service, and they developed a solid reputation for both." Their approach paid off, with sales and profits rising steadily.

Eventually the profits plateaued, then began to drop off. Booklet Binding reps spent most of their time haggling with customers over price. Patrevito and Kosowski considered downsizing and other cost-cutting measures to help stop the drain on profits. Before they took those steps, they made one last-ditch effort: they hired a professional sales trainer, Mark N. Landiak. Through Landiak they learned that they had never really articulated their vision for the company; they had never stated why they were in business or what they intended for their business to accomplish. They didn't have a creative strategy or plan—other than pricing and service—for gaining an advantage over the competition. They didn't even really know what their customers wanted.

With Landiak's help, Patrevito and Kosowski discovered that customers wanted sales reps who were true experts at helping them do better business. "Expertise is the better mousetrap," says Max Carey, founder and chief executive of Corporate Resource Development in Atlanta. "Rather than see you because of what you sell, customers see you because of what you know." Jim Morrissey, president of Market Share Catalysts, explains further, "The value added is not in the product anymore; it's in the relationship between the sales rep and the customer."

With Landiak's training, Booklet Binding's sales force developed ways to increase their expertise and get to know their customers better. They created an account profile, which told them as much as possible about a customer's overall business; they created a calendar log, which helped them preplan visits with customers; and they established a "red-alert" program, designed to lure business during the bindery's traditional slow period. "What you're doing is identifying the customers with the most potential, and understanding their business extraordinarily well," says Landiak.

Today, Booklet Bindery is on the mend. As you read this chapter, consider how important overall planning and strategy are to a company, at all levels. Everyone who works for a company needs to know why they are there and what the company wants to accomplish.

Source: Joshua Hyatt, "Hot Commodity," *Inc.*, February 1996, pp. 50–61. Adapted with permission, *Inc.* magazine, February 1996. Copyright 1996 by Goldhirsh Group, Inc., 38 Commercial Wharf, Boston, MA 02110.

Explore more at www.corpdyn.com/html/incquote.htm or by searching "Booklet Binding Inc." on the Web.

UNDERSTANDING CUSTOMERS
AND MARKETS

TWO

The one path to competitive advantage lies in continuously improving the value of your products in the minds of your customers.

Robert E. Drane, Vice President, Marketing Services and New Product Development,
Consumer Products Division, Oscar Mayer & Company

CHAPTER 5

Marketing Research: Information and Technology

CHAPTER 6

Consumer Behavior

CHAPTER 7

Organizational Buying Behavior

CHAPTER 8

Market Segmentation

Explore the Career Profiles on the Churchill and Peter Homepage at www.irwin.com/
marketing/value.

Experience what it is like to be a Marketing Research Manager on the Marketing Interactive:
Building Skills for your Career CD ROM.

Chapter Five

Marketing Research: Information and Technology

CHAPTER OUTLINE

Information for Effective Marketing
  Information versus Data
  Marketing Information Systems
  Sources of Information
  Primary and Secondary Data
The Marketing Research Process
  Formulate the Problem
  Plan a Research Design
  Collect Data
  Analyze and Interpret Data
  Prepare the Research Report
Applications of New Technology
  Geographical Information Systems
  Virtual Reality
  The Internet
Ethical Considerations
  Deceit and Fraud in Marketing Research
  Invasion of Privacy
Global Marketing Research
Summary

LEARNING OBJECTIVES

After completing this chapter, you should be able to:

1. Distinguish between *data* and *information,* and discuss the challenges of getting the type and amount of information needed.

2. Discuss how marketing information systems help marketers gather and analyze information.

3. Compare internal and external sources of information and primary and secondary data.

4. Identify the steps in the marketing research process.

5. Describe basic types of research design and approaches to collecting data.

6. Explain how marketing researchers go about analyzing and interpreting data.

7. Summarize principles for preparing a marketing research report.

8. Explain how modern technology has affected the process and use of marketing research.

9. Discuss ethical considerations of marketing research.

10. Describe issues that arise in international marketing research.

Fresh Express Farms

Salads are hot. That's what marketing research by the A.C. Nielsen company found. According to the study, Americans are eating plenty of salads—with a twist. They don't have the time to spend chopping, dicing, and grating their own vegetables for salads; they want someone else to do the chore instead. The study says that American salad eaters want plenty of variety and flavor, but without the work.

Fresh Express Farms, based in California, has responded to this research by giving consumers what they want. The company makes eight varieties of kit salads—packaged servings of dressings, croutons, shredded cheese, and other salad garnishes to add to lettuce or other greens. It also offers a line of specialty salads, which include more exotic types of produce.

Consumers are gobbling up the pre-made salads at a rate that has made Fresh Express Farms a leader in sales, with 48 percent of the kit salad segment and 47 percent of the specialty segment of the packaged salad market. (In one recent year, kit salads garnered nearly $85 million in nationwide sales.) Fresh Express Farms is not satisfied with the category's 54 percent household penetration and is hoping to increase it to 80 percent. The company plans to use innovative merchandising and promotional efforts to bring new customers into the category, such as tying the product to other category leaders used in conjunction with salads. As you read this chapter, think about how marketers can use information they gather about markets in order to create customer value by offering

consumers and other buyers the products they want.

Source: *Food Industry News*, November 1995, p. 44; Stephanie Thompson, "Beyond the Aisle," *Brandweek*, November 11, 1996, pp. 25–26.

Explore more at www.dole5aday.com/about/factory/factory.html.

marketing research
The function that links the
consumer, customer, and
public to the marketer
through information.

Chapter Overview

The story about Fresh Express Farms described how the company uses marketing research to determine what consumers want. The American Marketing Association defines **marketing research** as "the function that links the consumer, customer, and public to the marketer through information—information used to identify and define marketing opportunities and problems; generate, refine, and evaluate marketing actions; monitor marketing performance; and improve understanding of marketing as a process."[1] In other words, for marketers to anticipate or respond to customer needs, they need to know about their current and prospective customers and about the success of their own practices. They get much of this knowledge through marketing research.

Researching markets and topics of interest to marketers may be the responsibility of one member of the organization or of a marketing research department. At an organization that focuses on its core competencies, the best way to handle research activities may be to hire an outside firm that specializes in marketing research. Regardless of who performs the research function, the goal should be to provide information that improves marketing decisions.

This chapter provides an overview of what marketers can expect in working with marketing researchers and marketing research. It describes the kinds of information marketing researchers provide, the places they find it, and the ways computerized information systems help them organize and retrieve it. The chapter then details the steps in the process of marketing research. Next the chapter explores the impact of technology on marketing research and examines some ethical issues that may arise in conducting marketing research. The chapter closes with an introduction to the special challenges of international marketing research.

Information for Effective Marketing

Success threatened to choke the cellular phone industry several years ago, as growing usage inspired forecasts of a shortage in capacity. Cellular phone companies consulted with experts and decided to add capacity by adopting a new technology called digital modulation. At a cost of hundreds of millions of dollars, they developed the technology, installed it, and announced it to their customers. However, hardly anyone bought the new technology. Customers saw no benefit to switching from their existing phones, and marketers had to figure out ways to adjust the product and pricing to make the new phones more enticing.[2] The companies had acted based on information about industry trends, but they had failed to learn enough about customer wants and needs. They should have done marketing research to see if the new technology was perceived as a benefit by potential customers.

Marketers need information about their environment, especially information about customers and competitors. They need to know how target markets respond to a current marketing mix and how they would react to changes in it. They need to know how well competitors are doing and want to forecast what competitors plan to do next. Therefore, they turn to marketing research to provide information about all areas of marketing, especially their own and their competitors' market share, the market potential of current and potential products, and characteristics of the consumers and organizations in their markets. Table 5.1 lists some basic questions marketers wish to answer in order to help them plan marketing activities.

Information versus Data

data
Facts and statistics.

Marketers need information, not just data. **Data** are simply facts and statistics. Examples include the number of people living in Dallas, the average price of a new luxury car, or the number of calls received each day by the reference department of the public library.

T A B L E   5.1 Questions Marketing Research Can Help Answer

Questions about Markets		
Buyers	**Demand**	**Channels**
• What kinds of people buy our products? • Where do they live? • How much do they earn? • How many of them are there?	• Is demand for our products increasing or decreasing? • Are there promising new markets that we have not yet reached?	• Do channels of distribution for our products need changing? • Are new types of marketing institutions likely to evolve?

Questions about Marketing Mix			
Product	**Pricing**	**Placement**	**Promotion**
• Which product design is likely to be most successful? • What kind of packaging should we use?	• What price should we charge for our new products? • Should the price of existing products be changed?	• Where, and by whom, should our products be sold? • What kind of incentives should we offer the trade to push our products?	• How much should we spend on promotion? • How should our budget be allocated to products and to geographic areas? • What combination of media—newspapers, radio, television, magazines—should we use?

Questions about Performance		
Market Share	**Customer Satisfaction**	**Reputation**
• What is our market share overall? • What is our share in each geographic area? • What is our share by customer type?	• Are customers satisfied with our products? • How is our record for service? • Are there many product returns?	• How does the public perceive our organization? • What is our reputation with channel members?

Source: Adapted from p. 12 of *Basic Marketing Research,* Third Edition by Gilbert A. Churchill, Jr., © 1996 by The Dryden Press, reproduced by permission of the publisher.

information
Data presented in a useful way.

In contrast, **information** refers to data presented in a way that is useful for making decisions. Generally, this means that the data are presented to show the presence or absence of some trend, relationship, or pattern. A store's computer might produce data about how much of which items sold each day, week, and month. A researcher could evaluate these data to look for relationships such as the effects of coupons on demand for various products. The researcher could plot the sales of certain product categories on a month-by-month basis and look for seasonal changes. In these cases, the researcher is converting the data into information.

Such information, in turn, is useful for decision making. Thus, knowing that 50-cent coupons increase demand for Maxwell House Coffee by 17 percent helps determine the value of this strategy. Knowing sales trends could help with decisions such as when inventories should be increased or how often to order.

Before computers made it easy to record, sort, and analyze data, marketers generally had difficulty getting enough information to make decisions. Today, however, the typical marketer is overwhelmed with facts, reports, and analyses. The necessary information is available, but it can be hard to find. Marketers have five complaints about the information that crosses their desks:[3]

1. There is too much marketing information of the wrong kind and not enough of the right kind.
2. Marketing information is so dispersed throughout the company that great effort may be needed to locate simple facts.

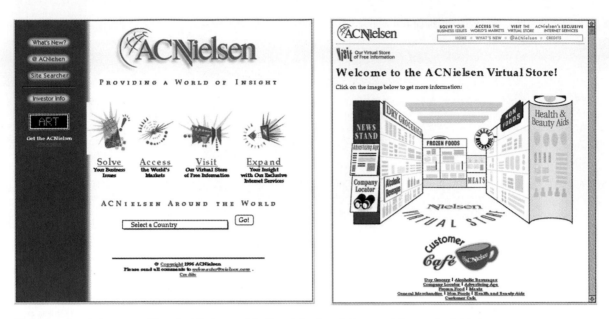

Marketers do not always need to collect their own data. Specialized market research firms collect data to provide to clients. The A.C. Nielsen Company is one of the largest, providing data on product movement for grocery and drug stores. Nielsen collects data, which are then analyzed for a particular customer.

3. Vital information is sometimes suppressed by other executives or subordinates for personal reasons.

4. Vital information often arrives too late to be useful.

5. It is often difficult to know whether information is accurate, and there is no one to turn to for confirmation.

The best defense against these problems is a thoughtful and thorough approach to conducting marketing research and to setting up and using a system for gathering, storing, and disseminating marketing information.

Marketing Information Systems

marketing decision support system
A coordinated collection of data, system tools, and techniques with supporting software and hardware by which an organization gathers and interprets relevant information and turns it into a basis for making management decisions.

Today, most organizations use computers to help them gather, sort, store, and distribute information to be used in making marketing decisions. A popular form of computerized marketing information system is the **marketing decision support system (MDSS),** "a coordinated collection of data, system tools, and techniques with supporting software and hardware by which an organization gathers and interprets relevant information from business and the environment and turns it into a basis for making management decisions."[4] Thus, the MDSS not only provides information, it does so in a form designed to assist the decision maker during the process of making a decision.

This means that the MDSS requires three types of software:

1. Database management software for sorting and retrieving data from internal and external sources.

2. Model base management software that contains routines for manipulating the data in ways that are of interest to marketers.

3. A dialog system that permits marketers to explore the database and use the models to produce reports that address their questions.

Figure 5.1 shows the basic setup of an MDSS. Typically an MDSS allows the user to conduct "what if" analysis. This means the user can ask the computer to show the likely outcome of changing a certain variable in a certain way. For example, marketers

F I G U R E   5.1
Basics of a Marketing Decision Support System (MDSS)

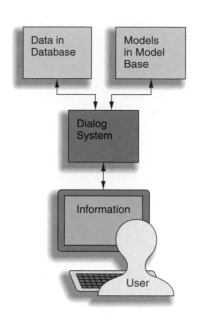

might ask what will happen if the advertising budget is doubled or if the number-three competitor drops out of the market.

A significant advantage of maintaining an MDSS over merely gathering information when requested is that the people who can use marketing information are able to get it quickly and easily. The information also should be up to date. United Airlines regularly asks a percentage of its flyers to fill out questionnaires concerning customer satisfaction, then stores the results in a computerized database. Managers routinely use the data to see whether the company's activities in a given area, such as baggage handling or food service, are satisfying its customers.[5]

Because an MDSS makes information readily available, it shifts expectations about what marketers and marketing researchers should do. Once marketing research emphasized data collection; today the emphasis is on analyzing and interpreting it. In the words of Joe Patti, Anheuser-Busch's senior director of retail planning and category management, "Today, you spend the majority of your time analyzing what . . . information means and how you can help . . . customers achieve their goals. It's a whole new and exciting era."[6]

An MDSS is most useful when its users see to it that they get the kinds of information they really need. Thus, marketing managers must be clear about the kinds of information that can help them make decisions. They must ask the designers of the system to include the capability of collecting and delivering these kinds of information. VeriFone, based in Redwood City, California, prepares a wide variety of reports, lets employees know how to find them on their computers, and tracks how often each type of report is looked up. The information on usage makes it possible to identify reports that may need to be modified, better promoted, or dropped altogether.[7]

Sources of Information

Marketing researchers can get information from inside and outside the organization. The Coca-Cola Company combines company data on the per capita consumption of its beverages in the countries it serves with external data on the population of each country to identify the countries with the greatest potential for sales growth. For example, China has a population of over 1 billion people and per capita consumption of 4 servings per year. This suggests significant growth potential compared to Canada, with a population 29 million and per capita consumption of 181 servings per year, and the United States, with a population 263 million and per capita consumption of 343 servings per year.[8]

T A B L E 5.2
External Sources of Data

Source	Examples
Business and industry publications	*Million Dollar Directory* (details about companies with assets over $500,000); *Directory of Mail or List Houses* (sources of mailing lists); *Sales & Marketing Management; The Wall Street Journal; Encyclopedia of Associations*
Research services	A. C. Nielsen Co., Arbitron Co., IMS International, Information Resources, Inc.
Trade groups	American Medical Association; National Association of Realtors; National Association of Retailer Dealers of America
Customer surveys	Mail surveys, telephone surveys, personal surveys (including mall intercepts, focus group interviews, and in-home interviews)
Government reports	Statistical Abstract of the United States; Survey of Current Business; state employment and economic data; United Nations Statistical Yearbook (worldwide data)
Computer databases	NEXIS (full text of articles from 125 periodicals); LEXIS (legal cases and documents); PATSEARCH (U.S. patents filed since 1975); CompuServe; Dow Jones News/Retrieval; Dialog; The Source; Mead Data Central

Internal Sources of Information   Marketers can find a wealth of data within the organization itself. For example, sales records indicate which products sell best and who is buying them. Accounting data can indicate which products are the most profitable. Inventory data can indicate how fast goods are moving off the shelves. By creating special discount programs for frequent shoppers, marketers can gather basic data about what kind of customers it has and where they are located.

When marketers determine that they need internally generated information, they should ensure that the organization's record-keeping systems provide it. Waste Management of Illinois West has tested trucks with on-board computers that record how long the truck spends at each stop, how much it collects, and comments about the site, including any problems the driver encounters. According to Frank McCoy, the division president and general manager, "The whole idea is to get closer to the customer and know his waste stream and the time it takes to handle it."[9]

External Sources of Information   Of course, marketers also need to know what is going on in the external environment. They need to know about the economy, the legal environment, their current and hoped-for customers, and much more. Such information can be obtained from business and industry publications, research services, trade groups, customer surveys, government reports, and computer databases (see Table 5.2 for examples). Spartan Motors, which builds chassis for heavy-duty vehicles, gathers information about customer needs, competitors, and technology by sending representatives to industry trade shows. Spartan designers at one show learned that fire fighters were falling out of speeding fire trucks, so the company introduced the first enclosed cab, now the industry standard.[10]

For companies that market consumer goods, an important source of external data is suppliers of single-source data. **Single-source data** refers to a single database containing data on sales by product and brand, coupon usage, and exposure to television advertising. The data on sales and coupon usage come from checkout scanners that read Universal Product Codes (bar codes), and the data on advertising exposure come from recording devices installed on the televisions of participating households. Figure 5.2 illustrates the process of collecting single-source data for a service known as Infoscan, offered by Information Resources Inc.

Single-source data can be useful for making a variety of decisions. The data on product sales can help producers and retailers learn which products sell best in particular locations. Tying sales data to coupon usage helps marketers decide whether coupon offers are effective in generating sales for particular products. If not, the marketer may wish to find other means to stimulate sales, or may consider making

single-source data
A single database containing data on sales by product and brand, coupon usage, and exposure to television advertising.

*Universal Product codes (**UPCs**) for each grocery item are scanned at checkout. Information sent from store to chain and on to Information Resources Inc. (IRI) via telecommunication systems.*

*   ***Household panel members*** *present an identification card at checkout, which identifies and assigns items purchased to that household. Coupons are collected and matched to the appropriate UPC. Information is electronically communicated to IRI computers.*

*   ***IRI field personnel*** *visually survey stores and all print media to record retailers' merchandising efforts, displays, and ad features. Field personnel also survey retail stores for a variety of custom applications (e.g., average number of units per display, space allocated to specific sections, and number of facings). Results are electronically communicated to IRI computers.*

*   ***Household panel members*** *are selected for television monitoring and equipped with meters that automatically record the set's status every five seconds. Information is relayed back to IRI's computers.*

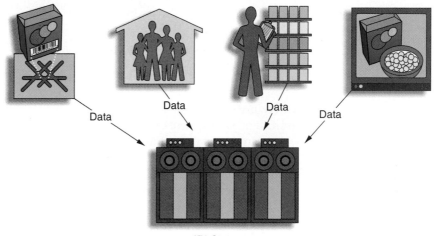

Data   Data   Data   Data

IRI Computers

Source: Adapted from William R. Dillon, Thomas J. Madden, and Neil H. Firtle, *Essentials of Marketing Research* (Homewood, Ill.: Irwin, 1993), p. 122.

the coupons worth more or publishing them in other media. Tying sales data to advertising exposure helps marketers evaluate the effectiveness of their advertising campaigns. Single-source data can be especially useful to marketers who see the information as a means to answer new questions. Instead of asking whether a coupon for a product was associated with greater sales volume, a retailer might ask how the change in sales volume affected profits in particular stores or which customers contribute the most to profitability.[11]

Furthermore, marketers can carry all of these efforts a step further by conducting experiments and using single-source data as a measure of the results. Thus, they can use different ad campaigns or coupon programs in different locations. They then compare the sales volume and profits in the locations to find which communications efforts seem most effective.

When using single-source data, marketers must bear in mind some limitations. Data for a single-source system are collected in limited geographic areas, so the results may not apply to the organization's entire market. Collecting single-source data also is costly and can overload marketers with more data than they can use productively. In the words of Tom Belle, executive vice president of Gage Marketing Communications, "Trying to use scanner data is like trying to drink from a fire hydrant."[12] Nevertheless, the speed of data collection and detail of information make single-source data a valuable tool when used appropriately.

Primary and Secondary Data

From internal and external sources, marketers can generate data to answer their own specific questions. For example, they might ask customers to evaluate the organization's services. Marketers may also look up reports of previous data-gathering efforts

Allan Ikawa, president of Big Island Candies, keeps up with changing customer preferences by conducting occasional surveys using a list of 8,000 customer names he has collected since opening the store 8 years ago. His research findings help him to change operations to accommodate both tourists and locals. For instance, when he learned that Japanese customers prefer chocolates and macadamia nuts and the local customers purchase more cookies, he placed candy on one side of the store and cookies on the other to facilitate traffic flow.

by the organization or outside sources. Marketers do this when they look up Census Bureau or Department of Commerce data about their target markets.

To carry out a marketing strategy based on value creation, consultant Mark Shonka advises a combination of data types. First, Shonka says, marketers should get to know their customers by researching publicly available data. For example, to serve organizational buyers, marketers can investigate organizations' strategies, strengths, and structure, as well as the identity and concerns of key decision makers. Next, Shonka advises setting up research meetings with customers to learn about their business, especially their plans and concerns.[13] This approach generates two basic kinds of data, known as primary and secondary data.

Primary Data   When marketing researchers conduct telephone polls, try selling a new service in a few selected areas, or listen to a group of consumers discussing what they look for in camping equipment, they are gathering primary data. **Primary data** are data "collected specifically for the purpose of the investigation at hand."[14] Katherine Barchetti, owner of K. Barchetti Shops in Pittsburgh, wrote letters to 3,000 former customers asking why they had stopped shopping at her stores. She used the 290 replies as the basis for personnel and pricing changes.[15]

primary data
Data collected specifically for a particular investigation.

Statistical Inference   Often primary data are used to infer something about a population, such as all small businesses or all teenage girls in the United States. Researchers question or observe a sample of the population, then use statistics to reach conclusions about the population. If 37 percent of the teenage girls surveyed say they plan to see a particular movie, a researcher might conclude that it is likely that 35 to 39 percent of all teenage girls in the United States would have the same intentions. This process of using data from a sample to draw conclusions about an entire population is known as **statistical inference.**

statistical inference
The process of using data from a sample to draw conclusion about an entire population.

Interestingly, statistical inference can be more accurate than a survey of the entire population (a "census"). The major reason is that surveying an entire population is such a big task that more errors can occur. Also, collecting the data can take so long that changes occur in the population during the research.

Sampling   For statistical inference to produce accurate results, the sample should be representative of the population. For example, if researchers want to know about all small businesses in the United States, the sample should not be limited to manufacturers or to businesses whose owners the researchers know. Likewise, if the organization wants to know whether its target market likes its products, it should not limit its research to existing customers. Doing so omits those who are so unimpressed with the product that they do not buy it.

Results of surveys that consist of an open invitation to register an opinion can be biased. Typically, the respondents use a fax machine or a 900 telephone number to send in their views on a particular topic, such as a political issue. Such methods usually do not generate representative opinions, but only responses from those who feel strongly enough to pay the phone or fax charge.

The usual way to make samples representative of populations is to use **probability sampling.** This is a process of selecting research subjects so that each member of the population has a known chance of being selected because they are selected randomly.

probability sampling
Selecting research subjects in such a way that each member of the population has a known chance of being selected because the subjects are selected randomly.

benchmarking
Identifying organizations that excel at carrying out a function and using their practices as a springboard for improvement.

Benchmarking   Many organizations seeking to create value have sought primary data through the practice of **benchmarking.** This involves identifying one or more organizations that excel at carrying out some function and using their practices as a source of ideas for improvement. For example, L. L. Bean is noted for its excellent order fulfillment. During one spring, the company mailed 500,000 packages, with every order filled correctly. Even during the busy Christmas season, the company fills 99.9 percent of its orders correctly.[16] Therefore, other organizations have sought to improve their own order fulfillment by benchmarking L. L. Bean.

Organizations carry out benchmarking through activities such as reading about other organizations, visiting or calling them, and taking apart competing products to see how they are made. In effect, benchmarking is an information source because the process generates ideas for improving marketing and other activities. The process of benchmarking varies according to the information needs of the organization and the resources available.[17]

Benchmarking can deliver results, but only under certain conditions. It is most useful for learning about existing rather than new products and about business practices, including ways of providing value to customers. Benchmarked organizations are less likely to reveal information about new products or to disclose their strategies to competitors.

Xerox is widely credited with the first benchmarking project in the United States. In 1979, Xerox studied Japanese competitors to learn how they could sell midsize copiers for less than what it cost Xerox to make them. Today many companies including AT&T, Eastman Kodak, and Motorola use benchmarking as a standard management tool. Pittsburgh's Mellon Bank started benchmarking to improve the way it handled customer complaints about its credit card billing. Mellon benchmarked seven companies, including credit card operations, an airline, and a competing bank, by visiting three companies and phoning four. By applying what it learned, the bank cut its time to resolve a complaint from an average of 45 days to 25 days.[18]

secondary data
Data gathered for some purpose other than the immediate study at hand.

Secondary Data   Sometimes researchers can obtain needed information—or at least narrow the search for it—by using data collected for some other purpose. The original purpose of the Census Bureau's count of the U.S. population each decade was to determine how many U.S. representatives each state should send to Congress. For that purpose, census data are primary data. However, many marketers use these population counts and other Census Bureau data to learn about the size and composition of markets (see Table 5.3). In this capacity, they are using the data as **secondary data,** that is, data "not gathered for the immediate study at hand but for some other purpose."[19] Government and industry organizations are key external sources of secondary data; internal sources might include sales records and documentation of product repairs.

Kenneth Seiff used secondary data to arrive at a basic marketing strategy for his company, Pivot Corporation, which makes golf-related sportswear. Statistics from the National Golf Foundation indicated to Pivot's founder that the largest age segment of U.S. golfers were in their twenties. Yet it was easy to see from current products that makers of golf apparel were targeting golfers over 50. Other data indicated that about half of all golfers play less than seven times a year. Together, these statistics told Seiff

T A B L E 5.3
Information Available from the
Population Census

Population	Housing
All Persons and Housing Units	
Household relationship	Number of units in structure
Sex	Number of rooms in unit
Race	Unit owned or rented
Age	Vacancy characteristics
Marital status	Value of owned unit or rent paid
Hispanic origin	
Sample of Persons and Housing Units	
Education—enrollment and attainment	Source of water and method of sewage disposal
Place of birth, citizenship, and year of entry	Autos, light trucks, and vans
Ancestry	Kitchen facilities
Language spoken at home	Year structure built
Migration	Year moved into residence
Disability	Number of bedrooms
Fertility	Farm residence
Veteran status	Shelter costs, including utilities
Employment and unemployment	Condominium status
Occupation, industry, and class of worker	Plumbing
Place of work and commuting to work	Telephone
Work experience and income	Utilities and fuel

that there was opportunity to produce youthful designs and make them available in department stores, rather than country club pro shops.[20]

Many types of secondary data are available at little or no cost. One of the most important sources for data about the United States is the U.S. Bureau of the Census. Every five years the Census Bureau conducts eight economic censuses, each describing an industrial sector (i.e., retail, transportation, utilities, etc.). Each business must report such basic operating statistics as number of employees, annual payroll, and the value of goods and services produced in the year of the census. Until recently, such extensive data were useful primarily to big organizations with mainframe computers. Today, however, a personal computer with a good-sized memory and a CD-ROM drive can get the information from CD-based software selling for about $1,000—well within the range of most small businesses.[21]

A few private sources of data include MRI, Simmons, and the *Buying Power Index.* The Prizm database (from Claritas/NPDC in Alexandria, Virginia) can identify clusters of consumers by a variety of criteria, including lifestyle and demographic segments. To learn about organizational buyers, a marketer might tap into Dun's Business Locator, an index on CD-ROM that provides basic data on over 10 million U.S. businesses.[22] In addition, on-line databases provide a wealth of secondary data.

Secondary data may be too dated or not focused enough to be used for a particular decision. However, because gathering secondary data tends to be less expensive than conducting primary research, an efficient research strategy is to begin by searching for secondary data. The information generated by this search can narrow the focus of any primary research and sometimes can even eliminate the need to obtain primary data.

The Marketing Research Process

Carrying out marketing research involves several steps. First, marketers and marketing researchers formulate the problem to be solved. Then the researchers determine a research design appropriate for solving the problem. Using the tools

F I G U R E 5.3 *Steps in the Marketing Research Process*

specified in the research design, researchers collect data. They then analyze and interpret the data, and communicate the findings by preparing and submitting a research report. Figure 5.3 summarizes this process.

Formulate the Problem

The marketing research process begins when someone in the organization has a problem that requires information. Marketers may want to evaluate new opportunities or improve current practices. Perhaps a product development team wants to know what price buyers will be willing to pay for a new car stereo with a given set of features. Perhaps an advertising manager wants to know whether an ad campaign is getting the anticipated results. A small-business owner might want to know whether her product was selling better in department stores or in specialty shops. Marketers use research to help them answer such questions.

When marketers need information, they should describe the problem and the kinds of information that might help them make a decision. For example, marketers might have to improve the performance of the sales force or decide the best distribution channels for a new product. In order to make such decisions, marketers and researchers need to work together to understand the decision and to specify the information that would be useful.

Sometimes marketers confuse problems with symptoms. A *problem* is a situation requiring some type of action, whereas a *symptom* is merely evidence that a problem exists. Thus, a number of years ago, Xerox was concerned that it was rapidly losing photocopier sales to Japanese competitors. That was the symptom. An investigation revealed that Xerox's marketers were focusing on what features they could add to their copiers to make them more desirable, whereas customers mainly wanted copiers that would break down less often. The problem was product quality. Xerox management realized that to compete, it would have to review data not just on sales and profits, but also on product performance and customer satisfaction.[23]

Focusing on symptoms rather than correctly formulating the problem can lead to vague, unhelpful research. In the case of declining sales, it is not enough to say that the purpose of the research is to improve sales. A marketer must find the problem, then investigate how to improve sales. However, in some cases, research is needed to help with problem formulation. In such situations, marketers might use exploratory research.

Plan a Research Design

"We need to do a survey." Often, when someone needs marketing information, this is the solution proposed. In the view of some managers, the core job of marketing researchers is to conduct surveys and interpret their results. However, the appropriate tools for getting particular information may not include a survey. To get the best information at the lowest cost, marketing researchers need to select the most appropriate research tools. The plan for how to collect and analyze data is known as a **research design.**

Researchers are in the best position to plan a research design when they work closely with marketers to define the problem and issues. A valuable role researchers

research design
The plan for how to collect and analyze data.

can play is to help managers or decision makers define the problem precisely so that research can help solve it.

Basic Research Designs   Based on the problem definition, researchers select one or more of the basic research designs: exploratory, descriptive, and causal research.

Exploratory Research   When researchers seek to discover ideas and insights, they conduct **exploratory research.** In general, exploratory research is used for generating hypotheses or tentative explanations and identifying areas to study further. For example, a researcher might ask consumers to describe their ideal vacation. The responses could give a travel agency ideas for assembling tour packages, or it could give an advertising agency ideas for images to test in planning an ad campaign for a resort.

Exploratory research gathers information from whatever sources are likely to provide useful insights. Thus, researchers tend to be less concerned with probability sampling and more concerned with opening communication lines to those with something to say. A case in point is the use of toll-free numbers and Web sites to learn about customer satisfaction. The Subway chain of sandwich restaurants has its phone number printed on its napkins. The 100 or so callers each week aren't necessarily a representative sample, but they do keep the company aware of what issues customers feel strongly enough to call about.[24] Some of these issues merit further investigation.

Descriptive Research   Studying how often something occurs or what, if any, relationship exists between two variables is called **descriptive research.** A researcher might want to know whether men or women more often select vacation destinations. A researcher might examine whether more people select a cruise package from a brochure whose front cover shows a photo of people swimming and dancing or one that shows bountiful buffets. In the latter case, the researcher is looking for a relationship between the brochure design and the success of the promotional effort.

As with exploratory research, the results of descriptive research may become the basis for further investigation. At Marsh Supermarkets, researchers on catwalks above the floor watched the movements of shoppers and learned that they tended to buy more from displays at the periphery of the store. Shoppers often avoided going up and down the aisles, where dry goods were stocked. So the researchers experimented with varying display space, repositioning various products, and installing TV monitors in the periphery that play ads for center-store items.[25]

exploratory research
Research that seeks to discover ideas and insights and to generate hypotheses.

descriptive research
Research that studies how often something occurs or what, if any, relationship exists between two variables.

Continental Airlines proudly advertises its top ranking in J.D. Power and Associates 1996 Domestic Airline Frequent Flyer Satisfaction Study, a survey that consisted of over 7,000 flight evaluations by frequent flyers. J.D. Power and Associates was the first marketing information firm to measure a customer's satisfaction after a sale—a type of descriptive research. Today, the Agoura Hills, California-based firm is doing business with every manufacturer that sells cars in the United States, as well as conducting research for other industries such as airlines, hotels, credit cards, telecommunications, and computer makers.

Perhaps now, certain luxury cars will start referring to themselves as the Continental Airlines of automobiles.

Continental
More airline for your money.

causal research
Research that looks for cause-and-effect relationships.

experiment
Research that involves manipulating one or more variables while keeping others constant, and measuring the results.

test marketing
A controlled experiment in a limited geographical area to test the impact of one or more proposed marketing actions.

Causal Research   The follow-up experiments at Marsh Supermarkets were a type of causal research. **Causal research** looks for cause-and-effect relationships. In other words, it doesn't just investigate whether there is a relationship between two variables, such as brochure design and vacation purchase. Rather, it seeks to find whether the design *causes* people to choose the cruise package. Cause-and-effect relationships are hard to demonstrate. In the case of the cruise brochure, one possibility would be to ask vacationers why they made the choices they did. In this case, the researcher would hope that vacationers really know what motivated them. Another possibility is to set up an experiment in which exposure to the brochure is systematically varied.

An **experiment** is a research design that involves manipulating one or more variables while keeping the others constant and measuring the results. Maritz Motivation Company conducted an experiment using eye-tracking equipment to test consumer responses to mailers printed in one, two, or four colors.[26] Many marketing experiments involve testing consumer reactions when a marketer varies the content of advertising for a particular product.[27]

Among the most common ways consumer goods marketers use experiments is in test marketing. To conduct **test marketing,** a product is offered in limited geographic areas, known as test markets, to see how customers respond to it. BirdsEye used test marketing to introduce the first frozen foods to consumers. In 1930 BirdsEye placed specially built storage cases for frozen foods in 18 grocery stores in Springfield, Massachusetts. Salespeople gathered data by interviewing customers in their homes to get detailed reactions to the first frozen products: chicken, haddock, sirloin steak, and strawberries. At the end of the 40-week test period, marketers concluded that frozen foods had strong potential.[28]

If the response in test markets is less than forecasted in the marketing plan, the marketing mix can be adjusted before offering the product to the entire target market. The results of test marketing can also influence other marketing decisions, such as the creation of advertising messages. Test marketing is an important way to forecast sales of a new product.

Problems with the research design can make the results of test marketing difficult to interpret. First, a researcher should select test markets that are representative of the total market to be served. If the total market is diverse, this may be difficult to do. Furthermore, uncontrollable events, such as bad weather or retaliation by a competitor, may make results unreliable. Finally, organizations may spend more in test markets than they will afterward. For example, marketers may be tempted to overpromote a new product during test marketing in order to make it look good and encourage a full-scale introduction.

Constraints on Research Design   In designing research, the amount of time and money available for collecting and analyzing the data needs to be considered. These are constraints on research. Generally, when the consequences of a decision are great, marketers spend more on research. The time available depends on the importance of the decision and on the consequences of delaying it. For example, if a competitor is likely to launch a new product quickly, the organization might want to act without doing complete market research.

Even when marketing research is expensive, the potential benefits can make it an important investment. This was the case with Biosite Diagnostics, a San Diego-based biotechnology company that spent $150,000 to hire a research firm to survey potential users of its planned first product, a disposable diagnostic test called Triage. The research showed that the target market—hospital emergency room physicians—was very interested in Triage, which enabled the unproven company to attract investment funds for production. Research results also helped the company refine its marketing strategy in two ways. First, the results showed that lab technicians, not doctors, made the purchase decisions for lab tests. Second, Biosite learned that the potential market was so big it should rely on distributors to handle selling activities. So Biosite

T A B L E 5.4
Basic Research Techniques

Technique	Advantages	Disadvantages
Observation	Accurate and objective	Limited to measurement of behavior and a few demographic characteristics; much time usually required
Surveys	Versatility; ability to uncover motivations, attitudes, beliefs; relative speed	Possible failure of subjects to report their attitudes, beliefs, behavior accurately; likelihood that some people will decline to participate

arranged with one distributor to sell Triage in the United States and another to handle European sales.[29]

Marketing research need not be sophisticated and expensive to be worthwhile. A survey of small to midsize companies conducted by *Inc.* magazine found that nearly 40 percent spent less than $1,000 to conduct their marketing research.[30] The top sources of information were current customers and colleagues.

Collect Data

Depending on the research design, collecting data may involve a variety of activities, from looking up articles on a computer database to watching a sample of consumers try out a product prototype to asking questions over the telephone. Whatever activities are involved, data collection requires personnel. They may be employees of the organization using the research, or the organization may contract with a research service. In either case, the accuracy of the data depends in part on hiring qualified people to do the collection and on supervising these people effectively.

Whenever a research project involves collecting primary data, some errors are bound to occur during data collection. For example, some members of a random sample may refuse to participate, survey respondents may check the wrong answers, or research staff may make mistakes when coding data to be entered into the computer. Researchers cannot prevent all errors but should have plans for reducing them.

Types of Data Needed   Given the information needed and budget constraints, researchers must decide whether to use primary data, secondary data, or some combination of the two. One common approach is to start the research effort by analyzing secondary data and using it to develop a plan for later gathering primary data. Thus, the collection and analysis of secondary data is used for exploratory research. When the research involves collecting secondary data, researchers should evaluate the sources of data to make sure that they are accurate.

If researchers decide primary data is needed, they select the technique or combination of techniques that is most suitable. The basic possibilities are observation and surveys. Table 5.4 lists advantages and disadvantages of each.

Observation   Sometimes people don't do exactly what they say they will, and sometimes users of a product can't fully describe their experiences with it. For these reasons, researchers may use **observation,** or the collection of data by recording actions of customers or events in the marketplace. Collecting data by observation includes walking through a competitor's store to observe operations and prices. Researchers might call their own company, posing as a customer, to observe the quality telephone service employees deliver.

Roger Kao, owner of the Golden Wok chain of Chinese restaurants in Mountain View, California, used observation to research the idea of providing home delivery. When Kao came up with the concept, he visited a Domino's Pizza outlet, ordered a pizza, then slowly ate it on the premises as he watched how the company worked. He learned tactics he wanted to apply to his own chain and identified aspects of the operation he could do better.[31]

observation
The collection of data by recording actions of customers or events in the marketplace.

Observation can be useful for learning about competitors and their products. Marketers can observe competitors' strategies, such as product offerings, advertising, outlets, and prices, and record this information in a database. Such a database also should include notes on what competitors' employees say in speeches to trade groups. Pamela Kelly, who operates Rue de France, a catalog company that sells lace curtains, places difficult orders with competitors and observes how those orders are handled.[32]

Observation is used to measure television viewing habits. To record what television shows are being broadcast in participating homes and who is watching, A. C. Nielsen Company uses a "people meter." Each member of the participating household has his or her own viewing number. Viewers are supposed to enter their numbers into the people meter whenever they turn on the set or change the channel. Nielsen uses the resulting data to produce the Nielsen ratings of TV shows. This type of observation has been extended to the use of personal computers. NPD Group's PC-Meter measures when home users work on their computers, what software and on-line services they use, and how much time they spend on line.[33]

survey
The collection of data through the use of a questionnaire.

Surveys   To learn the beliefs and thoughts of the people being studied, researchers use surveys. A **survey** is the collection of data by a questionnaire. Researchers can conduct surveys through the mail, by telephone, or in person.

Surveys are a major form of research in the United States. One study showed over 40 percent of respondents participated in a survey during the previous year. About three-quarters had participated in a survey at some time.[34]

Surveys are especially important for marketers seeking to create value for their customers because they can help identify what benefits and costs are significant to customers. The Fort Sanders Health System—six health care facilities serving the Knoxville, Tennessee, area—conducted a survey of customer satisfaction and learned that some of the measures of quality it considered most important were not what mattered most to hospital patients. Many hospitals tried to upgrade and promote their meals, but patients ranked food 32nd out of 34 items in terms of importance. Employees place importance on good clinical care, but patients take that for granted. What patients pay most attention to are the quality and degree of personal attention they receive from personnel in all areas of the hospital.[35]

Developing a Survey   When researchers' jobs include developing a survey, they can use several techniques to ensure that the survey will work as intended. One important step is to pretest the questionnaire. In a pretest, researchers ask a few people to answer the questions and check to see if they are confused by any of them.

It is also important to see whether people take longer to complete the survey than anticipated. The biggest objection people have to completing surveys is the amount of time involved. Refusal rates increase dramatically when surveys require more than 12 minutes to complete.[36] Therefore, researchers should consider this factor if they want people to participate. Ben & Jerry's uses short questions, multiple choices, and visuals to help ensure that its survey will work as intended. (See Figure 5.4.)

Researchers should compare the structure of the survey with the kinds of information to be provided by the research. To check whether the data will be relevant, researchers should plan the analysis and the format for reporting the data.

Mail Surveys   To reach a large number of widely dispersed people, a mail survey can be effective. Surveying people by mail is useful when they have to look up information or could be uncomfortable discussing the issues with strangers. For example, the review of a textbook manuscript is done by mail, enabling the reviewer to read the manuscript and refer back to it when making comments. On the down side, conducting a survey by mail can be time consuming. Subjects may not get around to replying for weeks or months, or may not respond at all.

FIGURE 5.4
A Survey That Takes
Less Than 2 Minutes
to Complete

Telephone Surveys

To get immediate responses, researchers use telephone surveys. This is an efficient way to contact a large group of people. Also, people are more apt to participate in a telephone survey because it is easier than filling out questionnaires.

Drawbacks of a telephone survey include the inability to show products over the phone or to reach people who have no phone or no listing of their number. Also, many consumers screen their calls, thanks to answering machines and Caller I.D. If many of them choose not to take calls from researchers, the research sample may not be representative.

Personal Surveys

To discuss issues in depth, researchers can use personal surveys that enable them to probe for further information. This type of survey is suitable for complex or emotional issues. It also allows the interviewer to present visual information such as a sample product or advertisement. However, personal surveys tend to be time consuming and expensive. Also, responses may be influenced by perceptions of the interviewer. Popular forms of personal surveys are mall intercepts, focus group interviews, and in-home surveys.

A **mall intercept** is a personal survey in which the interviewer stands in a shopping center, stops consumers, and asks them to participate. This is often an effective way to find potential purchasers. However, the sample of respondents may be biased. Only certain types of people may be willing to take the time to participate—notably, people with few other obligations. Also, interviewers may tend to ask certain kinds of people—say, those who look the friendliest or the least busy.

A **focus group interview** is a personal interview of a small group of people in which the interviewer poses open-ended questions and encourages group interaction. In a typical focus group interview, six to twelve people participate for one or two hours. Researchers may observe the interview through a one-way mirror or be present to participate in a dialogue with customers. The interview is often taped so that it can be studied later. Focus groups are useful for identifying issues to explore in more directed follow-up studies (see "Marketing Movers & Shakers: Martin McKendry and Charlie Bass/SoloPoint"). The success of focus groups depends on the ability of inter-

mall intercept
A personal survey in which the interviewer stops people in a shopping center and asks them to participate.

focus group interview
A personal interview conducted simultaneously among a small number of individuals that relies on group discussion to open ended questions.

Martin McKendry and Charlie Bass/SoloPoint

Charlie Bass has a mantra: "Markets, markets, markets, markets." He stuck to that mantra as he and Martin McKendry co-founded a company in California that was eventually called SoloPoint. In fact, Bass had to keep chanting his mantra, because SoloPoint didn't have anything else—no products, no technology, no customers—yet. Bass's point was that his company wasn't going to produce anything until they knew exactly what potential customers wanted. Perhaps his other mantra could have been, "research, research, research."

Of course, Bass and McKendry had an idea of where they wanted to head; they just needed to find out more. "I was intrigued by this individual-office phenomenon, and I did not see in it the elements of control, management, and sophistication I felt could be applied to it," recalls Bass. Thus, SoloPoint's market became individuals who work in small or home offices, called the SOHO market. Still, Bass and McKendry weren't certain how they could create a new product to serve those potential customers.

So they did research. First, they obtained data that told them there are workers in 40 million home offices and 5 million small offices. Then they conducted focus groups in which participants told Bass and McKendry that what they really needed was a "seamless phone system." In other words, they needed a product that could connect their business phone lines with their cellular phone lines and allow for screening without the aid of the phone company. They wanted a product that could also separate faxes from phone calls on the same line. McKendry calls all this "stupid phone tricks." But Bass and McKendry listened; and the result is SoloPoint's PCM, or personal call manager. The PCM is a little gray box that does those "stupid phone tricks."

Further research told SoloPoint's executives that the price threshold for SOHO individuals was around $400, the point at which potential customers would have to consult with someone else before making the purchase. If the product were priced at $200, they might just buy it off the shelf and try it; at $300, they'd want to investigate the product a little further (perhaps read a review) in order to know exactly what they were buying. So the PCM entered the market at $379. Finally, SoloPoint engaged in some test marketing, with about 100 units in the field. (*Inc.* magazine engaged in some marketing research of its own, conducting a reader's poll via e-mail or a toll-free number to find out if readers who were SOHO workers were interested in SoloPoint's product.) By then, the company had a mission: to become the "entry point of communications into the home office."

It is still too early to tell how well the PCM will fare in an industry where technology is constantly changing. But if McKendry and Bass keep listening to their markets, they should be able to give customers what they want—all in a little gray box.

Source: David Whitford, "Phone Improvement," *Inc.,* February 1996, pp. 68–75. Adapted with permission, *Inc.* magazine, February 1996. Copyright 1996 by Goldhirsh Group, Inc., 38 Commercial Wharf, Boston, MA 02110

Explore more at www.soloprint.com.

---

viewers to encourage the discussion and the ability of the researchers to interpret the results.

In-home interviews are surveys in which interviewers visit people in their homes. In Eastern Europe, Procter & Gamble researchers visited consumers and learned that many of the locally made detergents smelled terrible and worked so poorly that clothes had to be soaked all day. P&G concluded that consumers would be willing to switch to its Ariel detergent.[37] In-home interviews give researchers a chance to learn a lot about consumers. However, they depend on a representative sample being at home when the interviewer seeks them out, as well as on their willingness to talk to a stranger in their home. Because of these limitations, in-home interviews are the least-used type of survey.[38]

in-home interview
A personal survey in which the interviewer goes door to door to visit subjects in their homes.

Analyze and Interpret Data

To turn collected data into information, researchers must analyze it. When data are recorded on a questionnaire or other form, the researcher first reviews each form

coding
Assigning numeric symbols to the data collected.

tabulating
Counting the number of cases that fall into each category or combination of categories of response.

to make sure it has been filled out completely and properly. Then the researcher codes the data; **coding** means assigning numbers to the answers. Next, the data are **tabulated,** which means the number of cases that fall into each category or combination of categories of response are counted. For example, if the research involves watching people try out computer software, tabulation might include counting the number of users who do or do not consult the reference manual. If the research is a mail survey asking for demographic information about magazine subscribers, tabulation could include counting the number of subscribers in each income category broken down by age group.

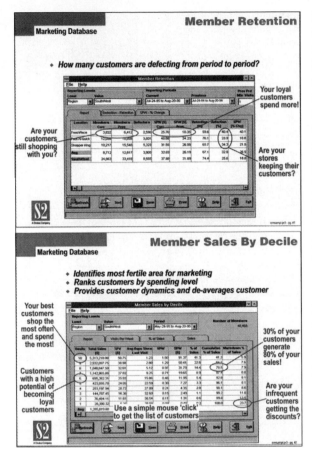

Statistical Analysis   When the data have been tabulated, researchers may perform various kinds of statistical analysis. The analysis may be as basic as computing the average response to a question or it may include a variety of sophisticated techniques. Modern personal computers are powerful enough to handle most types of data analysis. The selection of techniques should be based on which will produce the information that the research was designed to get.

Interpretation   Before preparing a final report, researchers need to determine what the data mean: What insights do they provide on the problem? Researchers also need to assess whether the results seem logical and reasonable. If not, part of the researcher's job is to review the assumptions behind the research as well as the process of arriving at the result. Researchers' logic and experience help them spot mistakes that could prove embarrassing and costly. Using sophisticated analytical techniques or state-of-the-art computer systems will not prevent errors from faulty assumptions, a poor research process, or even mistakes in data entry. At Oscar Mayer, researchers use data to generate models of what results to expect from various courses of action. If the results predicted by the model don't seem to make sense, researchers take another look at the model to find problems with it. If they don't see anything wrong with the model, they proceed with caution, perhaps testing the recommended course of action on a small scale.[39]

To help with statistical analysis and interpretation, marketers may use software such as Customer Relationship Marketing (CRM) from S2 Systems, Inc. in Dallas. Using data collected at stores, CRM computes statistics about stores' performance and shoppers' spending patterns. The program displays the data in formats such as the report shown here, to help marketers identify performance problems, target their biggest customers, and diagnose other marketing problems.

Evaluating the results can uncover situations where modifying further research could generate more helpful information. Campbell Soup Company set up a test panel in which consumers evaluated a proposed lower-sodium version of V-8 juice. The consumers in the test panel—men and women who had drunk a similar product in the previous six months—rated the new product unfavorably compared to their current product. However, the company was committed to developing a reduced-sodium version of V-8 and wanted to know how to market it successfully, so the researchers investigated further. They learned that most loyal drinkers of this type of product tended not to be very health conscious and therefore thought its high sodium content was just fine. The researchers set up another test panel, selecting consumers who used the type of product and also were sensitive to health issues. The modified test panel preferred the lower-sodium version, so Campbell targeted Light 'n Tangy V-8 juice to this type of consumer.[40]

Prepare the Research Report

Finally, researchers put the information generated by the study into a report. The report should begin with a concise summary of what the research was designed to do, what the results were, and what these results mean in terms of making marketing decisions. Supplementary information in the report then describes the research in greater detail, including the method and limitations. Statistical information, sample forms, and the like appear in an appendix at the end of the report. Besides a written report, marketers may request one or more oral reports.

A thorough research project may require much technical expertise and sophisticated statistical analysis. Nevertheless, marketers require that the report be understandable. If it is not useful as an aid to decision making, the report does not fulfill the goal of marketing research.

Applications of New Technology

Much as computer technology is enabling marketers to better tailor their offerings to create customer value, it also enables marketing researchers to meet the unique needs of individual users within the organization. The user of a personal computer in a network can retrieve data relevant to a particular problem and manipulate the data to provide a variety of types of information. Thus, one user might tap into the database to determine when to restock inventory, another might look up data to quote prices or delivery dates to a prospective customer, and a third user might identify the regions in which a new product was selling best.

Geographic Information Systems

geographic information system
The combining of various kinds of demographic data with geographic information on maps.

A useful tool that is helping marketers identify and learn about potential customers is computer mapping. Mapping software, which at its most sophisticated is called a **geographic information system (GIS),** combines various kinds of demographic data with geographic information on maps. The user can draw a map showing average income levels of a county, then zoom closer to look at particular towns in more detail. Most GIS programs on the market can show information as detailed as a single block; some programs can show individual buildings. Seeing the information on a map can be more useful than merely reading tables of numbers. At PepsiCo, a GIS enabled marketers to analyze traffic patterns and consumer demographics to identify the best sites for new Taco Bell and Pizza Hut restaurants.[41]

GISs once required mainframe computers and could cost more than $100,000, but today's applications are usually off-the-shelf programs that can run on personal computers. Microsoft's Excel, the popular spreadsheet program, contains a GIS function. Programs designed specifically for use as GISs include EasyStreet (by OverPlay Data Company), Maptitude (Caliper Corporation), Mapinfo (MapInfo), MapLinx (MapLinx), and GeoWizard (GeoDemX); some of these cost less than $500. Atlas Select (from Strategic Mapping) costs over $1,000 but includes data from the Census Bureau and Arbitron, among other sources.[42]

TerrAlign *is a geographical information system that allows marketers to examine statistics about their company's sales territories. For example, they can compare the number of customers in each territory, and the number of hours required to serve each territory. This information can help organizations adjust the boundaries of sales territories when needed to improve the performance of their sales force.*

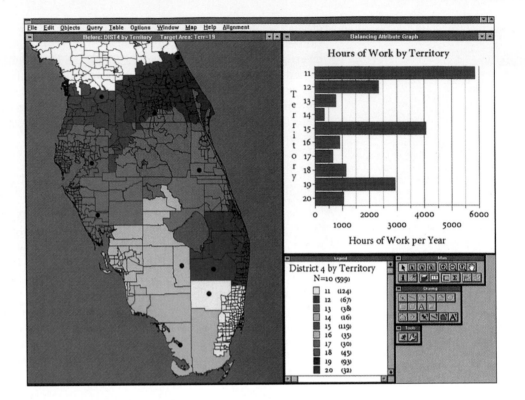

Virtual Reality

Another computer capability being applied to marketing research is virtual reality. This technology enables users wearing special goggles and gloves to see and manipulate objects in three dimensions, as if the objects were actually there. Virtual reality enables marketers to display potential new products or product displays without going to the expense of physically building them. MarketWare Corporation has developed Visionary Shopper software to use in consumer shopping experiments. The subject can remove products from the shelf, examine labels, and react to such variables as price or packaging by choosing whether to place the items in a shopping cart. The software developers hope that the results of experiments using Visionary Shopper will be more realistic than answers to a survey.[43]

technical-market research
Research incorporating customers by demonstrating a product on a computer screen and asking customers to evaluate it.

A major application of virtual reality to marketing research is known as **technical-market research**.[44] This type of research incorporates customers into the process of product design by demonstrating products on a computer screen and asking customers to evaluate them. The software shows the product in three dimensions, models how it will perform, and demonstrates how changes in the product's design affect performance. This process helps organizations find unmet customer wants. General Motors used this technology to test consumers' reactions to the view from the front seat of a new car.[45]

When companies use technical-market research, they bring together personnel from marketing and from research and development. The cross-functional team establishes goals, matches customer value with possible product attributes, develops computer models, and identifies target markets. Engineers and marketing researchers together interview targeted customers, using computers to show them what the potential product will look like and how it will perform, with and without modifications suggested by the customers. Such teamwork enables the organization to use the full potential of its technological expertise and to move quickly from concept to distribution of a product. In the tire industry, such a collaboration led to development of all-season tires, which free customers from changing their tires every winter and spring. In addition, Goodyear Tire & Rubber Company used technical-market research to work with automobile manufacturers to develop a variety of tire improvements.[46]

Virtual reality is used for many purposes—training, manufacturing, and even product development. The Cave Automatic Virtual Environment (CAVE) is a 3-D virtual reality chamber connected to powerful super-computers. In the photo, engineers at FMC Corporation are using their version of the CAVE, a virtual environments lab, to develop stronger deck structures that can withstand the battering of waves when a ship is moved near on oil production platform. The engineers stay dry in the virtual reality chamber while "ocean waves" pound a ship.

The Internet

The Internet is a research tool with extremely broad impact. Marketers can use this global computer network to tap into information on almost any topic (see "Put It into Practice: Surf the 'Net"). Directing search software to find references to particular words or phrases can send marketers to Web sites of competitors, customers, suppliers, and other key individuals and organizations. It can help marketers look up 10K reports detailing standard financial data on publicly held companies. Marketers can also search for references to the company, its products, competitors, or a category of needs the organization is interested in serving. The search might lead to relevant newsgroups on **Usenet,** the network of Internet "addresses" for electronic mail. When marketers identify relevant groups, they can post questions about their own or their competitors' products and get a high level of customer feedback. Organizations uncomfortable with this do-it-yourself approach can hire electronic clipping services such as CompuServe's Journalist and Clarinet Communications' ClariNews (which scans international wire services) to do it for them.[47]

There are many research opportunities on the Internet. Organizations can spot problems with products, likely moves by competitors, new customer wants, and more. Eric Anderson, chief executive of Art Anderson Associates, uses the Internet to locate potential customers for his organization, an engineering and architecture firm that designs ferry vessels and port facilities. Anderson looks up Web sites and newsgroups of foreign tourism boards to look for interest in developing industry or tourism in particular areas. When he sees a push for growth, he looks for the force behind it and tries to sell that organization his services.[48]

usenet
The network of Internet addresses for electronic mail.

Ethical Considerations

Information is so important to gaining competitive advantage that marketers may be tempted to overstep ethical boundaries to get it (see "You Decide: How Much Information Should Marketers Have about Consumers?"). One marketing research firm, Atkinson Research, was sued for using a survey questionnaire to solicit viewer response to programs for its client, KARE-TV. The survey asked respondents to watch a certain TV channel as often as possible. This may seem innocent enough, but the suit charged that the survey was deliberately conducted during a Nielsen ratings period in order to rig the ratings in favor of KARE-TV.[49] Also troublesome are so-called telephone surveys that become

Deceit and Fraud in Marketing Research

Suppose your boss asks you to do a survey of consumer interest in a potential new product that you know your boss is enthusiastic about. In fact, your boss has been speaking highly of this product to the company's other executives. Do you care what the results of the survey will be? Most likely, you hope that the results will support the boss's viewpoint, since that will please him or her. What if the results are ambiguous or show a distinct lack of interest in the new product? At such times, it can be tempting to make some "adjustments" so that the data produce the desired result. When time is running short and many research subjects have failed to respond, it can be tempting to compromise the integrity of the survey in order to produce a report that makes the research effort look complete. Bowing to such temptations, of course, would be unethical. Users of marketing information depend on researchers to provide accurate information for making informed decisions.

In other situations, researchers may be tempted to misrepresent the truth to participants. For example, researchers may promise participants that responses are anonymous when they aren't. Secretly marking questionnaires so participants can be identified violates anonymity.

Another kind of false claim is to ask people to participate in a research project that is really a front for a sales attempt. Such experiences can lead people to distrust marketing researchers and to avoid participating in research projects in the future. This poses a real problem for marketing research. Over the last decade, the proportion of people contacted who have refused to participate in a research study has more than doubled, to over 30 percent.[52]

Invasion of Privacy

If research is not handled carefully, it can invade people's privacy. In planning a research effort, researchers should identify ways in which privacy could be invaded and avoid doing so. For example, participants are likely to feel their privacy has been invaded if they haven't given consent to participate. Thus, it may be an invasion of privacy for a researcher to observe consumers shopping without first asking their permission. Two ways to minimize this type of invasion of privacy are to post notices stating that researchers are observing customers on the premises and to approach each consumer after the observation and ask for permission to use the data gathered.

Modern technology has made this issue increasingly relevant. For example, people who call an organization to gather information or place an order may be surprised to discover that the organization already has information about them via a Caller ID hookup to its computer.[53] Organizations that introduce such systems should ensure that customers get benefits (such as greater efficiency and accuracy of order taking) from them. Similarly, a survey of grocery shoppers found that many engage in shopping practices—such as paying by check, applying for a check cashing card or frequent shopper card, and using such a card—that enable the store to measure their buying behavior. However, almost half the survey participants indicated they were unaware that some or all of these behaviors could make them research participants. Most were unwilling, given the choice, to provide such information to researchers. Stores claim to fully disclose their policies for gathering and sharing information, but two-thirds of respondents said such disclosure had not been made.[54] In other consumer surveys, 90 percent of respondents said they wanted to be consulted before personal information was supplied to third parties, and 84 percent indicated concern about threats to personal privacy.[55] Together, these numbers suggest that marketing researchers need to constantly evaluate their activities to ensure they are acceptable.

Another type of invasion of privacy involves industrial espionage, or efforts to secretly determine what a competitor is doing. Some ways of learning about a competitor, such as reading magazine articles or taking apart and studying the competitor's existing products, are considered acceptable. Some organizations let competitors visit their facilities to benchmark areas of operation that are not considered proprie-

T A B L E 5.6
Selected Information Sources:
Secondary Data on
Global Markets

Information Source	Types of Data
The Export Connection, a National Trade Databank service of the U.S. Department of Commerce (Washington, D.C.)	Monthly series of CD-ROM disks containing data from 15 U.S. government agencies, including marketing research reports, information about specific countries and their economies, and a listing of foreign importers of U.S. products
Global Market Surveys	Detailed surveys for given industries such as graphics, computers, medical equipment, industrial equipment
Dun & Bradstreet's Principal International Business	Names, addresses, number of employees, products produced, and chief executive officer, up to 6 SIC classifications (4-digit) for each organization; over 144,000 business units classified by 4-digit SIC and alphabetical order
Moody's International Manual	Company histories, descriptions of business, financial statistics, management personnel
Overseas Business Reports	Monthly reports provide information for marketing to specific countries (e.g., "Marketing in Pakistan," "Marketing in Nigeria")
The Exporter's Guide to Federal Resources for Small Business (Washington, D.C.: U.S. Government Printing Office)	Reference guide to export assistance available from the U.S. government
Automated Trade Locator Assistance System (district offices of the Small Business Administration)	Results of current marketing research about world markets
Small Business Foundation of America, export opportunity hotline: 800-243-7232	Answers to questions from small businesses interested in exporting
Hotline sponsored by AT&T and seven other organizations: 800-USA-XPORT	Free exporter's kit and data on 50 industries and 78 countries
International trade fairs (sponsored by many industry organizations and national governments, including the U.S. Small Business Administration)	Products and needs of existing and potential buyers and competitors from around the world

Source: Giordano A. Chiaruttini, "Brave New World," *Entrepreneur,* May 1993, p. 156; George Gendron, "FYI: Foreign Affairs," *Inc.,* June 1993, p. 14; "Going Global: Canada," supplement to *Inc.,* June 1993; Aimee Stern, "Do You Know What They Want?" *International Business,* March 1993, pp. 102–103; Robert W. Hass, *Industrial Marketing Management* (Boston: PWS-Kent Publishing Company, 1989), p. 435.

tary. However, marketers should avoid collecting data through deceptive practices such as having a researcher pose as an employee of a competing organization. Likewise, it is unethical for researchers to share information about clients with other clients.

Here, too, technology is raising some new challenges. In particular, the free flow of information on the Internet gives marketers greater access to information about competitors. For example, asking about a competitor's product—or even a general class of products—can elicit feedback from competitors' customers or even from the competitors themselves. One possible solution is for marketers to identify the organization for which they are working.[56] Also, if an on-line search turns up documents that clearly were meant to be proprietary, the organization should avoid using them.

Global Marketing Research

The differences among countries make marketing research especially important when marketers consider targeting consumers or organizations globally. Global marketers often follow the research strategy of starting with secondary data and following up with primary research as needed. They use available secondary sources to study a country's laws, demographics, and culture. They also explore product needs and wants in the countries they plan to enter. Table 5.6 lists some sources of information about international markets.

The basic principles for conducting primary research are the same for foreign as for domestic markets. However, researchers should be aware of cultural differences relevant to research design.[57] For example, in Latin America, Russia, and China, telephone interviews are impractical because too few people have phones. In Saudi Arabia, door-to-door interviewing is illegal. To interview Saudi males, researchers can meet with them in their offices; to interview females, researchers can ask to be introduced to businessmen's wives and their friends.

Researchers also must be aware of cultural differences in communication styles. By mainstream U.S. standards, Italians, Spaniards, and Latin Americans may seem to be effusive and to overstate their answers. By the same standards, Germans and the English may understate their enthusiasm, and Asians may say what they think the interviewer wants to hear. In China, Gallup China Ltd. found that subjects were brought up short by follow-up questions asking why they had answered a previous question the way they had. After a pause, most subjects would reply, "Because it's true, that's why."[58]

In spite of the challenges, Procter & Gamble has used marketing research to help it enter the Russian market. For example, it hired local researchers to conduct door-to-door interviews about hygiene and household cleaning practices. P&G learned that Russians typically store detergent in their bathrooms, so the company made sure its detergent boxes could withstand water damage. P&G also gave samples to hundreds of Russian consumers, then interviewed them two weeks later, asking about the products and P&G's advertising. Among other information, the company learned Russians prefer that products be labeled in English alone, because they associate this with higher quality.[59]

Summary

Marketing research is the function that links consumers, organizational buyers, and the general public to marketers. Thus, the information that marketing research generates is a vital tool for marketers. Marketers need more than just data—facts and statistics; they need useful information that shows trends and relationships. Computer technology makes it easier to organize data into a marketing decision support system (MDSS), which brings together three types of software: database management, model base management, and a dialog system. Marketers can get information from internal sources (e.g., sales figures, accounting and inventory data) or external sources (e.g., business publications, research services, customer surveys). They can collect primary data through their own surveys or observations, including benchmarking. They can obtain secondary data from a multitude of published sources.

To be effective, marketing research begins with formulation of the problem. Next, researchers create a research design, using exploratory, descriptive, or causal research. Then researchers collect data through means such as checking secondary sources, or through observation or surveys. The next step is analyzing and interpreting data. Finally, the researcher prepares and submits a research report.

Modern technology has expanded marketers' access to detailed information. A geographical information system (GIS) provides maps linked to a variety of demographic data. Virtual reality enables marketers to test the use of expensive products without physically making them. Organizations may engage in technical-market research by demonstrating a product on a computer screen while asking customers to evaluate it. The Internet links marketers to a multitude of research sources, including potential buyers.

Many ethical considerations arise in the course of planning and conducting marketing research. These include instances when the organization may seem to profit from deceit, fraud, and invasion of privacy. Marketing researchers should evaluate whether their actions are ethical, and act accordingly.

When marketers consider serving customers in other countries, they also need marketing research. Just as in domestic research, global marketers usually start by using secondary sources to scan the environment. Then they follow up with primary research if needed. The research design, however, may have to be modified to reflect differences in values, customs, and technology. Many organizations have their international marketing research handled by firms that specialize in that type of work.

Key Terms and Concepts

marketing research (p. 112)
data (p. 112)
information (p. 114)
marketing decision support system
  (p. 114)
single-source data (p. 116)
primary data (p. 118)
statistical inference (p. 118)
probability sampling (p. 119)

benchmarking (p. 119)
secondary data (p. 119)
research design (p. 121)
exploratory research (p. 122)
descriptive research (p. 122)
causal research (p. 123)
experiment (p. 123)
test marketing (p. 123)
observation (p. 124)

survey (p. 125)
mall intercept (p. 126)
focus group interview (p. 126)
in-home interview (p. 127)
coding (p. 128)
tabulating (p. 128)
geographic information system (p. 129)
technical-market research (p. 130)
usenet (p. 131)

Review and Discussion Questions

1. Define *marketing research*. Using this definition, give three examples of how marketers might use marketing research to create greater value for their customers.
2. What are some of the complaints marketers often have about the kinds of marketing information they receive?
3. What are the three types of software necessary for a marketing decision support system (MDSS), and what do they do?
4. If you were a marketer in a company that was too small to hire an outside marketing research firm and your company was developing a new line of "healthful" dog food, what internal and external sources of information might you use to conduct your own marketing research?
5. What are the advantages and limitations of single-source data?
6. Suppose you wanted to conduct research about the market for wedding planning services. How might you use secondary data, then primary data to find the answers to your marketing questions?
7. What is benchmarking? How could it be used to improve a business school?
8. Why is it important for the marketing problem to be clearly formulated before marketing research begins? What is the role of exploratory research in this regard?

9. Suppose you work for a small manufacturer that wants to get a new product to a certain market quickly, to sell for a short time period (say, souvenirs for an event like the Olympics). You want to do some marketing research to determine whether the product will be successful. What constraints on research design would you have to consider?
10. If you were a marketer for a developer that was considering building a new shopping mall, how would you use observation as part of your marketing research?
11. Suppose you are conducting research for a movie distributor by preparing a survey that asks for demographic information about moviegoers in India.
   a. What types of data might be useful?
   b. What are some issues related to the marketing environment that you might need to consider?
12. Suppose you were asked to conduct a survey of potential users of a walk-in health care facility. What questions would you ask yourself to make sure your survey—and the information it provides you—is ethical?
13. What are three major technological innovations that are helping marketers conduct research, and how do they work?

Chapter Project

Imagine that you want to start your own business on campus. You might want to offer a service such as composing resumes, delivering late-night snacks, or childcare for students who are parents. Or you might think of a product that you are certain students (and perhaps professors) would need or use. (Your product might also incorporate service, such as homemade snacks delivered to the customer's door.)

Once you have selected a product or service idea, specify the information that you want to get with research. Then create a questionnaire designed to gather the data that you want. Put the questions in writing. Be sure to pose your questions in such a way that the data you gather will give you the information you need about your market. Test your questionnaire on a couple of classmates by asking them to answer the questions.

Chapter Six

Consumer Behavior

CHAPTER OUTLINE

The Consumer Buying Process
  Need Recognition
  Information Search
  Alternative Evaluation
  Purchase Decision
  Postpurchase Evaluation
Types of Consumer Decision Making
  Routine Decision Making
  Limited Decision Making
  Extensive Decision Making
Social Influences
  Culture
  Subcultures
  Social Class
  Reference Groups
  Family
Marketing Influences
  Product
  Pricing
  Placement (Channels of Distribution)
  Promotion (Marketing Communications)
Situational Influences
  Physical Surroundings
  Social Surroundings
  Time
  Task
  Momentary Conditions
Summary

LEARNING OBJECTIVES

After completing this chapter, you should be able to:

1. Define the steps in the consumer buying process.
2. Summarize how consumer behavior differs according to the type of consumer decision making.
3. Describe how culture, subculture, and social class influence consumer behavior.
4. Explain how reference groups influence consumer behavior.
5. Describe how family roles and the family life cycle can influence purchasing decisions.
6. Discuss how the marketing mix affects the consumer buying process.
7. Identify the major situational influences on consumer behavior.

The American International Toy Fair

Each year in February, thousands of toy buyers for retailers flock to the American International Toy Fair in the hope of finding the hottest toys that manufacturers have to offer. It might be a classic with a new twist, like a CD-ROM Barbie game. It might be a Disney movie tie-in, like figurines from *Pocahontas* and *Hunchback of Notre Dame*. It might be something completely new, like Parker Brothers' game Hot Potato. The Toy Fair isn't child's play; it is serious, competitive business. Buyers comb the exhibits for the toys that will give them the greatest profits while occupying the smallest amount of space in their stores. Exhibitors struggle to get buyers' attention and the advantage usually goes to the bigger companies. Companies will try just about anything to get attention. For instance, one year Playskool paraded huge renditions of its Potato People down Manhattan streets on opening day of the fair.

The buyers and sellers have these goals in common: to make products available to consumers and to influence consumers' decisions to buy. Doing so means first figuring out what consumers want and which toys consumers will believe provide the greatest value. "I tried to figure out what movies and TV shows will be hot around Christmas," says Deran Muckjian, a toy buyer for Bradlees Inc. "It's Disney." Understanding how consumers make decisions to buy products is one key to successful marketing. As you read this chapter, think about the buying decisions you make every day as a consumer. Then think about how you, as a marketer, would use that understanding to create greater value for the consumers of your products.

Source: Chris Reidy, "Much More Than Mere Child's Play," *The Boston Globe*, February 13, 1996, pp. 37, 42. Reprinted courtesy of *The Boston Globe*.

Explore more at www.toy-tma.com/index.html

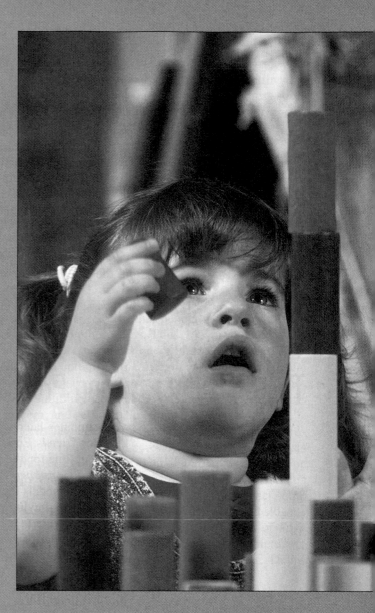

T A B L E 6.1
Characteristics of Three Types of Consumer Decision Making

Type of Decision	Consumer Involvement in Purchase	Characteristics of Consideration Set	Information Sources Consulted	Time Invested
Routine	Low	One or a few brands, sellers, and product characteristics evaluated	Internal sources used	As little as possible
Limited	Moderate	Several brands, sellers, and product characteristics evaluated	Internal and some external sources	Some time invested
Extensive	High	Many brands, sellers, and product characteristics evaluated	Internal and many external sources	Much time invested

In contrast, if customers decide that the benefits of a purchase were less than the costs, they may conclude that they received low value and become dissatisfied. Customers may then recognize that their needs are still unmet or met at too high a cost. This recognition leads buyers to try again to meet their needs—probably by purchasing a different product or brand.

Types of Consumer Decision Making

For many purchases, consumers do not follow all the steps of the buying process in detail. The way in which consumers decide whether and what to buy depends partly on the significance of the purchase. In general, consumers undertake a more formal, lengthy decision-making process when the following conditions exist:

* The purchase is important to consumers.
* The product's price is high.
* The product has features that are complex or new.
* There are many brands to choose from.

Thus, consumers give a lot more thought to buying a college education or a vacation trip than they do to buying cheese or a car wash. In general, there are three types of consumer decision making: routine, limited, and extensive. See Table 6.1.

Routine Decision Making

routine decision making
Decision making involving little search and purchasing effort.

To buy products that are simple, inexpensive, and familiar, consumers typically apply **routine decision making.** Consumers do not consider this type of purchase an important one and are not highly involved in it. This type of decision making usually involves considering one or a few brands, comparing them in terms of one or a few characteristics (such as price, color, or speed of delivery), and minimizing the costs of purchasing. Thus, few consumers are willing to run from store to store to compare the relative merits of shampoo, carrots, or dry cleaning.

Routine decision making may apply to other situations as well. For example, if an organization has cultivated positive relationships with customers, then customers are less likely to consider other alternatives for future purchases. Likewise, when consumers must fill a need quickly, such as a driver whose gas gauge reads "empty," they are apt to keep the search and evaluation process to a minimum.

To attract consumers who use routine decision making, marketers must know what characteristics consumers evaluate. For example, if some consumers choose whatever brand of bread or soda is cheapest, marketers may focus on setting a low price or

FIGURE 6.5
*Influences on
Consumer Behavior*

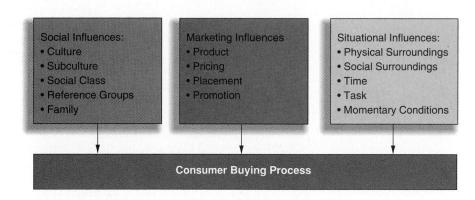

FIGURE 6.5
*Influences on
Consumer Behavior*

offering frequent discounts. Furthermore, since consumers do not go out of their way to find a brand for this type of purchase, marketers must make it widely available in a variety of stores and in some cases, vending machines.

Limited Decision Making

limited decision making
Decision making involving moderate search and purchasing effort.

Consumers engaging in **limited decision making** follow a moderate course. They consider several brands and sources of the product, such as when buying shirts or shorts, and they compare a few product features. They may get information about the product from several sources, such as advertising and a couple of friends. They are willing to spend a little time searching for value, but will keep down their time and effort costs.

To reach consumers in limited decision making, marketers may use eye-catching advertising and public relations messages to get their brands in the minds of consumers so that they will be in the consideration set.

Extensive Decision Making

extensive decision making
Decision making involving considerable search and purchasing effort.

When a product is complex or expensive, or when the product is unfamiliar or very significant to consumers, they tend to engage in **extensive decision making.** This type of decision making involves comparing many alternatives and evaluating them in terms of many characteristics. Consumers also consult a variety of information sources, perhaps researching the product in the library and interviewing salespeople and owners of various brands. The process of extensive decision making requires a significant investment of time and effort.

Compared to the other types, extensive decision making is less common. Many consumers use the process for buying a car, house, or computer; others limit their alternatives even for these high-stakes products. Some people just do not care to devote that much time to shopping. Marketers that cater to consumers making an extensive search can provide value in the form of marketing communications that compare various alternatives on key attributes. To serve consumers who think they should be doing extensive decision making but dislike the effort involved, retailers could deliver value by training salespeople to be knowledgeable about a number of brands so they could narrow the search for their customers.

Many variables affect not only which products consumers choose but which process they use to arrive at a decision. The remainder of this chapter focuses on three categories of influences: social, marketing, and situational. These are shown in Figure 6.5.

Social Influences

"Think for yourself." "Do your own thing." Many of us grew up hearing such sayings that uphold the importance of the individual. But no matter how much we emphasize the individual, the fact is that each person is influenced by various groups. Most notable are the broad groupings of culture, subculture, and social class, a person's reference groups, and family.

Those groups influence our behavior by providing direct and indirect messages about specific activities. For example, someone whose family and friends are football fans is likely to hear that sport described in glowing terms and is likely to buy tickets to football games or to watch them on television. Cultural, social class, and reference groups also influence consumer behavior indirectly by helping to shape the values and attitudes that influence purchase decisions. For example, a teenager whose social class values planning ahead and taking charge of one's life will believe it prudent to take college preparatory classes in high school and to save money for college.

Levi Strauss and Company has devised a marketing strategy that adapts to social influences in order to help it sell Dockers casual attire. Noticing a social trend—that many organizations (75 percent according to a recent survey of businesses) are trying a more casual dress code—Levi's creatively promotes its products as a way to participate in the trend while also pleasing the boss. To reach people through their employers, the company holds seminars, produces fashion shows, and distributes videos on how to dress appropriately but casually for office work (featuring the company's clothes, of course). The idea is that when consumers are deciding what to wear on casual days, they will select clothes that their employer and co-workers identify as appropriate. Buoyed by the success of this effort in the United States, Levi's has expanded it to European and Japanese cities.[14]

Culture

One of the most important means by which a society influences the behavior of individuals is through its culture. A **culture** is "the complex of learned values and behaviors that are shared by a society and are designed to increase the probability of the society's survival."[15] People express their culture in statements of what they value and in customs and practices that reflect those values. In mainstream U.S. culture, people value achievement, progress, individualism, and freedom.[16] Americans may express such values when they put work and working above family time or when they advocate equal opportunity for each individual. The society conveys information about such values and behaviors through the family and through religious and educational institutions.

This definition of culture emphasizes a culture's **core values,** the ones that are pervasive and enduring. Table 6.2 lists core values of mainstream U.S. culture. To understand the core values of the cultures they serve, marketers must research them, rather than assuming that the values listed in Table 6.2 are universal.

When serving foreign markets, marketers must be aware that the cultural values in other countries often differ from those held by the majority of Americans. For example, many other cultures do not value change as the U.S. does and may instead uphold long-standing customs and traditions. Likewise, while the dominant U.S. culture values individual achievement, most Asian nations and most Hispanic cultures tend to promote group harmony and frown on showing off. Procter & Gamble experienced the importance of value differences when it began marketing diapers in China and Korea. In those countries, P&G offers white unisex diapers, rather than the pink and blue versions popular in the United States, because consumers there don't want to show (by buying pink) that their child is a daughter.[17]

Cultural values are deeply ingrained, so marketers are most likely to succeed when they appeal to the cultural values of their target markets. The classic example of a promotional strategy appealing to individualism—nonconformity, self-reliance, being true to oneself—is the long-running series of Marlboro Man advertisements for the cigarette of that name. Of course, since Marlboro is the largest selling cigarette in the world, consumers are not standing out as unique by smoking them.

Recent Trends   Economic and social forces may cause cultural values to change. For example, in recent years more women have entered the U.S. workplace than in any period since World War II (17 million women were in the workforce in 1947, com-

culture
The complex of learned values and behaviors that are shared by a society and are designed to increase the probability of a society's survival.

core values
Values in a culture that are pervasive and enduring.

T A B L E   6.2
Summary of Mainstream
U.S. Cultural Values

Value	General Features	Relevance to Marketing
Achievement and success	Hard work is good; success flows from hard work	Acts as a justification for acquisition of goods ("You deserve it")
Activity	Keeping busy is healthy and natural	Stimulates interest in products that are time savers and enhance leisure-time activities
Efficiency and practicality	Admiration of things that solve problems (e.g., save time and effort)	Stimulates purchase of products that function well and save time
Progress	People can improve themselves; tomorrow should be better	Stimulates desire for new products that fulfill unsatisfied needs; acceptance of products that claim to be "new" or "improved"
Material comfort	"The good life"	Fosters acceptance of convenience and luxury products that make life more enjoyable
Individualism	Being one's self (e.g., self-reliance, self-interest, and self-esteem)	Stimulates acceptance of customized or unique products that enable a person to "express his or her own personality"
Freedom	Freedom of choice	Fosters interest in wide product lines and differentiated products
External conformity	Uniformity of observable behavior; desire to be accepted	Stimulates interest in products that are used or owned by others in the same social group
Humanitarianism	Caring for others, particularly the underdog	Stimulates patronage of firms that compete with market leaders
Youthfulness	A state of mind that stresses being young at heart or appearing young	Stimulates acceptance of products that provide the illusion of maintaining or fostering youth
Fitness and health	Caring about one's body, including the desire to be physically fit and healthy	Stimulates acceptance of food products, activities, and equipment perceived to maintain or increase physical fitness

Source: Leon G. Schiffman/Leslie Lazar Kanuck, *Consumer Behavior,* 5th ed. © 1994, p. 437. Reprinted by permission of Prentice-Hall, Inc., Englewood Cliffs, New Jersey.

pared to over 60 million in the mid 1990s).[18] Accompanying this trend, attitudes toward working women have become more positive. Since greater time and energy are required to run a single-parent or two-wage-earner household, the current appeal of "cocooning," or seeking the comforts of life at home rather than going out for entertainment is clearer. Table 6.3 summarizes some other major shifts that have been observed in common Western values.

Subcultures

subculture
A segment within a culture that shares distinguishing values and patterns of behavior that differ from the overall culture.

The population of the United States is becoming more and more diverse. One way to understand the diverse groups is in terms of various subcultures. A **subculture** is a segment "within a culture that shares distinguishing values and patterns of behavior that differ from those of the overall culture."[19] Table 6.4 shows some ways in which the population can be divided into subcultures.

These categories apply outside of the United States as well. For instance, Western Europe and the United States both have fast-growing Muslim communities, where many of the values are conservative and family oriented. Because each subculture has its own set of values and desirable behaviors, marketers might find that they can better meet the needs of particular subcultures than of the entire culture of a nation or region. Marketers may wish to adjust their strategies for various subcultures—say, distributing through different types of stores in Hispanic neighborhoods or using different advertising media to reach younger adults.

T A B L E 6.3
Major Shifts in Western Values

Traditional Values	New Values
Self-denial ethic	Self-fulfillment ethic
Higher standard of living	Better quality of life
Traditional sex roles	Blurring of sex roles
Accepted definition of success	Individualized definition of success
Traditional family life	Alternative families
Faith in industry, institutions	Self-reliance
Live to work	Work to live
Hero worship	Love of ideas
Expansionism	Pluralism
Patriotism	Less nationalistic
Unparalleled growth	Growing sense of limits
Industrial growth	Information/service growth
Receptivity to technology	Technology orientation

Source: Reproduced from "Changing Values: The New Emphasis on Self-Actualization," *The Futurist,* January–February 1989, p. 15, published by the World Future Society, 7910 Woodmont Ave., Ste. 450, Bethesda, MD 20814.

T A B L E 6.4
Types of Subcultures

Characteristics	Examples of Subcultures
Age	Adolescents, young adults, middle aged, elderly
Religion	Jewish, Catholic, Mormon, Buddhist, Muslim
Race	European-American, African-American, Hispanic-American, Asian-American
Income level	Affluent, middle income, poor, destitute
Nationality	French, Malaysian, Australian, Canadian
Gender	Female, male
Family type	Single parent, divorced/no kids, two parent/kids
Occupation	Mechanic, accountant, priest, professor, clerk
Geographic region	New England, Southwest, Midwest
Community	Rural, small town, suburban, city

Source: J. Paul Peter and Jerry C. Olson, *Consumer Behavior and Marketing Strategy,* 4th ed. (Burr Ridge, Ill.: Irwin, 1996), p. 415.

The U.S. subcultures representing various racial and ethnic groups are of particular interest to marketers because of their size. By 1992, one-quarter of the people in the United States were members of racial and ethnic minorities. That proportion is projected to increase to over one-third by 2020 and to one-half by 2050.[20] Recognizing this trend, General Mills Company used a computer to morph the photos of 75 diverse women and create a composite image for its latest incarnation of its Betty Crocker logo. The new Betty is darker than her predecessors and not as readily classified as a particular race.[21]

In describing subcultures, it is important to keep in mind that marketers identify general patterns of values and behavior; the descriptions do not necessarily apply to every individual within a subculture. Furthermore, because a person is a member of more than one subculture—for example, a young Jewish Easterner, a middle-aged Mexican-American Catholic—the degree to which each person is influenced by each subculture will vary. Thus, in reading the following descriptions of subcultures, bear in mind that these are overall patterns that do not apply uniformly to all members of the subculture.

European-American Consumers   The majority of people living in the United States today are of European descent. However, European-Americans do not typically think of themselves as a subculture. If they think of themselves as part of an ethnic group, it is more likely to be in terms of their roots in a particular country, say, Ireland or Italy. Because European-Americans are the dominant group, their values and practices tend to influence strongly the overall values and practices of the U.S. culture. This makes it easy to ignore or forget the fact that the European-American subculture is, in fact, a subculture. Thus, European-American teenagers would typically listen to different music and dress differently to go to a party than would their counterparts from other U.S. subcultures.

The majority of marketers are part of this subculture, so it is not surprising that marketing strategies often ignore the importance of subcultural differences. The most direct effect is that marketing efforts may reach only a portion of the customers they are intended to serve. Different subcultures may represent different target markets for organizations to try to serve.

African-American Consumers   The largest racial or ethnic minority subculture in the United States is African-Americans, with 30 million people in 9.3 million households.[22] While a relatively large share of African-Americans are poor, about two-thirds are not,[23] and in total black consumers are estimated to spend an impressive $280 billion a year.[24] Blacks tend to spend a higher proportion of their income than whites do, partly because they have less long-term debt and partly because, research shows, they worry less about economic uncertainty.[25]

Until recently, what little consumer research had been done on the buying patterns of blacks and whites showed mostly similarities between the two groups when differences in socioeconomic status were accounted for.[26] However, marketers have begun to research African-American consumers more carefully and have noted some distinctive characteristics. A study consisting of over 1,000 in-home interviews found that nearly half of blacks say they are "not too happy," more than three times the rate among nonblacks, a pattern that did not change when researchers adjusted for age and economic status.[27] This is significant to marketers because it suggests there are attitudes held in common by blacks, regardless of their class. Other differences uncovered by the survey are that African-Americans are more often willing to put up with a boring job in exchange for good pay, rely more heavily than others on advertising when they make product choices, and place higher value than others on religion, sense of duty, self-confidence, and individuality.[28]

In terms of consumer behavior, African-Americans spend more on clothing and personal-care products than the general population and make the majority of their charitable donations to their churches.[29] Blacks tend to watch television and listen to the radio more than whites, and a smaller percentage reads newspapers.[30] African-Americans are drawn to products and advertising that appeal to black pride and reflect their heritage. Thus, marketers do well to learn about and respect this subculture.

Two companies that did just that are Johnson Publishing Company, publisher of *Ebony* and other magazines targeting African-Americans, and Spiegel, the giant catalog retailer. The two entered into an agreement in which Spiegel uses ads in *Ebony* and the *Ebony* subscription list to promote and distribute a catalog called *E Style,* which offers clothing and accessories designed for black women. The clothing features dramatic design, warm and bright colors designed to flatter darker skin tones, and some items with an African flair. There's also a variety of hats, a fashion accessory purchased much more often by black women than by women of other subcultures. Research into the needs of the target market included not only focus groups but also measurements of 1,300 black women to ensure that the clothing would properly fit the proportions of these customers.[31]

Hispanic-American Consumers   With the largest growth in number of members among racial and ethnic groups in the United States, Hispanics are expected to become the biggest ethnic minority group in the United States by the middle of the next century.[32] Much of the future growth is expected to occur in California, Florida, New York, Texas, and the Southwest.[33]

This subculture includes people who trace their roots to Spanish-speaking countries, including Mexico, Puerto Rico, Cuba, Central and South America, and

In this ad from Hispanic *magazine, Astronauta Rodolfo Neri advises those in the broad Hispanic community that a successful life comes from educating themselves and doing their best each day. "¡Quién sabe qué tan lejos puedas llegar!" ("Who knows how far you are able to go!") Written in Spanish, the ad from the 25-year-old ITT Technical Institute is directed toward members of the Hispanic community who are fluent in Spanish but must be prepared to study in English: "Las clases son en Inglés."*

the Dominican Republic. By far the largest Hispanic group in the United States is Mexican-Americans. Because Hispanic Americans come from so many different nations, they actually represent many subcultures and even have language differences. They often think of their ethnic identity in terms of their national origin, rather than the broad umbrella of "Hispanic" or "Latino." However, these groups do share some common values, such as a strong family orientation.

In general, the socioeconomic status of Hispanic Americans is related to immigration.[34] About one-quarter of Hispanics in the United States are poor, but these are mostly recent immigrants. Those who have been in the United States for several generations are typically much better off economically. The Census Bureau found that 42 percent of Hispanics owned or were buying a home, for example. Furthermore, although the Spanish language is the basis for classifying Hispanic Americans as a single subculture, by their third generation in the United States, most speak only English.[35] Presumably, then, while Spanish-language advertising would reach many Hispanics, it would not be appropriate for marketing upscale products since many in this group may speak only English.

Asian-American Consumers   While Asian-Americans constitute the smallest of the three ethnic groups described here (6 million households), they are an important subculture to marketers, especially because their average educational attainment and household income are the highest among all groups, including whites.[36] This group is also experiencing the fastest rate of growth, having increased 108 percent during the 1980s.[37] Most Asian-Americans live in the West, particularly in California, and in urban areas.[38]

Like Hispanic Americans, Asian-Americans are highly diverse, tracing their ancestry to many different countries, including China, Japan, the Philippines, and Korea. This variety is made even more challenging by the fact that recent immigrants speak many different languages. However, some common traits include hard work, strong family ties, and a high value placed on education.[39]

Upper Americans: *Range from high-income elite to managers and professionals; value high quality, prestige, spending with good taste.*
Middle Class: *Average-pay, usually white-collar workers who live on the "better side of town," try to do what's proper, and emulate Upper Americans.*
Working Class: *Average-pay, blue-collar workers who depend heavily on relatives, have relatively limited horizons, and are concerned with pursuing ease of labor and leisure.*
Lower Americans: *May be poor or just above poverty; may or may not be employed; may or may not seek instant gratification.*

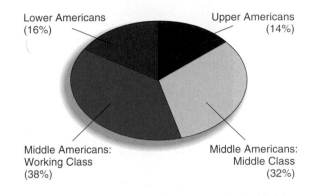

Source: Adapted with permission of the University of Chicago Press from Richard P. Coleman, "The Continuing Significance of Social Class to Marketing," *Journal of Consumer Research* (December 1983), pp. 265–280. © 1983 by the University of Chicago. See also Donald W. Hendon, "Class System Revisited," *Journal of Business Research,* 19 (1988), pp. 259–270.

Social Class

In spite of the value placed on equality in the United States, consumers here as well as in other countries are in different social classes. **Social class** refers to a national status hierarchy by which individuals and groups are classified in terms of esteem and prestige based on their wealth, skill, and power. The most reliable way to rate these is by occupation. Thus, a surgeon, a sales manager, and a data-entry clerk are likely members of different social classes. As a side note, the social class of a college student has more to do with the occupation of the student's parents and the student's career plans than with his or her part-time job flipping hamburgers.

While there is no hard-and-fast rule for identifying social classes in the United States, marketing analysts may divide the U.S. marketplace into the class groupings shown in Figure 6.6. These groupings show not only income differences, but also differences in values and behavior. For example, people in the lower classes tend to have a relatively strong focus on the short term, to think in relatively concrete terms, and to be relatively emotional in their decision making. Consumers in the upper classes, by contrast, tend to be more abstract and future oriented in their thinking.[40]

Given differences such as these, people of different social classes tend to make different choices regarding their clothing, home furnishings, use of leisure time, choice of media, and patterns of saving and spending. If marketers determine that their product is most likely to appeal to members of certain classes, they can develop a mix that takes into account some of these differences. An example is the advertising of luxury goods on classical radio stations.

Reference Groups

Besides sharing the values of a culture, subculture, and social group, consumers consider or consult with various groups when making purchase decisions. These groups serve as the consumers' **reference groups,** or people that influence consumers' thoughts, feelings, and behaviors. For example, teenagers typically use their friends as a reference group for deciding what clothes are attractive or whether it's smart to stay in school.

Who Makes the Buying Decisions in Your Family?

Important information for marketers is who makes the buying decisions—routine, limited, and extensive—in families. Consider your own family. Who makes most of the buying decisions in each category? Has it always been the same person (or people), or has the decision-making authority shifted as the family has gone through different phases of growth? If it has changed, what caused the change?

both sexes are involved in purchasing a variety of products. Especially in two-career households, the husband or both spouses together might do the grocery shopping. And although men are more likely than women to be patients in a recovery program for substance abuse, the person who actually purchases this type of service is more often a woman. Thus, one marketing strategy to promote such programs has been to advertise them on late-night television, when wives are waiting for substance-abusing husbands to come home.[41] Furthermore, thanks to busy parents and part-time jobs, children now do a significant share of the shopping. With so many differences, marketers have to research who the buyers and influencers are for specific products (see Put It into Practice: "Who Makes the Buying Decisions in Your Family?").

family life cycle
A set of stages families go through that influence needs and the ability to satisfy them.

Family Life Cycles   The needs of a family and the ability to satisfy those needs change throughout the various stages of the family's existence. Together these stages are known as the **family life cycle.** A traditional view of the family life cycle includes the following stages:

- Bachelor stage—young, single people living away from their parents
- Newly married couples with no children
- Young married couples with youngest child under six
- Young married couples with youngest child six or older
- Older married couples with dependent children
- Older married couples still in labor force but with children living independently
- Retired married couples with children living independently
- Solitary survivor in labor force
- Solitary survivor retired.

Of course, not every person or family passes through all these stages or passes through them in this order, especially given the various structures of the modern family. Figure 6.7 shows an attempt to portray a modern family life cycle in all its complexity. Even this diagram fails to cover all the possibilities, such as never marrying.

Despite its limitations, the family life cycle is a useful starting point for identifying ways in which needs change as families mature. For example, young married people tend to spend more on luxuries because usually both spouses are working and they don't have the expenses related to child rearing. As they get older and take on more responsibilities, their buying habits focus more on meeting children's needs and providing for a stable future. This change has presented a challenge for GM's Saturn division, which has built up a loyal following by delivering top-notch service along with its Saturn compact cars. But for Saturn buyers with growing families, loyalty to the brand conflicts with the limits of the car's size. Even customers devoted to the brand have to switch when they need a bigger car or minivan.[42]

Mike Bartusick/ Park Bench Cafe

The Park Bench Cafe, in Huntington Beach, California, sounds like the kind of place where people can relax outdoors with a cup of coffee, a glass of fruit juice, and a light sandwich or snack. It is. But it is also the kind of place where dogs can do exactly the same thing, as long as they are accompanied by their owners.

Mike Bartusick, owner of the outdoor cafe, noticed a couple of years ago that his patrons often stopped by with their dogs. The cafe was already popular with human customers because of the breakfasts and lunches it served in a tranquil setting. Those customers frequently fed their dogs scraps—a strip of bacon here, a bite of scrambled egg there. "I realized this was a potential health problem but also an opportunity, so I took charge." With the health department's permission, he added a doggie menu, entitled "Bone Appetit." Dogs may now be served their own meals— hot dogs, bacon, even vanilla ice cream. (All of this is served on disposable plates, in designated areas.)

Physical and social surroundings have played a huge part in the cafe's success, both before and after the addition of the doggie menu. Customers enjoy the beauty of the location—a serene park filled with eucalyptus trees, a tiny duck pond, freshly mowed grass. And they love the company not only of their own dogs, but of fellow dog lovers. "We don't have any kids, we just have our dogs . . . so we like to treat them well," explains Jane Smith, who visits the cafe with her black Labrador retriever, Saba. Even customers who don't own dogs seem to like the atmosphere at the cafe. "They provide a lot of energy and a

lot of life, and I like that," says Gene Turner, who visits the cafe because of its uniqueness. Tourists who have heard about the unusual ambiance stop by for the experience.

Recognizing his opportunity to further influence customers' decisions, Bartusick is expanding his Canine Cuisine menu to include new services: catered birthday parties for dogs.

Source: Adam Pertman, "Dog Dishes on Menu," *The Boston Globe,* April 27, 1996, pp. 1, 12. Reprinted courtesy of *The Boston Globe.*

Explore more by searching "Dog Treats" on the Web.

F I G U R E 6.7 *A Modern Family Life Cycle*

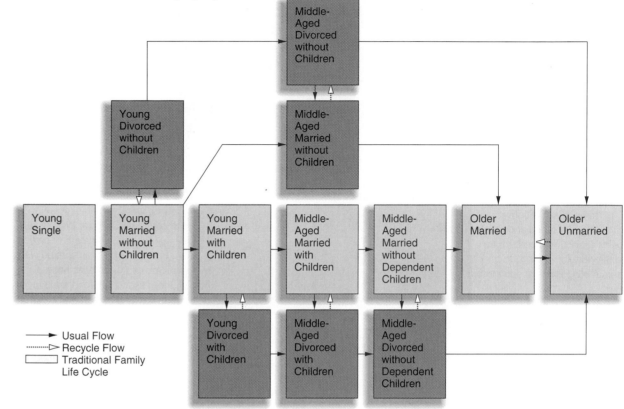

Source: Reprinted with permission of the University of Chicago Press from "A Modernized Family Life Cycle," by Patrick E. Murphy and William A. Staples, in the *Journal of Consumer Research* (June 1979): pp. 12–22. © 1979 by the University of Chicago Press.

---

surroundings that accompany shopping on-line or by catalog are likely to be quite different since customers do not have physical contact with merchandise available for sale. Jewel Food Stores' experience with the PeaPod on-line shopping system is that consumers spend freely but tend to skip impulse items such as gum, candy, and greeting cards.[48]

Some aspects of physical surroundings are not directly part of the marketing channel (such as the store), so they are beyond the marketer's control. Examples include the climate and weather. A study of Midwest supermarkets during a record heat wave found that the weather did indeed influence purchase decisions. Sweltering customers in July bought more products characterized as cold or refreshing, including bottled water and frozen juices, despite a lack of promotions for these items. At the same time, sales of coffee and cake mix dropped substantially, even though stores had been promoting both.[49] Besides determining which products consumers choose, the weather also can affect the way they go about choosing. For example, a consumer in March might conduct an extended search for the best value in air conditioners, but a consumer in the midst of an August heat wave might feel compelled to conduct a more limited search among the options still available.

Physical surroundings may influence consumers at various points in the decision-making process. An attractive display may influence need recognition by stimulating a desire to try something new. A warehouse-style store may stimulate purchases by conveying to customers that prices are low. A quiet, elegant bank lobby may signal that the institution is stable and professional, thereby stimulating a decision to open an account there.

As parents grow older, their financial position tends to improve, so they are more apt to spend money on leisure activities and home improvements. Older adults make purchases related to retirement and buy gifts for younger relatives. They also may be heavy consumers of health services.

When marriages don't last, one consequence is that household finances are often strained. Thus, the prevalence of divorce in modern society means that marketers can't count on the trend toward increased spending predicted by the traditional family life cycle. For example, Anne McBride found that because of her divorce, the need to save for her teenage son's college expenses, and the requirements of caring for elderly parents, she must do her shopping at discount stores.[43]

Marketing Influences

Since the objective of marketing is to create profitable exchanges, marketing activities also influence the consumer buying process. Each element of the marketing mix—product, pricing, placement (channels of distribution), and promotion (marketing communications)—has the potential to affect the buying process at various stages.

Product

Some aspects of the organization's product strategy that may affect consumer buying behavior are the product's newness, complexity, and perceived quality. A relatively new and complex product may require extensive decision making. Recognizing this, some marketers may wish to offer simpler, more familiar alternatives for consumers who avoid extensive searches.

Peapod, the virtual grocery store that takes your order by PC (http://www.peapod.com), uses its own special brand of one-to-one marketing to identify, track, and interact with individual customers. The service's database records customers' buying habits and remembers "your brand of peanut butter." Shoppers can view photos of products, check their nutritional content, add their bill at any time to check the total, select delivery dates and times, and determine the method of payment, all by using the graphical interface to select and highlight icons on screen. Peapod hopes that this focus on customer service will overcome the fact that customers have no physical contact with the merchandise or the company's physical surroundings.

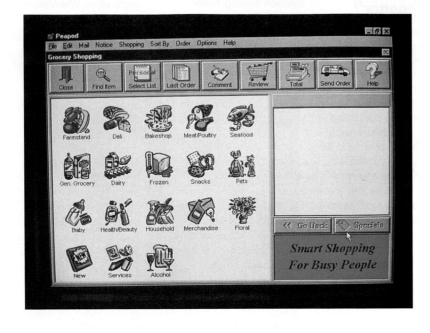

delivers greater value than competing products. Hearing such messages after a purchase may reinforce the purchase decision.

One power of communicating on-line is that consumers become highly involved and may look up information that can influence them at various stages of the decision-making process. Information about new products can stimulate a desire for those products, background information can influence evaluation and selection, and positive interaction with the organization can build satisfaction and loyalty. An organization that capitalizes on these benefits is American Express, whose ExpressNet service offers the ability to apply for a charge card, check account status, view photos of travel destinations, plan a trip, order a customized travel guide, and make reservations. As consumers use their American Express card repeatedly, the company can create long-term relationships with them.[46]

Situational Influences

Norman is health-conscious and a careful shopper most of the time. He studies nutrition labels before selecting food at the supermarket. However, while shopping before he was to baby-sit his young nephew, Norman grabbed a box of the sweetest, most chocolatey-looking cereal he saw, then hurried to the frozen-pizza case. As he later stood in the checkout line, he felt nervous about whether he had planned enough activities for his nephew. He impulsively added a coloring book and a couple of squirt guns to his cart.

In this example, Norman's shopping behavior is influenced by some of the circumstances surrounding this particular shopping trip. He is shopping for someone he assumes will have different food preferences from his own. Also, he feels nervous. Like Norman, consumers in general are influenced by characteristics of the situation. Major situational influences include the physical surroundings, social surroundings, time, the nature of the task, and momentary moods and conditions.[47]

Physical Surroundings

The physical surroundings that influence buying behavior are the easily observable features of the purchase situation. When a consumer is shopping in a store, those features include the location of the store, the way merchandise is displayed, the way the store is decorated, how well it is lit, the noise level, and so on. The physical

The working mother in this ad represents people who don't have time to bank. To help busy people, Chase Manhattan Bank promotes its "ChaseDirect" service that provides customers with direct access to their accounts and transactions by phone, fax, or PC. An added value is a free choice of software—Quicken® Starter Edition or Microsoft's Money® for Windows 95® and a $50 bonus for trying ChaseDirect for 3 months.

Social Surroundings

The social surroundings of a situation include other people, their characteristics, the roles they appear to play, and the ways they interact with one another (see "Marketing Movers & Shakers: Mike Bartusick/Park Bench Cafe"). For example, a consumer shopping with a friend may make different buying decisions than she would when shopping alone or with her mother. A frazzled father dragging two tired children down a supermarket aisle might add some purchases to placate the children—or skip some purchases in order to get out of the store faster. Chances are, he would engage in routine decision making for most purchases.

Other people besides shopping companions may be influential, as well. An overly crowded store or a customer arguing with a salesclerk may influence customers to make a quick selection—or simply to leave the area immediately.

Time

The influence of time on buying behavior can be measured in several ways. People may make different decisions based on when the purchase takes place: the hour of the day, the day of the week, or the season of the year. A shopper who slips into the store 15 minutes before closing or two days before school starts, for instance, is likely to engage in a shorter search of alternatives than one who has more time to shop.

The consumer behavior process also may be swayed by the length of time since the last purchase or until the consumer's next paycheck. For example, a consumer might justify the purchase of a restaurant meal on the grounds that he hasn't eaten out in two weeks. Someone who does not expect any income for three weeks might be exceptionally price conscious.

Finally, people are influenced by their perception of how much time they have available for shopping. A person under severe time constraints likely would make fewer purchases and would consider fewer brands and product attributes for the purchases that are made. Thus, someone juggling the responsibilities of a job, children, and aging parents may opt out of extensive problem solving more often than someone with fewer demands on his or her time.

Task

The task—that is, the general or specific reasons for collecting information, shopping, or purchasing—also influence consumer behavior. The task includes the uses for the product and the identity of the person to be using it. In the example that opened this section, Norman chose different types of cereal based on whether he or his nephew would eat it. Similarly, a consumer might select a different brand or style of a product to be given as a gift than she would pick for personal use.

Momentary Conditions

The momentary conditions of a buying situation that influence purchase are the moods and condition of the consumer at the time of the purchase. A person who is excited or angry may be unable to carefully consider many alternatives. Other relevant conditions include the consumer's health, energy level, and access to money. A tired consumer may derive greater value from an alternative that makes the purchase fast and easy. Consumers who are short on cash may place more emphasis on low price or shop only at stores that take credit cards.

Summary

To understand why consumers buy certain products and brands instead of others, marketers study consumer behavior—people's exchange activities and how they are shaped by various forces. These forces include social, marketing, and situational influences.

Consumers begin the buying process by identifying a need and then looking for information about alternative products and brands from internal sources, group sources, marketing sources, public sources, or experiential sources. They evaluate the alternatives and make a purchase decision. Once they have chosen a product, especially a big-ticket item, they evaluate their purchase. They also may experience cognitive dissonance, or second thoughts about their choice, but marketers can help overcome this with after-sales support. Postpurchase evaluation is the stage at which consumers determine whether they received value; if they conclude that they did, they may become loyal customers.

The consumer buying process ranges from routine to limited to extensive decision making. Consumers are most likely to use extensive decision making when the product is important, the price is high, the product is complex or unfamiliar, and there are many brands.

Social influences include culture and subculture, which send direct and indirect messages that shape values and related behavior. People also are influenced by their social class, the group of people who have similar esteem and prestige based on wealth, skill, and power. Reference groups are groups of people that influence consumers' thoughts, feelings, and actions. Consumers' families also influence their behaviors. Marketers are interested in knowing which family members make and influence buying decisions and which types of purchasing decisions are associated with various stages in the family life cycle.

Marketing influences on the consumer buying process include the effects of the marketing strategy. Product strategy can influence consumer evaluation of the product and its ability to provide value. Pricing strategy can influence the likelihood of selecting a particular product by increasing or decreasing the total cost of purchase. The marketer's strategy for place can influence selection based on how readily available the product is. Promotion can make consumers aware of a brand and bring it into their consideration sets.

Situational influences on consumer behavior include physical surroundings, social surroundings, time, the nature of the task, and momentary moods and conditions. These can change the consumer buying process and result in different brands being purchased.

Key Terms and Concepts

consumer behavior (p. 142)
motivation (p. 143)
utilitarian needs (p. 144)
hedonic needs (p. 144)
consideration set (p. 145)

attitude (p. 146)
cognitive dissonance (p. 147)
routine decision making (p. 148)
limited decision making (p. 148)
extensive decision making (p. 149)
culture (p. 150)

core values (p. 150)
subculture (p. 151)
social class (p. 154)
reference groups (p. 155)
family life cycle (p. 158)

Review and Discussion Questions

1. What are the five steps of the consumer buying process?
2. Summarize Maslow's hierarchy of needs. How can marketers use this theory?
3. If you were marketing a new development of condominiums, which information sources would you expect potential buyers to use in making their decision? How do you think they would use each one?
4. Name three ways a marketer might cultivate a favorable attitude toward a line of fat-free desserts.
5. Have you ever experienced cognitive dissonance— buyer's remorse—after purchasing product? If so, how did you deal with it?
6. What products have you bought in the last 48 hours that involved routine decision making? Note whether you bought them as a result of an emergency (out of gas), brand loyalty (same brand of shampoo), good relationship with a distributor or retailer (same restaurant), or low price.

7. If you were a marketer who planned to test a new line of baked goods in Santa Fe, New Mexico, what subcultures and social classes would be important for you to consider?
8. Suppose you wanted to promote a line of costume jewelry to middle- or upper-middle-class teenaged girls.
    a. What reference groups would you study to determine their influence on teens in the United States?
    b. Would your answer be different if you were interested in Japanese teenagers? Explain.
9. Name and describe the four elements of the marketing mix that influence buying decisions.
10. Consider a favorite store or restaurant. What aspects of the physical surroundings influence your buying decisions—what products to buy or how much time you'll spend in the store; whether to eat at the restaurant or what to order?

Chapter Project   Make Use of Reference Groups

Suppose you were a marketer for a clothing manufacturer that wanted to introduce a new line of "business casual" clothing targeted for your marketing classmates.

First, try to determine your potential customers' reference groups: primary and secondary groups, membership groups, aspiration groups, and even dissociative groups. Consider also family influences (do their parents still pay the bills, or are

some of your classmates married and supporting children?) and how they may affect your classmates' buying decisions.

Next, use that information to create a report for the executives at your company detailing tips and potential pitfalls they should be aware of in promoting the line of clothing. (For instance, a dissociative group might be people thought of as "nerds.")

Chapter Case   Fa(s)t Foods Are Selling Fast

Gone is the much-touted, low-fat McLean Deluxe burger (made partly from seaweed) from McDonald's menu, along with two of the restaurant's four salads. When its lower-fat menu failed to attract consumers, Taco Bell introduced its new Four-Alarm Double Decker Taco, backed by a $200 million ad campaign. Pizza Hut recently pulled its first steaming hot Triple-Deckeroni Pizza out of the oven. It has six kinds of cheese and 90 pieces of pepperoni—on one pie. What has happened? Where's the low fat?

Consumers aren't buying enough of the low-fat products, claim marketers for fast-food companies. They may *talk* about maintaining healthful, low-fat diets, but they are buying high-fat meals. "Forty to fifty percent of the population talks about healthy food," claims Ron Shaich, co-chairman of Au Bon Pain (which recently introduced a mozzarella-tomato-pesto sandwich that has 650 calories and 30 grams of fat). "Only about half that number actually eats it." Consumers— at least some of them—are changing their buying decisions again. For whatever reason, they feel that lower-fat foods are not giving them the good value.

"Consumers want value," notes Kim Miller, a spokeswoman for Burger King, which recently increased the sizes of its burgers and its breakfast sandwiches. "They want to fill up their stomachs without depleting their wallets." Indeed, fast-food restaurants are now engaging in "super sizing," or what they call "value meals"—meal combinations that offer more food for less money. "What we're seeing now is super-

sizing—pay an extra quarter and get twice as much food," observes Jayne Hurley, senior nutritionist at the Center for Science in the Public Interest. "It's hard for a lot of consumers to turn their back on a deal like that."

Self-deprivation is out. "Reward foods" are in. "This is about more taste, not bigger portions," says Ron Shaich of Au Bon Pain. Perhaps it is about both, and the fact that consumers need to feel they are getting more for their dollar— bigger portions, better taste, or both. Thus, pricing and product are major considerations in the creation of value for consumers of fast foods. Nutrition—for the moment—may no longer be an important consideration.

Questions

1. How might culture, social class, and reference groups influence consumers' decisions about buying the new fast-foods?
2. How might fast-food marketers focus on routine decision making to get consumers to visit their restaurants often?
3. Should marketers try harder to create value for consumers by offering more healthful food items, or should they create value by simply offering the higher-fat items that consumers seem to want? Explain your answer.

Source: Chris Reidy, "The Bulk Starts Here," *The Boston Globe*, April 25, 1996, pp. 1, 24. Reprinted courtesy of *The Boston Globe*.

Explore more by searching "Value Meals" on the Web.

Organizational Buying Behavior

CHAPTER OUTLINE

Organizational Markets
  Characteristics of Organizational Markets
  Categories of Organizational Buyers
  Business Classifications
  International Exchanges
Major Forces in Organizational Markets
  Demand
  Competition
  Technology
The Organizational Buying Process
  Types of Purchases
  Buying Criteria
  Characteristics of Organizational Buying
  The Nature of Organizational Exchanges
Interactions with Organizational Buyers
  Buyer-Seller Interactions
  The Buying Center
Summary

LEARNING OBJECTIVES

After completing this chapter, you should be able to:

1. Compare organizational and consumer markets.
2. Identify the categories of organizational buyers.
3. Discuss marketing issues related to the buying behavior of foreign organizations.
4. Explain how demand, competition, and technology affect marketing to organizational buyers.
5. Describe how organizational purchasing decisions are carried out.
6. Discuss the nature of interactions between marketers and organizational buyers.
7. Explain what buying centers are and how they affect the marketing effort.

Raptor Systems Inc.

The story reads like a high-tech thriller: computer break-ins at Harvard University, the White House, and the Pentagon; thousands of credit-card numbers stolen by a single computer hacker; Citibank's loss of $400,000 due to electronic theft. An Information Week/Ernst & Young survey revealed that 600 of the 1,200 respondents said their companies had suffered financial losses because of computer theft, and 20 said their losses were more than $1 million.

Enter Raptor Systems Inc., a small, Massachusetts-based software developer that offers "firewalls," software that can block these thefts. Creator David Pensak, president Robert Steinkrauss, and executive vice-president Shaun McConnon saw a weakness in the Internet (lack of security) and they attacked it. They provided organizations with security, then went several steps further to enhance value. They were the first to offer immediate notification of any suspicious activity and to offer security for remote access to networks via personal computer and modem, among other services. The company continues to design new products as well, responding to and anticipating the needs of their customers. "Raptor is a leading developer of firewall software in terms of the technology they're using and their marketing approach," notes David Readerman of Montgomery Securities in San Francisco.

Raptor's success didn't emerge overnight, but it could disappear quickly as technology changes. When David Pensak first developed the security software, most companies were barely aware of Internet opportunities or the threat of computer theft, so they didn't think they needed the software. It was only after they began to hear about or experience computer losses that they realized how valuable the firewalls could be. However, Raptor's dominant position could change as hardware manufacturers and other software developers begin

to build security into the systems they make, thus making the need for separate firewalls obsolete.

As you read this chapter, consider how important organizational buying decisions are—both to customers and marketers. Marketers who offer the best products or services to organizational customers create value for them by enhancing their profitability and enabling them to serve *their* customers better.

Source: Robert Keough, "Raptor Running Wild," *The Boston Globe*, April 10, 1996, pp. 33, 36.

Explore more at www.raptor.com

Chapter Overview

The story of Raptor Systems shows how that company created value for organizational buyers. In this and other ways, marketers seek to provide goods and services to organizations to help them carry out their own missions. Marketers who serve organizational buyers—in addition to or instead of consumers—must understand their behavior in order to offer them superior value.

This chapter provides an introduction to organizational buying behavior. It describes the nature of organizational markets and examines several basic categories of organizations. The chapter also considers how three forces—demand, competition, and technology—play a role in organizational buying decisions. Then the chapter describes the nature of purchasing decisions in organizations, including the types of purchases made and the ways organizational buyers decide to purchase. Finally, the chapter discusses the interactions among the people involved in organizational buying: first, the interactions between buyer and seller, and second, the interactions among the employees involved in making a purchase.

Organizational Markets

When we think of marketing, the first examples that come to mind usually involve consumer goods such as soap, televisions, and athletic shoes. However, the largest financial exchanges involve marketing to organizational buyers such as businesses and government agencies. Organizations buy goods and services to help them carry out their missions. For example, Ford Motor Company buys spark plugs in order to make cars, and all kinds of organizations pay for temporary secretarial help so that they can get work done when employees are away.

Characteristics of Organizational Markets

Organizational buyers vary enormously, from a tiny auto repair shop on a corner lot to a manufacturing giant like General Motors Corporation, from a small catering business to a massive government agency like the Social Security Administration. Nevertheless, some basic generalizations about organizational markets exist. These are listed in Table 7.1.

First, organizational markets consist of fewer buyers than consumer markets do. One reason is simply that in the population of any area—be it Japan, North Carolina, or the city of Los Angeles—there are more individuals (consumers) than there are organizations. The number of buyers is even less in the case of products that have specialized uses or are meant only for large organizations. For example, there are relatively few buyers of CAT scanners and even fewer buyers of space shuttles.

Organizational buyers also tend to place larger orders than consumers do. A household might buy a single personal computer; most organizations would purchase at least a few. Most organizations would outspend households on such things as phone calls, paper supplies, and cleaning services. In exchange for large quantity purchases,

TABLE 7.1
A Comparison of Organizational Buyers and Consumers

Characteristic	Organizational Buyers	Consumers
Number of buyers in market	Few	Many
Size of purchases	Large	Small
Decision criteria	Primarily rational	Rational and emotional
Interdependence between buyer and seller	Strong	Weak
Number of people involved in purchase decisions	Many	Few

CAUTION: Using InTouch MMI Software may result in excessive productivity

This ad for Wonderware In Touch MMI, "Industrial Strength Software That's Fun to Use," is directed to an organizational buyer in the manufacturing industry. It appeals to the buyer's need for rational decision making by promising that the software will improve productivity. In the ad's small print, it says that Wonderware is the industry leader and use of the software can lead to "significant productivity gains in both quality and quantity while lowering project and life cycle cost." The software is a graphical tool for monitoring and controlling manufacturing processes—industrial automation, process control, and supervisory monitoring.

organizational buyers expect lower unit prices and higher levels of service than may be available to consumers. For example, to get a contract to sell napkins and paper bags to McDonald's, Roses Southwest Papers worked with its own suppliers to get raw materials that would meet McDonald's requirements for 100 percent recycled paper. Roses also had to modify its methods for testing quality.[1]

The people who make organizational buying decisions have to answer to someone else (a boss or shareholders), so they need to show that their decisions are good for the organization. Therefore, organizational buyers know they must make decisions that are highly rational in the sense that they cost less or earn the organization a greater return than other alternatives. Of course, organizational buyers are human beings and subject to normal human biases, but marketers can help them make economically justifiable decisions. For example, marketers of home health care services appeal to cost-conscious managed-care organizations by demonstrating that home health care is less expensive than hospitalization.[2]

Organizational buying often involves greater interdependence between buyer and seller. From the seller's standpoint, the relatively small number of buyers and the relatively large size of each purchase make each organizational customer more important to the organization's success. From the buyer's perspective, many types of products often are required on an ongoing basis. A good mix of easy-to-purchase, high-quality, and low-price products from the same seller can enhance the organization's efficiency. A vendor that works closely with the organization to identify and solve problems also can help the organization improve its processes and strategy.

Organizational buying decisions tend to involve more people than consumer buying decisions do. Many consumer decisions are made by one individual or with a spouse or friend, but the group of buyers rarely gets any larger. In contrast, organizational purchases frequently involve a group of people.

Categories of Organizational Buyers

To appreciate the extent of organizational purchasing, it helps to think of organizational buyers in terms of four broad categories: producers, intermediaries, governments, and other institutions. Marketers serve these types of buyers in both domestic and foreign markets.

producers
Businesses that buy goods and services to produce other goods and services for sale.

Producers   When Detroit Edison sells electricity to Ford Motor Company or when a proofreader sells proofreading services to McGraw-Hill, they are selling to **producers,** also known as the industrial market. This type of organizational buyer consists of businesses that buy goods and services in order to produce other goods and services for sale. Thus, Ford uses electricity to produce automobiles to sell, and McGraw-Hill uses proofreading to produce textbooks to sell.

Producers are engaged in many different industries, ranging from agriculture to manufacturing, from construction to finance. Together they constitute the largest

Chapter Eight

Market Segmentation

CHAPTER OUTLINE

The Need for Market Segmentation
  What Is Market Segmentation?
  General Approaches to Serving Markets
Approaches to Segmenting Consumer Markets
  Demographic Segmentation
  Geographic Segmentation
  Psychographic Segmentation
  Segmentation Based on Thoughts and Feelings
  Segmentation Based on Purchase Behavior
  Multiple Bases for Segmentation
Approaches to Segmenting Organizational Markets
  Geographic Segmentation
  Segmentation Based on Customer Type
  Segmentation Based on Organizational Buyer Behavior
The Market Segmentation Process
  Analyze Customer–Product Relationships
  Investigate Segmentation Bases
  Develop Product Positioning
  Select Segmentation Strategy
  Global Implications
Summary

LEARNING OBJECTIVES

After completing this chapter, you should be able to:

1. Define market segmentation, and explain why marketers use it.
2. Compare various approaches to serving markets, from mass marketing to micromarketing.
3. Identify approaches to segmenting consumer markets.
4. Identify approaches to segmenting organizational markets.
5. Detail the steps in the market segmentation process.
6. Describe the basic alternatives for positioning products.
7. Discuss global issues related to market segmentation.

HMOs Try to Serve Two New Markets

Health maintenance organizations (HMOs) have been around for decades, serving consumers mostly in groups through their employers. But with the reform of different insurance regulations at the state level, two new groups of consumers are eligible for HMO services: Medicaid and Medicare patients. These two groups are covered by public funds, but their characteristics are very different. Medicare is the federally funded plan for senior citizens, regardless of financial need. Medicaid is both federally and state funded, and covers financially needy patients of all ages. HMOs are scrambling to determine how to create value for these two new groups of patients and still make a profit. Historically, these two groups have been only marginally profitable, but they do help cover fixed costs.

"There's a window of opportunity here," notes Barry Averill, vice-president for the Chicago operations of Louisville, Kentucky-based Humana Health Plan Inc. "We know other (providers) are coming in. We want to make sure we get our share of (the market)." In Averill's region alone, there are 50,000 Medicaid patients and 150,000 Medicare patients. Until now, most of them have not been enrolled in HMOs.

Humana and other HMOs like United Healthcare have been engaging in marketing efforts like direct

Free juice, coffee, rolls and a spiel: *Senior citizens at a Secure Horizons promotional session in Orange County, Calif.*

mail, telemarketing, and direct-response television advertising just to get their names to senior citizens who might be interested in their services. Then they follow up these efforts with informational seminars. "If (seniors) had a positive experience with the HMO, they have a great deal of loyalty," notes United HealthCare's senior director of marketing for Medicare and Medicaid, explaining these marketing tactics. The important thing is to get the right message to the right consumers—those who are eligible and interested. As you read this chapter, consider the importance of determining who potential customers are, what they need and want, and ultimately, how marketers can serve them.

Source: Joanne Cleaver, "Managed Care's New Markets," *Crain's Chicago Business*, March 6, 1995, pp. SR1, SR16.

Explore more by searching "HMO: Medicare" or "HMO: Medicaid" on the Web.

market
Individuals or organizations with
the desire and ability to buy
goods and services.

Chapter Overview

Health maintenance organizations like Humana and United Healthcare divide their total **market**—the individuals or organizations with the desire and ability to buy goods or services—into relatively homogeneous segments. This process is known as market segmentation. Based on the results, the company decides which of those segments to serve, and how.

This chapter discusses why and when organizations use market segmentation. It describes the process of market segmentation and the criteria used to select target markets to serve. This process includes positioning the product favorably relative to others in the minds of potential buyers. For marketers offering their products in more than one country, the process also includes deciding whether to serve all countries with a single marketing mix or to tailor it to individual country needs and wants.

The Need for Market Segmentation

Sometimes the road isn't a road at all...

Handle it!

℗ **DUNLOP TIRES**

For the Dunlop Dealer nearest you,
call 1-800-548-4714

Visit us on the World Wide Web
http://www.dunloptire.com

Radial Rover A/T OWL

Not everyone needs the same type of tire for their car. To satisfy diverse customer demands, the Dunlop Tire Corporation develops tires tuned precisely for many types of vehicles and road conditions. For example, Dunlop advertises its Radial Rover A/T Owl brand of tire for camping enthusiasts who might find that "Sometimes the road isn't a road at all . . . ."

One of the oldest and most commonly told stories of the need for market segmentation involves the early auto industry. By focusing on the economies of mass production, Henry Ford developed the Model T into a car intended to satisfy everyone. Said Ford, "They can have it in any color, as long as it's black." In contrast, General Motors' Alfred P. Sloan, Jr., had GM's engineers come up with several models, each designed to satisfy the needs and tastes of a different group of customers. This strategy helped GM become the nation's leading automaker.

Like Sloan, marketers have recognized for many years that a single marketing mix seldom is adequate to address the wants and needs of an entire market for a product. For example, not every consumer wants the same features in a home, nor does every business want to own the most advanced form of inventory management software. Similarly, buyers learn about products from different sources such as friends and coworkers, *Consumer Reports* magazine, and television commercials. They place different values on price; one organizational buyer might consider the latest technology to be a sound investment, whereas another is concerned with cutting costs. And different customers prefer to buy in different places (a catalog, a charming boutique, an outlet mall for consumers; over the phone, at a warehouse club, at a trade show for organizational buyers). Such variations among individual and organizational buyers are the main reason for market segmentation.

From the marketer's standpoint, serving only a portion of the total market is often the most efficient strategy. That is certainly the case when a portion of the market accounts for a disproportionate share of sales for a product. One reason that printer and catalog producer R. R. Donnelley failed in introducing a catalog to Japan was that it ignored this principle. Although Donnelley's catalog was in English, the company did not limit its mailing to Japanese consumers who knew the language. When the sales response to the catalog was disappointing, Donnelley shut down the project.[1] In contrast, an organization will more likely succeed if it focuses its marketing efforts on the portion of a market most likely to purchase from it.

What Is Market Segmentation?

Market segmentation is the process of dividing a market into groups of potential buyers who have similar needs and wants, value perceptions, or purchasing behaviors.[2] The individuals or organizations in each group, or market segment, may respond similarly to a particular marketing strategy. Businesses use the information to decide what segment(s) of the market they can serve most profitably; nonprofit organizations use it to help them be more efficient in reaching their goals. The particular market segment that an organization selects to serve is called a **target market.**

General Approaches to Serving Markets

In some cases, organizations find it advantageous to develop a single marketing mix to serve a single target market. This approach tends to be least costly and to give potential customers the clearest sense of the organization's specialty. Thus, although Fisher-Price markets over 400 products, the company focuses on moderately priced toys for children six and under[3]—a focus that is well known among toy buyers in the United States. Other organizations benefit more from developing several marketing mixes to serve several target markets. This approach is more complex and costly, but can enable the organization to appeal to more customers and generate larger profits.

Even when an organization decides to try serving an entire market with a single marketing mix, or not to enter a market at all, these decisions should only be made after a market segmentation analysis has been conducted. Only when marketers know about the size and profile of existing market segments can they select successful strategies. Table 8.1 summarizes the basic ways an organization can serve markets: mass marketing, segment marketing, and individual marketing.

Mass Marketing   In some cases, a single product appeals broadly to a market. Selling the same product to all customers with the same marketing mix is known as **mass marketing** or **undifferentiated marketing.** Today, few products and services are really mass marketed—most markets are segmented on some bases; however, some examples of things that approach mass marketing are phone services and Internet web pages.

Before deciding to use mass marketing, marketers need to carry out the research involved in market segmentation. They need to determine whether the conditions are right for mass marketing to be profitable. Besides looking for the conditions just listed, marketers must be able to appeal to a broad spectrum of buyers. When Western

market segmentation
The process of dividing a market into groups of potential buyers who have similar needs and wants, value perceptions, or purchasing behaviors.

target market
The particular market segment that an organization selects to serve.

mass (undifferentiated) marketing
The strategy of selling the same product to all customers with the same marketing mix.

T A B L E 8.1
Approaches to Serving Markets

Approach	Description	Examples
Mass marketing	A single marketing mix for the entire market	Phone service, Web pages
Segment marketing	A single marketing mix for one segment of the market	Women's Workout World (exercise facilities for women); American Association of Retired Persons (lobbying and membership services for people over age 50)
	Separate marketing mixes for two or more segments of the market	McDonald's (Happy Meals for young children, Big Macs for teens, Arch Deluxe for adults); Toshiba copiers (several sizes and features to meet different levels of business needs)
Individual marketing	A marketing mix customized for an individual or organization	Personalized amenities for repeat guests at Ritz-Carlton hotels; management consulting services tailored to an organization's needs

MANAGING AND DEVELOPING GOODS AND SERVICES

THREE

At General Mills, value is defined not only by superior product quality, but by superiority in the total product offering. Superior product is the cornerstone on which superior brand value and equity can be built.

P. Gayle Fuguitt, *Director of Marketing Research, Big "G" Division, General Mills, Inc.*

CHAPTER 9

Managing Existing Products

CHAPTER 10

Developing New Products

CHAPTER 11

Marketing Services

Explore the Career Profiles on the Churchill and Peter Homepage at www.irwin.com/marketing/value.

Experience what it is like to be a Product Manager on the Marketing Interactive: Building Skills for your Career CD ROM.

Managing Existing Products

CHAPTER OUTLINE

Product Classifications
  Consumer and Industrial Products
  Durables and Nondurables
The Product Life Cycle
  Introduction
  Growth
  Maturity
  Decline
  Evaluation of the Product Life Cycle
  Product Adoption and Diffusion
Branding and Brand Equity
  Benefits of Branding
  Types of Brands
  Selecting a Brand
  Protecting Trademarks
  Developing and Managing Brand Equity
Product Mixes and Product Lines
  Managing Product Mixes and Lines
Summary

LEARNING OBJECTIVES

After completing this chapter, you should be able to:

1. Identify ways in which products may be classified.
2. Describe the stages of the product life cycle.
3. Contrast renewed expansion, fashions, and fads with the basic product life cycle.
4. Summarize the process by which products are adopted by increasingly large numbers of buyers.
5. Define brands and describe issues marketers consider in devising a branding strategy.
6. Explain how marketers protect trademarks and manage brand equity.
7. Discuss basic types of decisions that marketers make with regard to product lines and product mix.

Chapter Nine

Pen Werks

Pens have been around for centuries. You probably have one in your pocket or purse right now, even if you're completely committed to your computer. So how can a company make pens seem new? That's exactly what Minnesota-based Pen Werks has done.

Products, like people, have life cycles. Pen products in general are at the mature stage of the life cycle, meaning that for them to continue to create value for consumers and profits for pen manufacturers, marketers need to breathe new life into the products. So Pen Werks has introduced its own brand of new pens that "offer a better price–value relationship and consumer-desirable features versus [the] competition," explains Jasmine Suljic, director of marketing at Pen Werks. Two of the pens are the Soft Stix, which through new technology offers a rubberized finger grip that is environmentally friendly, and the Perfect Pen, which was designed by German engineers to create the "perfect" ergonomic balance between fingers and pen.

Establishing a brand that consumers recognize and associate with value is crucial to a product's success. Pen Werks' marketers determined that there was no dominant brand in their industry segment, so they sought to build "consistent product quality and value coupled with consistent packaging layout" to give Pen Werks the competitive edge in branding, according to Suljic. Every Pen Werks package has the Pen Werks logo along with the depiction of Inky, Pen Werk's corporate mascot. Pen Werks uses Inky in direct-mail promotions, including one that offers a mouse pad featuring Inky on a surfboard. In addition, Pen Werks has a "Write Marks" program that allows consumers to collect points toward special offers.

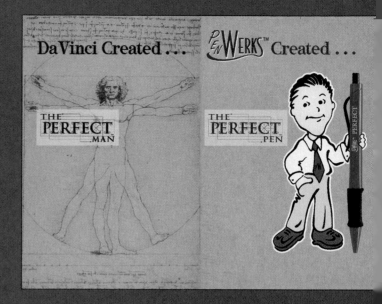

Finally, Pen Werks has expanded its product mix to include such items as the stick eraser called Erase-Err, which according to marketers has "a larger eraser, better design, and a value price to the consumer." Each of these tactics is designed to present a cohesive image to the public, so that people will recognize and remember the 12 different Pen Werks brands.

Pen Werks focuses on value. "Pen Werks has chosen to compete on the basis of value to consumers as it works to build a brand image," explains Jasmine Suljic. All these efforts make Pen Werks pens the kind you probably don't want to lend to someone, if you ever want to get them back.

As you read this chapter, think about how various products can be managed in order to prolong their lives. In addition to pens, what other consumer products could benefit from the ingenuity that Pen Werks has brought to its products?

Source: Interview notes from Jasmine Suljic, Director of Marketing, Pen Werks, October, 1996, "Perfect Pen" advertisement.

more by searching "PenWerks" on the Web.

Chapter Overview

As explained in Chapter 1, a *product* in the marketing sense includes not only goods or services, but also branding, packaging, customer service, and other aspects of the product that add value to customers. Products in this sense may be sold to consumers or organizations, and they may be largely tangible (goods) or intangible (services).

This chapter introduces product management, especially with regard to existing products. The chapter begins by defining broad categories of products. Next, it describes the typical life cycle of a product, from its introduction to its decline and possible removal from the market. Then the chapter turns to a discussion of brands, including ways in which branding can support product positioning and enhance customer value. The chapter closes by discussing issues concerning the organization's assortment of products.

Product Classifications

To help in planning the marketing mix, organizations classify their products in various ways. Two basic classifications consider whether the product is for consumers or organizations and whether it is a durable or nondurable.

Consumer and Industrial Products

consumer products
Goods and services sold to consumers.

industrial products
Goods and services sold to organizations.

convenience products
Products that are purchased frequently and with minimal time and effort.

shopping products
Products that are purchased after spending some effort comparing various alternatives.

specialty products
Products that are unique in some way, purchased infrequently, and usually expensive.

unsought products
Products that consumers do not seek out and may not even be aware of.

Marketers must consider whether their target market consists primarily of consumers or organizational buyers. Logically, goods and services sold to consumers are known as **consumer products.** Goods and services sold to organizations are known as **industrial products.**

Consumer Products   Goods and services targeted to consumers are as varied as cars and concerts, swimwear and CD players. Considering the breadth of possibilities, it can be helpful to group consumer products into categories. The usual classification is in terms of how consumers make purchase decisions:

• **Convenience products** are purchased frequently and with minimal time and effort. They are usually inexpensive. Examples include food, socks, and dry cleaning.

• **Shopping products** are purchased after spending some effort comparing various alternatives. For example, consumers typically do some shopping before buying electronic equipment, day care services, and many kinds of clothing. A major reason that consumers put more effort into selecting shopping products is that the consequences of a mistake are greater. For example, these goods and services tend to cost more than convenience products, and they are often more important to the consumer.

• **Specialty products** are unique in some way, purchased infrequently, and usually expensive. As a result, consumers are willing to make a special effort to obtain the exact product and brand they want. Examples include college educations, houses, and high-performance automobiles.

• **Unsought products** are products that consumers normally do not seek out and may not even be aware of. Consumers buy such products when marketers make them aware of their needs and the value of these products. A classic example of an unsought product is life insurance; other products that fit into this category are routine screenings for breast or prostate cancer. Since unsought products could be convenience, shopping, or specialty products, their characteristics vary.

The classification of a product may depend on its marketing strategy. For example, although writing pens are convenience products in most cases, some manufacturers have pens that are not. Paris-based Recife produces a line of environmentally friendly fountain, rollerball, and ballpoint pens encased in ebonite, a vulcanized rubber that is tapped harmlessly from trees in rain forests. The pens cost $78 to $200 each and are available in specialty stores and a few upscale department stores.[1] Thus, these pens are likely specialty products.

The Balance bicycle is an example of a shopping product. Since consumers may do some comparison shopping, Balance highlights its features, including limited production, handwelded frames, superlight tubing, special finish, and availability "at the greatest bike shops on earth."

Even the same product may fall into different categories for different consumers in varying circumstances. A Brooks Brothers shirt could be a convenience good for a business traveler whose luggage was lost en route to an important meeting, a shopping good for a comparison shopper preparing for a job interview, and a specialty good for someone who only wears Brooks Brothers pinpoint oxfords.[2] However, to devise a strategy that meets the needs of a target market, marketers must keep in mind how the product would be categorized for most consumers in the target market.

Knowing which of these categories their products fall into helps marketers devise an appropriate marketing mix (see Table 9.1 for these basic categories). If they are selling convenience products, marketers usually keep prices low and make the products widely available and easy to purchase. Attractive and informative packaging also is important for convenience products, since they often are selected at the point of purchase. Marketers selling shopping products offer them in fewer outlets and provide information on various product attributes that help consumers choose the right products for their needs. Marketers selling specialty products often sell in exclusive outlets and charge high prices to connote prestige.

Marketers can also find opportunities in changing the category of their products by changing product attributes. For example, Thor-Lo Inc. of Statesville, North Carolina, found success in selling athletic socks by creating sport-specific socks with dense padding in areas where the foot takes the most stress during the particular sport. Thus, the company turned its product from a convenience product into a shopping product which could be sold more profitably.[3]

Industrial Products Organizational buyers purchase raw materials, parts, machinery, and equipment to make their products, and supplies and services to operate their businesses. These are all industrial products. As with consumer products, it is useful to think of them in terms of basic categories:

T A B L E 9.1
Basic Categories of
Consumer Products

Category	Type of Purchase Decision	Price	Promotion	Placement or Distribution
Convenience	Routine decision making; low involvement; little decision time; little information sought	Relatively low	Mass media	Widely available
Shopping	Limited decision making; moderate involvement; more decision time; more information sought	Moderate	Mass media; some emphasis on personal selling	Selectively available
Specialty	Extensive decision making; high involvement; extensive decision time; lots of information sought	Relatively expensive	Mass media; more emphasis on personal selling	Exclusively available

The Mercedes-Benz automobile has traditionally been considered a specialty good, but this ad treats the car as a shopping product. Balancing the car's price of $29,000 or more against the functional benefit that the car will likely be valuable for many years, the ad emphasizes practicality rather than an image of prestige.

installations
Nonportable industrial goods that are major, and that are bought, installed, and used to produce other goods or services.

accessory equipment
Portable factory equipment and tools that are used in the production process but which do not become part of the finished product.

component parts and materials
Processed items that are made into finished products.

raw materials
Unprocessed items that are made into component parts or finished products.

supplies
Industrial goods that are consumed in the process of producing other products, but which do not go into the products.

business services
Services that support an organization's activities.

• **Installations** are "nonportable industrial goods such as furnaces and assembly lines that are major, and that are bought, installed, and used to produce other goods or services."[4] For example, Pitney Bowes's Mail Center 2000 is a computerized mailroom system that weighs, stamps, and prepares mail of any size or shape in a matter of minutes.[5]

• **Accessory equipment** consists of "portable factory equipment and tools that are used in the production process and do not become part of the finished product."[6] Examples include fork lifts, screwdrivers, and calculators.

• **Component parts and materials** are processed items that are made into finished products. Examples include switches, motors, and transistors. For example, Owens-Corning Fiberglas Corporation markets fiberglass walls and panels for refrigerators and water heaters.[7]

• **Raw materials** are unprocessed items that are made into component parts or finished products. Examples are wheat, copper, and cotton.

• **Supplies** are "industrial goods that are consumed in the process of producing other products." They facilitate the production process but do not go into the product itself.[8] Examples are light bulbs and pens.

• **Business services** are services that support the organization's activities. The trend among organizations is toward outsourcing, that is purchasing business services, ranging from marketing research and advertising to engineering and accounting, rather than doing these functions for themselves. In addition, organizations pay for a variety of more routine services such as cleaning and package delivery. Table 9.2 summarizes characteristics of these types of products.

As with consumer products, the category of industrial product influences the marketing mix. For example, installations tend to be very costly, so buyers make long, involved purchase decisions. Therefore, marketers of installations emphasize personal selling to help buyers make the right selection. For less costly, more routine purchases, personal selling is less important. Price is important for supplies and raw materials, where substitutes tend to be readily available. In contrast, many kinds of equipment and business services offer unique benefits for which customers will pay a premium.

Industrial products should be designed to help their buyers create value for *their* customers. For example, fiberglass walls are relatively expensive, but they provide

T A B L E 9.2
Basic Categories of Industrial Products

Category	Type of Purchase Decision	Price	Promotion
Installations	Complex; infrequent; lengthy; multiple members of buying center	Not as important	Personal selling
Accessory equipment	Less complex and lengthy; few members of buying center	May be important	Advertising
Component parts and materials	Less complex; frequent; several members of buying center	May be important	Personal selling
Raw materials	Frequent; complexity varies	Very important	Personal selling
Supplies	Simple; frequent; may be a single buyer	Important	Advertising
Business services	Varies	Varies	Varies

Ray-Ban sunglasses are nondurable goods—buyers expect to use them for less than three years. In this ad, durability takes a back seat to fashionability.

insulation as well as structure for refrigerators. Thus, manufacturers who purchase them don't need to use an extra layer of insulation and can create value for consumers by providing more storage space.[9] Industrial products also should be designed to help buyers reduce the cost of production and increase the quality of final products. This can often be done by producing assembled components requiring fewer moving parts or by substituting technologies. For example, when the price of remote keyless entry systems becomes lower, they could be substituted for mechanical locks on all automobiles. Thus, car manufacturers would save money purchasing and installing them and consumers would get a more convenient, higher-quality locking system.

Durables and Nondurables

durable goods
Products that are used over an extended period of time, typically three years or more.

When we buy some consumer goods, we expect them to last for years. For example, when we buy a car or mattress set, we expect to get years of use from it. These kinds of consumer goods which are "used over an extended rather than a brief period of time" are known as **durable goods**.[10] Typically, durable goods are considered to be those that are used for at least three years.

When we buy other goods, we don't expect them to last this long. In the case of some products, such as restaurant meals or gasoline, we might not even expect them to last for three days. Consumer goods that are used over a brief time period are called **nondurable goods**.

nondurable goods
Products that are used over a brief period of time, typically less than three years.

Marketing durable goods may involve different concerns than marketing nondurables. Buyers who expect to use the product over the course of several years will be concerned about the product's reliability and perhaps the seller's willingness to service the product. Because durable goods tend to be relatively costly, consumers tend to spend time researching these purchases. Therefore, personal selling usually plays a more significant role when marketing durable goods. In contrast, buyers of nondurables usually place greater emphasis on convenience and variety. Marketers of nondurable goods often focus on making them readily available to consumers in a variety of styles, colors, or flavors.

The Product Life Cycle

The marketing strategies that work best for newspapers are not the same as those for Internet search engines. There are many reasons for the differences, but an important one is that these products are at different stages of their life cycles. Products, like living beings, can be viewed as passing

FIGURE 9.1
The Product Life Cycle

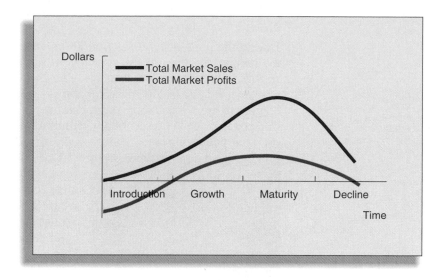

product life cycle
A model of the stages in a product's sales and profit history.

through certain life stages. The **product life cycle** is a model of the stages in a product's sales and profit history.

As shown in Figure 9.1, the four stages in the product life cycle are introduction, growth, maturity, and decline. The two curves in the figure show the pattern of industry sales and profits throughout these stages. During the final stage, marketers may try to stimulate demand or may stop offering the product.

Introduction

During the introduction stage of the product life cycle, a new product enters the marketplace. Sales start out slowly but begin to climb. Production costs are usually high because the producers lack experience in making the product. Marketing costs tend to be high because sellers must devote resources to educating target markets about what the new product is and how it will benefit them.

primary demand
Demand for the product class as a whole.

Marketing during this stage emphasizes building **primary demand,** or demand for the product class as a whole, such as electric garage door openers. In other words, marketers try to stimulate demand for the type of product, rather than for a specific brand. The objective is to make potential buyers aware of the product and to get them to try it.

Because costs are high and sales are only beginning to build, industry profits are usually negative at this stage. Thus, one of the biggest challenges of the introduction phase is to keep enough money coming in to cover the expenses of building demand. Depending on its size and reputation, the marketer also may have difficulty persuading resellers to handle the product. Fortunately, marketers in this stage of the product life cycle tend to face little competition. If they can protect some aspect of the product with a patent or copyright, they can maintain their position as sole producer of the product for years. The lack of competition, high costs, and the need for income often lead marketers to set a relatively high price at this stage.

An example of a product in the introduction stage in 1996 was smart phones. Colonial Data Technologies had introduced a phone that includes a display screen, magnetic card swipe, and keyboard. It can send pages or e-mail, download phone numbers from electronic directories, and tap into databases for shopping or banking. Colonial, which already marketed display boxes for Caller ID, offered its smart phones to phone companies for resale to consumers.[11]

Growth

During the growth stage, sales climb rapidly as more and more buyers begin trying the product. Profits also rise as sellers learn to make efficient use of their production facilities and distribution channels. The challenges of this stage include keeping up with demand and fending off competitors, who are attracted to the market because of its growth in sales and large profit margins. In general, competition causes marketers to emphasize building **secondary demand,** or demand for their brand, by lowering prices or enhancing brand image.

secondary demand
Demand for a particular brand.

With espresso bars no longer a West Coast oddity, Starbucks Corporation is enjoying its leadership in the growing coffee bar market. To sustain growth as the competition gets stiffer, the company is expanding into grocery stores with such products as coffee ice cream and a bottled version of Frappucino, a low fat, creamy, slightly sweet tasting coffee beverage.

One business in the growth stage in 1996 was search engines for the Internet. Search engines are needed because the Internet contains well over 10 billion words in documents that are not arranged for retrieval. Creators of search engines compile and index an electronic catalog of Web contents, then provide the software to search through the index for key words or concepts specified by the user. The search engine displays a list of documents containing the words or concepts. When the user clicks on an item in the list, the search engine retrieves the document. About a dozen major companies compete in the market, including Alta Vista, Yahoo!, and Lycos. Still more search engines are being developed, with their creators focusing on ways to differentiate their offerings. For example, Electric Library indexes only reliable sources such as newspapers, journals, *Compton's Encyclopedia*, and a world atlas. By serving as a gatekeeper for information, Electric Library offers for a monthly fee not just information, but information users can trust.[12]

Maturity

A product is mature when it becomes familiar to the market and when sales climb more gradually and then plateau. Because many buyers already own the product, sales growth slows and may even begin falling toward the end of this stage. For example, in the mature U.S. market for personal computers, sales growth fell in 1996 to about half the rate of the early 1990s.[13] Competition causes industry profits to level off. This is because prices are cut, while the cost of attracting buyers may increase.

It is common to seek new markets for products in the maturity stage. As prices of pagers fell from $400 to just $60 to $120, their appeal extended beyond business-people to consumers. For example, teenagers buy beepers so their friends can reach them while they are out. To further appeal to consumers, beepers now come in bright colors and are available in many outlets, including Kmart and some supermarkets.[14] When the U.S. market for shipping and trucking services started plateauing, Allied Van Lines, of Naperville, Illinois expanded into overseas markets that were still growing. Allied formed partnerships with companies in each target country and developed marketing communications for its foreign customers.[15]

Decline

Eventually the sales volume for most products begins to fall. There are many possible reasons for a sales decline. Perhaps new technology has led to a superior alternative. For example, in a recent year, CD players outsold turntables 8 to 1, and forecasts

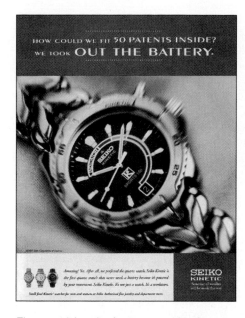

HOW COULD WE FIT 50 PATENTS INSIDE? WE TOOK OUT THE BATTERY.

SEIKO KINETIC

The potential market for quartz watches is mature, and Seiko is countering with innovation. Its Kinetic watch, shown here, is "the first quartz watch that never needs a battery because it's powered by your movement."

indicated that sales of turntables would continue falling.[16] Moreover, needs or values may change so that the product is no longer relevant or appealing. As a case in point, ticket sales for transatlantic flights on the Concorde have fallen, despite overall growth in international air traffic. Apparently, the jet's supersonic speeds do not make up for ticket prices, which are $2,400 higher than a first-class ticket on a standard jet from New York to London.[17]

Marketers may respond to the sales decline by seeking ways to keep the product profitable. One approach is to cut costs. In the case of turntables, makers did so by limiting the number of models they produced. If a niche market continues to demand a product, prices can be increased in some cases, as was also done with turntables.[18] In general, marketers can modify products and/or seek new uses or new markets to forestall decline, as will be discussed later in this chapter.

Evaluation of the Product Life Cycle

The product life cycle model is useful in a general way for helping marketers plan their strategies. For example, it reminds marketers of a new product with rapidly growing sales that they should anticipate increased competition and a need to adapt their strategy to maintain or increase sales and profits. In addition, there are general recommendations for strategy development for each stage of the product life cycle that can be helpful to marketers, as shown in Table 9.3.

However, the product life cycle does have limitations that require it to be used cautiously in developing strategy. For one thing, the length of time a product will remain in each stage is unknown and can't be predicted with accuracy. Thus, while each stage will likely occur for a successful product, marketers can't forecast when one stage will end and another will begin in order to adapt their strategies at the appropriate time. Related to this is the problem that marketers may misjudge when a stage is ending and implement an inappropriate strategy. For example, marketers who believe their products are ending the maturity cycle may cut their promotion costs and thus cause the product to decline, when the product could easily have continued to sell well if promotion had been altered.

Another limitation is that not all products go through the product life cycle in the same way. For example, many products are failures and don't have anything approaching a full life cycle. Several variations of the life cycle also exist, two of which are fashions and fads.

fashion
An accepted and popular product style.

Fashions are accepted and popular product styles. Their life cycle involves a distinctiveness stage in which trendsetters adopt the style, followed by an emulation stage in which more customers purchase the style to be like the trendsetters. Next is the economic stage, in which the style becomes widely available at mass-market prices, then eventually becomes phased out. This happened to the so-called grunge look. It moved from Seattle rock bands to college campuses. In a single year, U.S. sales of sturdy, no-nonsense Doc Martens shoes and boots—a staple of grunge—doubled.[19] When department stores began featuring flannel shirts and ripped jeans, musicians and students were ready to move on. Many fashions, such as skirt lengths and designer jeans, lose popularity, then regain it again. As in these examples, the fashion cycle is

TABLE 9.3
The Product Life Cycle's
Implications for Marketing
Strategy

Strategy Dimension	Introduction	Growth	Maturity	Decline
Basic objectives	Establish a market for product type; persuade early adopters to buy	Build sales and market share; develop preference for brand	Defend brand's share of market; seek growth by luring customers from competitors	Limit costs or seek ways to revive sales and profits
Product	Provide high quality; select a good brand; get patent and/or trademark protection	Provide high quality; add services to enhance value	Improve quality; add features to distinguish brand from competitors	Continue providing high quality to maintain brand's reputation; seek ways to make the product new again
Price	Often high to recover development costs; sometimes low to build demand rapidly	Somewhat high because of heavy demand	Low, reflecting heavy competition	Low to sell off remaining inventory or high to serve a niche market
Placement or Distribution	Limited number of channels	Greater number of channels to meet demand	Greater number of channels and more incentives to resellers	Limited number of channels
Promotion	Aimed at early adopters; messages designed to educate about product type; incentives such as samples and coupons to induce trial	Aimed at wider audience; messages focus on brand benefits; for consumer products, emphasis on advertising	Messages focus on differentiating brand from its competitors; heavy use of incentives such as coupons to induce buyers to switch brands	Minimal, to keep costs down

typical of clothing. Other products that follow this cycle are hairstyles and cosmetics. Tattoos, body piercing, and body branding also follow a fashion cycle.

Fads are products that experience an intense but brief period of popularity. Their life cycle resembles the basic product life cycle but in compressed form. It may be so brief that few competitors have a chance to capitalize on the fad. An example of a fad product is liquid-diet plans. Consumers rushed to them because they looked like an easy way to lose weight. Sales really took off in 1988 after talk-show host Oprah Winfrey credited use of Optifast with her loss of 67 pounds. But like Winfrey, most people failed to achieve long-term weight loss. The federal government began to investigate the claims made for the products and sales tumbled.[20] Some fads repeat their popularity after long lapses. That was the case with troll dolls, which were popular in the 1960s and again in the 1990s.

fads
Products that experience an intense but brief period of popularity.

Product Adoption and Diffusion

Throughout the product life cycle, a successful product enters the homes and workplaces of more and more buyers. In the 1950s, few households had television sets. Those that did had the discretionary income and innovativeness to buy the new technology, and their neighbors would gather to watch with the proud owners. As more and more consumers valued TV entertainment or wanted to emulate their neighbors and as TV prices fell, they bought sets of their own. Today at least one television is in virtually every American home, most of them color TVs.

The buyers who try the product early in its life cycle tend to have different characteristics than those who buy later. Also, the behavior of early buyers tends to influence those who buy later. The process by which new products spread through a population is called **product diffusion** (see "Put It into Practice: Do You Know What Kind of Buyers You Know?"). There are five adopter categories in the diffusion process, as shown in Figure 9.2.

The first category is **innovators,** who are the first to buy a new product. When innovators are consumers, they tend to be people who are venturesome and willing to take risks. For example, the first car owners to install neon lights on the underside of their vehicles were so impressed with the eerie effect that they were willing to risk generating some less than favorable reactions. Explains Pete Santoro, the Kansas City distributor for Motion Neon, "The police officers around here . . . when they see some car going down the street with lights underneath it, they freak out. The first thing they've got to do is catch it."[21]

When innovators are organizational buyers, they tend to be organizations that seek to remain at the cutting edge through use of the latest technology and ideas. Ingersoll Milling Machine Company, a maker of customized machines for heavy industry, is committed to the idea that using the latest machinery can improve its productivity. Ingersoll has a rule that when its machines reach 10 years old, they must be replaced unless someone can justify keeping them. This commitment to modernizing has enabled the company to double its output with half the number of machines.[22]

If the experience of innovators is favorable, **early adopters** begin to buy. These buyers are respected, and they influence the next group. Influenced by what early adopters have, the rest of the market begins to get interested in the product. The biggest category of buyers is divided into groups called the early majority and late majority. Members of the **early majority** tend to avoid risk and to make purchases carefully. Members of the **late majority** not only avoid risks, but are cautious and skeptical about new ideas. Eventually the product becomes commonplace, and even the laggards are ready to buy. **Laggards** are reluctant to make changes and are comfortable with traditional products, but may eventually purchase a well-established alternative.

Knowing that different types of customers buy at different stages may help marketers devise strategies that appeal to the group likely to buy at a given time. For example, first-time buyers of personal computers now are likely to be laggards. Marketers may need to convince this group that their products are easy to use, reliable, and widely acceptable in society.

product diffusion
The process by which new products spread through a population.

innovators
Consumers and organizations who are venturesome and willing to take risks.

early adopters
Consumers and organizations who tend to emulate innovators.

early majority
Consumers and organizations that tend to avoid risk and to make purchases carefully, typically after evaluating the experience of those who have previously purchased the product.

late majority
Consumers and organizations that tend to avoid risks and who are cautious and skeptical about new ideas and products, only buying them when their ownership becomes commonplace.

laggards
Consumers and organizations that are comfortable with traditional products and who buy new ones only when they become well-established alternatives.

Branding and Brand Equity

Buyers are usually concerned not with just types of products, but also with brands of products. Customers say, "I'd like to buy a Jaguar," or, "I have a craving for a Big Mac," or, "We could really improve our presentation if we use Powerpoint." It is clearly helpful to marketers of these brands that potential buyers are interested in a Jaguar, Big Mac, and Powerpoint, rather than just an automobile, a sandwich, and presentation software.

FIGURE 9.2
Adopter Categories

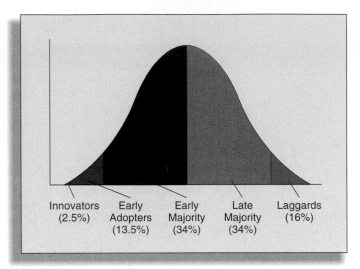

brand
A name, term, design, symbol, or any other feature that identifies one seller's good or service as distinct from other sellers.

brand name
That part of a brand that can be spoken.

brand mark
That part of a brand that cannot be spoken.

trademark
A brand that has legal status by virtue of its being registered with the federal government.

service mark
A brand for a service that has legal status by virtue of its being registered with the federal government.

trade name
The legal name under which a company operates.

brand extension
The practice of using an existing brand name for a new product.

family brand
The use of the same brand name for an entire product line.

Marketers brand their products to differentiate them from competitors and to help buyers make purchase decisions. A **brand** is "a name, term, design, symbol, or any other feature that identifies one seller's good or service as distinct from those of other sellers."[23] Examples include the name Cirrus for that network of automated teller machines and the symbol of the peacock for NBC. Even the appearance of a pill (its shape and color) can be protected as part of a brand.[24]

A variety of terms describe the elements of a brand more precisely. A **brand name** is "that part of a brand which can be spoken."[25] Thus, it consists of letters, numbers, or words, such as Clinique, Tylenol, and 7Up. A **brand mark** is that part of a brand that cannot be spoken.[26] It generally consists of a symbol or graphic design, such as the Golden Arches of McDonald's or the Nike swoosh.

To obtain the legal right to use a brand exclusively, its owner must register it with the federal government. Then the brand becomes a **trademark** or, if it refers to a service, a **service mark.** Finally, a **trade name** is the legal name under which a company operates. Thus, Ralston Purina Company is the trade name of a company that owns many brand names, such as Corn Chex.

Companies often market other products under a successful brand name in order to capitalize on the positive meanings customers already have for it. For example, when Honda introduced outboard motors under its name, many consumers had favorable attitudes about Honda engines from experiences with its automobiles. Using an existing brand name for a new product is called **brand extension.** In a recent year, 70 percent of the almost 16,000 new food, household, and personal-care products were brand extensions.[27] Brand extension can be effective if the brand is already successful and well-respected; extending a brand under such circumstances tends to grab more market share at a lower advertising cost than the marketer could by creating a new brand.[28] However, a brand extension strategy can fail and even damage existing products if the brand is used for products that are unrelated or when the brand's name or image doesn't fit the new product.[29]

When an entire product line uses the same brand name, it is called a **family brand.** Gillette Company uses the family brand Gillette Series for a line of men's shaving products, antiperspirant/deodorants, and aftershaves. To benefit from consumers' positive views of Gillette's Sensor razor, the company advertises the Gillette Series with the same slogan used for the razor: "Gillette. The best a man can get."[30] As in this example, a family brand is beneficial when the brand has a good reputation that can carry over from one product to another. A consumer who likes the Sensor razor, for example, might be favorably predisposed to try Gillette's other men's shaving products. Such a strategy can backfire if the organization fails to consistently offer value

Put It into Practice

Do You Know What Kind of Buyers You Know?

Consumers come in all shapes and sizes. They also have habits and attitudes that characterize their buying behavior. According to the model of product adoption, buyers fall into several categories—risk-taking innovators, influential early adopters, moderate early and late majority, and stubborn laggards. As a marketer, you want to know what adopter types will be interested in your products.

To get an idea, ask six to ten people you know for their permission to be interviewed—family, friends, co-workers, teammates, and the like (try to avoid interviewing classmates from this class). Make a chart with columns for each of the buying categories and enough space to mark the number of your interviewees who fall into each category as well as your own comments and observations. (Do not write down any of your interviewees' names.)

Ask your interviewees about their clothes buying habits. Do they buy the latest fashions? What influences what styles they were? How long does a look have to be around before they buy in? How long do they keep clothes after they buy them? Will they wear clothes that are out of style? Do they rely on popular brand names when making decisions? (You may come up with more questions on your own, but the interview need only last a few minutes.) When you are through, mark on your chart which adopter category you think your interviewee fits.

When your interviews and chart are complete, see if any patterns emerge. Did you have mostly innovators? Mostly laggards? Or were your buyers of all different types?

with all the products bearing the family brand; a negative experience with one product can harm buyers' opinions of the other products. Thus, an organization can most effectively use family brands if its products are related to one another and to the brand's image, and if the organization maintains the same quality for all its family-branded products.

Benefits of Branding

Using a brand is a way to distinguish products in the minds of potential buyers. They may put forth extra effort and spend additional money to buy a particular brand. Commitment to buy a particular brand is called brand loyalty. The majority of consumers are loyal to one brand when they purchase certain products, including cigarettes (such as Marlboro), mayonnaise (Hellman's), and toothpaste (Crest). (See You Decide: Does Sub-Zero Create Superior Value?) For other products, such as garbage bags and canned vegetables, only about one-quarter of consumers are brand loyal.[31] By protecting its brand with trademark or service mark status, the organization also creates an element of the product that competitors may not copy.

Branding benefits buyers as well as sellers. When they are comparison shopping, buyers can use brands to help them keep track of the various items they are evaluating. Thus, someone shopping for a used car might note that she particularly enjoyed test driving a Taurus. Furthermore, the brand images that people have help them make purchase decisions. They seek out brands for which they have positive images and avoid brands with negative images. In sum, brands can reduce the time and energy involved in shopping, as well as provide good feelings from positive associations with the brand.

Types of Brands

Branding can be done by manufacturers or resellers. Products also can be sold without brands. These are called generic products or generic brands. Figure 9.3 summarizes the possibilities.

manufacturer's brand
A brand that is owned and used by the producer of the product.

A **manufacturer's brand** is a brand that is owned and used by the producer of the product. For example, Warner-Lambert makes Listerine mouthwash, and American Home Products Corporation makes Advil ibuprofen. If the manufacturer wants customers' positive attitudes toward a brand to lead them to try the organization's other products, the manufacturer might use the same brand for several related products.

If manufacturers produce different versions of products to appeal to different target markets, they may use different brand names for each. Thus, General Electric makes both GE and Hotpoint appliances. Hotpoint appliances are designed to appeal to the price-conscious segment of the market, and GE-branded products are for the quality-focused segment. This strategy helps the company to differentiate its products and appeal to more consumers.

private brand
A brand that is owned and used by a wholesaler or retailer.

A brand that is owned and used by a reseller (such as a retailer or wholesaler) is called a **private brand** or private label. Wal-Mart stores sell a variety of items bearing its Great Value and Sam's American Choice brands. Most supermarket chains have private brands, such as Safeway's Party Pride, Manor House, and Canterbury. Sears private brands include Craftsman tools and Kenmore appliances. Department stores, too, use private brands. Saks Fifth Avenue's brand is called Real Clothes, and private brands at Bloomingdale's include Studio B. Private brands now account for over 18 percent of all units sold in supermarkets and almost 14 percent of dollar volume.[32]

Private-branded goods enjoyed a surge of popularity in the U.S. in the early 1990s. Observers explained the popularity by saying that the recession led consumers to try private brands. Many seemed to feel that manufacturers charged more for their brands

FIGURE 9.3
Branding Options

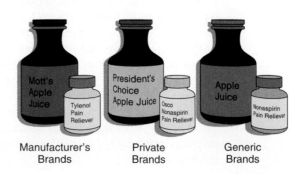

| Manufacturer's Brands | Private Brands | Generic Brands |

FIGURE 9.4
Product Sales by Type of Brand

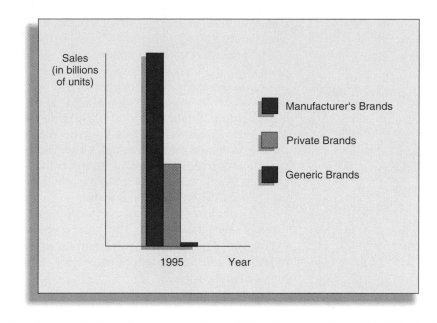

Source: Bob Gatty, "Private Label vs. National Brands: Battle Royal and Retailer Opportunity," *Grocery Marketing*, November 1995, pp. 6, 12 (citing data from Information Resources Inc. and the Private Label Manufacturers Association).

simply to cover the cost of advertising them, not because their branded products delivered more value.[33] Consumers' good experiences with private-brand products' quality led them to stick with the products.[34] By the mid-1990s, however, sales of private-label merchandise flattened as economic conditions improved and consumers returned to buying manufacturers brands.[35]

Private brands are popular in Europe and Japan. In one study, private labels accounted for an estimated 32 percent of British and 24 percent of French supermarket sales.[36] Prices of many goods in Japanese supermarkets fell when retailers increased the number of private-label alternatives.[37]

Many stores also stock some **generic brands** or **generic products,** defined as "products which are named only by their generic class."[38] Supermarket shoppers can find goods ranging from paper towels to dog food to peanut butter packaged as generic products. Their packages bear no brand names or other seller identification, simply the type of product and any required information, such as ingredients on food items. Buyers of medicine often can have prescriptions filled with a generic alternative.

Without brand names, products often are less expensive. However, many generic products have gained a reputation for lower quality. As a result, they are much less popular now than they were two decades ago. A recent survey found decreasing sales of generic brands, which accounted for well under 1 percent of total sales, sales dollars, and units sold (see Figure 9.4).[39]

generic (brands) products
Products that are named only by their generic class.

Strategies for Brand Types   Retailers enjoy several benefits from offering private and generic brands. Perhaps most important, these products often have higher margins and can be more profitable than manufacturers' brands because retailers may spend less to promote them. Also, retailers have greater control over the marketing mix, including product quality, promotion, and pricing. Finally, brand loyalty to a private brand benefits retailers directly because customers must buy from their stores in order to get the brand.

To counter the popularity of private brands, manufacturers have to demonstrate that their brands offer superior value. Since toy makers often convince children to ask for their products by brand, Toys "R" Us stocks only brand-name toys.[40] Coca-Cola's marketers point out to retailers that the customers who are attracted to stores carrying manufacturers' brands tend to spend a lot more on groceries than do buyers of private-label goods.[41]

Manufacturers also can compete with private and generic brands by cutting the price of their brand-name goods. Procter & Gamble responded to the popularity of private-brand and generic alternatives by lowering the price of its Tide laundry detergent. For similar reasons, Philip Morris cut the price of Marlboro cigarettes. Overall, manufacturers' brands are most likely to do well relative to private brands when they are priced close to private brand prices, when buyers don't want to risk quality (as in the case of baby food, for example), and when the products are innovative.[42]

Often the makers of manufacturers' brands also produce generic and private-label products. Why would they make generic and private brands to compete with their own brands? There are several reasons:

• A manufacturer may have excess production capacity, making it more economical to produce these goods. Merck decided to enter the market for generic drugs for that reason. At its plant in West Point, Pennsylvania, Merck makes the Dolobid brand of arthritis drug and its generic equivalent, diflunisal, thereby keeping product volume high and unit costs low.[43]

• Resellers of private and generic brands tend to place large and predictable orders. Therefore, they may be an important source of business.

• Choosing not to produce these products does not eliminate competition from them. The resellers that want private brands or generic goods will simply order them from someone else. When a brand-name company declined to make baby bottles for Toys "R" Us, Gloucester, Massachusetts-based NutraMax got the contract.[44]

Selecting a Brand

Decisions related to branding are critical to the success of marketing efforts. A good brand name can set the product apart from the competition and give rise to positive feelings such as trust, confidence, security, and strength.[45]

Selection Criteria   To select a brand name, marketers consider a variety of criteria that reflect the following five concerns:[46]

1. The brand name should imply the benefits delivered by the product. For example, Easy Off oven cleaner implies that the product will simplify this nasty chore; Sure deodorant connotes reliable protection.

2. The brand name should be positive, distinctive, and easy to say and remember. Examples include U-Haul truck rental and Nike Air Jordan athletic shoes.

3. The name should be consistent with the image of the product or organization. Thus, to position its Acura Legend to compete with luxury cars (which typically bear alphanumeric names like BMW 540i and Lexus LS 400), Honda renamed it the 3.5RL.[47]

4. The name should be legally permissible. This means that the name should not violate the trademark status of another organization's brand.

5. The brand name for a product to be offered globally should translate well. To speakers of other languages, the brand name should not be offensive or imply something negative about the product. To meet this objective, global marketers sometimes compromise on the first three criteria. By avoiding controversy, an easy-to-pronounce name with little or no meaning—for example, Exxon—may be more beneficial to an international company than a name with more meaning.

These criteria for choosing a brand imply that marketers need to understand the environment when creating a brand name. Thus, a crackdown by the Food and Drug Administration on foods making health claims has led to fewer applications for trademark status for names containing the words *heart, pure,* and *fresh*.[48]

Selection Process   One approach to selecting a brand name begins when members of the organization make name suggestions. The organization may also get suggestions from outside sources such as its advertising agency. Then the list is pared down. In the auto industry, the group that does this typically includes executives and ad agency representatives. When only a few names remain, the organization conducts marketing research to test how the names are perceived by consumers. When Mercury wanted to name a minivan, it was considering the name Columbia, hoping consumers would appreciate the connection to the space shuttle. But research showed that consumers linked the name to the country Colombia and that country's drug trade. So Mercury called its minivan the Villager instead.[49] As in this example, the organization uses research to further pare its list. It conducts legal research on the remaining ideas, weeding out any names that are trademarks or service marks. If more than one name survives, the final choice is based on experience and judgment.

Sometimes an organization seeks help in naming its brands from a brand-naming service such as Name Lab or Interbrand Group. For example, Nigerian Breweries (NB) asked Interbrand to come up with a name for a new beer, a stout that was to compete with Guinness in Nigeria. Through discussions and brainstorming, Interbrand came up with a number of possible names. The firm checked to make sure that none of them had a negative meaning in Swahili. Of the possibilities Interbrand suggested, NB approved 10. Interbrand checked the trademark status of these and conducted marketing research to see how consumers reacted to the names compared to Guinness. Finally, Interbrand recommended the name Legend because "it had global credibility."[50]

Protecting Trademarks

As mentioned earlier, organizations may obtain legal protection for their brands by registering them with the U.S. government. Registering the brand—making it a trademark or service mark—gives the owner the exclusive right to use it.

To further protect the trademark or service mark status of a brand, the organization should use it and identify it as a brand. The basic way to do this is to use the symbol ® following a trademark or service mark. When a brand is still being registered, the organization can use the ™ symbol to show that the brand is the organization's exclusive property. The brand name should always be capitalized, and the organization should never change its spelling.

In spite of these efforts, people may intentionally or unintentionally misuse the trademark. This is a particular problem in international trade, where 5 percent of all goods are counterfeit.[51] When misuse occurs, it is up to the owner to take legal action to protect its rights. Within the United States, the Federal Trademark Dilution Act of 1996 permits owners of well-known trademarks to file lawsuits against those who misuse the trademarks. For example, cosmetics marketer Avon successfully sued a woman who had registered to use "avon.com" as her address on the World Wide Web. Such cases may become more common, because people can choose any unused name for a Web site, and the number of commercial sites is growing at 8,000 a week.[52] Organizations can protect not only brand names, but also logos (as Brunckhorst Company, which markets deli foods under the name Boar's Head, did when G. Heileman Brewing Company introduced a beer called Boar's Head Red) or products' "trade dress"—their distinctive appearance when the public associates it with the product, as with a distinctive fashion design.[53]

Organizations that fail to take such measures risk having the brand lose its protection as a trademark or service mark. Some former brand names that have become generic are *aspirin, escalator,* and *thermos.* Sometimes the public uses a brand name as if it were generic, and the owner has to work hard to protect its rights to the

"The New Symbol For Eating Better" is a slogan being introduced by Good Humor-Breyers Ice Cream. The "eat better, eat well" symbol will appear on ice creams, yogurts and delicious frozen treats that have less sugar and/or fat. There is a ™ to the right of the symbol, which means that U.S. government registration has been requested and that the slogan is the exclusive property of the Good Humor-Breyers Ice Cream Company.

trademark. Such terms include Xerox, Coke, and Kleenex. The owners of these terms place advertisements reminding people to use the terms properly.

Developing and Managing Brand Equity

A good branding strategy is important because it helps marketers develop and maintain a positive image with buyers. A reputation for quality and value may attract new customers, as well as encourage existing customers to become loyal and to try other products with the same brand name. In this way, organizations can build sales at lower cost. Positive associations with a brand can even persuade people to give an organization a second chance when it slips up or encounters problems. Overall, strong brands can be an organization's most valuable assets.

brand equity
The value of a brand to an organization, including customer loyalty toward the brand, the brand's name awareness, perceived quality, and brand associations.

The value of a brand to an organization is called **brand equity.** As shown in Figure 9.5, brand equity includes customers' brand loyalty, name awareness, perceived quality, brand associations, and other proprietary brand assets. These components result from buyers' thoughts about the product, the organization, and other variables that affect exchanges for the product. Brand equity can be either positive or negative, depending on how consumers perceive the meaning of the brand.

When a brand has positive brand equity, the organization may receive value from it by (1) improving the efficiency and effectiveness of its marketing programs, (2) reinforcing brand loyalty, (3) enabling a premium to be charged for the brand,

Elements of Brand Equity

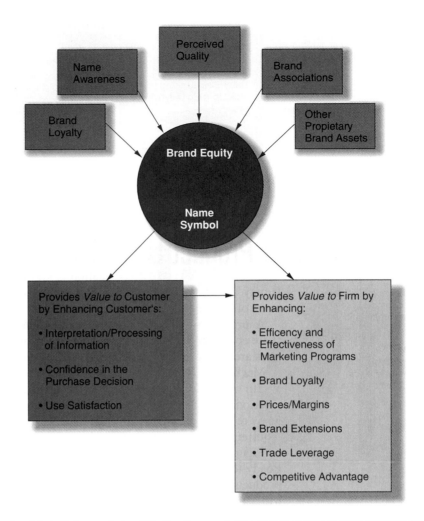

Source: Reprinted with the permission of The Free Press, a division of Simon & Schuster from *Managing Brand Equity: Capitalizing on the Value of a Brand Name,* by David A. Aaker. Copyright 1991 by David A. Aaker.

(4) providing a basis for brand extensions, (5) increasing leverage with others in the marketing channel, and (6) gaining a competitive advantage in the marketplace.

Brand equity provides value to customers by helping them interpret and process information about new and existing products. It gives them confidence in their decisions to purchase the brand, and adds to their satisfaction in making such purchases.[54] Such benefits were what Dennis Carter, vice president of corporate marketing for Intel, was referring to when he said, "In technology, where products change rapidly, the brand is doubly important—more important than in packaged goods, where a product may be more understandable because it's stayed the same for a long time."[55]

Given its value, marketers work hard to develop and protect brand equity. They do this through trademark protection and through strategy efforts to enhance brand images. Intel sued to obtain trademark protection for its 386 microchip, widely known simply as the "386." However, the company lost the case. To protect its brand equity, Intel focused on promotion. Modifying a slogan that had worked in Japan, the company adopted "Intel inside" and granted advertising allowances to computer makers who included the phrase in ads for computers containing the Intel chip. Among consumers who own personal computers, the new ad campaign caused awareness of Intel's microchips to soar from around 20 percent to over 80 percent.[56]

Coca-Cola, too, enjoys substantial brand equity. Its red-and-white logo is familiar around the world. In fact, executives claim that if all of the company's physical assets were destroyed in a disaster, it could immediately borrow $100 billion to rebuild; its brand name alone would be enough collateral.[57]

Product lines and the products within them must be evaluated on a regular basis in order to make these decisions. Operationally, an organization has four options. First, it could use a continuation strategy in which it keeps the same products and lines with no changes. Second, it could use a product modification strategy in which products or whole product lines are changed. Third, it could use a product addition strategy in which new products are added to lines or new lines are added to the product mix. Finally, it could use a deletion strategy in which products or lines are removed from the product mix.

Continuation Strategy   This strategy involves keeping the same products and product lines in the product mix with no changes. An organization may want to do this if it cannot keep up with demand for its current offerings so it has successful products but lacks the resources to expand. However, since the product life cycle has shortened for many products because of intense competition and rapid technological change, most firms cannot survive long without some changes in their product mix.

Product Modification Strategy   At a minimum, most organizations try to improve the competitive position of some of their existing products or lines on a regular basis. Marketers can improve the product (say, by adding features or improving quality), find new uses for the product, or find new markets to serve with it (reposition the product) to increase sales and profits (see "Marketing Movers & Shakers: Harvey McLeod & Chris Freeman/Devil Sticks"). A classic example of finding new uses for a product is baking soda. Originally developed as a food product, baking soda is now used to deodorize refrigerators as well as drains. In another example, Himmel Nutrition Inc. found new markets for Ovaltine milk modifier, a chocolate-flavored powder popular during the 1940s. Himmel communicated the fact that, unlike competing products such as Nestlé's Quik, Ovaltine was fortified with vitamins, thus positioning the product to appeal to health-conscious consumers. Sales have jumped in response to the effort, and Himmel is researching ways to improve the product to stimulate even more demand.[62]

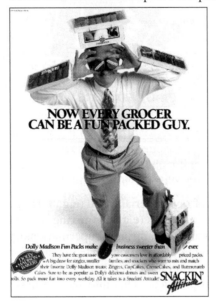

Interstate Brands Corporation's Dolly Madison Bakery, manufacturer of sweet baked treats such as Zingers, CupCakes, CremeCakes, and Buttercrumb Cakes, developed Fun Packs—smaller low-priced packs—to build its market share with single people, smaller families, and snackers who want to mix and match their treats.

When marketers are looking for new customers, global markets often are appealing. However, marketers must be careful to avoid assuming that people in another nation or culture will understand what the product is and how to use it. A firm that introduced baby food to several African nations evidently didn't consider that there could be more than one explanation for what is in a jar with a picture of a baby on it. Consumers in those nations reached the logical but disturbing conclusion that the jars contained ground-up babies.[63]

Addition Strategy   Organizations can add new products to existing lines or can add new lines to their product mixes. These strategies increase the depth and width of a product mix and are designed to increase market share, sales, and profits.

In some cases, the organization adds products because customers ask for them. Consulting firm Step Associates, based in Laramie, Wyoming, conducts surveys of clients who attend its seminars. Clients at seminars on facilities management asked for training in management skills, so Step added those services. Then participants in

Harvey McLeod & Chris Freeman/ Devil Sticks

Kids of all ages have been playing with them—college students, high school students, elementary school students. And of course, adults. They are devil sticks, one of the hottest-selling toys in the United States and Canada at stores ranging from Toys "R" Us to F.A.O. Schwarz. Devil sticks are decidedly low-tech. They don't require a computer to operate and don't come with umpteen parts to lose or break. Devil sticks are just three sticks. To play, you just juggle them. Here's the best part: It's fun.

Devil sticks aren't a new toy. But two young guys from Canada rediscovered their appeal. "The exact origins have been lost, but most people seem to agree it started in the Orient, probably China . . . and predated Christianity," says Harvey McLeod. Harvey drew more attention to his t-shirt booth in Hampton, New Brunswick, with a set of his brother's devil sticks than with his admittedly mediocre t-shirts. Customers wanted to buy the sticks, not the shirts. So he tried making a few sets by himself and sold 20 the first week, at $10 apiece. Four months later, he had sold 800 sets. He happened to sell his first set to Chris Freeman, a friend who helped him tinker with the design—eventually the sticks became lighter, more flexible, and wrapped with colorful tape for grip and friction. After moving to Montreal, the pair secured financing from two Canadian businessmen.

The toy turned into a multimillion-dollar success almost immediately. "They're an absolutely huge hit," says Amanda Gronich of F.A.O. Schwarz. "That's the way it was with Frisbees and hackey sacks. It's very special when an item comes along that's so appealing and fun." Gronich predicts that this fad will evolve into a classic, staple toy—like the Frisbee—rather than fading back into obscurity. Thus, the centuries-old product, while enjoying some faddish popularity, may very well pass from a high-growth phase into maturity and have a classic renewed product life cycle.

Devil sticks (whose name, by the way, has nothing to do with Satan—*devil* is a translation of the Greek word *diablo*, which means "toss across") deliver value to both kids and parents. First, they cost less than $20. Second, kids enjoy them—and parents approve of the time spent developing balance and coordination. "A lot of the mainstream toys are just things to accumulate," says Terri Bernsohn, whose 11-year-old son received a set of devil sticks for his birthday and plays with them for hours instead of watching TV or playing computer games. "I think these have a lot of play value. He can use them inside or outside. And there's no right or wrong, no winning or losing. He can just get better at it," explains Terri.

Frank Reysen, editor of the toy trade magazine *Playthings,* agrees. "It's not dependent on a hit movie. It's not like Barney that you outgrow in a few years. You don't exhaust its possibilities the first few times you play with it. Essentially, there's an awful lot of fun in the toy." Perhaps that's the secret to an idea that has lasted for so many centuries. It's challenging. "Kids will stand there all day until they get it right," says McLeod. It's fun also. It's still fun, the twentieth, two-hundredth, or two-thousandth time you play.

Source: Tracy Dell'Angela, "Even High-Tech Toy Industry Gives Devil Sticks Their Due," *Chicago Tribune,* March 25, 1996, sec. 1, p. 12.

Explore more by searching "Devil Sticks" on the Web.

---

the training seminars started asking for consulting services, and Step again responded by broadening its product mix.[64] Assuming the organization can maintain high quality and acceptable profits, adding goods and services customers ask for makes good marketing sense.

The new products may be line extensions or they may be a whole new product line. When an organization sees a need for a particular product that serves an existing target market or is related to an existing product, a line extension is probably most appropriate. When the organization needs more diverse offerings, it focuses on adding new product lines. Mr. Coffee has been focusing on new product development to allow the company to diversify beyond coffee makers. Heavy competition for coffee makers has made that market less attractive, so the company added a water-filter pitcher that filters two quarts of tap water in up to one minute.[65]

In determining whether and how to add products to the product mix, marketers should consider using brand extensions. General Mills has done this by sweetening and flavoring Cheerios in various ways, creating Honey Nut Cheerios and Apple Cinnamon Cheerios.[66] Similarly, Kellogg Company has modified Rice Krispies to create Cocoa Krispies, Fruity Marshmallow Krispies, Frosty Marshmallow Krispies,

T A B L E 9.4
Deciding Whether to Delete a
Product: Some Questions to
Answer

Area of Concern	Questions
Sales trends	How have sales moved over time? What has happened to market share? Why have sales declined? What changes in sales have occurred in competitive products, both in our line and in those of other manufacturers?
Profit contribution	What has been the profit contribution of this product to the company? If profits have declined, how are these tied to price? Have selling, promotion, and distribution costs risen out of proportion to sales? Does the product require excessive management time and effort?
Product life cycle	Has the product reached a level of maturity and saturation in the market? Has new technology been developed that poses a threat to the product? Are there more effective substitutes on the market? Has the product outgrown its usefulness? Can the resources used on this product be put to better use?

Source: J. Paul Peter and James H. Donnelly, Jr., *A Preface to Marketing Management,* 7th ed. (Burr Ridge, Ill.: Irwin, 1997), pp. 117–118.

and Rice Krispies Treats cereal.[67] Assuming the new product fits the brand's image and targets the same buyers, brand extension benefits the organization by using customers' good associations with the existing brand to persuade them that the new product also delivers value.

Deletion Strategy   Before removing a product or product line from the organization's mix, marketers should consider whether doing so will be more beneficial than some other strategy. Marketers should have a set of criteria for making such decisions. As a start, marketers can consider whether sales and profits are likely to improve and where the product is in its life cycle. Table 9.4 provides some specific questions to answer. For example, if new technology has made a product obsolete and higher costs have all but eliminated profits, the product is probably not worth keeping.

Deleting products can have great impact on an organization. Customers may be disappointed that the organization has stopped offering a product that they want and like. When Volkswagen dropped its popular Bug in 1975, its sales went on a decline that the company is now trying to reverse by introducing a new version of that car.[68] Discontinuing a product may also mean laying off the employees who produced and sold it. Furthermore, discontinuing a product does not necessarily free a company from all expenses related to that product. For example, the organization may still need to offer customer service to owners of the product, and it may need to provide a supply of replacement parts.

Nevertheless, deleting products allows the organization to devote more resources to more profitable products. When the organization is no longer spending as much money to support a poor performer, its overall profitability may improve. This is the aim of Procter & Gamble in reducing the variety of products it offers. Through such changes as eliminating the White Cloud brand of toilet tissue in favor of Charmin Ultra and Puritan oil in favor of Crisco, P&G hopes to reduce production and marketing costs.[69]

Summary

Depending on their major target market, products may be consumer or industrial products. Consumer products fall into the categories of convenience, shopping, specialty, and unsought products. Industrial products may be installations, accessory equipment, component parts and materials, raw materials, supplies, and business services. Goods may be either durable (lasting at least three years) or nondurable (lasting less than three years).

Differences also arise because products pass through stages of a life cycle at different rates and times. During the introduction stage, a new product enters the marketplace with little or no competition, and marketers must convince the target market that it meets their needs and wants. During the growth stage, sales climb rapidly as more buyers try the product and competitors enter with new brands. When a product reaches maturity, it is familiar to its widest group of buyers and has attracted many competitors. When sales begin to fall, the product enters decline and marketers may delete it. The product life cycle has limitations, but it is useful as a general framework for developing a marketing strategy. Some products also follow fashion or fad cycles. A fashion is an accepted and popular style; a fad is a product that experiences intense and brief popularity.

Buyers who make purchases at different stages of a product's life cycle tend to have varying characteristics. Innovators are venturesome and the first to try a new product. Early adopters follow innovators and influence the next group. Most buyers are either the early majority (who avoid risk and make their purchases carefully) or the late majority (who are more cautious and skeptical). Laggards resist making changes; they are more comfortable with tradition.

A brand is a word, design, symbol, or other feature that distinguishes a seller's product from its competitors'. By developing positive meanings for their brands, marketers seek to make customers loyal to their brands. Types of brands are manufacturer's brands (owned and used by producers of a product), private brands (owned and used by resellers), and generic brands (goods or services named only by generic class, without a brand name or brand mark). In choosing a brand, marketers consider several criteria: (1) it should imply the benefits delivered by the product; (2) it should be positive, distinctive, and easy to say and remember; (3) it should be consistent with the product's and organization's image; (4) it must be legally permissible; and (5) it should be appropriate in the languages of any global markets where it will be offered. Effectively selecting brands, delivering value, and protecting trademarks help the organization maintain its brand equity—its most valuable asset.

Marketers must manage products not only individually but in terms of their relationship to other products in the line and mix as well. When considering whether to continue as is, modify, add, or delete products and lines, marketers should keep in mind the relationships among them. A line extension is a way to capitalize on the organization's brand equity and its expertise in producing and marketing a category of products. Marketers describe an organization's product mix in terms of its width, depth, and consistency. Modifying a product, its uses, or markets may help increase sales. Adding products is an important source of growth, if doing so does not weaken the brand's or organization's image or ability to maintain high quality. Deleting a product from a mix may allow an organization to devote its resources to more profitable products. However, deletion may disappoint loyal customers, require employee layoffs, and force the company to continue to provide service to customers who already own the product.

Key Terms and Concepts

consumer products (p. 230)
industrial products (p. 230)
convenience products (p. 230)
shopping products (p. 230)
specialty products (p. 230)
unsought products (p. 230)
installations (p. 233)
accessory equipment (p. 233)
component parts and materials (p. 233)
raw materials (p. 233)
supplies (p. 233)
business services (p. 233)
durable goods (p. 234)
nondurable goods (p. 234)

product life cycle (p. 235)
primary demand (p. 235)
secondary demand (p. 236)
fashion (p. 237)
fads (p. 238)
product diffusion (p. 239)
innovators (p. 239)
early adopters (p. 239)
early majority (p. 239)
late majority (p. 239)
laggards (p. 239)
brand (p. 240)
brand name (p. 240)
brand mark (p. 240)

trademark (p. 240)
service mark (p. 240)
trade name (p. 240)
brand extension (p. 240)
family brand (p. 240)
manufacturer's brand (p. 242)
private brand (p. 242)
generic (brands) products (p. 243)
brand equity (p. 246)
product mix (p. 248)
product line (p. 248)
line extension (p. 249)

Review and Discussion Questions

1. What is the major difference between consumer and industrial products? What are the four different types of consumer products? What are the six different types of industrial products?

2. Decide whether each of the following is a durable or nondurable good.
   a. a week's vacation in the Caribbean
   b. a refrigerator
   c. two pounds of coffee
   d. a rocking chair
   e. a CD
   f. the Sunday newspaper

3. Think of a product that is clearly in the mature stage of the product life cycle (it may be a cereal, an appliance, or a vehicle). As a marketer, what steps would you take to keep sales of the product going? In what ways might you be able to increase the value your product offers to consumers?

4. Suppose you are a marketer for a manufacturer that produced manual lawnmowers (not powered by gas or electricity). You have decided there might be renewed interest for the product because it does not burn fuel or use electric power and has minimum impact on the environment.
   a. What steps might you take to market these lawnmowers?
   b. In what countries do you think your product strategy might be effective?

5. Think of a fad you have observed or experienced in your lifetime. Briefly describe the product, what it was used for, approximately how long its popularity lasted, and why you think it was popular.

6. What are the characteristics of the five adopter categories? Which type of buyer are you in general? Are you always one type of buyer, or do you change categories depending on the type of purchase you are making?

7. What are the differences between manufacturer's brands and private brands? How do they differ in the value they offer consumers?

8. Find two advertisements for different brands of the same product (such as shirts, soaps, or automobiles). Compare them for differences in quality, features, and design. Which brand would you buy, and why?

9. Compare the brand names of the two products you evaluated in question 8. How effective are they? Do they imply benefits delivered by the product? Are they positive and distinctive? Are they consistent with the image of the product or company?

10. What are the five components of brand equity? In what ways does brand equity provide value to customers?

11. What are the difficulties involved in deleting a product from a line?

Chapter Project   Develop a Private-Label Brand

Imagine that you are a retailer—a department store, a home-improvement store, a grocery store, or another type of store of your own choosing. You have been asked to come up with ideas for a line of products under a private-label brand that could compete with the manufacturer's-brand products your store already sells.

First, go to a store that is representative of the type you have chosen, and note which manufacturer's brands are on the shelves. Next, choose an area in which you want to concentrate your line (for instance, you might want to propose a line of private-label hand tools for a home-improvement store).

Then determine ways in which your private-label products could create greater value for consumers than the competing manufacturer's-brand products (lower prices? more features? association with the store's reputation?). Note any fashions your product line might capitalize on, as well as the type of buyers who would be most interested in it (innovators, early majority, etc.).

Finally, think of a brand name and brand mark for your product line. Put your project in writing, with a graphic for the brand mark.

Chapter Case   The Tupperware Corporation

Tupperware. The brand name conjures up housewives of the 1950s in each others' homes at the famous Tupperware Home Parties, buying and selling plastic containers with snap-on lids. It conjures up refrigerators and pantry shelves stuffed with those plastic containers. Tupperware was founded in 1946 by Earl Tupper, a chemical engineer. The products, offered only at "home parties" by representatives who sold directly to consumers, were known for their high quality. Their relative exclusivity (consumers couldn't get them at supermarkets or department stores) made them attractive to buyers who would be considered innovators, and then, through the influ-

ence of early adopters, the early and late majority buyers. Consumers knew that the company specialized in one type of high-quality good, thus offering a product of value.

Eventually, however, sales declined. As more women entered the work force, they didn't have time or didn't want to attend parties. The brand's image faded not due to declining quality but due to its association with the declining image of homemakers and housework. In addition, consumers could find competitors' products at stores like Wal-Mart for less money.

Instead of discontinuing the product, however, Tupperware's parent company, Premark, pushed for renewed expansion by entering markets overseas. By the mid-1990s, Tupperware was hosting 13 million parties in 100 countries around the world. Foreign sales accounted for 85 percent of its total revenue of $1.36 billion and it began selling in two major international markets, China and India.

The Orlando, Florida-based Tupperware does face competition overseas. Rubbermaid has bought plastics manufacturing companies in Poland and France, and has begun to make its presence felt, though its sales of about $337 million are way below Tupperware's. "I don't think it's going to be as good a business as it has been," predicts Matthew Roswell, a consumer products stock analyst with Legg Mason.

Recently, Premark spun off The Tupperware Corporation as an independent company with its own offering on the New York Stock Exchange. The company is planning to remove the responsibility of storing products from the sales representatives (who are often stuck with piles of product in their garages, family rooms, and basements) so that they can concentrate on recruiting and sales. Tupperware is not giving up on either the domestic or foreign markets. Perhaps, with persistence, the 50-year-old company will see renewed expansion of its products. After all, those little plastic Tupperware containers are durable goods that last a long, long time—if you don't lose the lids.

Questions

1. What steps might Tupperware marketers take to promote renewed expansion of their products in the United States?

2. How might Tupperware increase brand equity?

3. What steps might Tupperware take to create value for consumers in India and China?

Sources: Kurt Badenhausen, "Tupperware: Party On," *Financial World,* September 16, 1996, p. 24; Jon E. Hilsenrath, "Is Tupperware Dated? Not in the Global Market," *The New York Times,* May 26, 1996, p. 3; Gene Marcial, "All This and Free Tupperware Too," *Business Week,* May 27, 1996, p. 140; Raju Nariesetti, "Corporate Focus: Can Rubbermaid Crack Foreign Markets?," *The Wall Street Journal,* June 20, 1996, p. B1.

Explore more at www.tupperware.com

Developing New Products

CHAPTER OUTLINE

Types of New Products
The New Product Development Process
  Idea Generation
  Idea Screening
  Business Analysis
  Product Development
  Test Marketing
  Commercialization
Selecting New Product Characteristics
  Quality Level
  Product Features
  Product Design
  Product Safety
Packaging and Labeling New Products
  Packaging
  Labeling
  Global Implications
Reducing New Product Failures
  Why New Products Fail
  Organizing for Success
  Shortening Development Time
Summary

LEARNING OBJECTIVES

After completing this chapter, you should be able to:

1. Explain what makes a product "new."
2. Identify the steps in developing a new product.
3. Discuss how various characteristics of products play a role in marketing.
4. Describe the role of packaging and labeling for new products.
5. Give reasons why many new products fail.
6. Describe ways in which companies organize to carry out the product development effort.
7. Summarize approaches to shortening the time required for developing new products.

Smart Cars: Zexel USA Corporation and Avis Inc.

The days of trying to read a map while driving, haggling with your front seat passenger over directions, or searching for your destination late on a rainy night along a winding road may be coming rapidly to a close. Zexel USA Corporation would like them to, anyway. If the way cars equipped with the company's high-tech system are rolling off Avis' car rental lot is any indication, so would consumers.

Michigan-based Zexel has developed a revolutionary new computer program that makes "smart cars," that is, cars that can navigate themselves to your destination through computer technology. Here's how it works: An optical disk drive located in the car's trunk contains a disk with a detailed map of a local area. A group of 24 satellites orbiting a few hundred miles above the earth's surface acts like the computer's central nervous system, communicating with the car to locate a destination accurately within a few feet. The computer located in the car then plots a coordinate on an electronic map mounted on the dashboard. Once you tell the computer where you want to go, a series of beeps and computer-voice instructions tell you where to turn, stop, and so forth. Even if you're a little vague—say, you just want to know where the nearest gas station is—all you have to say to the computer is, "nearest gas station."

The smart car system is a natural for business and vacation travelers who arrive in unfamiliar cities and want to know how to get around. So Avis Inc. test marketed the product in a number of cities, including Atlanta, Los Angeles, Miami, Chicago, Denver, Houston, and Indianapolis. Avis has 1,000 such vehicles in operation, offered to customers at no extra charge. Competition is looming—Hertz and National are launching a similar campaign. In addition, consumers can actually purchase the system on some new cars (such as the Oldsmobile 88) for the relatively low price of $1,995. Demand for the product is high, and Zexel is doing its best to get the systems to market. "We're working as hard as we can to get it out as quickly as possible," says Mike Rice, sales and marketing manager with Zexel.

Even so, the smart cars in operation aren't yet considered smart enough. Technology continues to improve, and marketers are looking for more and more ways to serve customers who want the system. Soon a system called Safety Security Communication (SSC) will be available, which will provide services such as automatically activating 911 if a car's airbag is deployed. With radar, SSC can also "sense" an object (such as a bicycle or pedestrian) in a car's path, as well as warn you if a car or anything else has traveled into your blind spot. If you are on a collision course with another vehicle, you'll receive both audio and visual warnings.

Does all this take the fun out of driving? Not necessarily. Unless, of course, you are interested in the car being developed by the Carnegie Mellon Robotics Institute, which *actually drives itself.* The car has already done a test drive from Washington, D.C. to San Diego, California.

As you read this chapter, consider the vast opportunities for the development of new products, especially in a global market. Consider also the importance of testing new products to be sure that they are what consumers and organizational buyers want. Don't forget to think about the ways new products can become successful by creating value for customers.

Sources: Tom Dellecave Jr., "Lost in New York," *Sales & Marketing Management,* May 1996, pp. 98, 103; TV broadcast, "CBS This Morning," June 20, 1996.

Explore more by searching "Smart Cars" on the Web.

Chapter Overview

Zexel USA Corporation's ability to develop high-quality products has been an important ingredient in its success. Like Zexel, organizations need to develop **new products** to survive and prosper. Because of stiff competition from around the world, organizations that fail to innovate will lose ground to those that find better ways to create value for customers.

The industry leaders in terms of sales growth and profitability get almost half their revenues from products developed within the preceding five years. In contrast, the least successful companies get only 11 percent of their sales from new products.[1] Because new products are so important, many organizations set sales objectives for them. For example, Gillette requires that over 40 percent of sales every five years must be from new products, so the company must develop about 20 new products each year.[2]

This chapter discusses issues related to developing new products and determining whether and how to market them. The chapter begins by identifying the characteristics that make a product "new." It describes the process of new product development, as well as decisions about a product's quality, features, design, safety, packaging, and labeling. It then turns to a discussion of why new products fail. The chapter ends by examining ways in which organizations seek to minimize new product failure through organizational structure, technology, and efforts to speed up the development process.

Types of New Products

There are many ways to classify new products. For example, they can be continuous innovations, that is, changes in existing products, or discontinuous innovations that are completely new. They can also be technology-driven innovations that come from R&D or customer-driven innovations that come from analyzing customer needs and wants.[3] From a company-level viewpoint, one useful classification, shown in Figure 10.1, includes the following categories:

1. *New-to-the-world products.* These products are inventions that did not previously exist. They include such products as television, computers, global positioning

FIGURE 10.1
Types of New Products

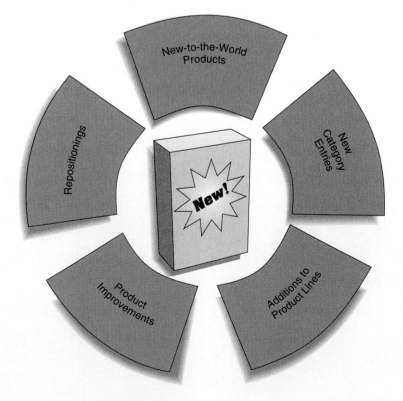

systems, and laser printers. Such new products are often revolutionary and can change the way people live and work.

2. *New category entries.* These products are new to a company but not new inventions. They include Procter & Gamble's first shampoo, Oscar Mayer's line of turkey products, and Levi's belts and shirts.

3. *Additions to product lines.* These products are line extensions such as Tide Liquid detergent, Bud Light, and the Ford Expedition.

4. *Product improvements.* These are products that are new in the sense that they are changed versions of a company's existing products. Examples include fuel-injected Harley-Davidson motorcycles, Panasonic VCRs that can be programmed to record shows from numbers designated in the TV Guide, and Rollerblade's Metroblade skates that have a removable athletic shoe liner.

5. *Repositionings.* These products are retargeted for new uses or new markets. Examples include Arm & Hammer baking soda's use as a refrigerator deodorant, Skintastic skin lotion as a bug repellent, and Gillette Sensor razors for women as well as men.[4]

Of course, other changes can be made to a product that can make it new in some sense. For example, a product could be new because of improved packaging (toothpaste in a pump container or pudding in easy-to-open, single-serve cans) or because of a new method of manufacture (stamped rather than cast auto parts or products made from recycled materials).

The best type of new products for a company to focus on depends on many factors. Companies like Merck Pharmaceuticals, Microsoft, and 3M have the research and development (R&D) capabilities and resources to develop new-to-the-world products; such products can be highly profitable. Companies who have mature products may seek to purchase or develop other product lines to ensure survival; Levi's Dockers line of casual clothes and Oscar Mayer's line of Lunchables are two examples. Companies that have strong brand equity, such as Kellogg's and Budweiser, often find that line extensions and product improvements are the best way to improve profits. Repositioning products also can be an effective strategy. Repositioning coffee as an iced drink, orange juice as an anytime beverage, and aluminum foil for cleaning barbecue grills could be cost-effective ways to make them new and increase sales.

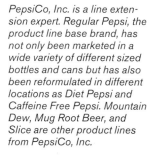

PepsiCo, Inc. is a line extension expert. Regular Pepsi, the product line base brand, has not only been marketed in a wide variety of different sized bottles and cans but has also been reformulated in different locations as Diet Pepsi and Caffeine Free Pepsi. Mountain Dew, Mug Root Beer, and Slice are other product lines from PepsiCo, Inc.

FIGURE 10.2
*The New Product
Development Process*

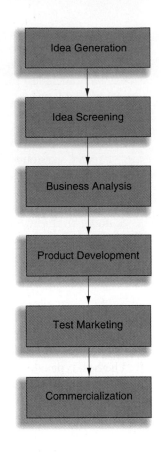

The New Product Development Process

New products are a key to a company's growth and success. Consider the case of ConAgra. After Charles M. Harper, president of the company, suffered a heart attack, he directed his R&D staff to explore the idea of developing a line of foods with reduced sodium, fat, and cholesterol levels that would also taste good. The company developed the line and named it Healthy Choice. It selected green packaging that would stand out in grocery frozen-food cases. After a year of work, ConAgra's employees had a line of products ready for test marketing.

Consumers were impressed with the taste. ConAgra distributed Healthy Choice in traditional grocery stores rather than health food stores. Within four years, the brand was enjoying a 40 percent share of the market for frozen dinners and entrees. ConAgra didn't stop there, but rather continued to develop new products to carry the Healthy Choice label.[5]

There is no way to guarantee that all new products will succeed as the Healthy Choice line did. However, being systematic about developing new products increases the chances of success. Figure 10.2 shows a logical process for developing new products.

Idea Generation

New products start as ideas. According to estimates, an organization needs 60 or 70 ideas to come up with one viable new product. This means that marketers must constantly seek ideas. Good ideas may come from the organization's sales force, other employees, research and development activities, and outside sources such as customer suggestions, competitors' products, advertising agencies, and inventors (see "Put It into Practice: Generate Your Own Ideas for a New Product"). Some of the techniques marketers use for generating ideas are brainstorming, employee suggestion boxes, and customer surveys. David Blohm, who heads MathSoft, a software company in Cambridge, Massachusetts, gets ideas from participating in industry conferences.

Generate Your Own Ideas for a New Product

As a consumer, you are one of a marketer's best sources for ideas for new products. So generate some ideas of your own. Think of something you need for which there does not seem to be a good or service—or at least, nothing in your region. For instance, suppose all the dry cleaners in your area open at 6:00 AM and close at 6:00 PM. But you leave for work or school before they open and return after they close. Why couldn't there be a dry cleaning establishment open 24 hours a day? Say that you really like the taste of ginger ale but prefer the energy boost of a cola. Would there be a market for ginger ale with caffeine?

Try to come up with at least 10 ideas (remember, the average organization needs 60 or 70 new ideas to come up with one viable new product). Narrow it down to two or three that you think have the best possibilities. Then try your ideas out on a few friends, family members, and classmates, writing down the responses. Discuss your ideas—and people's responses—in class.

Attending the meetings enables him to efficiently keep up to date on new technology.[6] Table 10.1 describes some of the techniques marketers use to generate product ideas.

The search for new ideas should start with customers' wants and needs. John Deere Company did this when it asked farmers to describe their ideal tractor. Then the company gave them what they asked for: strong and safe machines with sound-proof cabins, seats offering back support, more headlights for improved night vision, and more glass for greater visibility.[7] Customer complaints about existing products also can generate ideas for new ones. For example, 3M consumers complained that steel scouring pads were apt to rust and splinter after just a few uses. The 3M Company responded with a new soap-filled scouring pad, Scotch Brite Never Rust.[8]

Learning about customers and their needs is especially important in devising a product strategy to serve international markets. Differences among countries may dictate some basic product modifications. For instance, electric appliances used in Europe must operate on different voltages than in the United States, and cars driven in Japan and England require steering wheels on the right side. The fact that most countries, unlike the United States, use the metric system makes it necessary to modify many U.S. goods. Services, too, may require modification. An example is checking accounts, which would be structured differently in Greece (where checkbooks are rarely used) than in the United States.[9]

In some cases, organizations invent new products to serve the needs of a global market. For example, because tastes in food vary so widely, food producers often must create products that match local eating habits. To serve the Ivory Coast, Nestlé developed Bonfoutou, a version of a local yam dish.[10]

Another important source of new product ideas is the organization's research and development) activities. Organizations that develop new products often focus on specific technology. Corning's R&D staff conducts research to make the company a leader in all aspects of glass technology. The company spent millions of dollars to fund research in such areas as methods to make high-quality car windshields. The results of that project led to the development of glass for the flat-panel displays used in laptop computers. Furthermore, Corning's R&D staff continuously seeks ways to improve these displays and the other products it has developed.[11]

Sometimes the investment in R&D is the source of an organization's competitive advantage. Reebok's R&D department includes an Advanced Concepts Group, which designs products for the future. An example of a product developed by this group is the Pump Fury, which lightens a runner's load by removing 25 percent of the weight

T A B L E 10.1
Techniques for Generating Ideas

Technique	Description
Delphi method	A panel of experts fills out a questionnaire; a researcher tabulates the results and sends them to panel members. Repeat the process until the panel reaches a consensus or an impasse.
Benefit analysis	List all the benefits customers receive from the product under study. Think of benefits that are currently missing from the list.
Use analysis	Ask customers how they use the product under study. List the various uses.
Relative brand profile	Ask target markets whether the brand name makes sense for other product categories under consideration. A stretch of the brand name that makes sense to potential buyers can be the basis for a new product.
Unique properties	List all the properties held in common by a product or material currently on the market. Look for unique properties of the organization's product.
Achilles' heel	List the weaknesses of a product or product line (for the organization and its competitors). Prune the list to the one or two weaknesses most likely to inspire a response from competitors. Identify product concepts that could result from correcting these weaknesses.
Free association	Write down one aspect of the product situation—a product attribute, use, or user. Let the mind roam, and jot down every idea that surfaces. Repeat the process for other aspects of the product situation.
Stereotype activity	Ask, "How would _____ do it?"—referring to how a member of some group or a particular person would use the product. Example: What type of bicycle would a senator ride? Can also ask what the stereotype would *not* do.
Study of other people's failures	Study products that have failed. Look for ways to solve the problems that led to failure

Source: Adapted from C. Merle Crawford, *New Products Management,* 4th ed. (Burr Ridge, Ill.: Irwin, 1994), pp. 444–451.

of each shoe, including the middle third of the midsole, the laces, and most of the upper. What keeps these shoes on your feet? A bladder inflated with a Pump button or a CO_2 cartridge.[12]

Marketers must decide whether to set up R&D facilities in one or several locations. To serve consumers in over 140 countries, Procter & Gamble has chosen a middle route by operating technical centers in the United States, the United Kingdom, Belgium, Germany, Venezuela, and Japan.[13] When setting up research facilities overseas, an organization must recognize the strengths and weaknesses of the foreign country's engineering and science talent. To serve the rapidly growing Chinese market, Motorola hires hundreds of engineers there but has found that Chinese graduates are much stronger in basic sciences than in technological applications. As a result, Motorola provides its Chinese engineers with extensive training at its facilities in the United States, Singapore, and Hong Kong.[14]

Besides coming up with ideas through their own primary research, R&D personnel can generate ideas by learning from their colleagues at other organizations. Scientists can share ideas with others in the field when they write or read articles in journals, attend conferences, or communicate on the Internet. Thus, Samuel H. Fuller, vice president for corporate research at Digital Equipment Corporation, says, "We treat university research as a virtual research lab."[15] An organization that cannot afford its own research laboratory may form alliances with others that specialize in research or copy the technology of a competitor. Of course, new technology is often patented to protect it from being used by competitors.

Idea Screening

Next the organization must evaluate and screen the ideas that have been generated, deciding which are worth pursuing further. This step involves determining whether the product idea will help achieve the objectives of the organization. Marketers should

TABLE 10.2
Checklist for Evaluating New
Product Ideas at Johnson Wax

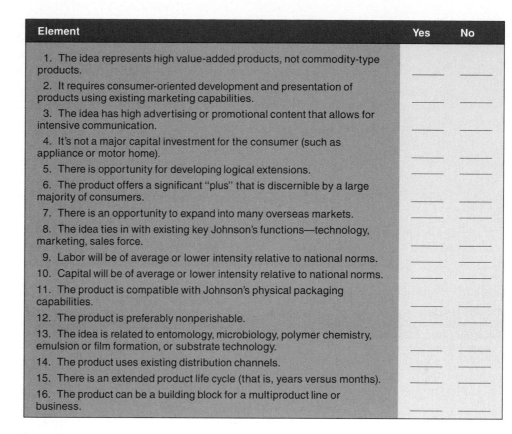

Element	Yes	No
1. The idea represents high value-added products, not commodity-type products.	____	____
2. It requires consumer-oriented development and presentation of products using existing marketing capabilities.	____	____
3. The idea has high advertising or promotional content that allows for intensive communication.	____	____
4. It's not a major capital investment for the consumer (such as appliance or motor home).	____	____
5. There is opportunity for developing logical extensions.	____	____
6. The product offers a significant "plus" that is discernible by a large majority of consumers.	____	____
7. There is an opportunity to expand into many overseas markets.	____	____
8. The idea ties in with existing key Johnson's functions—technology, marketing, sales force.	____	____
9. Labor will be of average or lower intensity relative to national norms.	____	____
10. Capital will be of average or lower intensity relative to national norms.	____	____
11. The product is compatible with Johnson's physical packaging capabilities.	____	____
12. The product is preferably nonperishable.	____	____
13. The idea is related to entomology, microbiology, polymer chemistry, emulsion or film formation, or substrate technology.	____	____
14. The product uses existing distribution channels.	____	____
15. There is an extended product life cycle (that is, years versus months).	____	____
16. The product can be a building block for a multiproduct line or business.	____	____

Source: Adapted from Rodger L. DeRose, "New Products—Sifting through the Haystack," *Journal of Consumer Marketing* (Summer 1986); p. 83. Reprinted by permission of Marketing Journals Publishing Company.

consider whether pursuing the idea draws on the organization's strengths and allows it to capitalize on environmental opportunities. AT&T seeks to identify innovations that enable it to market all kinds of communications terminals, from telephones to televisions to computers. Such innovations enable the company to make the most of its vast communications network.[16] If an idea is outside the organization's area of expertise but meets its customers' needs, the organization might consider pursuing a strategic alliance with another firm.

Idea screening should cover a variety of other issues as well. Table 10.2 shows a checklist of criteria used for evaluating new product ideas at Johnson Wax. Marketers will want to consider whether the product idea is really innovative and whether it can be protected with a patent or copyright. Marketers also need to consider legal and ethical issues, such as whether the product will be safe to use. The safety issue has been prominent in evaluating possible new products for use with microwave ovens. For example, researchers explored the development of massage creams and hair oils that could be warmed in the user's microwave. However, because the ovens heat products unevenly, companies were concerned that consumers could easily burn themselves.[17]

Business Analysis

Usually only a few ideas survive the screening stage at any particular time. Marketers then conduct a rigorous analysis of these ideas, to see whether they could be commercially successful. Marketers may get help in this process from decision-making software, such as Quick Insight (by Business Resource Software), which asks 60 or more questions about the business potential of the product. After the user has described such factors as the regulatory environment, the nature of the competition, and the planned marketing strategy, the program calculates a score recommending that the marketer either proceed with, modify, or abandon the new product.[18]

Since marketers need to know whether new products are likely to be profitable, they develop forecasts of sales and costs under different strategy assumptions. Marketers should continue to develop a product idea if it has the potential to meet the organization's profit objectives and does not violate any ethical or legal constraints.

Forecasting Sales   Marketers need an idea of the sales a new product could generate. Forecasting demand for a new product can be difficult, since little or no historical data is available. As a case in point, many companies have been interested in the economic potential of interactive television, and some have set up trials to assess it. In one trial, consumers used an interactive-TV service to rent an average of 2½ movies a month, which at $3–$4 a movie, would generate sales of $90–$120 a year. That's not much, so other sources of revenue have been considered. Advertising seemed a logical source of revenue, and the cable industry has experience that could be used as a basis for making sales forecasts. However, cable television has generated less than 20 percent of its revenue from advertising,[19] so other sources would be needed to make this product idea profitable.

To assess demand for a possible new product, marketers often use **concept testing.** This involves having potential customers evaluate pictures, mockups, or written descriptions of the product. For complex products, marketers and designers may work together to present computer models of the product and make changes to the model in response to customer feedback. Concept testing usually focuses on getting reactions from the ultimate consumers of a product, but marketers should test the concept with resellers as well.

Marketers use concept testing to identify product ideas for which there is potentially strong demand. Makers of ready-to-eat cereal have extended their product lines to snacks, introducing products such as Fingos, Chex Snack Mix, and Rice Krispies Treats. One reason is that many consumers already eat cereal as a snack food. Another is that Americans spend more than three times as much on snacks as they do on cereal.[20] Thus, the potential for snack products made from cereal is huge.

Forecasting Costs   To predict whether the product can be produced and marketed profitably, marketers must forecast the expected costs and subtract them from potential sales. In the case of interactive television, marketers weighed the revenues of $90–$120 per household per year that might be generated by video-on-demand plus the amount generated by advertising against the initial cost to provide the service: $500–$1,000 per home. Not surprisingly, enthusiasm for marketing interactive TV has been waning.[21]

Marketers must determine the product's features to estimate production costs. Will new components be needed to produce the product? Will existing personnel and facilities be sufficient? Marketers also must estimate marketing costs. To do so, they must have a general plan and forecasted budget for packaging, channels of distribution, advertising, and so forth. For example, 3M launched Scotch Brite Never Rust scouring pads with a $9 million advertising budget.[22]

In some cases, quality can be improved and cost reduced by outsourcing or joint ventures. IBM decided it should use a technology called advanced liquid-crystal displays in its computer screens. To keep costs under control, the company entered into a joint venture with Toshiba Corporation. IBM contributed its expertise in materials, Toshiba its superior manufacturing capabilities.[23]

Product Development

If business analysis results in favorable forecasts, the product concept is further developed. Marketers and other members of the new product development team begin by developing specifications for the product. These spell out in detail what materials

---

concept testing
Having potential customers evaluate pictures, mockups, or written descriptions of the product.

Zenith Electronics Corporation has pioneered the development of digital high-definition television (HDTV) products. Its new front-projection monitor displays high-definition images in both regular and wide-screen formats. Zenith's initial target markets for HDTVs are schools and commercial users, which evaluated prototypes.

Zenith's new front-projection monitor displays high-definition images and can provide exciting new ways to enhance the educational experience, such as this classroom CD-ROM application.

and components will go into the final product. For tangible products, the specifications would include such information as materials, size, weight, and performance requirements.

Many organizations have realized that they can benefit from linking product design (what the product will be like) with manufacturing engineering (how it will be made). Combining these tasks through teamwork is a practice known as **concurrent engineering,** which can increase production efficiency. Organizations that use concurrent engineering often can make goods faster and at a lower cost than their competitors. Invacare Corporation, an Elyria, Ohio, maker of home medical devices, uses such an approach. At the concept stage of the development process, Invacare assembles a team of employees from its marketing, quality, manufacturing, purchasing, engineering, and financial functions. The group evaluates product specifications and manufacturing requirements together, thereby developing a more efficient system while getting the product to the manufacturing stage faster.[24]

concurrent engineering
Linking product design with manufacturing engineering so that the tasks go on simultaneously.

Product development also includes building and testing a prototype. Actually building and testing the product is the surest way to see whether it works as planned. Thus, Chrysler tested a prototype of its battery-powered minivan by having engineers drive it from Detroit to Los Angeles. Along the way, engineers were able to identify ways to improve the minivan. The project also generated publicity for Chrysler's efforts to produce an environmentally friendly product.[25] For most consumer goods, marketers also need to prepare samples of the packaging to be used.

Marketers may have a sample of potential customers test the prototype by using it in natural settings. This can be a useful way to keep product development focused on customer value. It also tests the product's performance in real-life situations. To this end, General Motors enlisted 1,000 consumers to test-drive its 30 prototype battery-powered cars for periods of two to four weeks.[26]

Test Marketing

During the preceding steps of the development process, the organization usually tries to keep its new products' concepts a secret. Eventually, the organization needs to know whether customers will actually buy the product. Test marketing is used to obtain this knowledge without the costs of a full-scale introduction.

In test marketing, new products are offered for sale in a limited geographic area for a specified time and sales and costs are measured. Marketers evaluate the product and the marketing strategy used to sell it. The results of test marketing help marketers determine whether the product should be launched full scale, and if so, whether adjustments are needed prior to launch.

Test marketing was used by Citibank, Chase Manhattan, MasterCard, and Visa to investigate the potential of a smart card, a plastic card that looks like a credit card but contains a micro chip. When a purchase is made at a participating convenience store, fast-food outlet, movie theater, taxicab, or other cash-oriented retailer, the customer swipes the card through a terminal (or slot in a vending machine), and the amount of purchase is credited to the seller from the buyer's bank account. The two banks issued smart cards to 50,000 New York customers to determine who used them and whether the rate of usage would generate enough money to make them profitable.[27]

Test marketing can be an expensive and time-consuming stage of the development process. For General Mills, testing and refining its chain of Olive Garden restaurants required five years and about $28 million. For another restaurant concept, a chain of Chinese-American restaurants called China Coast, the company opened test restaurants in Orlando, Florida. This city was selected because the large number of tourists gave management a chance to gauge reactions from a broad cross section of the U.S. population. Customers completing taste tests and questionnaires allowed the company to distinguish between consumers' stated preferences and their actual behavior. For example, consumers said they favored light, healthful dishes but tended to order the menu items highest in fat, sugar, salt, and sauces.[28]

Types of Test Markets   An organization may set up test marketing in a variety of ways. A **standard test market** involves a marketer offering a new product through normal distribution channels in a limited area, as General Mills did to test its restaurant concepts.

A variation of this is to arrange for an outside service to set up a **controlled test market.** The service pays an agreed-upon set of retailers for the privilege of setting aside shelf space for the product in a desirable area of the store. The service may also use electronic data-gathering techniques by issuing identification cards to a panel of shoppers; each shopper's card is scanned whenever he or she makes a purchase. The standard approach better represents how retailers will handle the new product, but by ensuring that consumers will see the product, the controlled approach helps the organization test consumer reactions to it.

A third variation is **simulated test marketing (STM).** These are essentially experiments in which a sample of consumers has an opportunity to select products from mock grocery shelves. In a typical experiment, interviewers ask consumers in a shopping mall whether they use a particular class of product. Those who do are invited to the purchase laboratory, where they are asked about their product usage and preferences. The consumers see sample advertisements for the new brand and competing brands, then receive money, which they may use to buy this type of product from the mock grocery shelf. Those who buy the test product answer further questions about the reasons for their purchase. All the data are fed into a computer simulation model that forecasts consumer behavior on a broader scale. STM allows an organization to gauge consumer reactions to a new product without tipping off competitors. However, this approach does not provide information concerning the support producers would get from others in the marketing channel, and the results are only as good as the simulation model and the assumptions underlying it.

Regardless of the type, test markets should reflect the target markets for the new product. For this reason, organizations seeking to serve markets throughout the U.S. are interested in knowing which cities have populations most like that of the country as a whole. A study by Donnelley Marketing Information Services found that the most typical American cities in terms of age distribution, racial mix, and housing prices are those shown in Figure 10.3. Topping the list was Tulsa, Oklahoma. This city is especially attractive as a test market because Tulsans are more likely than other Americans to agree to participate in a marketing survey. Consequently, an increasing number of

standard test market
The practice of offering a new product through normal distribution channels in a limited area.

controlled test market
The practice of offering a new product through a set of retailers who have been paid to set aside shelf space for the product in a desirable area of the store.

simulated test market
An experiment in which a sample of consumers has an opportunity to select products from mock grocery shelves.

F I G U R E 10.3
*The Most Typical
American Cities**

*Based on a study of cities with more than 50,000 people by Donnelley Marketing Information Services. "Typical"
means they come closest to meeting the national averages for age distribution, racial mix, and housing prices.
Source: Steve Lohr, "Test It in Tulsa—It'll Play in Peoria," *Chicago Tribune,* June 7, 1992, sec. 7, p. 3.

marketers are testing their products there. However, many still prefer the older approach of favoring medium-sized cities in the Midwest that they feel are typically American.[29]

Uses of Test Marketing   Because test marketing is expensive and can provide early information to competitors about a company's new products, organizations use it only in certain cases. It is commonly used for products that are expensive to market. Thus, if a consumer product requires extensive distribution and a nationwide television advertising campaign, it makes sense to try the product in a few local markets to see whether consumers respond as expected. In contrast, test marketing should not be used when competitors could make a few quick modifications to the product and launch a superior competing product. For products that are truly innovative, it may be risky to skip test marketing unless the product is clearly superior in value to existing alternatives. Test marketing is also useful for staple products for which the brand name is the primary differentiating feature.

Commercialization

commercialization
The stage in which management commits to introducing the new product into the marketplace.

Product development ends with the launching of the new product. During this step, known as **commercialization,** the organization commits to marketing the product and starts full-scale production, distribution, and promotion. During commercialization, marketers may still need to make adjustments to the marketing mix. For example, problems that result from full-scale production may require changes in product design or new channels may have to be developed to reach the market.

Commercialization does not have to be a headlong plunge into the marketplace. Especially when the costs of marketing a product are high, the organization might choose to gradually roll it out. This means the organization introduces the product city by city or region by region until the whole market is being served. Frito-Lay first sold its Doritos Tortilla Thins exclusively in Tulsa and Omaha, then expanded distribution to the rest of the United States months later.[30] Procter & Gamble launched its disposable training pants in Holland and the United Kingdom, expanding from there to Canada and the United States.[31]

The Sled Dogs Co. in Minneapolis, Minnesota, recently used the National Sporting Goods Association Expo at McCormick Place in Chicago to commercialize their new product: snow skates, a "hot new means of playing fast and loose with gravity." The response was enthusiastic. The company also has a Web site (http://www.sleddogs.com) on which you can see product demonstrations, learn about the sport, and see it in action. With a marketing strategy aimed at the sports segment who twist in and out of crowds and other obstacles on in-line skates during warm weather months, the new snow skates are expected to "fly high in sales" during the snow season.

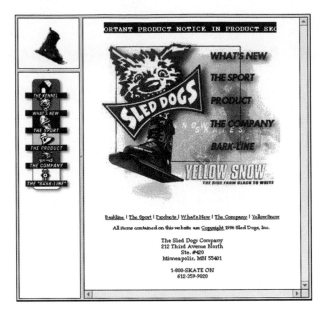

The way the organization handles commercialization can influence responses from the target market and from competitors. Marketers might actively promote their forthcoming products so that targeted buyers are aware of and interested in them before they hit the market. This is often done with new movies or TV shows. Alternatively, marketers might try to downplay new products under development so that competitors are caught off guard when commercialization begins. In the case of the Newton palm-top computer, Apple Computer oversold its capabilities and underestimated how long it would take to get to market. Initial reviews and sales of the product were disappointing, and competitors had made progress on developing alternative products by the time the Newton was launched. In contrast, Apple's earlier development of the Macintosh personal computer had been cloaked in secrecy and surprised competitors. The market responded favorably to its capabilities.[32]

Selecting New Product Characteristics

In developing new products, marketers have a variety of decisions to make about the characteristics of the product itself. Four of these are quality level, product design, product features, and product safety levels.

Quality Level

Consumers and organizational buyers usually consider the level of product quality when making purchase decisions for new and existing products. At a minimum, customers want products that will perform the functions they are supposed to and do so reasonably well. Some customers are willing to accept lower quality if product use is not demanding and price is lower. For example, some homeowners prefer Sears brand hand tools over the higher-quality Craftsman brand since they are lower priced and may be used only occasionally. Organizational buyers for nuts, bolts, and electrical connectors for automobiles seldom buy the high quality, expensive fasteners used in aircraft since cars are used in less demanding situations. Lower quality may also be accepted because the difference in products is relatively small. For example, consumers buy Planter's cashew halves at a lower price than whole nuts. Apparently, one dimension of perceived quality for this product is the product form.

In designing new products, marketers must consider what criteria potential customers use to determine their perceptions of quality. While these vary for different products, customers and situations, eight general criteria include:[33]

The high quality and performance of the new Pilot electronic address book and calendar by U.S. Robotics has earned it recognition as one of Business Week's "Best New Products." The magazine praised the product's portability and ease of use: "Place it in its cradle, hit a button, and the data in the device are synchronized with the information on your PC." Such favorable publicity helps enhance the product's image of quality.

- *Performance*—How well does the product do what it is supposed to do?
- *Features*—Does the product have any unique features that are desirable?
- *Reliability*—Is the product likely to function well and not break down over a reasonable time period?
- *Conformance*—Does the product conform to established standards for such things as safety?
- *Durability*—How long will the product last before it will be worn out and have to be replaced?
- *Serviceability*—How quickly and easily can any problems be corrected?
- *Aesthetics*—How appealing is the product to the appropriate senses of sight, taste, smell, feel, and/or sound?
- *Overall Evaluation*—Considering everything about the product, including its physical characteristics, manufacturer, brand image, packaging, and price, how good is this product?

An important indicator of a number of these criteria is the presence and extent of a new product **warranty.** A warranty is the producer's statement of what it will do to compensate the buyer if the product is defective or does not work properly. Lanier Worldwide offers its customers a refund if its copiers do not meet their guaranteed uptime of 98 percent, that is, if the copiers are out of order more than 2 percent of the time.[34] In many instances, the courts also hold that businesses have implied warranties or unstated promises to compensate buyers if their products fail to perform up to the basic standards of the industry or to the level promised. Of course, like Lanier, an organization that wants to emphasize high quality will offer customers more than implied warranties enforced by the courts.

Many marketers offer a guarantee instead of or in addition to a warranty on new products. A **guarantee** is an assurance that the product is as represented and will perform properly. Typically, if the product fails to perform, the organization making the guarantee replaces the product or refunds the customer's money. Guarantees imply to some customers that the manufacturer is confident of the new products' quality.

Customers tend to have a more favorable view of products with generous guarantees and warranties. Thus, to keep its customers, Lanier offers a 100 percent uptime guarantee for its digital dictation systems.[35] McDonald's tries to build a quality image with a guarantee of hot food, fast and friendly service, and accuracy of drive-thru orders. The company promises, "If you're not satisfied, we'll make it right. Or your next meal is on us."

Product Features

Häagen-Dazs Triple Brownie Overload ice cream contains chocolate ice cream, pecans, fudge, and pieces of brownie. It also contains over 20 percent more calories than plain chocolate Häagen-Dazs ice cream.[36] These are examples of this product's features. A **product feature** is "a fact or technical specification about [the] product."[37]

Marketers select new product features by determining what it is that customers want their products to offer. For example, two companies—Haas Automation

warranty
The producer's statement of what it will do to compensate the buyer if the product is defective.

guarantee
An assurance that the product is as represented and will perform properly.

product feature
A fact or technical specification about the product.

Weight Watchers advertises the features of Kung Pao Noodles and Vegetables, one of 12 products in its new International Selections *food line. The ad mentions "a delicious Asian dish of dumpling noodles, green beans, bok choy and bamboo shoots in a sauce fragrant with soy, sherry and a dash of chili spice." The product's features of appetizing and healthy ingredients provide the consumer with an opportunity to "form a healthy relationship with pleasure."*

and Fadal Engineering, both based in California—successfully served small machine shops by developing new computer-controlled machine tools with just basic features. In contrast, Japanese manufacturers (which once controlled the U.S. market for machine tools) added so many features and increased the price so much that only large manufacturers could afford their products. By making an affordable product, Haas and Fadal each captured about one-third of the market for vertical machining centers, which are used for cutting tools.[38]

Value-driven organizations attempt not only to ask potential customers what they want, but to learn what these customers are likely to *need*. Marketers in such organizations may identify a need for new features that target markets have not yet thought of and may not yet even understand. This worked in the toothbrush industry, where producers added a variety of new features to stimulate a 30 percent increase in sales despite higher prices. For example, SmithKline Beecham's Flex toothbrush added a tiny spring in its handle to help prevent overly vigorous brushing from damaging gums. Gillette Company's Oral-B toothbrushes include a patch of blue bristles that gradually fade to white, indicating that it's time to replace the brush.[39]

An important feature of some new products is the color or colors they come in. A product's color can influence how people perceive its value and whether they buy it. Igloo Products Corporation attributes an increase in sales of its coolers to adding new colors. Color consultant Patricia Verlodt told the company that its red and blue coolers were boring, and she suggested that the company add turquoise- and raspberry-colored products. After changing colors, sales rose 15 percent.[40]

Product Design

Many well-designed products are easy to use as intended and pleasing to the senses. Designing new products for both ease of use and aesthetic appeal can be difficult, but it can differentiate new products. For example, one reporter found a new version of Honda's CRX automobile practical, exquisite in its engineering, and fun to drive with the top removed and packed away.[41] OXO International, a maker of kitchen utensils, designs new products that succeed with virtually no advertising. Despite their moderate price, OXO tools are a pleasure to use and are striking to look at.[42]

Good design can add to the value of a new product. For example, Ingersoll-Rand Company learned that half the people using wrenches on an auto assembly line were women, so it recognized a need for a new tool that could be used by workers with a wide range of hand sizes. The result was a two-size, variable-grip wrench. Not only did the wrench meet the needs of U.S. workers, but it turned out to be popular in Japan, where hands tend to be smaller.[43]

A well-designed product can please customers without necessarily costing more to make. This is especially likely when the organization uses cross-functional teams to develop its products. If employees from engineering, marketing, and manufacturing

Even a cutter used by retail food store employees can have "world class safety." The Handy Safety Cutter S2 is "used by the largest retailers in the world ... ergonomically designed ... [and] is safe and comfortable to use." Advertised in Grocery Equipment *magazine, Pacific Handy Cutter promotes the product's safety benefits to the retail buyer—it reduces "accidents and carpal tunnel syndrome, damaged goods, [and] puncture wounds with a new patented Safety Point Blade."*

work together on what the product will look like and how it will operate, they can create a design that is easy and economical to make as well as use.

Westinghouse once faced declining sales of a mature product line, electrical panel-board and switchboard products sold to electrical contractors. The products also had become expensive to make because customers selected from over 2,400 possible components in many different configurations. To revamp the entire product line, Westinghouse set up a team of employees from its engineering, manufacturing, marketing, process planning, and information systems departments. The team redesigned the product, improving it by making the units smaller and using half the number of possible components. The team also researched customer needs and learned that just eight configurations would satisfy over 90 percent of the market's requirements. This knowledge helped the team improve the efficiency of purchasing, stocking parts, manufacturing, and processing orders.[44]

Product Safety

Marketers must develop new products that have a reasonable level of product safety. Safety is both an ethical and a practical issue. Ethically, the prevailing view is that customers should not be harmed by using a product as intended. The practical issue is that when users get harmed by a product, they may avoid buying it in the future, may tell family and friends to avoid the product, and may perhaps sue the company that made or sold it. Lost sales and a damaged reputation are hard to reclaim. It is also expensive to defend and pay damages in a product liability lawsuit in which the user seeks compensation for injuries resulting from using the product.

Many products are inherently dangerous and can result in injury to users. However, it may be so expensive to make them safer that buyers could not afford them. Such products include automobiles, farm and other machinery, and guns. Other products such as patented medicines can harm a small portion of the product's users. However, the help such products offer are considered to outweigh the risks to a small group.

Packaging and Labeling New Products

Marketers must make decisions concerning the packaging of new products, as well as the labeling that identifies and describes them. Although marketers may make improvements to existing packages and labels, decisions about these issues are most common when a product is new.

Packaging

Packaging serves several purposes that add value for customers. First, packaging is functional. Many kinds of products, such as soup, laundry detergent, and lubricating oil, must be carried in some type of container. Besides protecting and containing the product, the package may provide the customer with convenience—say, a cap for measuring liquid detergent, plastic cups that portion yogurt into single servings, or bottles of motor oil with necks that allow it to be poured easily into the engine. Packaging can also provide a degree of safety in that it protects the product from damage in shipping or from tampering. In some cases, packages have antitheft devices, such as a magnetic strip or plastic tag to be deactivated by a sales clerk.

Packaging can also be used to promote the product. This benefits the customer by providing information and the seller by drawing attention to the product. Colorful, attractive packaging helps a product stand out in the eyes of buyers. Coca-Cola has long identified its product by its curvy "contour" bottle. According to marketing research, older consumers associate the shape with quality, while young consumers see it as distinctively modern.[45] In contrast, Seckinger-Lee's original packaging for its gourmet cookies was too dull. The cookies sold briskly when stores offered samples but otherwise they sat on the shelf. After redesigning the package into eye-catching tins featuring pictures of the cookies inside, sales picked up dramatically.[46]

Dole Food Company's Lunch For One™ product line is an example of functional packaging that provides consumers with the safety of a sealed plastic bag and the convenience of having lunch provided in one container that fits their needs. Lunch For One "comes complete with regular or fat free dressing and even breadsticks, garlic cheese toast or melba toast. It's so easy, you may never brown bag it again."

Introducing Dole® Lunch For One. Wherever You Go, A Great Lunch Is In The Bag.

Choose from four delicious varieties of fresh salads that come complete with regular or fat free dressing and even breadsticks, garlic cheese toast or melba toast. It's so easy, you may never brown bag it again.

Finally, packaging can distinguish products from those of competitors. This is the case with fancy perfume bottles designed to reflect the image of a particular fragrance. On a more mundane level, Kimberly-Clark Corporation introduced a line of Kleenex Expressions tissues in a variety of boxes featuring graphics that match styles of home decor, including country, Southwestern, and Victorian. The idea was that consumers who care about the aesthetics of tissues boxes would be inspired to place Kleenex throughout their homes.[47]

The use of packaging to distinguish a product may be an important part of the marketing mix for reaching certain target markets. For example, to target elderly consumers, marketers might use packages that are easy to open. To target single people, food marketers might offer smaller or single-serving packages. To target families with children, marketers might use child safety containers for dangerous products like medicine or lye.

In selecting packaging, marketers must consider the costs of various alternatives. Making packaging as attractive, protective, convenient, or safe to use as possible could be prohibitively expensive. Therefore, marketers must determine the costs of various packaging alternatives and select packages that satisfy customer needs at low cost.

With noncost issues as well, marketers must respond to customer wants and needs. In the case of soft drinks, U.S. consumers have become unwilling to drag returnable bottles back to the store for a deposit. Although glass bottles may be environmentally desirable and attractively priced, they are no longer accepted by U.S. consumers who prefer cans. In Egypt, however, 90 percent of Coke products are sold in refillable bottles, as are 99 percent in the Philippines.[48] Figure 10.4 offers 10 tips for developing effective packaging.

Overflowing landfills attest to the fact packaging can have a major impact on the environment. Thus, marketers must somehow choose between using more packaging to keep products safer and less packaging to reduce the amount of garbage. Marketers

FIGURE 10.4
Ten Tips for Developing Effective Packaging

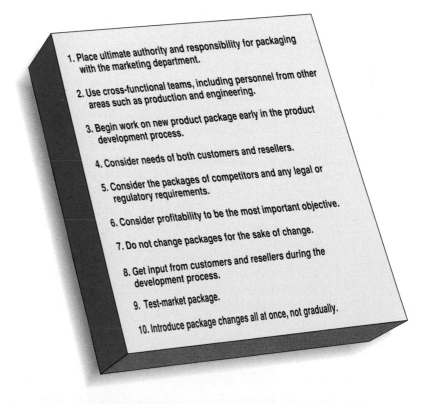

1. Place ultimate authority and responsibility for packaging with the marketing department.

2. Use cross-functional teams, including personnel from other areas such as production and engineering.

3. Begin work on new product package early in the product development process.

4. Consider needs of both customers and resellers.

5. Consider the packages of competitors and any legal or regulatory requirements.

6. Consider profitability to be the most important objective.

7. Do not change packages for the sake of change.

8. Get input from customers and resellers during the development process.

9. Test-market package.

10. Introduce package changes all at once, not gradually.

Source: Adapted from *Business Horizons*, January–February. Copyright 1988 by the Foundation for the School of Business at Indiana University. Used with permission. Reported in Steven J. Skinner, *Marketing* (Boston: Houghton Mifflin Co., 1990), p. 262.

also have choices as to the packaging materials to use. For example, aseptic packaging, such as used for juice boxes, is convenient and protects the product well but has been criticized because it is made of materials that are difficult to recycle.

Packaging decisions increasingly reflect concern about their impact on the natural environment. Many consumers and organizational buyers are concerned about environmental issues, as are many marketers and packaging manufacturers. Many packages and bags now are made of recycled paper that is labeled with the arrows in a circle that symbolize recycled materials. Aluminum cans are also recycled, as are plastic bottles and jugs. Aerosol cans that hurt the ozone layer have been replaced by more environmental-friendly containers. Styrofoam packages that do not easily decompose in landfills have been replaced by recyclable paper cartons in fast-food restaurants. Overall, many marketers have responded in a socially responsible manner to the environmental problems with packaging.

Labeling

An important part of most packages is some kind of label. A label can be as small and simple as a sticker on an apple identifying it as a Royal Gala from New Zealand, or it can be as complex as the information taped to the window of new cars. Labels can support the marketing effort by promoting the product and by adding value to customers by providing information to help with product selection and use.

Labels support the organization's promotional effort by drawing attention to products and their benefits. If promotion emphasizes certain product features or quality messages, these can be reinforced on the labels. Many food products attract health-conscious consumers with labels that trumpet "fat free" or "low-fat." Skillful label writers choose words carefully to promote product benefits, not just product features. To announce that Doritos were in a larger bag and more heavily seasoned, Frito-Lay printed "More Great Taste!" on the front of the bag. Even expiration dates can be appealing: "Enjoy by Sept. 10," says a six-pack of soda.[49]

universal product code (UPC)
A code imprinted on a product or product package that identifies its type, manufacturer, and other characteristics such as its size or flavor.

The information on labels can be helpful to both resellers and end users of a product. For example, resellers of many products expect that labels will carry a **universal product code (UPC)** or bar code. The UPC identifies the product by inventory number and size or weight and is used for scanning prices at the checkout counter. Consumers, in turn, expect that labels will help them make buying decisions by indicating product features. For example, food products contain lists of ingredients and parts for appliances or office machines indicate which models they are designed for. Labels may contain instructions to help buyers use the product correctly, as in the case of washing instructions on detergent boxes. Labels may also explain how to care for products, such as cleaning instructions on clothing labels.

For some products, the government requires that labels contain specific information. Clothing labels must indicate fiber content, and the labels on prepared foods must list the ingredients in order of weight. Under the Nutrition Labeling and Education Act of 1990, the Food and Drug Administration (FDA) allows labels to make health claims only when they are scientifically valid. For example, a manufacturer of frozen entrees may not claim they prevent heart disease simply because they have less saturated fat than competing brands. Furthermore, labels may not make vague claims such as "light"; any claims about nutrients must meet criteria specified by the FDA. The challenge of meeting such regulations has provided opportunities for companies such as Baltimore's Label Check, which analyzes food labels to make sure they conform to the law.[50]

Global Implications

In developing packages and labels for international markets, marketers must consider a number of issues. One is that the package may have to be durable enough to withstand transportation over greater distances or via a less reliable infrastructure than in

Do Eco-Labels Really Create Value for Consumers?

Labels can have a profound effect on the success of a product. Labels that provide information such as fat content or potential side effects can make or break a sale to some consumers. These labels can create value for consumers by providing information to help them make intelligent purchases.

Now there's another kind of label: the eco-label or "green" label, which tells consumers whether products are environmentally safe or benign. A wide range of products bear this label—from linens to detergents to paper products. In order to receive one of these labels, a product has to be tested or rated by certain standards. In the United States, these ratings are provided mostly by two organizations, Green Seal, Inc., and Scientific Certification Systems. However, in the United States, neither consumers nor marketers have been clamoring for the labels.

Overseas, however, "green consumerism" is a hot issue and eco-labels are sought out by consumers. In Germany, consumers look for the Federal Environment Office's blue angel on packages. In Sweden, it's the image of the white Nordic swan. Even in India, where environmental issues are critical because of the large population and still-developing infrastructure, consumers look for a seal that guarantees a product's manufacture, use, and disposal is supposed to be as harmless as possible. The European Union, whose eco-label depicts a flower with twelve stars for petals, has strong regulations regarding pollution, recycling, forest management, and other issues. The European Union is also a large market, one in which marketers from all over the world would like to succeed. Thus, it makes sense for marketers from the U.S. and elsewhere to conform to EU's standards.

Not everyone sees the issue this way, however. Some believe that the eco-labels represent a kind of trade protectionism. "Eco-seals potentially create barriers to trade," complains Scott Stewart of Procter & Gamble. Others believe that the labeling idea is noble, but the practice itself may prove to be flawed. "It's a very pure idea," observes Phil Evans of Britain's Consumer Association. "The problems come in the actual practice." For example, whereas recycling may be practical in a small, densely populated country like Holland, it may prove more costly and use more resources in a large, sparsely populated country like Canada. Does that mean that Canada's products, which may not meet the criteria for an EU label, are less environmentally sound than those of Holland? Still, proponents such as Norman Deal of Green Seal, put the issue this way: "It's a consumer right-to-know issue." Do you agree with the idea of providing eco-labels for products that meet standardized criteria on a global basis? Why or why not? Do you think that the labels create value for consumers? Why or why not?

Sources: Pan Demetrakakes, Michael Bordenaro, and Mark Spaulding, "A Look Back, A Look Ahead," *Packaging*, March 1994, pp. 8–14; Thomas Gloria, Theodore Sadd, Magalie Braville, and Michael O'Connell, "Life-Cycle Assessment: A Survey of Current Implementation," *Total Quality Environmental Management,* Spring 1995, pp. 33–50; Michael Roberts, "Eco-Labels Live Again," *Chemical Week,* May 10, 1995, p. 20; James Braham, "Don't Rush Into ISO 14000," *Machine Design,* January 11, 1996, pp. 38–42; Marc Levinson, "Seeing Red Over Green," *Newsweek,* June 17, 1996, p. 55.

Explore more by searching "Eco-Label" on the Web.

---

the United States. Also, marketers must take into account language differences. When global markets speak different languages, it may be more efficient to use several languages on one package or label than to print separate versions for each. To market candy in Europe, for instance, M&M Mars prints as many different languages on each wrapper as will fit.[51] Freeman Cosmetic Corporation, based in Beverly Hills, California, has learned that many Mexican consumers like products that look as though they are from the United States, so the company prints the front label in English and the back label in Spanish.[52]

Packaging should be consistent with local wants and tastes. Phoenix-based Penn Racquet Sports had trouble selling its tennis balls in Japan until the company realized that customers there didn't like buying three balls in a can, the standard packaging in the United States. The company did much better with a two-ball canister.[53] Many consumers in China consider Procter & Gamble's shampoo a luxury, so the company successfully markets single-use pouches of shampoo priced at the equivalent of 14 cents apiece.[54]

In the European Union, there are regulations designed to encourage the use of environmentally friendly products and packaging.[55] Under the eco-label program, products deemed friendly to the environment qualify to bear a special label (see "You Decide: Do Eco-Labels Really Create Value for Consumers?"). Also, a proposed EU regulation seeks to protect the environment by, among other things, setting packaging requirements that will make packaging materials easier to recycle. Since the environmental concern of many Europeans is mirrored by Americans, many U.S. marketers already have experience in this area that can help them compete in Europe.

Reducing New Product Failures

The effectiveness with which organizations introduce new products varies widely. Regardless of effort, however, many new products fail in the marketplace. According to estimates, failure rates for new products range from 33 percent to 90 percent.[56]

Despite the commonly held perception that markets are dominated by the company that got there first, being a pioneer is no guarantee of success. A study of 50 markets found that the pioneer wound up with the largest market share in only 11 percent of the cases. In fact, almost half the pioneers in these markets did not even survive. For example, although Procter & Gamble is reputed to have pioneered disposable diapers, a brand called Chux pioneered the market over two decades before P&G did but failed.[57] Organizations need to not only generate new products, but new products that succeed.

Motorola, in contrast to many companies, is a pioneer that has achieved long-term success. The company's SCR 536 hand-held wireless radio (pictured at left in the ad) provided flexible communication to soldiers in World War II. Today, Motorola leads in the modern wireless technology market with cellular phones, including the MicroTAC Ultra Lite™, also pictured in the ad.

One reason people assume that pioneers grab the most market share is that the market leader does tend to be an innovator. The market leader is typically the first company to appeal to a large market by improving quality, lowering price, and broadening applications. For example, Ampex developed VCR technology in the 1950s, but the U.S. company sold only a few machines at $50,000 apiece. In contrast, three Japanese companies—JVC, Matsushita, and Sony—spent years developing a $500 version of the VCR, then captured most of the market for it.[58] More recently, Prodigy Services, the pioneer in on-line computer services for consumers, failed to adapt its product to consumers' desire to use on-line services as a route to the Internet. Prodigy lost its lead to America Online, and its long-term success depends on whether the company can figure out how to deliver enough value to recapture lost sales.[59]

Why New Products Fail

Research into marketing practices has found that the primary reason for the failure of new products is the inability of the selling company to match its offerings to customer needs and wants.[60] Organizations lack this ability when they do not thoroughly research customer needs, do not stick to what the organization does best, or do not provide better value than competitors. The organization may be so focused on costs or technology that it forgets to ask how it can create value for customers. These mistakes can lead to problems such as poor-quality products, too-small target markets, and misunderstood customers. For example, in Hungary, marketers unfamiliar with the habits of consumers launched a two-in-one shampoo and conditioner. However, most Hungarians were unfamiliar with the idea of using a conditioner; they couldn't figure out how the new product would save them time, since they were only using shampoo anyway.[61]

Sometimes new products fail because the organization didn't bring them to market fast enough. A competitor may have a similar idea or learn of the organization's plans and beat it to market. Buyers then become loyal to the competing product before the organization has a chance to develop its market position. Market conditions could also change so that the new product is no longer valued by customers. Groveland Trading Company, a supplier of natural foods, had this problem when it took a year and a half to introduce a new product; the company moved too slowly to catch the peak of the turkey hot dog fad.[62]

Marketers can't prevent every problem that leads new products to fail, but they can take actions that reduce the chance of failure. As mentioned earlier, one of these actions is to be systematic about new product development. However, methodically following the steps of the development process may take too much time in rapidly changing industries.[63] In such situations, marketers may need to streamline the process to shorten development time.

Organizing for Success

The work of developing a new product typically is handled by several departments in the organization including marketing, R&D, engineering and operations. Other organizations such as suppliers, advertising agencies, and research laboratories also may be consulted.

Successful new products often come from companies that emphasize planning, organization, and cooperation among various functions.[64] One way to put this emphasis into action is through the use of cross-functional teams. At Fuji Xerox, development of the successful 3500 Copier brought together the efforts of corporate planners, design and manufacturing engineers, parts suppliers, and marketing, sales, and services personnel.[65]

Organizational Forms   As shown in Figure 10.5, there are at least five ways to organize new product development:[66]

* A *functional* organization is one in which employees carry out particular functions, such as marketing or finance. The company assigns employees from the necessary functions to spend part of their time working on tasks related to developing a new product. They may be assigned to serve on a new product committee, which regularly meets to review progress on one or more products under development. The functional organization typically is used for relatively minor innovations such as product improvements or new package sizes.

* In a *functional matrix,* people from various functions are assigned to represent their department on a team or committee charged with developing the new product.

* With a *balanced matrix,* employees report to both a functional manager and a project manager. They are responsible for both the project and functional contribution to the organization. Of course, this situation may lead to uncertainty about which type of combination should take priority.

* When the company wants greater loyalty to the project, it can use a *project matrix.* This is a variation of the matrix arrangement in which employees are told to focus on developing the new product.

F I G U R E   10.5

Organizational Forms for New Product Development

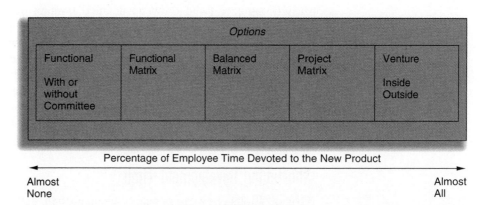

Source: Adapted from C. Merle Crawford, *New Products Management,* 4th ed. (Burr Ridge, Ill.: Irwin, 1994), p. 411.

T A B L E 10.3
Performance of the Basic
Organizational Forms for
New Product Development

Organizational Form	Percent of Projects	Percent Rated Successful	Percent Rated Either Successful or Marginally Successful
Functional	13%	32%	63%
Functional matrix	26	41	79
Balanced matrix	17	58	88
Project matrix	28	62	92
Venture	16	62	94
Total	100%		
Total projects: 540			

Source: Reprinted by permission of the publisher from "Organizing for Product Development Projects," Erik W. Larson and David H. Gobeli, *Journal of Product Innovation Management,* September 1988, pp. 180–190. Copyright 1988 by Elsevier Science, Inc.

• With a *venture* or *venture team,* the company charges employees to work full time on the new product. The venture may operate as part of the company, or it may be set up as a separate division—maybe in a separate part of the building or even in another city or state. The cost of setting up a venture and dedicating employees' time to a new product can be high, but it can get employees to focus their efforts on the new product's success.

Which organizational form is best? It depends on the type of new product desired. In an organization that is content with its product mix but wants to make some minor adjustments, a functional approach is the least costly. If a major new product is sought, more commitment to it can be obtained by moving toward a venture.[67] Companies where innovation is viewed as a key to success often set up some type of venture organization. As shown in Table 10.3, the venture organizational form produced the highest percentage of successful new products in one study.

Using Venture Teams   Organizations are increasingly using venture teams to develop new products. A **venture team** is a cross-functional team responsible for all tasks involved in the development of a new product. The team may turn over responsibility for the product following commercialization, or it may assume responsibility for managing the product as a separate business. Companies that have used venture teams include Exxon, IBM, Motorola, and Xerox.

Venture teams operate independently of the organization's functional departments. A typical venture team includes engineers for designing the product and developing a prototype. Staff from the marketing department develop tests of the product concept, conduct test marketing, forecast sales, and plan the marketing mix. Accountants analyze costs and evaluate profitability. At 3M Corporation, a venture team was charged with developing a mechanical splice for optical cables. The team included a senior design engineer (who drew up detailed product designs), a senior engineer (who produced molds, dies, and prototypes), an advanced physicist (who handled product testing and evaluating), and a sales and marketing manager (who figured out how to sell the splice, including arranging for a demonstration at a trade show).[68]

Venture teams are especially useful for developing products that are completely new to the company or that involve new technology. Successfully launching such products typically requires more time and money than managers of existing products often are willing to risk. In contrast, the leader and members of the venture team should be fully committed to the success of the new products.

venture team
A cross-functional team that is responsible for all the tasks involved in the development of a new product.

Shortening Development Time

Organizations often can boost the chances their new products will succeed by shortening the time spent developing them. Getting products to market faster gives com-

Bill Gates & Doug Rowan/Corbis Corp.

Photography isn't new. Even the idea of converting photographic images into electronic files isn't new. However, the idea of providing a service that turns photographic negatives into electronic images and sending them to customers via the Internet is new for Bill Gates. His latest venture, Corbis Corp., intends to capture as much of this potentially huge market as it can.

Gates' first try in the market failed because he did not tune into the wants of the professional photographers whose work he sought. Photographers, along with their agents and lawyers, immediately rejected the contract terms Gates offered them; word spread, and his pool of potential acquisitions quickly dried up. So he retreated and refocused on artists' concerns, hiring professional photographers, photo editors, art historians, and copyright lawyers. He put Doug Rowan, a computer industry marketing expert, in charge of the new company called Corbis (Latin for "woven basket"). In doing all this, he was making his company better prepared to meet the wants of his potential customers—publishers and editors, as well as consumers such as a sixth-grade student who might want to include a photograph in a school report.

Corbis Corp. then bought the entire Bettmann Archive—16 million images for $6 million. The collection includes famous photographs such as Dorothea Lange's Depression-era family, the exploding Hindenburg, and Marilyn Monroe in her swirling skirt. In addition, Corbis has sent its own photographers out to cover historic events in the making. Rowan and Gates' mission for the Bellevue, Washington-based company is hardly modest: "[To] capture the entire human experience throughout history," says Rowan.

Corbis already has plenty of competition. Picture Network International, an online graphics service based in Virginia, offers stock photos, illustrations, sound effects, and more on its Web site. Liaison International offers 2,400 of its 4 million photos on its Web site. Photodisc offers 15,000 images on its Web site and customers can use a credit card to make purchases. Corbis' collection is much larger than these, and the company also produces CD-ROMs of certain images that will eventually be available online. The CD-ROM collections include works of great artists such as Leonardo da Vinci. This inclusion illustrates well the marriage of old and new technology to create new products; the work of da Vinci endures, in a new medium.

Will Rowan and Gates rule the universe of digitized images? Will they, in fact, capture electronically all of the human experience? "Regardless of how much Corbis acquires, they can't compete with the whole rest of the world," comments Josh Bernoff, senior analyst with Forrester Research at the Library of Congress. Perhaps not. But they can try.

Sources: Jennifer Sucov, "Digital Archives Bank on Publishing Biz," *Folio: The Magazine for Magazine Management,* January 1, 1996, p. 47; "Bettmann's Pix," *Advertising Age,* January 29, 1996, p. 16; "Gates' Corbis Corp. Purchase Swells Its Historical Image Archive," *CD-Rom Professional,* February 1996, p. 16; Katie Hafner, "Picture This," *Newsweek,* June 24, 1996, pp. 88, 90; Thane Peterson, "Cezanne & Co. on CD-Rom," *Business Week,* August 19, 1996, p. 18.

Explore more at www.corbis.com

---

petitors less time to beat the organization to market. Also, the conditions leading to a new market need or want are less likely to have changed if new products hit the market quickly. Major ways to shorten product development time are to use cross-functional teams, apply technology, delegate authority, and build on a base of specialized knowledge.

Use Cross-Functional Teams The ability to handle functions simultaneously and get consensus is a major benefit of cross-functional teams. By having team members from different functions work together on new products from the idea generation stage forward, they are more likely to discover and solve problems than with a more sequential approach.

Chrysler uses teams to shorten the development process and has built the Chrysler Technology Center (CTC) so that all employees working on product development can work in one location.[69] 3M Corporation also built a product development facility. It has two wings, one for the research department, the other for marketing. Where the wings meet, there are large conference rooms intended to encourage meetings between members of the two departments.[70]

Apply Technology   Modern technology can be used to speed up communication and analysis of product designs, product tests, business analysis, and test marketing data and bring a product to market faster. Computer software called groupware enables people to share information about the projects they are working on. Food supplier Groveland Trading used the groupware product called Lotus Notes to develop an organic turkey-and-chicken potpie in just eight months. With Lotus Notes, each person involved was able to keep the project moving since they were up-to-date on all developments. For example, a sales representative researched which ingredients would be acceptable to natural-food stores. As soon as he entered the results into his computer, they were available to decision makers responsible for obtaining ingredients and running taste tests. When chefs recommended using sugar, a quick check of the Notes file indicated that this ingredient was not acceptable to retailers, so the team avoided wasting time on unacceptable recipes.[71]

Other technology can speed the process of testing prototypes. Speedy product development is essential for BrainWorks, a company that sells playful computer accessories featuring licensed characters from shows such as *The Flintstones* and *Star Trek*. To save time at the prototype stage, the company uses a computer to create three-dimensional models of the products. The 3D images enable a contractor to create plastic models within hours. The company's machinists in Taiwan use the computer models to set up tooling to produce the product. So far, the company's fast and continuous innovation has kept competitors away from the market.[72]

Delegate Authority   Large organizations can usually move more quickly when decision making is delegated to lower levels of management. Middle managers at Johnson & Johnson have power to make some new product decisions. Even if top managers are unimpressed with a new product idea, middle managers often can pursue it. If the idea fails, these managers are not punished. Explains Ralph S. Larsen, the company's chairman, "Growth is a gambler's game."[73] Such delegation of authority is one reason for the company's many successes, which include disposable contact lenses and Retin-A skin cream.

Build on Specialized Knowledge   Another way to shorten new product development time is to devise marketing strategies that involve building and taking advantage of a base of specialized knowledge.[74] Through specialized knowledge of technology, target markets, and its own strengths or weaknesses, an organization can focus its new product development efforts. One way marketers gain this knowledge is by involving target markets in designing new products.

An organization using this strategy also might involve suppliers and other outside organizations in the development approach. In some cases, even a venture team lacks some of the know-how or experience needed to successfully introduce a new product. To compensate, an organization may form a partnership with another company. In a survey of over 400 fast-growing companies, half formed partnerships with outside organizations to develop new goods or services. These companies generated over 20 percent more products than companies that worked alone.[75]

That approach paid off for Joseph Jarke, who wanted to develop a product to ease the challenge of airline travel for wheelchair users like himself. Jarke took his product concept, a wheelchair that can fold up to the size of a briefcase, to United Airlines for input on usage problems and to GE Plastics for expertise in selecting materials. Both companies were impressed with Jarke's SeatCase Travel Chairs and were willing to help him. SeatCases are now available on a dozen airlines and on Japan's bullet trains.[76]

Building on a base of specialized knowledge can speed new product development by reducing the time it takes for the organization to figure out what customers need and want and what products will satisfy or perhaps even delight them. As the organization builds its expertise, it gains insights that can improve product design. The product expertise of Rollerblade's engineers and the skill of the top boot designers at Italy's Nordica made a strong team to improve the safety of the braking system for in-line roller skates. Skaters using Rollerblade's Active Brake Technology stop by rolling the boot forward, not the whole skate, which moves a lever that lowers the brake. Theoretically, this method of braking is easier and more natural than the original method.[77] Such specialized knowledge creates value for customers and a competitive edge for marketers.

Summary

A new product is an addition to an organization's product mix that was not previously marketed by it. There are at least five types of new products: new-to-the-world products, new category entries, additions to product lines, product improvements, and repositionings.

Companies can enhance their chances of success with a new product if they are systematic about developing it. The process of development begins with idea generation. Ideas for new products can come from many sources, including customers, the sales force, and other employees. The organization must screen ideas to be sure that they meet the objectives of the company. Next marketers conduct a business analysis to see whether forecasted sales and costs are acceptable. If so, the process continues with development of the product and other elements of the marketing mix. Usually the organization test-markets the product to see whether it is received and used as expected. If the results of test marketing are acceptable, the development process ends with commercialization.

In devising a product strategy, marketers consider characteristics of the product, including quality, features, design, and safety. Product features, the technical specifications of a product, should meet the buyer's wants and needs. Many well-designed products are easy to use as intended and pleasing to the senses. Product safety has ethical as well as practical implications.

Other decisions for new products include packaging and labeling. Packaging should be protective, convenient, safe, and attractive, but at a reasonable cost. Packaging for many products includes UPCs and antitheft devices. Out of a commitment to social responsibility and to meet increasingly stringent laws worldwide, many marketers try to reduce the negative impact of used packaging on the natural environment. Labeling provides information that can help customers with product selection and use and help marketers with promotions.

Although there is no way to guarantee the success of new products, companies that emphasize planning, organization, and cooperation among various functions may reduce the rates of failure. The people responsible for product development may have responsibility along functional lines, project lines, or some balance between the two (such as a matrix structure). An increasingly popular way to organize is to use a venture team, a cross-functional team responsible for all the steps in the development of a new product. Ways to shorten new product development time include the use of cross-functional teams, technology, delegation of authority, and specialized knowledge.

Key Terms and Concepts

new product (p. 258)
concept testing (p. 264)
concurrent engineering (p. 265)
standard test market (p. 266)

controlled test market (p. 266)
simulated test market (p. 266)
commercialization (p. 267)
warranty (p. 269)

guarantee (p. 269)
product feature (p. 269)
universal product code (UPC) (p. 274)
venture team (p. 278)

Review and Discussion Questions

1. Name the five ways a product might be considered "new."
2. Why is it important for marketers to ask domestic and global customers for ideas for new products?
3. Why is research and development important?
4. A company that produces cameras has an idea for an entirely new and superior type of film, but business analysis shows that the cost of taking it to market is prohibitive. How might the company be able to go ahead with the product? Elaborate on how this might work.

5. How might a manufacturer of bicycles use concurrent engineering to come up with a new product?
6. When is test marketing most effective? What are the shortcomings of test marketing? How can they be avoided?
7. What are the eight general criteria that consumers could use to evaluate the quality of new products? Think of an important purchase you made recently. Which of the criteria did you use? Which one was *most* important to you?

8. Why is emphasis on high quality important for global markets?

9. Choose a specific convenience product—a toothbrush, a marker or pen, snack food, or the like. List all the product features that you can. In what ways does it meet your wants and needs?

10. Assume a U.S.-based company markets a line of outdoor clothing, specializing in clothes for skiing and hiking. The company wants to expand its market to serve Japan, China, and Western Europe. As a marketer, what steps would you take to prevent failure of a new product line for these countries?

11. What are the five ways to organize people for new product development?

Chapter Project   Design a Package and Label

Packages and their labels serve important functions for marketers. As you learned in this chapter, packages and labels also create value for consumers—by including safety features, providing information on ingredients or how to use the product, and so forth.

Choose a product—your own idea for a new product, your private-label product from the Chapter 9 project, or an existing product that you think could benefit from some significant changes. Then design a package for your product, taking into consideration any protection, convenience, safety, and promotion features the package should have. You can design your package on paper, or on a computer, or you can make an actual model. Finally, create a brand name and an attractive, appealing label for the package.

Chapter Case   Pleasant Company

About a decade ago, Pleasant T. Rowland founded a company based on her idea:"To provide girls with beautiful books, dolls, and pastimes that celebrate the experience of growing up as an American girl. . . . The American Girls Collection was created to give girls an understanding of their past and a sense of pride in the traditions they share with girls of yesterday." Thus, a company with several product lines was launched.

Selling only through mail-order catalogs, the Middleton, Wisconsin-based Pleasant Company originally offered four dolls, each representing a period in American history. Along with those dolls came an incredible array of accessories—from holiday clothes to miniature furniture, china, toys, even dolls for the dolls. Each doll also had its own collection of historical books, in which the doll was featured as the main character in a story. With a high price (the dolls alone go for $82 apiece, and the entire ensemble for one doll can run up to nearly $1,000), the dolls were targeted at upper-middle-income families and above. They sold like crazy.

Why? Perhaps because attention to high quality in the design and features was—and is—evident in every product sold by the company. The dolls are durable and realistic looking. The clothes are stitched well, with historically correct details. The books are well written, even carried by many bookstores and public libraries. Some parents, like public affairs manager Julia Prohaska, feel that the products have "lasting value" and are thus willing to pay the price. Others pay the price reluctantly. "The quality is fabulous, but it's just another doll," comments one parent. Another admits, "You pull chairs out of the trash for yourself, and here you're spending $65 on chairs for a doll! At some point I had to pull in the reins."

Even the packaging is of high quality. The boxes for the dolls and clothes are sturdy. Each product is wrapped gently in tissue paper, and the box has a tiny cardboard "bow" with the logo.

The success of the original dolls has prompted Pleasant Company to offer several product line extensions. One is the Bitty Baby Collection—four baby dolls of differing races, with the same high-quality accessories. The price tag for these is lower, at $38 per doll (the dolls are smaller and do not have the realistic hair of the larger dolls) and the outfits and accessory sets start at around $20 each. Another is a line of 20 contemporary dolls, each with a different combination of skin, hair, and eye color, so a parent can choose one that closely matches a daughter's looks. These sell for $82 each. Accessories for these dolls include in-line skates, a ballet outfit, a swim outfit, even a complete set-up (including patio furniture) for an American Girl birthday party. The idea for this line, called "American Girl of Today," came from customers' suggestions. "Letters urged us to expand our vision from the past to the present to help girls address the challenges of growing up in the '90s," writes Rowland in her catalog.

Then there is the line of real-girl clothes, outfits designed after those worn by the dolls, but sized to fit their owners. There are also American Girl activities—cookbooks and craft books, sewing and craft kits. Finally, there are the "mini" American Girl dolls, miniatures of the original historical figures.

Pleasant Company stays in touch with consumers by organizing social events like American Girl tea parties and fashion shows and soliciting ideas via telemarketers. Eight months after launching the Bitty Baby Collection, catalog customers were called and asked for ideas for new outfits and other accessories, as well as to give them a chance to voice any complaints or other suggestions. "My sense is that the Pleasant Company does a phenomenal promotion and marketing effort," says Rob Mitchell of Harvard Bookstore in Cambridge, Massachusetts. "And the books are accepted by discriminating adults, both teachers and parents." They are also accepted by the girls lucky enough to have them. "I think of them as real people, I don't think of them as dolls," says one eight-year-old.

Questions

1. Why do you think Pleasant Company has been so successful with each new product it has offered?

2. What new products would you recommend for Pleasant
   Company?

3. Do you think Pleasant Company could have success with
   a new line of dolls at more moderate prices? Why or why
   not? What steps might the company take to find out?

Sources: Cynthia Dockrell, "Dolls and Cents," *The Boston Globe*, June 10, 1996,
pp. 34, 38; Pleasant Company Spring 1996 catalog, p. 1; conversation with
Pleasant Company telemarketer, June 1996.

Explore more at www.pleasantco.com

Marketing Services

CHAPTER OUTLINE

The Service Economy
  Reasons for Growth
The Nature of Services Marketing
  Characteristics of Services
  Classification of Services
  The Marketing Environment for Services
The Marketing Mix for Services
  Developing Services
  Pricing Services
  Distributing Services
  Promoting Services
Nonbusiness Services Marketing
  Nonprofit Organizations
  Government Agencies
  Political Groups
Summary

LEARNING OBJECTIVES

After completing this chapter, you should be able to:

1. Discuss the importance of marketing in the service economy.
2. Define characteristics of services.
3. Identify ways marketers classify services.
4. Explain how consumers and organizations make decisions about purchasing services.
5. Summarize characteristics of the marketing environment for services.
6. Describe issues that arise in devising a marketing mix for services.
7. Discuss how nonbusiness organizations market services.

The Boston Athletic Association

To many people, the Boston Marathon is not just a road race. For runners all over the world, competing in the race garners prestige. For fans and locals who turn out to cheer the runners each year, the race is a source of pride. For the Boston Athletic Association, the nonprofit organization that administers the race, it is a reason for being. And when the 100th Boston Marathon was run in 1996, making it the oldest continuously run marathon in history, all those feelings reached a fever pitch.

So did the marketing surrounding the race. Retailers hawked everything from T-shirts to commemorative wine. Hotels charged top rates for rooms. When the take was tallied, Metropolitan Boston had raked in over $136 million from 37,500 runners and their guests as well as 1.5 million spectators.

But the Boston Athletic Association (BAA) faced some difficult challenges and criticism for its marketing approach. In fact, many people felt that the organization did not do enough to promote itself or the event. For many, a marathon is an experience whose success depends on the service it provides—from accommodations for out-of-towners to how the race itself is organized. Tourists and runners alike expect the experience to be good if they are going to spend their hard-earned money to be a part of it. The BAA was touted for doing a tremendous job of organizing the experience for everyone; however, critics charged that they did not do enough to promote it and missed opportunities to raise money that could be poured back into the sport of running and/or community charities.

Unlike the New York Road Runners Club Inc., which stages events year around and is a master marketer, the BAA is too cautious about marketing, some people say. "The BAA could make another $3 million easily and pour it back into the community," says David F. D'Alessandro. D'Alessandro has a stake in BAA's marketing because his company, John Hancock Mutual Life Insurance Co., put up $1.4 million toward the race. For instance, the BAA could establish running programs in area schools. "Running is a superb sport for children who don't have a lot of money," says Frances Mosely, president of the Boys and Girls Clubs of Boston Inc. "It doesn't take a lot of equipment."

D'Alessandro offers four ways that the BAA could market itself and its services more successfully. He suggests that the BAA take over running the annual Sports & Fitness Expo in Boston and take control of merchandising related to the marathon. He suggests selling pieces of the finish-line tape as souvenirs, and highly recommends establishing a relationship with the travel industry.

The prestige and pride of an event like the Boston Marathon is not lost on D'Alessandro. "I happen to think, as a consumer, it's kind of neat to see some event in this country that's noncommercial. But you can still make more money off this event and be perceived as noncommercial." As you read this chapter about marketing services, consider the broad range of services that are available—from sporting events to entertainment and travel to healthcare. Consider also how important marketing services is to both commercial and nonprofit organizations.

Sources: Jerry Ackerman and Kathy McCabe, "Advertisers, On Your Marks, Get Set . . . ," *The Boston Globe*, April 12, 1996, pp. 41, 50; David M. Halfinger, "Marketing the Marathon," *The Boston Globe*, April 7, 1996, pp. 71, 73; morning broadcast, WCVB-TV, June 2, 1996.

Explore more at www.baa.org

PRICING PRINCIPLES AND STRATEGIES

FOUR

Value is more than price. It is the combination of product quality, world class customer service, and a fair price.

Lands End Inc. Fact Sheet, Internet Web Site, http://www.landsend.com, July 17, 1996

CHAPTER 12

Fundamentals of Pricing

CHAPTER 13

Pricing Goods and Services

Explore the Career Profiles on the Churchill and Peter Homepage at www.irwin.com/marketing/value.

chapter Twelve

Fundamentals of Pricing

CHAPTER OUTLINE

Economics of Pricing
  Demand Curves
  Marginal Analysis
Approaches to Pricing
  Pricing Based on Cost
  Pricing Based on Competition
  Pricing Based on Customer Value
Legal and Ethical Issues in Pricing
  Government Regulation of Pricing
  Ethics of Pricing
Summary

LEARNING OBJECTIVES

After completing this chapter, you should be able to:

1. Describe the role of pricing in the marketing mix.
2. Explain the economic principles that link price to sales and profits.
3. Describe approaches to pricing based on cost, competition, and customer value.
4. Compute prices based on markup and markdown pricing.
5. Execute a breakeven analysis.
6. Discuss legal and ethical issues surrounding pricing.

Nordstrom Inc.

The Nordstrom name is synonymous with customer service, which is the way the Seattle-based department store distinguishes itself in creating value. Nordstrom's service has helped the company generate the highest sales per square foot of any department store chain in the United States. Now the store is creating value in another way—by offering some of its merchandise at lower prices in its own off-price stores called Nordstrom Rack. Instead of jamming sale items into regular departments, Nordstrom has decided to offer the items in separate stores around the country. Nordstrom has 61 retail stores and 20 Rack stores in 16 states nationwide. Half of the merchandise in Rack stores comes from Nordstrom department stores; the other half is bought specifically for the discount chain.

Is Nordstrom raiding its own closet, cannibalizing sales from its department stores? Not according to Bob Middlemas, Midwest general manager. "The Rack is really for the discount shopper," he observes. "They really don't compete with the full-line store." Discount shoppers are looking for quality merchandise, but at a price that is lower. Their purchasing decisions may be based more on price than on other considerations, such as how long it takes to drive to the store or in what colors certain clothing items are available. Thus, Nordstrom managers don't worry that the Rack stores may be located within several miles—or blocks—from the parent department stores. In fact, market researcher Leo Shapiro, founder of Chicago-based Leo J. Shapiro & Associates Inc., says,

NORDSTROM RACK DIVISION

NORDSTROM RACK

20 Stores

"There's nothing wrong with having a Rack store close to the full-line store. If I were Nordstrom, I would put it right next-door."

Skeptics may assume that Nordstrom's trademark service is cut back at Rack stores. Not so. Fitting rooms are spacious, alterations are offered, and some locations even have coffee bars. Because of continued attention to service, Rack stores can maintain the Nordstrom reputation and compete with other off-price stores by offering low prices *and* superior service. All of this adds up to value for customers. As you read this chapter, note how pricing decisions influence the marketing mix and contribute to customer value.

Sources: Mark Veverka, "Discount Stores Yield Value for Nordstrom," *Crain's Chicago Business,* May 27, 1996, p. 11; "How to Make Extraordinary Effort the Rule Rather than the Exception," *Total Quality Newsletter,* February 1994, vol. 5, no. 2, p. 1.

Explore more at www.nordstrom-pta.com

price
The amount of money, goods, or
services that must be given up
to acquire ownership or use of a
product.

Chapter Overview

Nordstrom Inc.'s success with its off-price Rack stores shows that high-quality products, superior service, and good prices can be a formula to marketing success. A **price** is the amount of money, goods, or services that must be given to acquire ownership or use of a product. International advertising agency DMB&B bought 30 episodes of the Taiwanese television series, "Judge Pao," in order to exchange them to Chinese TV stations for advertising slots.[1] In most cases, however, a price is stated in terms of money—say, $12 for a haircut or $10,300 for a Saturn car.

Price is only part of the total costs customers pay in an exchange. The total costs of an exchange include time and mental and behavioral effort, as well as the product's monetary price.

Price plays two major roles in the marketing mix:

1. It influences whether purchases will be made and, if so, how much of a product consumers or organizations purchase. In general, potential customers seek a price that will result in positive value from the exchange. They may also consider the price relative to that of competitive offerings.

2. It influences whether marketing products will be sufficiently profitable. Even small price changes can dramatically influence profits. For example, a price decrease of 3 percent by the average Standard & Poor's 1000 company knocks profits down from 8.1 percent of sales to 5.1 percent, a 37 percent decrease.[2]

A price consistent with the other elements of the marketing mix is important for positioning products. Nissan Motor Company's Altima is positioned as an excellent value—as well made as a luxury car but selling at a much lower price. Initially priced at $13,000 for the base model, the Altima was soon attracting more sales than had been forecasted. In the words of Christopher W. Cedergren, senior vice president of the marketing research firm AutoPacific Group, "Nissan's hit a home run, and the reason is price."[3]

This chapter introduces the basic principles of pricing that marketers use to make pricing decisions. It begins with a general look at the role of price in the marketing mix. The chapter then describes economic pricing concepts. Next, the chapter discusses the basic approaches to pricing including cost, competition, and customer value. Finally, the chapter addresses legal and ethical issues in pricing decisions.

Economics of Pricing

To determine appropriate prices, marketers may apply economic concepts such as demand curves and marginal analysis.

Demand Curves

demand curve
A graphical representation
of the quantity of a product
demanded at various prices.

To select the most profitable price, marketers can research demand at various price levels. By plotting the quantity demanded at various prices, marketers can create a demand curve for their products. A **demand curve** is a graphical representation of the quantity of a product demanded at various prices. Each product has its own demand curve, and most follow the general pattern of sloping downward, as shown in Figure 12.1. This suggests that at lower prices, the quantity demanded increases. For example, when Disneyland Paris cut admission fees by 20 percent, attendance rose by 20 percent,[4] and when Kraft cut cheese prices 8 percent, sales volume increased 5 percent.[5]

The shape of a demand curve for an individual firm is influenced by the market structure in which the organization is operating. As described in Chapter 2, a market structure may be a pure monopoly, an oligopoly, monopolistic competition, or pure competition.

In a pure monopoly, a single firm sells a product for which there are no good substitutes. The firm has the market for the product to itself, so the demand curve for

F I G U R E   12.1
Sample Demand Curve

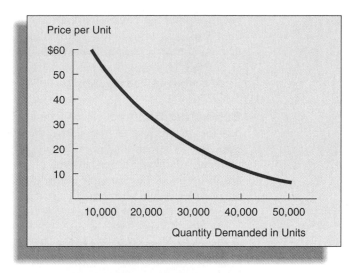

Price per Unit

Quantity Demanded in Units

The market for beef is characterized by pure competition. So, supply and demand determine price. Because greater demand enables them to sell more at a higher price, beef producers benefit from joining together and running ads such as this one by the Beef Industry Council.

the industry is identical to the demand curve for the firm. Thus, the monopolist typically is able to control the product's price and the quantity demanded.

In an oligopoly, the number of sellers is small enough for the activities of a single seller to affect other firms and for the activities of other firms to affect it. While the products the firms sell can sometimes be differentiated from one another, they are still good substitutes for each other. Because of the availability of attractive substitutes, the demand curve for oligopolists is relatively flat.

With monopolistic competition, there are many sellers of the product, but the product of each seller is in some way differentiated in customers' minds from the product of every other seller. This product differentiation gives the firm some discretion in setting price and output. However, the availability of similar products limits pricing discretion and makes the demand curve relatively flat throughout its relevant range.

With pure competition, there are many firms selling identical products, and no one firm is large enough to influence market price. Under these circumstances, the firm can sell its entire output at the prevailing market price, and nothing above that price. It has virtually no pricing latitude and simply accepts the prevailing market price as a given. Furthermore, the price is lower when supplies of the product are great and higher when only a small quantity is available. For example, in 1996 when many countries' wheat harvests were poor, wheat prices rose by 40 percent.[6]

Life Cycle   A product's demand curve is likely to undergo changes throughout the life of the product. Effective promotion can shift the demand curve to the right, meaning that more of the product will be demanded at any relevant price. The entry of new competitors into the market can change the slope of the demand curve. This is because potential buyers will be reluctant to buy at a high price when they can take their business elsewhere. Changes in tastes and technology also lead to shifts in demand curves as customers' interests change. For example, a surge in the popularity of the paintings of Latin American artists such as Fernando Botero, Diego Rivera, and Frida Kahlo resulted in record prices for their works.[7]

Estimating Demand   How do marketers know what the demand will be at each possible price? The answer is that they don't know with certainty; rather, they make estimates. Their estimates are based on research into demographic and psychological factors of their target markets and on estimates of how sensitive sales of the product are to its price. For example, surveys may provide demographic and psychographic data, and test marketing may provide information about price sensitivity. These demand factors affect the shape of the demand curve for a particular product.

When Powerfood considers demographic factors in demand estimates for its PowerBar, a snack designed to provide athletes with low-fat fuel, the potential demand by runners surely looks encouraging. The popularity of the sport of running is increasing. In 1970 the New York City Marathon, the largest spectator sporting event in the United States, had 55 total finishers; in 1995, 26,754 runners finished. Even the President of the United States runs an 8-minute mile.

Demographic Factors   Knowing the demographics of target markets can be useful in estimating demand. These data can indicate how many potential buyers there are and whether they have the resources to buy at a particular price. Some specific questions marketers ask in this regard include:[8]

- How many potential buyers are in the market?
- What is the location of potential buyers?
- Are they organizational buyers or consumers?
- What is the consumption rate of potential buyers?
- What is the financial condition of potential buyers?

Marketers also look at trends in the industry. For example, pharmaceutical companies study trends in drug purchases. They know that purchase decisions have shifted from individual physicians to large buyers such as health maintenance organizations and mail-order drug retailers.[9]

Psychological Factors   In addition, marketers consider psychological factors, that is, how potential buyers perceive various prices or price changes (see "Put It into Practice: Consider Psychological Factors in Pricing as a Consumer"). They ask questions such as the following:[10]

- Will potential buyers use price as an indicator of the product's quality?
- Will potential buyers be favorably attracted by odd pricing such as 99 cents instead of $1, or $177 instead of $180?
- Will potential buyers perceive the price to be too high relative to what the product offers?
- Are potential buyers concerned enough with prestige to pay more for the product?
- How much will potential buyers be willing to pay for the product?

In the case of marketing drugs, pharmaceutical companies have noted that buyers are placing more importance on low price. The traditional marketing strategy was heavy

Consider Psychological Factors in Pricing as a Consumer

When marketers set a price for a product, they should take into consideration psychological factors that are important to consumers. In order to understand how these factors work, choose two products that you purchased recently: one product should be a convenience product, the other should be a shopping or specialty good. In order to better understand psychological factors in pricing, ask yourself the following questions. For these purchases, did I use price as an indicator of product quality? Was I influenced by odd pricing? Did the prestige of the brand name lead me to pay a higher price? Did I view the price of alternatives too high to offer me value?

spending on salespeople who visited doctors to explain particular drugs' advantages and drop off free samples. Since the doctors didn't have to pay for the drugs they prescribed, they made purchase decisions primarily on drug performance. In contrast, HMOs and mail-order pharmacies seek lower prices.[11]

price elasticity
A measure of the sensitivity of demand to changes in price.

Price Elasticity   Estimating demand also involves price elasticity. **Price elasticity** is "a measure of the sensitivity of demand to changes in price."[12] Stated mathematically, it is the percentage change in the quantity demanded divided by the percentage change in price:

$$\text{price elasticity} = \frac{\text{percentage change in quantity demanded}}{\text{percentage change in price}}$$

$$= \frac{\text{change in quantity/original quantity}}{\text{change in price/original price}}$$

When price elasticity is greater than 1, demand is said to be *elastic*. This means that a small change in price results in a large change in the quantity demanded. When price elasticity is less than one, a small change in price yields a smaller change in the quantity demanded, and demand is said to be *inelastic*.

Demand for a product is likely to be inelastic if the product has few substitutes, is a necessity, and costs relatively little. Examples are gasoline and telephone service; most people keep driving and making phone calls even when prices go up. In contrast, if the cost of a European vacation were to rise, many consumers might decide that this is the year to vacation closer to home. Demand for a European vacation is elastic then. Figure 12.2 shows these relationships.

Knowing the product's price elasticity helps marketers predict patterns in total revenue. In general, for a product with *elastic* demand, total revenue increases when the product's price *declines*. Thus, for a decline in the price of European vacations, the increase in the number of tourists would be great enough to generate more total revenue, even though the average tourist would spend less. If a product has *inelastic* demand, total revenue increases when the product's price *increases*. Thus, if the price of a loaf of bread goes up by a dime, most consumers will keep buying about the same amount of bread, and the company's total revenue increases. Table 12.1 shows an example of how changing price elasticity affects total revenues. When the price of the product goes from $50 to $75 a unit, demand is inelastic enough that the company earns more at the higher price. But when the price rises to $100, demand is more

F I G U R E   12.2 *Demand Curves Showing Different Price Elasticities*

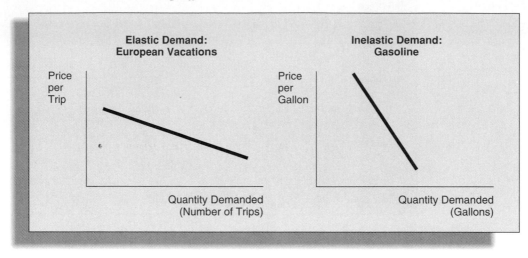

elastic; sales volume falls more than proportionately, and the company earns less at the higher price.

Sometimes marketers conduct research to learn about the price elasticity of their products. When Approach Software, based in Redwood City, California, prepared to introduce its first product, a database program, marketing director Jaleh Bisharat interviewed 30 prospective customers. Bisharat learned that they expected to pay at least $149. Then she sent a mailing to 50,000 prospects, offering different groups the software at either $99, $129, or $149. Sales at the top price almost equaled those at $129, so the company tested an even higher price, $199. At that price, demand fell off. So Approach launched the software at an introductory price of $149.[13]

Often, conducting this type of research to determine price elasticity is considered too costly and time consuming. How can marketers estimate price elasticity without offering the product at many different prices? One approach is to look at historical data and see how the quantity purchased varied as the product's price changed. When Bernard Chaus Inc. raised the prices of its women's clothing to match those of Liz Claiborne, sales revenues declined 20 percent, and the company went from generating profits to losing money. Chaus later lowered prices and found that unit sales went up more than enough to make up for the lower price per unit of clothing.[14] Another approach is to compare data from markets where different prices are charged. While these estimates have limitations, they can give marketers a sense of how potential customers will respond to different price levels.

Estimating Revenue   Demand curves and the theory related to them help marketers estimate the revenue that products are likely to generate at various prices. In making these estimates, marketers use three basic measures of revenue: total revenue, average revenue, and marginal revenue.

T A B L E   12.1
Changing Price Elasticity
for a Product

Unit Price	Quantity Demanded	Total Revenue (Price × Quantity)
$ 50	2,700 units	$135,000
$ 75	2,200 units	$165,000
$100	1,300 units	$130,000

FIGURE 12.3
Sample Total Revenue Curve

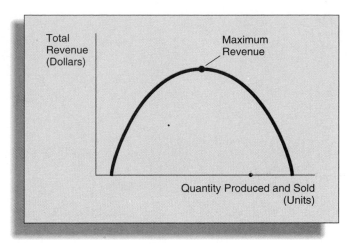

Total revenue refers to the total amount of money received from the sale of all units of a product. To find the total revenue (TR) associated with a given price, the price (P) is multiplied by the number of items sold (Q):

$$TR = P \times Q$$

At some price, represented by the peak of the curve in Figure 12.3, revenue reaches its maximum amount. Assume that a shoe store could sell 1,000 pairs of shoes a week at $5 each, 100 pairs of shoes a week at $75, and 10 pairs of shoes a week at $500. Multiplying quantity by price gives total revenues of $5,000, $7,500, and $5,000, respectively. Of these three pricing choices, $75 would yield the greatest revenues—$2,500 more than if the shoes were priced at either $5 or $500. From this example, you can see why cutting prices does not always generate greater revenues, even when more of the product is sold. This concept is important for marketers to remember when considering price changes.

Average revenue is the average amount of money received from the sale of one unit of a product. Assuming that the product sells at a single price, the average revenue would equal the price of one unit. However, if units are sold at different prices, average revenue (AR) can be determined by dividing total revenue (TR) by the quantity of units sold (Q):

$$AR = TR/Q$$

Marginal revenue (MR) is the change in total revenue (ΔTR) that results from producing and selling additional units of a product (ΔQ):

$$MR = \Delta TR/\Delta Q$$

If a museum that has sold 5,000 membership subscriptions can sell one more for $50, its marginal revenue would be $50 (that is, 50/1). To sell 5 million more subscriptions, the museum would probably have to set a lower price, so marginal revenue for each additional membership would be lower. Thus, the marginal revenue curve slopes downward because to sell more and more of a product, the organization has to offer it at lower and lower prices.

Marginal Analysis

The measurements just described are important for identifying the price at which the organization will earn the greatest profit. A business's **profit** is the positive difference between the total revenues it generates and the total costs it incurs:

Profit = Total Revenues − Total Costs

total revenue
The total amount of money received from the sale of all units of a product.

average revenue
The average amount of money received from the sale of one unit of a product.

marginal revenue
The change in total revenue that results from selling additional units of a product.

profit
The positive difference between total revenues and total costs.

F I G U R E 12.4
*Marginal Analysis
Relationships*

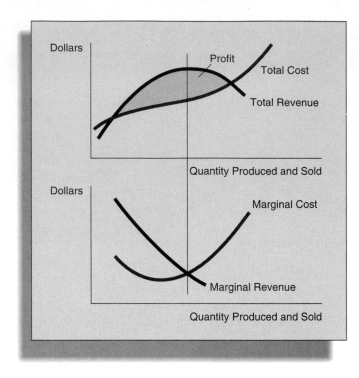

If the organization sells a number of units at the same price, its total revenue equals the number of units sold times the price per unit. For this situation, the profit equation can be stated as follows:

Profit = (Number of Units × Price per Unit) − Total Costs

Suppose an office-cleaning service charged its customers $12 per hour and handled 100 hours of work in one week. If its total costs for that week were $1,000, its profits for the week would be (100 hr. × $12/hr.) − $1,000 = $200.

A basic economic principle is that businesses should seek to maximize profits. Raising the price higher and higher would have this effect if such changes did not affect the amount sold or the expenses incurred. However, the problem is more complex because price does affect the other quantities in the equation. Recall that demand curves slope downward; a lower price means that more units will be sold. Also, the more units sold, the greater the total costs of production and marketing.

At what level of sales (and price) will the organization earn the greatest profit? One way to determine the answer is to use **marginal analysis,** a technique for finding the greatest profits by measuring the economic effect of producing and selling each additional unit of product. To conduct marginal analysis, marketers begin by looking at how total costs and total revenues change at various levels of production and sales.

As shown at the top of Figure 12.4, total costs increase along with an increase in the quantity produced and sold. Costs increase fastest when the quantity is small (because of high start up costs and learning) and when the quantity is very large (because the organization uses more expensive resources, such as personnel working overtime). Total revenue rises to a peak and then falls off, because to sell the largest quantities, the organization would have to charge lower prices. Profits are maximized when total revenue is the farthest above total cost.

The bottom portion of Figure 12.4 shows how this pattern is reflected in marginal analyses. Profits are maximized at the point where marginal cost equals marginal revenue. Thus, if marketers estimate the organization's marginal cost and marginal revenue, they will be able to identify the quantity at which profits will be the

marginal analysis
A technique for finding the greatest profits by measuring the economic effect of producing and selling each additional unit of product.

FIGURE 17.1
The Communication Process

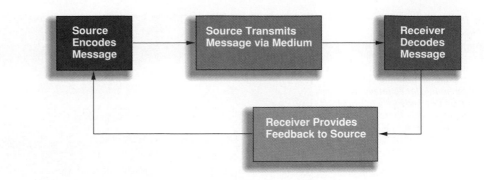

receiver
The person or group for whom the message is intended.

decode
The process of converting the group of symbols to the images or concepts contained in a message.

noise
Physical sounds, misunderstandings, or other distractions that cause a receiver to fail to decode a message properly.

feedback
The receiver's response to a message.

The receiver's response to the message provides **feedback.** In a sense, feedback begins the communication process all over again: The receiver now becomes the sender, and the sender becomes the receiver. A basic type of feedback for marketing communications is a purchase by the receiver. The receiver of marketing communications may also respond in other ways, such as recommending the product, requesting product information, or accepting the image the organization seeks to convey.

The communication process can be illustrated by considering a marketing example. When Universal Pictures was about to release the film, *Independence Day,* it had to communicate with moviegoers to get them to buy tickets. It featured clips from the film as a coming attraction on movie screens, sent clips and actors to TV talk shows, got publicity from movie reviews on TV and in newspapers, and ran TV commercials. The clips shown on movie screens and TV commercials included a voice-over to explain the overall plot and featured loud background music to generate excitement and attention. Given the media it used to transmit its message, Universal reached its target market of moviegoers. Moviegoers received the message loud and clear and made the film a huge box-office success. In sum, a source (Universal pictures) encoded messages (words, pictures, music, action) about its exciting product (the film), transmitted them through various media (movie screens, television, newspapers), which were decoded (received and understood) by receivers (moviegoers), who in turn provided positive feedback (purchases of movie tickets).

All of the stages of communication are important to the marketing effort, and a breakdown in any one of them can cause havoc in the communication between an organization and its market. For instance, marketers encode messages with their choices of words, including product names. In the perfume industry, creators of a new cologne decided to call it Santa Fe, banking on positive associations about the Southwest: its rugged, open country and artsy sophistication. The company hoped that potential customers who received this message would send positive feedback by purchasing the cologne. Such issues apply equally to serving foreign markets. Although many Japanese consumers love anything to do with the American West, they might not be familiar with Santa Fe. "Texas" might have conveyed a clearer message for them.[6]

The AIDA Model

Marketers want receivers of messages to respond by buying the products or brands being offered. However, to get this result, communication must first influence customers in several ways. As shown in Figure 17.2, one way of analyzing communication efforts is to view them as influencing customers' attention, interest, desire, and action.

Marketers need to create communications that break through the clutter of other messages so that the target market will at least attend to them. Messages are most likely to be attended to when they are distinctive and relevant to the audience. Thus, marketers who segment properly and focus on customer value are in the best position to create messages that generate attention.

greatest. By referring to the demand curve for the product, marketers can identify the price at which this quantity will be demanded.

Approaches to Pricing

While marginal analysis is the appropriate way to price products from an economic standpoint, gathering the information needed can be difficult and costly. Further complicating the task, there are more variables than this analysis considers. As a case in point, when Compaq lowered the prices of its computers across the board, many customers traded up and bought more powerful computers rather than purchasing the cheaper models.[15] Apparently value to them was not just a matter of paying the lowest price, but of getting a deal on a more powerful computer. Such shifts in demand are not easily accounted for by marginal analysis.

Given the challenges of using marginal analysis, marketers in practice approach pricing decisions in various ways. The basic approaches are based on cost, competition, and customer value. These approaches are not mutually exclusive, and sound marketing practice requires that the organization consider all three in pricing. In other words, pricing should take into account the amount needed to cover costs and earn a profit, competitors' prices, and customers' perceptions of value. A simplified version of this approach is used by the Vermont grocery store owner who told one of his suppliers' salespeople, "What you charge tells me how low I can go. What my competitor sets prices at is how high I can go. I just pick a place in between, and that's my price."[16]

Pricing Based on Cost

fixed costs
The costs that remain the same over a wide range of quantities produced.

variable costs
Costs that change along with changes in quantity produced.

As a general rule, the price of a product must be high enough to cover the total cost of production and marketing. The total cost includes fixed and variable costs. **Fixed costs** are the costs that remain the same over a wide range of quantities produced. A major fixed cost is the production facility. Only after production increases by a very large amount will an organization build another factory or service facility. **Variable costs** are the costs that change along with changes in quantity produced. For example, materials and labor costs are greater when the organization produces more goods or services.

Failure to cover total cost means the organization will lose money. In an effort to ensure that revenues cover costs, marketers use some form of cost-oriented pricing. These techniques involve determining the cost to produce and market a product, then making sure the selling price is higher.

markup pricing
A pricing approach that adds a percentage to the product's cost in order to arrive at a selling price.

Markup Pricing   To use **markup pricing,** marketers add a percentage to the product's cost in order to arrive at a selling price. There are two basic ways to state the markup percentage:

1. The easiest markup percentage to understand is a markup stated as a *percentage of the cost* to the reseller. If the reseller pays $9 for a compact disc and sells it for $15, the markup of $6 is 66.7 percent of the cost ($6/$9 = .667).

2. Often, however, the markup percentage is stated as the *percentage of the selling price* that is added to the cost to get the selling price. In the case of the compact disc, the markup as a percentage of the selling price is $6/$15 = .40, or 40 percent. Table 12.2 shows some average markup percentages for various products, stated as a percentage of selling price.

A variation of markup pricing is to add on a dollar amount rather than a percentage to arrive at the selling price. For example, a contractor might set a price for a project $10,000 above the expected cost. This variation of markup pricing is called *cost-plus pricing.*

Markup pricing is common among resellers. This approach is simpler and more practical than analyzing the market forces for each of hundreds or thousands of products.

T A B L E 12.2
Typical Markup Percentages

Type of Purchase	Markup Percentage*
Shoes	49%
Women's dresses	47
Men's wear	38
Small appliances	30
Sporting goods	29
Books and magazines	28
Auto accessories	27
Records and tapes	25
Large appliances	15
Tobacco	13
Automobiles	10

*Percent of original retail price.
Source: Gene A. German and Debra J. Perosio, *Operating Results of Mass Retail Stores* (Washington, DC: International Mass Retail Association, 1989–1990), p. 67; Elif Sinanoglu, "Want a Markdown? Lower the Markup," *Money* 25 (February 1996) p.166.

To support the image of its main product line, audio systems for cars and trucks, Monsoon uses its World Wide Web site (http:// www.monsoonpower.com) to offer a "Complete line of Audiowear"–clothing with the Monsoon logo. The pricing strategy of charging one price for sizes M-XL and a greater price for sizes XXL or XXXL reflects the greater cost of producing the largest sizes. Not only does each unit of XXL or XXXL clothing require more raw materials (raising variable costs), but these sizes incur a greater share of fixed costs because a smaller quantity is manufactured.

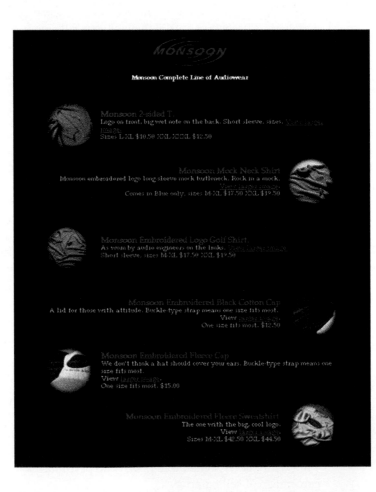

rate-of-return pricing
A pricing approach that involves determining total costs and then adding a desired rate of return to them to determine the selling price.

Rate-of-Return Pricing   A variation of cost-based pricing commonly used by manufacturers is **rate-of-return pricing.** This pricing technique involves determining total costs and then adding a desired rate of return on investment to them to determine the selling price. The marketer may add either a percentage return or a particular dollar amount. For example, return on investment (ROI) is the profit as a percentage of the capital invested in the operation.

F I G U R E   12.5
Breakeven Analysis

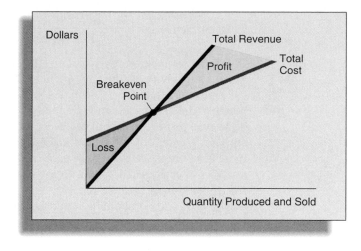

To apply rate-of-return pricing, marketers use a formula such as this:

$$Price = \frac{Total\ Cost + ROI}{Number\ of\ Units}$$

The total cost per unit includes both the variable costs to make each unit (notably, the labor and materials devoted to producing it) and a share of the fixed costs. Suppose a manufacturer produced 10,000 skateboards at a cost of $60,000. The required investment to fund this operation is $450,000, and the company seeks a 25 percent return on its investment. The company could compute the price to charge resellers as follows:

$$Price = \frac{\$60,000 + \$450,000(.25)}{10,000} = \$17.25/Unit$$

Breakeven Analysis   A common technique for identifying profitable prices is **breakeven analysis,** which involves determining the sales volume needed to cover all costs at a specific price. The level of sales at which total revenues equal total costs is called the **breakeven point.** Rhino Records has a breakeven point of just 15,000 copies of an album. It keeps its costs low by focusing on reissues while its big competitors are trying to go platinum with new recordings.[17]

To conduct breakeven analysis, marketers can construct charts such as the one shown in Figure 12.5. *For a given price,* marketers estimate the sales revenues (price × quantity) that would be earned at various quantities. Then the marketer graphs the total costs of producing and marketing various quantity levels. This chart makes some assumptions commonly used to simplify breakeven analysis. First, it assumes that the curve for total revenues will be a straight line; in other words, each unit is sold at the same price. It also assumes that the total cost curve will be a straight line. In other words, the cost to produce each additional unit is the same. The point at which these two lines intersect is the breakeven point. Marketers would want to offer the product at a specific price only if they expect to sell more than the quantity at the breakeven point at that price.

An alternative to using charts is to use the following formula for computing a breakeven point (in units):

$$Breakeven\ Point = \frac{Fixed\ Costs}{Selling\ Price - Variable\ Costs}$$

Thus, in the skateboard example, assume that the total cost of $60,000 to produce 10,000 units included fixed costs of $17,500 and variable costs of $4.25 per unit. At a price of $18.25, the breakeven point would be computed as follows:

breakeven analysis
A technique for determining the sales volume needed to cover all costs at a specific price.

breakeven point
The level of sales at which total revenues equal total costs.

$$\text{Breakeven Point} = \frac{\$17,500}{\$18.25 - \$4.25} = 1,250 \text{ units}$$

If the cost estimate were correct and the organization in fact sold 1,250 units, it would break even, having neither a profit nor a loss.

Once marketers have estimated the breakeven point, it's necessary to forecast whether they could sell enough units to at least break even. They might compare the breakeven points for several prices to see which the organization could likely meet or surpass. The more familiar marketers are with the demand curve for the product, the more accurate this analysis can be. Thus, marketers combine breakeven analysis with analysis of customer demand. In the case of Disneyland Paris, an analyst estimated that the company had not reached breakeven and needed to increase the number of annual visitors by about 8 million—about the populations of London and Paris combined.[18]

Of course, marketers don't want merely to cover costs and break even; they want to make profits. Marketers can incorporate a specific profit objective into breakeven analysis. To do this, they add the desired level of profits to the total fixed costs in the breakeven equation. In the previous example, suppose a $21,000 profit is sought. The equation would be revised as follows:

$$\text{Breakeven Plus Profit} = \frac{\text{Fixed Costs} + \text{Desired Profit}}{\text{Selling Price} - \text{Variable Costs}}$$

$$= \frac{\$17,500 + \$21,000}{\$18.25 - \$4.25} = 2,750 \text{ Units}$$

As this example shows, the organization has to sell 1,500 more skateboards at a price of $18.25 to meet the objective of earning a $21,000 profit. If marketers want to know the level of sales dollars that are needed to break even or to earn a specific profit, they can multiply the breakeven volume by the selling price. In the example above, $22,812.50 (1,250 × $18.25) in sales are needed to just break even; to earn a profit of $21,000, sales of $50,187.50 (2,750 × $18.25) are required.

Advantages and Limitations of Cost-Based Pricing   In general, cost-based pricing is relatively easy to use. This makes it popular among marketers who handle many different products. The emphasis on covering costs also makes it appealing for pricing nonroutine jobs such as construction and the development of military weapons. AutoResearch Laboratories Inc. (ALI) uses a cost-based approach to set prices for its customized testing services. When preparing to bid on a job, ALI conducts a detailed analysis of all the costs it expects to incur. It then adds a profit percentage to the total cost. If the result is higher than competitive prices for services of the same quality, ALI considers adjusting the profit percentage it adds to its costs. However, ALI rarely lowers the percentage below what it considers its base profit margin.[19]

Perhaps the most important limitation of cost-oriented pricing techniques is that they do not consider the effect of price on customer demand. Thus, marketers might find that a price high enough to cover costs and deliver a comfortable profit is so high that buyers turn to competing or substitute products.

Cost-oriented pricing also fails to take into account competitors' prices. To compete profitably, marketers might have to cut costs rather than charge higher prices. However, when marketers offer distinctive products that customers value, they can often charge higher prices.

Pricing Based on Competition

One way to overcome some of the limitations of cost-based pricing is to take competition into account when making price decisions. Marketers must be able to meet or beat competitors' prices or show why their products offer greater value if a higher

Doris Christopher, owner of The Pampered Chef, uses a simple pricing strategy. The Pampered Chef is a direct retailer of classy kitchen utensils. A decade and a half of experience has taught Christopher she can make a profit by charging double what she paid for each item. However, this strategy does not necessarily lead her to the most profitable price.

price is charged. Competitors' prices are especially important to consider under the following conditions:

- There are several competitors with quality products.
- At least some competitors are financially strong.
- Product features are easily copied and products are hard to differentiate.
- Competitors have access to distribution channels.
- Competitors have high levels of marketing knowledge and skills.
- Competitors have similar cost structures.

In the headline of this ad, Hewlett-Packard claims that "Compaq and IBM haven't decided whether to put value pricing ahead of features or vice versa. With HP PCs, you don't have to ask which comes first." Instead, HP claims in the ad's small print it offers "the very best prices on the very best PCs," not just on the "low-end boxes." This competition-based strategy of promising more for less is appropriate for a market like that for personal computers, where competitors are aggressively trying to grab market share.

Marketers may set prices below, at, or above competitors. Pricing below the competition can be an effective way to grab market share when price elasticity is high. Marketers may attract new customers with price cuts, or keep prices the same when competitors raise prices. Pricing below competition can be an effective way to attract price-conscious buyers, particularly when marketers have lower costs than competitors. For example, Campbell's has long dominated the canned soup market because it is the low-cost leader and can prosper even with small margins.

Alternatively, the organization may match competitors' prices and distinguish itself in other ways. Following any price changes made by the industry leaders is typical of an oligopoly (a few suppliers serving the entire market). For example, when one airline lowers fares, the others tend to follow suit.

If customers believe that a marketer offers greater value than competitors, it may be able to charge higher prices. For example, marketers can charge more for products that are higher quality, or more prestigious, convenient, or reliable than competitors' offerings. Klöber GmbH, a German manufacturer of office furniture, offers a line of deluxe office chairs under the brand Cronos for $1,100 to $3,000. About 10,000 customers have paid these prices, which are 10 times that of a basic chair. They value a Cronos chair's elegant design and a mechanism in the seat that adjusts to the user's weight and tilt, providing sound ergonomics even when the user shifts body position.[20] To price above competition, marketers must know which components of the value equation are critical to customers.

A final type of pricing relative to competition is *sealed-bid pricing,* in which a buyer asks sellers to state a price for a particular project. For relatively complex, specialized products, each bid also includes information about the seller's capabilities and the way it will carry out the work. The buyer usually selects the seller making the lowest bid. However, there is often room for the seller to demonstrate how it can create value in other ways. Competitive bidding is common for government projects and for construction work. For example, several companies bid on developing a new space shuttle system. The bid was won by Lockheed.

Advantages and Limitations of Competition-Based Pricing   Taking competitors' prices into account is a practical and essential aspect of pricing strategy in most cases. When customers can choose from more than one marketer, they have the opportunity to choose an alternative with the highest value. Marketers must consider how to offer superior value to customers and price below, above, or at competition to enhance it.

Competition-based pricing has limitations, however. Since it does not include cost information, it leaves open the question of whether a profit can be generated at a given price. If a company's costs are higher than competitors', it may not be able to price at or below competition and survive. In addition, competition-based pricing does not directly explore customer value. For example, if customers use price as an indicator of quality, they may avoid products priced below competition.

Pricing Based on Customer Value

No matter what the organization's costs, no matter what competitors are charging, potential buyers may not purchase the product if they don't think they are getting their money's worth. Therefore, pricing decisions should take into account customer perceptions of the value of an exchange. This means that marketing research is needed to learn about customer perceptions of value and price (see "Marketing Movers & Shakers: The New Bike Manufacturers").

Marketers should try to find out what customers expect to pay for a product and what price range they consider acceptable. The answers are sometimes enlightening. When Michael D. Mondello and a colleague were planning a mortgage evaluation service, they described the idea to recent homebuyers and asked them what they would expect to pay for such a service. Respondents indicated they were willing to pay two or three times more than the planned fee.[21]

When investigating customer perceptions about price, an important piece of information is the customer's **reference price.** This is "the price that buyers use to compare the offered price of a product or service."[22] The idea is that customers have a price or price range in mind about what something should cost. Buyers tend to think a price is a good value if it is less than their reference price. Baker's, an Omaha, Nebraska, supermarket chain, charges $.99 to $1.99 for one-day video rentals. The chain set these prices because they generate a profit and may look irresistible to customers who use the price of a trip to a movie theater (perhaps $6.50 per person) as a reference price.[23]

reference price
The price that buyers use to compare the offered price of a product or service.

The New Bike Manufacturers

You can still buy a ten-speed road bike. You can probably even buy a three-speed, if you look hard enough. But you'll be making both of these purchases at sports swaps or yard sales. Bike design and manufacturing have moved way past these models to the new basic bike—the mountain bike—and beyond, to high-performance, handmade models. Mountain bikes, which were once thought to be a fad, now account for 65 percent of the 12.5 million bicycles sold in one year, according to the National Bicycle Dealers Association. "It's replaced the road bike as the bike for the masses," says Steve Frothingham, executive editor at *Bicycle Retailer and Industry News.*

What does the new trend have to do with price? It means that there is an opportunity for small, innovative bike design and manufacturing firms to find a niche in the market—at the high end of the price range. Several have managed to do this successfully. Merlin Metalworks makes titanium bike frames, which are lighter and better shock absorbers than traditional steel frames. Merlin prices its frames at $1,500 to $5,000 (that's without pedals, wheels, gears, and so forth). "We build the best bike imaginable and see if people want to buy it. Our overall attention to detail in terms of how a bike feels while someone is riding it sets us apart," notes Merlin's president, Guy Parsons.

Independent Fabrication, an employee-owned company, is another example. The manufacturer hand-builds chromoly-steel frames that, once fully equipped, sell for about $1,800. The company only sells about 600 per year in the United States and abroad. "It's one of the smallest niches in the market . . . but we believe there are people out there who desire a frame built by hand, as opposed to those built off a production line," explains Steven Elmes, vice president of sales and marketing.

Finally, there's Rhygin Racing Cycles, which makes hand-crafted steel and aluminum frame high-performance mountain bikes. The company has three employees, ships completed bikes directly to customers and sells frames through 18 dealers. The frames run from $2,300 to $2,500. "What I like about not being a big company is that we can do [bicycles] that fit people's needs," says Christian Jones.

All three of these companies share some common characteristics with regard to price. First, their bikes are

targeted for riders who want top materials and high performance. Second, they are small companies that sell a limited number of frames. Third, their bikes are hand-built. All of these factors translate to a high cost of manufacture and higher prices than the average mass-produced bike, which ranges from about $200 to $500. These companies illustrate that a high price is not necessarily a deterrent to buyers. Instead, the high price allows the companies to create value for customers in other ways—through attention to detail in manufacturing and design, expensive materials, and hand-construction. Merlin Metalworks, Independent Fabrication, and Rhygin Racing Cycles have managed to ride on top of the changing bicycle market.

Source: Kathy McCabe, "Olympic Peddling," *The Boston Globe,* June 4, 1996, pp. 37, 42. Reprinted courtesy of *The Boston Globe.*

Explore more at www.merlinbike.com, www.wheelworks.com/if, and www.rhygin.com

---

demand-backward pricing
A pricing approach that involves setting a price by starting with the estimated price consumers will pay and working backwards with retail and wholesale margins.

Manufacturers of consumer goods take customer perceptions into account when they use **demand-backward pricing.** This pricing strategy involves "setting a price by starting with the estimated price consumers will pay and working backwards with retail and wholesale margins."[24] Marketers start with the list price consumers will be likely to pay, say, 50 cents for a candy bar or $10 for a toy. Then the markups that the resellers of these products customarily take are subtracted. The result is the manufacturer's selling price, if it is still profitable enough. Compaq has used this approach to price its computers.[25]

Marketers can carry this approach further to aid in planning. Subtracting marketing expenses and profit from the manufacturer's selling price yields the amount the manufacturer can afford to spend on production. If production costs more than this amount, the organization will need to find ways to cut costs. At Compaq, managers of the materials, engineering, manufacturing, and marketing departments must allocate the funds that remain after subtracting the dealer's markup and Compaq's profit margin from the list price. The company's pricing strategy thus calls for a cross-functional team approach to develop pricing strategy.

Value Pricing   Customers purchase on the basis of value, that is, the difference between perceived benefits and perceived costs of an exchange. As emphasized in this text, this relationship is shown in the equation:

Value = Perceived Benefits − Perceived Costs

From this equation, you can see that value is greater when customers perceive greater benefits or lower costs than competitive or substitute products or both. To respond to the interest in value, marketers may engage in **value pricing.** This approach involves setting prices so that the exchange value is higher than the value of competing exchanges. Because many components enter into the value equation, setting a low price is only one possible means of value pricing. If other costs are relatively low or the perceived benefits relatively high, a price may be higher than that of competitors. The key is to analyze all relevant benefits and costs.

Quality inspectors at J. C. Penney compared the store's girls' turtlenecks with similar sweaters from Lands' End, The Gap, and L. L. Bean and found Penney's sweaters were inferior. Designers at Penney's responded by setting more stringent specifications for fabric, fit, and construction. Then the store priced the improved turtlenecks 38 percent below the ones sold at The Gap. As a result, sales tripled. Similar tactics throughout the store caused its sales growth to outstrip that of competitors at the time.[26]

value pricing
A pricing approach that involves setting prices so that the exchange value is higher than the value of competing exchanges.

A common approach to value pricing is the one promoted by Target in this ad: offering a reliably good product at a relatively low price. This strategy is reflected in Target's emphasis on both beauty (the photo) and price (shown prominently at the center of the ad). The theme is repeated in Target's slogan at the bottom of the ad, "Expect More. Pay Less."

$24.99

Stop and smell the bargains.

These delightful floral-patterned table linens and accessories

are a great way to celebrate spring. The 52x70" tablecloth

shown is just $24.99. The bargains are in full bloom at Target.

⊙ **TARGET**
EXPECT MORE. PAY LESS.

As noted, higher-priced products are sometimes perceived as having higher quality and paying a higher price may benefit customers in feelings of prestige and admiration. Thus, high-priced products may offer superior value to customers in some cases, particularly for public products like cars, clothing, and jewelry.

Advantages and Limitations of Value Pricing   Focusing on customer value can enable an organization to give customers what they want, perhaps even at a comfortable markup. Value pricing is especially advantageous if the organization can find a match between what it does well and what a market segment values. Thus, if the organization excels at creating pleasurable exchanges and an image of prestige, it can set high prices yet create value for a market segment that wants these things. Similarly, an organization that can deliver a good basic product at a low price can create value for price-conscious customers.

As with the other approaches, value-based pricing does not work well in a vacuum. Marketers must be aware of their costs; they cannot be profitable delivering customer value at an unprofitable price. Likewise, even if marketers set prices that customers consider a good value, they may go elsewhere if competitors offer an even better deal in terms of the total value equation. In sum, marketers need to consider all three elements—their costs and profit objectives, competitive pricing strategies, and customer value—when making pricing decisions.

Legal and Ethical Issues in Pricing

Besides considering their profits and costs, competitors, and customers, marketers must set prices within legal and ethical constraints. The government has created a number of laws and regulations that limit pricing activities. In addition, pricing involves ethical considerations that concern marketers.

Government Regulation of Pricing

To promote fair trade, federal and state governments impose limitations on pricing decisions. As summarized in Table 12.3, the U.S. government has limited price fixing, deceptive pricing, price discrimination, and dumping. State laws and the laws of other countries also constrain pricing in different ways. Therefore, marketers should consult lawyers familiar with regulation of prices in the states and countries where they seek exchanges.

price fixing
Illegal agreements among competitors to set the price of a product.

Price Fixing   Marketers may not legally make agreements about the price of products with competitors. Such practices are known as **price fixing.**

Some companies previously have used a form of price fixing known as "resale price maintenance." This involves forming agreements with retailers under which they must sell the manufacturer's products at set prices. Manufacturers have argued that resale price maintenance enables them to maintain a price that supports the product's positioning strategy. However, it also limits the ability of retailers to compete

T A B L E   12.3
Laws Limiting Pricing Practices

Law	Pricing Practices
Sherman Antitrust Act	Price fixing
Consumer Goods Pricing Act	Resale price maintenance
Federal Trade Commission Act	Deceptive pricing practices
Robinson-Patman Act	Price discrimination that lessens or damages competition; discrimination in the use of promotional pricing
Laws of most countries	Dumping

on the basis of price. For that reason, resale price maintenance was declared illegal under the Consumer Goods Pricing Act.

Outside the United States, the legal picture may be different. For instance, some European countries have laws requiring retailers to sell books at the price set by the publisher. The laws are intended to protect the profits of publishers so that they can afford to invest in specialized literature that might not generate big sales. Countries that protect fixed book prices include France, Norway, and Germany; others, including Britain and Sweden, have no such limits. Some countries have international agreements. Germany and Austria require that each country's booksellers follow the prices set by publishers in the other.[27] Keeping track of the various laws clearly poses a challenge for publishers and booksellers interested in serving European markets.

Deceptive Pricing   The Federal Trade Commission Act prohibits deceptive pricing practices. **Deceptive pricing** involves misleading customers about the relative goodness of an asking price. An example would be to mark goods with an extremely high price, then announce a "price reduction" and sell the product at the normal price. Likewise, a retailer may not advertise that it sells products at less than the "manufacturer's suggested retail price" unless others are actually charging that price.

Price Discrimination   Other restrictions have to do with charging different prices to buyers that do not reflect cost differences to the seller. Such a practice is called **price discrimination** (see "You Decide: Are Women Being Taken to the Cleaners?"). Price discrimination that lessens or damages competition is prohibited by the Robinson-Patman Act.

This prohibition applies only to goods, not services, and covers products of the same grade and quality. For example, a seller that uses promotional pricing, such as special discounts, free goods, or merchandising service, must offer them to all customers on equal terms in proportion to the size of their purchases.

Predatory Pricing   Setting prices at very low levels in order to hurt competitors is called **predatory pricing.** When the intent of predatory pricing is to drive competitors out of business, it is illegal. Predatory pricing is usually a short-term strategy; prices are then raised when competitors are bought out or go out of business.

deceptive pricing
An illegal pricing tactic that involves misleading customers about the relative goodness of an asking price.

price discrimination
The practice of charging different prices to buyers that do not reflect cost differences to the seller.

predatory pricing
A pricing approach that involves setting very low prices in order to hurt competitors.

Consumers who don't perceive a cost difference to the seller often object to price differences as being discriminatory. To avoid such suspicion of unethical pricing, a growing number of dry-cleaning stores, tailoring shops, and hair salons have adopted unisex pricing. It does cost more to clean women's blouses that are smaller than a men's size 14 or 14-1/2 because they are too small for the dry-cleaning equipment. However, as Washington, D.C., shop owner Brian Grozbean (photo) pointed out, "Extra-large shirts over men's size 18-1/2 don't fit the pressing machines either, but people are afraid to tell a big man to pay more. . . . We decided [unisex] pricing would net us more money in the long run," by keeping customers happy.

Are Women Being Taken to the Cleaners?

If you are a woman, does your haircut cost more than your boyfriend's or husband's, at the same place? When you pick up the dry cleaning, have you been charged more for your shirts than he has? Do department stores offer him free alterations, while you have to pay? If so, you may be subject to price discrimination. Price discrimination—charging different prices to different customers without a cost difference for the seller—is illegal.

Price discrimination by gender seems to be particularly pervasive in the dry cleaning business. In California, for instance, a woman might pay $4 to have a blouse cleaned, whereas a man would pay $1.99 for a laundered shirt. Thus, California became the first state in the country to pass the Gender Tax Repeal Act, making it illegal for any business (not just dry cleaners) to charge different prices to men and women for the same services, if the cost of providing the service to each is the same. Breaking the law carries a $1,000 fine. But enforcing price discrimination laws isn't always easy; in fact, some laws don't even have a specific statute for enforcement. Instead, they just open the door for lawsuits. "Women are going to have to fight back through lawsuits—block by block, dry cleaner by dry cleaner," observes women's rights attorney Gloria Allred. Indeed, one California dry-cleaning customer observed, "I haven't noticed a change."

In Massachusetts, the attorney general's office reports that, although there is not a state law in place, actions like injunctions against specific establishments have had some success. "We really embarked on an educational campaign," says Barbara Anthony, chief of the attorney general's public protection bureau, speaking about the state's strategy. The Massachusetts Board of Cosmetology now has regulations against price discrimination in haircuts.

Even so, Frances Cerra Whittelsey, author of *Women Pay More,* argues that price differences persist nationwide because of a "broad societal bias" in favor of men. Whittlesey has also established a World Wide Web site (http://www.sis.org) that includes surveys for women to inform her about price discrimination violations. If you are a woman, have you been subject to price discrimination (that you are aware of) due to your gender—at the dry cleaners, hair salon, car mechanic, and so forth? If you are a man, have you been aware of such price discrimination? Do you think there should be more widespread legislation against price discrimination? Why or why not?

Source: Jane Meredith Adams, "Getting Taken to the Cleaners," *The Boston Globe,* April 5, 1996, p. 57. Reprinted courtesy of *The Boston Globe.*

Explore more at www.sis.org

---

dumping
The practice of pricing a product below its costs or below the going rate in a market.

Dumping A related pricing tactic is **dumping,** the practice of pricing a product below its costs or below the going price in the market. A foreign company might use dumping to gain market share in a different country, thereby taking business and jobs away from domestic manufacturers. Imports are subject to antidumping laws in the United States and most other countries. In fact, the General Agreement on Tariffs and Trade preserves the right of member nations to act on complaints of dumping.

In some cases, forbidding dumping results in customers paying higher prices. The U.S. International Trade Commission (ITC) found that steel imports from 16 countries were priced unfairly. As a result, steel from some countries was subject to stiff import duties. The higher costs resulting from this decision could cause U.S. consumers to pay as much as $1 billion in higher prices.[28]

In some cases, domestic companies respond to dumping by developing superior alternatives. Around the time Japanese firms were being accused of dumping microchips in the United States, Intel and other U.S. companies began developing more sophisticated "design-rich" chips to meet special needs. This gave U.S. firms the lead in the high-profit end of the market for microchips.[29] Likewise, Motorola once faced a plunge in the price of Japanese pagers to a level so low that Motorola's managers were convinced their foreign competitors were dumping. Motorola responded by meeting its competitors' prices and by working with its employees and suppliers to aggressively cut costs. Rather than cutting costs by sacrificing quality, Motorola discovered it could save money by eliminating defects.[30]

Ethics of Pricing

The laws just described ban a number of pricing tactics. For the most part, these tactics are illegal in the United States. However, some pricing tactics are legal but of dubious ethical value.

Prices that confuse customers may be unethical. For example, some prices, such as air fares, have such a complex structure that they can be overwhelming. If potential customers can't figure out how to get a lower price, they may spend more than they have to. Pricing structures may also encourage customers to buy features they don't really need. For instance, car rental companies used to add on a charge for insurance, even though most renters would already be covered by insurance on their own cars.

Customers may interpret claims of low prices more literally than they may be intended. Thus, Wal-Mart once used the slogan "Always the low price. Always." Concern that customers might take this statement literally as a legally binding promise that Wal-Mart would have the lowest price on every item in the store helped to motivate management to tone down the wording. Wal-Mart now says, "Always low prices. Always."[31]

Sometimes marketers set a high price as an indicator of quality and exclusivity. But what if the product isn't really superior to those of competitors? Is the high price misleading? Are customers getting anything extra for the greater expense? If not, perhaps customers are being cheated.

At the other extreme, some stores advertise very low prices for certain products in order to attract customers to the store. Then the store's salespeople tell the customers about the limitations of the low-priced products and steer them to higher-priced models or brands. The salespeople may even report that the lower-priced models are out of stock. This promotion and pricing practice is called **bait and switch.** Bait-and-switch tactics are illegal as well as unethical.

On a more positive note, there are many ways to use pricing as an effective marketing tool. Pricing may even be an extension of social responsibility. After Hurricane Andrew devastated South Florida, Home Depot stores refused to raise prices, even though some suppliers reacted to the intense demand for building materials by jacking up prices as much as 40 percent. By refusing to take advantage of their customers' plight, Home Depot was practicing relationship marketing—focusing on building long-term relationships with customers rather than simply the profit to be derived from individual transactions. Observed Kerry Herndon, a flower grower in Homestead, Florida, "If they had spent $50 million on advertising, they couldn't have bought the good will they got" by holding the line on prices.[32]

bait and switch
An illegal tactic by which customers are attracted to a store by an advertised low-priced product that is then reported to be out-of-stock or disparaged in order to sell a more expensive product.

Summary

Price plays two major roles in the marketing mix. It influences whether purchases will be made and, if so, how much of the product customers will purchase. It also influences whether marketing products will be sufficiently profitable. Of course, price should be consistent with other elements of the marketing mix.

Marketers try to find out the demand for products at various prices. The demand curve illustrates the relationship between price and quantity demanded. Marketers try to estimate demand based on demographic and psychological factors that affect price elasticity and total demand. The demand curve also helps marketers estimate the revenue a product is likely to generate, including total revenue, average revenue, and marginal revenue. Estimates of revenues and costs help marketers determine potential profits; profits are greatest when total revenue exceeds total cost by the largest amount. This occurs when marginal cost equals marginal revenue.

Pricing can be based on cost, competition, or customer value, but all three should be considered. Pricing based on cost includes markup pricing and rate-of-return pricing. Breakeven analysis is a cost-oriented approach which determines the breakeven point, where total revenue just equals total costs. Marketers may price below the competition to appeal to price-conscious buyers. They may also price at or above competition and compete on other factors. Finally, pricing based on customer value involves learning as much about customers as possible in order to set a price that represents what customers think the product is worth. To do this, marketers can use demand-backward pricing or value pricing.

Of the legal and ethical issues that surround pricing, many are strictly regulated by the government: the Sherman Antitrust Act and Consumer Goods Pricing Act were passed to curtail price fixing, the Federal Trade Commission Act forbids deceptive pricing, and the Robinson-Patman Act prohibits price discrimination. Other practices that may be illegal are predatory pricing and dumping, both of which involve setting prices very low to drive out competitors. In addition, pricing strategies designed to trick buyers—for example, prices that are overly complex, promoted in misleading ways, or part of bait-and-switch tactics—are considered unethical. In contrast, marketers that focus on customers' needs and wants in setting prices can improve value and build long-term relationships.

Key Terms and Concepts

price (p. 310)
demand curve (p. 310)
price elasticity (p. 313)
total revenue (p. 315)
average revenue (p. 315)
marginal revenue (p. 315)
profit (p. 315)
marginal analysis (p. 316)

fixed costs (p. 317)
variable costs (p. 317)
markup pricing (p. 317)
rate-of-return pricing (p. 318)
breakeven analysis (p. 319)
breakeven point (p. 319)
reference price (p. 322)
demand-backward pricing (p. 323)

value pricing (p. 324)
price fixing (p. 325)
deceptive pricing (p. 326)
price discrimination (p. 326)
predatory pricing (p. 326)
dumping (p. 327)
bait and switch (p. 328)

Review and Discussion Questions

1. What is the role of price in the marketing mix?
2. According to the general pattern of demand curves, would demand be relatively high or low for the following products?
    a. Diamond earrings that cost $2,000
    b. Single-serve nonfat yogurt with a price recently cut by 5 percent
    c. Cowboy boots that cost $75, in a region where there is a surge of interest in country music and dancing
    d. A guided tour of several national parks, after an effective advertising campaign
    e. Office furniture, six months after several new competitors have entered the market
3. Imagine you are a marketer responsible for pricing an organic deterrent to garden pests (insects or rodents).
    a. What demographic and psychological factors might you consider in estimating demand for your product?
    b. How would you expand your analysis if you were targeting Britain and Canada as well as the United States?
4. For each of the following examples, compute the price elasticity and indicate whether demand for the product is elastic or inelastic.
    a. Dr. Koo is a family physician in rural West Virginia. When his insurance costs went up, he raised his basic charge for an office visit from $20 to $25. The number of patients who came for office visits in a month declined from 200 to 180.
    b. When ABC Supermarkets marked one-pound bags of M&Ms candies down to $1.50 from $2.50, sales rose by 65 percent.
5. An office-supply catalog lists cork bulletin boards with oak frames for $60 each. Last year it sold 480 of these.
    a. What was the retailer's total revenue from the bulletin boards?
    b. What was the average revenue?

    c. What was the marginal revenue at 450 bulletin boards?
6. How do marketers determine a price based on cost?
7. As a consumer, do you think that markup pricing creates value? Why or why not?
8. Which basis for pricing (cost, competition, or customer value) would you use for the pest-control product in question 3? Explain your choice. (Remember that you can use a combination of approaches if you think that works best.)
9. A hardware store buys padlocks for $4 each and marks them up by 25 percent of cost.
    a. What is the selling price for the padlocks?
    b. What is the percentage markup based on selling price?
10. A clinic provides the immunizations required for Americans who want to travel abroad. It calculates that its total cost to provide this service to 1,000 patients is $9,000, including $4,000 in fixed costs and average variable costs of $5 per patient.
    a. At a price of $20 per patient, what would the clinic's breakeven point be?
    b. Assume the clinic wants to earn a $10,000 profit on this service. Compute a breakeven plus profit point.
11. Name and describe briefly the four basic approaches to setting prices relative to the competition.
12. How does determining customers' reference price for a product help marketers to price based on customer value?
13. What are the advantages and limitations of value pricing?
14. What is price fixing? Are there global laws prohibiting the practice?
15. How might an advertisement for a "storewide sale" be misinterpreted by consumers? How might an advertisement like this be considered unethical?

Chapter Project   Price a Product to Create Value

There are several approaches to pricing products. For your project, you should combine them to offer the appropriate price to make profits and offer customer value.

Choose the service that you developed and targeted for the project in Chapter 11 or some other potential new product that interests you. Estimate the costs of providing the product or service. Study competitive prices. Does your product have many competitors? Are they financially strong and have a lot of marketing savvy? Is it difficult to create distinctive differences between your product and your competitors'? If your product does not yet have competition, be assured that it will eventually if it is successful.

After studying the competition, study your potential buyers. What psychological factors will contribute to their decision to buy your product (review the section in the chapter on "psychological factors")? How does your product stack up against the competition with regard to these factors? What is your customers' reference price? At what price can you give customers the greatest value? Use this combination of approaches to set your price. Finally, estimate revenue and profits and explain your reasoning in writing.

Chapter Case   Fixed-Price Shopping at Used-Car Superstores

Thomas Eggleston is the president of a new kind of store. The store is Driver's Mart, a chain of 10 superstores backed by nine of the country's largest and most powerful automobile dealerships. It's a new approach to car shopping—and pricing.

At Driver's Mart and other stores like it, salaried (not commissioned) sales staff will show you "nearly new" and "off-lease" cars at fixed prices. That means you don't have to negotiate the price, trying to outwit the salesperson, trying to get the best deal you can. Some shoppers might say this takes the fun out of car shopping, but Driver's Mart is betting that most will prefer the new method.

Driver's Mart isn't the only used-car superstore on the block. H. Wayne Huizenga, founder of the Blockbuster video group, is opening a similar chain, called AutoNation USA, based in Ft. Lauderdale, Florida. And there's CarMax, a division of Circuit City stores of Richmond, Virginia. CarMax sales reached $280 million in one year with just four stores open in several southern states. The division planned to open 50 more stores nationwide. "Our target is to clearly be the market share leader everywhere we operate," says Austin Ligon, CarMax chief executive.

Why the sudden switch to this new type of pricing and shopping for cars? American drivers have created an increased demand for used cars. Since the average new American car costs around $20,000, car shoppers are looking for lower prices and better value. In one survey, they revealed that they would rather buy a used car, with more features, for less money, than fork over the money for a new car that depreciates so quickly. Dealers also recognize where their profits lie. Believe it or not, many make no more than $100 profit on a new car; but they can make $300 to $500 on a used car.

New car makers have even joined up with superstores. Chrysler Corp. awarded a new-car franchise to the CarMax showroom in Norcross, Georgia. Chrysler president Robert Lutz takes a hard line in defending the company's action. "[This] is a wake-up call for dealers," he says. But Justin Todd, a Chrysler dealer in Wyoming complains, "We feel betrayed."

Many of today's used cars represent good value. They have low mileage (around 40,000), a low price, extended warranties, even money-back guarantees. The superstore showrooms also have a greater selection of brands and models to choose from than traditional dealers do.

The new pricing strategy is something of a revolution in a business that hasn't changed much during its first 100 years of operation. Jay Ferron of Coopers & Lybrand predicts, "The reality is, when the dealers change, they'll change the manufacturers." So if haggling is your style, you'll have to go somewhere else to buy your next car.

Questions

1. Do you think that the new approach to pricing used cars represents greater value for customers? Why or why not?

2. Using the questions listed in the text, which psychological factors do you think will be important for marketers to consider as they develop their auto superstores?

3. What aspects of the competitive environment must marketers for auto superstores keep in mind?

Sources: Paul A. Eisenstein, "Cruising the Auto Mega Mart," *World Traveler*, May 1996, pp. 60–62; Jesse Birnbaum, "No Need to Kick the Tire," *Time*, February 19, 1996, p. 50.

Explore more at www.drusmart.com

Chapter Thirteen

Pricing Goods and Services

CHAPTER OUTLINE

Pricing Objectives
  Segmentation and Positioning Objectives
  Sales and Profit Objectives
  Competitive Objectives
  Survival Objectives
  Social Responsibility Objectives
Pricing Strategies
  The Pricing Process
  Pricing New Products
  Pricing Existing Products
  Pricing Product Lines
Adjusting Prices
  Discounting
  Psychological Pricing
  Geographic Pricing
  Strategies for Global Marketers
Evaluation and Control of Pricing
  Competitor Responses
  Customer Responses
  Controlling the Price Level
Summary

LEARNING OBJECTIVES

After completing this chapter, you should be able to:

1. Summarize the major categories of pricing objectives.
2. Identify the steps in the pricing process.
3. Describe pricing strategies for new and existing products and for product lines.
4. Outline the basic methods of discounting.
5. Explain how marketers use psychological pricing.
6. Define techniques for adjusting prices to reflect cost differences of serving buyers in different locations.
7. Discuss how marketers adjust prices to serve international markets.
8. Explain how marketers evaluate and control pricing strategy.

Cereal Wars: Post, Kellogg's, and General Mills

The announcement probably affected more households than any other sensational headline could: Post, the nation's third-largest cereal maker (a subsidiary of Philip Morris Cos.), was slashing its cereal prices by an average of 20 percent. Not just some prices on some cereals for a limited time; all prices, on its entire line of Post and Nabisco cereals, indefinitely. "It's an important strategic move for the company," said Burt Flickinger, director of Management Horizons, a division of Price Waterhouse. "It's also a gutsy move, given that the price of raw materials will probably be increasing in the upcoming crop year."

Perhaps the move was gutsy. But marketers saw it as necessary. Consumers were not only reluctant, but downright outraged at cereal prices, which had crept up to $5 a box in some cases. They weren't buying. "Consumers say they don't want to pay $5 for a box of flakes," noted Chris Jakubik, equity analyst for SBC Warburg Inc. in New York. "That's the thrust of it." Jakubik also pointed out that profit margins for cereal had been upwards of 20 percent. Although for decades, cereals had been marketed as a food that delivered value—good nutrition for very little money (about 25 cents per serving)—consumers decided they had had enough. "There are not many foods you get for 25 cents a serving, including the price of milk," argued one industry spokesman. "With a large family, there can't be a larger value." But consumers disagreed. Sales fell.

So Post reduced its prices. About two months later, Kellogg's followed suit, with the first major price cut in its 90-year history. Frosted Flakes, Froot Loops, Raisin Bran, and Smacks were reduced by 19 to 28 percent, depending on the brand. General Mills, instead of reducing prices at the same time, pointed to its own, previous price reductions. "Philip Morris's and Kellogg's recent decision to follow our lead should make the entire cereal category an even more attractive value for consumers," read the company's official statement. Quaker ducked the issue altogether because its cereals are distinctive enough that they don't compete directly with the mainstream brands offered by Kellogg's, Post, and General Mills.

Would the price reduction actually be passed on to consumers?, asked skeptics. Marketers for the cereal manufacturers answered with an emphatic yes. "The actual cost savings to consumers is going to be between 70 cents and 80 cents a box," predicted Chris Ahearn, corporate communications manager for Food Lion in Salisbury, North Carolina. "We would expect to see increases in volume of cereal as a result of the decreased prices." Thomas Knowlton, executive vice president of Kellogg also noted that "We've protected the profits for each box a retailer sells. If it's a $4 box and the retailer makes 75 cents, and if it goes to $3 a box, it will still stay 75 cents for the retailer." This way, retailers would be encouraged to pass the entire savings on to consumers.

A price war like this is not without its casualties. Employees at some subsidiaries were laid off almost immediately in order to cut costs. Investors were sure to back off, causing stock prices to fall. But many experts believed that the price adjustment was long overdue. "Kellogg calls this a victory for the consumer," said Terry Bivens of Donald & Co. Securities in New York. "It tells me they priced cereal too high over the years, and the chickens are coming home to roost."

As you read this chapter on pricing goods and services, consider how important pricing is in creating value for consumers. Consider also how consumer response to the price of an item can influence any future adjustments to the price that marketers may make. Finally, think about how competition affects price, and how a price war within an industry may affect the survival of its companies.

Sources: Bob Bauer, "Post Reduces Cereal Prices, Changes Couponing Strategy," *Supermarket News,* April 22, 1996, pp. 1, 126; Casey Bukro, "Kellogg Serves up Price Cuts," *Chicago Tribune,* June 11, 1996, sec. 3, pp. 1, 3.

Explore more by searching "Cereal Price Wars" on the Web.

PLACEMENT: DISTRIBUTING GOODS AND SERVICES

FIVE

Winning in tomorrow's global markets isn't going to be a matter of scoring points but of creating value with customers, clients, suppliers, and colleagues in innovative ways.
Michael Schrage, "Manager's Journal: Notes on Collaboration," *The Wall Street Journal,*
June 19, 1995, p. A10

CHAPTER 14
Managing Distribution Channels

CHAPTER 15
Wholesaling and Physical Distribution

CHAPTER 16
Retailing

Explore the Career Profiles on the Churchill and Peter Homepage
at www.irwin.com/marketing/value.

Chapter Fifteen

Wholesaling and Physical Distribution

CHAPTER OUTLINE

The Role of Wholesaling in Distribution

Major Types of Wholesalers

  Merchant Wholesalers

  Agents and Brokers

Marketing Strategies for Wholesalers

  Strategies to Attract Producers

  Strategies to Attract Retailers

Trends in Wholesaling

Physical Distribution

  The Physical Distribution Process

  Managing Physical Distribution

  Trends in Physical Distribution

Summary

LEARNING OBJECTIVES

After completing this chapter, you should be able to:

1. Describe the role of wholesaling in distribution.
2. Define basic categories of wholesalers.
3. Describe marketing strategies used by wholesalers.
4. Discuss trends in wholesaling.
5. Identify the tasks in the physical distribution process.
6. Explain how marketers evaluate and control the physical distribution process.
7. Summarize trends in physical distribution.

Creating Customer Value

Gotcha Covered Wholesale

In the early hours of each Friday morning, Courtney Young and his father Dick hop into the cab of their refrigerated truck and drive the six hours from Las Vegas to their warehouse in Capinteria, California. On Saturday morning, they begin to visit the 50 or so flower growers who supply them with fresh-cut flowers. They fill the truck with their fragile, fragrant cargo between Saturday and Monday morning, then head back to Las Vegas where florists are waiting for the flowers to sell to consumers.

The Youngs, owners of Gotcha Covered Wholesale, are wholesalers—they link products (in this case, fresh flowers) to retailers (florists). Ultimately, of course, the flowers will go to consumers for weddings, anniversaries, birthdays, and other occasions. In order to create value for their customers, the Youngs must be able to keep the flowers fresh, which means they must be able to transport their flowers rapidly. They also must be able to deliver the types of seasonal flowers that florists need in order to satisfy consumers. Technology helps them do this.

With a laptop Compaq computer, Courtney Young enters the flower growers' invoices into the system while his father drives the truck across the Nevada desert. The truck also is equipped with a telephone, so customers can call the Youngs and order more flowers while they are on the road. Courtney can enter a customer request into the computer and determine immediately if he can fill it from this week's inventory. Once the truck gets to Las Vegas, retail florists come aboard to choose the flowers they want. Young punches the type and number of flowers bought by each customer into the computer and immediately comes up with a price and an invoice. The system also maintains a database of past purchases, so all florists know what they have bought during the month, or even the year. Young creates further value for his customers by being able to tell them exactly what they purchased previously during heavy ordering times—such as Valentine's Day or Mother's Day. This helps customers make better ordering decisions. "We just call up the order on the computer and print out last year's invoice," boasts Young. "That impresses the hell out of some of our customers."

Gotcha Covered Wholesale illustrates how a small business can create value for customers by linking them with the products they need. As you read this chapter on wholesaling and physical distribution, think about how important these aspects of distribution are.

Source: Courtney Young, "Coming Up Roses," *Inc. Technology*, November 14, 1995, p. 105. Adapted with permission, *Inc.* magazine, November 14, 1995. Copyright 1995 by Goldhirsh Group, Inc., 38 Commercial Wharf, Boston, MA 02110.

Explore more by searching "Gotcha Covered Wholesale" on the Web.

Chapter Overview

Many producers rely on wholesalers and retailers to get their products to consumers and organizational buyers. They must decide not only whether to use these intermediaries, but also which specific types and specific companies to use. Furthermore, the wholesalers and retailers themselves must devise marketing strategies.

The specifics of these decisions vary somewhat depending on whether the intermediaries involved are wholesalers or retailers. In distinguishing types of intermediaries, keep in mind that some serve both roles. For example, Smart & Final operates over 100 retail stores that sell food and food-related products to consumers. It looks like a retailer. However, over 60 percent of Smart & Final's sales are to small businesses, community organizations, and church groups.[1] Because the majority of its sales are to organizational buyers, Smart & Final is primarily in the wholesaling business. Similarly, the Staples chain of office-supply stores targets small businesses (wholesaling) but also sells to consumers (retailing).

However, most intermediaries are either wholesalers or retailers. This chapter focuses on wholesalers and the process of physical distribution. It begins with a formal definition of wholesalers, then identifies some of the different types of wholesalers. The chapter also considers wholesalers' marketing strategies to attract both suppliers and buyers. Next, the chapter discusses current and future trends in wholesaling. When the product is tangible, wholesalers and other channel members physically move goods to users. Thus, the chapter ends by discussing physical distribution concepts.

The Role of Wholesaling in Distribution

wholesaler (distributor)
A business that buys, takes title to, stores, and resells goods to retailers or to other organizations.

A **wholesaler** is a merchant that "is primarily engaged in buying, taking title to, usually storing and physically handling goods in large quantities, and reselling the goods (usually in smaller quantities) to retailers or to industrial or business users."[2] Wholesalers also are called **distributors** in some industries, particularly when they have exclusive distribution rights. Although most consumers have little contact with wholesaling, it is a major industry. According to the Census Bureau, approximately 492,000 wholesale establishments operate in the United States and they employ roughly six million people.[3]

Wholesalers create value for both suppliers and buyers by performing distribution functions. For example, they may transport and warehouse goods, exhibit them at trade shows, and tell store managers which products are selling best. Retail stores and chains deal with wholesalers because they make goods available from a variety of producers. Producers use wholesalers to more easily reach large markets. Bob Trinchero, chief executive of Sutter Home Winery, says an important factor in his company's success has been the ability to choose and work cooperatively with wholesalers.[4]

Wholesalers create value when they handle distribution functions more efficiently and effectively than producers or other channel members. Table 15.1 lists some ways in which wholesalers may increase value. They may lower costs for the other channel members by efficiently carrying out such activities as physically moving goods to a convenient location, assuming the risk of managing large inventories, and operating during hours convenient to their organizational buyers. Such efficiencies can translate into lower prices for final customers.

Moreover, wholesalers' expertise may not only save money but may also help develop new and better ways to distribute products. In Europe, so-called smart distribution centers are serving business customers by providing assembly or customization of products, testing, repairs, and multilingual hot lines—whatever customers need to make products work.[5]

T A B L E 15.1
Ways Wholesalers Can
Create Value

For Producers	For Retailers	For End Users
Providing greater ability to reach buyers	Providing information about industries and products	Reducing monetary costs by efficiency and expertise contributed to channel
Providing information about buyers	Reducing monetary, time, and activity costs by providing a variety of goods	Improving product selection by providing information to retailers about the best products to offer end users
Reducing monetary costs through greater efficiency and/or knowledge	Reducing monetary costs through greater efficiency and/or expertise	
Reducing potential losses by assuming risks		

FTD, a 23,000-member florist that delivers retail customers' orders electronically. To provide its members with more up-to-date information, FTD is replacing its 2,500-page membership directory and its catalogs of floral arrangements with a modern information system. JavaStations, small computers that use the new Java computer language by Sun Microsystems, will provide credit card authorization, banking services, customer profiles to aid sales forecasts, and inventory control, as well as illustrated on-line directories and catalogs. At the retail level, the JavaStations will also double as kiosks for customer browsing. Flower arranging, however, will still be provided at the retailer and by human hands.

A wholesaler is behind the success of the video rental department of the Omaha-based chain of Baker's supermarkets. The wholesaler, Video Home Theater, provides Baker's with a leasing package that includes videos, fixtures for displaying them, training of Baker's staff, computer systems, setup, and promotion of the video department. Louis Stinebaugh, general merchandise director at Baker's, says, "We believe we have the best of all worlds—very little risk, minimal investment, excellent service, and access to lots of expertise."[6]

Major Types of Wholesalers

There are two main types of wholesalers: merchant wholesalers, and agents and brokers. Table 15.2 identifies these types and defines a number of subcategories under each. Because the mix of services provided by different wholesalers varies, certain wholesalers are common in some industries but not in others. Therefore, producers selecting wholesalers should learn what types are common in their industries.

T A B L E 15.2
Major Types of Wholesalers

Type	Definition
Merchant wholesalers	Wholesalers that take title to the products they sell
Full-service wholesalers	Wholesalers that perform all the channel functions
General merchandise wholesalers	Wholesalers that carry a variety of goods in several distinct and unrelated lines of business
Specialty wholesalers	Wholesalers that stock a narrow range of products
Limited function wholesalers	Wholesalers that perform only some of the distribution functions
Rack jobbers or service merchandisers	Wholesale intermediaries operating principally in the food trade, supplying certain classes of merchandise that do not fit into the regular routine of food store merchandise resource contacts; commonly place display racks in retail stores, provide an opening inventory on a consignment or guaranteed-sale basis, periodically check the stock, and replenish inventories
Cash-and-carry wholesalers	Wholesalers that carry a limited selection of products and do not provide transportation for the goods they sell; customers must pay cash and transport their purchases
Drop shippers	Wholesalers that deal in large lots shipped direct from the factory to the customer of the drop shipper, take title to the goods, assume responsibility for the shipment after it leaves the factory, extend credit, collect the account, and incur all the sales costs necessary to secure orders
Truck jobbers	Wholesalers that operate a small warehouse and stock trucks that carry the goods to retailers, where they are sold in their original packages to the retailers
Agents and brokers	Wholesalers who do not take title to goods
Agents or manufacturers' representatives	Business units that negotiate purchases, sales, or both but do not take title to the goods in which they deal
Brokers	Intermediaries that serve as "go-betweens" for buyer or seller, assume no title risks, do not usually have physical custody of products, and are not looked upon as permanent representatives of either the buyer or seller

Source: Most definitions from Peter D. Bennett, ed., *Dictionary of Marketing Terms,* 2nd ed. (Chicago: American Marketing Association, 1995).

Merchant Wholesalers

When marketers discuss wholesalers, they are usually referring to merchant wholesalers. **Merchant wholesalers** are independent businesses that take title to the products they handle. Merchant wholesalers are by far the largest category, accounting for over 80 percent of all wholesaling establishments (see "Marketing Movers & Shakers: Nanci Mackenzie/U.S. Gas Transportation"). When selecting merchant wholesalers for a channel, manufacturers need to consider the wholesaler's level of service and the number of companies the wholesaler represents.

Level of Service   Producers selecting a merchant wholesaler must consider how many distribution functions these intermediaries handle. **Full-service wholesalers**

merchant wholesaler
A wholesaler that takes title to the products it sells.

full-service wholesaler
A wholesaler that performs all distribution functions to some degree.

Nanci Mackenzie/ U.S. Gas Transportation

"My role models were always women who worked," recalls Nanci Mackenzie, founder and head of U.S. Gas Transportation, a Colorado-based merchant wholesaler. The company buys natural gas from producers—independent drillers as well as the larger corporations—and then distributes it through rented pipeline space to organizational customers such as utilities and towns.

USGT can be considered a specialty wholesaler because it provides one type of product to its customers. It is also a value-driven company. Anyone can transport gas through a pipeline, from one location to another; USGT provides extra benefits. For instance, USGT reps and gas controllers "have laptops, and the scheduler can reroute gas by computer," explains Mackenzie. "It can be at the utility within four hours of the initial call." USGT can even guarantee it. This is crucial for utilities and towns that depend on it. The small wholesaler gains an edge over its larger competitors by focusing on customers. "We do it with TLC, with things the big companies no longer do," says Mackenzie. "We do a lot of listening to customers."

Indeed, USGT has only 20 employees, and Mackenzie practices hands-on management, helping out wherever she can, including the oil-and-gas trading desk. Mackenzie is also looking for opportunities for her company to expand. The wholesale electricity business is becoming deregulated and she is considering entering the market. However, she is quick to admit that she is not willing to take on too much—or to risk USGT's current success, just to plunge into a new market. "I prefer not to be the leader. I'd rather let the rough spots smooth out," she says. This way she can determine what works and what doesn't through observation rather than through costly mistakes. In the meantime, she'll keep working, providing the service her customers value so much. "Work is not a chore for me," she says. "I enjoy working like other people enjoy taking vacations."

Source: "Cookin' with Gas," *Working Woman*, May 1996, p. 45.

Explore more by searching "Gas Transport" on the Web.

---

general merchandise wholesaler
A wholesaler that carries a variety of goods in several distinct and unrelated product lines.

specialty wholesaler
A wholesaler that carries a narrow range of products.

limited-function wholesaler
A wholesaler that performs only some of the distribution functions.

service merchandiser (rack jobber)
A wholesaler that performs many distribution functions in addition to providing and stocking racks for merchandise.

cash-and-carry wholesaler
A wholesaler that carries a limited selection of products and does not provide transportation for the products.

drop shipper
A wholesaler that takes title to products but does not handle physical distribution.

perform all distribution functions to some degree. They may be **general merchandise wholesalers,** which carry a broad range of products such as hardware, drugs, or clothing. Other full-service wholesalers are **specialty wholesalers** that carry a narrow but deep product mix, such as wholesalers for automobile parts or health foods.

As their name implies, **limited-function wholesalers** perform only a limited number of distribution functions. There are four main types. **Service merchandisers** or **rack jobbers** perform many distribution functions. Rack jobbers get their name because they stock the racks (shelves) on which the merchandise is displayed in stores. Rack jobbers supply supermarkets and other stores with products such as magazines, hosiery, and health and beauty aids. Rack jobbers deliver these goods, set them up on racks, and keep track of inventory.

Cash-and-carry wholesalers offer a limited selection of products and do not provide transportation for the goods they sell. Their customers, primarily small retailers, come to them, pay cash, and transport their purchases. These wholesalers commonly handle office supplies, hardware, electric supplies, and some grocery items.

Drop shippers take title to the products they carry but do not handle physical distribution. They get orders from retailers and arrange for producers to deliver the merchandise directly. They may sell goods that are expensive to transport, such as coal, grain, and lumber. By eliminating the costs of transporting these bulky goods to warehouses and keeping them in inventory, drop shippers reduce costs and lower prices.

truck jobbers
A wholesaler that operates a small warehouse and trucks that carry products to retailers.

Truck jobbers (also called truck wholesalers) operate small warehouses and a fleet of trucks. The trucks carry the goods to retailers and other organizational buyers (such as hotels, restaurants, and hospitals), where they are sold in their original packages. These wholesalers typically handle perishable or fast-moving items such as baked goods, meat, and fresh produce.

Number of Producers Represented   An important consideration is whether a merchant wholesaler will represent one, a few, or many producers. From the manufacturer's standpoint, wholesalers that sell for only a few other producers give products greater selling effort. Also, producers usually prefer wholesalers that do not carry competitive product lines. Reef Brazil, which exports sandals targeted to surfers, has had the greatest success in countries where it had wholesalers new to the business. The reason is that these new intermediaries generally handled fewer product lines, so they worked harder for Reef Brazil.[7]

On the other hand, retailers often prefer to work with wholesalers that represent many producers. For example, Lotus Light Enterprises, based in Silver Lake, Wisconsin, handles 7,500 different natural foods and health and beauty aids for about 400 companies. Lotus Light's sales and marketing coordinator, Michael Charney, says, "Our most important service is providing a forum for our customers' [manufacturers'] products. We show their products to retailers and exhibit them at trade shows."[8] Lotus Light also provides such services as shipment of orders within 24 hours and a toll-free phone number retailers can call to place orders.

Agents and Brokers

Some wholesalers that sell to retailers and organizational buyers do not take title to products. Often, they do not take possession of the goods either. Instead, their role is to bring together producers and other intermediaries by negotiating purchases and sales. These intermediaries are called **agents, manufacturers' representatives,** or **brokers,** with the exact title varying from one industry to another.

agent (broker, manufacturer's representative)
A wholesaler that negotiates purchases, sales, or both but does not take title to the goods.

Agents and brokers provide value because their specialized knowledge of a product line or market makes exchanges simpler for buyers and sellers. Companies that cannot afford to hire and train their own sales force, or that are entering a new market, often benefit from the use of an agent or broker. Advanced Hardware Architectures, a Pullman, Washington, maker of semiconductor devices, uses agents to serve international markets. By selecting agents who have good selling skills and familiarity with local markets, Advanced has been able to adapt to cultural differences and make 40 percent of its sales outside the United States.[9]

Agents and brokers earn their income by charging producers a fee or commission. Agents are commonly used in the distribution of services, including the sale of air travel, insurance, and securities to business customers.

Some agents or brokers represent several producers. Contracts with each producer spell out terms such as prices and arrangements for processing orders. Other agents and brokers

Agents for Baird & Warner, the largest real estate broker in Illinois, are known as professional sales associates. Operating out of 31 branch offices, they bring together buyers and sellers of real estate. The company maintains a site on the World Wide Web (http://www.bairdwarner.com), where it provides information on residential and commercial properties, relocation services, mortgages, and the company's history and career opportunities.

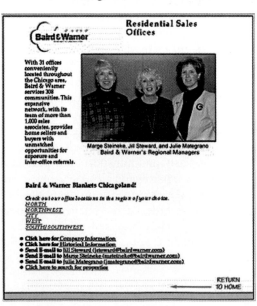

FIGURE 15.1
Marketing Strategies for Wholesalers

sell on behalf of a single producer. In effect, the agent serves as a wholesale sales department for the producer. Agents and brokers may represent the seller for a single transaction, or they may have an ongoing relationship with the producer.

Marketing Strategies for Wholesalers

As shown in Figure 15.1, as an intermediary between producers and retailers or other resellers, independent wholesalers need to develop two different types of marketing strategies. First, they need to develop a strategy to attract producers to use their services and build long-term relationships with them. Second, they need to develop a strategy to attract retailers and other buyers and build long-term relationships with them, too. Both are needed for successful wholesaling.

Strategies to Attract Producers

Wholesalers need to attract producers to use their services in order for them to have something to sell and make profits. Just as producers often seek wholesalers in developing channels, wholesalers seek producers that have successful products and product lines to increase their own sales and profits. Wholesalers can attract producers by offering to perform all of the distribution functions or tailoring their services to include only the functions that producers do not have the ability to perform effectively. Typically, relationships between producers and wholesalers begin with discussion of the responsibilities of each company and the appropriate pricing of products.

The Deli Gourmet kiosk shown here is a creation of Wittco Foodservice Equipment of Milwaukee, Wisconsin. By developing this product, Wittco moved beyond simply providing foodservice equipment to helping its customers compete against the foodservice offerings of chain stores. The Deli Gourmet kiosk offers numerous foodservice items and can be tailored to specific regional tastes.

Wholesalers may also attract producers by offering to distribute products and perform distribution functions cheaper than competitive wholesalers. Of course, wholesalers with excellent track records, locations, reputations, expertise, and relationships with major retail customers can more easily attract manufacturers of successful products. Also, wholesalers that effectively serve large markets may be more attractive since producers may be able to reduce the number of wholesalers needed.

However, wholesalers that carry a number of competing products and brands, particularly those of market leaders, may have a more difficult time attracting other producers. Because their sales would likely be a small percentage of the wholesaler's total, these smaller producers might believe that their products would not receive sufficient marketing effort. If another wholesaler were available, it may be selected or the producer may use a different type of channel altogether. In some cases, a wholesaler selling strong competitive products may still be selected if it aggressively markets all of its products and brands or is the only or best wholesaler available.

Wholesalers as well as producers benefit from developing long-term relationships with each other. These relationships depend on trust, doing a good job for one another and open communication about opportunities and problems.

Strategies to Attract Retailers

Wholesalers need to attract retailers and organizational customers to buy products from them. In many cases, wholesalers have exclusive contracts to distribute producers' goods in a particular trading area. For popular products and brands with large market shares, the wholesaler's task is simplified because retailers want to carry them. For example, wholesaler bottlers of Coke and Pepsi can attract retailers easily because the products sell so well and consumers expect to find them in supermarkets, drugstores, convenience stores, and restaurants. Retailers without these brands would be at a competitive disadvantage.

However, for new or small-market-share products and brands, particularly those of less well-known manufacturers, wholesalers may have to do considerable marketing to get retailers to stock them. Wholesalers may get placement in retail stores and retail chains because they have developed strong, long-term working relationships with them. They may offer same-day service on orders and guarantee deliveries with extended payment terms. They may point out that the manufacturer is going to advertise the product extensively and only sell it to selected retailers. They may also attract retailers by offering better profit margins than established brands and special introductory offers and deals. For example, sporting goods wholesalers offer special deals on displays for pocket knives and other products.

Trends in Wholesaling

The survival of wholesalers depends on their ability to recognize and meet the needs of both sellers and buyers and to do so efficiently. The principles of target marketing and value orientation are as essential to wholesalers as to other marketers. Wholesalers can build long-term relationships with other channel members to create value for them and end users.

Many producers are using shorter channels, often eliminating wholesalers. Moreover, it is predicted that wholesalers' share of products sold in the United States is likely to continue to decrease.[10] Wholesalers likely to survive are the ones that offer a level of service difficult to obtain through other channels—in other words, those that create value in channels and build strong relationships (see "Put It into Practice: Help a Wholesaler Survive").

One way wholesalers create value is by developing cutting-edge distribution technology. Distributor W. W. Grainger, Inc., offers same-day delivery of 53,000 different

Help a Wholesaler Survive

You are a marketing consultant for wholesalers. A mid-size wholesaler of athletic shoes comes to you for advice on how to survive these extremely competitive times. Develop and write out a strategy for the wholesaler, concentrating on ways that the wholesaler could create value. Note what manufacturers and retailers the wholesaler should try to attract and how they could be convinced to do business with the wholesaler.

maintenance, repair, and operating supplies. The computer technology that makes this possible includes one system for more accurately forecasting sales and another for closely tracking the movement of products from suppliers to regional distribution centers to branch locations to customers. Through a satellite network, Grainger branches can share information about inventory availability. Also, an Electronic Catalog on CD makes it easier for Grainger's customers to locate and order the items they need. Customers using a system called Grainger Express can link with Grainger branch computers to learn products, prices and availability, place and check the status of orders, and leave messages for Grainger branch employees.[11]

Wholesalers that focus on creating value can help their customers by providing useful information. Darter Inc., which wholesales products such as mill, paper, and janitorial supplies, sends manufacturers' representatives to factories to show them how to cut costs using Darter-distributed products.[12]

Physical Distribution

One of the major activities that takes place in channels of distribution is the physical movement of goods to end users. This process, called **physical distribution,** includes transportation, warehousing, inventory management, and order processing.[13]

physical distribution
The process of handling orders and moving and storing goods to get them efficiently to customers.

The physical distribution process makes exchanges possible, and is a source of value for customers. Consumers and organizational buyers alike want to purchase products easily and replace them when needed; they do not want a long wait for delivery, or delivery of the wrong product. Reliable physical distribution is critical for business customers that use just-in-time inventory management systems. Getting exactly what they need, when they need it, enables business customers to cut costs and create value for their customers. As channel members carry out the tasks of physical distribution, they create a chain of value for end users.

The Physical Distribution Process

As noted, physical distribution includes transportation, warehousing, inventory management, and order processing (see "You Decide: Can Truckers and Wholesalers Establish a Better Relationship?"). These functions occur in a process such as the one shown in Figure 15.2. To carry out this process, producers and intermediaries may use other organizations such as transportation companies, public warehouses, insurance companies, and fulfillment companies.

F I G U R E 15.2
The Physical Distribution Process

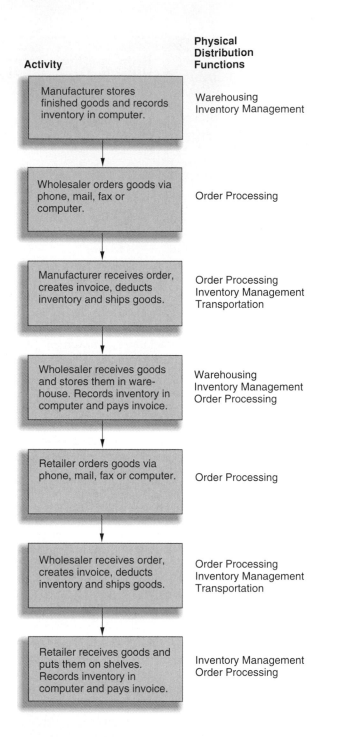

Activity

Physical Distribution Functions

Manufacturer stores finished goods and records inventory in computer.

Warehousing
Inventory Management

Wholesaler orders goods via phone, mail, fax or computer.

Order Processing

Manufacturer receives order, creates invoice, deducts inventory and ships goods.

Order Processing
Inventory Management
Transportation

Wholesaler receives goods and stores them in ware-house. Records inventory in computer and pays invoice.

Warehousing
Inventory Management
Order Processing

Retailer orders goods via phone, mail, fax or computer.

Order Processing

Wholesaler receives order, creates invoice, deducts inventory and ships goods.

Order Processing
Inventory Management
Transportation

Retailer receives goods and puts them on shelves. Records inventory in computer and pays invoice.

Inventory Management
Order Processing

mode of transportation
The class or type of carrier used.

Transportation   Transportation involves actually moving goods from sellers to buyers. The basic choices, or **modes of transportation,** are motor carriers (trucks), railroads, air carriers, water carriers, and pipelines. Figure 15.3 shows the proportion of goods transported by each of these modes.

To select a mode of transportation, marketers consider factors such as the relative costs, speed, and flexibility to carry different types of products. Table 15.3 on page 402 summarizes how each mode stacks up on these criteria. In general, motor carriers are a good choice when speed and flexibility are needed. Railroads offer a lower cost,

Can Truckers and Wholesalers Establish a Better Relationship?

Physical distribution—moving products from one place to another—causes its share of headaches for people who do it. Recently, truck drivers who deliver goods to wholesalers have been voicing serious complaints, to the point where they are refusing to drive for certain producers. Trucking companies are refusing to transport the goods of certain producers because of the way their drivers are treated at the wholesale and retail levels. "They are abusive, uncooperative, unreasonable, and nasty," says one driver about the dockmasters with whom he deals in the supermarket industry. "They forget that everything they sell in their stores comes to them in a truck—mine or somebody else's." This driver and others complain that they are asked to do jobs for which they were not hired, such as unloading goods, and are treated poorly in the bargain. "It's like they are trying to save money and cut corners, so they take it out on the drivers," he continues. "They want us to do their jobs as well as our own. Sometimes they're like little tin gods."

Lana Batts, president of the Interstate Truckload Association, echoes these complaints. "[The driver] makes an appointment to deliver, shows up, and then . . . sits there for hours. The wholesaler or distributor thinks his time is free." On the unloading issue, she says, "That's not their job. They are drivers, and they want to drive. They are not usually being paid to unload."

As we have stressed throughout this course, creating value is of prime concern to everyone in business, and building good relationships is part of creating value. Thus, it is clear that something must be done about this problem. One large producer, Procter & Gamble, has taken a formal

step in this direction. Steven N. David, vice president of U.S. sales, notes that removing physical distribution inefficiencies could save the grocery industry up to $11 billion. So the incentive to improve is overwhelming. Through P&G's new "Streamlined Logistics II" program, customers who meet certain criteria will receive hefty discounts. Some of those criteria involve relationships in physical distribution.

Loads must be picked up on schedule, unloaded in less than two hours, and a specific type of "single pallet" must be used in deliveries. P&G has prepared display-ready units which "allow for easy crossdocking and delivery straight to the selling floor," says Dean Skadberg, director of industry affairs. "If we are shipping, we want a two-hour turn with no carrier touch," he continues. That means, the carrier does not have to unload. "We want to make it easier to load and unload trucks." Customers can also get discounts by ordering full rather than partial truckloads from the plant, or by accepting shipment through regional distribution centers where their orders are commingled with others.

What do the carriers think of Streamlined Logistics? "That's what the carrier wants," comments Batts. "We'd love it. It's no touch freight. It means our drivers can drive and not be forced to unload, reconfigure pallets, and do all of the other things the receiver should be doing." Procter & Gamble has taken the first step in improving this important relationship in the distribution channel. What other steps might producers, wholesalers, and trucking companies take to improve their relationships? How might the use of technology help?

Source: Bob Gatty, "The Big Truck Pile Up," *Grocery Marketing,* October 1995, pp. 16, 18.

Explore more by searching "Streamlined Logistics" on the Web.

as well as great flexibility, but are slower. When speed is the most important consideration, air carriers meet that need. Water carriers and pipelines can keep costs down, but they are practical only for certain types of products and are limited geographically.

The selection of transportation mode is simpler when the shipment is small. For example, marketers aren't going to be choosing between trains and boats to ship a

FIGURE 15.3
Proportion of Goods Carried for Each Mode of Transportation*

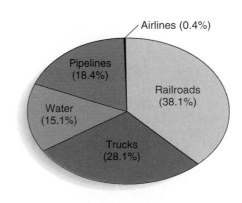

*As measured in ton-miles.

Source: U.S. Department of Commerce, *Statistical Abstract of the United States,* 115th ed. (Washington, D.C.: U.S. Government Printing Office, 1995), p. 626.

TABLE 15.3
Transportation Mode Selection Criteria

	Cost	Speed	Load Flexibility
Motor carriers	High	Fast	Moderate
Railroads	Moderate	Moderate	High
Air carriers	Very high	Very fast	Low
Water carriers	Very low	Very slow	Very high
Pipelines	Low	Slow	Very low

When speed is the most important factor in the delivery of goods internationally, marketers often choose air transportation such as this Korean Air Cargo carrier. In this ad, Korean Air Cargo calls itself the world's largest Asian transpacific cargo carrier. The fine print says the company "maintains one of the largest all-cargo fleets, including Boeing 747 freighters and Airbus 300 freighters" and is ranked "third among worldwide international airlines in cargo tonnage carried."

You're looking at the world's largest Asian transpacific cargo carrier.

The fact is, Korean Air maintains one of the largest all-cargo fleets, including Boeing 747 freighters and Airbus 300 freighters. Not only that, IATA Statistics now ranks Korean Air 3rd among worldwide international airlines in cargo tonnage carried. Which means? We have all the expertise needed to carry the one load that really matters: yours. For bookings, call 1-800-421-5822 (Western U.S.) or 1-800-221-6272 (Eastern U.S.).

KOREAN AIR CARGO
Fly the spirit of dedication.

manuscript, a report, or a computer diskette— or, for that matter, the small packages sent out by a catalog retailer such as Lands' End or Smith & Hawken. For small packages, marketers use motor and air carriers like the mail or Federal Express.

Owning versus Contracting For a selected mode of transportation, marketers must choose a specific carrier. Sometimes, marketers evaluate whether to own the mode (say, a fleet of trucks), or to contract with an independent carrier to transport the goods. Marketers may also compare various suppliers of transportation services in terms of costs, quality, and areas of specialization. For instance, Martinair Holland is a specialist in transporting animals. It offers customized shipping of animals, from cattle to whales to ostriches.[14]

Intermodal Transportation Marketers may also need to select some form of **intermodal transportation,** that is, transportation combining more than one mode. One version is **piggyback service,** whereby a railroad picks up truck trailers, loads them onto flatcars, and carries them to a station near their ultimate destination. The trailers are then delivered by truck to the buyer. Water carriers offer similar services. Intermodal transportation can offer a degree of flexibility and efficiency unavailable with individual modes of transportation. This is important for Robbins Company, which ships large machinery and needs to move machines quickly to its customers around the world. In a typical month, Robbins ships three or four containers of parts by train from Kent, Washington, to New York. There the containers are loaded onto ships, which deliver them to Liverpool, England. From there they travel by truck to the company's assembly plant.[15]

Many businesses that serve global markets use intermodal transportation to handle the complexities of international physical distribution. Intermodal systems have become increasingly reliable, thanks in part to strategic alliances among transportation companies and fast electronic access to information. For example, Lufthansa Airlines, the Maersk Inc. steamship line, and San Francisco-based Aeroground Inc. work together to carry containers from Asia to Europe by air, sea, and truck.[16]

Freight Forwarders For companies with small shipments, it is often advantageous to use a **freight forwarder.** Freight forwarders gather small shipments from various organizations and then hire a carrier to move them as larger lots. Besides the cost advantage, freight forwarders offer pick up and delivering services.

The expertise of freight forwarders in obtaining export licenses and taking care of foreign banking activities makes them popular for handling international shipments.

intermodal transportation
Transportation that combines several modes.

piggyback service
Intermodal transportation of truck trailers via train to a station near their ultimate destination.

freight forwarder
A company that gathers small shipments from various organizations and hires a carrier to move them as larger lots.

Freight forwarders can solve a range of problems, as in the case of a load of pipes to be flown to Saudi Arabia. There seemed to be no way to fit the pipes on the plane until freight forwarder Union Transport suggested removing the plane's front windows. The pipes were loaded through the cockpit and into the cargo area.[17]

warehousing
The storing of products while they await sale or transfer.

Warehousing   After transportation, the most costly function of physical distribution is **warehousing,** or holding a stock of the product while it awaits sale or transfer. Besides making the product available within a reasonable distance of the intermediary or end user, warehouses provide a location for sorting and consolidating goods. Organizations warehouse goods when it is more efficient to produce or buy large quantities, rather than use just-in-time inventory systems. They also need to warehouse goods that can be produced during only part of the year, as in the case of crops. Conversely, some goods can be produced year-round but need to be warehoused because they are purchased only during part of the year. Examples include swimming pool filters and artificial Christmas trees.

To plan for storage, marketers must decide how many warehouses will be needed and where they should be located. These decisions depend on customers' needs for rapid delivery. Although holding inventory is costly, losing sales because goods are unavailable can damage a company's reputation and its chances for survival. In selecting the locations for warehouses, marketers need to consider the most efficient transportation routes for the goods.

Buyers and sellers can benefit from working together to set up a warehouse system. GE Supply, a distributor of electrical products, worked with a building contractor to set up mini-warehouses in trailers at construction sites. A computerized catalog in each trailer lists the various materials available, including a picture and description of each. When workers need supplies, they walk to the trailer, select them from bins, and use a scanner to read the bar code on each. Each day the computer system creates reports of product usage, which GE Supply uses to determine what to deliver the next morning. The contractor has estimated that this approach saves about 20 percent over a more traditional warehousing system.[18]

public warehouse
A business that offers space and inventory support services for a rental fee.

Another warehousing decision is whether to use public or private warehouses. **Public warehouses** are businesses that offer space and inventory support services for a rental fee. This approach is flexible because the renter pays only for the space and services used. However, many organizations find it more efficient to own their warehouses. Private warehouses give their owners greater control over warehouse operations. Also, some products, such as hazardous or sterile materials, are not suitable for public warehouses.

Inventory Management   Most producers and resellers of tangible goods carry some inventory. One reason is that they don't want to risk being out of stock when a customer wants to buy. Another reason is that production can be more efficient when a large lot of one type of good is produced before switching over to something else. The organization may also inventory products to protect against supply problems, such as strikes or equipment breakdowns.

Balanced against these advantages are the costs of carrying inventory, which include storage space and insurance for the goods. Additionally, the money tied up in inventory is unavailable for investment in other ventures. Organizations therefore seek to manage inventory by maintaining just enough to provide the benefits they seek (see Figure 15.4). At the Quaker Oats Company, this trade-off between inventory and other costs is one of the issues monitored by its Supply Chain Management program. Supply Chain Management is a continuous effort that examines the whole production and distribution process and identifies ways to improve quality and lower costs.[19]

To keep track of inventories, organizations often use Universal Product Codes (UPCs), commonly called bar codes. A scanner reads the black-and-white stripes of bar codes and translates the information into a computer code identifying the product.

In this ad, GE Information Services points out that although inventory is an asset, holding it too long is costly. In the fine print, the company explains that it can help organizations meet basic objectives of inventory management, including faster turnover of inventory and elimination of out-of-stock occurrences. GE's services include advice in setting up electronic links with suppliers, manufacturers, and distributors.

This process is much faster than keeping written records. However, an inventory management system based on UPCs requires that these codes be accurate. Anyone who has stood in a checkout line while a clerk struggles to get the price of an item with a faulty bar code knows how frustrating such mistakes can be. Many retailers, including Kmart and Wal-Mart, therefore, set quality standards for UPCs and fine the supplier whenever a bar code is missing or inaccurate.[20]

Order Processing   To process an order, it must be received and entered into the processing system. The order may come via phone, fax, or mail, or a customer's computerized inventory control system may automatically transmit an order whenever supplies reach some minimum level. However the order is received, the order-processing system notifies production or warehouse personnel to fill it. Inventory is checked and if the goods are in stock, the order is filled. If not, the goods must be produced and the customer must wait for them. In the meantime, the buyer's credit may be checked and an invoice prepared. Funds received are deposited.

Order processing is commonly handled with a computer system. Computerization speeds up the process and makes information about transactions readily available for correcting mistakes, for inventory planning, and for marketing research. Thus, a well-designed, properly used order-processing system can create value for customers by increasing the speed and accuracy with which their orders are filled and by improving the supplier's ability to identify their wants and needs.

Value-driven organizations develop order-processing systems that solve customer problems. The McKesson Drug unit, for example, surveyed its customers and learned that the service improvement they most wanted was faster credit for returned merchandise. So McKesson Drug challenged its employees to find ways to speed up that process, and they did, cutting credit-processing time from 19 days to 7.[21]

FIGURE 15.4
*Costs of Too Much or
Too Little Inventory*

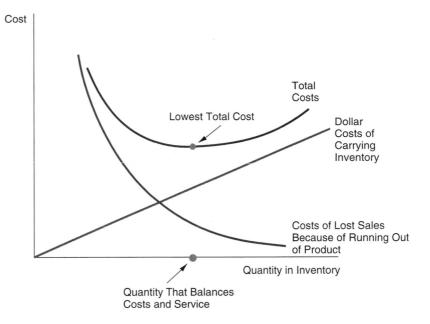

"The Fresh 1," a fruit and vegetable marketer, creates
value for its retail customers by adding labels that provide
information for use at the checkout. Bulk produce
receives stickers with standard PLU (price look-up)
numbers. Packaged items are labeled with UPCs
(universal product codes, or bar codes). Using these
codes speeds up work by checkout clerks and enables
the retailer to collect data electronically.

Some organizations cut costs by hiring outside services to process orders. Team Logistix, a logistics and courier company in Austin, Texas, provided such service for GTE Mobilnet in a reverse channel. GTE Mobilnet, a marketer of cellular phones, found that many customers changed their minds after the salesperson left their home. The challenge was to process the cancellations and recover the phones. Team Logistix set up Lotus Notes groupware linking its service representatives directly to GTE. When a customer phoned, GTE transferred the call to Team Logistix, where a representative looked up customer information, confirmed the address, and arranged to have the phone picked up.[22]

While reducing the expense of order processing through the use of outside parties like Logistix can reduce costs and increase profits, it can also cause customer service to suffer. When the producer's or intermediary's employees process orders, greater control and closer contact with customers is maintained. The seller can identify unmet needs and build long-term relationships. Thus, if outside services are hired to handle order processing, marketers need to develop ways to maintain close contact with their customers.

Managing Physical Distribution

Marketers rely on physical distribution to help make their products available to customers when and where they are ready to buy. Since a major channel objective is to minimize total distribution costs for a particular level of market coverage, physical distribution costs must be analyzed. Trade-offs may be made between physical distribution costs and other costs. For example, a faster, more expensive transportation mode may be selected to reduce total distribution costs by reducing the cost of lost business. While offering superior physical distribution services may increase monetary costs, it may also be a way to develop value for customers and a competitive advantage for marketers. For example, superior customer service has been the key to success for Micro Warehouse, which sells computers and software through mail order. If customers have a problem or change their mind about an order, the company gives them a shipping number to have the product returned at no charge.[23] This service helps Micro Warehouse reduce customers' concerns about buying products through mail order and can build long-term relationships.

Value-Driven Physical Distribution   To deliver greater value, organizations look for ways to increase the speed and reliability of physical distribution while holding the line on costs (see Table 15.4). For some organizations, the solution is to use the expertise of a contract logistics company, such as Airborne Express, FedEx, or UPS. Organizations already spend about $25 billion a year on contract logistics, with the total expected to double by 2000.[24]

Many examples illustrate the potential benefits. For example, Nike has used Airborne Express for more efficient physical distribution, from warehousing to inventory management to transportation via air, ground, or water.[25] Similarly, Intel has FedEx distribute its Pentium computer chips, which are produced in Southeast Asia. FedEx cut delivery time from two to three weeks to just two or three days. The efficiencies of FedEx's operations enable Intel to lower costs for warehousing and transportation, while at the same time promising customers fast delivery.[26] Chevron and other organizations doing business in the former Soviet Union have benefited from contracting

T A B L E 15.4
Ways Physical Distribution Can Create Value

For Producers	For Intermediaries	For End Users
Getting goods to buyers when and where they will buy them	Making goods available when and where customers want them	Making goods available when needed or desired
Making the producer a dependable and/or fast source of goods	Maintaining the necessary level of inventory; replenishing stock quickly and reliably	Making goods available where needed or desired
Distributing goods efficiently so that they can be priced so as to deliver value	Providing the goods at a low enough cost to be priced profitably	Making goods available that are undamaged in transit and priced reasonably
Providing information about the availability of goods and their status during distribution	Providing information about the availability of goods and their status during distribution	Providing information about the status of goods during distribution

with Fritz Companies, Inc. (FCI). FCI has cut through complicated legal restrictions and learned to cope with the limited infrastructure to develop a full range of services, including warehousing, transportation, packaging, and a system for tracking the status of shipments.[27]

Cross-Functional Decision Making   A cross-functional view of physical distribution can help lead the organization to the best trade-offs between cost and customer service. In the past, the norm was to divide responsibility for the different aspects of physical distribution. Thus, one person might handle inventory management and another person shipping, without the two being responsible for seeing how those functions affect one another or the organization's total costs. In contrast, forward-thinking organizations link responsibility for these activities with one another and with other functions. This cross-functional approach ensures that the physical distribution system supports the overall strategy of the organization.

As a case in point, McKesson Water Products Company assembled a cross-functional team to study inventory control. The team introduced the use of hand-held computers that allow sales representatives to keep track of their inventory. The system is more accurate than the previous paper-and-pencil approach and saves hundreds of hours of record-keeping time.[28]

Trends in Physical Distribution

One trend in physical distribution is to integrate it into a system, rather than a series of discrete functions. Procter & Gamble views physical distribution as a source of customer value and rewards channel members for delivering it. P&G has a program called Streamlined Logistics II, which grants lower prices to channel members who meet certain conditions. They must: (1) use electronic data interchange to automate order processing; (2) agree to procedures for timely pickup and unloading of deliveries; (3) use special display-ready loads for popular items that can be moved directly to the store's selling floor; and (4) participate in "co-marketing" with P&G through a company-published magazine that highlights retailers and P&G products.[29]

Other trends focus on ways to improve the efficiency of physical distribution. Many firms are taking advantage of the ability of computers to process a lot of information quickly and easily. Computer technology helps firms conduct more sophisticated planning and control of the distribution effort.

just-in-time (JIT) inventory management
A system of holding little inventory and requiring suppliers to provide the exact quantity needed according to a precise schedule.

Just-in-Time Inventory Management   Many organizations have sought to hold down inventory costs by adopting **just-in-time (JIT) inventory management.** Brought to the United States from Japan by auto and other manufacturers, JIT consists of holding little inventory and requiring suppliers to provide the exact quantity needed according to a precise schedule. By receiving products just as they are needed, the buyer minimizes the cost of carrying inventory. The supplier shoulders the responsibility for delivering acceptable-quality products on time—perhaps even several times a day for large buyers.

For JIT to deliver the benefits of low cost and high quality, buyers have to be able to accurately predict how much of what products they will need and when. Suppliers must be able to provide fast, reliable delivery. The quality of their products also must be high, because a JIT schedule does not allow time for replacing defective goods. To achieve such goals, channel members using JIT often build strategic alliances and use relationship marketing.

JIT works best when suppliers are located near the buyer. For example, Toyota's plant in Kentucky sends trucks to pick up parts from some local suppliers as often as 16 times a day. Clearly, this is practical only because some suppliers are close at hand. Along with geographic proximity, teamwork with suppliers also helps a JIT system run smoothly. California-based Kingston Technology Corporation has developed a strong reputation for integrity in dealing with its suppliers. Companies that supply parts to Kingston, which makes product upgrades for computers, give Kingston preferred service—even shipping products to Kingston ahead of other customers. "We will deal with a vendor only as a long-term partner," explains David Sun, one of the company's founders.[30] Also, the buyer should be certain that the reduction in warehousing costs is greater than the increased cost of frequent, fast deliveries.

Applications of Computer Technology   Modern computer technology helps marketers carry out the detailed planning and coordination needed for physical distribution strategies involving JIT inventory. It also provides other forms of useful information. Marketing decision support systems routinely include information about physical distribution—what products have been ordered, what orders have been shipped, what items are on back order, and the inventory level of each product. United Parcel Service, for example, uses bar codes to regularly update data on the location of each package it handles.

Perhaps most important, computer technology can make many distribution functions more efficient, increasing profits and making it possible to better serve small customers. When Timberland realized that small boutiques were selling more Timberland shoes, the company used technology to make these customers more profitable to serve. By using scanners to track inventory and create shipping bills, Timberland cut the cost of small shipments. By setting up a system for customers to send electronic orders via computers, Timberland increased the speed and lowered the cost of order processing.[31]

Electronic Data Interchange   Electronic data interchanges enable channel members to share information quickly and inexpensively. **Electronic data interchange (EDI)** is the "intercompany, application-to-application exchange of business transactions in a standard data format."[32] Instead of sending one another paper documents,

electronic data interchange
A communication system that allows direct electronic transfer of information among companies.

Matson Navigation Company, Inc., is a principal cargo carrier between the U.S. Pacific Coast and Hawaii. Use of electronic data interchange at the company's Phoenix, Arizona, customer service facility allows customers access to Matson's entire freight information network. Customers with all sizes of shipments can call one toll-free number, and Matson's customer service representatives have the hardware and software to help them arrange for transport of their cargo. In the photo is Matson's S.S. Manulani, which provides weekly service between Los Angeles and the ports of Seattle and Vancouver, B.C.: an alternative to truck and rail services along the West Coast.

such as purchase orders and shipping reports, channel members that use EDI make the information available electronically. This gives EDI users information that is more flexible and up-to-date. Warehouse managers can check on orders being processed by manufacturers. Wholesalers can check the computer system of their trucker or air carrier to see where a particular shipment is and when it is likely to arrive.

Two common uses of EDI are inventory control and order processing. Intermediaries share sales data with suppliers via EDI so that they can schedule production and shipping. Companies can transmit purchase orders and invoices electronically. Electronic data transmission can update accounting systems automatically, thereby avoiding the risks of a document being lost in the mail or entered into the other company's system inaccurately. Wal-Mart is linked electronically with over half of its 5,000 suppliers, and Kmart with 2,600 of its 3,000 suppliers.[33]

The convenient and continuous flow of information supports the trend toward close and cooperative relationships among channel members. In Framingham, Massachusetts, stereo-speaker producer Bose Corporation arranged for a steamship line, a domestic

When Associated Grocers of New England, a cooperative wholesaler, expanded its territory, drivers were no longer able to return to the warehouse each night, and routing became very complicated. The solution was to find outside expertise. Associated turned over its transportation needs to Ryder, a technologically advanced transportation company that offers a dedicated logistics program covering the entire distribution chain, from drivers to software.

When Associated Grocers of New England, a cooperative wholesaler, expanded its territory, they chose to partner with Ryder, leaving to them the worry about trucks, drivers, insurance and fuel.

trucker, and a freight forwarder to set up an integrated EDI system linked to Bose. The companies also supply Bose's plant with staff to monitor and expedite the movement of cargo. This arrangement has allowed Bose to minimize inventory levels and achieve an exceptional rate of on-time deliveries.[34]

Bose also has similar links with its suppliers. G&F Industries, which makes plastic molding, has an employee stationed at Bose's main facility, where he uses Bose's information system to identify when to place orders with G&F. Products from G&F are delivered directly to Bose's manufacturing facilities according to production schedules, so Bose does not need to keep an inventory of G&F products. Using this system, G&F supplies Bose operations in the U.S., Canada, Mexico, and Ireland.[35]

To lower the costs and improve the reliability of shipments from foreign vendors, London-based Woolworth PLC set up an arrangement with P&O Containers Ltd. P&O had experience with EDI and was willing to tailor a system to Woolworth's needs. P&O manages cargo logistics from order to delivery, and has employees working full time in Woolworth's British offices and in its production facilities. In its first year, this setup saved Woolworth $1.5 million.[36]

Impressed by the potential benefits, big retailers often insist that their suppliers adopt an EDI system. Such requests are routine for big producers and wholesalers, but they may challenge small firms. However, as the use of EDI has grown, so have the sources of help for setting up electronic systems. A number of consultants specialize in EDI systems, and organizations contract with them to set up order-processing and inventory management. For example, when Federated Department Stores told Belly Basics, a New York City maker of maternity clothing, that it must begin using EDI, Belly Basics arranged for a company called Intercoastal Data to handle Federated's purchase orders and invoices.[37]

Decision-Making Software   Another way computers are modernizing physical distribution is through software that helps users select the optimal solution to a complex problem. Software such as Roadshow by Routing Technology Software identifies the delivery route that offers the best combination of speed and low cost. Simulation software can help managers with the design and layout of warehouses. Other packages help users compute the necessary inventory levels for providing a given level of customer service.[38]

To help control physical distribution, satellites make it possible to navigate and communicate with carriers worldwide. On-board computers provide a record of the carrier's performance. Such advances are particularly important for distributing goods to customers that use JIT inventory management. These and other advances in information technology have enabled channel members to handle distribution more efficiently and create value for end users by offering faster, more reliable service.

Summary

A wholesaler is a business that buys, sometimes stores, and resells goods to retailers or organizations. Wholesalers are used when they can handle distribution functions more efficiently and effectively than producers or other channel members.

There are two basic types of wholesalers: merchant wholesalers, and agents and brokers. Merchant wholesalers, which are independent of producers, are the largest category, accounting for about 80 percent of all wholesalers.

Wholesalers often have to develop two different types of marketing strategies, one to attract suppliers to use their services and one to attract buyers to do business with them.

Economic and technological changes have made wholesaling increasingly competitive. Because many producers sell directly to retailers, wholesalers are being eliminated. To survive, wholesalers must create value in channels by applying technology to share information or by cultivating partnerships to address customers' wants and needs.

Physical distribution is the moving and storing of goods from producers to end users. It includes transportation, warehousing, inventory management, and order processing. Marketers must make decisions for each of these. For trans-

portation, marketers must decide whether to own or contract these tasks. They also must decide the mode of transportation (motor carriers, railroads, air carriers, water carriers, or pipelines) and whether intermodal transportation and freight forwarders will be used. For warehousing, decisions have to be made concerning the number of warehouses, their locations, and whether to use public or private warehouses. For inventory management, marketers must decide the size of inventory to carry and how to keep track of it. For order processing, marketers must decide the system to use, the degree to which it will be computerized, and whether to hire an outside service to handle it. Marketers must assess the cost of each activity and the benefits it provides to develop a physical distribution system that profitably creates value for customers.

Some organizations use just-in-time (JIT) inventory management systems and electronic data exchange (EDI) to improve the efficiency of physical distribution. JIT inventory management systems cut the cost of holding inventory but require a close working relationship between organizations. EDI is used in some physical distribution systems to allow information to be shared among channel members quickly to improve customer service.

Key Terms and Concepts

wholesaler (distributor) (p. 392)
merchant wholesaler (p. 394)
full-service wholesaler (p. 394)
general merchandise wholesaler (p. 395)
specialty wholesaler (p. 395)
limited function wholesaler (p. 395)
service merchandiser
   (rack jobber) (p. 395)

cash-and-carry wholesaler (p. 395)
drop shipper (p. 395)
truck jobber (p. 396)
agent (broker, manufacturer's
   representative) (p. 396)
physical distribution (p. 399)
mode of transportation (p. 400)
intermodal transportation (p. 402)

piggyback service (p. 402)
freight forwarder (p. 403)
warehouse (p. 403)
public warehouse (p. 403)
just-in-time (JIT) inventory
   management (p. 407)
electronic data interchange
   (EDI) (p. 408)

Review and Discussion Questions

1. In what general ways do wholesalers create value for producers?
2. Name and describe briefly the different types of wholesalers.
3. If you were a marketer for a line of trendy, brightly colored socks, what type of wholesaler should you choose and why?
4. If you wanted to become a merchant wholesaler for sporting goods, what factors would you consider in developing a product strategy?
5. Economic and technological changes in the marketing environment have made wholesaling highly competitive. What steps must modern wholesalers take in order to survive?
6. For each of the following products, what mode(s) of physical distribution do you think would be most efficient? Why?
   a. apples bound from Washington State farms to Midwestern supermarkets
   b. blood samples being analyzed by a genetics laboratory in another state
   c. natural gas being delivered to homes and workplaces around a major city

7. In what ways do value-driven physical distribution and cross-functional physical distribution create value for customers?
8. What are some benefits and pitfalls of just-in-time inventory management? Would you recommend it for a computer wholesaler serving North America and the Pacific Rim? Why or why not?
9. How is computer technology influencing physical distribution?
10. Prior to taking this course, you may or may not have been aware of the effect that physical distribution has had on you as a consumer. Think of a time when physical distribution affected your purchase decision— perhaps one product was unavailable, so you bought a competing product instead, or you had to wait a long time for a delivery from a mail-order house. Describe how your experience affected your buying decision and how it affected your perception of value in the product you purchased—and, if appropriate, the product you did not purchase.

Chapter Project Become a Value-Driven Wholesaler

Being a successful wholesaler means creating value for producers and other intermediaries. That is, you must be able to create value by offering superior service for a reasonable price. You also create value by linking customers with the products they want to buy.

For your project, choose a familiar product, perhaps cosmetics, fishing gear, pet food, hand-knit sweaters, or snacks. Then work up a proposal to be a wholesaler for it. Based on what you have read in this chapter as well as what you know

about the product's current distribution (such as where the manufacturer is located and in what type of stores the product is sold), develop a proposal to offer value to the producer for selecting you as a wholesaler (concentrate on service and other benefits; it will be difficult for you to calculate costs). As part of your proposal, state how hiring you as a wholesaler would create value for consumers (which should make your services attractive to the producer).

Chapter Case Corporate Express

The very name of Jirka Rysavy's company evokes not only his past but the mission of his business. Before he founded Corporate Express, Rysavy was an international hurdler for his native Czechoslovakia. He later left his homeland and settled in the United States. Corporate Express, now based in Colorado near Rysavy's mountain retreat, gets office products from manufacturers to corporate customers—fast.

After fleeing Czechoslovakia through sports connections that got him an exit visa, Rysavy traveled around the United States, doing small jobs for a little cash. "I ate bread," he recalls. "I slept outside in parks or in airports or bus stations." He returned to Czechoslovakia where he spent time alone, in the mountains. "To learn to be alone without being lonely is very important," Rysavy says. After earning a master's degree in engineering, Rysavy made his way back to the United States to start his new life. His previous experiences—as an athlete and as a recluse—all helped shape his approach to business.

After starting up and selling several small businesses, Rysavy bought an office-supply store from a neighbor in downtown Boulder, Colorado. He installed a computer system to track customers and sales. After reviewing the accounts, Rysavy determined that future success lay in focusing on organizational buyers instead of retail sales. This decision helped increase sales eightfold. Then Rysavy did more research and found that office supplies could be distributed more efficiently by eliminating wholesalers and improving physical distribution. He also learned that $30 billion a year was spent by large companies on office supplies. He decided that if he moved fast and offered greater value to these companies, he could develop a loyal and profitable customer base.

Rysavy began to buy up small office-supply companies that were in trouble. He reviewed the way they filled orders, held inventory, and shipped products. Then he developed a plan that allowed Corporate Express to bypass wholesalers and purchase office supplies directly from producers. He cut down the number of products offered, listing about 5,000 in-stock items in his catalog instead of the customary 25,000, and got them to customers faster. Corporate Express claims that it can deliver 99 percent of all orders by the next business day; no other competitor does this. At competing companies,

explains Rysavy, "salespeople have to call customers and explain why the order isn't being filled quickly. That adds lots to costs, and it's a frustration for customers." By filling orders so quickly, Corporate Express also cuts inventory carrying costs, By focusing on customers that place large orders for standard suppliers, Corporate Express can make bulk purchases from supply manufacturers at lower prices. By passing these savings on to customers, Corporate Express builds customer value.

None of this efficiency could take place without the right computer system. Rysavy hired his childhood friend, Pavel Bouska, to develop a software system that could handle all aspects of office-supply order processing and inventory management. Says Bouska, "Every night the computers look at everything in inventory. They try to make sure we don't run out of things—but not at any price. We stock only as deep as is cost-efficient."

The computer system analyzes everything from purchasing patterns to future demand. Bouska can ask it questions, such as whether the company should overstock during certain seasons. The software provides answers such as "the free freight will more than make up for the overstocking." Bouska can then give the system the go ahead to act on the recommendations. With the ingenuity of two entrepreneurs, Corporate Express has managed to turn the business of selling paper clips and rubber bands into a $1 billion enterprise, the largest company in the industry.

Questions

1. Why is the reliable physical distribution that Corporate Express provides for its business customers so valuable to them?

2. Why is inventory management so important to Corporate Express's success?

3. Is there any way a wholesaler could compete with Corporate Express? If so, how? If not, why not?

Source: Stephen D. Solomon, "New World, Ordered," *Inc.*, December 1995, pp. 68–79. Adapted with permission, *Inc.* magazine, December 1995. Copyright 1995 by Goldhirsh Group, Inc., 38 Commercial Wharf, Boston, MA 02110.

Explore more at www.corporate-express.com

Chapter Sixteen

Retailing

CHAPTER OUTLINE

The Role of Retailing in Distribution
Major Types of Retailers
  Store Retailing
  Nonstore Retailing
Marketing Strategy Decisions for Retailers
  Product Decisions
  Pricing Decisions
  Placement Decisions
  Promotion Decisions
  Store Image and Atmospherics
Changing Environment of Retailing
  Changes in the Types of Retailers
  Technological Changes in Retailing
  Global Scope of Retailing
Legal and Ethical Issues in Retailing
Summary

LEARNING OBJECTIVES

After completing this chapter, you should be able to:

1. Explain how retailers can contribute to the process of creating value.
2. Distinguish store retailing and nonstore retailing.
3. Define basic categories of retailers.
4. Summarize marketing strategies used by retailers.
5. Describe how the mix of retailers is changing.
6. Identify ways in which technological developments have influenced retailing.
7. Assess the effect of globalization on retailing.
8. Discuss legal and ethical issues in retailing.

Virgin Megastore

Imagine a store that is the size of one and a half football fields. Imagine one million CDs, one thousand listening booths, 21,000 videos, and more than 200 workers—all in the same store. This description fits the Virgin Megastore in New York City. It is the largest record store in the world—larger, even, than Virgin's other megastores in Paris, London, and San Francisco.

The store represents retailing at its largest. It also represents some other aspects of retailing. The store is an example of a category killer, or a huge store that sells just one category of merchandise. Category killers "kill" off smaller competitors by offering a deep product selection at low prices. To succeed, they must create value for consumers.

The Virgin Megastore has a 110-seat cafe, a bookstore, software store, and a movie theater that is only accessible through the record store. "This isn't simply a record store," says Brian Regan, the company's marketing director. "It's an environment." Ian Duffell, president of the Virgin Retail Group, expands on Regan's comment: "Tower [Records] has a record-warehouse sort of feel. HMV, at least originally, was like a club. We're trying to make the Megastore a grand place to visit —an event." Each section of the store has its own atmosphere—music videos in the rock section; quiet ballads and show tunes in the jazz and Broadway sections; a classical pianist playing live in the classical section.

Virgin executives had to build their stores in the right places. So far, their preference has been "landmark locations" where tourists visit. In Paris it was the Champs Elysees and in London it was Oxford Street; in New York, it's Times Square. Thousands of people pass through Times Square every day; Virgin hopes that most of them will take a detour through its store. Once they do, they may

spend up to two hours browsing inside. If they don't stop at the cafe or movie theater, they can always relax on one of the soft-pillowed couches that are placed exactly where shoppers are apt to want to take a rest.

As you read this chapter, consider the ways in which retailers create value, and the ways in which retailing has changed during your lifetime and how it may change in the future.

Source: Fred Kaplan, "A World Record Store," *The Boston Globe,* April 19, 1996, pp. 85, 88. Reprinted courtesy of *The Boston Globe.*

Explore more at www.virginusa.com

Chapter Overview

Consumer goods are distributed through retailers. These intermediaries are a link between producers and consumers that make exchanges more efficient. Retailers may also add value by making exchanges fun—like the Virgin Megastore—or by other ways.

This chapter introduces the role of retailers in adding value in the chain from producers to consumers. The chapter begins by formally defining retailers and discussing their role in value creation. Then, the chapter explores the many types of retailers and examines the types of decisions retailers make. The chapter then turns to a discussion of trends in retailing, including the effects of competition, technology, and globalization of markets. The chapter closes with a look at legal and ethical issues in retailing.

The Role of Retailing in Distribution

retailer
An intermediary that sells
primarily to ultimate consumers.

A **retailer** is an intermediary "engaged primarily in selling to ultimate consumers."[1] Retailers buy from manufacturers or wholesalers. Intermediaries that sell to consumers are engaged in retailing, whether or not they operate stores. For example, Audrey Evans sells troll dolls and collectable dolls from a kiosk located in the Gurnee Mills mall in Gurnee, Illinois.[2] Anyone Can Whistle uses a catalog to sell user-friendly musical instruments and related products such as wind chimes. Consumers who want to hear what the instruments sound like before purchasing can request a free 30-minute cassette tape of them.[3] In these examples, both Audrey Evans and Anyone Can Whistle are considered retailers.

Retailing is even bigger business than wholesaling. Over three times as many people work in retail trade as in wholesale trade.[4] Total retail sales of approximately $2 trillion amount to roughly $7,700 for each person in the United States.[5] Figure 16.1 shows which types of retailers accounted for the largest segments of the total.

Retailers deliver benefits to both suppliers (producers and wholesalers) and consumers. They offer suppliers an efficient way to make products available to consumers. Especially with the information-gathering capabilities of modern technology, retailers can provide suppliers with useful market research information. Retailers also help forecast sales and assume risk in purchasing products that are perishable or become obsolete. Some retailers also take part in physical distribution.

From the buyer's perspective, retailers can create value by making products available at convenient hours and during the desired seasons or times of day. Retailers try to operate in convenient locations and some even come to consumers' homes. Retailers

FIGURE 16.1
Sales by Major Types of Retailers

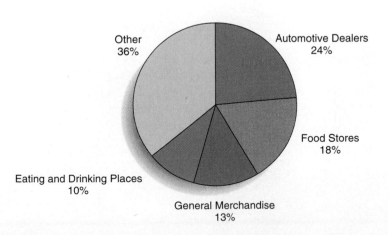

Source: U.S. Department of Commerce, *Statistical Abstract of the United States,* 115th ed. (Washington, D.C.: U.S. Government Printing Office, 1995), p. 782.

T A B L E 16.1
Ways in Which Retailers Can
Create Value

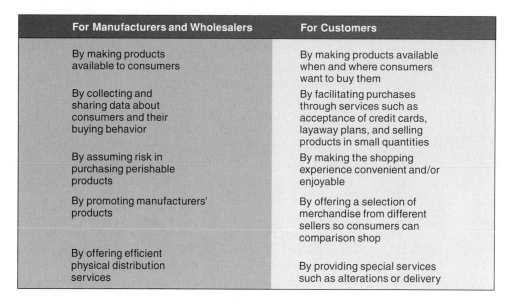

For Manufacturers and Wholesalers	For Customers
By making products available to consumers	By making products available when and where consumers want to buy them
By collecting and sharing data about consumers and their buying behavior	By facilitating purchases through services such as acceptance of credit cards, layaway plans, and selling products in small quantities
By assuming risk in purchasing perishable products	By making the shopping experience convenient and/or enjoyable
By promoting manufacturers' products	By offering a selection of merchandise from different sellers so consumers can comparison shop
By offering efficient physical distribution services	By providing special services such as alterations or delivery

make exchanges easier by accepting credit cards, offering layaway plans, and selling in relatively small quantities or packages. They may make the shopping experience enjoyable by offering a pleasant atmosphere, helpful service, interesting product information, and other amenities. Teach & Play Smart, a retailer of educational toys and supplies, has displays where shoppers can try out products, including art supplies, computers, and building materials. This service makes the store so appealing that some people have called to learn the store's (nonexistent) admission charge.[6] Retailers also may modify products to make them more valuable to consumers, such as by monogramming luggage or slicing salami.

Retailers also create value for consumers by meeting their needs and wants. Commuter Cleaners meets commuters' desire for a truly convenient way to get their clothes to and from the dry cleaners: Rather than simply opening at a busy street corner, Commuter Cleaners operates trucks that meet commuters at the train station each morning and evening.[7]

To create value for consumers, retailers must offer benefits they care about. When the small Fleagle Foods supermarket chain in Waterloo, Iowa, faced new competition from low-priced Sam's Club, Fleagle held a focus group to learn how it could serve customers better. By implementing the suggested changes, Fleagle not only prevented a loss of customers to Sam's Club, it added noncustomers. And when the neighborhood demographics around Christy and Nada Spoa's Ellwood City, Pennsylvania, supermarket changed to include a high percentage of food stamp recipients, the Spoas changed their pricing strategy and product mix to cater to these customers. They cut most of their promotion expenses to keep costs down and offered 50-pound bags of potatoes at the beginning of each month, when customers received their food stamps and wanted to get the most out of their limited budgets.[8] Table 16.1 summarizes some of the many ways retailers can create value for their suppliers and their customers.

Major Types of Retailers

It is important that products be sold through the right types of retailers to reach consumers and build market share. For example, Yaleet Inc., a shoe marketing company based in Syosset, New York, distributes its retro, Sixties-style Naot sandals and shoes through health food stores, in-line skating stores, bike shops, and surf shops, as well as through shoe stores. By using nonshoe retailers, the company reaches its typical customers, who tend to be interested in health and the environment.[9]

In contrast, Huffy Corporation used the wrong type of retailers when it launched its Cross Sport, a combination of sturdy mountain bike and lightweight racing bike.

Huffy distributed the Cross Sport through its usual channels—mass merchandisers such as Kmart and Toys 'R' Us. Since the bikes were more expensive than the rest of Huffy's line and were targeted to an older market, they required more sales support than the stores could provide. A year after the Cross Sport was launched, Huffy cut back production by 75 percent.[10]

In general, retailing occurs either in stores or through a variety of types of nonstore retailing, ranging from Web sites to catalogs. Some organizations use both. The National Cheerleading Association (NCA), for instance, offers cheerleading-related merchandise in catalogs and in the NCA Super Center stores it owns in Houston.[11]

Store Retailing

Marketers divide stores into a number of types based on characteristics such as assortment, price level, and convenience. Manufacturers try to distribute their products through the types of stores that support their positioning strategies. Retailers develop store types that they think will best meet the shopping preferences of their target markets and be profitable. Three general types of retail stores are specialty stores, mass merchandisers, and convenience stores. These are described in Table 16.2.

T A B L E 16.2
Major Types of Store Retailers

Type	Definition	Examples
Specialty Stores	Stores that handle a deep selection in a limited number of product categories	Coconuts Music and Video
Limited-line stores	Stores that offer a large assortment of a few related product lines	The Gap
Single-line stores	Stores that emphasize a single product line	Batteries Plus
Category killers	Big, low-priced, limited-line stores featuring deep selection but also some breadth	Toys 'R' Us, Sports Authority, Circuit City
Mass Merchandisers	Retailers offering a wide but somewhat shallow mix of products	Sears
Supermarkets	Large, departmentalized retail establishments offering a relatively broad and complete stock of dry groceries, fresh meat, perishable produce, and dairy products, supplemented by a variety of convenience, nonfood merchandise and operated primarily on a self-service basis	A&P, Safeway, Kroger
Department stores	Retail establishments which carry several lines of merchandise, such as women's ready-to-wear and accessories, men's and boys' clothing, piece goods, small wares, and home furnishings, all of which are organized into separate departments for the purpose of promotion, service, accounting, and control	Macy's, Nordstrom, Marshall Fields, J. C. Penney
Catalog showrooms	Retail outlets that consumers visit to make actual purchases of articles described in catalogs mailed to their homes	Service Merchandise
Superstores	Large stores that feature low prices and carry more items than most supermarkets	Cub Foods

Specialty Stores   When consumers seek a deep selection in a particular product category or want to draw on the expertise of salespeople, they tend to shop at **specialty stores.** These stores handle one or a few product categories and compete on their expertise and selection within them. Coconuts Music and Video specializes in CDs, cassettes, and videotapes, but it offers an extensive number of titles.[12] Consumers use specialty stores to gather information about product choices and to compare products and brands.

Specialty stores may be either single-line stores (which offer only one product category) or limited-line stores (which offer a few related product categories). Some of the most successful retailers have been big, limited-line stores featuring low prices. These stores are called **category killers** because their deep assortment and low prices make them tough to compete with in the product categories they offer. Other limited-line and single-line stores may charge higher prices in exchange for their expertise and large selection of sometimes hard-to-find items.

Mass Merchandisers   In other situations, consumers want the convenience of being able to buy several kinds of products at the same store. **Mass merchandisers** are retailers that offer a wider, but usually shallower, assortment of products than do specialty stores. Supermarkets, department stores, and catalog showrooms

specialty store
A store that handles a deep selection in a limited number of product categories.

category killer
Big, low-priced limited-line store featuring deep selection but also some breadth.

mass merchandiser
A retailer offering a wide but somewhat shallow mix of products.

T A B L E   16.2
Continued

Type	Definition	Examples
Hypermarkets	Unusually large limited-service combination discount store, supermarket, and warehouse under a single roof; typically sells both food and nonfood items at 10 to 15 percent below normal retail prices	Bigg's, American Fare
Discount stores	Large retail stores which incorporate aspects of supermarket merchandising strategy to a high degree, attempt to price merchandise at a relatively low markup, carry stocks, and render only limited customer service, usually on the basis of a specific extra charge	Wal-Mart, Kmart, Target
Warehouse stores	Retailers that offer certain types of merchandise, particularly groceries, drugs, hardware, home improvement products, and home furnishings in a warehouse atmosphere; facilities are typically in low-rent, isolated buildings with a minimum of services offered, and the consumer performs the bulk of the functions in a self-serve mode	Price Club, Sam's Warehouse
Variety stores	Establishments selling a variety of merchandise in the low and popular price range, such as stationery, gift items, women's accessories, toilet articles, light hardware, toys, housewares, and confectionery	Woolworth
Off-price retailers	Retailers that offer lower price for goods late in the season or with a limited selection of colors and sizes	T. J. Maxx, Filene's Basement
Convenience Stores	Retail institutions whose primary advantage to consumers is locational convenience; high-margin, high-turnover retailers	7-Eleven, Stop 'N' Go

Source: Most definitions based on Peter D. Bennett, ed., *Dictionary of Marketing Terms,* 2nd ed., (Chicago: American Marketing Association, 1995).

Most supermarkets offer a wide variety of goods, but Bashas' Supermarkets in Arizona is carrying the idea further than many by teaming with Wells Fargo & Co. Wells Fargo's location at Bashas' are staffed by full-time banking officers. They offer not only deposits and withdrawals, but CDs, investments, and loan applications.

compete primarily by offering different product categories while the other types listed in Table 16.2 also compete on the basis of low prices. Mass merchandisers attract larger numbers of customers who make both planned and impulse purchases from a variety of product categories.

Mass merchandisers featuring low prices differ according to the types of products they offer and the level of service they provide. A retailer of general merchandise might operate variety stores (such as Woolworth) or discount stores (such as Wal-Mart or Kmart). They provide the basic services of a store retailer, such as displaying merchandise, letting consumers buy in small quantities, and ringing up sales, but keep prices down by operating efficiently and buying large volumes of goods at discount prices. Other mass merchandisers keep prices low by limiting service. For example, at warehouse clubs consumers may have to buy bulk quantities and forgo services. Moreover, such stores are typically plain structures in low-rent locations.

Convenience Stores   Time pressures have caused some consumers to emphasize convenience over other criteria in assessing value. Since many of these consumers are two-earner families, they are willing to pay higher prices to save time by shopping at convenience stores like 7-Eleven. **Convenience stores** stock the kinds of products people want in a hurry—milk, batteries, magazines, sandwiches, and so on—and receive a price premium on many goods for making them so convenient to purchase. Some convenience stores attract more customers by including self-serve gas pumps at their locations.

Nonstore Retailing

Not all retailing takes place in stores. Consumers also buy merchandise from catalogs, from television offers, from vending machines, and increasingly from computers. The two basic types of **nonstore retailing** are vending machines and direct marketing. Table 16.3 provides definitions for the types of nonstore retailing.

Vending Machines   The practice of selling through **vending machines,** sometimes called "automatic merchandising," is useful for products that can be sold via credit card or for relatively small amounts of cash. Some products sold this way are soft drinks, snack foods, stamps, photocopies, and telephone calls.

A relatively new type of vending machine is an Internet kiosk, which consists of a computer terminal that will connect a user to the Internet for a price. A company

convenience store
A retailer whose primary advantage is location.

nonstore retailing
A form of retailing in which consumer contact occurs outside the confines of a retail store.

vending machine
A machine that delivers a product when the buyer inserts payment.

TABLE 16.3
Types of Nonstore Retailing

Type	Definition	Example(s)
Vending machines	Machines that deliver a product when the buyer inserts payment	Coin-operated photocopiers, soft-drink vending machines
Direct marketing	Marketing efforts that use personal selling or various advertising media to solicit orders from consumers where they live or work	Telephone sales calls, catalogs
Direct selling	Personal explanation and demonstration of a product, with an opportunity to buy	Tupperware or Discovery Toys party
Direct-mail marketing	Mailing of brochures, letters, and other materials that describe a product and solicit orders	Letter inviting the consumer to subscribe to *Time;* catalog for Johnny's Selected Seeds
Tele-marketing	Telephoning prospects, describing the product, and seeking orders	Phone call from a theater inviting the consumer to buy season tickets
Direct-action advertising	Advertisements containing ordering information	Magazine ad or television info-mercial with a toll-free number for placing an order
On-line marketing	Computer display of product information providing ordering via modem	Web site that invites visitors to use a credit card to place orders
Integrated direct marketing	Combining several types of direct marketing into a single effort	Direct mail offer coupled with follow-up phone calls

called CafeNet has set these up in coffee shops. Users drop in a quarter for three minutes of time on-line, or they may set up an account with CafeNet. Given the reception these kiosks have received, CafeNet plans to set them up in other kinds of locales, including airports, bookstores, and shopping centers.[13]

Vending machines' major source of value is their convenience; consumers can use them at any time. This makes vending machines particularly appealing for products demanded around the clock, especially those that do not require sales help or the need to closely inspect the merchandise before purchase. On the down side, the machines can be expensive to maintain, driving up prices.

direct marketing
Marketing efforts that use personal selling or various advertising media to solicit orders from consumers where they live or work.

Direct Marketing   **Direct marketing** consists of marketing efforts that use sales-people or impersonal media to solicit orders from consumers where they live or work. Direct marketing once consisted mainly of brochures and catalogs mailed to consumers, but now also includes phones, magazines, radios, televisions, and computers.

Direct marketing creates value in several ways. It offers consumers convenience because they can make purchases and receive products without leaving home. It is especially useful for serving consumers who have difficulty shopping in stores because they are disabled, need to care for children, or have other responsibilities. A benefit to sellers is that consumers who are likely to be interested in certain products can be well targeted. For example, sellers can purchase mailing lists of people who own complementary products and market to them, such as software offers to computer owners. Because the seller can keep records of all the customers who received a mailing or phone call, response rates can be measured and the effectiveness of the

Midnight Waltz Barbie, a limited-edition Barbie Collectible doll, is available exclusively from the Barbie Shoppe, which is accessed through the Barbie Collectibles Internet site on the World Wide Web (http://www.barbie.com). The collectible doll is advertised only on the Web site and can be ordered by a choice of two direct marketing methods: an 800 number or via mail using an order form provided by computer printout. The Barbie doll is one of the most successful consumer product brands of all time and special-edition dolls such as Midnight Waltz Barbie, as well as direct marketing by informercials and magazine advertising, have helped boost the Barbie adult collector business to 1995 sales of more than $175 million.

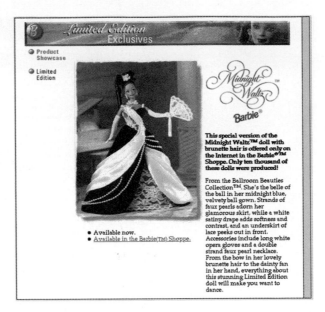

direct marketing effort can be assessed. Direct marketing is useful for test marketing as well as for full-scale marketing efforts.

The uses of direct marketing often are quite sophisticated. In Japan, Amway has become the fastest-growing foreign firm by setting up a network of 700,000 independent agents armed with fax machines, computers, and telephones. They sell about 150 household items, most imported from the United States. Using its three automated distribution centers, which have on-site customs inspection, Amway can deliver orders in only two days.[14]

direct selling
A personal explanation of a product by a sales representative with an opportunity to buy.

Direct Selling   Direct marketing through **direct selling** occurs when a sales representative gives consumers a personal explanation and demonstration of the product, often in their homes or at work. In the United States, direct selling accounts for almost $17 billion in annual sales.[15]

Tupperware, Amway Corporation, and Mary Kay Cosmetics use direct selling for their products. So does Avon, the world's largest cosmetics company, which generates more than half of its sales outside the United States. In Brazil, Avon sells through "320,000 Ladies," including 60,000 in the Amazon. In some Brazilian river villages, Avon products arrive by kayak, and the Avon Ladies arrange barter deals—say, 20 pounds of flour for a bottle of cologne. More often, payments are in the form of gold nuggets or powder.[16]

direct mail marketing
Mailing of brochure, letters, and other materials that describe a product and solicit orders.

Direct Mail   **Direct mail marketing** is the mailing of brochures, letters, and other materials that describe a product and ask consumers to order it. Geerlings & Wade, a direct-mail retailer of wine, sends its customers a four-page brochure and order form every few weeks describing a type of wine and the vineyard where it is produced.[17] Sales resulting from direct mail have grown fast in Japan, where marketing via mail works particularly well for fashion accessories, jewelry, cameras, ladies' wear, and furniture.[18]

Catalogs are a common form of direct mail retailing. In the United States, the catalog industry mails out well over 12 billion catalogs a year.[19] They are sent by giant retailers like Spiegel and Lands' End as well as by such entrepreneurs as Thanksgiving Coffee Company, based in Ft. Bragg, California, which sells gourmet coffee blends.[20]

Whether by catalog, brochure, or newsletter, direct mail can be an effective way to sell products to consumers who enjoy the convenience of shopping from home. Unlike direct selling, however, direct mail does not give consumers a chance to handle or try out products. To ask questions, consumers have to be motivated enough to contact the company. Beverly LaBadia, who manages a women's specialty clothing store in Flemington, New Jersey, maintains that catalogs cannot completely replace store retailing for clothing because they do not show what the clothes will look like on the buyer. Women's clothing, in particular, has no standard sizing; the dimensions of a jacket size, for example, can vary considerably.[21] Retailers who use direct mail address such limitations by offering sizing information in their catalogs and by having helpful customer service representatives, a liberal return policy, and a good reputation.

telemarketing
The practice of telephoning prospects, describing the product, and seeking orders.

Telemarketing   Selling by telephoning prospects, describing products, and asking for orders is called **telemarketing.** Telemarketing allows for more personal contact than direct mail or catalogs. Thus, it can be useful when consumers have specific questions. However, this form of retailing is less effective if consumers need to see the product or want to compare several options. It therefore does not make sense for purchases that consumers view as involving high risk.

direct-action advertising
Advertisements containing ordering information.

Direct-Action Advertising   For low-risk purchases, such as a trial offer, some marketers use **direct-action advertising.** These advertisements include ordering information, such as a number to call or an address to which to send an order. Direct-action advertising may be displayed on billboards, broadcast on radio or television, or printed in newspapers or magazines. Broadcast media have become increasingly important in direct-action advertising. Home shopping television channels broadcast shows that demonstrate products and provide a phone number to call with an order. Some TV commercials also include information for ordering products. Interactive TV may soon allow viewers to skip the phone call and simply place orders using their remote controls.

on-line marketing
Computer display of product information including how to order via modem.

On-Line Marketing   Computer networks, including the Internet, also offer information about a variety of products. With **on-line marketing,** consumers can use a modem to place orders and pay by credit card. On-line marketing is likely to grow in importance as more consumers become comfortable with purchasing this way. One problem that is being overcome is providing for the secure transmission of credit card numbers or other funds transfer. One successful on-line marketer is PC Flowers of Oakton, Virginia. By enabling users of the Prodigy service to have flowers delivered, PC Flowers has become one of the biggest florists in the United States. One reason given for the success of this business is the fact that men—the major users of on-line services—are also major buyers of flowers.[22]

Integrated Direct Marketing   Of course, manufacturers are not limited to direct selling, direct-action advertising, or any single form of direct marketing. In fact, combining several modes of direct marketing can improve the performance of the

integrated direct marketing
The combination of several types of direct marketing into a coordinated effort.

overall marketing effort. The combination of several modes of direct marketing, used in a coordinated effort, is called **integrated direct marketing.**[23] For example, marketers know that a small percentage of consumers receiving a direct-mail piece will place an order. By adding toll-free telephone numbers, training staff to handle calls, and using follow-up phone calls, purchases can be greatly increased.

Marketing Strategy Decisions for Retailers

In the market for clothes for adults under 30, Urban Outfitters defines itself as the antithesis of the Gap. In contrast to the Gap's neat khakis and T-shirts, Urban Outfitters offers an eclectic mix of worn-looking but artsy clothes. Some employees call it a "high-class thrift shop." The company prides itself on being ahead of fashion trends (a view shared by editors of fashion magazines) and often brings in a new selection of merchandise each week. Whereas the Gap generates billions in sales from its multitude of locations, Urban Outfitters has chosen to grow slowly, locating in large urban areas with major colleges while planning to limit its U.S. presence to 35 stores, plus stores in Canada and possibly in Japan and Europe.

To appeal to its counterculture clientele, Urban Outfitters sets up stores in former factories or garages, and plays music mainly from independent recording labels. It hires young employees who share the retailer's sense of style. Rather than using standard advertising formats, Urban Outfitters promotes itself in a newspaper called *Slant,* available at the store as well as at clubs and coffee houses. Together, these elements of Urban Outfitters' marketing strategy meet the wants of young adults who, in the words of *Fashion Network Newsletter* editor Alan Millstein, "[don't] want to be Gapped."[24] Urban Outfitters' marketing mix is much different than the Gap's, yet both are successful retailers. One of the reasons for their success is that both Urban Outfitters and The Gap have consistent marketing strategies. They combine the right product, price, placement, promotion, and store image to create value for their customers.

Product Decisions

One of the marketing decisions retailers must make is the merchandise assortment they will offer consumers. In addition, they must decide what services and how much of them to provide consumers to create value.

Merchandise Assortment   Retailers must decide the depth and breadth of the merchandise assortment to be offered. A deep assortment includes may variations of product types. A broad assortment includes many different types of products. For example, Table 16.4 depicts the breadth and depth of bicycles carried in three different types of stores: a local bicycle shop (a specialty store), Toys 'R' Us (a category specialist), and Wal-Mart (a general merchandise discount store). Wal-Mart has fewer models, or less depth, than Toys 'R' Us, which in turn carries fewer types and models than the bicycle shop. While the bicycle shop has the deepest product line, it also has the narrowest line; it carries only bicycles and bicycling supplies, while Toys 'R' Us carries other toys and games as well. Wal-Mart has the broadest product line in that it carries a great many other products, too.

Some retailers offer greater value than their competitors by offering a broader or deeper merchandise assortment. Others offer lower-priced, private-label merchandise or items that are of higher quality or are hard to find. Still others may match their competitors' decisions about merchandise assortment and deliver greater value through additional services or an exclusive store image.

Merchandising decisions also involve adding new products and categories, such as supermarkets offering carryout foods. Not only do these offerings broaden a

T A B L E 16.4
Three Retailers' Variety and
Assortment of Bicycles

Types of Bicycles	Retailer		
	Bicycle Shop	Toys 'R' Us	Wal-Mart
Adult road	Trek Ross Mongoose Bridgestone Specially-built (27 SKUs) $195–$4,000	none	Murray (2SKUs) $93
Adult hybrid	Trek Ross Mongoose Bridgestone Specially-built (29 SKUs) $190–$1,079	Murray Huffy Roadmaster Nice Magna (9 SKUs) $88–$200	Murray Huffy (10 SKUs) $96–$130
Mountain	Trek Ross Mongoose Bridgestone Specially-built (77 SKUs) $130–$3,080	Murray Huffy Roadmaster Pacific Rand Trendy Dynacraft Range Union (26 SKUs) $88–$200	Murray Huffy Roadmaster (9 SKUs) $96–$150
Child	Ross Mongoose Jazz Specially-built (36 SKUs) $57–$320	Murray Huffy Roadmaster Pacific Rand Trendy Dynacraft Range Union Rallye Paragon Kent (38 SKUs) $53–$160	Murray Huffy Roadmaster (7 SKUs) $90–$100

Source: Michael Levy and Barton A. Weitz, *Retailing Management,* 2nd ed. (Chicago: Irwin, 1995), p. 31.

supermarket's merchandise mix, they also appeal to consumers who are pressed for time. Similarly, catalog retailer L. L. Bean expanded its merchandise mix by including children's clothing as an addition to its adult clothes and sporting goods.

Other merchandising decisions involve deleting products from the merchandise mix. Thus, to maintain Crate & Barrel's position as a specialty store with stylish offerings, its managers change up to 40 percent of its selection of housewares and furniture each season.[25]

Service Level A high level of retail service can contribute to customer value by reducing the money, time, and effort required and by making the shopping experience more pleasant. Retailers offer services that include personal selling, product information, easy returns and exchanges, free delivery, credit, gift wrapping, and product modifications such as alterations of clothing. Depending on the target market and merchandise mix, additional services may be appropriate. For example, full-service retailers may offer gift registries, play areas for children, and delivery and installation of merchandise. For a nonstore retailer, a high level of service may include knowledgeable order takers who can help with purchase decisions, enough inventory to ship

orders right away, and a policy that makes returning unwanted merchandise easy. Lands' End offers 24-hour-a-day operators to take phone orders, "specialty shoppers" to help customers who want advice, and full refunds with no questions asked.

Consumers don't want to spend a lot of time waiting in line to pay for their purchases and want to be treated well by store employees. Thus, the level of service offered by a retailer involves the number of personnel available to help customers, their training, and their authority to make decisions related to satisfying customers. The retailer's policy for accepting returns and exchanges also affects the service level. At the Value Village chain of resale stores, goods that still have a price tag attached may be returned for store credit within seven days of purchase. This policy is based on what the chain's owners learned from Nordstrom department stores: For every dollar Nordstrom refunds for returned merchandise, the customer spends another three dollars.[26]

Exceptional service may be the basis of a retailer's competitive advantage. At Galloway Lumber in Kirksville, Missouri, when a customer reports a problem, one of the Galloways calls later the same day to make sure the problem is being solved to the customer's satisfaction. While other businesses in town are closing, Galloway's Lumber continues to expand.[27] Thus, retailers must select the best level of service to meet their target markets shopping preferences.

Pricing Decisions

Retailers typically use markup pricing. The percentage used to mark up merchandise must be sufficient to cover overhead and contribute to profits but not be so high as to make the store non-competitive.

Retailers also must decide if and when to discount or mark down the price of merchandise. Markdowns are common when retailers seek to move out merchandise that is perishable in some sense. For example, because of changes in fashion as well as changes in season, sellers of clothing frequently slash prices to make room for new merchandise. However, predictable patterns of marking down merchandise may encourage consumers to delay purchases until a sale comes up.

forward buying
The practice of buying a big
supply to take advantage of a
reduced price from a supplier.

diverting
The practice of reselling
products bought from a supplier
at a reduced price in another
part of the country where the
supplier is not offering the same
deal.

Retailers also must decide whether to use forward buying and diverting. Through **forward buying,** retailers buy a big supply of a product when the supplier offers it at a reduced price. Suppliers do this in some cases to get retailers to sell at a lower price to consumers. Retailers sell some of the product at the special low price, but when the promotion is over, they mark the remainder of the merchandise up to the full price, enjoying greater profits. Through **diverting,** retailers buy more than they need when a supplier offers a deal, then resell what they don't need at a profit to channel members in another part of the country where the supplier is not offering the deal. As a consequence of these practices, retailers are more profitable, but consumers don't get the full impact of the price reductions producers are trying to offer. This works to the disadvantage of higher-priced, brand-name products relative to their private-label competition, which is why some big producers such as Procter & Gamble encourage every-day low pricing.[28]

Placement Decisions

Manufacturers and retailers must decide whether to offer products in stores or through nonstore retailing. Retailers also must select sites for stores and for the operations of nonstore retailing businesses.

Store versus Nonstore Retailing   Manufacturers and retailers must decide whether to distribute products through stores or nonstore retailing or through some combination of the two. Retailing using a store format is useful when consumers want to see and handle products, when a store is the traditional place for purchasing particular products, and when additional impulse purchases are common. Store retailing is also an appropriate choice for selling products that customers want to use right away.

Nonstore retailing can be used when consumers are willing to wait to have their products delivered and can make purchase decisions without physically handling the products. This placement strategy also makes sense for retailers that create value through convenience or lower prices. Nonstore retailing also allows consumers to purchase products not available locally and to purchase any time they want.

Manufacturers may choose nonstore retailing when they cannot afford to build stores to serve scattered markets or cannot get effective distribution through channels that use stores. For example, buyers of highly specialized products may be geographically dispersed and place such small orders that building stores is not cost effective. Established retail stores and chains may be reluctant to carry products that are slow moving or for which there is not established demand. In these cases, direct marketing may be used to build enough demand to persuade stores to carry the products. For example, Intuit Inc. initially could not persuade retailers to stock its personal finance software, called Quicken. So Intuit sold Quicken directly to consumers by placing ads in computer magazines. This approach was so successful that retailers started stocking Quicken.[29] Similarly, small recording companies use direct marketing when they can't get their products sold in retail stores. Subscribers to *Nautilus,* an electronic monthly published on compact disc, can hear samples of music available from Windham Hill Records. To order CDs of the music they like, they simply enter a command on their computers.[30]

site selection
The decision of where to locate
a retail store.

Store Location   For store retailers, one of the most important placement decisions is **site selection,** or deciding where to locate stores. Table 16.5 summarizes issues to consider in selecting a retail site. One of the most creative companies in terms of site selection is PepsiCo, which developed nontraditional sites for its Taco Bell, Pizza Hut, and KFC restaurants. For example, the company opened a kiosk in a Moscow subway station to sell Pepsi's soft drinks along with food from Taco Bell.[31]

When locating stores, retailers consider how many consumers desiring their products are located within the area served by particular sites, as well as what competitors are already serving that area. Nearby competitors can be a plus for products for which

T A B L E 16.5
Issues to Consider When
Choosing a Retail Site

Type of site
- Is site near the target market?
- Is the type of site appropriate for the store?
- What is the age and condition of the site?
- What is the trade area?

Accessibility
- What are the road patterns and conditions surrounding the site?
- Do any natural or artificial barriers impede access to the site?
- Does the site have good visibility from the street?
- Is there a good balance between too much and too little traffic flow?
- Is there a good balance between too much and too little parking?
- Is there a good balance between too much and too little congestion of cars and people?
- Is it easy to enter/exit the parking lot?

Locational advantages within a center
- Is the site adjacent to important tenants?
- Will adjacent tenants complement/compete with the store?

Terms of occupancy
- Are the terms of the lease slanted in favor of the landlord or retailer?
- Is the type of lease favorable to the retailer?

Legal considerations
- Does the site meet requirements of the Americans with Disabilities Act?
- Does the site meet environmental standards?
- Is the site zoning compatible with the store?
- Does the store's architectural design meet building codes?
- Are the store's external signs compatible with zoning ordinances, building codes, and shopping center management?
- Can the store acquire special licenses (e.g., liquor license) for the site?

Source: Michael Levy and Barton A. Weitz, *Retailing Management,* 2nd. ed. (Chicago: Irwin, 1995), p. 205.

consumers prefer a wide selection, such as a variety of fast-food restaurants or shoe stores. The presence of many stores can attract consumers looking to purchase from a product category. For other products, such as gasoline, a nearby competitor may be less desirable. When book superstores were poised to enter the St. Louis market, The Library, Ltd., moved to an alternative site and built a large store so that it could establish itself as the area's giant bookstore. The Library has since expanded even further into a huge 53,000-square-foot location, making it among the largest bookstores in the United States. It features seven, themed reading rooms, including a mystery room decorated with a fireplace, Oriental rug, mahogany paneling, and wingback chairs. Unlike most independent booksellers, it continues to hold its own against big players in the industry.[32]

A desirable location is one that will attract consumers interested in the types of products being offered. Thus, for fast-selling products, retailers often seek convenient, easy-to-find locations. For specialty items, on the other hand, a convenient location is often less important than the merchandise mix. The Kaleidoscope Room is located off a main street in Evanston, Illinois, just north of Chicago. It survives off the beaten path because kaleidoscope collectors will go out of their way to find the unusual store, often traveling there from other states. Because collectors are willing to seek out the store, it makes sense to locate where rents are relatively lower.[33]

When low prices are key, retailers often choose more remote locations in order to reduce their building and rental costs. Bargain-hunting consumers are drawn to out-of-the-way outlet malls, where sales have outpaced those at more traditional malls.[34] In fact, some department stores have opened clearance centers in outlet malls to carry unsold merchandise from their other stores. Nordstrom, for instance, locates some of its Nordstrom Rack discount stores in outlet malls located away from their regular stores in traditional shopping centers. This not only keeps costs under control but prevents the discount stores from cannibalizing the full-line stores and makes them more accessible to shoppers who are seeking discount goods.[35]

Issues of convenience include how easy it is to travel to stores and find parking (see "Put It into Practice: How Convenient Is Your Local Mall?"). Access to parking may make a suburban mall or a strip shopping center more desirable than an inner city central business district. Another way to achieve convenience is to locate stores in heavy traffic areas of cities or malls. For example, Eateries Inc., locates its Garfield's restaurants near mall attractions such as movie theaters.[36] Locating in shopping centers helps draw customer traffic because consumers come to them to purchase many different products—the majority of consumer shopping trips are for multiple purposes.[37]

Malls and business districts offer promotions or entertainment to attract consumers. The 78 acres of Minneapolis's Mall of America include a miniature-golf course, a 14-screen theater, and an amusement park called Camp Snoopy.[38] Even larger is the West Edmonton Mall in Canada—a tourist draw as the world's biggest shopping mall. A mall can be an expensive store location, but some big developers offer assistance programs to small retailers in an effort to create a varied mix of tenants.[39]

Even for nonstore retailing, marketers must select the site or sites from which they will conduct business. Sites are selected to keep operations costs down, including mail and shipping charges.

This ad for the Diehard battery promotes both "motorcycle batteries only at Sears" and the company's new image as an exciting place to shop. Sears, Roebuck and Co., with 800 full-line department stores and 1,500 off-the-mall stores, is one of North America's leading retailers of apparel, home, and automotive products. The promotion of Sears's new image has been a success as measured by the rate of sales increase—as much as 8.9 percent during the past three years.

Promotion Decisions

Retailers promote both themselves and the merchandise they carry. Marketing communications seek to build an image of the retailer that will be attractive to its target market. These messages also provide information such as a store's hours and location. Messages about the merchandise mix inform members of the target market about brands and models offered and specials on them.

Many retailers focus more on promoting merchandise than on promoting the store itself. This tendency is common among certain types of retailers, such as supermarkets. The main form of promotion used by supermarkets is weekly advertisements inserted in newspapers or distributed to homes in the store's trading area that focus on sale prices for featured items. This strategy rein-

T A B L E 16.6 Some Dimensions of Atmospherics

Dimensions	Descriptions	Examples
Architecture	Imposing room heights and elegant details; period architecture such as colonial look; small or large rooms; modern or old fashioned	Warehouse look of stores emphasizing low price; waterfalls, pillars, and mosaics in upscale department store
Layout	Basic grid of straight aisles; clustering of related goods into "boutiques"; main aisle as a loop with merchandise along walls and in center	Grid pattern of most supermarkets for efficient shelving; boutique pattern of upscale gift shops to encourage browsing
Lighting	Bright or dim; purely functional or attention getting	Bright lights to stimulate sales in a supermarket; dim lighting with special effects to create an exciting atmosphere in a nightclub
Color scheme	Warm colors to draw in customers and stimulate quick decisions; cool colors to relax customers	Fast-food restaurant decorated with heavy use of red and yellow; elegant restaurant decorated in blues and grays
Sounds	Music (loud or soft, fast or slow); high or low noise level	Pianist playing soft music at Nordstrom to create sense of elegance; loud music to generate excitement and fast turnover at Hard Rock Cafe
Merchandise display	Huge volumes of merchandise stacked high on displays; few product items well spaced in store	Large quantities of canned goods in supermarkets to suggest good sellers, abundance, and low prices; less merchandise and wide open spaces in Nordstrom to suggest affluence and exclusivity
Odors	Pleasant smells like cologne, chocolate, leather, fresh produce, pizza	Food smells can generate hunger in groceries or restaurants; other odors can attract consumers to stores or products such as perfume or leather goods
Salespeople's appearance	Well-dressed and well-groomed salespeople for store selling expensive luxuries; costumes for theme restaurant and stores	Athlete's Foot sales personnel wear referee outfits to look athletic and knowledgeable about shoes

forces a view that people should make shopping decisions based on price, a view that does not necessarily build store loyalty. As supermarkets have broadened their understanding of how to deliver value, some are using other forms of promotion, including radio and television advertisements aimed at positioning stores. Fleming Companies encourages its IGA retailers to focus on building an image apart from low price. Many IGA stores have adopted a theme of "Hometown Proud," in which they participate in local events and let consumers know how the stores serve community needs.[40]

Store Image and Atmospherics

As part of their marketing strategy, both store and nonstore retailers attempt to create images for their operations.

store image
Everything consumers think about particular retail stores and chains.

Store Image   **Store image** involves everything consumers think about particular retail stores and chains. These perceptions are based on the physical characteristics of a store, its merchandise, prices, advertising, and salespeople, and include emotional feelings as well.

In planning and evaluating store images, retailers should bear in mind that from a customer's standpoint, image is not a collection of unrelated characteristics. Consumers usually do not mentally measure the aisles, note the type of shelving used, evaluate the color scheme, and so on. Rather, consumers form general impressions of what a store is like and judge it relative to other stores.[41] For example, most consumers probably have an image of Wal-Mart as low-priced stores and Nordstrom as exclusive outlets.

An understanding of store image requires retailers to think beyond the specific tactics they use to create and adjust an image; they also should consider the perception their target market has for the particular store (see "You Decide: Does Wal-Mart Need a New Face?"). In the case of a hot dog stand, the operator should know that people who come to it expect to find features such as simple decor, condiments, a

Does Wal-Mart Need a New Face?

In the eyes of many marketers, Wal-Mart could do no wrong. The world's largest retailer, with annual sales of $94 billion, seemed to outgrow itself year after year by offering wide selection and low prices to consumers everywhere. But recently, Wal-Mart's growth has slowed. Competitors are eating into profits. Midwest-based Meijer Inc., Kohl's Corp., and Target, along with category killers such as Toys 'R' Us and Home Depot, have been giving the company a run for its money. But Wal-Mart is not giving up the store, and is fighting back mightily on a variety of fronts.

Wal-Mart CEO David Glass believes in supercenters—huge discount stores that combine food and general merchandise under one roof. Although food is generally acknowledged to be less profitable than apparel, Wal-Mart spokesman Jay Allen says that general merchandise business increases up to 30 percent when food is added to the mix. "We have a 42 percent share of the discount store business," says Allen. "If we achieve half that percent in food—that's success. And, we've just begun." At the supercenters and its other stores, Wal-Mart will continue to push its already successful apparel lines, including McKids and Kathie Lee Gifford, without raising prices.

In addition to the new supercenters, Glass sees many opportunities overseas, particularly in South America and Asia; Wal-Mart stores have already opened in Sao Paulo, Brazil, and Shenzhen, China. But these expansions have their own difficulties. "They've run into competitors in South America, players they've never dealt with that are not pushovers," explains Steve Johnson, a managing partner at Andersen Consulting in Chicago. "And they've had resistance from suppliers who have loyalties to other retailers." In China, says Johnson, "The excitement about Wal-Mart's arrival is there, but whether customers can take advantage of that is questionable. Wal-Mart, which has long had a reputation for being able to throw its weight around, will have to learn about cultural differences and lifestyles in the new countries it wants to serve.

Finally, back at home, Wal-Mart is gearing up a third new approach to business. It has opened 374 Home Town stores, which sell merchandise that is appropriate for customers in specific geographic areas. For instance, one store in Oklahoma sells cattle feed and ranch supplies. Several stores in Missouri, Texas, and Arkansas offer free grocery delivery for a low, flat fee. Steve Johnson sees these as good moves. Wal-Mart, he says, needs to venture into "any mass market product—home improvement, books, auto parts—but operating out of the down-and-dirty big-box formula."

In addition to fighting competition, Wal-Mart has had to fight residents and small businesses that do not want Wal-Mart stores in their towns. The fact that Wal-Mart hurts local businesses has tarnished the company's image somewhat. How might Wal-Mart expand its market coverage while enhancing its image, both domestically and abroad? Do you shop at a Wal-Mart regularly? Why or why not?

Source: Genevieve Buck, "A Jarring Wake-Up Call for Sam Walton's Empire," *Chicago Tribune*, June 23, 1996, sec. 5, pp. 1, 7.

Explore more at www.wal-mart.com (see Newsroom).

---

limited menu, and low prices. If they find something with these or similar characteristics, they are likely to be satisfied.

One basic way store retailers create and maintain positive store images is through creating a unique store atmosphere (see "Marketing Movers & Shakers: John L. Morris/Bass Pro Shops"). Retailers' decisions about store atmosphere involve **atmospherics,** or "store architecture, layout, lighting, color scheme, temperature, access, noise, assortment, prices, special events, etc., that serve as stimuli and attention attractors."[42] Table 16.6 summarizes some dimensions of atmospherics. These dimensions work together in a well-planned store to generate positive feelings about it and about shopping there.

Atmospherics can influence any of the senses. To entice shoppers to visit its in-store bakery, for example, one supermarket set up a fan in the bakery to blow the mouth-watering smell of fresh bread into the rest of the store.[43] Many stores consider the music they play part of their retailing strategy. Some play enjoyable music, encouraging shoppers to linger in the store and shop casually. Those that do so are trying to appeal to shoppers like paralegal Jaime Barthmare, who says she'll stay in a store to hear the end of a tune she especially enjoys. Some stores hire music consultants to regularly select and send out music recordings or broadcasts.[44]

Store layout can also influence purchasing. The Gap positions a table inside the front door angled to appear as a diamond. This positioning is intentional, based on research that indicates customers entering the store turn right 80 percent of the time. At the Gap, consumers are guided by the table's angle to a collection of full-priced, newly arrived clothing.[45]

Nonstore Image Nonstore retailers must be concerned about their images, as well. For nonstore retailers, such things as the quality of the paper a catalog is printed on or the design of a Website can influence their overall image.

atmospherics
Factors such as architecture, lighting, and layout that attract attention and stimulate sales.

John L. Morris/ Bass Pro Shops

"Fishing is like a game of chess.... It's a fascinating and ever-changing adventure," explains John L. Morris, who is talking about his passion in life and his business. Morris, an avid fisherman, is also founder and CEO of Bass Pro Shops, the largest fishing and sporting retail operation in the world. Based in Springfield, Missouri, Bass Pro Shops is a specialty retailer. Even so, the company casts a broad net over a variety of fishing-related activities. In addition to Outdoor World, the 170,000-square-foot flagship store that lures four million visitors through its doors each year to purchase all kinds of gear, Morris's company has a 400-page, full-color catalog offering 30,000 items; a lakeside vacation lodge for fishing tourists, a fleet of charter boats, and more than 7,000 independent dealers that sell the firm's own brand-name fishing equipment.

The Outdoor World store makes heavy use of atmospherics designed to make shopping fun and to entice shoppers to buy. The store contains a huge aquarium, a gently winding trout stream, and even a waterfall that cascades to the ground floor from four stories up.

None of this would be possible without John Morris himself. When he founded Bass Pro Shops, his goal was to "develop a reputation for being the place for people who enjoyed fishing—especially bass fishing—to come for the best assortment and most specialized service in the area." He has far exceeded his original goal, but continues to base all of his business on a personal love of fishing, which ultimately creates value for shoppers. "Being a specialty retailer, it's been invaluable for us to stay close to our customers," says Morris.... "We can relate to our customers and their needs because we're from the same group ourselves."

Ethics and social responsibility also play heavily in Morris's business. Morris is active in a variety of

conservation efforts, having chaired or won awards from organizations such as the National Fish and Wildlife Association, the Wildlife Legislative Fund of America, and the International Game Fish Association.

"There's a lot more to fishing than just tying up the boat and waiting for the fish to take your hook," he says. That statement seems to reflect not only how Morris fishes, but his business and his life, as well.

Source: L. B. Gschwandtner, "The Perfect Bait," *Selling Power,* March 1996, pp. 80–84.

Explore more at www.basspro.com

In the case of vending machines, retailers should maintain them so they are clean and attractive, easy to use, and in good working order. Retailers also must consider where the machines are located and ensure that they are stocked regularly.

With regard to direct marketing, creating and maintaining an image depends on the types of media used. Sales representatives who contact consumers in person or over the phone should be well trained and professional. Written materials used in direct marketing should be attractive, and their message should be clear. Creating a catalog that is appealing to its target market is essential to success. High-quality pictures and graphics and useful product and ordering information are critical. In the case of the catalog retailer for Thanksgiving Coffee, an observer of the direct-mail industry wrote, "With warm introductions to the [owners] and their employees, personable copy and an appealing design, the . . . catalog provides more ambiance than most retail stores."[46]

Changing Environment of Retailing

Shifts in the environment have brought about significant changes in the way retailers operate. Economic and demographic changes have made many consumers busier and more value-conscious, bringing about shifts in the popularity of various types of retailers. Technology has brought retailers new opportunities and challenges, and globalization has made many retailers international companies.

Changes in the Types of Retailers

The types of retailers in business have changed in recent years. Most notable has been the decline in the number of department stores and supermarkets and the increase in low-priced mass merchandisers. Although individual stores have closed and some chains have gone out of business, there are still a lot of places to shop. In the United States, the amount of retail sales space per person doubled in a 15-year span to 18 square feet for every U.S. citizen, making competition in retailing more intense.[47]

Creating Value with Lower Prices　The main reason consumers shop less at department stores and supermarkets is that they believe they can get better value elsewhere. According to retail consultant Elizabeth Eagles, "Shoppers believe that by walking into a department store they are automatically going to have to overpay for their purchases."[48] Among retailers of food, drugs, and household items, supermarkets have lost half their market share to their bigger, often lower-priced competition. The major winners have been discount stores, most notably Wal-Mart and Target.[49] This change has occurred not only in the United States, but also in Europe and Japan.[50]

Other winners have been the category killers like Barnes & Noble, Home Depot, Circuit City, Sports Authority, and Toys 'R' Us. However, the category killers have competitive pressure from other retailers that are even more specialized, such as Baby Superstores (specializing in a narrower age segment than Toys 'R' Us) and Noodle Kidoodle (specializing in a narrower product line, high-end "educational" toys). Other challengers are even deeper discounters, which are undercutting even the category killers' prices.[51]

In the meantime, some big manufacturers are helping midprice retailers, such as supermarkets, look for ways to keep costs down so they can offer lower prices. These efforts, called efficient customer response, include Scott Paper Company's efforts to help supermarkets reduce inventory. Keyes Fibre helped supermarkets by developing multi-unit "family packs" of paper goods that are smaller than those sold at warehouse clubs yet big enough for families, while selling at a low price.[52]

Creating Value with Special Products and Services　Fortunately for some retailers, consumers don't measure value strictly on the basis of price. Industry analysts have observed that consumers increasingly are choosing to shop either at a discount store *or* at a high-end retailer offering special goods or services.[53] Thus, many retailers find success by offering better service and special merchandise.

With fewer families having a full-time homemaker, time and convenience are increasingly valued by shoppers. Some stores employ a greeter who stands at the door to welcome customers and provide directions to help consumers find products quickly. Strip shopping centers, where consumers can hop out of the car to buy a bagel or rent a video, are reviving in cities and suburbs. To meet demand for fast, tasty home dinners, retailers like Emily's Market in Arizona, Eatzi's in Dallas, and Harry's in a Hurry in Atlanta offer selections of prepared meals, prepackaged salads, and uncooked items to quickly feed a family at home. They will even send a chef to customers' homes to do the cooking.[54]

Nonstore retailers, which allow consumers to shop from home, benefit from this demand for convenience, too. According to the Direct Marketing Association, more than half of the adult population in the United States orders products by mail or phone, and the number of catalog shoppers has grown much faster than the population.[55] Mail-order sales of personal computers, for example, have grown twice as fast as the overall PC market.[56]

Nevertheless, catalog retailers need to continue to focus their efforts on containing costs, improving efficiency, and creating customer value. Paper and postage expenses represent one-quarter of the cost of marketing through catalogs, and costs have risen at double-digit rates.[57] Many catalog retailers have reduced catalog size, paper quality, and the number of names on their mailings lists to cope with spiraling costs. They also are using information technology to more precisely target customers and focus mailings. This can enhance relationship marketing by enabling the retailer to know its customers' preferences better.

Other retailers are competing by offering benefits that make shopping more enjoyable. This was the strategy adopted by a number of retailers in Bath, Maine, when they learned Wal-Mart planned to open a nearby store. Knowing that they couldn't beat Wal-Mart's price on high-volume goods, they sought other sources of competitive advantage. For example, Gediman's Appliance Store set up a room where people can sit in easy chairs to watch and compare televisions. It also eliminated the low-priced end of its inventory where Wal-Mart is most competitive.

The Wheel of Retailing   An early and widely quoted attempt to explain the changes in retailers across time is the **wheel of retailing** shown in Figure 16.2. According to this model, many types of retailers begin by featuring low margins, low prices, and a low-status image. By charging lower prices than the established types of retailers, these retailers attract a sizable base of customers. As they generate profits, they enter a phase of trading up: upgrading their facilities, adding services, and raising prices. They then become vulnerable as new types of retailers emerge to compete with them by offering lower prices.

wheel of retailing
A theory of retail institutional change that explains how new forms of retailing will emerge and how others decline in popularity.

This model illustrates the experience of department stores, supermarkets, discount stores, and off-price retailers. Department stores moved to the vulnerability phase of this model over the course of a century. The wheel has turned faster for more recent categories of retailers, such as catalog showrooms, which entered the vulnerability phase after about a decade. However, the wheel of retailing doesn't work for all types of retailers. Some, including fashion boutiques, did not start out offering low prices and no frills, and some low-price, no-frills establishments have never traded up. Overall though, the wheel of retailing does have an important message for retailers: A successful retailing approach will not remain successful unless it continues to create value better than other approaches.

Technological Changes in Retailing

Modern technology, especially information technology, has dramatically changed retailing in recent years. Some of the most significant ways in which technology has helped in value creation are by increasing the amount and quality of information

FIGURE 16.2
The Wheel of Retailing

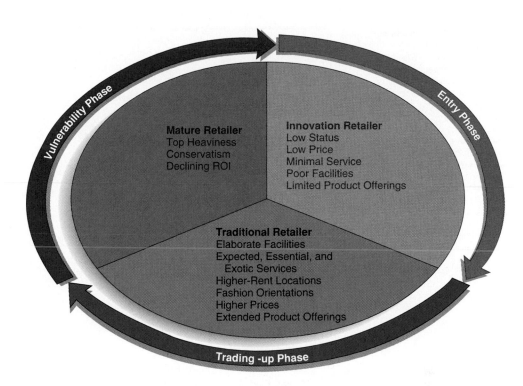

Source: Reprinted by permission of Merrill, an imprint of Macmillan Publishing Company, from *Retailing*, 4th edition, by Dale M. Lewison. Copyright © 1991 by Merrill Publishers.

available to retailers and other channel members, making shopping more convenient for consumers, and increasing the ways retailers can target promotional messages to consumers.

Information Availability   The most significant technological advances affecting modern retailing have to do with gathering and sharing information via electronic systems.[58] Geographic information systems (GIS) help even small retailers select sites with heavy concentrations of targeted consumers. GIS software, such as Maptitude, Mapinfo, or MapLinx, can provide detailed information about potential sites. GISs may even track sales performance and profitability of various locations *within* a store.[59]

Many retailers use scanners to keep track of sales, enabling them to order merchandise as needed. Coupled with frequent-shopper, check-cashing, or debit cards, the scanner systems can also help retailers learn about who their customers are and what products and brands they select. **Frequent-shopper programs** are incentive programs offered by retailers to reward customers and encourage repeat business. The reward is usually based on purchase volume or number of stores visited. Roundy's supermarkets used data from its frequent-shopper program to target a promotional effort to a group of consumers who had discontinued shopping there. The effort succeeded in luring back an impressive number of that group.[60] Many retailers are not yet fully benefiting from the technology, however. For example, since few retailers update customer profiles, they don't know when customers' value perceptions have changed.[61]

Kmart has long applied technology to retailing.[62] Satellites transmit sales data nightly from each store to the company's headquarters in Troy, Michigan. The company uses the data to adjust prices, place orders, and adjust inventory levels at the chain's regional distribution centers. Kmart stores also have tested ceiling-mounted scanners that track the number of customers entering and leaving the store. The scanners are part of a system that notifies personnel when a particular department needs more sales personnel or cashiers in the checkout lanes. Also, by measuring overall store traffic each day, the system provides evidence for whether promotional efforts are succeeding.

frequent-shopper programs
Incentive programs offered by retailers to reward customers and encourage repeat business.

Big retailers are not the only ones able to use information technology. The costs of information technology have fallen so dramatically that even a small company like County Fair Food Stores, a two-store chain, can take advantage of it. County Fair pays a monthly fee to use a satellite system to receive manufacturers' broadcasts of advertisements and discount information tailored to the stores' offerings. The system plays the broadcasts over the stores' speakers, helping to keep items moving off the shelves. With computers and laser printers, County Fair prints signs for products on sale; the system now prints signs in a few minutes that were once made by hand over the course of several hours.[63]

Modern technology also provides a means for improving cooperation among channel members. A notable application is electronic data interchange. Many channel members apply this technology to **quick-response inventory management,** a system in which channel members cooperate to reduce the lead time for receiving merchandise. By scanning bar codes, the retailer collects sales information through point-of-sale terminals and transmits it to distributors and manufacturers who ship inventory daily in small lots in order to time product delivery closer to actual demand.[64] Quick-response systems provide value for retailers and other channel members by reducing the costs and risks of carrying inventory. They provide value for consumers by reducing out-of-stock items.

quick-response inventory management
A system in which channel members cooperate to reduce the lead time for receiving merchandise.

Shopping Convenience   Technology can also add to shoppers' convenience. For example, the technology is available for service-oriented retailers to use portable terminals to ring up sales anywhere in the store. The store employee uses a scanner on a portable terminal to read product bar codes and the magnetic stripe on customers' credit cards. The terminal then produces receipts. Using this system, customers don't have to wait in line at a checkout counter. Car rental companies use this system widely at some airports.

Convenience also may be enhanced with modern communications technology, including voice mail, electronic mail, and fax machines. A number of supermarket chains, for example, let consumers fax them a grocery list; store personnel then fill the order. On-line shopping makes the process even more convenient for consumers who have the right hardware and software. For example, users of the Peapod shopping service set up a list of their most frequently purchased items. They scan the list and mark the items they want to include in a particular purchase, then add any other items they desire and transmit the list via modem. A Peapod employee picks out the items at a Jewel supermarket and delivers them to the shopper's kitchen.

Finally, technology can help nonstore retailers better target direct marketing efforts. Modern printing technology makes it possible not only to tailor mailing lists, but to produce several versions of a catalog or other written materials to match the needs and interests of various groups. Distribution technology can provide new mechanisms for displaying and ordering merchandise.

Targeted Communications   The data obtained from modern information technology enable retailers to target their marketing messages more effectively. For example, some supermarkets have installed kiosks where frequent shoppers can swipe their cards through a scanner and receive coupons that are targeted to them based on their purchase history. At Pick 'n Save Stores, shoppers can obtain a list of product discounts, customized on the basis of their purchasing history. The company found that shoppers are more likely to take advantage of the listed offers than to use old-fashioned coupons.[65]

video selling system
A system that uses video screens located near checkouts or kiosks to advertise products and services.

The kiosks may be part of a **video selling system.** Such systems use video screens near checkouts or in kiosks to present a variety of marketing communications, including advertisements, lists of products on sale, and user information for store services, such as refunds or film development. Some video selling systems, such as a system in Florsheim Express shops, also allow customers to place orders for merchandise.[66]

The Global Scope of Retailing

Globalization has become a fact of life for retailers. In the past, many retailers only imported products to offer for sale. Today, however, retailers also are expanding their markets globally. U.S. retailers especially are driven to look to other countries because many U.S. markets are saturated.[67]

U.S. retailers have some advantages in foreign markets because they offer American products admired by consumers in other countries. U.S. retailers also have experience serving a diverse population within the United States, and they can apply this experience to foreign markets. Moreover, in countries where retailers have been relatively protected from competition, retailers' experiences in the mature U.S. marketplace can help them attract consumers with lower prices or better merchandising. Toys 'R' Us, for instance, has been successful in marketing reasonably priced, brand-name toys to Western Europe and Japan.

Direct marketing can quickly position retailers in foreign markets, especially if they are savvy enough to overcome differences in language and culture. In industrialized countries, communications and transportation systems have advanced to the point where geographic distance is not the barrier to global retailing that it once was. The desirability of American goods have made U.S. catalog retailers successful in Japan. When the Commerce Department offered 125 catalogs in its Osaka office, Japanese consumers lined up to *pay* for the catalogs even though they were free.[68]

Entering some foreign retail markets can be difficult, however. The bureaucracy of Eastern Europe is notoriously cumbersome since some Western European countries restrict retailing operations, including the hours of business and types of stores. For example, France once imposed a six-month ban on opening new stores measuring more than 300 square meters.[69] Japan, too, has limited the opening of large stores. Because of this limitation, the retail market in Japan has been served primarily by an extensive array of small retailers.

At the same time foreign markets are offering greater opportunity, retailers are seeing more foreign competition in their home markets. The relative size and wealth of U.S. markets has made them attractive to retailers based in other countries. A number of foreign businesses have entered the U.S. market by acquiring U.S. firms,

Cyrillus, a French designer of clothing for women, men, and children, offers its products throughout the world via its mail-order catalog. The coupon at the bottom of this ad is for requesting a free catalog. A message at the bottom of the coupon reads, "Our catalog is sent worldwide."

including the A&P supermarket chain (owned by a German firm) and Saks Fifth Avenue (owned by a company funded primarily by Arab investors).[70]

Legal and Ethical Issues in Retailing

Like all marketers, retailers are subject to the laws of the countries and localities where they operate. For example, U.S. retailers must avoid price fixing as well as deceptive pricing practices such as bait-and-switch tactics.

Retailers also face a number of ethical issues. Consumers expect that any claims retailers make—for example, that clothes are "Made in America" or that produce is organically grown—are supportable. They may also want retailers to buy only products made in accordance with certain values they hold. For example, they may disapprove of a retailer selling products made with child labor or tested on animals. Moreover, retailers may have problems if they sell counterfeit or stolen merchandise. Retailers, like other marketers, must appreciate their customers' values and do business legally and ethically.

Because retailers sell to the public, they also must consider legal and ethical issues in their choices of target markets. Targeting certain segments of the public may be good business strategy, but refusing to sell to a would-be customer because of that person's appearance or other characteristics may lead to charges of illegal discrimination, along with hefty doses of bad publicity and lost sales. On the other hand, there are some situations where legal and ethical behavior may call for a refusal to sell. Examples include refusing to sell cigarettes to minors or to serve alcoholic drinks to patrons who are already drunk and likely to endanger themselves and others. Whenever they contemplate avoiding or refusing a sale, retailers should weigh the legal and ethical implications of their decisions.

Another legal and ethical concern involves direct selling when it is used to disguise a pyramid selling scheme. A pyramid scheme involves developing a hierarchical network of salespeople who sell products to others for resale. The idea is to load up the pyramid of sellers with products, with little concern for actually selling them to consumers. The people at the top of the pyramid often unload products and make money but those lower down end up with inventory for which there is no demand. To avoid any charge of setting up a pyramid scheme, retailers interested in direct selling should get advice from lawyers with expertise in the area.[71] In addition, focusing on value creation and long-term relationships helps retailers build strategies that are sound and legally and ethically correct.

Summary

A retailer is an intermediary that sells primarily to ultimate consumers. Retailing is much larger than wholesaling, employing about three times as many people and generating sales of about $2 trillion in the United States. Retailers create value for wholesalers and manufacturers by providing an efficient way to make products available to consumers, gathering and sharing information about consumer behavior, assuming risk, and providing efficient physical distribution services. They create value for consumers by making products available at convenient times and places, facilitating purchases, and offering amenities to make shopping more pleasant.

The two major categories of retailing are store retailing and nonstore retailing. Store retailers differ according to the types of products they offer and their means of creating value. The three major types of stores are specialty stores, mass merchandisers, and convenience stores. Nonstore retailing includes vending machines and direct marketing. Direct marketing has many forms, categorized according to the medium through which products are offered: direct selling, direct mail (including catalogs), telemarketing, direct-action advertising, and on-line marketing. A planned combination of direct marketing methods is called integrated direct marketing.

Retailers have to make a set of marketing strategy decisions. Product decisions include which goods and services to offer and what additional services should be provided to consumers. Pricing for retailers involves figuring out the markup percentage to be used, and making decisions about discounting and the use of forward buying and diverting. Placement decisions include the choice of store and/or nonstore retailing and the location of their operations, be they stores, vending machines, or distribution centers. Retailers need to make promotion decisions concerning both the products they sell and the retail organization itself. Finally, retailing strategy includes decisions about how to build a positive image, such as the store image conveyed by atmospherics or the image of a nonstore retailer conveyed by the quality of a catalog.

Major trends affecting retailers include changes in the types of retailers, technological changes, and the effects of globalization. The number of supermarkets and department stores has declined while the number of discount stores and category killers has increased. Retailing analysts believe that consumers will continue to do business with those retailers that create superior value in one way or another. A popular model to explain changes in retailers is the wheel of retailing.

Information technology allows retailers to gather and share crucial information that helps get products to consumers more efficiently. Information technology also enhances shopping convenience for consumers and helps retailers to better target communications. Globalization offers opportunities to retailers to expand into less saturated markets.

Retailers are subject to legal and ethical constraints. Consumers may demand that the products carried by retailers meet certain criteria, such as not being made with child labor. In addition, legal and ethical issues may arise when retailers decide whether or not to sell to particular customers. Some situations call for turning down sales, such as selling cigarettes to minors; other situations require avoidance of discrimination. Finally, retailers need to be cautious about pyramid schemes.

Key Terms and Concepts

retailer (p. 414)
specialty store (p. 417)
category killers (p. 417)
mass merchandiser (p. 417)
convenience store (p. 418)
nonstore retailing (p. 418)
vending machine (p. 418)
direct marketing (p. 419)

direct selling (p. 420)
direct mail marketing (p. 420)
telemarketing (p. 421)
direct-action advertising (p. 421)
on-line marketing (p. 421)
integrated direct marketing (p. 422)
forward buying (p. 425)
diverting (p. 425)

site selection (p. 425)
store image (p. 428)
atmospherics (p. 429)
wheel of retailing (p. 432)
frequent-shopper programs (p. 433)
quick-response inventory management (p. 434)
video selling system (p. 435)

Review and Discussion Questions

1. In what ways do retailers contribute value to manufacturers and consumers?

2. Why is choosing the right kind of retailer important for manufacturers?

3. Category-killer stores, like Toys 'R' Us, Crown Books, and Circuit City have been very successful in recent years. Think of your own idea for a new category-killer retail chain. What steps would you take to offer value to consumers at your store?

4. Name and define the two basic types of nonstore retailing. Give examples of products sold through each. (Try to think of some not mentioned in the text.)

5. As a consumer, how do you respond when you receive calls from telemarketers? Why do you respond this way? If you respond negatively, are there any steps that telemarketers might take to get a more positive response from you?

6. If you were the agent for several young artists (sculptors and painters) who wanted to sell more of their work to the public, would you approach one of the home shopping channels? Why or why not?

7. Assume you own a local appliance shop (selling TVs, dishwashers, washing machines, microwaves, air conditioners, and small appliances such as vacuums and food processors). One of the large category killers (like Circuit City) recently opened just a few miles from your shop. What steps would you take in order to remain competitive?

8. As the owner of a gift shop, what would you do to reduce the time customers wait in line to pay for purchases and improve employee contact with customers?

9. In which of the following locations would you place a kiosk selling moderately priced gloves and hats, and why?
   a. inside a shopping mall, a few paces from the entrance to a major department store
   b. on a busy urban street corner where a lot of commuters walk by every day
   c. at a ski resort

10. What type of image should be presented by a sales representative who practices direct sales for financial services such as investments?

11. Think of your favorite store. How does the store use atmospherics to make your shopping experience a positive one?

12. Supermarkets and department stores have decreased in sales and popularity. What steps might either of these (choose one) take to survive by creating greater value for consumers?

13. Consumers don't always equate low prices with high value. If a retailer cannot or does not want to compete using low-price strategy, what could be done to offer greater benefits to shoppers?

14. What is the wheel of retailing? What important message does it have for retailers?

15. What are the most significant technological advance affecting modern retailing? In what ways can retailers use this advance to create value?

Chapter Project Site and Design a Mall

This is your chance to design the shopping mecca of your dreams. Shopping malls, which once enjoyed huge popularity, have recently fallen on hard times, mostly because many of them no longer offer consumers what they really want. For your project, you are to design your own mall. First, determine your target market. Then, decide where the mall should be sited and make a drawing of it with spaces for stores.

Choose what types of stores and the specific retailers that belong in your mall and where they should be located. Finally, write a proposal to go with your drawing, describing your target market, your choice of stores (and why), and how you would use atmospherics to offer consumers a positive shopping experience. Describe any other steps you would take to create great value for customers.

Chapter Case Virtual Vineyards

Are your tastebuds ready for virtual wine? Don't worry, they don't have to be. But Virtual Vineyards, an on-line wine seller, is hoping you are ready to order wine via your computer. Founders Robert Olson and Peter Granoff watched the retail wine industry grow and change. Consumers wanted wine, but they wanted it at low prices, without a lot of confusion about what to buy. Some retailers responded to this demand by building superstores to sell high volume at low prices. Instead of hiring wine experts to serve consumers, they hired general clerks and paid them less. The smaller wineries suffered; they produced high-quality products, but in limited quantities—and not for low enough prices to be stocked by the superstores. Eventually, some consumers realized that they were getting lower quality wine and no service at the superstores. Olson and Granoff stepped in.

Virtual Vineyards is an on-line wine retailer that brings together vineyards and wine drinkers. Consumers can browse its Web site and order from a list of 250 top-quality wines, from 50 specialty wineries, at low prices. But that's where value just begins: Virtual Vineyards also offers consumers the knowledge of Peter Granoff, a master sommelier (wine expert). The site offers information about wine, a wide choice of wines not available at many stores, and personal interaction. Consumers like to buy wine from someone who knows the product. "Every time we sharpen the authorial presence, people respond," notes Olson. While other on-line retailers act as a clearinghouse for consumers to get information from other sources, Virtual Vineyards offers its own, in-house expert. Virtual Vineyards has an advice column that covers subjects ranging from how to buy wines for investment to how to choose wine glasses. It also offers a portfolio of wines and even a "tasting chart," in which Granoff evaluates the different qualities of wines against each other. Last but not least, the Web site is easy for consumers to use.

All of these benefits to consumers have made Virtual Vineyards a successful nonstore retailer. Olson and Granoff plan to continue enhancing the value they create for their customers by compiling records of past purchases, personal preferences, and the like. By making smart purchases on what consumers want, they can lower their own costs and pass the savings on to customers.

After only a couple of years in business, Virtual Vineyards' annual sales are at about $1 million (the company has seen growth of about 20 percent per month). That's pretty good money for some virtual newcomers.

Questions

1. Given the constraints and freedoms of on-line nonstore retailing, what other services and benefits could Virtual Vineyards offer consumers?

2. How does Virtual Vineyards use atmospherics to enhance the shopping experience of its customers?

3. Where does Virtual Vineyards fit into the wheel of retailing? How might Olson and Granoff use the model to maintain a competitive edge?

Source: Fred Hapgood, "What Makes Virtual Vineyards Rule?", *Inc. Technology*, 1996, no. 2, pp. 76–79. Adapted with permission, *Inc.* magazine, 1996. Copyright 1996 by Goldhirsh Group, Inc., 38 Commercial Wharf, Boston, MA 02110.

Explore more at www.virtualvin.com

PROMOTION: INTEGRATED MARKETING COMMUNICATIONS

SIX

Superior value resides in the minds of customers. Superior communication puts it there.

Anonymous

CHAPTER 17
Managing Marketing Communications

CHAPTER 18
Advertising, Sales Promotion, and Publicity

CHAPTER 19
Personal Selling and Sales Management

Explore the Career Profiles on the Churchill and Peter Homepage at www.irwin.com/ marketing/value.
Experience what it is like to be an Advertising or Sales Manager on the Marketing Interactive: Building Skills for Your Career CD-Rom.

Chapter Seventeen

Managing Marketing Communications

CHAPTER OUTLINE

Goals of Marketing Communications
  Create Awareness
  Build Positive Images
  Identify Prospects
  Build Channel Relationships
  Retain Customers
Understanding Marketing Communications
  The Communication Process
  The AIDA Model
  Communication with a Target Market
Elements of the Communications Mix
  Advertising
  Personal Selling
  Sales Promotion
  Publicity
  Integrated Marketing Communications
Managing Communications Strategy
  Setting Communications Objectives
  Selecting the Communications Mix
  Setting Communications Budgeting
  Implementing and Controlling the Communications Strategy
  Implications for Global Marketers
Legal and Ethical Issues in Marketing Communications
  Regulation of Communications
  Socially Responsible Communications
Summary

LEARNING OBJECTIVES

After completing this chapter, you should be able to:

1. Describe major functions of marketing communications.
2. Summarize the process of communication and how it can influence behavior.
3. Identify the elements of the communications mix.
4. Explain the use of integrated marketing communications.
5. Discuss how marketers select communications mixes.
6. Explain methods for creating a communications budget.
7. Describe how marketers evaluate and control communications efforts.
8. Discuss social and ethical issues in marketing communications.

Jessica Brackman and Barbara Roberts sell snapshots of history. Founded 60 years ago by Brackman's father, Freelance Photographers Guild (now FPG International) has become a venerable clearinghouse for the licensed use of photographic images, especially its esteemed "Real Life" collection, which depicts Americans in all walks of life. In order to create value for the thousands of organizational customers who purchase FPG's images for use in everything from textbooks to annual reports, chairwoman Brackman and president Roberts must find ways to communicate with them.

Value starts with the first call to FPG. "Customers will always get a human voice when they call here—that's a real value," says Brackman. The FPG receptionist has immediate access to the right account executive for each customer. "This helps clients feel as if they matter right away," notes Roberts.

FPG emphasizes personal selling by telephone—telemarketing—in its communications efforts. "To be successful in marketing, you need to hit the client three times in a three-month time frame," suggests Roberts. "For outbound telemarketing, we'll do three calls in six months. We want our customers to feel we're a friend they can count on. We first ask if it's okay to call back in a few months, even if the client may not need us. The second call shows our reliability and gives us another chance to ask if the client needs a catalog. The third call again asks the customer if we can keep in touch." These calls help build lasting relationships. They also provide helpful information for customers. For instance, one telemarketing and direct mail campaign let customers know about FPG's hours of operation so that customers in different time zones would know when to call.

FPG also communicates with customers and potential customers through advertising and sales promotions. For instance, when a customer places an order for the first time, FPG sends a personalized note and a pencil. "That pencil is an important extra," explains Roberts. It is something that competitors don't offer. Repeat customers may receive anything from a desk calendar to a T-shirt.

Director of marketing Jill Grafflin explains how FPG reaches people via catalog: "We mail catalogs to people who are ongoing clients, but we also mail them to names that have been added to [our]

more by searching "FPG International" on the Web.

database but haven't made a purchase." Gary Elsner, director of sales, explains further: "When people respond to direct mail tests, we assign those names; establish accounts, and get product catalogs out. The initial promotions and catalogs are major seeds. With those seeds planted, it's then the salesperson's job to grow that prospect [potential customer] into a plant or flower."

The quality of FPG's marketing communications is respected throughout the industry. "FPG's marketing is original and the look of their catalogs and print ads is breaking new ground," admits competitor Daniel Pierce, director of marketing and collection development at Bettmann Archive, a photography stock house that specializes in historical images. "Their work is sharp and eye-catching." This is exactly how Brackman and Roberts want it to be.

As you read this chapter, focus on the many ways marketers communicate with customers and how these communications create customer value.

Source: Lambeth Hochwald, "Picture This," *Sales & Marketing Management*, April 1996, pp. 65–69.

Chapter Overview

FPG International uses a number of methods to inform potential buyers about the quality of its goods and services. Before consumers or organizational buyers can purchase a product, they need to know what the product is, how it offers value, and where they can find it. Providing this information is the goal of the marketing mix element traditionally known as promotion. More often today, marketers call it **marketing communications,** defining it more broadly to include all the ways marketers communicate with current and potential customers.

marketing communications
The various ways marketers communicate with current and potential customers.

This chapter introduces marketing communications. It begins by describing major goals of this element of the marketing mix. Then the discussion moves to the process of communication itself—what it is, how messages are transmitted, and how they can influence behavior. Next, the chapter defines the elements of the communications mix—advertising, personal selling, sales promotion, and publicity—and explains why it is important to integrate them. Then the chapter explores activities involved in managing a domestic or global communications effort, and closes with an overview of ethical and social issues in marketing communications.

Goals of Marketing Communications

In general, marketers use communication to try to increase sales and profits or accomplish other goals. To do so, they inform, persuade, and remind customers to buy their products and services or do other things. To increase sales, marketers communicate their products' superior benefits, lower costs, or some combination of benefits and costs that customers want. By communicating the special benefits of their products, marketers may get potential customers to want them and buy them. For example, short-hitting golfers may buy HP2 Titlest golf balls because they have been advertised as a long-distance ball. By emphasizing new uses of their products, marketers may get current customers to buy more of them. For example, Campbell's increases the sales of its soup products by featuring them as ingredients in recipes.

Marketers can also increase sales and profits by promoting lower costs to customers. This is commonly done in advertising and by salespeople who offer lower prices for a limited time. For example, Marshall Field's promotes a 13 Hour Sale with reduced prices. Marketers may also promote use of their services at off-peak times to increase sales and profits. For example, Subway restaurants offer double frequent-buyer stamps on its subs on Tuesdays to try to increase sales on this day.

Nonprofit organizations also use communications to achieve their goals. For example, the Peace Corps uses advertising to attract workers and The United Way uses it to attract donations.

Communication is also used by marketers to accomplish specific strategic goals. A number of these are summarized in Table 17.1 and discussed below.

TABLE 17.1
Some Strategic Goals of Marketing Communications

Strategic Goal	Description
Create awareness	Inform markets about products, brands, stores, or organizations
Build positive images	Develop positive evaluations in people's minds about products, brands, stores, or organizations
Identify prospects	Find out the names, addresses, and possible needs of potential buyers
Build channel relationships	Increase cooperation among channel members
Retain customers	Create value for customers, satisfy their wants and needs, and earn their loyalty.

Create Awareness

Imagine that you are planning to drive across the country. Your parents advise you to sign up with the Triple A Motor Club so that you can get help if your car breaks down. A friend recommends that you visit Jiffy Lube to have your car's oil changed. A newspaper article recommends that travelers carry credit cards in case of emergencies. These sources of information make you aware of goods and services that can make your trip safer and more economical. Marketers, too, use communication to generate awareness of their products. For example, Triple A, Jiffy Lube, and Mastercard all use advertising to inform customers about their services. Marketing communications designed to create awareness are especially important for new products or brands. Creating awareness is also important for global expansion of existing products.

Build Positive Images

When products or brands have clear images, they help potential buyers better understand the value that is being offered. Positive images may even create value for customers by adding meaning to products, such as the prestige of a Mercedes Benz (see "Put It into Practice: Observe How a Product's Image Is Created"). Retail stores and other organizations also use communications to build positive images. A major way marketers create positive images is through communications. Panduit, a marketer of wiring and communications products used for electronic data interchange, established a Web site as a way to support a high-tech image in the minds of its technology-savvy business customers.[1] To build an authentic Italian image, Ragú set up a Web site "hosted" by a warmhearted Italian Mama who tries to interest visitors in Italian cooking and Ragú products. Mama offers recipes, Italian lessons, and a tour of Little Italy, and urges visitors to fill out a survey.[2]

Bayer Corporation is best known for its brand-name aspirin, but the company actually produces more than 8,000 products. This ad seeks to cultivate an image of Bayer as a diversified and innovative company. The fine print begins, "If you think Bayer only means aspirin, you'll be surprised to know how much more we bring to your life," then goes on to detail the types of products made by Bayer. The company's Web site (http://www.bayerus.com) supports this message with details on the company, its business segments, research efforts, and more.

Identify Prospects

Marketing communications can be directed toward identifying potential buyers and creating relationships with them. Future communications between the organization and these prospects could then clarify prospects' wants and needs and how the organization can satisfy them. This approach is common for exchanges involving extensive information search by customers. For example, an organization that markets industrial equipment could run ads in trade magazines and include a coupon that readers could send in for more information. A catalog could be sent and salespeople could contact these prospects to provide more information and learn about their needs and wants. Salespeople frequently search for prospects by asking their current customers for leads.

The city of Memphis uses advertisements, bumper stickers, and signs to get out the word that it is "America's Distribution Center." The city is home to Federal Express Corporation, as well as several major rail lines and over 200 truck lines, and

Observe How a Product's Image Is Created

Choose a product that you recently became aware of—a certain make of car, a restaurant, a tourist destination, a college or university, a type of soft drink, or the like. Jot down what messages you received about the product. Do you remember the media used to transmit these messages to you, such as television ads or brochures in the mail?

Based on these communications, what do you think the product's image is? Do other people share your perception of the product's image?

is located on the Mississippi River. The ads offer an information packet with guaranteed next-day delivery to demonstrate the city's distribution prowess. In return, the city gets the names and addresses of those interested organizations, likely prospects for building the city's economy.[3]

Identifying prospects is becoming an increasingly important use of marketing communications because modern technology makes information gathering much more practical, even for big consumer markets. Retailers and producers alike can maintain records of consumers who have expressed an interest in a product, then direct future communications to them. For example, organizations can use Web sites to gather information about people interested in their products. Supermarkets can use kiosks or point-of-sale terminals to dispense coupons selected on the basis of a customer's past purchases. Advertising for Snapple drinks included a toll-free telephone number that consumers could call to receive a coupon for a free bottle. Requiring the phone call gave the company an opportunity to gather information about interested consumers so it could better target them.

Build Channel Relationships

Marketing communications build relationships among channel members. For example, when producers use marketing communications to stimulate demand for their products, they are also helping their resellers. This is especially true for marketing communications that mention that a product is available through particular resellers. Manufacturers may arrange with retailers to distribute coupons, set up special displays, or hold promotional events in their stores, all of which can increase store traffic and purchases. Retailers support manufacturers when they feature brands in their ads to attract buyers. Through such efforts, all members of the channel can benefit from increased sales. Cooperating in these communications efforts can build stronger channel relationships.

Retain Customers

Marketers usually want customers to make repeat purchases from them. Marketing communications can support efforts to create value for customers and satisfy them so they become loyal. Information about frequent-shopper or frequent-user programs, such as those offered by airlines, hotels, and retail stores, can get customers involved in them. These programs can include mailings that invite frequent shoppers to special events or inform them about discounts offered to them alone. For example, Northstar-at-Tahoe, a California ski resort, has a frequent-skier program called Club Vertical. Members wear special wristbands embedded with microchips that record the number of vertical feet they have skied. The wristbands give them access to members-only

HMV (His Master's Voice), "the world's most famous music store," uses brochures at its retail outlets, such as this one obtained at London's Heathrow Airport, to gather information about prospects for its retailing catalog. Besides advertising HMV direct service, the brochure includes a catalog request form that obtains name, address, phone number, and preferences for various categories of music. HMV can use this information to target future communications.

lines at ski lifts, an easy way to charge services, and the ability to receive electronic messages while skiing.[4]

Interactive modes of communication—including salespeople and Web sites—can play an important role in retaining customers. These modes can serve as sources of information about product usage and products in development. They can also gather information from customers about what they value, as well as their experiences in using products. This two-way communication can help marketers increase the value offered in exchanges. Greet St.'s Web site markets greeting cards and maintains a database of each customer's purchases, which it uses to make recommendations when the customer next visits the site to shop. Greet St. even e-mails properly timed reminder notices to customers who have entered special occasions on its electronic calendar.[5]

Understanding Marketing Communications

communication
The transmission of a message from a sender to a receiver, such that both understand it the same way.

source
The sender of a message.

encode
The process of converting a message to a group of symbols that represent images or concepts.

communication medium
The mode that carries the message, such as television, radio, print, live speech, or music.

Communication is the transmission of a message from a sender to a receiver, such that both understand it the same way. Thus, a print advertisement, coupon, television commercial, or other marketing communication must be created to clearly convey the intended meaning.

The Communication Process

As shown in Figure 17.1, communication involves a process. The **source** (such as a company or an individual) determines what information is to be communicated and **encodes** the message in appropriate symbols such as words or pictures. Through a **communication medium**—such as television or radio, written words, photographic images, live speech, and musical sounds—the source transmits the message to the **receiver,** the person or group for whom the message is intended. The receiver then **decodes** the message by interpreting its meaning. If the receiver does not or cannot decode the message to mean what the source intended, then there is **noise** in the communications system. Noise can take the form of physical sound—such as radio, telephone, or television static—or it can be the receiver's misunderstanding of the sender's language or symbols, a printing error, or a distraction such as a customer's dislike of a salesperson's mannerisms or dress.

F I G U R E 17.2 *The AIDA Model*

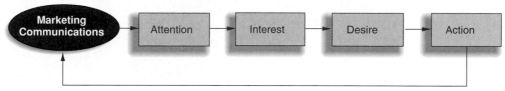

Next, the communication aims to generate interest in the organization and/or its products and brands. In general, this means letting receivers of the message know how the organization or its products can deliver value to them. A basic way to do this is to focus on benefits, not just on features. Thus, a promotional letter in which a marketing research company says, "We can help you know your customers and their needs" (a service benefit) should generate more interest than one that says, "We have a powerful computer for doing sophisticated statistical analyses" (a service feature). If the information about benefits is successfully presented, receivers may develop a desire for the products described.

The last stage of the AIDA model—action (particularly purchases)—is the one that most directly affects the organization. However, it also can be the hardest step to achieve. Potential buyers may resist buying even if they agree they will be better off with the good or service; after all, some costs are involved. For this reason, marketing communications often include incentives to stimulate a purchase by reducing costs. Coupons, for example, reduce monetary costs and free coffee at a bank makes the trip there a bit more pleasant. Whether customers purchase or not provides feedback concerning the success of both marketing communications and the overall marketing strategy. Of course, customers can also communicate with marketers in other ways, such as with compliments and complaints about products.

Communication with a Target Market

Effective communication is designed so that it is understandable and appealing to the target market. This means that marketers must understand what words will be clear to members of the target market. Marketers also must understand how the target market interprets pictures, images, and sounds used in the message.

In addition, marketers should study the media members of the target market use. Do targeted customers watch television? Which programs? Do they clip coupons? Read labels on packages? Do targeted organizational buyers attend trade shows? Do they read trade magazines? Do they have time to meet with a salesperson? Answering questions such as these can help marketers select the appropriate communications media to reach the market.

Elements of the Communications Mix

communications mix
The blend of advertising, personal selling, sales promotion, and publicity that makes up a communications strategy.

The **communications mix** blends together four different elements to create the overall marketing communications strategy. The elements of this mix are advertising, personal selling, sales promotion, and publicity. These elements can be more generally categorized as *personal selling* and *nonpersonal selling*. Personal selling is conducted on a person-to-person basis, whereas nonpersonal selling encompasses advertising, sales promotion, and publicity.

Advances in communications technology have blurred the distinction between personal and nonpersonal selling in some cases ("see Marketing Movers & Shakers: Jason and Matthew Olim/CDnow"). For example, Internet software called SalesNET enables the user to create customized electronic catalogs. These catalogs lead each customer through an interactive sales process based on interests and buying history, selecting and displaying items targeted to the customer's tastes and needs.[7]

Jason and Matthew Olim/CDnow

If music is the message, twentysomething twins Jason and Matthew Olim are playing it loud and clear—and people are hearing it. The Olim twins aren't musicians themselves, but through their young company's Web site, CDnow, they sell plenty of music. They don't have a paper catalog, and they don't have a personal selling staff. But technology does allow them to blur the lines between personal selling and nonpersonal selling.

Jason and Matthew recognized music CDs as an excellent product to be sold on-line. Shoppers don't need to touch the CD or try it on. The CDs themselves can come from various suppliers rather than CDnow's own warehouse. The Web site is an excellent place from which to advertise, conduct sales promotions, and disseminate other messages of interest to consumers. The Olims have made good use of the site.

They have purchased the electronic rights to publish material from *The All Music Guide,* which publishes reviews and biographies of musicians; they have purchased digitized artwork so that shoppers can call up album covers, virtually "flipping" through them the way they do in actual record stores; and they have offered special sales promotions. One of these was a contest that gave shoppers the chance to win a trip to meet Clint Eastwood by correctly identifying Eastwood's hat and gun as they cybertoured his new CD-ROM. In another promotion developed especially for Geffen Records, CDnow offered this message to college students: "Hey, you! The college kid in front of the screen. Get 10 percent off on all Geffen titles." If a student ignored the message but kept surfing the site, he or she got a follow-up message, perhaps not suitable for the over-30 classical set, but tailored for the average university student: "Hey! We asked you nicely the first time, now get . . . in here!"

CDnow even offers advertising; the Olims charge advertisers 4 cents each time a shopper clicks on an ad. "Advertising is going to be very critical to us," notes Jason. He predicts that CDnow's advertising revenues will top $3 million within 12 months.

Jason and Matthew have continually looked for ways to add value to their site. "The rule I've kept applying is, if it adds value, you can do it," emphasizes Jason. He believes that adding service and other benefits will boost sales volume, and ultimately profits. They'll have to keep up the value approach, in order to stay ahead of competitors such as Music Boulevard and 1-800-MUSIC NOW, run by MCI.

The Olims expect to have a million shoppers a month soon. They believe they have the technology—and the savvy—to handle all that business. "Every week is a revolution," says Jason. Maybe not the kind of revolution John Lennon had in mind. But it's a revolution, nonetheless.

Source: John Grossman, "Nowhere Men," *Inc.*, June 1996, pp. 63–69. Adapted with permission, *Inc.* magazine, June 1996. Copyright 1996 by Goldhirsh Group, Inc., 38 Commercial Wharf, Boston, MA 02110.

Explore more at www.cdnow.com

Marketers should strive for the most effective and efficient communications mix. There are advantages and disadvantages to each type of communication. For example, advertising reaches many people at once, but its costs are high and feedback can be difficult to evaluate. Publicity, in contrast, is virtually free but difficult to control.

Advertising

advertising
Any announcement or persuasive communication placed in the mass media in paid or donated time or space by an individual, company, or organization.

When people think of marketing messages, they usually think of advertisements. **Advertising** is "any announcement or persuasive message placed in the mass media in paid or donated time or space by an identified individual, company, or organization."[8]

When deciding how advertising fits into the communications mix, marketers consider issues such as which media to use—television, radio, print, direct marketing, or outdoor (billboards)—and what messages to send. Each medium has its advantages and disadvantages, and the medium, or blend of media, that is most appropriate for one product may not be suitable for another. For instance, a national television commercial can reach most U.S. households at once—not an efficient way to advertise a

sale at a local department store. When choosing when, where, and how to advertise, marketers should select the method that will communicate most effectively and efficiently.

Personal Selling

personal selling
Selling that involves personal interaction with the customer.

Personal selling is selling that involves personal interaction with the customer.[9] Personal selling can take place face to face, by phone (telemarketing), or by fax or computer—in other words, through any medium that allows direct, personal interaction between seller and buyer. Personal selling provides immediate feedback to marketers, which allows them to adjust communications to meet the needs of the situation. Thus, if a customer does not understand how a particular feature on a lawn mower works, a salesperson can demonstrate its use. If a telemarketer calls a potential customer at an inconvenient time, the phone call can be rescheduled.

On the downside, personal selling usually costs more per customer contact than other types of marketing communications, and salespeople are sometimes poorly trained and annoying. Also, some salespeople are clearly better at their job than others, making market coverage inconsistent.

Sales Promotion

sales promotion
Media and nonmedia marketing pressure applied for a predetermined, limited period of time at the consumer, retailer, or wholesaler level in order to stimulate trial, increase consumer demand or improve product availability.

When marketers want quick sales increases from their communications efforts, they often use some form of sales promotion. **Sales promotion** is "media and nonmedia marketing pressure applied for a predetermined, limited period of time at the level of consumer, retailer or wholesaler in order to stimulate trial, increase consumer demand or improve product availability."[10] For instance, a free sample of toothpaste encourages consumers to try it. Note that sales promotions may be directed toward intermediaries or end users.

At the consumer level, sales promotions include coupons, limited-time discount offers, free samples, tie-in "gifts," two-for-one offers, rebates, contests or sweepstakes, special events, or similar efforts. Sales promotion usually takes place in conjunction with advertising or personal selling. For example, a coupon may appear in a newspaper ad or in a piece of direct mail.

Sales promotions directed toward intermediaries are called *trade promotions.* These activities include providing displays for products, awarding intermediaries prizes based on sales performance, and displaying products at trade shows. Manufacturers may also stimulate channel sales with price breaks in the form of trade allowances.

Sales promotions usually are designed to boost sales quickly and, hopefully, to create loyalty. However, if conducted on a continuous basis, they may become ineffective. A perpetual "sale," frequent coupons with no expiration dates, or the continuous offer of the same gift with a purchase, may cause potential buyers to ignore the promotions.

Publicity

publicity
Nonpaid communication of information about the company or product, generally in some media form.

The communications mix may also include efforts to generate publicity. **Publicity** is "non-paid-for communication of information about the company or product, generally in some media form."[11] Publicity can appear in a variety of forms. The most common are news stories about new products or companies' successes or failures. Other types of media coverage include reviews (say, of a restaurant, hotel, sports teams, or music recording) and broadcasts of speeches. To get media coverage, marketers may use press releases, press conferences, and other events intended to draw attention. When McDonald's introduced the Arch Deluxe hamburger, it staged events in dozens of American cities linked by simultaneous press conferences held in New York, Los Angeles, and Toronto. The company landed a front-page story in *USA Today,* but other media outlets were not convinced that a new hamburger was headline news. Phyllis Schwartz, news director at Chicago's WLS-TV, called the announcement merely "a good 20-second business story" about targeting a new market.[12]

Although it is "free advertising," publicity has its downside. Marketers have little or no control over what is said and what audience receives the information. Since marketers usually do not participate in the process of editing a news story, press conference, or review, certain remarks may be taken out of context, creating confusion, misunderstanding, or a poor view of the organization or its products. Also, noise is difficult to control and coverage is usually short-lived.

Because marketers do not control the content of publicity, audiences are more likely to believe the information is more objective. Thus, for a new or small company or a nonprofit organization with a tight communications budget, favorable publicity can be critical for promoting goods or services. For example, Virtual Vineyards, which markets wine via a site on the World Wide Web, received extensive publicity when it started up because the concept of marketing over the Internet was novel. According to Robert Olson, the company's president, this publicity has been more effective than the company's advertising, perhaps because Internet users may disregard advertising messages.[13]

Table 17.2 summarizes the strengths and weaknesses of the four elements of the communications mix.

Integrated Marketing Communications

integrated marketing communications (IMC)
The coordination of the elements of the communications mix into a consistent whole so as to provide greater clarity and marketing impact.

If marketers combine all the elements of the communications mix in a systematic way, they are likely to achieve greater impact than if the communications are uncoordinated or haphazard. This is the aim of **integrated marketing communications (IMC)**—an approach that combines the elements of the communications mix into a consistent whole so as to provide greater clarity and marketing impact.[14] Some

T A B L E 17.2
Elements of the
Communications Mix

Element	Strengths	Weaknesses
Advertising	• Reaches many potential customers • Effective way to create images • Flexible in terms of time and markets • Variety of media to choose from • Relatively low cost per person exposed to message • Appropriate for achieving many types of communications objectives	• Reaches many people who are not potential buyers • Ads are subject to much criticism • Exposure time is usually short • People tend to screen out advertisements • Total cost may be high
Personal selling	• Salespeople can be persuasive and influential • Two-way communication allows for questions and other feedback • Message can be targeted to specific individuals • In some situations, such as for complex products, buyers may expect personal sales	• Cost per contact is high • Salespeople may be hard to recruit and motivate • Presentation skills vary among salespeople • Poor presentations may damage image as well as lose sales
Sales promotion	• Supports short-term price reductions designed to stimulate demand • Variety of sales promotion tools available • Effective in changing behavior • Easy to link to other communications	• Risks inducing brand-loyal customers to stock up while not influencing others • Impact may be limited to short term • Price-related sales promotion may hurt brand image • Easy for competitors to copy
Publicity	• Total cost may be very low • Media-generated messages seen as more credible than marketer-sponsored messages • Potential buyers may be less apt to screen out publicity messages	• Media may not cooperate • Competition for media attention is heavy • Marketer has little control over message • Messages tend not to be repeated

marketers advocate that the use of IMC extend to all communications between an organization and its market, including things such as the impressions the organization sends by its choice of distribution channels.

Disney uses IMC to reinforce the image of its offerings as safe, reliable, and fun family entertainment. Its movies get advertising on the Disney Channel, in its stores, and through licensed products such as toys and clothing. The toys and clothing in turn generate attention, interest, and desire to see the movies. A *Fortune* article reports, "A Disney project of any sort has the ability to flash on the collective consciousness up to 425 million times in a three-month period through the company's parks, stores, films, TV programs, videos, games, and music or on the Internet, according to an internal company survey."[15]

IMC begins when the organization first establishes its marketing objectives and decides how each element of the communications mix can support these objectives. In doing so, marketers consider how customers come into contact with the organization, its products, and its messages. For example, they may ask what media their current and potential customers use and when they are most receptive to receiving messages about particular products.

The idea of looking at the communications mix as a total package with common objectives may sound obvious, but is not always the norm. In some cases, especially at big companies, different personnel and strategies are employed for advertising, personal selling, sales promotion, and publicity. While an advertising manager might be trying to get a big budget to buy television spots to support a prestige image for the organization's products, a sales manager might be lobbying for price cuts so that the sales force could cut more deals.

IMC has arisen in part to correct the dysfunctional consequences of marketers working at cross-purposes within organizations and also to respond to changes in the

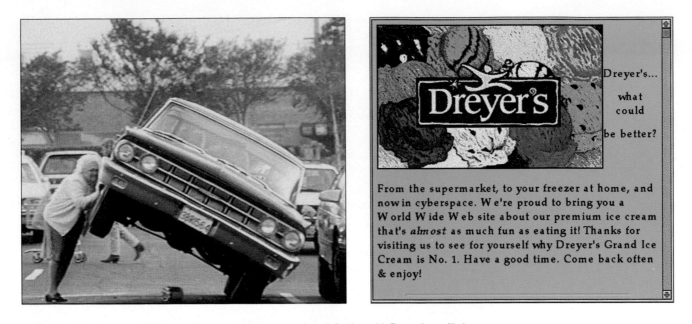

In the television commercial illustrated here, an elderly woman's satisfaction with Dreyer's vanilla ice cream is so "strong" that when she drops her carton of ice cream under her car, she stoops down, lifts the car, and with her free, white-gloved hand, snatches the carton from the ground. Having rescued the ice cream, she drops the car. The announcer states, "Dreyer's. Evidently, its not your normal ice cream." This humorous television commercial is part of Dreyer's Grand Ice Cream's integrated marketing communications (IMC). Dreyer's IMC efforts include television advertising, coupons, point-of-sale merchandising, and a home site on the World Wide Web (right). The Web site (http:// www.dreyers.com), for example, supports the television ad's image of Dreyer's ice cream by leading off with the slogan "Dreyer's . . . what could be better?"

marketing environment. Stronger, global competition has forced marketers to look closely at how well they communicate with customers and deliver value to them. Organizations are relying more on targeted, value-driven techniques such as personal mailings, phone calls, and interactive on-line messages to communicate better with customers and create more value for them by customizing products and services. Moreover, technological developments have made these more customized approaches practical for a growing number of organizations. IMC is a way to approach the challenge and complexity of communicating effectively with customers in highly competitive markets.

Managing Communications Strategy

Managing a communications strategy involves planning, implementing, and controlling it. Planning includes the three interrelated tasks of setting communications objectives, selecting a communications mix, and setting communication budgets. Implementing and controlling involve putting the communications strategy into action, evaluating results, and changing the strategy if necessary.

Setting Communications Objectives

As with other types, communications objectives should be clear, specific, and challenging, but achievable. Communications objectives should also support overall marketing objectives. If the overall marketing objective is to increase sales 20 percent and profits 10 percent, then the communications objectives must include reaching enough potential customers to achieve these goals. This might mean setting a higher sales force commission rate for sales to new customers or increasing advertising exposures for high-growth products by 40 percent.

Communications objectives include consideration of the basic messages and images to be used. If the marketing objectives involve expanding market share to 14 percent for a mature product, the communications objectives might include developing messages that explain why the product is better than competitive offerings. The message might also emphasize that a lower price, or availability in more convenient outlets, makes the product a better value. If the marketing objectives include positioning the product as a prestige item, messages should be designed to convey this image.

Selecting the Communications Mix

Keeping in mind that communications elements should work together, marketers must select the right mix. To do so, marketers evaluate the contributions that advertising, personal selling, sales promotion, and publicity can make to achieving communications objectives, as well as overall marketing objectives. Marketers also should research whether the communications strategy is sound. Marketers can ask a sample of the target market to evaluate a storyboard for an ad or react to a planned sales promotion. Publishers of new magazines often research the impact of two or three different cover designs by distributing them in different geographical areas and monitoring market response.

Nature of the Market Knowledge of the size of a target market, its characteristics, and its geographic distribution can help determine the best communications mix. The larger the market, the more the organization may have to rely on impersonal communications such as advertising to stimulate demand or identify prospects. Personal selling will likely play a more important role when a target market is relatively small and geographically concentrated, as is often the case for markets consisting of

The market for cellular phones is huge, so advertising is appropriate to reach the target market. Also, cellular phones are no longer in the introduction stage of the product life cycle, so advertising makes comparisons among brands. In this ad, Ericsson stresses features of its cell phone, such as light weight ("weighs a barely noticeable 8.7 ounces") and ease of use ("fits easily in your pocket . . . menu-driven operation"). The company also promises "reliability and dependability you can count on."

organizational buyers. Furthermore, the characteristics of people in a target market may influence whether they will be more receptive to different elements of the communications mix. Economic and technological influences can broaden or limit opportunities to communicate via telephone, television, radio, or electronic links. Because Virtual Vineyards targets Internet users who, the company believes, are skeptical about advertising claims, the company limits its advertising on on-line service providers such as America Online and Prodigy. The company places more emphasis on publicity, such as interviews with CNN, National Public Radio, and major newspapers, and on sales promotions, such as discount offers for gifts "because gifts get two people [aware of the company] instead of one."[16]

For marketers targeting consumers in the United States, several trends influence the success of communications strategies.[17] One is that many consumers feel inundated by advertising. By one estimate, typical U.S. consumers encounter up to 3,000 marketing messages a day.[18] On television, the shift to 15-second commercials has caused the number of ads to increase, and consumers are zapping them with their remotes, tuning them out, or confusing which ads are for which products. A noteworthy example is the series of ads for Eveready batteries that feature a marching rabbit. Critics and consumers alike praised these ads, but almost half of consumers surveyed thought they were for Duracell—and Duracell's market share grew.

For global markets, marketers often must tailor their communications to reflect cultural differences. When Coca-Cola introduced its Coca-Cola Light reduced-calorie soda in China, its communications efforts ran into trouble. While the appeal of a "light" or "diet" Coke in the United States and Western Europe was obvious, it wasn't so in China, where food supplies are limited and Coke is a status symbol. In China, "less" Coke was less appealing to consumers, and the availability of two similar Coke products was confusing. These problems led the company to return to selling just Coca-Cola Classic in China.[19]

Nature of the Product   The product itself also affects the most effective communications mix. For starters, whether a product is a good or a service will make a difference. Because potential buyers cannot see, hear, touch, taste, or smell services before purchasing them, marketers try to use communication elements that make benefits tangible and provide confidence in a purchase decision. For example, television ads can show beautiful, well-manicured lawns that could result from using Tru Green lawn services. Often service communications focus on building a good image or reputation, because customers sometimes purchase on this basis.

Highly complex, technical, or specialized products may require communications that enable marketers to explain them and their benefits in detail. Often, such products are sold to organizations, and a sales force may be divided on the basis of products so that salespeople become specialists in selling particular items. When complex products are sold to consumers, manufacturers may provide sales training to resellers so that they can provide support. In most cases, high-price offerings such as homes need personal selling. Some marketers also use less expensive ways to communicate about complex, technical products, such as providing detailed information on computer diskettes or Web sites. The information might include a demonstration or a series of questions that tailor the presentation to customers' needs.[20]

Most consumer products do not need personal selling. Convenience goods and many shopping goods usually do well with advertising and sales promotions. For products with highly seasonal demand, such as air conditioners or outdoor concerts, advertising may be more efficient than a year-round sales force. For products that are difficult to differentiate from their competitors, publicity may help generate favorable images.

F I G U R E **17.3** *Two Marketing Communications Approaches*

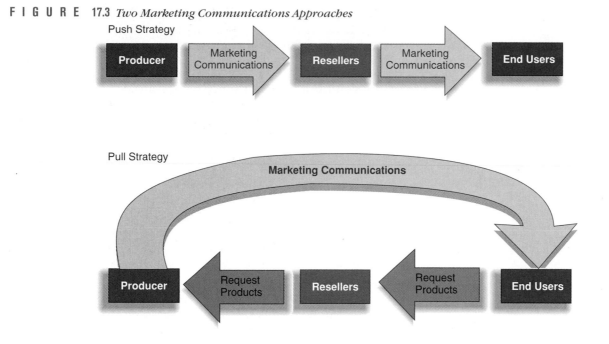

Push versus Pull Strategy   Marketers evaluate whether a push or a pull communications strategy is better for particular goods or services. As shown in Figure 17.3, a **push strategy** directs marketing communications to other members of the marketing channel, such as wholesalers or retailers. When Procter & Gamble discontinued Citrus Hill orange juice, Coca Cola's Minute Maid brand sought to take over Citrus Hill's shelf space through a push strategy. Minute Maid offered incentives to grocers to get them to increase their stock of the product. Minute Maid also offered special promotions, such as free samples, when Citrus Hill bowed out.[21]

A **pull strategy** builds product momentum the opposite way—by communicating directly with end users. By stimulating final demand for products, channel members respond by carrying it. Tropicana used a pull strategy in its response to the demise of Citrus Hill. Just weeks after P&G announced the product's withdrawal, Tropicana sent coupons to households that were likely users of Citrus Hill. Tropicana also boosted its spending on TV ads by $1.2 million to create more end-user demand for its juice.[22]

In many cases, marketers rely on both push and pull strategies, although emphasis may be placed on one or the other depending on the nature of the market, the product, and so forth. However, in the market for many consumer goods, technology increasingly favors a pull strategy. As retailers use point-of-sale terminals to monitor sales of individual products, they can help manufacturers determine which communications are most effective and which products are most profitable. Increasingly, retailers are basing ordering decisions on consumer demand generated in part by marketing communications from manufacturers.[23]

Setting Communications Budgeting

Some marketers still set budgets separately for each element of the marketing mix, with, say, the advertising budget developed separately from the budget for personal selling. However, given the logic of integrated marketing communications, it makes sense that all elements of the communications mix should be considered together

push strategy
Directing marketing communications to other members of the marketing channel.

pull strategy
Directing marketing communications to end users.

when budgeting. There are a number of approaches to setting communications budgets. These include the percentage-of-sales method, the fixed-sum-per-unit method, competition-based method, the all-you-can-afford method, and the objective-and-task method.

Percentage-of-Sales Method

percentage-of-sales method
Establishing a communication budget based on a specified percentage of actual or estimated sales.

Percentage-of-Sales Method   With the **percentage-of-sales method,** the communications budget is based on a specified percentage of either actual or estimated sales. Assume a company decides to spend 5 percent of forecasted sales on marketing communications. If the company forecasts $500,000 in sales for a product during the coming year, it would allocate $25,000 (that is, .05 × $500,000) to marketing communications.

This simple method can be useful when a product is in the growth or maturity phase of its life cycle. If sales are growing or have stabilized at a fairly high rate, the increased allocation of resources to communications can help a company be more competitive.

The method has its drawbacks, however. In a sense, it suggests that the tail wag the dog, that is, that higher sales result in higher budgets for communication rather than the other way around. Marketing communications are designed to increase sales, so setting budgets as a percentage of sales reverses this logic. Furthermore, sales may not meet forecasts, and may dip and rise unexpectedly. If sales drop due to new competitors entering a market, it doesn't make sense to lower communication spending. This would likely help competitors gain market share. A final weakness is that the percentage-of-sales method doesn't provide a way to allocate resources among the elements of the communications mix.

fixed-sum-per-unit method
Allocating a fixed sum to the communications budget for each unit to be sold or produced.

Fixed-Sum-per-Unit Method   Marketers using the **fixed-sum-per-unit method** allocate a fixed sum for communications based on each unit of product sold or produced. Imagine that a producer of bicycles decides to spend $20 on communications for each mountain bike it sells. The company predicts it will sell 80,000 mountain bikes, so it budgets $1.6 million ($20 × 80,000) for marketing communications.

While this method gives marketers a place to start with a budget, it has the same limitations as the percentage-of-sales method. For example, it doesn't take into account the role of marketing communications in building sales. However, if the market is easily identified and the product has a clear position in that market, the fixed-sum-per-unit method can be a simple way to track and control costs for marketing communications.

Competition-Based Method   Some marketers spend communication dollars based on competition. They determine how much competitors are spending and then budget the same amount or some proportion of it. However, competitors don't always reveal exactly how much they are spending on communications, or they may reveal an overall budget (possibly to intimidate competitors) but decline to discuss specifics such as how much the budget for particular products has changed. When Chesebrough-Pond's relaunched its Vaseline Intensive Care lotion, the leading skin lotion, with 28 percent of the $683 million market, the company announced that it would be spending $38 million in advertising and $21 million in sales promotions. However, it wouldn't reveal the percentage of increase these figures represented.[24]

Like the previous methods of budgeting, meeting the competition doesn't focus on communication objectives or the product's communications needs. Following competitors' budgets can lead to escalating communication spending by all competitors that doesn't help any of them.

all-you-can-afford method
Spending all the organization can afford on communications.

All-You-Can-Afford Method   Another approach to communication budgeting is the **all-you-can-afford method.** This method consists of deciding what the organization can afford to spend on communications, then allocating that amount among the various elements of the communications mix. The all-you-can-afford method is common among small companies with new products.

This type of budgeting does help keep a company from overspending. However, it doesn't take into account how much money is necessary to achieve marketing objectives, such as breaking into a new market or building market share. On the other hand, this way of budgeting may help a company focus its limited spending on the most effective communication elements. For example, Jenny Johnson, a Mary Kay sales representative who works out of her home, wanted to increase her sales but had limited funds. So on Halloween she gave trick-or-treaters not only candy but also a gift for mom: cards with eye shadow samples attached. By giving the samples to children who had walked to her door, Johnson indicated to consumers that she was conveniently located in the neighborhood; she generated five new clients with her low cost promotion.[25]

objective-and-task method
Quantifying communication objectives, determining the communications mix required to meet those objectives, and budgeting the cost of that mix.

Objective-and-Task Method   The **objective-and-task method** is based on the communications objectives and is custom designed to meet the communications needs of products. Figure 17.4 shows how it works. To use the objective-and-task method, marketers first define the objectives of the communications mix, such as a 30 percent increase in brand awareness or a 20 percent increase in new accounts. Once objectives have been quantified, marketers evaluate each element in the communications mix and decide what tasks each should perform. Money is then allocated to accomplish each task; the total amount is the communications budget.

The objective-and-task method does have shortcomings. For one thing, determining the communications mix necessary to meet objectives and the tasks each element performs best can be difficult. Moreover, the method provides no basis for setting priorities among objectives. Finally, this method may result in a communications budget that is too expensive to be funded. If so, objectives may have to be cut back or less expensive ways of achieving them will have to be found. However, even if changes have to be made, a budget method such as this that explicitly considers communication objectives makes the most sense.

Table 17.3 summarizes the advantages and disadvantages of each method of budgeting money for communications.

Implementing and Controlling the Communications Strategy

Implementing communications strategies involves a variety of activities, depending on which elements of the communications mix are included. Advertising involves working with ad agencies, creating ads, and getting them scheduled in appropriate media. Personal selling involves hiring and training salespeople, changing sales territories, and evaluating compensation methods. Sales promotion involves preparing promotions and scheduling them. Publicity involves getting news releases prepared and sent to the media.

Marketers use a number of tools to monitor the communications effort. They track sales to look for changes that could be responses to their communications and watch for reactions in their competitors' communications activities. They also conduct research to learn whether members of the target market have received their communications, what they recall about them, and whether the communications have affected their beliefs, attitudes, purchase intentions, and buying patterns.

F I G U R E   17.4 *Budgeting with the Objective-and-Task Method*

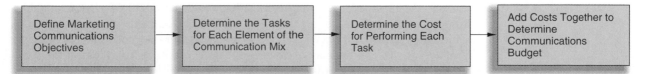

| Define Marketing Communications Objectives | Determine the Tasks for Each Element of the Communication Mix | Determine the Cost for Performing Each Task | Add Costs Together to Determine Communications Budget |

Method	Advantages	Disadvantages
Percentage of sales	• Simple to use	• Budgeting based on expected sales implies communications can't improve sales performance
Fixed sum per unit	• Marketer likely to benefit from increasing the budget during times of rising sales	• Decreasing the communications budget during periods of falling sales could be disastrous in some cases
Competition-based	• Takes into account competitors' activities • Amounts budgeted will be reasonable if competitors are budgeting effectively	• Can be difficult to get competitors' budget information • Can lead to ever-increasing communications budgets • Assumes competitors have the same objectives
All you can afford	• Takes into account limited resources • May stimulate creativity in making funds work hard	• Doesn't consider marketing objectives • Borrowing may be worthwhile to fund some communications strategies
Objective and task	• Based on achieving communications objectives • Focusing on objectives uses funds most efficiently	• No basis for setting priorities among objectives • Treats all objectives as equally worthy of funding • Hard to estimate what it will cost to achieve a particular objective

Sales Changes   Changes in sales are one indication of whether communications are working as intended. Sales below forecasted levels indicate a problem—and so might higher-than-expected sales. As a case in point, Hoover Ltd., a British unit of Maytag Corporation, suffered from an overly enthusiastic response to its offer of free airline tickets to qualified buyers of its appliances. So many consumers applied for the tickets that Maytag had to report a $30 million charge against its earnings to cover the unexpected costs.[26]

The cost of communications also should be compared with sales results. Janene Centurione used to rely on advertising for her Great Harvest Bread bakeries in the Michigan cities of Ann Arbor and Birmingham. However, since this cost her $80 per new customer, Centurione switched to mailing postcards to her most loyal and enthusiastic customers with information and special offers. At a cost of only $7 per customer, this approach brought in about $200 in sales per customer, with most new customers resulting from recommendations among friends.[27]

Nabisco is one of the more advanced companies in terms of evaluation and control of marketing communications. The company markets Oreos, Chips Ahoy!, Fig Newtons, Ritz crackers, and other name-brand snacks. Nabisco's 2,800 sales reps not only stack the company's products on store shelves, they also carry hand-held computers to collect sales data and use laptop computers to help retailers strategically place products on the shelves. Thus, up-to-date information about sales and promotional efforts is available at all times, not only to Nabisco but to the company's retailers, helping both to adjust promotional efforts.[28]

Sales data from scanners also can be combined with customer demographics, advertising and in-store sales promotions information. Marketers use this to measure the success of their communications strategies by quantifying consumer response to ads and sales promotions, and to measure the profitability of these efforts.

Marketing Research   Another way to evaluate the effectiveness of marketing communications is to do marketing research. A simple approach is to just ask customers how they learned about the organization and its products. Marketers can mail out surveys or set up conferences called *customer roundtables* with consumers, organizational buyers, or wholesalers and retailers. Marketers ask customers how they view products in general and about price, packaging, and product features to see what respondents remember from marketing communications. Marketers also ask questions about various types of communications used to see what respondents remember and think about them.

Other types of marketing research focus on customer purchase intentions and purchase behavior based on communications. For example, the Barn Nursery & Landscape Center, located in Cary, Illinois, printed coupons for the items featured in its monthly newsletters which are sent in response to customer requests. By tracking the number of coupons redeemed, the store could determine the number of sales generated by the newsletter. One month, the Barn promoted tree wraps in its newsletter. Sales for that month equaled the usual sales for an entire year.[29] Thus, the coupons were considered an effective communication.

To measure the sucess of its marketing communications, Pier 1 Imports—America's largest and fastest-growing specialty retailer of home furnishings, gifts, and related items imported from 44 countries—used focus groups, exit interviews, surveys, and personal contacts. After analyzing its media mix, the company changed its focus, which traditionally used color newspaper ads, and launched a television campaign to reach younger, upwardly mobile consumers. The company reported that implementation of this plan was followed by double-digit sales gains.

Implications for Global Marketers

In devising a global communications strategy, marketers also must consider differences in foreign markets. For example, foreign language differences can change communications strategies. Foreign publications are unlikely to bother with publicity materials unless they are in the right language; publishers may even be insulted if marketers haven't bothered to translate a press release. Web browsers may soon be able to use interactive catalogs that first identify their language, then automatically translate catalogs.[30] For many marketing messages, mere word-for-word translations often lead to mistakes in intended meaning. Marketers need to use people who are fluent in both the languages and cultures of countries to translate messages effectively.

Marketers must ensure that messages reflect the culture of the country and its people. Again, mistakes can be embarrassing. For example, although Muslims and Jews are forbidden from eating pork, promotional materials for refrigerators being introduced into Middle Eastern countries used a photo of a refrigerator whose contents included a large ham.[31]

Some political actions to control advertising include the work of the Center for Science in the Public Interest. This organization issues annual "awards" for the ads it deems most unfair, misleading, and irresponsible. "Winners" in one year included Old Milwaukee beer's "Swedish bikini team" ads, for linking beer drinking to sexual conquest, and Whittle Communications' educational poster on how the heart works, which included ads for fast food and candy bars directly alongside.[42]

Marketing communications directed to children present special problems. The basic reason is that children often lack the cognitive ability to evaluate marketers' messages. Young children usually are literal; they do not always understand when what they are seeing or hearing is meant to be a fantasy or metaphor. They also may not grasp the costs involved in an exchange. Even in adolescence, many children have not fully developed the critical thinking skills necessary to decide whether or how a message is biased. Thus, they may not have the ability to properly evaluate communications made by a parent, advertiser, news reporter, or teacher. A minimum ethical standard for marketers is to make communications to children straightforward, literal, and honest.

The average American child watches more than 20 hours of TV each week and sees more than 20,000 commercials a year.[43] Thus, children are aware of many products and want some of them. Some children's advocacy groups have lobbied to limit marketing efforts, such as cartoon programs that require the use of interactive toys, arguing they are thinly veiled ads for the toys that appear as characters in the cartoons.

Some advertising that children see has raised health and safety concerns. Two characters that appeal to youngsters—Spuds Mackenzie, the former mascot for Budweiser beer, and Joe Camel, the mascot for Camel cigarettes—are major examples. Both companies came under attack for their portrayal of drinking and cigarette smoking in a way that is appealing to young consumers; both denied that the characters were created to entice young people.

Finally, the creation of Channel One has brought TV, and its advertising, to the school classroom. Channel One, a for-profit cable television company owned by Whittle Communications, provides a 12-minute videotape each weekday to participating schools representing an audience of millions of children. The tape contains a 10-minute newscast of current events, with 2 minutes of advertising for snack foods, candy, and similar products.[44] Because the Channel One contract requires schools to guarantee that a certain percentage of students will watch the program each day, the company's marketers can approach potential advertisers with a clearly targeted market and a guaranteed audience. Critics complain that even if students benefit from the current events broadcast, advertising's place in the classroom is questionable.

"Because human need never ends, neither does our commitment to meeting that need," states the ad from the Dayton Hudson Corporation, which owns several major retail chains. The ad goes on to explain that the company donates 5 percent of pretax profits to programs for the arts, social services, and the environment. For example, Target, a Dayton Hudson company, is among the largest corporate partners of Habitat for Humanity, a nonprofit organization that builds and makes home ownership possible for low-income people. Target has sponsored Habitat homes in market areas it serves.

Socially Responsible Communications

Marketing communications can be socially responsible by conveying accurate information about how the organization can deliver value through goods and services that meet a legitimate need. Many corporations use marketing communications to support worthy causes as well. They may use sales promotions to sponsor events such as walk-a-thons, telethons, and bicycle rides to benefit charities. Some companies also engage in socially responsible advertising for products that have risks. For example, beer companies now advertise on television with slogans such as "Friends Know When to Say When," promoting the idea of a designated driver and not driving after drinking.

Some companies combine promotion with socially responsible activities. For example, supermarkets around the United States have made their stores available to the Visiting Nurse Association's (VNA) flu vaccination program. Nurses for the nonprofit organization gave flu shots to tens of thousands of shoppers 18 years and older at a cost of $6 to $15 per shot. In this way, participating grocery stores provide a valuable community service while generating good publicity. Such efforts enable organizations to create value for the public as well as for customers.

Summary

Through marketing communications, organizations seek to inform their target markets and influence their attitudes and buying behavior. Effective marketing communications may increase sales or profits or help accomplish other objectives, such as making people aware of the organization and its products, building positive images, identifying prospects, building channel relationships, and retaining customers.

Communication is the transmission of a message from a source to a receiver such that both understand it the same way. Elements of the communication process include the source, or sender of the message; encoding, or converting the message to a group of recognizable symbols; a communications medium, such as television or print; a receiver, that is, the person or group for whom the message is intended; noise, or distraction from the message; and feedback, or the receiver's response to the message. In the case of marketing communications, this process is intended to stimulate attention, interest, desire, and action.

The communications mix includes four elements: advertising, personal selling, sales promotion, and publicity. Advertising is any announcement or persuasive message placed in the mass media in paid or donated time or space by an identified individual, company, or organization. Personal selling is selling through personal interaction with customers. Sales promotion is media and non-media marketing efforts applied for a predetermined, limited period at the level of the consumer or intermediary in order to stimulate trial, increase demand, or improve product availability. Publicity is non-paid-for communication of information about the organization or product, generally in some media form. Today many organizations combine these elements in integrated marketing communications, which combines the elements of the communications mix in a way that provides clarity, consistency with the entire marketing mix, and greater impact.

To manage communications strategy, marketers begin by setting objectives. These objectives should support overall marketing and organizational communications. To achieve the objectives, marketers then select a communications mix. In doing so, marketers consider the nature of the target market, the nature of the product, and the decision to use a push strategy or pull strategy. Marketers also develop communications budgets, using the percentage-of-sales method, the fixed-sum-per-unit method, competition-based method, the all-you-can-afford method, or the objective-and-task method. To implement and control communications strategies, marketers put the strategies into action and use sales changes and marketing research to evaluate their effectiveness. For global communications strategies, marketers should adapt to differences in languages, meanings, and availability of media. Many global marketers prefer ad agencies with international experience.

Marketing communications involve a number of legal and ethical issues. Problems such as misleading advertising and communications directed at children cause some members of the public to be wary of marketing communications. Honest communications coupled with socially responsible service announcements are a positive use of marketing communications.

Key Terms and Concepts

marketing communications (p. 444)
communication (p. 447)
source (p. 447)
encode (p. 447)
communication medium (p. 447)
receiver (p. 447)
decode (p. 447)
noise (p. 447)

feedback (p. 448)
communications mix (p. 449)
advertising (p. 450)
personal selling (p. 451)
sales promotion (p. 451)
publicity (p. 452)
integrated marketing communications
   (IMC) (p. 452)

push strategy (p. 457)
pull strategy (p. 457)
percentage-of-sales method (p. 458)
fixed-sum-per-unit method (p. 458)
all-you-can-afford method (p. 458)
objective-and-task method (p. 459)

Review and Discussion Questions

1. Name and describe briefly the major goals of marketing communications.
2. What are the elements of the communication process?
3. Name and describe the four elements of the AIDA model. Give an example of each.
4. Name and describe the four elements of the communications mix.
5. In what ways has technology blurred the distinction between personal and nonpersonal selling?
6. If you were a marketer for a new line of solar-powered hand tools, would you choose a communications mix that emphasized personal or nonpersonal selling? Why?
7. How might a marketer try to get publicity for an electric car? What special challenges would it face in seeking publicity in foreign countries?

8. Most consumers today feel inundated by advertising. As the marketer for a new movie thriller, how would you use the nature of your target market and the nature of your product to determine what types of communication you should use?
9. Which method of budgeting matches the budget to the communication objectives? Do you think this is the most effective method of budgeting? Why or why not?
10. What are some of the communications problems marketers face in global marketing?
11. If you were a marketing manager at Channel One, how would you answer criticisms of the type of advertising it presents?

Chapter Project Establish a Value-Driven Marketing Mix

Integrated marketing communications (IMC) is becoming more popular in response to changes in the marketing environment. Value-driven marketing techniques are often part of integrated marketing communications.

Choose an existing product with which you are familiar (the car you drive, the brand of jeans you wear, the pizza you like to eat, and so forth). Imagine that you have been ap-

pointed the new marketing manager for this product. Using the IMC approach, set objectives and select the elements you think should be used in your communications mix. Choose an approach to budgeting (such as percentage of sales) and explain why you chose it. Finally, describe how you plan to implement and control the marketing communications strategy.

Chapter Case Levi Strauss & Co.

"Dressing down," or casual business wear, has become popular at offices around the country. For some companies, the new dress code applies only on Fridays; for others, it is a week-long thing. Some employees, such as those at the conservative Charles Schwab & Co., at first took the relaxed rules to such an extreme that they showed up in sweat suits and ripped jeans. So managers decided that a new—albeit casual—dress code needed to be implemented. Enter Levi's, the company that has been dressing Americans in casual wear for a century.

In a marketing communications effort, Levi's positioned itself as something of a fashion consultant to businesses. When Schwab called Levi's for help, Levi's provided all kinds of marketing information for Schwab's employees: brochures showing how to dress casually but neatly (in Levi's clothes, of course); lists of other companies that had successfully made the transition to casual attire; even a video fashion show that Schwab played for its employees in the cafeteria and at meetings. Although Levi's thinks it was careful in the way it communicates—no overt advertising—employees were quick to pick up on the intention of the messages. "People asked whether we were pushing Levi's merchandise," says Julius James, human resource director at Schwab.

Before developing the program it offered Schwab, Levi's conducted a nationwide study to see whether, in fact, casual wear had become a real trend in offices. Once that was supported, the company sent a newsletter to 65,000 human resource managers; since then, it has sent the fashion video to

more than 7,000 companies. In addition, Levi's offered fashion shows at the workplace and made a presentation to the New England Employee Benefits Council in an effort to help human resource managers outline new dress codes for their companies.

All of these messages are designed to stimulate demand. Helping companies design a new dress code stimulates demand for casual wear in general; fashion shows, videos, and other presentations of course encourage people to buy Levi's clothes. Some experts believe that Levi's has, in fact, hastened the move toward casual wear; more than 75 percent of businesses now allow workers to "dress down" at least once a week, as opposed to 37 percent just a few years ago. Levi's consumer marketing director for North America, Daniel M. Chew, is more modest about the company's role. "We did not create casual business wear," he remarks. "What we did was identify a trend and see a business opportunity." While the marketing message is clear, people do not seem to be resisting it; in fact, they perceive it as providing value. "It's a very good marketing ploy," says Lea P. Davies, a human resource director at Nynex. "It helps Levi's and gives us good practices for how to dress."

The budget for Levi's efforts is fairly small, considering the amount of money it makes. The company has spent $5 million, but could easily sell an additional 11 million pieces of casual business clothing a year.

Levi's intends to take its message global with an $8 million marketing campaign it calls "The Mission." It has planned a

32-page advertisement for newspapers in London, Manila, Milan, New York, and other cities worldwide. The promotion includes a tongue-in-cheek "Guide to Casual Science," and Levi's has even hired actors to stage mock demonstrations against old-fashioned, conservative business clothing. "Levi's is capitalizing on its brand name and teaching men how they should look," observed Janet J. Kloppenburg at Robertson, Stephens & Co. Kloppenburg doesn't mention women, but we assume that Levi's has plenty of marketing messages for them, too.

Questions

1. In what ways does Levi's success with its new casual business wear depend on creating awareness and building an image?

2. Which options in the communications mix will probably be most successful in the new campaign as Levi's takes it global? Why?

3. Do you think Levi's faces any ethical or social issues in its marketing communications for casual business wear? If so, what might they be?

Sources: Louise Lee, "Some Employees Just Aren't Suited for Dressing Down; Corporate 'Casual Day' Rules Can Be a Formal Hassle," *The Wall Street Journal,* February 3, 1995, p. A1; Alice Z. Cuneo, "Dockers' Mission Sweeps Forward," *Advertising Age,* April 1, 1996; pp. 3, 61; Linda Himelstein and Nancy Walser, "Levi's Vs. the Dress Code," *Business Week,* April 1, 1996, pp. 57–58; Kate Walker, "Dress for Success and Comfort," *HR Magazine,* June 1996, pp. 56–60.

Explore more at www.dockers.com

Chapter Eighteen

Advertising, Sales Promotion, and Publicity

CHAPTER OUTLINE

Advertising
  Types of Advertising
Developing and Managing Advertising Campaigns
  Review Advertising Goals and Budgets
  Create Messages
  Select Media
  Pretest Ads
  Evaluate Advertising Effectiveness
  Adjust Advertising as Needed
  Legal and Ethical Issues in Advertising
Sales Promotion
  Consumer Promotions
  Trade Promotions
  Legal and Ethical Issues in Sales Promotion
Publicity
  Types of Publicity
  Managing Negative Publicity
  Ethical Issues in Publicity
Summary

LEARNING OBJECTIVES

After completing this chapter, you should be able to:

1. List major functions of advertising.
2. Identify basic types of advertising.
3. Discuss legal and ethical issues in advertising.
4. Describe how marketers manage an advertising campaign.
5. Identify major techniques for sales promotion.
6. Explain how sales promotion can create value and be used ethically.
7. Summarize basic types of publicity and ways that marketers generate publicity.
8. Describe how marketers manage bad publicity.
9. Evaluate ethical issues surrounding publicity.

When Microsoft's Windows 95 hit the market, the whole world knew about it. That's the way Chairman Bill Gates wanted it. This world party was also the most expensive new product introduction in history; Bill Gates didn't seem to mind that, either. Between advertising and publicity, news of the new graphical operating system software spread around the world from the United States to Britain to Western Europe to Eastern Europe to Japan in rapidfire succession. The cost of this promotion? Somewhere between $100 million and $200 million.

Bill Gates, known for his creative marketing, orchestrated the campaign so that Windows 95 became a phenomenon around the world. In England, Microsoft bought up one entire edition of the *Times of London* for about $500,000 and agreed to distribute all 1.5 million copies free to readers that day. In turn, Microsoft ran several ads and a 24-page supplement in which newspaper staff and public relations writers praised the new product. The cost was only a fraction of what Microsoft planned to spend on advertising in the United Kingdom (more than $30 million), and the publicity—nonpaid-for communication with the market—generated by the stunt was "worth several million," according to Bob Offen, managing director of Mediastar in London. Of course, Gates had his critics, but he brushed them off. "I like what we're doing . . . I think we're buying advertising," he said.

In another unusual agreement, the Rolling Stones agreed to allow Microsoft use their song "Start Me Up" as a theme song in commercials for Windows 95. This was the first time Mick Jagger and Keith Richards had allowed the commercial use of their songs (other than in advertising related to their own concert tours). Microsoft also planned a half-hour infomercial in conjunction with Coca-Cola Co., Eastman Kodak Co., Compaq Computer Corp., and CompUSA. The infomercial was hosted by Anthony Edwards, star of television's "E.R." "It's a big event," noted Bob Bertini of Coke. "We are always looking for different and innovative ways to engage our consumers."

Around the world, a four-story Windows 95 box sailed on a barge into the harbor at Sydney, Australia. In Britain, Microsoft painted farmers' fields with the Windows 95 logo so airplane passengers could see it. In Poland, Microsoft marketers took journalists underwater in a submarine to illustrate what it would be like to live "in a world without Windows."

Bill Gates himself did not remain on the sidelines. In eight days he visited six countries, attending promotional meetings and festivities. Two hundred fans greeted him at the airport in Budapest (later, thousands packed the State Opera House at a special event); ten thousand guests attended a glitzy affair in France. Of course, all of these appearances made the news, generating more publicity for Windows 95. As you read this chapter, consider the impact that advertising, sales promotion, and publicity have on how customers perceive a product and the ultimate success or failure of the product. Consider also how these elements of marketing create value for the customer. Do they provide valuable information or cloud the important issues?

Sources: Richard L. Hudson, "Windows 95 Sales Are Disappointing for Some in Europe," *The Wall Street Journal,* November 10, 1995, Sec. B, p. 7; Dana Milbank, "Marketing & Media: Microsoft Purchases an Entire Edition of Times of London," *The Wall Street Journal,* August 24, 1995, Sec. B, p. 5; Don Clark, "Marketing: Windows 95 Buzz Will Get Even Louder," *The Wall Street Journal,* August 18, 1995, Sec. B, p. 1; "Technology & Health: Europeans Roll Out Many Red Carpets for American Icon," *The Wall Street Journal,* September 5, 1995, Sec. B, p. 2.

Chapter Overview

Advertising, sales promotion, and publicity all have important roles to play in creating value for customers. These tools create value by providing customers information for making good purchase decisions and improving their lives. They can create value by lowering monetary, time, and effort costs.

This chapter discusses these nonpersonal elements of the communications mix. It explains what advertising does and what basic types of advertising are available. Then the chapter discusses the steps involved in managing a domestic or global advertising campaign and explores legal and ethical issues in advertising. Next, the discussion turns to sales promotion: types of sales promotion, its sources of value, and ethical considerations. Finally, the chapter examines publicity, first exploring the types of publicity and then ways to generate it. The chapter closes with discussions of methods for managing negative publicity and ethical issues surrounding it.

Advertising

As noted in the last chapter, advertising is any announcement or persuasive message placed in the mass media in paid or donated time or space by an identified individual, company, or organization. Advertising serves a number of functions, both for marketers and their customers.

The overriding function of business advertising is to inform potential customers about products and persuade or remind them to buy. It can also convey information about the organization itself or issues important to the organization. Advertising can inform a large number of customers at the same time. Good advertising can create or enhance perceptions of the quality or reliability of a product, thus encouraging customer loyalty and repeat purchases.

Advertising costs money. Although advertising costs less per person reached than personal selling, the money spent on advertising is sizable. One estimate of annual spending on advertising by U.S. companies alone totaled $174.1 billion.[1] The country's leading advertisers, companies like Procter & Gamble, Philip Morris, General Motors, Ford, and Sears spend over $1 billion on advertising a year.[2]

Types of Advertising

As shown in Table 18.1, there are many types of advertising. Knowing the basic types can help marketers select the best ones for meeting their communications objectives.

T A B L E 18.1
Types of Advertising

Term	Definition
Product advertising	Advertising that focuses on creating demand for goods, services, places, persons, or events
Service advertising	Product advertising of services
Institutional advertising	Advertising that promotes the name, image, personnel, or reputation of a company, organization, or industry
Pioneering advertising	Advertising that attempts to develop primary demand for a category of product
Competitive advertising	Advertising that attempts to develop selective demand for particular brands of products
Comparative advertising	Advertising that compares a brand with competitor's or with previous formulations
Advocacy advertising	Institutional advertising that supports particular positions, activities, or causes
Corrective advertising	Advertising involving a company running new ads that correct a deceptive or unfair advertising message previously disseminated

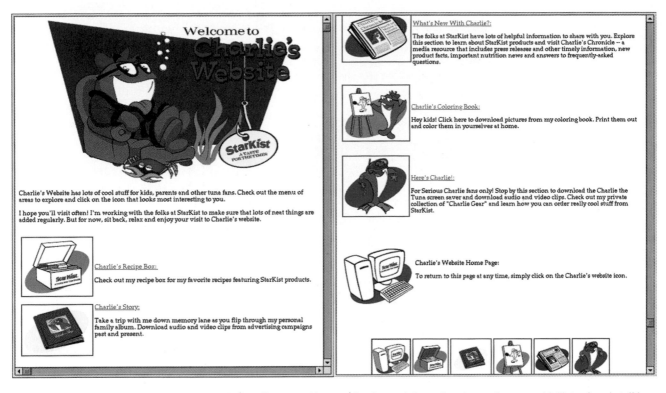

The StarKist Foods site on the World Wide Web (http://www.starkist.com) is a happy, informative place to browse, with "lots of cool stuff for kids, parents, and other tuna fans." Charlie the Tuna, the famous trademark owned by StarKist, invites site visitors to "sit back, relax and enjoy" StarKist recipes from "Charlie's recipe box." The Web site also offers advertising campaign video clips, product information, a coloring book, an audio/video screen saver, and an opportunity to order "really cool stuff" from StarKist.

product advertising
Advertising that attempts to create demand for goods, services, places, persons, or events.

institutional advertising
Advertising that promotes the name, image, personnel, or reputation of a company, organization, or industry.

pioneering advertising
Advertising that attempts to develop primary demand for a category of product.

competitive advertising
Advertising that attempts to develop selective demand for particular brands of products.

Product advertising focuses on creating demand for goods or services. For example, televised demonstrations of the No Mess Dough Disc on QVC spurred sales of over 200,000 of the cloth-covered kitchen gadgets.[3] Product advertising can also be for places, persons or events.

In contrast to product advertising, **institutional advertising** promotes the name, image, personnel, or reputation of a company, organization, or industry.[4] An example is Chevron Corporation's Web site. By providing in-depth information about the organization's extensive operations plus background information about the oil industry, the Web site helps position Chevron as an expert in fuel. Moreover, by being one of the first companies to develop a strategy for communicating via the Web, Chevron positioned itself as aware of the latest technology.[5] Of course, Chevron also hopes that its positioning strategy will help sell more fuel. In general, objectives for institutional advertising include improving public relations through positive messages, helping the organization's salespeople gain access to customers (resellers or end users), and providing reseller support by enhancing the image of the brands carried by the reseller.

Pioneering advertising seeks to develop primary demand, that is, demand for a product category—say, dairy products, beef, or plastics—rather than a specific brand. Pioneering advertising is especially important for introducing an innovative product or one that is new to a target market. In Russia, for example, consumers had little access to the wide variety of goods available from Western companies for many years. As a result, some global marketers to Russian consumers had to explain what their products were and how they were to be used.[6]

Competitive advertising attempts to develop selective demand—demand for a particular brand of product. Britain's Virgin Atlantic Airways distinguishes itself from the competition through ads describing Virgin's amenities, including roomy seating, individual videos to watch, and limousine transportation to and from the airport.[7]

This ad by the National Fluid Milk Processor Promotion Board is pioneering advertising that seeks to develop primary demand for milk, rather than for a particular brand. When this campaign began, milk sales had been in a three-decade slump. This ad and the others in the campaign have proved amazingly effective in boosting milk's image and its sales.

Guilty or not? Do you cross out the waist size on your jeans? Listen, it's totally pathetic, but how can we not? Everyone talks about losing weight. My advice? 1% milk. 3 glasses a day. It has all the calcium you need and less fat. Now there's a fashion statement.

MILK
Where's your mustache?

comparative advertising
Advertising that compares a brand with competitors' or with previous formulations.

Comparative advertising usually involves a brand being compared with that of a named or unnamed competitor and being shown to be superior on particular attributes.[8] For example, Burger King advertised that in taste tests, its Whopper is preferred to McDonald's Big Mac. Comparative advertising also describes ads that focus on the superiority of a new product formulation over the old one. For example, Duracell advertised that its batteries were the best it had ever made, suggesting that they were superior to previous types. Many brands of prepared food products advertise that they are lower in fat or calories than previous formulations.

advocacy advertising
Institutional advertising that supports particular positions, activities, or causes.

Advocacy advertising is placed by businesses and other organizations and is intended to communicate a viewpoint about a controversial topic relating to the social, political, or economic environment.[9] For example, Budweiser and Miller Brewing run ads promoting responsible drinking.

Developing and Managing Advertising Campaigns

When marketers decide their communications mix should include advertising, they develop and manage an *advertising campaign*. Doing so requires teamwork. In small companies, the advertising staff might be one or two people working with the owner. Large organizations often have an advertising group within the marketing department. Members of the advertising group include researchers, artists and designers, copywriters, and media analysts. Marketing managers and top executives also are involved in advertising decisions. Other employees with input include product and finance personnel, who provide inputs on product functions and budgeting.

Often marketers use other companies to help them develop marketing communications. They call on **advertising agencies** to help plan and prepare advertising campaigns. The agency and the client work as a team to develop advertising that is effective and consistent with the rest of the communications mix.

advertising agency
A firm devoted to planning and preparing advertising campaigns for other organizations.

Advertising agencies seek to meet marketers' needs by offering a variety of services (see "Marketing Movers & Shakers: Michael Bronner/Bronner Slosberg Humphrey Inc."). Working with marketers, agencies study products to identify attributes and benefits that could be highlighted in ads. They analyze markets for products and develop general strategies for advertising them. When the strategy is approved by the client, advertisements are designed and produced, media are scheduled, and the ads are pretested. In some cases, advertising agencies may help plan and implement the whole communications mix in an integrated communications effort.

Michael Bronner/ Bronner Slosberg Humphrey Inc.

"Mass marketing is like defoliating Vietnam," quips Mike Slosberg, vice chairman and creative director of Boston-based Bronner Slosberg Humphrey Inc., the fifth largest direct marketing firm in the country. That's an extreme statement. Yet it sums up the antithesis of what his company, founded by colleague Michael Bronner, is all about: customized direct marketing.

While still in college at Boston University (BU), Michael Bronner came up with the idea of producing a coupon book filled with coupons from local businesses catering to college students—pizza joints, record stores, laundromats, and the like. He slipped the coupon book into the 14,000 mail boxes of BU students, and his success began.

Direct marketing used to be considered a poor cousin to advertising. Traditional advertising, through mass media, could reach a lot more people and it was glitzy and glamorous. With advertisers and advertising agencies now taking more of a value-driven approach, both have realized the tremendous potential of direct marketing that can be tailored to meet the interests and needs of specific customers.

With a client list that many agencies would envy—AT&T, GM, IBM, L.L. Bean, American Express, Federal Express, and Fidelity Investments—Bronner Slosberg Humphrey elevated direct marketing to an art. "It's only junk mail if the message is irrelevant to the customer who receives it," says Michael Bronner.

Bronner specializes in making the message relevant to each customer. For instance, in a customized print campaign created for L.L. Bean, the agency compared Bean's customer base to the subscription lists of 20 national magazines. Ads placed in these magazines were customized based on whether subscribers were already on Bean's catalog list or not. Bronner Slosberg was able to segment the list further by looking at Bean's customers' buying habits, such as how often they shopped and what types of items they bought. The ads were targeted so precisely that two people living in the same apartment building, receiving the same magazine, could get two different ads. This method allowed "us to give the ads a high level of personalization," explained Slosberg. "A long-time customer might not know that they can now buy Rollerblades and mountain bikes from Bean as well as khaki trousers and chamois shirts. The ad would let the customer know that. In essence, the ad becomes direct mail, and the magazine is the envelope."

This was an expensive test for Bean, but it paid off. "We wanted to get back a read on our investment, and Bronner Slosberg devised this one-time test," noted Chris McCormick, Bean's president of advertising. Based on the results, Bean doubled its advertising budget. McCormick felt that the agency provided real value for his organization. "They really understood how our business worked and that every dollar had to be justified," he says. "They approach you more like a management consultant than a creative person from an ad agency."

Pretty sophisticated stuff for a former college kid who started by stuffing coupon books in students' mailboxes. Bronner's agency now employs nearly 600 people and is billing more than $500 million in fees each year. "We're cramming and jamming," says Bronner.

Source: Chris Reidy, "Taking 'Mass' Out of Marketing," *The Boston Globe*, June 16, 1996, pp. 47, 53. Reprinted courtesy of *The Boston Globe*.

Explore more by searching "Bronner Slosberg Humphrey" on the Web.

To be most effective, an advertising agency should have complete knowledge of its client's product, competitors' products and advertising strategies, and media available for disseminating ads. The agency also needs to understand its client's philosophy, objectives, and image, as well as its target markets. Understanding local markets can give small agencies an edge over the global giants. For example, big international agencies eagerly moved into Eastern Europe when markets opened up there, but were not well prepared. Eastern Europeans did not see the irony in a Lipton tea commercial in which Tom Selleck portrayed a tough guy standing on a mountaintop sipping tea. When Hungary's telecommunications firm, Matav, insisted that ad agencies make their presentations in Hungarian, global agencies found themselves at a disadvantage to a local company, which won the contract.[10]

Once work has begun with an ad agency, marketers must formally and informally evaluate how well the two organizations work together. Sometimes it takes several trials before an agency develops a campaign that pleases the client. Nevertheless, marketers consider whether the relationship results in effective, timely

FIGURE 18.1 *Checklist for Evaluating Ad Agencies*

Rate each agency on a scale from 1 (strongly negative) to 10 (strongly positive).

General Information
- ☐ Size compatible with our needs.
- ☐ Strength of management.
- ☐ Financial stability.
- ☐ Compatibility with other clients.
- ☐ Range of services.
- ☐ Cost of services; billing policies.

Marketing Information
- ☐ Ability to offer marketing counsel.
- ☐ Understanding of the markets we serve.
- ☐ Experience dealing in our market.
- ☐ Success record; case histories.

Creative Abilities
- ☐ Well-thought-out creativity; relevance to strategy.
- ☐ Art strength.
- ☐ Copy strength.

- ☐ Overall creative quality.
- ☐ Effectiveness compared to work of competitors.

Production
- ☐ Faithfulness to creative concept and execution.
- ☐ Diligence to schedules and budgets.
- ☐ Ability to control outside services.

Media
- ☐ Existence and soundness of media research.
- ☐ Effective and efficient media strategy.
- ☐ Ability to achieve objectives within budget.
- ☐ Strength at negotiating and executing schedules.

Personality
- ☐ Overall personality, philosophy, or position.
- ☐ Compatibility with client staff and management.
- ☐ Willingness to assign top people to account.

References
- ☐ Rating by current clients.
- ☐ Rating by past clients.
- ☐ Rating by media and financial sources.

Source: William F. Arens, *Contemporary Advertising,* 6th ed. (Burr Ridge, Ill.: Irwin, 1996), p. 93.

communications with their customers. If not, one of the benefits of using an agency is that, if the results are disappointing, it is relatively easy to end the relationship and find another one. To evaluate agencies to work with, marketers use a number of criteria such as the ones shown in the checklist in Figure 18.1.

A small ad agency may consist of only a few staff members doing a variety of jobs. But large advertising agencies employ creative staff, production staff, account executives, and marketing services personnel. Account executives set up contracts and make arrangements with clients. The creative and production services groups prepare the actual advertisements. The marketing services group selects media and places the ads, and may conduct various types of research as well.

Global marketers need to be familiar with the practices of advertising agencies in other countries. In Japan, the biggest advertising challenge is getting a share of limited ad space, so ad agencies with close links with the media are in demand. The need to stand out from the clutter of many short commercials has resulted in Japanese ad agencies preparing bizarre commercials. In an ad for Giga television, for example, a man sits in a dark house, eating a banana and staring at a static-filled TV screen. Similarly, in an ad for a food product, a tribe chases a moa (a giant extinct bird) to the edge of a cliff. The moa jumps into the air and the tribesmen rush off the cliff. An announcer proclaims, "Hungry? Cup Noodles!"[11]

Whether ad campaigns are developed in-house or with the help of an agency, they must be managed. This includes planning, implementing, and controlling the campaign. Planning involves four tasks: reviewing advertising goals and budgets, creating messages, selecting media, and pretesting ads. Implementing includes scheduling ads and running them. Controlling includes evaluating advertising effectiveness and improving the ad campaign, if possible. These tasks are sequenced in Figure 18.2.

Review Advertising Goals and Budgets

In integrated marketing communication, the goals and budget for advertising are tentatively set when marketers develop the communications mix strategy. While changes could occur during the development or execution of an ad campaign, at this

F I G U R E 18.2
*The Process of
Managing Advertising*

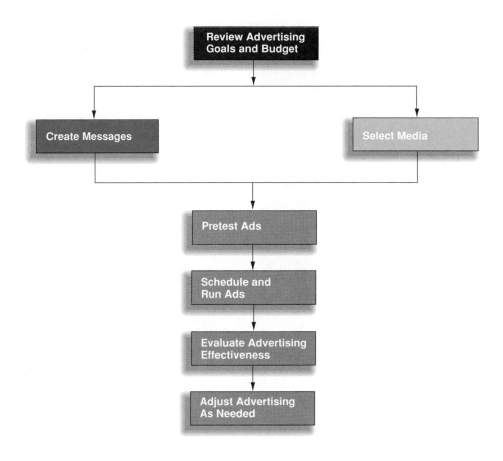

The target audience for this advertisement consists of corporations that need telecommunications systems in the Asia-Pacific region. Telstra is an Australian telecommunications provider of services for call and data management; e-mail systems; products that can integrate voice, data, text, and image transmissions; cellular telephones; and pay phones and phone cards. To reach its audience, Telstra placed this ad in The Economist, *a business magazine with extensive global coverage. The photo (Asian businessmen enjoying cable-car spas) depicts a custom of a region served by Telstra and implies that companies might need help in understanding foreign cultures. The heading reads, "Not too familiar with all the customs in Asia? Talk to the Australian telecommunications company that knows its way around."*

stage marketers review the goals and budget set for advertising.

The goals are necessary for providing guidelines for advertising strategy. For example, Robert Olson, president of Virtual Vineyards, noted that the design of its Web site would differ depending on whether its goals were stated in terms of the number of sales, the number of visitors to the site, or the company's image.[12] Goals also are needed to ensure that the effectiveness of a campaign can be evaluated. Additionally, marketers review previous advertising and its effects, and any changes in the environment that could affect advertising strategy.

Marketers must also consider the *target audience* for the ads. This is the group to which advertising will be directed, which is typically the same as the target market. Different ads may be developed to serve different target audiences. For example, when Chevron set up its Web site, it created different pages to meet the information needs of investors who seek financial data, reporters who want news-related facts, and students and teachers looking for background details about the industry.[13]

Create Messages

"Just do it" (Nike); "It's the real thing" (Coca-Cola); "Celebrate the moments of your life" (General Foods International Coffees); "We run the tightest ship in the

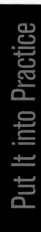

How Many Slogans Do You Remember?

We hear thousands of slogans during our lifetime as consumers. A slogan is part of an advertising campaign, the catch phrase about the product or company that you are supposed to remember. Some slogans are more memorable than others—Nike's "Just Do It" and the Beef Council's "Beef: It's What's for Dinner" come to mind.

Brainstorm five slogans, jotting them down as you go. Try to remember the product—and company—those slogans represent and write them down, too. Try to determine what made each slogan memorable to you. Was it the choice of words? Was it an image? A musical jingle that accompanied it? A memorable character?

If possible, share your list of slogans with the class. Were there any slogans for which you could not name both product and company? Did you get any wrong?

shipping business" (UPS). All of these famous advertising slogans contain messages that marketers want customers to remember and understand (see "Put It into Practice: How Many Slogans Do You Remember?"). Nonprofit advertisers also rely on memorable slogans, such as "This is your brain on drugs" (Partnership for a Drug-Free America).

Of course, advertising is more than catchy slogans. It is information that target audiences care about—the name and location of a good restaurant, the benefits of a new product, the current exhibit at an art museum. Advertising may contain words, pictures, actions, images, and symbols that marketers use to influence customer perceptions and behaviors. In general, advertising messages contain various types of appeals.

A *rational appeal* focuses on the measurable benefits of selecting the product or brand. For example, ads for Taco Bell focus on the extreme value—tasty, large portions of food at a low price—customers get by eating there. Rational appeals also are common in ads for organizational products that could help a company be more efficient or effective.

Emotional appeals try to create good feelings about products or make customers experience other emotions. For example, Pillsbury ads for biscuits and cookie mixes often show preparers receiving love and appreciation from family members. One Harley-Davidson TV ad depicted an old man's regrets for not having bought a Harley when he was younger.

A *fear appeal* is a type of emotional appeal that arouses fear by demonstrating the consequences of not purchasing and using particular products. For example, one insurance company ran a TV commercial showing a young man going to a dead-end job. He is thinking out loud that he was supposed to go to college and that his dad had planned for everything—except that he didn't plan on dying with no insurance.

Sex appeals suggest that using a product will make the consumer more attractive and sexy. Products such as makeup, shampoo, jeans, and exercise equipment often use these appeals. They also are used for automobiles, beer, liquor, cigarettes, and even real estate.

Humor appeals rely on the target audience's sense of humor. In general, they can be effective, but only for a short time. Part of the success of a humor appeal is its surprise; once consumers have seen or heard the commercial or read the ad, the humor decreases rapidly.

Chrysler Corporation uses humor in this advertisement for a Jeep 4x4 that appeared on the back cover of National Geographic *magazine. The small label on the back end of the elephant states, "If you can read this your Jeep is too close." Besides grabbing the reader's attention, this ad makes that point that a Jeep can drive in places that are inaccessible to many vehicles.*

A *moral appeal* tries to convince an audience that using or accepting an idea is the right or moral thing to do. Ads opposing abortion often use moral appeals.

Usually, creating messages and appeals is the job of copywriters and creatives at ad agencies. These people try to convey product benefits and images in ways that catch and hold people's attention and develop their interest and desire. While this demands creativity, it also requires that copywriters understand the overall communications strategy and the profile of the target audience. Thus, ads should use words and pictures understandable by and interesting to the target audience, feature benefits and other stimuli important to it, and support the client's strategy.

Likewise, the message needs to reflect the product's concept or intended image. For example, Bob Devlin and Barbara Hogan Devlin wanted an image for their real estate agency that it is customer focused and knowledgeable of the community. To develop this image, the Devlins set up a Web site offering detailed information about local schools, hospitals, commuting, weather, demographics, and much more, as well as real estate information.[14]

Select Media

Marketers try to choose the best media to reach their target audience with their advertising message. Often, they use a mix of various media to communicate. To select different media vehicles (specific newspapers, magazines, TV programs, etc.), marketers evaluate them on criteria such as:

- **Reach**—the number of different persons or households exposed to a particular advertising media vehicle or a media schedule during a period of time.[15]
- **Rating**—the percentage of the total potential audience who are exposed to a particular media vehicle.[16]
- **Frequency**—the average number of times a person, household, or member of a target audience is exposed to a media vehicle or an advertiser's media schedule within a given time period.[17]
- **Cost per thousand**—the cost of using a media vehicle to reach 1,000 people or households.
- **Gross rating points (GRPs)**—a measure of the total advertising exposures produced by a specific media vehicle or combination of them during a specified time. A GRP is determined by multiplying reach percentage by frequency.

Decisions about which medium or media to use must be based not only on cost but on the location and media habits of target audiences. Marketers also must consider which media best suit the positioning of products. For example, some products require extensive explanation and may need print ads; others require high-quality color graphics and may be limited to magazines and TV commercials. The major media choices are television, radio, print (newspaper, magazines, Yellow Pages), direct mail, outdoor advertising, and the Internet.

Television   Television can reach the most people simultaneously. Indeed, properly placed television commercials could reach most of the households in the United States. Furthermore, they appeal to both sight and sound senses through the use of words and pictures as well as music, voices, and other sounds. Through the effective use of sights and sounds, an audience can almost smell a Big Mac and feel the baby blanket softened in Downy fabric softener. Marketers can communicate on television by purchasing standard 15- or 30-second commercials, running an infomercial for a half-hour or longer, or obtaining space on a home-shopping channel. To get on a TV home-shopping program, marketers can pay for ads in publications such as *TV Products Showcase,* a trade magazine read by decision makers in the home-shopping industry.[18] Television advertising can generate attention and has a low cost per exposure.

A relatively new twist on television advertising is the **infomercial.** These 30-minute blends of information and advertising enable marketers to explain products in greater depth than standard TV commercials. Thus, they make television advertising suitable for more products and messages. McDonald's aired an infomercial on Black Entertainment Television to provide information about the company's efforts to be socially responsible to the African-American community. Explains Stephanie Skurdy, McDonald's director of communications, "[African-American consumers] want to know what we are doing to support the community, and you can't tell it in 30 seconds."[19]

Television has its downside, however, most notably its high cost. Not only do networks charge more than $100,000 for a 30-second spot in prime time, there are production costs as well, which can be in the range of a million dollars.[20] Although television's cost per thousand can be reasonable compared to alternative media, its wide coverage can also be a drawback. Marketers must pay to reach everyone who is watching, instead of just the target audience. A viewer's exposure to a television commercial is short—usually 15 or 30 seconds and the life of a commercial usually isn't very long—perhaps a few months. Part of the appeal of a new television commercial is its freshness and surprise, which quickly fade. Television is not available in some countries, or is only available on a limited basis or to a limited share of a market. Finally, consumers often "zap" commercials with their remotes.

Television advertising is particularly useful when marketers want to draw attention to products that are widely purchased and simple to understand. That is one reason marketers of personal computers have begun using television advertising in place of print media, since many people are now familiar with the product and marketers are mainly trying to create demand for their brands.[21]

Radio It may seem that radio is being replaced by television. However, there are many more radio stations in the United States than there are television stations. It costs much less to advertise on radio than it does on television, and advertisers are much more apt to reach their target audience—say, listeners who like country music, late-night talk shows, or business news. Radio often is effective for local businesses, from car dealerships to hardware stores, and is widely available throughout the world.

Radio commercials lack the visual effects of television, but a great deal of drama and illusion can be created with voices, music, and other sounds. Like television commercials, radio ads live a short life, and it is difficult to convey information that is abstract or complex using them. Also, radio rate structures are unstandardized and listeners often pay little attention because they are doing other things—like driving their car—while listening.

Print Newspapers and magazines, depending on their content and circulation, can provide either broad exposure or exposure to a very specific market. Also, print ads allow detailed information on complex products so customers can study them and understand product benefits. Daily newspapers allow retailers to advertise immediate events such as one-day sales, and airlines can advertise short-notice fare changes. Weekly special sections on travel or food carry advertisements for restaurants, hotels, and the like that appeal to readers. The reach for newspaper advertising can be very good, but frequency depends on how often an ad is run as well as how often the newspaper is published (daily or weekly). Cost for local newspaper ads is relatively low although ads in nationally circulated newspapers such as *U.S. Today* cost more.

Magazines have large and varied audiences. Marketers can reach thousands of readers in magazines like *Time* or *People,* or they can more

The Art Institute of Chicago advertised its exhibit "Degas: Beyond Impressionism" in Newsweek. While the magazine is distributed nationally, it publishes geographically defined editions, one of which reaches the Chicagoland market, where this ad appeared.

precisely target a category of consumers with specific interests in magazines like *Antique Monthly, Popular Photography,* and *Golf Digest.* Trade publications such as *Electrical Contractor* and *Convenience Store News* offer a way to target organizational buyers in particular industries.

National magazines also allow marketers to target specific audiences. When national magazines publish special advertising sections, an audience interested in the particular topic can be reached. Marketers can reach selected geographic segments by running ads in zoned or geographic editions of national magazines. Because only some copies of the magazine carry the ads, marketers pay less and avoid some wasted circulation.

Magazines can reproduce colors well and have larger pass-along audiences than newspapers. In addition, marketers can insert attention-getting gimmicks such as pop-ups or sample packets of products such as hand lotion in magazines. However, magazine advertisements must be submitted weeks or even months in advance of publication, and marketers usually have little control over where the ad is placed. A magazine ad usually costs more than a newspaper ad or radio commercial.

A form of print advertising that can be effective for organizations serving a local market is the Yellow Pages. One advantage of advertising in the Yellow Pages is that individuals and organizations hang on to their copies for a year—far longer than they keep looking at a magazine or newspaper. Another is that when people look in the Yellow Pages, they are generally planning to make purchases. Marketers can also target their audience by more than geography; many specialized listings are available. Members of the Yellow Pages Publishers Associations publish directories in a variety of languages, including Chinese, Farsi, Korean, Russian, and Spanish.[22] A major disadvantage of Yellow Pages advertising is that it is hard to create an ad that stands out from the many others on the same page.

Direct Mail   With direct mail, marketers can precisely target advertising to a market. Direct mail advertising is a daily event for many consumers who receive catalogs, invitations to join nonprofit organizations, campaign flyers, newsletters, and advertisements for everything from credit cards to power tools. A direct mail ad can contain more information than a standard television commercial or magazine ad, so the medium is useful for describing complex or big-ticket items. Although many people consider direct mail to be "junk mail," more than 90 million consumers in the United States responded to a direct mail offer in one year and spent more than $180 billion on mail-order products.[23] Direct mail also has advantages since there are no competing products advertised and its effectiveness can be more easily measured by marketers. Competitors, on the other hand, have a difficult time monitoring direct mail activities.

A downside of direct mail is high cost. Paper and postage expenses—which together account for about one-fourth of the cost of catalog advertising—have risen dramatically in recent years. These expenses have made contacting customers electronically or by phone relatively more attractive. Direct mail also lacks other information, such as TV shows or magazine articles, to attract attention. Delivery time and dates also cannot be guaranteed.

Outdoor   Outdoor advertising includes billboards, signs on buildings, hot air balloons, banners, and posters such as those found on buses, cabs, and in subway tunnels. It once was considered the most effective way to reach American consumers in rural regions. During the late 1960s, Ladybird Johnson's campaign to "beautify America" and eliminate billboards, along with corporate consolidations and restrictions on liquor and tobacco advertising, caused outdoor advertising to decline. Billboards and transit ads, however, remain popular in some cities, with many of them placed by retailers, marketers for regional tourism, and the entertainment industry.[24] Billboards and signs have the advantage that they can be placed away from signs for competitive products and close to stores selling the product.

A poster or billboard can reach many people, repeatedly, but it rarely can target an audience, except by geographic location. A good billboard should be eye-catching to drivers without completely distracting them, and since drivers see it for only a few seconds, written copy should be kept to a minimum. Moreover, a cleverly placed sign can overcome some of the limitations. On a three-story apartment building behind the right-field wall of Wrigley Field (home of the Chicago Cubs) stands a sign visible to the millions of baseball fans who attend games—and also to those watching the game on broadcast and cable television.[25]

Billboards are not cheap. Depending on location as well as the complexity of the board itself, such as if it has lights or moving parts, billboards can cost as much as a television commercial. Universal Studios in Florida has some billboards that cost $100,000 each: one with King Kong shaking his fist and another on which E.T.'s finger lights up and his eyes roll around.[26] Because of the expense of billboards, many outdoor ads are simple posters in cabs and buses.

The Internet   The Internet has become an advertising medium for a number of organizations. Marketers use the World Wide Web to combine words, pictures, and even sound and video to reach domestic and global marketers. Marketers advertise on their own Web sites or with messages on other sites.

Marketers can control advertising content by establishing their own Web sites. Moreover, they can also control their costs through the type of site they establish. With modern software, they can convert word-processing documents to Web pages, a very inexpensive alternative. However, paying for a sophisticated site design can be well worth the cost. Nicole Miller paid a consultant $10,000 to set up a site that turned out to be dull and disappointing. The company then turned to another contractor, who charged more but created a site that generated much more traffic with exciting graphics, music, and clips from fashion shows.[27]

Marketers can also pay for their names or logos to be included on other organizations' Web sites. Unlike ads in traditional media, users can click on the name or logo and link to the marketer's own Web site. In this way, the marketer's site can easily be visited by people interested in the company. Rates for Web advertising on other sites vary tremendously; at the high end, an advertiser might pay $100,000 a quarter for an ad on ESPN's SportsZone site or $20,000 per month for an ad on Yahoo!, a popular search engine for the World Wide Web. Some observers predict that ad rates will plunge as the market for Web advertising matures.[28]

Embratur, the Brazilian Tourist Board, offers information at its Web site (http://www.embratur.gov.br). The Web site's home page offers information in Portuguese and English and the opportunity to select state and city sites where you can view beautiful photos and obtain information such as maps, current events, and travel tips on clothing, restaurants, rental cars, and places to stay. As use of the Internet becomes widespread, more and more organizations are including Internet addresses in their print advertising.

Another approach is to sponsor non-advertising Internet programming. Such programming might include magazines such as *HotWired*, celebrity interviews, or even Web soap operas. The first serial drama launched on the Web was *The Spot*, which follows the story of seven roommates in Santa Monica, California. The tens of thousands of people from over 50 countries who visit the site each day see ads for Hugo Boss, Honda, K-Swiss, and C/Net.[29] Ideally, marketers select sites where the programming is interesting enough to attract many visitors who can be told about the organization or its products.

The Web offers many benefits to marketers. First, organizations of all sizes can establish a basic site for a nominal cost that is accessible to Web browsers around the world at any time. Information at a Web site may be customized to the browser's buying history and stated preferences. Moreover, the ability to gather information on customers gives marketers a good source of marketing research data. Marketers can arrange payments to Web publishers based on particular results. For example, Procter & Gamble has arranged to pay Web publishers according to the number of people who use a P&G ad to click to a P&G Web site, not just the number of people who click to a Web site displaying a P&G ad.[30]

Disadvantages of Internet advertising include language differences in global audiences and the fact that customers must have the necessary hardware and software. The latter problem is shrinking as more and more people go on-line. For an organization serving high-tech consumers or organizational markets, access to the Internet is not usually a problem. Audiences must also seek out information on the company and its products rather than being exposed to it in normal day-to-day activities. Another disadvantage is that the quality of images seen by the audience varies according to the capabilities of each person's hardware and software. Finally, anyone can post an Internet message about anything, so hackers may add noise to the communication process by setting up Web site look-alikes with humorous or even hostile messages. During the 1996 presidential campaign, someone set up a site at the Web address www.dole96.org and linked the Republican candidate to the fruit company of the same name. Messages included offering "position papers" on the candidate's favorite fruit.[31] Table 18.2 summarizes the advantages and disadvantages of the major media.

Other Media   Creative marketers have options other than the major media. A familiar alternative is to place the company's name or logo on athletes' uniforms or their equipment. According to one estimate, placing a logo on a NASCAR race car gets the sponsor "exposure time" equivalent to over $200 million in advertising.[32] Another alternative is videocasettes. To announce the opening of a store in Sunnyvale, California, J. C. Penney sent local households a 4½-minute videocassette showing off the store.[33] And a British company called Van den Bergh Foods developed a video game starring its Peperami snack sausage.[34]

Pretest Ads

pretest
Researching a test's audience
reactions to an ad before
launching the campaign.

Once the goals and budget have been reviewed, the messages created, and the media selected, marketers often **pretest** advertisements. This involves researching a test audience's responses to ads before launching the campaign. If the target audience for the pretest doesn't respond well, marketers can modify the ads and pretest them again before running them in the media.

Marketers can choose from among several types of pretests. In a *portfolio test*, participants read a portfolio that contains the ad along with other ads and written material. The researcher asks them questions about the ad such as: Was it memorable? and Was it informative? In a *jury test*, a panel of consumers views an ad and then rates it according to how attractive and informative it was, as well as how successfully it caught their attention. *Theater tests* are a little more involved. Consumers watch television shows or movies in which the new ads are also shown, then indicate their reactions to the advertisements with small recording devices or fill out questionnaires after the preview.

Schedule and Run Ads   Advertising strategy also includes scheduling ads in media. Marketers have three basic choices for the scheduling pattern of their ads: a continuous media pattern, flighting, or pulsing. In a *continuous media pattern*, ads are scheduled continuously throughout the period of the campaign.[35] In a *flighting pattern*, ads are scheduled on and off for different time intervals.[36] In a *pulsing pattern*, ads are scheduled throughout the period, but spending is heavier for some time intervals.[37] Decisions as to which pattern to use depend on the nature of demand for products. A continuous media pattern is commonly used for products for which demand does not vary much throughout the year. A flighting pattern is common for

T A B L E 18.2
Relative Merits of Major
Advertising Media

Medium	Advantages	Disadvantages
Television	• Reaches a broad audience • Provides both audio and visual information • Can generate attention • Low cost per exposure	• High network charges and production costs • Limited ability to target customers • Short exposure time in most cases • Limited availability • Can be zapped by consumers with remotes
Radio	• Less costly than television advertising • Messages can be fairly well targeted for consumer markets • Widely used in many parts of the world	• Messages are short • Inability to convey visual information • Lower attention than television • No standard rate structures • Audience engages in other activities while listening
Print	• Can provide broad or targeted exposure • Cost can be low • Reader can study an ad and review detailed information • Broad acceptance • High believability • Magazine reproduction quality is high • Some pass-along audience	• Some print media require submission well in advance of publication • Some print media do not effectively reproduce color • No guarantee of ad's position • Ads in widely read magazines and newspapers may be costly • Frequency limited by publication schedule
Direct mail	• Messages can be narrowly targeted • Messages can be relatively long and detailed • No competing ads within medium • Performance can be measured relatively easily • Difficult for competitors to monitor results	• Relatively high cost • Poor image of medium among many customers • Usually lacks nonadvertising material to attract readers • Delivery time and date cannot be guaranteed
Outdoor	• Inexpensive (in the case of posters) • High repeat exposure • Low competition • Can be placed near point of sale	• Targets an audience only by geographic location • Message viewed very briefly • Expensive (in the case of billboards) • Negative image among environmentalists
Internet	• Messages can be customized • No additional cost for reaching global markets • Message can include words, pictures, sound, and video	• Not all users speak the language used in the ad • Quality of images varies • Audience limited to Internet users interested in the company or product

products with seasonal demand. A pulsing strategy is used to stabilize demand, support sales promotion, and introduce new products.

Evaluate Advertising Effectiveness

posttest
Testing that evaluates the success or failure of an ad after it has run.

Marketers evaluate advertising effectiveness with several types of **posttests.**[38] With *aided recall* or a *recall test,* marketers show consumers an ad, then ask where they have seen it in the past: Was it something they read? Something they heard? Something they saw? A popular service for aided recall is the *Starch Readership Report.* Interviewers for Starch ask readers of selected magazines whether they remember certain ads in them. Interviewers may ask about specific parts of large ads, using a copy of the magazine as an aid when doing so. The results of the Starch Readership Report are presented as scores reflecting the percentage of respondents who read the ad as a whole and each part of it. An example of a Starch report is shown in Figure 18.3.

With *unaided recall,* marketers ask participants what ads they saw recently. In a quarterly survey, Video Storyboard Tests asks consumers, "What is the most

FIGURE 18.3
Starch Readership Report

Noted %
w 51
Associated %
49
Read most %
27 –
Read %
w 48
Seen %
w 51
Read some %
w 35
Signature %
w 49

outstanding TV commercial you've seen in the last four weeks?" The answers enable marketers to determine whether participants remember ads without being prompted. Unaided recall can make it harder for marketers to gather reactions to a particular ad, however, because many participants may not recall it. Also, with both types of recall tests, marketers are not measuring the ad's effect, if any, on actual buyer behavior.

Attitude tests are designed to measure how effective advertising is in creating a favorable attitude toward products or organizations. Marketers can conduct surveys asking members of the target audience to rate the organization and its products relative to competitors. This can be done before and after ad campaigns, and the results can be compared to see if advertising led to more favorable attitudes.

To more directly measure the effects of advertising on buying behavior, marketers can use *inquiry tests.* In these, marketers include offers requiring some type of response in the ad. Offers might include coupons, a phone number or address to get free information, samples, or other promotional items. The number of inquiries (or sales, in the case of coupons) that result is used as a measure of the ad's effectiveness in generating a response. On the Internet, the usual measure is the number of "hits," or the number of visits to a particular site. A drawback of this measure is that it fails to sort casual browsers from interested prospects. Edelman Public Relations Worldwide set up a Web site that received 600 hits a day in its first few months on-line but generated only one new client.[39] Given these limitations, savvy Internet users have begun setting up sites to gather more useful information. Windham Hill Records, for instance, gathers data on which ads at its site people look at, how long they look, and what products they download to sample. These data show Windham Hill which artists are most popular and in which cities.[40]

Sales tests involve an effort to find links between adverting and sales. Marketers can conduct experiments using different media in different locations to see which ones generate the most sales. Marketers can run two different versions of an ad in the same media in different cities, or they can compare old and new ad campaigns and compare differences in sales. Of course, such tests cannot control differences in all of the variables that can affect the results. For example, differences in weather patterns or local economies can lead to shifts in sales that are unrelated to advertising campaigns.

Another type of sales test combines advertising with sales promotion to allow marketers to link responses to the ads. For example, Direct Tire Sales, located near Boston, promised in its radio ads that it would donate 3 percent of all radio-generated sales to a local charity. Customers were happy to help the charity by telling Direct that they were responding to the ads.[41]

Adjust Advertising as Needed

After evaluating advertising, marketers may decide to make some changes. If posttests show that consumers aren't affected by ads in a particular media, marketers can change spending on that media, change ads, or schedule them differently. If tests show advertising messages aren't understood, marketers may rework the ads or scrap them and start again with a new message. If tests show that magazine ads are the most effective, marketers may shift the budget to this medium.

Legal and Ethical Issues in Advertising

Because advertising can influence customers, marketers have legal and ethical responsibilities to use it appropriately. In designing ad campaigns, marketers should consider laws regulating advertising, social attitudes about advertising, and industry guidelines.

In the United States, advertising is regulated by the Federal Trade Commission (FTC). The FTC's domain includes guarding against unethical, unfair, or deceptive advertising as well as regulating advertising targeted to children. Thus, when Eggland's Best advertised that its eggs did not contain cholesterol, the FTC required the company to stop making this claim because studies revealed that the eggs were no different. If the FTC finds an advertising claim is misleading, it may require corrective advertising. **Corrective advertising** involves a company running new ads that correct a deceptive or unfair advertising message previously disseminated.[42]

corrective advertising
Advertising involving a company running new ads that correct a deceptive or unfair advertising message previously disseminated.

If FTC regulations seem strict, they are much more relaxed than those of some other countries. To illustrate, Sweden and Canada have banned all advertising targeted to children. Switzerland does not allow an actor to portray a consumer. Both Switzerland and New Zealand place limits on TV political ads.

Besides issues of accuracy, laws govern organizations' use of intellectual property such as trademarks and copyrighted works of art. Thus, when planning an ad for any medium, be it a newspaper ad, Web site, or infomercial, advertisers must secure permission before using anyone's name, photograph, song, and so on. Marketers also should be aware of laws that help them protect their own intellectual property—for example, they should register with the government their trademarks, including the domain name (address) of their Web sites.

Although government regulations give marketers guidelines to follow in deciding what advertising practices are legal and ethical, social attitudes also influence what is acceptable. Calvin Klein overstepped this boundary when it ran a series of ads in which an off-camera voice asked provocatively clad teenaged models a series of questions loaded with sexual innuendo. A public outcry resulted, and the FBI announced it would investigate whether the advertising violated laws against child pornography. After considerable publicity, Klein withdrew the ads but maintained that the company had done nothing wrong.[43]

The National Advertising Division (NAD) of the Council of Better Business Bureaus offers guidelines for marketers to follow. Consumers, other marketers, and government agencies are all encouraged to complain to the NAD about possible unethical advertising practices. The NAD cannot force companies to withdraw ads it challenges, but most do so; if not, the NAD informs the appropriate government agency. For many years, the NAD has policed print and television advertising, and now also checks on Internet advertising. Its first action against Internet advertising criticized Infinity Distribution for making unfounded claims about a vitamin supplement. Infinity removed the claims from its Web site.[44]

Sales Promotion

Marketers often think of sales promotion as a supplement to other elements of the communications mix. *Sales promotion* is media and nonmedia marketing pressure applied for a predetermined, limited period of time at the level of consumer, retailer, or wholesaler in order to stimulate trial, increase consumer demand, or improve product availability.[45] One example is a sweepstakes advertised in the Kawasaki *Good Times* publication in which the prizes were a Nissan 4x4 SE-V6 King Cab and a Kawasaki motorcycle or Jet Ski SuperSport Watercraft.

Sales promotions often generate quick sales—in most cases, much faster than advertising. Scanner-generated data have enabled stores to recognize and show producers the practical, often substantial impact of a sales promotion. Furthermore, a unique sales promotion may be hard to copy and can lead to enormous success, imprinting the product's name in customers' minds. Entrepreneurs can make valuable use of sales promotions on a tight budget, as did Ken Meyers, creator of Smartfood popcorn. Meyers hired skiers to dress in giant popcorn bags and ski the slopes of several New England resorts while he handed out free bags of Smartfood popcorn at the base.

Sales promotions also have their drawbacks. They are short-lived and may be more effective at generating more immediate sales from already loyal customers rather than generating sales from new customers. Because many sales promotions involve short-term price breaks, they may erode brand loyalty and brand equity by encouraging

This ad for subscriptions to Men's Fitness *magazine details a sales promotion. The basic offering is a "special gift rate." Purchasers also receive a "designer gift card" to announce the gift. In both the headline and the small print, the ad points out that the reduced rate will be offered for only a limited time.*

FIGURE 18.4
Expenditures on Media Advertising, Trade Promotions, and Consumer Sales Promotions

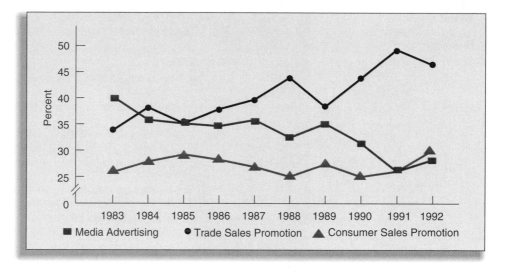

Source: William F. Arens, *Contemporary Advertising*, 6th ed. (Burr Ridge, Ill.: Irwin, 1996), p. 93.

customers to make selections based on price, cheapening the image of brands as a result. This view was supported when the increased use of price-related promotions decreased consumers' brand loyalty.[46]

Sales promotions may be consumer oriented (aimed at end users) or trade oriented (aimed at intermediaries). As Figure 18.4 indicates, marketers historically have spent more on trade promotions than on consumer sales promotions. In either category, marketers may choose from a variety of techniques, each of which may have a different impact on the value equation.

Consumer Promotions

consumer promotion
Sales promotion directed toward consumers of a good or service.

There are a variety of types of sales promotions that can be used to influence consumer behavior. Moreover, **consumer promotions** can be used to accomplish a variety of communication objectives, as shown in Table 18.3, although increasing sales is the primary one. Many of these can also be used to attract organizational buyers.

Coupons   Coupons are one of the most common types of consumer promotions.[47] In a recent year, U.S. consumers redeemed 6.2 billion coupons, with an average face value of 63 cents.[48] Marketers commonly use coupons in the United States and in many other countries, including Canada and the United Kingdom. In contrast, coupons are rarely worth using in Germany, where the law limits coupon discounts to 1 percent of the product's value.[49] Because coupons offer a price break, they are particularly effective for generating sales from price-conscious consumers.

For consumers, coupons require the work of clipping and remembering to use them. Perhaps because of these activity costs, coupon redemption rates have been on the decline.[50] From the marketer's standpoint, the major disadvantage of coupons is that they focus attention on price, not the benefits the product offers. For these reasons, marketing giant Procter & Gamble planned to phase out its use of coupons by the late 1990s.[51]

Many coupons are printed on freestanding inserts, the glossy sheets that fall out of the Sunday newspaper. Others are distributed in packaging, in magazines and newspapers, and in stores. When the objective of coupons is to get consumers to switch brands, in-store distribution can be effective. Some checkout systems are programmed to print coupons whenever the scanner reads that a competing brand is being purchased. Coupons can also be sent in the mail. "Direct mail to your local area is probably the best way to reach local customers," claims Bob Bennett, vice

T A B L E 18.3
Communications Objectives
of Major Types of
Consumer Promotions

Type	Communication Objectives
Coupons	Stimulate sales by short-term price reductions; obtain trial for new products
Deals	Stimulate sales of products, visits to stores; increase quantities purchased
Premiums	Attract new customers to existing products; build goodwill; offer greater value
Contests and sweepstakes	Attract attention; create goodwill; increase sales; generate publicity
Free samples	Encourage usage by consumers so they can experience product benefits
Free trials	Stimulate sales by lowering risk of product being unacceptable after purchase; provide experience of product's performance
Point-of-purchase displays	Make products more prominent in stores; increase chances of impulse purchases; introduce new products
Rebates	Encourage purchases, particularly for big ticket items; get customer information for databases
Continuity plan	Reward customer loyalty; support relationship marketing efforts; increase sales volume
Trade shows	Generate attention and awareness of an industry's products, identify prospects, make sales
Specialty promotions	Generate awareness of company, products and locations; get repeated exposures to messages; create goodwill

president of marketing at Promotion Fulfillment Corp. in Camanche, Iowa.[52] However, this method is expensive. Marketers with tight budgets can leave coupons on the windshields of parked cars, slip them onto doorknobs, or hand them to customers who walk into stores.

In general, coupons that offer large savings generate more sales but are more costly for marketers. "Nothing works as well as the word *free,*" notes Bob Bennett. "Offers of 'buy one, get one free' or 'buy one, get french fries free' get the best response."[53] According to NCH Promotional Services of Lincolnshire, Illinois, the largest coupon processor and promotion information manager in the world, coupons that grant cents off on the product should offer at least a 40 percent savings if the goal is to get consumers to try something new.[54]

Marketers that use coupons should track redemption rates so that the impact of various coupon amounts and methods of distributing them can be evaluated. Many retailers scan coupon bar codes and store the information in their databases. Quaker Direct, the direct marketing arm of The Quaker Oats Company, took a sophisticated approach to coupon tracking. Quaker included a number on each coupon that identified the household to which it was sent. Within a few months, Quaker could track coupon usage by individual households. This information enabled the company to better tailor its future mailings.[55] Many manufacturers arrange for coupon service bureaus to handle the tasks of processing coupons and collecting redemption data.

An important issue in using coupons is whether the coupon generates sales from new customers or merely enables existing customers to buy at a lower price. According to one study, 99 percent of households surveyed reported using a coupon in the preceding year. Of these, 90 percent used them for products they usually buy, and only 32 percent used them to try new brands.[56] Thus, while coupons can increase sales, they may not be the best method for generating trial of existing products by new buyers.

Deals   Deals are special inducements to get consumers to perform shopping and purchasing behaviors. Special offers, such as "buy three tires and get the fourth one free," or "no interest charges for one year" are designed to increase demand for stores and possibly their financing services. Special sales, such as "25 percent off all merchandise marked with a red tag," or "20 percent off all Rubbermaid products," are used to encourage shopping at particular stores and buying particular merchandise.

Price packs or *price offs* are deals marked on packages such as "25 cents off" or "20 percent off" which can encourage trial or a brand switch. Deals include limited-time, specially-packaged "two for one" offers or *bonus packs* with extra amounts in them such as "two ounces of coffee free" which make the purchase more attractive. Deals also include special packaging containers, such as cookies or crackers in old-fashioned collector tins, offered for a limited time. Given the variety of deals available, it is clear that they are flexible. In addition, deals can be very effective and many of them, particularly deals offered by retailers, are relatively easy to implement.

Premiums   Another sales promotion technique is to offer other merchandise for free or at a low price with the purchase of the product. These free or low-priced items are called *premiums*. For example, Motor Guide offered a free jacket with the purchase of one of its trolling motors, and Direct Tire Sales offered a premium of $80 in ski lift tickets with the purchase of a set of new tires.[57]

Contests and Sweepstakes   Although both give consumers a chance to win prizes, contests and sweepstakes are different. To be eligible to win a prize in a *contest,* consumers must complete a task, such as answering trivia questions or drawing a picture. In Calgary, Alberta, Melitta, a producer of coffee makers, sponsored a contest in which a radio station broadcast actors speaking lines from famous movies. Callers who identified the name of the actor and movie were eligible to win Melitta products. To enter a *sweepstakes,* on the other hand, consumers need only complete an entry form; the sweepstakes is purely a game of chance that attracts attention to a company and its products. The Publishers Clearing House runs a well-known sweepstakes annually that promotes the sale of magazines.

Contests and sweepstakes in the United States are regulated by the Federal Trade Commission. FTC regulations are designed to ensure that contests and sweepstakes are fair, that the odds for and against winning are presented clearly, and that prizes are actually awarded to winners.

Samples   Most consumers have received free samples of products in the mail, such as shampoo, toothpaste, laundry detergent, cereal, and even diapers. In addition, magazines often contain tiny packets of makeup or perfume attached to advertisements. These samples are included so consumers can try products, like them, remember them, and buy them. To reach college students, many marketers provide samples at party-style marketing events with names like College Fest and Campus Fest, where students can enjoy live music along with sales presentations.[58]

Sampling can be expensive. Therefore, marketers usually give away samples of products that are new, cost little to produce, and are purchased frequently. For example, when Barry Potekin started Gold Coast Dogs, a hot dog chain featuring top-of-the-line ingredients, he hopped into a cab each day with about 50 hot dogs that were delivered free to a company he selected. Along the way, he told cab drivers about Gold Coast Dogs, then tipped them $5 and invited them to come in and try the food. His original store has since grown to three plus 18 franchise outlets.[59] Marketers can increase the effectiveness of samples by offering them near a display of the product in stores and by giving out coupons. Coupling samples with personal selling can also increase effectiveness. For instance, deli employees can offer samples and discuss them with customers rather than merely leave them out on a tray.[60]

Free Trials   For expensive products, sampling is impractical. Marketers of these products may instead reduce the risk of buying a product by offering a free trial. Car dealers do this by allowing potential buyers to take cars for a test drive. Software makers may offer diskettes that enable customers to try them out before purchase or an on-line service may offer a short time at no charge.

Point-of-Purchase Displays   To draw shoppers' attention to products in stores, marketers use *point-of-purchase (POP) displays*. These are special in-store signs, bins, or other devices that stock and advertise products at the same time. Sometimes the displays are accompanied by an in-store demonstration or coupons, or free samples for products such as crackers, appetizer dip, soft drinks, or frozen pizza.

Point-of-purchase displays help products stand out from competitive items. According to a study by Information Resources Inc., POP displays boosted sales of laundry detergent by 207 percent, frozen dinners by 245 percent, and soft drinks by 138 percent.[61] POP displays introducing Doodle O's cheese snacks were so effective they sometimes had to be refilled daily rather than weekly, as expected.

Rebates   *Rebates* are a return of money with proof of purchase of products. Manufacturers of everything from autos to hair dryers to light bulbs use rebates to increase sales. Buyers are apt to take advantage of large rebates on big-ticket items, such as automobiles. However, they don't always bother to clip a proof-of-purchase seal, fill out a mailing label, and spend money on postage to mail in for a small rebate on inexpensive, frequently purchased products such as shaving lotion or film. While this saves manufacturers rebate money, it doesn't get customers' names and addresses for marketing databases.

Continuity Plans   To build loyalty and repeat business, marketers may use some form of *continuity plans,* which reward customers for accumulated purchases. Continuity plans are also called patronage awards and continuity programs. Airlines' frequent-flyer programs reward customers based on the number of miles they fly. Customers in these programs can get free air fares, upgrades to first-class travel, or free merchandise. Other users of patronage plans include hotels, supermarkets, and car rental agencies.

Organizational Buyer Promotions   When the target market is organizational buyers, other types of sales promotions are commonly used. However, some of the tools used for consumer promotions, such as patronage awards and free trials are also used with organizational buyers.

Trade Shows   Marketers in many fields participate in *trade shows,* events that are designed to bring marketers and customers together in one location over a short period of time—usually three or four days. Thousands of such events take place each year in the United States alone. At trade shows, marketers exhibit their goods and services to potential customers. Trade shows are useful for reaching organizational buyers, especially for marketers of big-ticket items. In addition, marketers working at a trade show have a chance to see what their competitors are doing. Although generally thought of as a sales promotion tool for organizational buyers, some shows also target consumers.

According to the Trade Show Bureau (TSB), people attend these events to update their knowledge in the industry and to shop for the goods and services they need.[62] Although exhibiting in trade shows can be expensive and marketers should choose carefully in which shows to exhibit their products, they are a major promotional method for some industries.

Specialty Promotions   *Specialty promotions* (also called specialty advertising) involve printing promotional messages on a wide variety of give-away items. These include such things as coffee cups, calendars, pencils, golf balls, hats, mouse pads, key chains, T-shirts, watches, knives, and refrigerator magnets. Marketers may have salespeople leave the specialties with organizational prospects they call on, or they may give the items to consumers in stores or by mail. Whenever customers use the specialties, they may be reminded of the organization and its products. The most effective specialties are those that are used often and support the desired image of

As described in this ad, a recent year's trade shows included one sponsored by the American Pet Products Manufacturers Association, Inc. The show featured exhibits by 450 U.S. manufacturers of pet products such as pet food and accessories. Retailers who attended the show could update their knowledge of industry trends and products.

companies and their products. For example, while Oscar Mayer gives away inexpensive hot-dog whistles to children, such a specialty would not be appropriate for Mercedes automobiles.

Trade Promotions

trade promotion
Sales promotion directed to intermediaries to increase channel demand or support for manufacturers' products.

Trade promotions are sales promotions directed to intermediaries to increase channel demand or support for manufacturers' products. Many companies spend more on trade promotions than they do on consumer promotions or advertising. Many types of consumer promotions can also be used at the trade level. For example, Fuji Photo ran a contest for retailers in which prizes were awarded for the best display featuring its products and the theme "Image of Excellence."[63] However, trade allowances or trade discounts and cooperative advertising payments are for intermediaries only.

Trade Allowances or Trade Discounts   Trade allowances or discounts are short-term offers made to intermediaries based on various criteria. *Merchandise allowances* are paid to retailers for special promotion of products in-store. *Case allowances* are discounts on each case of a product ordered by wholesalers and retailers during a specified time period. Manufacturers may also sell cases at full price but offer a free case for purchasing 10 or some other number for a limited time. A *finance allowance* is paid to retailers for handling consumer promotions. Many retailers also receive *slotting allowances* for carrying new products on their shelves.

Trade allowances and discounts can be used to build stronger channel relationships and increase marketing effort by channel members. They can also be used to improve the efficiency of manufacturers. For example, case allowances offered during periods of low demand can keep production running smoothly as well as lower inventory and distribution costs.

cooperative advertising payment
Funds paid by manufacturers to get their products featured in local retail ads.

Cooperative Advertising Payments   **Cooperative advertising payments** are funds paid by manufacturers to get their products featured in local, retail ads. Manufacturers sometimes route these payments through their wholesalers, who determine which retailers will get them and how much they will be given. Manufacturers do not always pay these in cash but prefer to pay in free goods or credit memos.

Manufacturers or their ad agencies provide ad copy, pictures, and film clips that retailers put in their stores' ads or commercials. Cooperative advertising can benefit both manufacturers and retailers by leading to sales for both the products and the stores. They can also reinforce both brand and store images. For example, a Nordstrom ad featuring Salvatore Farragamo shoes could enhance the prestige of both companies.

Legal and Ethical Issues in Sales Promotion

As with advertising, sales promotion in the United States is regulated by the Federal Trade Commission. The FTC regulates sweepstakes and contests for fairness and legitimacy. As with other areas of marketing, avoiding legal problems is a minimal standard. The appropriate ethical standards are often difficult to judge for sales promotions. For example, when Pepsi ran a promotion offering a deal on Motorola beepers, some people complained that the use of beepers by teenagers is associated with drug dealing. Pepsi retorted that the program promoted responsible beeper use. Others noted that if grown-ups complained, it could only benefit the product's image with teenagers.[64]

Marketers using premiums should keep in mind that the items they offer are sometimes products sold by others for profit. Using videocassettes as a premium, for example, cuts into normal video sales and rentals. McDonald's once offered cassettes of *Dances with Wolves* for $7.99 to customers who bought meals at its restaurant, which cut normal sales of the cassettes.[65]

Sampling can pose ethical problems if access to products should be limited. Sampling of cigarettes poses obvious problems because minors can get them. Similar issues arise with other products that many feel should have limited access, such as over-the-counter medicines or previews of R-rated movies.

In the case of rebates, an ethical issue arises when marketers promote them and get consumers to buy, but make it so inconvenient or complicated to redeem them that many consumers don't bother. In some cases, consumers may have been misled to believe that the rebate was simple to obtain.

Publicity

Whether or not they think of it as part of the communications effort, all organizations are concerned about their public relations and the kind of publicity the companies generate. *Publicity* is non-paid-for communication of information about the organization or product, generally in some media form. Publicity should be planned, implemented, and controlled as part of integrated marketing communications efforts.

Because it is not paid for by marketers and is reported by the media as news, publicity often is believed and trusted by the general public. Good publicity can greatly enhance the image and sales of a company while negative publicity can cause real damage.

Types of Publicity

Publicity comes in many forms. The most common are news stories and public service announcements. News stories initiated by the media allow marketers little direct control over the communication. However, information for such stories often comes from interviews with company officials, so company spokespeople must be able to think on their feet and answer questions honestly. Companies can also send out stories about their progress or products to various media.

Marketers can generate news stories to attract favorable media coverage. One approach is to circulate press releases or video clips to the media. Other approaches include hosting news conferences and staging attention-getting events.

Press Releases   A *press release,* also called a news release, is an article written by company members and distributed to the media—newspapers, magazines, television, and radio stations. A press release is a company-produced news story that

The northern Illinois chapter of the Make-A-Wish Foundation generated favorable publicity when Michael Jordan appeared at one of its events. The participation of the well-loved basketball star made the event especially newsworthy. The Make-A-Wish Foundation uses donors' contributions to meet the special wishes of children suffering from life-threatening illnesses. At the event shown, Jordan chatted with 10 children who attended a lunch at his restaurant. Organizations such as the Make-A-Wish Foundation hope that when people learn about what they do, more will want to contribute time and money.

provides the media with information about the organization or its products and the names and phone numbers of company personnel who can be contacted for further details. For a television station, marketers may also provide video clips to include in news programming.

A press release gives marketers some control over news coverage by allowing them to decide when to make a public announcement and what information to include. This does not, however, guarantee that the media will publish or broadcast the story, nor does it guarantee that it will be presented in its original form.

Some organizations hire outside publicists, but even in these cases the publicity should be coordinated with the rest of the communication mix. In preparing a press release, marketers can get better results by following these tips:[66]

- Keep it short. A single page is best.
- Use clear, concise language, and avoid jargon.
- Polish up the lead (first sentence or paragraph) so that it grabs the reader's attention.
- Cite major facts or statistics.
- Include the name and phone number of the person on the publicity team who can be contacted to verify the story.

Because reporters receive many more press releases than they can use, marketers should try to make their press releases stand out. To get publicity for his Great Scott! fudge, Jim Scott included a sample with the press releases. The fudge has been featured in *Bon Appétit, Food & Wine, Chocolatier, The Los Angeles Times,* and *The New York Times.*[67]

News Conferences   Marketers can also communicate with the media through *news or press conferences.* In these, marketers invite reporters to the conference location and usually provide them with advance information. A spokesperson for the organization may read a prepared statement, answer questions from the media, or both. News conferences give the company some control over coverage, but there is no guarantee that reporters will attend or will ask appropriate questions.

Activities and Events   The media are deluged with stories about new products, company practices, and newly hired executives. To break through the clutter,

Summary

In general, advertising informs, persuades, and reminds customers about products, and builds images and trust in organizations. Product advertising focuses on creating demand for goods and services, places, persons, or events. Institutional advertising promotes the name, image, personnel, or reputation of a company, organization, or industry. To develop primary demand, marketers may use pioneering advertising; to develop selective demand, marketers may use competitive or comparative advertising. Advocacy advertising is used to support a viewpoint.

A company may produce its own advertising or work with an outside advertising agency. Either way, marketers should first review the goals and budget for advertising. Next, messages are created that often have a particular appeal. Then, media are selected from television, radio, print, direct mail, outdoor, the Internet, or other options. Before the ad campaign is launched, marketers conduct pretests to make sure customers respond well to it. If so, ads are scheduled in the media. Finally, after ads have been run, posttests are conducted to measure effectiveness and determine whether changes are needed to improve the ads.

Advertising should be done ethically, with messages that are truthful and not misleading. Organizations that run misleading ads may be required by the Federal Trade Commission to run corrective advertising.

Sales promotion is media and nonmedia marketing pressure applied for a predetermined, limited period of time at the level of consumers, retailers, or wholesalers in order to stimulate trial, increase consumer demand, or improve product availability. Sales promotion may be directed to consumers, and organizational buyers, or to trade intermediaries. Consumer promotions include coupons, deals premiums, contests and sweepstakes, free samples, free trials, point-of-purchase displays, rebates, and continuity plans. Organizational buyer promotions include trade shows, specialty advertising, and trade promotions. Trade promotions include trade allowances or trade discounts and cooperative advertising payments. Like advertising, sales promotion is regulated by the FTC.

Publicity is non-paid-for communication of information about the company or its products, generally in some media form. The most common forms of publicity are news stories and public service announcements. Marketers can generate publicity by distributing press releases, hosting news conferences, and staging special events. However, the media decide whether and how to cover a story. Because publicity is not paid for by marketers, many consumers believe in and trust it as valid information. Negative publicity can be damaging to an organization's image, but often it can be managed effectively.

Key Terms and Concepts

product advertising (p. 470)
institutional advertising (p. 470)
pioneering advertising (p. 470)
competitive advertising (p. 471)
comparative advertising (p. 471)
advocacy advertising (p. 472)
advertising agency (p. 472)

reach (p. 478)
rating (p. 478)
frequency (p. 478)
cost per thousand (p. 478)
gross rating points (GRPs) (p. 478)
infomercial (p. 478)
pretest (p. 482)

posttest (p. 483)
corrective advertising (p. 485)
consumer promotions (p. 487)
trade promotion (p. 491)
cooperative advertising payment
    (p. 491)

Review and Discussion Questions

1. What are the main functions of business?
2. What type of advertising does each of the following represent?
   a. an advertisement for vacations in Alaska
   b. an advertisement in favor of bans on cigarette smoking
   c. an advertisement for a new luxury car
   d. an advertisement that evaluates two different brands of ketchup
   e. an advertisement for a health maintenance organization (HMO)
3. Do you think regulations governing comparative advertising should be stricter in the United States or more relaxed than they already are? Why?
4. In what ways can an advertising agency create value for advertisers?
5. What type of appeal do you think would work best for a new line of frozen yogurt? Why?

6. Create a slogan for a new line of frozen yogurt that captures the appeal you selected in question 5.
7. Which media would you choose for your frozen yogurt campaign? Why?
8. What are some advantages and disadvantages of the following advertising media?
   a. television
   b. newspapers
   c. outdoor
9. When you receive direct mailings (for credit card applications, department store sales, political candidates, and the like), do you read them or throw them away? Do you sort through these mailings and only read the ones that interest you? What types of appeals and messages attract your attention?
10. How do posttests help ad campaigns?
11. Imagine you are a marketer for a chain of sporting

goods stores. Your communications objective is to increase sales by bringing in new customers.

   a. What types of sales promotions would you use? Why?

   b. In what ways could you generate good publicity about the sporting goods store to bring in new customers?

12. An accounting firm targets small businesses in a local community. How might it use advertising, sales promotion, and publicity to generate business?

Chapter Project   Write a Press Release

Writing a press release can be a marketing task. A press release may be intended to generate positive publicity about a new product or an event involving a company, or to try to mitigate negative publicity about a company or its products.

For your project, first look through the business pages of a major newspaper, such as the *New York Times,* the *Boston Globe,* the *Chicago Tribune,* or the *Los Angeles Times.* Choose a story about a company or product that interests you. For instance, a small computer company might be launching some new software; a manufacturer might be facing allegations of employee discrimination; a hotel chain might have recently opened a shelter for battered women and children. All of these organizations could benefit from a well-written press release.

After you have chosen your story, write a press release designed to generate good publicity about the organization. Follow the tips for writing good press releases listed in the chapter. Remember to be accurate about the facts.

Chapter Case   Three-C Body Shop

Bob Juniper, second-generation owner of Ohio-based Three-C Body Shop, fixes cars. In recent years, through a relentless image and advocacy ad campaign, he has accomplished a lot more. During the early 1990s, auto insurance companies began to establish "direct repair programs," or DRPs. In these programs, they set up relationships with auto repair shops in which the insurers would "recommend" them to customers who needed car repairs. The shops, in turn, would charge the insurance companies less. The arrangement sounds ethical enough. In fact, auto owners received value when they did business with participating shops, since they did not have to get repairs preauthorized by the insurance company.

But Bob Juniper recognized quickly that both the auto shops and consumers got the short end of the deal. "You can't charge 20 percent less without taking shortcuts. The consumer would be losing." In fact, insurance companies requested that shops forgo cosmetic repairs and the use of expensive manufacturers' parts. Sheila Loftus, editor of the trade magazine, *Hammer and Dolly,* concurred with Juniper's early observation. "I think he was early to see that DRPs would be the death of the collision-repair industry as we know it," she notes. "He also saw a marketing opportunity."

Indeed, Juniper saw a huge opportunity: He could be an advocate for consumers, beat the competition, and grow his business. So he launched an advertising campaign unprecedented in the industry. He began running radio ads intended simply to get people to recognize the Three-C name. He appeared on a public service radio ad about drunken driving. Then he wrote ads against DRPs, funneling them to local radio-station ad salesman Tom Hughes, who re-wrote them for the air. One ad began, "This is Bob Juniper. There's a growing problem in the collision-repair industry that seriously affects every vehicle owner in Ohio." It got people's attention—not only consumers, but competitors and insurance companies as well. Insurance agents called and made threats to the business. Competitors called the radio station demanding "equal time"; they didn't receive it, however, because Juniper's ad was paid for by him.

Juniper's ad ran 36 times on nine radio stations for a week, then went off the air. A new ad returned, with the same airing schedule. During the campaign, "we hit 76 percent of the Columbus [Ohio] radio audience three times or more," says Juniper.

With the success of the campaign, business was so good that Three-Cs had to add a second shift, and by year-end, sales had doubled, to $2.7 million. Juniper grew more confident and his ads grew more aggressive. He and Hughes developed a hot-pink, neon logo and bought ad space on one of the new city buses and a dozen billboards. They flew hot-air balloons and airplane banners above city events and Ohio State football games, and printed a free brochure for customers called "Ten Things to Know Before Having Your Car Repaired." Then they ran another ad, this one featuring a picture of Juniper in a leather jacket with neon eyes and the slogan, "Auto insurers make me see pink."

Juniper sent competitors direct-mail pieces that read, "If you want to be number one in collision repair . . . you'll have to go through me." Juniper admitted that he "burned whatever bridges I still had with that."

The budget for all this advertising was high: Three-C's averaged around $500,000 per year compared to the average body shop which spent about $4,500. Juniper felt that the increased business and gratification of getting his message across to consumers justified the expense.

The advertising effort was so successful that Juniper and Hughes started a separate company, Jupiter Marketing & Advertising. Vaughn Owens, an executive with the new company said, "We're probably the only collision-shop-focused marketing agency in the world." More than 30 other shops in 15 states came to the agency for help with marketing in the first year. Jupiter Marketing creates value for shop owners like Tom Rompel of Factory Paint & Body because the agency knows and understands the auto-repair business. "The marketing approach was brilliant, I thought," says Rompel. "Just take the issue to the consumers and let them make the choice." Then take the results to the bank.

Questions

1. What legal and ethical issues does Bob Juniper face with his ad campaign? Do you think he took the right approach? Why or why not?

2. Juniper's campaign generated a tremendous amount of publicity, most of it good. How might the publicity have backfired and become negative?

3. In what ways can Three-C's offer greater value to consumers than shops that participate in DRPs?

Source: Leslie Brokaw, "Rebel with a Cause," *Inc.,* June 1996, pp. 80–90. Adapted with permission, *Inc.* magazine, June 1996. Copyright 1996 by Goldhirsh Group, Inc., 38 Commercial Wharf, Boston, MA 02110.

Explore more by searching "Bob Juniper" on the Web.

Chapter Nineteen

Personal Selling and Sales Management

CHAPTER OUTLINE

The Nature of Personal Selling
  The Role of Personal Selling
  Activities of Salespeople
  Relationship Selling
Steps in the Selling Process
  Prospect for Customers
  Prepare for Sales Calls
  Approach Qualified Prospects
  Make Sales Presentations
  Handle Objections
  Close Sales
  Build Long-Term Relationships
Sales Management
  Organizing Sales Forces
  Recruiting Salespeople
  Training and Supervising Salespeople
  Motivating and Compensating Salespeople
  Evaluating and Controlling Salespeople
Ethical Issues in Personal Selling
  Manipulation of Prospects
  Bribery
  Accuracy of Reports
Summary

LEARNING OBJECTIVES

After completing this chapter, you should be able to:

1. Discuss the role of personal selling in the organization.
2. Define the various tasks involved in personal selling.
3. Explain the importance of relationship selling to organizations that practice value-driven marketing.
4. Identify the steps in the selling process.
5. Describe the activities involved in managing a sales force.
6. Discuss ethical issues in personal selling.

Avon Products, Inc. Track-and-field star Jackie Joyner-Kersee sprints along the beach. She's fit, she's famous, she's a champion. As you watch this TV commercial, you're thinking that it's probably for running shoes or some new sports drink. But then the caption across the screen reads: "Just another Avon Lady." The ad doesn't say whether Joyner-Kersee is an Avon representative; it doesn't really have to. The point is made: Avon cosmetics and skin-care products are for the strong, the beautiful, the accomplished.

The Avon Lady is still calling. For more than a century, sales representatives have offered personal service to customers and potential customers, delivering quality products at affordable prices. "It's these women who have been the bread and butter of our company," says Brian Connolly, Avon's vice president of U.S. sales. The company expanded the definition of an "Avon Lady" to include any of the savvy customers who sell or—in the case of Diane Von Furstenberg and Josie Waton—even design Avon products. As a global company, Avon prides itself on addressing the needs of women. And, of course, the majority of Avon's sales representatives are women (2 million representatives worldwide).

Although things have changed at Avon—many representatives now make calls at customers' workplaces rather than their homes—some things remain the same. First, the products are priced more affordably than those of competitors such as Mary Kay Cosmetics. Thus, an Avon representative can get started in the business for less: about $20 for a starter kit, as opposed to several hundred dollars to become a Mary Kay rep. Second, the products are high quality. The representatives use them and like them, so it is easy to persuade customers to try them. "A friend of mine was using the products and her skin just looked beautiful," says sales rep Fran Raffetto. Raffetto tried the products, loved them, and became a rep herself. Third, the sales job offers autonomy and flexibility for women who want careers outside of traditional offices.

Avon also has ventured overseas. The company has representatives in Japan, China, Eastern Europe, Brazil, Mexico, and Argentina. Women in

developing countries such as China and Brazil are experiencing new-found independence as sales representatives. "The whole concept is economic empowerment," explains Avon's Connolly. "Women are out there earning money and able to be more independent. That's exactly what's happening in new markets." As you read this chapter, think about the role of personal selling in marketing goods and services. How does personal selling create value in dynamic domestic and global markets?

Source: Pamela Reynolds, "Avon Still Calling," *The Boston Globe,* August 21, 1996, pp. C1, C5. Reprinted courtesy of *The Boston Globe,* and interview with Alex Mendes, Avon Products, February 14, 1997.

Explore more at www.avon.com

Chapter Overview

The personal selling element of the communications mix involves direct interaction between salespeople and customers, face to face or by telephone. This chapter describes the nature of personal selling—its role in marketing, the different tasks involved, and the increasing importance of it in developing long-term relationships with customers. The chapter also describes the steps involved in personal selling. The chapter then discusses management of domestic or global personal selling efforts and concludes with an examination of some ethical issues.

The Nature of Personal Selling

Gone is the Avon sales force that called exclusively on U.S. homemakers to sell cosmetics. Gone is the Electrolux salesperson who relied on the tried-and-true sales tactic of dumping dirt on carpets and suctioning it up with a high-powered Electrolux vacuum cleaner. Yet both companies are still in business and both rely heavily on their sales forces. Today, Avon representatives sell to career women in the workplace, as well as in their homes both in the United States and abroad. Electrolux salespeople sell a variety of appliances in the United States and Europe as well, so its sales force must be able to meet the needs of diverse groups of customers and create value for them.[1]

Salespeople create value for both their employers and their customers. Salespeople create value for their employers by collecting information on customer needs, wants, and problems so that the company can create better products. They also find new customers, service accounts, handle transactions, and increase sales and profits. Salespeople create value for customers by providing useful information to help them make good purchase decisions. They also can make shopping and purchasing more enjoyable and lower transactions costs by reducing the time and effort involved. By handling customer problems or complaints effectively, they can build long-term relationships that benefit both their customers and their employers. Figure 19.1 shows how business-to-business salespeople spend their workweek serving both.

Personal selling is a challenging and exciting career that can provide excellent training for people who want to pursue other management positions. About 60 percent of marketing graduates in the United States begin their marketing careers in sales.[2] And nearly 30 percent of the top executives in the 1,000 largest U.S. corporations have spent at least part of their careers in sales and marketing.[3]

FIGURE 19.1
How Business-to-Business Salespeople Spend Their Time

The average salesperson spends over five hours a day on some form of selling, including sales calls.

Breakdown of an Average 46.9 Hour Workweek

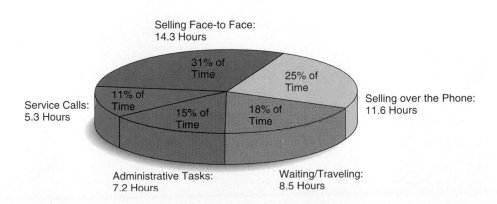

Selling Face-to Face: 14.3 Hours — 31% of Time

Selling over the Phone: 11.6 Hours — 25% of Time

Service Calls: 5.3 Hours — 11% of Time

Administrative Tasks: 7.2 Hours — 15% of Time

Waiting/Traveling: 8.5 Hours — 18% of Time

Source: "Dartnell's 29th Sales Force Compensation Survey," 1996–1997. Courtesy of the Dartnell Corporation, Chicago 1996.

The Role of Personal Selling

Personal selling can be an organization's largest operating expense and is often the largest marketing expense. Because the average cost of a business-to-business, face-to-face sales call is over $300[4], salespeople must get results. Many organizations have recognized the value of personal selling. Most businesses have sales forces and even professional services have learned selling skills. For instance, sales trainers and salespeople are helping lawyers ask clients about their businesses, to see whether the firm can address any unmet needs. Training by The Law Firm Development Group includes how to ask for client feedback, discuss fees as a way to help clients feel they are getting their money's worth, and identify what is involved in providing good service.[5]

In global markets, salespeople must understand customers' languages and cultural nuances. For example, French customers tend to be put off by boasts that a product is the biggest or greatest and by salespeople who address them by their first name. They tend to respond well to salespeople who focus on the big picture first, then move on to the details. Business lunches are typically reserved for celebrating the closing of a sale after the salesperson has worked with the customer for a long time.[6]

Salespeople also get information about competitors from talking with customers. Salespeople may be the first in a firm to hear about competitive innovations or communications strategies. Thus, salespeople not only generate sales, they also play a role in marketing research. This information commonly is included in sales call reports.

Salespeople often formulate their own selling strategies. This requires knowledge of their strengths and weaknesses and the approach that customers are most likely to value. For example, does a customer want a no-nonsense exchange of information or a casual discussion? Salespeople decide when and how to work with customers after a sale to help them use products effectively or quell doubts about purchases.

In organizations that empower their employees, salespeople may have some authority to adjust prices or payment schedules or to offer customers other benefits. Such decisions require salespeople to forecast customer responsiveness to various deals and their impact on relationships and profits.

Activities of Salespeople

Table 19.1 lists a number of activities and responsibilities involved in personal selling. While not all sales jobs involve all of these tasks, most are common in organizational or business-to-business selling. In general, salespeople have three basic tasks: order

I.B. Nuts & Fruit Too has developed a unique form of personal sales: No more impersonal vending machines for employees of the 400 companies on the company's sales routes in Columbia, Missouri. Twice a month salesmen deliver pound bags of healthy snack mixes such as "Nacho Average Mix" directly to workers at their desks. All snacks are mixed at the company's store. They cost less per ounce than regular vending machine products, and according to founder David Hockett (at right in the photo with employee Shane Whittaker), "you don't have to kick our guys to get your change back."

TABLE 19.1
Activities and Responsibilities
in Personal Selling

1. Selling function • Plan selling activities • Search out leads • Call potential accounts • Identify decision makers • Prepare sales presentations • Make sales presentations • Overcome objections • Introduce new products • Call new accounts	**6. Attending conferences/meetings** • Attend sales conferences • Attend regional sales meetings • Work at client conferences • Set up product exhibitions • Attend periodic training sessions
2. Working with orders • Write up orders • Expedite orders • Handle back orders • Handle shipping problems • Find lost orders	**7. Training/recruiting** • Recruit new sales reps • Train new salespeople • Travel with trainees
3. Servicing the product • Learn about the product • Test equipment • Supervise installation • Train customers • Supervise repairs • Perform maintenance	**8. Entertaining** • Entertain clients with golf and so forth • Take clients for dinner • Take clients out for drink • Take clients out for lunch • Throw parties for clients
4. Managing information • Provide technical information • Receive feedback • Provide feedback • Check with superiors	**9. Traveling** • Travel out of town • Spend nights on the road • Travel in town
5. Servicing the account • Stock shelves • Set up displays • Take inventory for client • Handle local advertising	**10. Distribution** • Establish good relations with distributors • Sell to distributors • Handle credit • Collect past due accounts

Source: Adapted from William C. Moncrief III, "Selling Activity and Sales Position Taxonomies for Industrial Salesforces," *Journal of Marketing Research* (August 1986), pp. 266–267, published by the American Marketing Association. Reprinted with the permission of the American Marketing Association.

getting, order taking, and order delivery. In addition, support salespeople also assist in selling tasks.

order getting
The process of developing business by seeking out potential customers, providing them with necessary information about products, and persuading them to buy.

Order Getting   When people think of personal selling, the activities that most often come to mind are those involved in order getting. **Order getting** is developing business by seeking out potential customers, providing them with necessary information about products, and persuading them to buy. Order getters may be positioned inside a store (such as an appliance salesperson for Sears) or outside (such as a sales rep for Snap-On Tools, who visits auto mechanics at their shops).

Good order getters fully understand the products they are selling, how to find out their customers' needs, and how to solve customers' problems better than competitors. Winning over buyers of competitive products requires selling skills. According to one survey, buyers are reluctant to switch suppliers even when there are good reasons to change.[7] Overcoming this challenge requires salespeople to convince buyers that they offer superior value.

"Buyers like to be sold," notes Pam Lontos, a sales trainer based in California. "They will buy, but you've got to help them get beyond their indecision and fears."[8] In organizational selling, effective order getters address customers' general business concerns as well as their specific purchasing concerns and help them make good buying decisions. In consumer selling, order getters address specific benefits such as the safety of a car, the power of a snowblower, or the durability of a carpet fabric. Helping buyers make decisions that meet their needs and wants is part of value-driven marketing.

As use of the Internet grows, electronic orders are supplementing face-to-face interaction. Amazon.com Books' Web site (http://www.amazon.com) is an online bookstore in which customers can browse a database of over a million books by title, author, subject, or keyword. If customers find a book they want to buy, they can put it into their virtual shopping basket and order on-line, choosing the mode of shipment and whether they want gift wrapping. To pay, they submit a credit card number on-line (online payments are protected by encryption), or they can provide the last five digits and the expiration date on-line, then call or fax Amazon.com Books to provide the remainder of the credit card number. If they have questions, they can read instructions provided on the pages or get answers by phoning or e-mailing Customer Service Representatives.

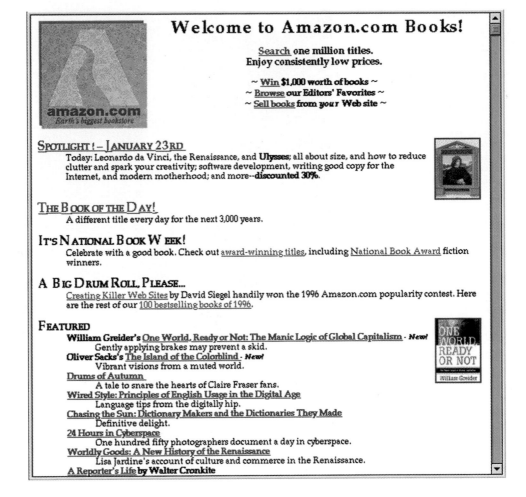

order taking
The routine completion of transactions after customers have already decided to buy.

Order Taking   Order taking is the routine completion of transactions after customers have already decided to buy. Order takers must be able to answer questions, make price or payment adjustments, handle complaints, and inform customers of changes in products or supporting services. Well-trained order takers alert their companies to possible new business. Order takers may also be order getters, as in the case of phone sales representatives for mail-order catalogs such as Lands' End or L. L. Bean. The manner in which these order takers handle phone calls can influence whether a customer decides to buy not only a sweater or pair of boots, but perhaps a wool hat or socks. Mail-order catalog companies often have special deals that are offered to callers after a phone order has been taken.

order delivery
The activities involved in getting products to customers and enabling them to be used.

Order Delivery   When customers place orders, salespeople may be involved in completing the exchange by performing tasks related to **order delivery,** that is, getting products to customers and enabling them to be used. Salespeople perform a number of order delivery tasks. These include activities such as:

- Preparing products for delivery (for example, wrapping candles in tissue paper and placing them in a bag).
- Installing products (for example, setting up a home entertainment system).
- Providing instructions (for example, showing how to load film into a camera).
- Handling products under warranty (for example, giving a replacement for a defective phone).

In addition, salespeople often are called first when questions or problems arise with a new purchase. For example, they are often called when products are not delivered on

As an agronomist for Pioneer Hi-Bred International, Inc., the largest seed company in the world, Florence Sidoine (right) is a technical specialist. She helps Pioneer salespeople by giving customers advice on how to achieve the genetic potential of the company's products, thus making the products more valuable to customers. In the photo she advises farmer François Vanier on his farm near Lindron in France.

time. Thus, salespeople must be prepared to handle a variety of tasks related to order delivery, such as checking on orders and arranging deliveries. Skillful and tactful handling of such tasks can create value for customers and build successful long-term relationships.

Sales Support

support salespeople
Salespeople who help order getters and order takers in a variety of ways, but who do not conduct actual sales transactions.

Support salespeople help order getters and order takers in a variety of ways but do not conduct actual sales transactions with the organization's customers. There are two main types of support salespeople: missionary salespeople and technical specialists.

missionary salespeople
Support salespeople who work for manufacturers and call on channel members and end users.

Missionary salespeople work for manufacturers, calling on channel members and end users and performing promotional activities. These salespeople perform tasks that help stimulate greater demand for their products. Examples include representatives of brewers, who call on bar owners and encourage them to order a particular brand of beer from the local distributor, and medical "detailers," who call on doctors as representatives of pharmaceutical manufacturers. These people do not, however, take orders for the products.

technical specialists
Support salespeople who provide order getters with technical assistance.

Technical specialists (called *sales engineers* in some industries) provide salespeople with assistance in the form of technical expertise. Technical specialists are important to pharmaceutical companies, environmental engineering firms, manufacturers of building products, and other marketers of complex goods and services. At Ebasco Services, geologists, chemists, and engineers serve as technical specialists in a team marketing effort.

Other Selling Arrangements

Rather than having salespeople meet or call on potential customers alone, many organizations use other selling arrangements. Two of these are team selling and seminar selling.

team selling
The use of a team of sales professionals who work together to sell and service an organization's major customers.

Team Selling

In **team selling,** a team of sales professionals works together to sell and service an organization's major customers. A selling team may include order-oriented salespeople as well as missionary and technical support people, along with employees from other parts of the company, including finance and operations. Black & Decker has increased sales to Wal-Mart and Home Depot since it set up teams to serve these big customers. Each team includes salespeople, a marketer, an information systems expert, a sales forecaster, and a financial analyst, all of whom collaborate on selling and promotional activities for their client.[9]

Personal selling by pharmacists—including Walgreens pharmacy manager Bill Bruckner, shown here at a Walgreens store in Memphis, Tennessee—consists of verifying prescription orders, counseling patients on the appropriate use of prescriptions, and advising over-the-counter remedies. To help pharmacists provide better service in these areas and develop trust, Walgreens Drugstores is installing a workflow/computer system called Intercom Plus. The system helps pharmacists process orders more efficiently so that they can shorten customers' waits and spend more time answering their questions.

Team selling is very effective for products that are complex and require support following the sale. Some team members help prospective buyers understand products and how they are used, and others provide after-sales support. Team selling is useful for serving organizations that use teams for making purchases, as is often the case when buying organizational computer hardware and software systems.

seminar selling
An educational program designed to reach a group of people interested in a topic related to the organization's products or services.

Seminar Selling Organizations offering innovative or complex products may use seminar selling. **Seminar selling** is an educational program designed to reach a group of people interested in a topic related to the organization's products or services. Seminar selling helps organizations make initial contacts with prospects and begin the formation of relationships that can continue through more customized follow-up. In general, people attend seminars to gather information, rather than to shop, so this selling arrangement is used less for closing sales.

The specifics of seminar selling depend on the nature of products and customers. A seminar may inform organizational buyers' technical staffs about product innovations. The technical staff may then try to persuade those with purchasing authority to buy. An organization also may use seminar selling to educate consumers about services. Experience has taught Cowan Financial Group that seminars on topics such as estate planning can be effective for reaching large numbers of interested prospects in one selling effort. However, their effectiveness depends on contacting prospects afterward. Says Cowan's marketing director, Victoria Chorbajian: "If you spend $5,000 to $10,000 on a seminar, and you aren't willing to follow up within a few days, it's a waste."[10]

Relationship Selling

relationship selling
The development of long-term, mutually beneficial relationships between salespeople and their customers.

Many firms practice **relationship selling,** in which salespeople develop long-term, mutually beneficial relationships with customers. Customers often value more involved relationships than simple order taking. They want to collaborate with trusted salespeople who offer in-depth counseling on purchasing decisions, help find imaginative solutions to problems, support them within the salespeople's companies, and have high ethical standards.[11] Such relationships are especially valued by organizational buyers, who turn to partnership relations with vendors as a means to gain competitive advantage (see "Marketing Movers & Shakers: Stuart Levine/Dale Carnegie & Associates").

Stuart Levine/ Dale Carnegie & Associates

The late Dale Carnegie founded his now-famous training institute on the premise that salespeople and business leaders could learn "how to win friends and influence people." Heading into the twenty-first century, that focus has changed somewhat. With the advent of information technology and the pressure of global competition, business executives have recognized that the best way to attract and retain customers is by building relationships with them. In fact, Dale Carnegie & Associates Inc. learned the lesson itself: Suffering from a major drop in market share, the service organization had to find a way to turn itself around by offering greater value to its customers.

That's where CEO Stuart Levine came in. "After years of continued success, we noticed that market share started to decline. And when you have a decrease in sales, you take it personally." So Levine and a cross-functional team comprised of salespeople, trainers, customers, and sponsors hammered out a plan to redesign the Dale Carnegie Sales Course. The new course is now called the Sales Advantage program, and the most important emphasis of the new program is building relationships. "Although over one-half million people had graduated from the Dale Carnegie Sales Course, worldwide research showed that selling had shifted from the traditional track-driven concept, where salespeople relied on memorized lines, to a relationship-driven process where the customer is at the controls," explains Levine. He continues, "That's why we have developed a more dynamic model . . . In the new course we don't talk about closing hard and early. We don't use memorized language . . . If a salesperson insults your intelligence by giving you a memorized pitch that's not based on your individual needs, you'll show that salesperson to the door in about six seconds."

Levine believes that the explosive development in information technology has created a greater need for building personal relationships. "Technology has had a huge impact on our business day," he relates. "We're entering into what is called a demassified society, and as a result, people often feel less connected to one another. While technology drives our business environment, the substance of business is driven by relationships."

So the new Sales Advantage program emphasizes strategies such as building rapport and trust (with customers); understanding the questioning process; presenting solutions instead of products or services; becoming a powerful communicator; and addressing customers' buying motives. In the course, salespeople spend a great deal of time learning how to listen to customers and communicate their message clearly and effectively. "Prospects and customers today want you to communicate your message clearly, succinctly, and in terms that highlight their interests," notes Levine. He points out that all of these changes still emphasize the customer's point of view, which is something that the Dale Carnegie organization has always tried to do. And which, after all, is how to win friends and influence people.

Source: Bob Alexander, "How To Succeed in a Changing World," *Selling Power,* March 1996, pp. 13–14, 16, 19–20.

Explore more by searching "Dale Carnegie" on the Web.

Relationship selling is not new, but it is becoming more popular because of intense global competition. Consumers appreciate relationships with salespeople they can trust to help them make purchases over time, such as for appliances or clothing. Organizational buyers value relationships with suppliers that can help them be more efficient.

As an illustration of relationship selling, Bose, a $500 million manufacturer of acoustic speakers, asked that G&F, a small manufacturer of molded plastic parts, assign a full-time employee to work at the Bose plant. This arrangement eliminated regular sales calls by G&F and allowed Bose to cut buying and planning costs. It solidified the relationship between G&F and Bose and it changed the way G&F viewed personal selling. According to G&F president John Argitis, "Instead of spending time trying to get new accounts, we concentrate solely on servicing and pricing. You don't really sell, you look for opportunities."[12]

Steps in the Selling Process

The process of personal selling involves seven steps. As shown in Figure 19.2, these steps are: prospect for customers, prepare for sales calls, approach qualified prospects, make sales presentations, handle objections, close sales, and build long-term relationships. Sales-

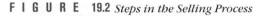

F I G U R E 19.2 *Steps in the Selling Process*

| Prospect for Customers | → | Prepare for Sales Calls | → | Approach Qualified Prospects | → | Make Sales Presentations | → | Handle Objections | → | Close Sales | → | Build Long-Term Relationships |

people do all of these steps, but the boundaries between them can be blurry (see "Put It into Practice: Identify Your Own Personal Selling Experience"). Furthermore, research by Dale Carnegie & Associates has found that customers are most receptive to selling activities adapted to them, rather than "canned approaches" that sequentially go through the selling process. Thus, a memorized presentation with a dozen closing techniques is less effective than building relationships with customers based on identifying and meeting their needs.[13]

Prospect for Customers

prospecting
The process of identifying potential customers.

Personal selling begins with **prospecting,** or identifying potential customers. Salespeople must locate individuals or organizations that could be buyers for their products. These potential buyers can be put into three categories:

1. *Leads*—individuals or organizations that are potential customers.
2. *Prospects*—individuals or organizations that have an interest in the product.
3. *Qualified prospects*—individuals or organizations that are willing to buy, can afford to buy, and have the authority to purchase the product.

Obviously, the last category includes the best bets for salespeople, but they are the hardest to identify. Salespeople often start out with a long list of leads, narrow it down to prospects, and narrow it further to fewer qualified prospects.

Sources of Prospects   Salespeople get leads and prospects from a number of sources. Popular sources include mailing lists, databases, trade shows, previous customers, suppliers, and personal contacts. Referrals from existing customers are often the best prospects and can be found just by asking. Creative salespeople use these and other sources. For example, a book called *Cole's Directory* uses U.S. Census Bureau

E. Rachel Hubka is president of Rachel's Bus Company, whose regular business is transporting children to and from school. To increase her business for private groups, Hubka trained the bus drivers, who have the closest relationships to the customers, to recognize prospects for the new business and to sell to them. She provides all drivers with business cards, helps them with personal appearance and manners, and teaches them how to talk with customers and ask for their business. She also adds a sales incentive—an opportunity to earn more. Some drivers have earned as much as two-thirds of their paychecks from new business, and the company's revenues from private jobs have risen to about 15 percent of total revenues.

Identify Your Own Personal Selling Experience

Each of us is already a personal seller. We have all made a sales presentation to someone at some point in our lives. It might have been to our parents, trying to convince them we needed a car. It might have been to our childhood neighbors, trying to sell them our services as a lawn mower or pet sitter. It might have been to a college recruiter, trying to convince him or her of what we could contribute to the school as students.

Think of a situation in which you have practiced personal selling. Note how you prospected, prepared, approached the "customer," presented your argument, addressed and overcame objections, "closed" the deal, and ultimately built or enhanced a long-term relationship. In what areas were you strongest? Weakest? What parts of the experience might you apply to a job as a professional salesperson?

statistics and other data to classify streets and neighborhoods in the United States based on income levels. The average income on what the directory calls an "$A" street is in the top 20 percent for that particular region.[14] Salespeople for luxury products would focus on these streets and neighborhoods.

In addition, salespeople may try **cold canvassing** (or cold calling) by simply getting lists of names. To reach consumers, they might pick names and addresses from a phone book. Sellers to organizations might turn to Dun's Market Identifiers, an information service of Dun & Bradstreet. Figure 19.3 shows an example of the type of information provided by this service available on a computer file. Generally, the refusal rate with cold canvassing is high, but some salespeople use it successfully.

In Japan, however, cold canvassing is difficult because formal introductions and relationship building are important there. One U.S. company found that Japanese consumers resented sales calls from strangers even in response to a request for information. To reach Japanese businesses, marketers sometimes try sending direct-mail advertising first to serve as an introduction.[15]

cold canvassing
Locating leads and prospects from a phone book or other source and calling on them.

Qualifying Prospects   **Qualifying** prospects involves determining whether they are indeed likely to buy. Qualifying is important because not every prospect meets the criteria to be a buyer. For instance, prospects who want to buy luxury automobiles may not be qualified because of low income. Employees who want personal computers at their desks may not be authorized to make such purchases.

qualifying
Determining whether a prospect is in a position to buy a product.

Prepare for Sales Calls

Preparation means the salespeople find out more about their qualified prospect and, if necessary, make certain they know the technical aspects and benefits of their products. Salespeople who want to engage in relationship selling with organizational buyers also learn about their clients' industries, their strengths and weaknesses, and strategic objectives. Such preparation continues throughout a value-driven selling process yet it begins during this stage.

preparation
Learning more about qualified prospects and how to create value for them.

Salespeople can accumulate information about customers directly from prospects as well as from outside sources. For John Holmes at Pacific Bell, preparation to sell advertising to the owner of a tile company began with examining records related to the client's ad buying history. Holmes learned that the client was already advertising in 10 of the company's directories, including four that would soon stop taking ads for the year. Holmes concluded that he needed to meet with the client to discuss advertising in those four directories so he gathered additional information about advertising rates.

FIGURE 19.3

*Sample of Information
from Dun's Market
Identifiers*

```
    9/5/1
    0213235      DIALOG File 516:  D&B Duns Market Identifiers
    Allied Warehousing Service Inc
    Abbott Labs
    20 26th St
    P O Box 1700
    Huntington, WV  25703-1233

    TELEPHONE: 304-523-2131
    COUNTY: Cabell       MSA: 3400   (Huntington-Ashland, WV-KY-OH)
    REGION: South Atlantic

    BUSINESS: Public & Contract Warehousing

    PRIMARY SIC:
      4225        General warehousing and storage, nsk
       42250000   General warehousing and storage, nsk
       42259901   General warehousing

    LATEST YEAR ORGANIZED:  1980    OWNER CHANGE DATE:           NA
    STATE OF INCORPORATION:  WV    DATE OF INCORPORATION: 09/26/1980
    ANNUAL SALES REVISION DATE: 01/02/1994
                                       LATEST          TREND        BASE
                                        YEAR           YEAR         YEAR
                                                      (1992)       (1990)

    SALES         $     2,700,000E  $      NA   $        NA
    EMPLOYEES TOTAL:             41          41            50
    EMPLOYEES HERE:             20

       SALES GROWTH:  NA %  NET WORTH: $         NA
       EMPLOYMENT GROWTH:  -18 %

    SQUARE FOOTAGE: 650,000  RENTED
    NUMBER OF ACCOUNTS: NA
    BANK: Twentieth Street Bank (Inc)   BANK DUNS: 00-794-5066
```

Source: Used by permission of Dun and Bradstreet Information Services.

Approach Qualified Prospects

approach
Initial formal contact with
the qualified prospect.

Once salespeople have completed preparations, they plan an **approach** or initial contact to the qualified prospect. The goals of the approach are to learn more about the customer's needs, gain attention, and stimulate interest. The most foolproof way to get prospects' attention and interest is to have a potential solution for their problems.

During the approach, salespeople ask questions and gather information from the potential customer. Some salespeople establish rapport in a friendly manner, use a pleasant voice, and offer an opportunity to chat before getting down to business. Some salespeople push too hard during an approach. For example, when John Holmes greeted the tile company owner, the client was dismayed to see Holmes carrying four phone directories and said, "We aren't going to handle all of them today, are we?" When Holmes replied that they should at least get started on them, the client added, "And I suppose you're going to tell me there's a rate increase." Holmes confirmed the rate increase and was thrown out of the office.[16] This was an information-gathering approach, so perhaps Holmes should have left the directories in his car until the client's wants and needs were discussed.

Make Sales Presentations

sales presentation
Communication of the sales
message to the customer.

The **sales presentation** communicates information to customers, with the goal of stimulating further interest. The traditional approach is for salespeople to describe and demonstrate specific product attributes and to explain how they can benefit the prospect.

In addition, value-oriented selling requires that communication flow in both directions. Salespeople often begin a presentation with open-ended questions that help uncover information about prospects' wants and needs. Salespeople can help build long-term relationships, rather than merely completing a single sale, by identifying not only how a particular product can help, but how the organization could work with its clients. Dan Kosch of RCP, Inc., a Connecticut-based consulting and training firm, applies this principle to business-to-business selling: "Salespeople typically spend their time on finding a product fit, but to sell value you have to look beyond the product to a strategic business match."[17]

Types of Presentations   Salespeople use three main types of presentations: stimulus–response, formula selling, and need satisfaction.

Stimulus–Response   In a **stimulus–response presentation,** salespeople try to offer the appropriate information (stimulus) at the right time to get the customer to buy (response). One form of stimulus–response presentation is *suggestive selling,* in which salespeople ask customers if they would like particular information. For example, a catalog sales rep could ask a telephone customer if he or she would like to hear about a special offer, or a restaurant waiter could ask patrons if they would like to see the dessert menu. Furniture-kit manufacturer Cohasset Colonials practices a form of suggestive selling through its catalog pages by offering "go-togethers"—two or more of its products sold at a slight discount.

Formula Selling   The **formula selling presentation** is somewhat more rigid, based on the idea that product information must be provided in a thorough, lockstep format. Although the sales information is conveyed sequentially, good salespeople are flexible enough to answer questions or stop during the presentation to explain product features that customers don't understand. An advantage of this type of presentation is that it reduces the risk of omitting important information. The Ohio-based Longaberger Basket Company uses formula presentations to sell its baskets in customers' homes.

Canned presentations, which are memorized or read and presented without variation, are often used by telephone salespeople. Many prospects dislike canned presentations, but telemarketing consultants believe this is due to poor scripting and delivery. Judy Lanier, a partner at Softel Systems in California and author of *The 11 Best Kept Secrets of Successful Scripts,* says goal setting is just as important in writing sales scripts as in other aspects of marketing. "You really have to know your objective before you start writing," she emphasizes. She comments further, "Presentation is everything." In other words, the best-written script will fall flat with a bad delivery.[18]

Need Satisfaction   The **need-satisfaction presentation** emphasizes asking questions and listening to customers' answers in order to nail down their needs and desires. Once salespeople have identified these, they present the benefits of their products or organizations and how these can satisfy needs and solve problems. Need-satisfaction presentations are geared to identifying and solving problems for customers, so they are most consistent with value-driven marketing principles. However, salespeople who use other presentation types can still focus on value by listening to their customers.

At Pacific Bell, John Holmes had to schedule a new appointment in order to make his presentation to the tile company owner, and he selected a need-satisfaction approach. He concluded that the owner had been upset because Yellow Pages advertising was so valuable to him that he was stuck with the rate increase. Focusing on that need, Holmes did some more preparation, devising a new package of ads targeted toward the client's marketing needs. On his next visit, Holmes astonished his client by suggesting that in one directory, his business could maintain its dominant position with an ad half its previous size. The flabbergasted client, pleased with the $1,800 savings, was then prepared to listen to the rest of the presentation. Client and salesperson focused on advertising objectives and Holmes was able to demonstrate how, in another directory that represented a potential area for growth, the client's business would benefit from running a larger ad.[19]

stimulus–response presentation
Sales presentation that provides a stimulus with the goal of influencing the customer to buy the product.

formula selling presentation
Sales presentation of product information in a thorough, lockstep format.

canned presentation
A memorized, standard presentation given without variation to all prospects.

need-satisfaction presentation
Sales presentations that include asking questions and listening to customers' answers in order to identify their needs and desires.

Salespeople can use various types of need-satisfaction presentations. In *adaptive selling,* the salesperson adjusts the presentation to fit the selling context, which dictates whether more questions should be asked or solutions offered. In *consultative selling,* the salesperson acts more directly as an expert who can recognize and solve a customer's problems. Carla Alley, who sells sales support systems for 3M Corporation, starts presentations by learning about prospective clients. She asks about company strategies such as plans to enter new markets or introduce products, sales force organization, and the experience of the sales force. Based on what she learns, Alley helps prospects analyze the sales process and identify ways to improve it with 3M's computer systems.[20]

Presentation Formats   Salespeople can make presentations in person or over the phone.

Selling Face-to-Face   When selling in person, physical appearance is important. Prospects often form impressions of salespeople and their organizations based on appearances. In addition, salespeople should bring along materials for explaining products and their benefits. Salespeople should acknowledge and greet everyone attending the presentation, clearly describe the product and its benefits, and encourage prospects to discuss how products might be relevant to their situation. Successful salesperson Paul Sherlock notes, "There is something more important than what you are saying—that is, what the customer has to say."[21]

Selling over the Phone   Organizations can lower the costs of sales calls by having salespeople make their presentations over the telephone. Such selling efforts are called **telemarketing.** Salespeople using telemarketing can reach more customers, at a lower cost, in less time, than with face-to-face selling. This makes telemarketing attractive to organizations that cannot afford personal selling.

telemarketing
Conducting sales presentations over the phone.

The efficiency of telemarketing enables organizations to provide levels of service that might otherwise be too expensive. Summit Racing Equipment, which sells performance auto parts, takes orders over the phone 24 hours a day. This enables U.S. consumers to order parts when they work on their cars at night and allows overseas customers to reach Summit at times convenient for them.[22] Union Pacific Railroad began serving its 20,000 smallest accounts with telemarketing from Omaha. The telemarketers can interact with these customers much more than traveling sales reps, and a higher proportion of customers are impressed with the service they receive.[23]

However, telemarketing is viewed as a nuisance by many potential customers. Complaints about abuses of telemarketing have led to various restrictions. In the United States, the Telephone Consumer Protection Act of 1991 requires that telemarketers maintain a "no solicitation" list and avoid any wire solicitation—such as by telephone, fax, or computer modem—of anyone on the list.[24] In addition, many states have restrictions, such as requiring that telemarketers obtain licenses.

Salespeople who use telemarketing make their initial impression by using good telephone etiquette. Telemarketers should have a confident and pleasant manner and should speak clearly in a style appropriate to the audience.

Handle Objections

objections
Prospects' reasons for not making purchases.

In the sales situation, **objections** are prospects' reasons for not making purchases. Objections are based on costs, benefits, or both. They also may occur because prospects do not see a need or want for products.

Skilled salespeople know when objections are valid and show respect for prospects' wishes by backing off; perhaps that prospect will become a customer in the future. But the same salespeople also recognize when objections become an opportunity to further showcase the product's benefits. For instance, if prospects compare the salesperson's products unfavorably with the competition, salespeople can show ways in which they are better suited to the prospects' needs. Salespeople can explain how a weakness in a product is outweighed by other strengths. If prospects are concerned about prices, salespeople could demonstrate that the product is priced competitively or is of higher quality than competing products.

At Pacific Bell, John Holmes used the tile company president's objections to a price increase for Yellow Pages ads as an opportunity to show that he would work with the client to improve advertising effectiveness. In fact, he sold a four-directory advertising package at an overall price increase. Instead of feeling manipulated or angry, the client, in Holmes's words, "was happy because he felt I had given him recommendations not based on what was going to be best for me, but based on his needs and what ultimately was best for his business."[25]

In some situations, prospects use objections as a negotiating tactic to lead salespeople to sweeten the deal. Such customers exist around the world, but it can be helpful for global salespeople to be familiar with typical negotiating tactics in particular countries. In France, for example, business customers are known as clever and dramatic negotiators. The successful salesperson is patient and demonstrates interest in, but not an overwhelming need for, the client's business.[26]

Close Sales

closing
Asking for orders and getting prospects to commit to purchase.

Closing involves asking for orders and getting prospects to commit to purchase. In most cases, salespeople initiate closing. This may seem obvious, but according to marketing experts, many sales are lost because salespeople don't ask for orders. In the words of Michael LeBoeuf, author of *How to Win Customers and Keep Them for Life,* "How can you get the order if you don't ask?"[27]

There are a few standard techniques for closing. In the *trial close,* salespeople ask prospects to make decisions about particular aspects of purchases, such as the color of a car or the model of a refrigerator. In the *assumptive close,* salespeople discuss issues such as financing or delivery, presuming that the prospect is going to buy. In the *urgency close,* salespeople impress upon the prospect the need for an immediate decision, because, say, interest rates are increasing, airfares are going up, or the popularity of the item means it may go out of stock. Other tactics are to encourage prospects to try out products before making commitments or to imagine themselves using the product and receiving its benefits. These tactics can build prospects' involvement with products and help them appreciate the product's value.

Salespeople with a value orientation use these techniques only when they are appropriate to the situation. For example, travel agents should use urgency closes only if they have accurate information that airfares or hotel rates are indeed going to increase. Appliance salespeople should use the assumptive close only when it is clear that new homeowners need and want appliances. Otherwise, these techniques are questionable and backfire because they are perceived as high-pressure tactics.

Moreover, closing techniques are less important if prospects appreciate that the exchange is in their best interest. When prospects believe that salespeople are collaborating with them to create value, making purchases is simply the logical next step. At Pacific Bell, when John Holmes focused on what was best for the tile company business, he closed a sale and began a relationship that would help him in closing future sales.

Build Long-Term Relationships

In relationship marketing, the closing is not the end of a sale. Instead, value-driven salespeople continue building long-term relationships with customers. Relationship-

follow-up
After-the-sale activities to make sure the customer is satisfied with the product purchased.

building activities, including **follow-up** sales calls, are geared toward making sure customers are satisfied with their purchases. Effective follow-up contributes to a customer's evaluation that an exchange was beneficial and delivered value. Customers who make such evaluations about an exchange are more likely to become repeat buyers.

Building relationships may involve phone calls to learn whether products were delivered on time and undamaged, to find out if they are functioning properly, and to be sure that customers are satisfied. It also is helpful to provide written information on how to get the most from products or to offer training programs for users. Salespeople may ask customers to complete a brief survey to assess their satisfaction and identify any problems that can be resolved.

Building long-term relationships with customers is especially important in the case of expensive purchases, particularly when customers have doubts about the purchase decision (called "buyer's remorse" or "post-purchase dissonance"). Effective follow-ups can alleviate such feelings. Some research suggests that conducting the follow-ups necessary to obtain repeat sales from existing customers costs about half the amount needed to close a sale with a new customer.[28]

Sales Management

The efforts of a sales force need to be managed and are driven by a **sales plan,** or formal statement of selling goals and strategies. Designing and managing sales plans are the basic activities of **sales management.**

sales plan
A formal statement of selling goals and strategies.

sales management
The planning, directing, and controlling the personal selling activities of the organization.

In the typical medium-sized or large organization, sales management is the responsibility of sales managers. Sales managers typically perform the functions of recruiting, training, organizing and supervising sales forces. In companies that use team selling or other types of cross-functional teams, sales managers' roles are particularly important because they need the knowledge and skills to create effective teams. In large companies engaged in selling globally, vice presidents of sales coordinate sales forces from different parts of the world.

Organizing Sales Forces

sales territories
Groups of present and potential customers assigned to particular salespeople, branches, dealers, or distributors.

Senior marketing managers and sales managers must decide how sales forces should be organized. To get the most from their salespeople, sales managers set up sales territories. **Sales territories** are groups of present and potential customers assigned to particular salespeople, branches, dealers, or distributors.[29] As shown in Figure 19.4, most companies organize their sales forces by geography, by product, or by customer.

In a geographic structure, individual salespeople are assigned geographic territories to cover. A salesperson calls on all prospects in the territory and usually represents all of the company's products. For example, a salesperson might be assigned to cover business buyers in Chile, the southwestern United States, or a smaller region such as metropolitan Miami. A geographic structure provides the practical benefit of limiting the distance each salesperson must travel to see customers.

In a product structure, each salesperson is assigned to prospects and customers for a particular product or product line. A product structure is beneficial when the sales force must have specific technical knowledge about products in order to sell effectively. However, this structure can result in a duplication of sales efforts because more than one salesperson can call on the same customer. For this reason, it tends to be expensive.

A customer structure assigns a salesperson or selling team to serve a single customer or single type of customer. It works best when different types of buyers have large or significantly different needs. When this structure involves devoting all of a salesperson's time to a single customer, it is expensive, but can result in large sales and satisfied customers. For example, when G&F assigned a full-time salesperson to work at the Bose speaker plant, it could thoroughly meet Bose's needs. In the five

FIGURE 19.4
Common Ways of
Organizing a Sales Force

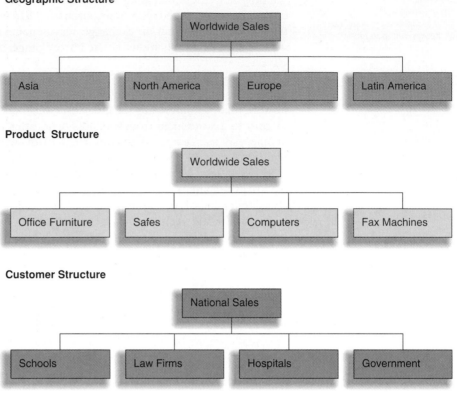

Geographic Structure

Worldwide Sales

Asia | North America | Europe | Latin America

Product Structure

Worldwide Sales

Office Furniture | Safes | Computers | Fax Machines

Customer Structure

National Sales

Schools | Law Firms | Hospitals | Government

years after making the arrangement, G&F's annual sales grew from $3 million to $15 million.[30]

In a variation of the customer-organized structure, a company may employ **major account management,** or the use of team selling to focus on major customers to establish long-term relationships. Procter & Gamble, whose sales force used to be organized by product, shifted to major account management, which the company calls Customer Business Development. P&G management believed that assigning resources to particular customers was a more flexible and customer-focused structure.[31]

The customer-organized structure is well suited for the use of cross-functional teams and value-driven marketing. Nevertheless, geographic and product territories can also be managed with a focus on value. For this to happen, sales management and the sales force must concentrate on learning and meeting customers' wants and needs better than competitors.

major account management
The use of team selling to focus on major customers to establish long-term relationships.

Recruiting Salespeople

How does a sales manager recruit salespeople who are bright, creative, motivated, and willing to stay on the job? The recruitment process involves a number of activities, from deciding whether to hire salespeople or contract with independent representatives to selecting the specific individuals for sales positions.

Independent Reps versus Company Sales Force   Marketers and sales managers must decide whether to use independent sales representatives or hire their own sales forces. **Independent sales representatives** are professional salespeople who act as independent contractors and who are paid on commission. Examples are the sales consultants for companies like Mary Kay Cosmetics and the Longaberger Basket Company.

independent sales
representatives
Professional salespeople who act as independent contractors, paid on commission.

Using independent reps has advantages in a variety of situations. It quickly establishes a sales force for smaller companies and those that are just starting out. According to Bill Kinard, owner of a California-based manufacturing company, contracting with reps "enables you to get fairly rapid coverage without the heavy initial outlay of money needed to support a direct sales force."[32] In addition, companies that sell in foreign countries can benefit from local reps' understanding of the country's business culture and avoid the mistakes that can result from entering global markets without sufficient cultural knowledge. However, sales managers have less control over the performance of individual salespeople when independent reps are used.

Hiring its own sales force gives a company more control over the selling of its products. This can be especially important for highly technical or proprietary products where the sales force needs detailed technical knowledge. To market its sophisticated motion control products in 58 countries, Parker Hannifin Corporation operates sales offices in locations from Prague to Taipei.[33] However, staffing a sales force requires much work and money. A company has to figure out what kinds of people are likely to sell its products effectively and how to identify those people. It has to hire, train, and supervise them, which can be difficult. If certain salespeople don't work out, the company has to bear the frustration and expense of dismissing them and looking for more suitable replacements.

Search for Candidates Whichever route the organization follows in setting up a sales force, sales managers must find salespeople to represent the organization's products. Sales managers may start the search simply by asking their industry contacts for suggestions. To find experienced independent reps, managers may prospect at trade shows or run classified ads in trade journals. Some organizations, including Amway and Shaklee, use **network selling,** also known as multilevel selling. Under this arrangement, independent reps can increase their own earnings by recruiting and supervising other sales reps.

There are many ways to identify candidates for sales positions. A good place to start may be to ask current employees for suggestions. Employment agencies, which prescreen applicants, are another source of candidates. Colleges and universities can provide the names of candidates who are educated in marketing, enthusiastic, and ready to be trained.

Sales Candidate Profile Before sales managers can evaluate job candidates, they need a clear sense of the type of person they are looking for. A systematic approach is to start by understanding the selling job. The sales manager conducts a job analysis and prepares a job description. A job analysis is an investigation of the activities, tasks, responsibilities, and environmental influences involved in the job. A job description is a detailed report of these findings.

Based on the job description, the sales manager can create a sales candidate profile—a description of ideal characteristics or qualifications. Typically, these characteristics include indicators of ability such as intelligence, verbal and math skills, and some measure of sales aptitude. In addition, many organizations look for certain personality traits thought to be related to success in selling. These organizations might look for someone who is responsible, sociable, creative, and has high self-esteem. Finally, the profile might specify certain skills, such as technical product knowledge, ability to make an effective sales presentation, and interpersonal skills. A variety of tests are available to estimate these criteria. These help predict the ability to carry out the responsibilities in the job description and help sales managers locate the right people for the sales job.

The criteria to include in the profile depend in part on the nature of the product being sold. Selling highly technical products, for instance, requires knowledge of the product and its applications. However, research by Acumen International has found that the most successful salespeople have a focus that balances people and task skills. They are competitive and enjoy challenges, but they also are warm, creative, and able

network (multilevel) selling
The practice used by direct selling companies to have independent agents serve as distributors and resell merchandise to other agents who eventually make sales to consumers.

to relate well to others.[34] In the words of Dirk Beveridge, president of Beveridge Business Systems of Illinois, the ideal salesperson builds a good emotional relationship with the customer, knows the product thoroughly, can identify the customer's needs from the customer's point of view, and ultimately becomes "like an unpaid member of your customer's staff."[35]

The optimal criteria for salespeople may vary according to the countries in which they work. Personality traits or selling skills that work well in one country may be a hindrance in another. For example, a salesperson with a casual and friendly style may put U.S. customers at ease but insult prospects in a country that places more importance on formality and respect. Selection criteria that are acceptable and even encouraged in one country, say, ethnic background in Malaysia, may be inappropriate or even illegal in others, as is ethnic background in the United States.[36]

Screening Candidates   When sales managers have identified candidates and decided on the criteria for selecting them, they are ready to screen them. The basic techniques are to review résumés or job applications, administer aptitude and/or personality tests, and conduct interviews.

Many sales managers have their own tactics for screening candidates. Some call candidates back for a more thorough interview outlining territory, responsibilities, and so forth, then ask the candidates to outline what they expect to accomplish in the job over a certain period of time.[37] Others provide candidates with product and company information, asking them to give a sales presentation a week later. Some managers have candidates travel with company representatives on sales calls for a day, then ask their reps to report on the candidates' skills, attitude, motivation, and so forth.[38]

All of these tests are designed to see candidates in action in order to evaluate how well they will do on the job. These situations also give candidates a chance to decide whether they indeed want the job. In the end, both sales managers and sales candidates want a good match.

Training and Supervising Salespeople

Once salespeople have been hired, sales managers must train and supervise them. These activities are important even for experienced salespeople.

Training Salespeople   Training can get new recruits up to speed and improve experienced salespeople. However, training costs an organization money and salespeoples' time, so both want it to be effective. Sales managers want the sales force to be unified, whether in team or individual sales efforts. Training helps achieve this goal. Sales training involves more than learning the steps in the selling process. According to one study, average training programs spend 35 percent of their time on product information, 30 percent on sales techniques, 25 percent on market and general company information, and 10 percent on topics such as ethical selling practices.[39]

Training for new sales recruits often comes on the job, sometimes in "apprenticeship" with experienced salespeople. But many organizations go further, sending salespeople to seminars, classes, or workshops, and providing training with videos and interactive computer programs. Some organizations have their own sales training staff; others hire outside firms that specialize in sales training. WilTel, an Oklahoma-based company that employs telephone salespeople, sends each new hire to Washington University in St. Louis for a two-week course in telecommunications technology. Then trainees spend two days at the University of Tulsa to polish up their writing and presentation skills.[40]

Many salespeople are not experienced in team selling. As such, organizations that use teams need to train sales and other employees to work in this manner. Kraft General Foods trains its salespeople to take a customer focus by having teams play a computer simulation game in which they pretend to sell to a traditional supermarket

Some organizations obtain sales training from outside firms, such as Xerox Worldwide Education and Learning. Xerox's sales skills training program was originally developed to train the company's own sales force. Xerox has also provided the training to its suppliers and customers. In this ad, the company is offering the training program to any interested organizational buyer.

chain, a discounter, and a distributor that serves independent grocers.[41] Cross-functional training is beneficial not only for companies involved in team selling, but also for firms that simply want their sales force to be linked closely to the rest of the organization. Robinson Brick Co., a Denver manufacturer of residential brick, requires that salespeople take one other employee into the field with them each month.[42]

Supervising Salespeople   In many cases, ongoing training of salespeople is part of supervising them. The job of supervision entails enabling salespeople to do their jobs and seeing that the work gets done up to standards. Thus, supervision also includes motivation, compensation, evaluation, and control. John Sample, CEO of Business Interiors, notes, "Salespeople, especially successful ones, are entrepreneurs. And they are used to doing things on their own and having control of what they do, and they like to look at a job from start to finish."[43] Through supervision, sales managers rein in salespeople and make them more team oriented.

Some management experts advise that a sales manager in a customer-driven organization be not a gatekeeper for the sales force, but rather an advocate for the customer.[44] Others emphasize the importance of managers staying in touch with the sales force by traveling with it: "Sales management is a field job," writes Jack Falvey, contributing editor of *Sales & Marketing Management*.[45] Falvey explains that by talking with salespeople and accompanying them on visits to customers, sales managers learn how their organizations can help salespeople do their jobs well. In sum, to supervise the sales force effectively, sales managers should stay in contact with both the sales force and its customers.

Motivating and Compensating Salespeople

motivation
The positive or negative needs, goals, desires, and forces that impel an individual toward or away from certain actions.

Motivation is "the positive or negative needs, goals, desires, and forces that impel an individual toward or away from certain actions, activities, objects, or conditions."[46] In terms of salespeople, motivation is the drive that keeps them productive year after year. How do successful salespeople stay motivated? "The answer is that they enjoy the challenge of working with customers and being paid well for their ability to produce business through creativity, knowledge, trust, and integrity," writes Falvey. "To motivate such salespeople, managers must treat them as contributors."[47] Such efforts have the most impact if they include the sales support staff as well as those directly engaged in selling. *TV Guide,* for instance, gives two annual awards to recognize sales support staff with a cash bonus, a plaque, and a speech honoring them at the publication's national sales meeting.[48]

Sales managers look for self-motivation in new recruits before hiring. Salespeople also must be presented with clear performance standards and be rewarded for obtaining them. Good sales managers know how to challenge and stimulate sales forces in sluggish economies or declining markets.

To meet the expectations of sales management, salespeople need to know what those expectations are. The most basic way to communicate these expectations is with

Sales Criteria	
• Total sales • Quota attainment • Sales of new products • Total profits	• Number of orders • Average size of orders • Number of canceled orders

Account Criteria	
• Customer satisfaction • Number of active accounts • Number of new accounts	• Number of lost accounts • Number of overdue accounts • Number of prospective accounts

Calling Criteria	
• Number of calls • Number of planned calls	• Number of unplanned calls

Time and Time Utilization Criteria	
• Days worked • Calls per day (call rate)	• Selling time versus nonselling time

Expense Criteria	
• Total • By type	• As a percentage of sales • As a percentage of quota

Nonselling Activity Criteria	
• Letters written to prospects • Telephone calls made to prospects • Number of formal proposals developed • Advertising displays set up • Number of meetings held with distributors/dealers • Number of training sessions for distributor/dealer personnel	• Number of calls on distributor/dealer customers • Number of service calls made • Number of customer complaints received • Number of overdue accounts collected

Source: Adapted from Gilbert A. Churchill, Jr., Neil M. Ford, and Orville C. Walker, Jr., *Sales Force Management*, 5th ed. (Burr Ridge, Ill.: Irwin, 1997), p. 657.

a clear job description. The organization should spell out the activities salespeople should do and how their performance will be measured. The activities specified might include those listed earlier in Table 19.1. Table 19.2 provides examples of common performance criteria.

Dan Vena, director of sales at Da Vinci Systems, a marketer of electronic mail systems, took a fresh look at expectations after four months of sales far below targeted levels. First, he asked each salesperson to describe his or her responsibilities and learned that none of them really knew what was expected. Next, Vena asked each employee for three suggestions as to how they could be more effective. Finally, he made sure that the goals he set were measurable. Following those actions, sales rose almost immediately.[49]

Expectations and company policies for salespeople must not only be clear; they also must be fair. Many salespeople are eager to meet challenges, but an impossible goal is more likely to discourage than to motivate. Salespeople want to feel that they have a chance at the rewards the organization offers. Two ways to motivate salespeople are financial compensation and performance recognition.

Financial Compensation   The usual ways to compensate salespeople are to pay a straight salary, a straight commission, or a combination of salary and commission.

T A B L E 19.3
Comparison of Major
Compensation Methods

Compensation Method (Frequency of Use)	Especially Useful	Advantages	Disadvantages
Straight salary (12%)	• When compensating new sales reps • When firm moves into new sales territories that require developmental work • When sales reps must perform many nonselling activities	• Provides sales reps with maximum amount of security • Gives sales managers large amounts of control over sales reps • Easy to administer • Yields more predictable selling expenses	• Provides no incentive • Necessitates closer supervision of sales reps' activities • During sales declines, selling expenses remain at same level
Straight commission (5%)	• When highly aggressive selling is required • When nonselling tasks are minimized • When company cannot closely control sales force activities	• Provides maximum amount of incentive • By increasing commission rate, sales managers can encourage reps to sell certain items • Selling expenses relate directly to sales resources	• Sales reps have little financial security • Sales managers have minimum control over sales force • May cause reps to provide inadequate service to smaller accounts • Selling costs are less predictable
Combination (83%)	• When sales territories have relatively similar sales potentials • When firm wishes to provide incentive but still control sales force activities	• Provides certain level of financial security • Provides some incentive • Selling expenses fluctuate with sales revenue • Sales managers have some control over reps' nonselling activities	• Selling expenses less predictable • May be difficult to administer

Source: Gilbert A. Churchill, Jr., Neil M. Ford, and Orville C. Walker, Jr., *Sales Force Management,* 5th ed. (Burr Ridge, Ill: Irwin, 1997), p. 508.

salary
A fixed payment made to an employee on a regular basis.

commission
Payment tied directly to the sales or profits from sales that a salesperson completes.

A **salary** is a fixed payment made to an employee on a regular basis (say, at the beginning and the middle of each month). A **commission** is payment tied directly to the sales or profits from sales that a salesperson completes. Table 19.3 summarizes uses, advantages, and disadvantages of each of these compensation methods.

Commissions are usually paid on a percentage of sales basis. For example, if a sales rep who earns a 5 percent commission closed a $50,000 sale, the sales rep would earn a commission of .05 × $50,000, or $2,500. Laws governing compensation of sales representatives vary from state to state, and sales managers must be familiar with them. Generally, state laws cover the way commissions are computed, when the commission must be paid—including payment upon termination—and the penalties for late payment.[50]

In the case of team selling, compensation can become a bit complicated. If the whole team does well, does everyone deserve equal compensation? Likewise, if the team does poorly, should every member suffer? Traditionally, people in the service and support area are paid less than order-getting salespeople. However, organizations

What's the Best Way to Motivate Sales Support Staff?

Salespeople are used to the motivational perks that come with their job—bonuses, trips, gifts of jewelry or cars, and/or recognition in the form of announcements, plaques, and other awards. But sales support people—those who coordinate and service accounts, handle customer service, call on channel members and perform other promotional activities—rarely get the limelight. Usually, they get their yearly raise and a pat on the back for a job well done, and nothing more.

At some companies, that is changing. Every year now, *TV Guide* awards two bonuses to sales support achievers in the marketing and research departments. The employees are selected by ballot at the national sales meeting and are recognized in a speech. "It's nice to have the recognition of your co-workers," says Mindy Nathanson, who won the $2,500 award recently. Suzanne Grimes, *TV Guide*'s publisher, personally recognizes a sales support person each month by awarding the employee dinner for two at his or her favorite restaurant. "Everyone wants to be recognized—you can pay any top consultant to tell you that," explains Grimes.

At General Electric, sales support employees can choose to assign 5 percent of their base pay to an incentive plan that operates on team sales goals. Many choose this option, and those who do often earn 25 percent of their base pay as a bonus. George Danko, GE general manager notes, "If you believe that your sales support organization is important to your growth, I think it's very easy to take the next step to make sure you have a plan in place to support them."

Some experts warn that managers should think carefully about the types of awards they offer people. Edward Ford, an expert on recognition, conducted independent research showing that people assign little value to gifts bearing a company logo, in fact, when given a choice, almost 96 percent chose gifts without a logo. Even gifts that are expensive to purchase—such as gold or diamond jewelry—are perceived to have less value if they bear a company logo; Ford observes that some form of cash carries the greatest value among employees. What do you think are the most effective and valuable forms of recognition and reward? Why?

Source: Michele Marchetti, "Toasting Sales Support Staffers," *Sales & Marketing Management*, April 1996, pp. 33–34.

Explore more by searching "Employee Recognition" on the Web.

---

that recognize the efforts of the total team in the sales effort have found ways to even out the compensation. One approach is to pay straight salaries, with bonuses based on the organization's profits. Mine Safety Appliances, based in Pittsburgh, has a more complex structure designed to recognize that individual contributions may vary. Mine Safety, which has 28 sales teams, pays each salesperson a base salary, bonuses linked to revenues, plus bonuses tied to other objectives. Base salaries are set at one of seven levels based on the performance evaluations of managers and team members.[51]

Performance Recognition   Providing recognition and appreciation of excellence on the job fosters motivation to do what is rewarded (see "You Decide: What's the Best Way to Motivate Sales Support Staff?"). Recognition may come in the form of tangible compensation such as money, travel, or merchandise, or it may be public appreciation of a salesperson's contribution to the sales effort, such as being named salesperson of the month. In many cases, recognition is a combination of both money and appreciation. Table 19.4 lists some of the major ways companies recognize outstanding sales performance.

On a day-to-day basis, there are many ways to motivate salespeople. One with high potential for success is to empower salespeople. To do this, sales managers can ask for and actively listen to sales reps' opinions, praise sales efforts that are in progress, and acknowledge staff for hard work and positive results. For example, each week at Dale Carnegie & Associates, the CEO sends a personal letter of recognition to an employee nominated by someone in the organization. The letter is accompanied by a check for $250 and a copy of the nomination letter.[52]

Evaluating and Controlling Salespeople

The measures for evaluating and controlling the sales force include both objective and subjective criteria. The most popular objective criterion is salespeople's performance versus their **sales quotas** or sales goals.[53] Sales quotas may be expressed in dollars, units, or points (in that a predetermined number of points may be allotted for each dollar or unit sale).

The sales manager's job usually includes setting sales quotas, perhaps in a joint effort with the salespeople who are expected to meet those quotas. Because they are

sales quota
Sales goal used for managing selling efforts.

T A B L E   19.4
Types of Salesperson Recognition

• Public announcement of outstanding performance	• Advanced training and career development opportunities
• Compliments from management	• Special perquisites for outstanding performance
• Participation in goal setting and strategy development	• Contest prizes

supposed to motivate salespeople, quotas should be challenging but achievable. This usually means they should be set at least as high as the sales forecast for the salesperson's territory, but lower than the total potential sales if all customers purchased in the time period.

Whether or not salespeople meet their quotas has a strong influence on the commission, bonus, or raise they receive. Consequently, from a management perspective, it is crucial that sales quotas are stimulating the kinds of activities desired. At an organization that claims to emphasize customer value, high quotas without measures of customer satisfaction can actually work against it. One company set quotas for selling service agreements along with its goods. Salespeople secretly included service agreements in most customers' contracts, knowing that they would meet their quota even if the customers later called to have the agreements voided.[54] The company said it cared about serving customers, but what it evaluated was the level of its sales.

Measuring Value in Selling   At an organization concerned with value creation, sales volume is not the only measure of a salesperson's success. Value-driven organizations place at least as much emphasis on retaining customers and building loyalty. They need to know such information as satisfaction of existing customers and the number of customers who have stopped buying.

The Raymond Corporation manufactures and sells narrow aisle forklifts. It recently claimed record orders, shipments, revenues, and profits. Raymond dealerships are part of a "DART" (Dealer Alliance for Recruiting and Training) program. With an intensive 14 weeks of technical training for dealer salespeople and the support of on-line access to the 24-hour guaranteed parts distribution center in East Syracuse, New York (photo), customers receive better service. Also, Raymond's continuing customer audit program provides immediate feedback from customers, which helps the company meet their needs. The feedback is also used in evaluation of a salesperson's performance.

Customers are more likely to be repeat buyers if they are delighted not only with the product itself, but also with the service they receive from salespeople. Measuring customer satisfaction with the sales effort is especially important in serving organizational buyers, who often rely on salespeople to provide information and help them solve problems. The challenge is that customer satisfaction can be difficult to quantify. The organization may rely on information from customer surveys, or it may track measures such as the number of merchandise returns and the number of customer complaints received. In either case, when customer satisfaction is part of the basis for rewarding employees, employees usually put more effort into it.[55]

Performance Appraisals   Most organizations require sales managers to conduct periodic performance reviews of each sales representative. Typically, these judgments are secured by having sales managers subjectively rate salespeople on each of a number of

F I G U R E   **19.5** *Salesperson Evaluation Form*

	Poor	Fair	Satisfactory	Good	Outstanding
Knowledge of work	☐	☐	☐	☐	☐
Degree of acceptance by customers	☐	☐	☐	☐	☐
Amount of effort devoted to acquiring business	☐	☐	☐	☐	☐
Ability to acquire business	☐	☐	☐	☐	☐
Amount of service given to customers	☐	☐	☐	☐	☐
Dependability—amount of supervision needed	☐	☐	☐	☐	☐
Attitude toward company—support given to company policies	☐	☐	☐	☐	☐
Judgment	☐	☐	☐	☐	☐
Resourcefulness	☐	☐	☐	☐	☐

Source: Gilbert A. Churchill, Jr., Neil M. Ford, Orville C. Walker, Jr., *Sales Force Management,* 5th ed. (Burr Ridge, Ill.: Irwin, 1997),

attributes using some kind of rating scale. Figure 19.5 is an example of the kind of scale that is used. The attributes more commonly evaluated using merit rating forms are:

- Sales results, including such things as total volume, sales to new accounts, and selling the full product line.
- Job knowledge, including knowledge of company policies, products, and prices.
- Management of territory, including such things as planning of activities and calls, controlling expenses, and handling company reports and records.
- Customer and company relations, including the salespeople's relationships with their customers and their standing with other employees in the company.
- Personal characteristics, including initiative, personal appearance, personality, and resourcefulness.

The emphasis given to each of these attributes varies by company. The emphasis also seems to depend on the purpose for which the evaluation is being used. Sales performance measures tend to be more important in termination and compensation decisions, whereas product knowledge and customers relations seem to be more important in transfer and promotion decisions.[56] Performance evaluations give salespeople and sales managers a chance to discuss achievements, areas that need improvement, performance objectives for the future, and career goals.

Ethical Issues in Personal Selling

Since personal selling is based on interactions and relationships between people, it is not surprising that this area of marketing gives rise to many ethical issues. Generally speaking, ethical dilemmas involve conflicts between the immediate sales a salesperson can generate by taking advantage of prospects and the benefits of building positive relationships with prospects. The reason these areas come into conflict is that sometimes the benefits of deceptive practices are immediate, whereas the benefits of ethical behavior may come more gradually, over the long run.

No matter how tempting the immediate rewards of unethical selling tactics, unethical behavior is unwise on practical as well as moral grounds. Research supports the commonsense notion that buyers are more likely to make purchases from organizations whose representatives behave ethically.[57] FMC's Alan Killingsworth has made the following observations about running that company's petroleum equipment group:[58]

In my tenure internationally, I never lost an order because we refused to compromise our ethics. I will say we had to sell a little harder in some cases and had to continue to focus the customer on the benefits and features of our product, services, and company. We sold to an organization and not to an individual. This limited any attempt by an individual making a purchasing decision to evaluate FMC on anything but our features and benefits.

As more and more organizations focus on delivering customer value, salespeople increasingly should find that unethical tactics are not tolerated, much less rewarded. This requirement is both a personal challenge to salespeople, who must make ethical decisions routinely, and a management challenge to their employers, which must ensure that they monitor and reward ethical behavior, not sales at all costs.

Manipulation of Prospects

Many people have a negative view of personal selling because some salespeople use manipulative tactics. Most of us have at some time encountered an overeager salesperson who tried to push us into buying something we weren't sure we really wanted. Some salespeople make outrageous claims for their products. Broadly speaking, when a salesperson makes a false claim about a product's features or benefits, the salesperson's behavior is illegal as well as unethical.

An example of a false claim would be to say a stock market investment is sure to earn the investor at least 10 percent a year. In fact, the returns on most kinds of investment aren't guaranteed, as many investors in Prudential-Bache energy partnerships once learned the hard way. Pru-Bache salespeople were accused of using the Prudential name, and its image as solid and dependable, to lead investors to believe the partnerships were a safe investment. However, as limited partnerships of this type tend to be, these were risky, and some investors lost their retirement savings. Without admitting wrongdoing, Prudential agreed to pay well over $300 million to settle investors' claims.[59] Some observers have criticized not only the salespeople themselves, but also their managers for creating a climate in which such behavior is viewed as normal and for rewarding earnings without examining the behavior that generates them.[60]

Sometimes a salesperson's claim is clearly an exaggeration. For example, a salesperson for a food processor might say, "This is the last appliance you'll ever need to buy for your kitchen." Such claims are considered a selling tactic called *puffery* and are used in advertising and personal selling. Puffery is legal, but it may leave prospects wondering whether they can believe anything the salesperson says.

A salesperson should not try to manipulate prospects into buying, especially if it is clear that the sale will not deliver value to them. In the end, such tactics can generate ill will and undermine the reputation of salespeople and their employers. Thus, neither customers nor salespeople benefit in the long run.

Bribery

bribery
Giving money, goods, or favors in exchange for purchases or influence.

In many instances, salespeople give gifts to customers or receive gifts from them. However, this practice may border on a practice unethical and illegal in the United States, that of taking or giving **bribes**—money, goods, or favors given in exchange for purchases or influence. Even if a gift is not intended as a bribe, it may be perceived as one, so salespeople should consider their actions carefully. For example, sending holiday greeting cards to customers is a friendly gesture that should not be misconstrued as a bribe. However, presenting expensive gifts of food, liquor, entertainment, or even cash might very well get both parties into trouble.

Many salespeople have felt pressure to use bribery because competitors do so. If competitors are giving purchasing agents cash kickbacks to buy from them, salespeople might fear that the prospects will not want to do business with them unless they do the same. In such situations, sales managers can do much to encourage ethical behavior by making the organization's standards clear, using rewards for delivering satisfaction as well as sales, and fostering a climate in which customer value is everyone's top priority.

Part of the difficulty in avoiding bribery is that the difference between a friendly gesture and a bribe is unclear and varies from one situation and one country to another. As in other areas of marketing, however, if there are doubts about the ethics of an action, it should be evaluated and discussed with colleagues to determine its ethical standing.

Accuracy of Reports

expense accounts
The listing of a salesperson's work-related expenditures for a given time period.

Organizations generally require their salespeople to complete regular reports that help the organization evaluate the costs and benefits of the salespeople's work. **Expense accounts** report the salesperson's work-related expenditures for a given time period. Such reports include mileage estimates for a salesperson who travels by car, as well as the cost of meals and lodging while traveling. Some salespeople are tempted to "pad" these reports by inflating their expense figures somewhat. They might add in some extra miles spent running personal errands, a meal that was really with friends, not clients, or a slightly larger fare than they actually paid the cab driver. Some salespeople justify these actions on the grounds that the excessive charges are minor or that the practice is common. However, by definition, padding an expense account is dishonest.

call report
A report summarizing the activities of a salesperson for a given time period.

Similarly, **call reports** can be a tempting place to distort the truth. Many organizations require these reports as a means for salespeople to report their activities: the number of prospects called on and the number and amount of sales closed in a particular time period. Some salespeople are tempted to "fudge" these reports by inflating the amount of work they did during the time period. Salespeople who do not keep careful records may make generous estimates because they simply do not remember. Like padding an expense account, fudging a call report is dishonest, whether or not the immediate cost to the organization seems to be great. In fact, the longer-run cost may be a climate of distrust and dishonesty, which tends to result when such practices are common.

Summary

Personal selling involves direct interaction between salesperson and customer—face to face or by telephone. Salespeople inform customers about the organization's products and their benefits, learn about customer wants and needs, and get news from customers about competitors.

There are several basic sales tasks. Order getting involves developing business by seeking out potential customers, providing them with product information, and persuading them to buy. Order taking is the routine completion of sales to customers who have already decided to buy a product. Order delivery consists of the tasks required to get the product to the customer and enable the customer to use it. Support salespeople assist order getters and order takers but do not conduct sales transactions themselves. In team selling, a team of sales professionals works together to sell and service a company's major customers. Many value-driven organizations practice relationship selling, in which salespeople and customers develop long-term, mutually beneficial relationships.

The personal selling process begins with prospecting, or identifying potential customers. Then it moves to preparing a sales call, or learning more about a prospect's wants and needs. Next is the approach, or initial contact with a qualified prospect. Then the salesperson makes a presentation, communicating with prospects about their wants and needs, the product's benefits, and the organization's capabilities for working with the client. At some point, the salesperson may have to handle prospects' objections, or resistance to making a purchase. The next step is the close, or the point at which prospects make a commitment to purchase. Finally, the process is completed with activities used to cement a long-term customer relationship.

Management of the personal selling effort is the job of a sales manager. This job begins with organizing the sales force, typically by dividing responsibilities into geographic, product, or customer sales territories. The sales manager must also ensure that there is a skilled and motivated sales force. The manager may hire independent sales representatives or a full-time sales force. Doing so involves specifying the characteristics of the job and the employee, then identifying and screening candidates for the position. Training new recruits is important in unifying the sales force; it also is expensive for the company, so training efforts must be effective. Ways to motivate the sales force effectively include fair treatment, clear expectations, and fair compensation. Evaluation and control of the sales force can include a comparison of sales to quota, measures of customer satisfaction, and the use of other objective and subjective criteria. Periodic performance reviews offer a chance to discuss performance, objectives, and career goals.

Ethical issues are especially important in personal selling because of the personal interactions and relationships involved. A major area in which ethical issues arise is the temptation to manipulate prospects into buying. The salesperson can do this by providing misleading or inaccurate information. Salespeople sometimes are tempted to use bribery to induce prospects to buy. Such tactics may offer short-term benefits, but they detract from the effort to build a mutually beneficial relationship with customers by creating value for them. Salespeople are sometimes tempted to provide their employer with inaccurate information in expense accounts and activity reports, but such practices are dishonest.

Key Terms and Concepts

order getting (p. 504)
order taking (p. 505)
order delivery (p. 505)
support salespeople (p. 506)
missionary salespeople (p. 506)
technical specialists (p. 506)
team selling (p. 506)
seminar selling (p. 507)
relationship selling (p. 507)
prospecting (p. 509)
cold canvassing (p. 510)
qualifying (p. 510)
preparation (p. 510)

approach (p. 511)
sales presentation (p. 511)
stimulus–response presentation (p. 512)
formula selling presentation (p. 512)
canned presentations (p. 512)
need-satisfaction presentation (p. 512)
telemarketing (p. 513)
objections (p. 513)
closing (p. 514)
follow-up (p. 515)
sales plan (p. 515)
sales management (p. 515)
sales territories (p. 515)

major account management (p. 516)
independent sales representatives
   (p. 516)
network (multilevel) selling (p. 517)
motivation (p. 518)
salary (p. 521)
commission (p. 521)
sales quota (p. 522)
bribery (p. 525)
expense accounts (p. 526)
call reports (p. 526)

Review and Discussion Questions

1. In what ways do salespeople create value for their employers and customers?
2. Name and define the three basic sales tasks.
3. If you were a sales manager for a company that manufactured equipment for office phone systems, how would you use team selling to sell the product? Do you think conference selling or seminar selling would work? Why or why not?
4. As the owner of a small firm that writes and produces direct-mail marketing material for other companies, how would you use relationship selling to build your business?
5. As the owner of a small company that does historic restoration and renovation of commercial and residential buildings, what sources might you use in prospecting?
6. Once you found good potential customers for your renovation business, what steps might you take to prepare and approach them?
7. What type of sales presentation would you give a qualified customer for your renovation business? Why?
8. What qualities must a telemarketer exhibit in order to increase the chances for success?

9. As a salesperson, in what instances might you decide to accept a prospect's objections and not try to close the sale?
10. Why is follow-up an important part of the selling process?
11. In what ways are sales forces usually organized? How does technology affect the organization?
12. If you were a sales manager, what methods would you use to determine whether a potential sales recruit was right for the job?
13. Suppose you are a sales manager for a sales force that has been fighting a sluggish economy and has been plagued by low sales and low morale.
   a. What steps would you take to motivate your sales force?
   b. Suppose your sales force served business clients in Japan and Germany as well as the United States. How would this affect your approach?
14. What are the measures for evaluating and controlling efforts made by the sales force?
15. What ethical issues arise with regard to personal selling?

Chapter Project   Interview a Salesperson

A good salesperson is adept at communication; the best are both good speakers and good listeners. For your chapter project, choose a salesperson whom you know personally or with whom you have had at least a few dealings as a customer (someone who works for a bank, a department store, a car dealership, a real estate office, a hair salon, or the like). Ask the salesperson if you may interview him or her about his or her job. Arrange a meeting time and place, then prepare questions for your interview.

Determine what type of selling the person does—order getting, order taking, order delivery, sales support, or some combination of these. Find out what the person's role is within the organization and how the person builds relationships with customers. Ask what steps the person might take to create value for customers. Also give the person a chance to add any other pertinent comments about the job. Later, write up the interview with any conclusions or observations you wish to make about personal selling, based on your conversation.

Chapter Case Service Professionals Are Selling Too

It used to be that service professionals—doctors, dentists, lawyers, accountants, and so forth—not only avoided selling, they actually disdained it. "Accountants think of salespeople as used-car salesmen," explains Mark Strawser, a business-development director at McGladrey & Pullen, an accounting firm in Davenport, Iowa. "They think of them as guys who would sell you anything, whether you need it or not."

But that view is changing. In an environment that is increasingly competitive, service professionals must find new ways to attract clients and meet their needs. Thus, even the accountants at McGladrey & Pullen are learning how to sell. The difference is that "selling" is not the same old concept it used to be. Instead of prospecting for customers and looking for the immediate close, selling involves helping customers determine their needs and then meeting them, creating value for them in new ways. For instance, at McGladrey & Pullen, business-development director Gary Lindgren and Terry Wisner, an audit partner, team up to make calls on customers together. Wisner helps a customer identify auditing needs and Lindgren, a former stockbroker, helps the same customer determine other ways the firm can help the customer's business grow.

The same change is taking place among law firms. "A decade ago, you would never talk about marketing inside a law firm," notes Deborah Brightman Farone, director of marketing and public relations at the law firm of Debevoise & Plimpton in New York. The fact that her job exists at all speaks volumes. The Boston-based law firm of Mintz, Levin, Cohn, Ferris, Glovsky and Popeo now has a director of practice development who organizes training programs that teach lawyers how to sell their services. Jim Durham, the director, is also director of a subsidiary—The Law Firm Development Group—which conducts similar training on a nationwide basis for other firms.

Sales training for service professionals, by its very nature, must focus on relationship building because the services themselves are based on relationships. "The new sales model applies building trust, identifying needs, presenting solutions, closing, and confirming," explains Julie A. Eichorn, president of Paragon: Professionals Training Professionals, of Austin, Texas. Both Durham's group and Eichorn's group focus on teaching professionals how to showcase the services they can provide that will help business customers grow. "It's not making pitches," Durham notes. Durham conducts seminars on listening, asking for business, networking, cross-selling, responding to requests for proposals, giving presentations, managing client relationships, and communicating.

Slowly but surely, these sales techniques are catching on. Yet the idea of sales and salespeople still bears a stigma; professionals who are involved in sales at service firms are usually called business developers, business consultants, or the like. But they are still engaged in sales; they just have to come to terms with the fact that there is nothing wrong in that.

Questions

1. In what ways might a business developer for a health maintenance organization (HMO) create value for the HMO's customers (both the organizations that are its customers and the patients who use the services)?

2. In what ways can trainers like Jim Durham and Julie Eichorn help diminish the stigma of sales to professionals?

3. In what ways could sales training benefit service professionals who want to enter global markets?

Source: Linda Corman, "Look Who's Selling Now," *Selling*, July/August 1996, pp. 49–52. This copyrighted material is reprinted with permission from *Selling Magazine*, Institutional Investor, Inc., 488 Madison Ave., New York, NY 10022.

Explore more at www.ljx.com/firmmktg/index.html

EVALUATING MARKETING EFFECTIVENESS

SEVEN

'We've got a lousy track record with quality, service and cleanliness relative to our competition,' McDonald's USA President Edward H. Rensi complained during a recent videoconference with the company's restaurant operators. 'We're falling further and further behind.'

Franchisees were told to aim for at least an 88 percent customer satisfaction approval rating next year . . . The company didn't indicate during the conference what the current level of satisfaction is, but a McDonald's spokesman said yesterday that '100 percent customer satisfaction is our top corporate priority.'

Goals include filling orders within 90 seconds, and having no one wait more than 3½ minutes, including the drive-thru line. To monitor performance, company representatives will make surprise visits to restaurants each quarter . . .

Richard Gibson, "McDonald's Resolves to Improve Service, Acknowledging a 'Lousy' Track Record," *The Wall Street Journal,* December 28, 1995, p. A4.

CHAPTER 20

Implementing and Controlling Marketing Activities

Explore the Career Profiles on the Churchill and Peter Homepage at www.irwin.com/marketing/value.

Chapter Twenty

Implementing and Controlling Marketing Activities

CHAPTER OUTLINE

Organizing Marketing Activities
    Organizing Marketing within a Company
    Organizing Marketing across Companies
Implementing Marketing Plans and Strategies
    Staffing Marketing Positions
    Coordinating Marketing Activities
    Communicating Ideas and Information
    Motivating Employees
Controlling Marketing Plans and Strategies
    The Control Process
    Sales Analysis
    Profitability Analysis
    Customer Satisfaction Analysis
    The Marketing Audit
Summary

LEARNING OBJECTIVES

After completing this chapter, you should be able to:

1. Describe the basic ways in which marketing groups can be organized.
2. Summarize techniques for coordinating marketing activities.
3. Explain how marketing managers can motivate their employees.
4. List principles for communicating effectively.
5. Identify the steps in the control process.
6. Explain how marketers evaluate performance in terms of sales, profits, and customer satisfaction.
7. Discuss the use of marketing audits.

Transmedia and Dining a la Card

Lower prices and convenience are the primary values offered to customers by two dining services, Transmedia and Dining a la Card. These two companies have alliances with restaurants (6,500 for Transmedia and 6,000 for Dining a la Card) to give discounts to customers.

Here's how it works. For a fixed annual fee, Transmedia offers a credit card that entitles customers to a 25 percent discount (before tax and tip) on all meals eaten at restaurants in the alliance. When customers receive their monthly bills, the discount is already computed. Dining a la Card customers use their MasterCards or Visas and pay the full price but receive reimbursement checks covering the discounts. Dining a la Card marketers argue that their program offers greater value because no one at the restaurant, including dining companions, knows that the customer is getting a discount.

Both companies "prebuy" meals from member restaurants at a considerable discount. For example, Transmedia usually pays $5,000 for $10,000 worth of meals from a participating restaurant. After giving customers a 25 percent discount, the company still makes the remaining $2,500. Prebuying meals creates value for restaurants by providing them ready cash and guaranteed sales. This is extremely important for new restaurants and also helps them develop a clientele.

Diner discount programs have one major problem: Diners who use them go to restaurants on the same nights that regular customers do. "It would be wonderful if the card holders would go to the restaurants on Mondays, Tuesdays, or Wednesdays," says restaurant consultant Saul Garlick. "The problem is when discount customers

come in on Fridays and Saturdays and take the seat of a customer who would be paying full price." However, if the discounts were only offered on certain nights, customer value and discount sales would decrease.

As you read this chapter, consider how implementing and controlling marketing activities increases customer value and achieves organizational goals. How could Transmedia and Dining a la Card change their strategies to overcome the problem created for restaurants?

Source: Alison Arnett, "Dining at a Discount," *The Boston Globe*, August 21, 1996, pp. D1, D2. Reprinted courtesy of *The Boston Globe*.

Explore more at www.transmediacard.com or www.dalc.com

Chapter Overview

Transmedia and Dining a la Card create value for both restaurants and diners. They do this by offering the service, managing its day-to-day operations, and changing it to improve performance. In general, marketing managers are responsible for assuring that the activities called for in marketing plans are performed appropriately and changed when needed.

This chapter introduces basic issues related to the implementation and control of marketing activities. It begins by explaining ways in which marketing personnel are organized so that strategies can be implemented. Then the chapter describes the staffing, coordination, communication, and motivation needed to make implementation succeed. Once the marketing effort is under way, marketing managers are responsible for seeing that the activities focus on achieving objectives. Thus, the last section of the chapter describes how managers evaluate and control activities.

Organizing Marketing Activities

In order to successfully implement marketing plans and strategies, personnel must be organized appropriately to create value and achieve objectives. Marketing activities must be organized within a company, including relationships with supporting companies such as advertising agencies and marketing research firms. In addition, marketing activities must be organized across companies that are engaged in strategic alliances and other types of joint ventures.

Organizing Marketing within a Company

Marketing activities within a company are carried out by an organization's employees as well as those of support companies such as the advertising agencies and marketing research firms with which they work. Within an organization, marketing activities can be organized in a variety of ways. For example, they can be organized by function, wherein a manager and staff are assigned various functions such as marketing research, sales, and product planning. Marketing activities also can be organized by geographic area in which each territory, region, country or continent has its own marketing group. However, two market-focused ways to organize are by products and by customer types.

Organizing by Product   Companies may organize their marketing activities to focus on particular products. In this way, managers can develop greater knowledge and skills in marketing products to particular customer groups. These positions require the management of various product categories, product lines, products, or brands. How a company organizes by product depends on how many different products and brands it has and how different they are.

Many different titles are used to describe various managers in product-based organizations, including category managers, product managers, and brand managers.[1] In general **category managers** have profit responsibility for all of the brands in a particular product category, such as sliced meat, coffee, or toothpaste. These managers report to the marketing manager or the vice president of marketing. **Product managers** are responsible for particular product lines or products and may report to the marketing manager, group product manager, or category manager. **Brand managers** are usually responsible for a particular brand of a product and may report to any of the other types of managers listed above. The terms product manager and brand manager are often used interchangeably.

Regardless of the titles and assigned responsibilities, managers in these types of organizations have several things in common. First, they typically do not have line authority over other functional areas in marketing or in the company and must use their communication and people skills to get functional managers to work with them. Second, they have their own staff to manage and to assist them in accomplishing the

category manager
The person responsible for the marketing of several brands falling under a particular product category.

product manager
The person responsible for marketing a particular product or product line.

brand manager
The person responsible for marketing a particular brand of a product.

development, implementation, and control of marketing plans and strategies. Third, most of them do not have responsibility for developing new products, but may have authority to offer suggestions for line extensions and product improvements.

A product- or brand-based organization has some advantages. Marketers can become experts in their product and the needs of its target market, and product or brand managers are committed to the success of their particular product or brand. Also, because these managers must handle a variety of responsibilities, the organization develops management talent. However, product or brand managers must compete for the resources of other functional groups, and they may be rewarded for focusing on short-term sales rather than long-term customer satisfaction.

Organizing by Customers   To tackle the competitive pressures generated by new technology and increased global competition, some companies organize their marketing activities on the basis of specific customers, customer types, and industries served. For example, companies selling to large organizational buyers such as government agencies and large channel members such as Wal-Mart or Toys 'R' Us may have marketing teams devoted to serving these specific customers. Other companies may divide the market based on whether customers are organizational or consumer buyers, as well as subgroups among these. Companies serving organizational markets may organize into groups based on the industries served.

Organizing in this way has several advantages. First, employees can become experts in the exact needs and wants of customers and can help develop superior value for them. Second, employees can develop superior knowledge of customer purchase and consumption behavior. Third, this approach helps a company build long-term relationships with its customers.

Organizing Marketing across Companies

Many companies have recognized the value of working with other companies to develop new products and market them throughout the world. To build relationships and profitable projects, companies work together in joint ventures that require coordination of business and marketing activities.

strategic alliances
Long-term partnerships designed to accomplish the strategic goals of both parties.

Strategic Alliances   Working with other companies requires organizing personnel to build strong relationships. To do so, organizations form **strategic alliances,** in which they work jointly to pursue common objectives. For example, in managing Honda and Chrysler's joint effort to market four-wheel-drive Jeeps in Japan, Mitsuru Sato had to get managers from both companies to appreciate each other's problems. In particular, Sato worked hard to convince Chrysler to make quality improvements and to win over Japanese car dealers so that they would give the cars favorable treatment.[2] A survey of fast-growing companies found that 72 percent of the companies with sales of $5 million or more have used strategic alliances with suppliers, and many have formed other kinds of partnerships.[3]

core competencies
The processes and activities that the organization does best and that are central to its success.

In well-planned strategic alliances, each company contributes its **core competencies**—the processes and activities that it does best and that are pivotal to its success. In this way, the alliance gets the best that each member has to offer and can achieve results no single company can match. Genentech's core competency is advanced genetic research, and it forms strategic alliances with firms such as Corning to apply the results of its work.[4] Apple Computer combined its easy-to-use software, but shortage of manufacturing facilities, with Sony Corporation's skills in manufacturing and miniaturization. Sony made 100,000 PowerBook notebook computers for Apple under its strategic alliance.[5]

The differences in marketing from one country to another often make strategic alliances attractive to global marketers. Rather than building expertise and relationships in each target country, marketers find organizations with local expertise and relationships. It arranges for those organizations to handle the marketing functions

The New Pig Corp., is a 10-year-old, 300-employee firm in Tipton, Pennsylvania, that manufactures contained absorbents (see the product with the team in the photo)—sock-like bundles of absorbent materials used to soak up industrial spills. Because New Pig Corp. also sells 3,000 products through the company's catalog, it formed strategic alliances with 30 of its largest volume suppliers. The goal of the alliances was to improve communications and foster continuous improvement and problem solving. In the 18 months after the program was put in place, several joint projects with suppliers led to improved processes and reduced costs; one shipping method change produced savings of hundreds of thousands of dollars.

network organization
An organization of independent business units interacting with one another.

virtual corporation
A network of alliances in which each member shares its expertise in a particular area.

for which their local presence gives them an edge. The use of such global strategic alliances increased 20 to 30 percent during a recent period.[6]

Network and Virtual Organizations   An organization that seeks flexibility and expertise by extensively using strategic alliances may take the form of a **network organization.** As shown in Figure 20.1, the operations of a network organization are carried out by independent business units interacting with one another.[7] Their degree of cooperation may range from simple buying and selling arrangements to strategic alliances. The individual firms in networks often have only a few layers of management. This allows them to be flexible so they can adapt rapidly to changes in customers, competitors, and other environmental forces.

Taking the network organization and its flexibility a step further is a structure called the **virtual corporation,** a network of alliances in which each member shares its expertise in a particular area. In the purest form of a virtual corporation, the member organizations are small and streamlined, contributing only their core competencies. The virtual corporation may form quickly in response to a market need and end when that need disappears.[8]

To move quickly, share risks, save money, and bring together creative people, Paul Farrow set up Walden Paddlers as the core of a virtual corporation. Farrow, Walden's only employee, saw a need for a high-quality kayak designed for beginners and made of recycled plastic. He arranged a manufacturing alliance with Hardigg Industries, a plastics molding business that was seeking to do custom work and had the necessary facilities. He also contracted with Jeff Allott of General Composites, a design firm that wanted to position itself as a specialist in sporting goods, to design the kayak. Until he could create an alliance with a major national distributor, Farrow built relationships with local dealers by supplying each with a demo kayak for 30 days. The dealers quickly sold the first 100 boats produced. Walden Paddlers also relied on the expertise of an outside banker, lawyer, and packaging designer.[9]

Implementing Marketing Plans and Strategies

Whatever way marketing activities are organized, marketing personnel must implement plans and strategies. Marketing organizations with a value orientation continuously look for ways to execute marketing plans and strategies to please customers and achieve goals. For example, a team developing a new product would focus on creating value for

FIGURE 20.1
A Network Organization

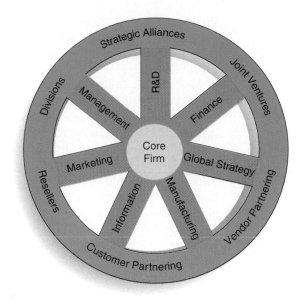

Source: Frederick E. Webster, Jr., "The Changing Role of Marketing in the Corporation," *Journal of Marketing* (October 1992), p. 9. Reprinted with permission of the American Marketing Association.

customers by giving them more benefits and lower prices than expected. Employees involved in physical distribution would try to identify ways to ensure that orders are filled quickly and without errors. Salespeople would focus on providing excellent service so that prospects become repeat customers. Successful implementation depends on staffing, coordinating work, communicating with people inside and outside the organization, and motivating employees.

Staffing Marketing Positions

To implement marketing plans and strategies, organizations need people with a clear understanding of marketing mixes, customers, competitors, and the environment. They should be able to work in teams, use modern technology, and be adaptable enough to meet new customer needs as they arise. Staffing the marketing group includes identifying people with these talents, hiring, and then adequately training them. As an example, when Hawaii's saturated market for art galleries was struggling in a recession, Bill Wyland made a success of his Wyland Galleries Hawaii by staffing it with people knowledgeable about both art and marketing. Wyland provides each employee with ongoing monthly training through an outside firm.[10]

Those responsible for staffing must appreciate that talented marketing people are a diverse lot. Indeed, Workforce 2000, a report by a policy research organization called the Hudson Institute, forecast that 85 percent of the net growth (new hires minus people leaving) in the U.S. labor force during the 1990s would be among women, racial minorities, and immigrants.[11] As the population ages, more retired people take part-time jobs or launch second careers. In addition, an increasing number of people with disabilities are able to participate in the work force, thanks to technological developments that have helped them overcome physical limitations, as well as the institution of the Americans with Disabilities Act, which requires employers to make their workplaces accessible.

Organizations can benefit when their marketing staff and outside marketing experts reflect the diversity of the markets they serve. A diverse workforce brings a variety of insights and strengths that can add creativity to decision making and problem solving. In addition, when marketers are diverse, they can better recognize and interpret the needs of more of the population and tailor the features of the marketing mix to customers.

McDonald's Corporation is noted for its appreciation of the value of a diverse workforce.[12] When the chain of restaurants expanded into cities from its original suburban locales, McDonald's continued its policy that each store should reflect the community in which it operates. McDonald's hires and trains people of every race as well as people with disabilities. Through its McMasters program, the company recruits older people, mostly retirees, to work with young crew members and mold values of caring and courtesy. The company also provides sensitivity training to help its diverse employees work together. When businesses burned in the 1992 Los Angeles riot, no McDonald's restaurant was set afire. Explains Edward H. Rensi, president and CEO of McDonald's U.S.A., "Our businesses [in South Central Los Angeles] are owned by African-American entrepreneurs who hired African-American managers who hired African-American employees who served everybody in the community, whether they be Korean, African-American, or Caucasian." [13]

Coordinating Marketing Activities

Even the most brilliant and hardworking marketing experts need help in carrying out their marketing plans and strategies. Companies large and small need employees or contractors to handle marketing activities—say, designing a logo or distributing goods. In addition, the success of the marketing effort depends on cooperation from nonmarketing personnel. Thus, implementing marketing plans and strategies requires marketing managers to coordinate the work involved by setting priorities, scheduling activities, and building cooperation.

Setting Priorities   Because employees in various departments have different or even conflicting concerns, priorities can be difficult to agree on. For example, production managers can reduce mistakes and increase productivity when the company makes a moderate amount of the same product. However, sales managers can boost earnings by offering a variety of products. Even within marketing departments, there are disagreements over priorities. If the head of marketing research is convinced that spending more on research will enable the company to target its product so well that it can afford to cut back spending on promotion, the head of promotion may object.

Marketing managers can either impose priorities or lead the group in reaching a consensus to resolve conflicts. The latter approach can be more difficult and tends to require more patience, but it is likely to result in greater commitment to the agreed-on priorities. Whether managers set priorities alone or lead others in doing so, the focus should be on doing what is necessary to achieve the objectives of marketing and the organization.

Scheduling   Implementing any marketing plan requires carrying out many activities. To make sure that they are done on time, marketing managers must schedule them or support team efforts at scheduling. Scheduling requires identifying what needs to get done, who will perform each task, how long each task will take, and when it must be completed. For example, a company launching a new service may want the bulk of its advertising to take place around the time the service is to be introduced. If the company advertises too far in advance, people may become discouraged when they can't buy the service and may lose interest by the time it is available.

Scheduling activities is easier when managers use efficient techniques and tools. One such tool is the **Gantt chart,** which lists the activities to be completed and uses horizontal bars to graph how long each is to take. Figure 20.2 shows a sample Gantt chart of the type used by AutoResearch Laboratories Inc. (ALI), a company which conducts tests to measure the performance of petroleum products. By looking at the

Gantt chart
A chart that lists the activities to be performed and uses horizontal bars to graph the time allotted to each.

F I G U R E 20.2
Sample Gantt Chart

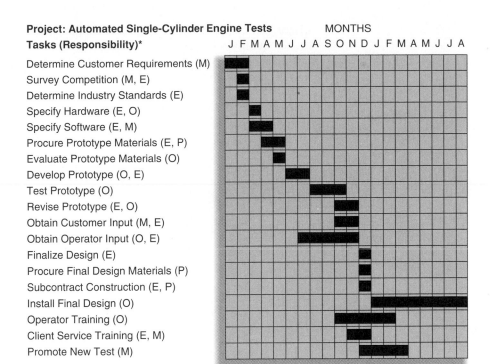

Project: Automated Single-Cylinder Engine Tests

Tasks (Responsibility)*

MONTHS

J F M A M J J A S O N D J F M A M J J A

Determine Customer Requirements (M)
Survey Competition (M, E)
Determine Industry Standards (E)
Specify Hardware (E, O)
Specify Software (E, M)
Procure Prototype Materials (E, P)
Evaluate Prototype Materials (O)
Develop Prototype (O, E)
Test Prototype (O)
Revise Prototype (E, O)
Obtain Customer Input (M, E)
Obtain Operator Input (O, E)
Finalize Design (E)
Procure Final Design Materials (P)
Subcontract Construction (E, P)
Install Final Design (O)
Operator Training (O)
Client Service Training (E, M)
Promote New Test (M)

*M = Marketing; O = Operations; E = Engineering; P = Purchasing

Source: Auto Research Laboratories, Inc.

chart, managers can easily see what needs to be done at any given time. In this example, upgrading a service involves four functional areas—marketing, operations, engineering, and purchasing—so the chart is coded to show which function(s) are responsible for each activity.

Another way to schedule activities is to use the **critical path method (CPM).** To do so, managers create a network with circles representing the tasks that must be completed and arrows between the circles representing the activities required to carry out each task. The time available for tasks is written on the arrows. The sequence of tasks that requires the greatest amount of time is called the critical path. For the project to be completed on time, the manager must make sure that activities along the critical path do not fall behind.

Another resource for scheduling is computer software. Today, a variety of project management programs are available to help with scheduling on a personal computer. These include Superproject for Windows, Project Scheduler 5, and Time Line. Among other uses, these programs allow users to create and update Gantt charts, look at cost-and-time graphs, and schedule multiple projects, allowing for the relative priority of each project.[14]

Building Cooperation   To implement plans and strategies, managers and employees alike need the cooperation of others. In general, people are more likely to cooperate when they understand their role and when they respect the person seeking their cooperation. Thus, a general guideline for building cooperation is to make sure others understand what it is you are trying to do and why. For example, when requesting help from the company's accountant in developing sales and cost records for each product line, a marketer could explain, "This kind of information helps us make sure we are selling only profitable products."

Cooperation also is enhanced when managers are aware of the concerns and goals of employees in different functional areas and understand how marketing activities affect them. For example, for Corning to meet the sales objective of keeping Ford

critical path method (CPM)
A method using a network of circles and arrows to chart the schedule of activities.

Motor Company, one of its biggest customers, the production department had to meet higher quality requirements. This created more work for the production department but turned out to be so successful that Corning had to reopen a previously closed factory to meet demand.[15]

Coordinating Teamwork   Coordination is especially important when marketing activities are done by teams. In organizations that rely on teamwork within and across departmental and organizational lines, success depends on the ability to work cooperatively.

As western regional sales manager for Fila Sports, Pete Davis supervised 15 reps and 6 sales agencies to build a winning record: in three years, sales in his region more than tripled. According to Davis, the secret of his success is his experience with team sports as a basketball player at Michigan State and for the New York Knicks. Sports taught Davis teamwork skills, including the need for preparation, hard work, and follow-through. In an interview Davis explained that his role as a point guard required him to make his teammates better players, to be able to play every position on the floor, and to execute in pressure situations. That is how he sees his role as a sales manager for Fila.

For team members to coordinate their work, they need to understand what they can and should be doing. They need to know the objectives and performance criteria of the team and of the organization. Management and the team leader must work together to ensure that this information is disseminated.

Because team members depend so heavily on one another to achieve their objectives, teams need to evaluate their progress. Team leaders need to make sure that team members are participating in meetings and other work. Signs that team members are working well together are open debate and disagreement on issues coupled with comfort in working toward resolution of the issues.

To develop effective teams, team leaders often act as coaches, rather than as bosses telling team members what to do. When problems arise, team leaders help employees find solutions by asking questions to keep the discussion moving forward, rather than simply issuing directives. Teamwork is most likely to succeed when there are cooperative goals and open discussion of opposing viewpoints.[16] Thus, team leaders should try to keep team members focused on a common objective, such as creating customer value.

Communicating Ideas and Information

To implement and control plans and strategies effectively, marketing managers need to communicate with several groups. First, they must communicate with customers about the benefits of products and services, where purchases can be made and how much the offerings cost. Second, they must communicate with upper management concerning their plans and the budgets they request to implement them. Third, they must communicate with managers and employees in other functional areas and in other companies to coordinate activities and elicit support. Finally, they must communicate with their staff to ensure that tasks are done effectively and plans are implemented on schedule.

To communicate effectively with these groups, marketing managers need several skills (see "Marketing Movers & Shakers: Small Business Counselors"). First, they must be able to speak effectively so that others understand them and can respond. Similarly, they need to write messages that are understandable and can elicit the desired actions. Marketing managers use written communication in preparing marketing plans; company memos, e-mails to suppliers, their staff, and channel members;

Small Business Counselors

Communication is a foundation of marketing. Marketers must communicate with employees and customers, co-workers, and even competitors. Some experts have started their own organizations (both commercial and nonprofit) to help marketers get the most out of communication.

One such counselor is Carol Pietrus, who with her partner, Caryn Amsters, runs a marketing consulting firm based in Wheaton, Illinois, called Marketing Coaches. Marketing Coaches charges corporate clients $90 an hour for their services, but gives a break to entrepreneurs who can take a three-hour seminar for $45. One plumber implemented just two suggestions from a seminar, which brought him a $40,000 annual increase in sales.

Mark King, manager of the enterprise development division of the Chicago Neighborhood Initiative, tells marketers, to "know thyself" and to engage in the fine art of networking—in other words, communicate as part of the marketing effort.

Deborah Hawkins, a Chicago-based corporate training consultant advises, "If you want to meet decisionmakers who aren't in your field, go where they go for their own purposes—business classes, retreats, where you can just get to know them."

All of these counselors rely on good communication skills to help create value for the entrepreneurs and other marketers who come to them for help. In turn, they stress the importance of reaching out and communicating with marketers in other businesses. Kimberly Stansell, a Los Angeles-based small business specialist, publishes a quarterly newsletter, "Bootstrapping Entrepreneur." When she was researching the possibility of starting her own mail-order jewelry business, Stansell turned to the Service Corps of Retired Executives (SCORE) for advice on whether the opportunity made sense. The SCORE director in turn introduced her to the retired head of catalog operations for Sears Roebuck & Co., who was able to give Stansell invaluable advice free of charge. All Stansell had to do was practice good listening skills.

"Think outside the lines," advises Joanne Stone-Geier, who hired a technology assessor to help her determine what technology she would need to market her business, America's Treasures Gallery. Stone-Geier's knowledge lies

in the arts; she needed help figuring out what technology would help her marketing efforts, and she needed someone who could explain things to her in terms she could understand.

All of these marketers understand the importance of communication to their marketing efforts as small business owners. "People like to do business with people they like to work with," notes Deborah Hawkins. And that takes communication.

Source: Joanne Cleaver, "A Springboard to Success," *Crain's Small Business Resource Guide,* May 1996, p. R3.

Explore more by searching "Marketing Small Business" on the Web.

advertising and sales promotions for customers; and other messages to members of various groups.

Second, marketing managers need good listening skills to understand the messages they receive when developing and implementing plans and strategies. Marketing managers must be sure that they understand upper management's reactions and suggestions concerning plans and their results, customer responses to advertising and marketing research questions, and questions and information from other managers, employees, and their own staffs. Failure to understand the meaning of messages can lead to poor strategic planning, implementation, and control.

Third, marketing managers need to understand nonverbal communication cues. Nonverbal communication includes such things as posture, gestures, facial expressions, eye contact, voice tone and inflection, clothing, and distance between speakers

Communication skills are essential to the marketing strategy of Brooks O'Kane of ClearVue Products, Inc., which markets glass cleaner and disinfectants. O'Kane stimulates interest with an attention-getting mailing. He follows up with phone calls in which he listens to prospects' needs and suggests how his company can help. After calling, he demonstrates respect for customers' time with an old-fashioned touch: a prompt thank-you note.

and listeners. All of these can influence the effectiveness of managers in sending and receiving appropriate messages.

Motivating Employees

Through effective communication, marketing managers make sure employees know what they need to do to implement plans and strategies effectively. If they have the proper training and education, the employees also should know how to carry out their tasks. In addition, for implementation to succeed, marketing managers must motivate employees, that is, inspire them to work in appropriate ways.

For example, to attract a loyal and committed workforce, Starbucks Coffee Company offers an exceptionally good employee benefit package. All employees, even those who work part-time, receive health insurance, stock options, training programs, career counseling, and product discounts. Howard Schultz, the chief executive of Starbucks, explains the benefits of this approach: "More than half of our retail sales force is part-time workers. That tells me that the majority of our customers are coming into contact with part-timers. How we treat our people is directly related to how we treat our customers and the quality of our product."[17]

Wal-Mart expects its greeters, positioned near the entrance of each store, to send customers a positive nonverbal message. Here, the open stance, friendly smile, and wave of a greeter named Coeen signal a friendly "Welcome."

To motivate employees, marketing managers should recognize that different people respond to different things at different times. One employee may want to earn a lot of money, whereas another is more interested in professional growth. According to various theories of motivation, some of the incentives that motivate employees are money, security, interesting work, relationships with co-workers, esteem, the opportunity to realize one's potential, and opportunities to be creative or to be promoted. Marketing managers' behaviors also can motivate employees to work hard to implement plans and strategies effectively. Employees are more likely to be motivated when they see that their boss works hard. Marketing managers can also motivate by treating employees with respect and by communicating what is expected of them.

To help motivate employees, organizations offer different rewards. Money, professional growth, security, and opportunities for creative assignments can all be incentives. In this ad, Incentive Partnerships and Western Motivational Incentives Group offer employers incentive programs in which employees are rewarded with gift certificates from more than 3,700 retail stores, including Foot Locker, Kinney Shoes, and Lady Footlocker.

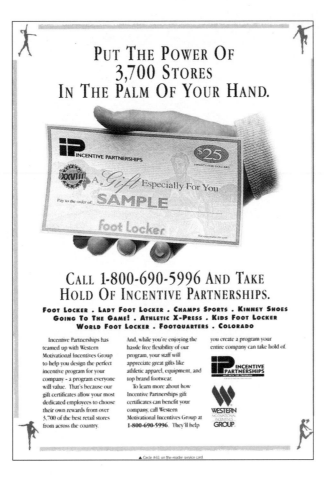

One study of work teams found that many were not as effective as desired because compensation and rewards were based solely on individual, rather than group, performance.[18] To motivate employees to work as a team, marketing managers could offer rewards for group achievements, not just for individual accomplishments. A **group incentive system** is a compensation method based on paying a bonus to members of a group that achieves specified objectives. Thus, after a team launches a new product on time and under budget, each team member might receive a bonus representing a share of the first year's profits generated by the new product.

group incentive system
A compensation method based on paying a bonus to members of a group that achieves specified objectives.

Controlling Marketing Plans and Strategies

After plans and strategies are implemented, marketing managers need to know whether they are obtaining the expected results (see "You Decide: Can Businesses Control the Direction of Technology?"). The Danish Pharmaceutical Association, a network of 300 privately owned pharmacies, devised a strategy to reposition Danish pharmacies as a comprehensive source of healthcare information and services, rather than just a place to buy drugs and related goods. To implement this strategy, the pharmacies expanded their product mix, started an antitobacco campaign that included stop-smoking classes and sale of anti-smoking chewing gum, and developed packages of healthcare supplies for patients discharged from hospitals. Unfortunately, other healthcare providers thought many of the tactics infringed on their businesses, brought pressure on the pharmaceutical association, and forced it to change course.[19]

When a marketing strategy does not perform as expected, marketers need to find out the reasons why and make changes to bring performance and objectives into line. The process of evaluating performance against objectives, plans, and strategies and making changes is called **control.**

control
The process of evaluating performance against objectives, plans, and strategies and making changes when and where needed.

Can Businesses Control the Direction of Technology?

Smart cards—cards that look like credit cards but allow all kinds of other services, such as debit, electronic transfer of funds or benefits, and so forth—are making an impact on business. Industries ranging from food retailing to banking to human resources are banding together to figure out how to apply the technology of smart cards to create value and increase profits. The Smart Card Forum, based in Tampa, Florida, examines applications and control measures involved with the use of smart cards. Its members include banks, government agencies, technology vendors, card issuers, processors, and a few retailers. The Forum's new Retail Work Group, which charges companies a hefty $15,000 to join as voting members, meets regularly to try to determine the future of the new technology.

Each member has something to gain from smart card applications, and wants to make certain it can cash in. Don Friddle, manager of corporate cash resources for Marsh Supermarkets of Indiana notes, "It looks like we're going to be impacted fairly quickly. There are a lot of questions to be answered yet." This is especially true in the case of retrofitting supermarket store equipment to accept smart cards without foul-ups.

Friddle and colleague Joy Nicholas, pricing manager at Ralphs Grocery Co. in California, are interested in smart card technology for frequent shopper programs. "That's why I'm [in the group]—to watch the trends and applications that are being discussed and try to provide our industry with updates on the timetables for smart card launches within the retail environment. It's my role representing FMI to keep tabs on those pilots so that if there is anything that is getting ready to explode, we are aware of it and can participate in the direction it takes."

Each industry—and individual business—that uses new technology such as smart cards must be prepared to take advantage of opportunities, but must also be able to put controlling measures in place. If supermarket customers don't like using the new cards, for instance, then value is not created for either the store or its customers. Do you think that interest groups such as the Smart Card Forum and its Retail Work Group can effectively shape the direction of technology applications? Why or why not? If so, how?

Source: Christine Dugas, "Heavy Hitters Join Smart-Card Effort," *USA Today*, December 5, 1996, p. 1B; George Graham, "Electronic Money," *The Financial Times*, November 25, 1996, p. 12; Jane Bryant Quinn, "The Uncertain Value of 'Smart Cards,'" *The Washington Post*, November 24, 1996, p. H2; Denise Zimmerman, "Retailers Are on Deck to Set Smart Card Pilot Programs," *Supermarket News*, April 22, 1996, pp. 25, 33.

Explore more by searching "Smart Cards" on the Web.

The Control Process

Controlling involves several steps, shown in Figure 20.3. First, marketing managers measure the results obtained from implementation. Then, they compare the results with the objectives that have been set in the marketing plan. Finally, when performance is close to or superior to the objectives, managers evaluate whether performance could be improved. When performance is significantly below the objectives, managers should evaluate whether the objectives were too lofty, whether the strategy was poor, whether the strategy was good but poorly implemented, or some combination of these. In any case, when problems arise, corrective actions should be taken.

As a case in point, Michael Hough saw the need for corrective action when attendance plummeted at the trade shows hosted by his Exton, Pennsylvania, company, A/E/C Systems International. Revenues had plunged by half, so Hough decided to make his marketing communications more efficient through better use of information technology. Hough developed a database of 50,000 current and potential clients that could be sorted on up to 39 criteria, such as type of organization and trade shows previously attended. The database enabled Hough to target his promotional mailings so precisely that they generated more business than ever before at a much lower cost. Seeing the benefits, Hough continued to refine and use his database. The targeted communications created value for prospects by providing trade show information likely to interest them.[20]

The types of action to take in response to performance below objectives depends on the type of problem causing it. The basic causes of unacceptable performance are problems with objectives, with plans, with the way plans were implemented, or some combination of these.[21] Objectives may be unrealistic or changes in the environment may make previously good objectives become unrealistic. In such situations, managers need to review and modify the objectives. Problems with plans arise when they were not well thought out or changes in the environment require changes in them.

Problems with how plans were implemented arise for several reasons. Perhaps not enough resources were used, or employees didn't understand what they were sup-

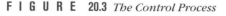

FIGURE 20.3 *The Control Process*

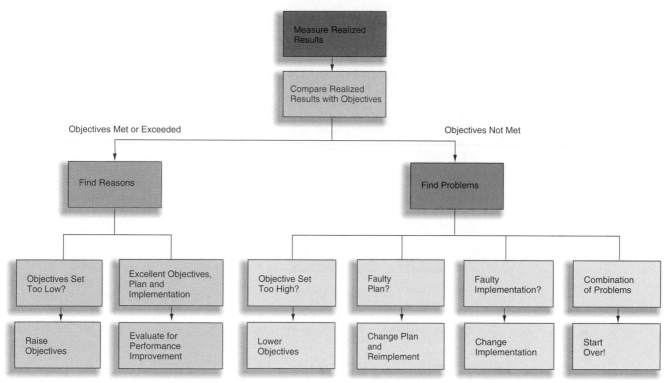

posed to do or didn't put forth enough effort. A problem at Enrich International stemmed from poor communication between the product development and order-processing departments. The company told its distributors about new products, but forgot to tell order processors about them. When orders for the new products came pouring in, the order takers were annoyed and confused.[22]

When performance suffers from problems with implementation, these problems must be solved quickly. For Enrich International, this included creating a communications team with members from both departments. The team prepared a schedule of new product rollouts and became a forum for ideas on how order processors could promote other products when they handled calls.

When there are problems with both plans and their implementation, managers must start the planning process from the beginning. At Sears, Roebuck and Company, for example, management responded to declining sales and profits by changing a number of things, including closing many stores, redefining its target market to women with families rather than men, returning more decision-making power to store managers, increasing the share of the business devoted to apparel, and abandoning the attempt to use every-day low pricing.[23] These changes resulted in a remarkable turn-around for the company.

The need to start over with a fresh strategy should be rare, especially in organizations that focus on customer value. Such organizations should be making continuous improvements, rather than waiting for major problems to occur. With input from customers, employees, and others, marketing managers should be continually fine-tuning their plans and strategies and the process of implementing them. Control should not happen only after implementation is completed. Instead, objectives, plans, strategies and implementation should be improved continually.

Much of marketing control focuses on analyzing financial results—that is, the money spent and generated by marketing. If marketing expenditures bring about-

To ensure that it is creating value for its customers, Caterpillar's Building Construction Products Division continually seeks feedback from them. By asking contractors about such matters as product advancements, operating environment, service support, and parts availability, Caterpillar can adapt its equipment and services to customer needs. By applying information obtained from customers, Caterpillar has made its equipment easier to use and more versatile.

desired financial results, they are often considered effective. Financial results are evaluated by doing sales and profitability analyses. However, financial analysis is not the only way to evaluate marketing efforts; customer satisfaction is also a goal of marketing.

Sales Analysis

One method for evaluating the effectiveness of a plan and its implementation is to conduct **sales analysis.** This type of analysis consists of "gathering, classifying, comparing and studying company sales data."[24] The analysis can begin by looking at total revenues, such as shown in Table 20.1. The table shows that sales increased from 1995 to 1996, then declined in the following year. In addition, realized sales were greater than forecasted sales for the first two years, but below forecast for the third year. This suggests a need to analyze carefully changes in the environment, objectives, plans, and strategies, and their implementation to understand the reasons for the short fall in the third year.

Sales analysis requires planning the kinds of information marketing managers will use in the control process. This information should include records of what goods were sold and what services were performed. The records also should include any other information needed to classify sales data, such as price and place of purchase. At most organizations, this information will be computerized so that marketing managers and others can retrieve and analyze it as needed.

After the organization has a system for gathering relevant sales information, marketers can classify, compare, and study it. Marketers break sales down in a variety of useful ways:

- By product, package size, model, grade, or color.
- By customer type.
- By geographic region.
- By price or type of discount.
- By method of sale, such as store sales or mail order.
- By method of payment, such as cash or charge.
- By size of order.
- By salespeople.
- By reason for purchase.

sales analysis
Gathering, classifying, comparing, and studying company sales data.

T A B L E   20.1
Sample Information for Sales Analysis

	1995	1996	1997
Forecasted sales	$65,000	$80,000	$90,000
Actual sales	66,200	87,100	81,000
Difference	$ 1,200	$ 7,100	($ 9,000)

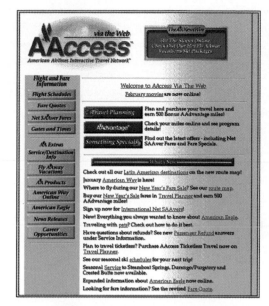

American Airlines gathers sales data by destination and uses that information to sell on the Internet. Each week, American analyzes the sales data and identifies which flight destinations have too few passengers. Then it sends e-mail offering subscribers to its Net SAAver program low fares to those destinations. Travelers subscribe to the Net SAAver at American's Web site (http://www.americanair.com) by clicking on the "Something Specials" key (right). In this way, American uses sales data to sell more seats without lowering regular fares.

Each of these classifications can be used to help understand markets and strategies. For example, by classifying sales according to customer type, catalog retailer Talbots learned that sales of its children's clothing were growing at around a 15 percent rate in a recent year, faster than its companywide sales increase of 9 percent.[25] This suggests that the children's clothing line should be expanded.

Classifying sales helps marketers identify problems to solve or opportunities to explore. For example, total sales at the Northshore men's clothing store in Rumson, New Jersey, were down, but an analysis of sales by product indicated that rugby jerseys bearing the letters and colors of various colleges were selling well. So the store's owner, Brian George, created new products branded Varsity Raggs. The products bearing this name include school blankets, towels, varsity jackets, sweaters, and caps, sold mostly through colleges. These products were responsible for increases in sales and profits at George's company.[26]

Measurement of Sales   There are several ways to measure sales, each of which provides only a partial picture of the organization's performance. The most common measures of sales are unit volume, dollar volume, and market share.

To determine unit volume, marketers total up the number of goods or units of service that have been sold. Following the launch of SnackWell's Devil's Food Cookie Cakes, for example, the company reported consumers were buying more than one million cookie cakes a day.[27] Unit volume is useful for identifying the organization's most popular products and for measuring overall demand for each. When unit volume is increasing, marketers often conclude that their strategies are effective, although this may not be true. For example, unit volume could be increasing but the market could be growing at a faster rate.

Total unit-volume measures alone cannot indicate whether the organization is making a profit or growing as fast as its competitors. If costs are too high or the price too low, the organization can sell a lot of products and actually be losing money. If competitors are growing faster than the organization, it may be losing market share even while unit sales increase.

Another way to measure sales is to calculate dollar volume, or total sales in dollars. Michael Hough at A/E/C Systems International concluded that the targeted mailings for his trade shows were working well because dollar volume rose from $230,000 to $300,000 in the first year after implementing this strategy. A few years later, dollar volume had doubled and was still climbing.[28] To find total dollar volume, marketers multiply unit volume by the revenue received for each unit.

Whereas unit volume indicates the number of products sold, dollar volume takes into account different revenues received for products. For example, the number of wills prepared at a family law practice might be much greater than the number of

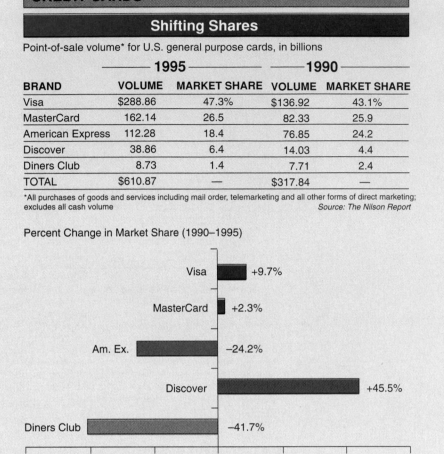

CREDIT CARDS

Shifting Shares

Point-of-sale volume* for U.S. general purpose cards, in billions

	1995		1990	
BRAND	VOLUME	MARKET SHARE	VOLUME	MARKET SHARE
Visa	$288.86	47.3%	$136.92	43.1%
MasterCard	162.14	26.5	82.33	25.9
American Express	112.28	18.4	76.85	24.2
Discover	38.86	6.4	14.03	4.4
Diners Club	8.73	1.4	7.71	2.4
TOTAL	$610.87	—	$317.84	—

*All purchases of goods and services including mail order, telemarketing and all other forms of direct marketing; excludes all cash volume

Source: The Nilson Report

Percent Change in Market Share (1990–1995)

Visa +9.7%
MasterCard +2.3%
Am. Ex. −24.2%
Discover +45.5%
Diners Club −41.7%

−60 −40 −20 0 20 40 60

Source: Adapted from Laurie Hays, "American Express Sizes Up Rivals, Turns Green," *The Wall Street Journal*, May 3, 1996, pp. B1, B2. Reprinted by permission of *The Wall Street Journal*. © 1996 Dow Jones & Company, Inc. All rights reserved worldwide.

divorce cases negotiated. However, the dollar volume of handling divorces is usually higher because they generate greater revenue individually.

Marketers can also measure sales volume in terms of market share. To compute market share, total sales of the company's product is divided by the total sales of the product by all competitors. As an illustration, the upper part of Figure 20.4 shows the market share for five brands of general-purpose credit cards. Market share figures show how well a product is selling relative to competitors.

Organizations can evaluate changes in market share over time for its products and services or compare market shares with that of competitors to help control their strategies. The decline in market share for the American Express card relative to bank credit cards shown in the lower part of Figure 20.4 indicated to American Express Company that it needed new ways to build customer relationships. One way would be to build strategic alliances with the banks.[29]

Controlling with Sales Data   To use sales data in the control function, marketing managers compare sales results with sales objectives or forecasts. If managers want to see if salespeople have met their quotas, for instance, data can be broken down by

TABLE 20.2
Sample Information for
Profitability Analysis

	1995	1996	1997
Revenues	$66,200	$87,100	$81,000
Costs	60,900	81,000	74,500
Profit	$ 5,300	$ 6,100	$ 6,500
Profit margin	8.0%	7.0%	8.0%

salesperson. If sales objectives are set for products or geographic regions, sales figures can be broken down by these criteria.

Marketing managers compare the realized sales with sales objectives to identify areas for corrective action. In evaluating salespeople, members of the sales force will have earned rewards for meeting their quota. Sales by product might show that the reason an organization has exceeded its total sales target is that one product performed much better than expected. With demand for SnackWell's Devil's Food Cookie Cakes greater than supply, Nabisco had to consider new strategies such as investing in more factories to make the cookie cakes or communicating with consumers to persuade them to try other kinds of SnackWell's cookies.

Profitability Analysis

The best economic measure of a company's or strategy's success is its profitability—how great the difference is between sales revenues and the costs to produce them. For controlling purposes in marketing, it is useful to calculate profitability by customer groups. For example, marketing managers at General Mills might compare the profitability of a new cereal brand with that of Cheerios, or managers at Humana might compare the profitability of hospitals located in different regions of the United States.

A useful measure of profitability is profit margin, which is calculated by dividing profits (revenues minus expenses) by revenues. For example, in Table 20.2 the profit margins for each of the three years are 8.0% ($5300 ÷ $66200), 7.0% ($6100 ÷ $87100) and 8.0% ($6500 ÷ $81000).

Profit margins that are growing or are greater than competitors' are usually a sign of financial health and marketing efficiency and effectiveness. Starbucks Coffee originally sold only coffee beans. Adding brewed coffee boosted profit margins by 5 percent, confirming that this was a profitable direction in which to expand.[30]

Just as they do when analyzing sales, marketing managers often break down profit margins in various ways, such as by product or by customer. They use this information to decide which products or target markets should receive more selling effort. Managers can use profit margins to adjust marketing mixes—say, to raise the price of products with low profit margins or increase distribution of products with high profit margins. U.S. machine tool makers had problems when they sold products to Toyota's auto plant in Georgetown, Kentucky. Because they had not carefully estimated their profit margins, they quoted prices that were below their costs.[31]

To assess profitability, organizations must know their costs. To do so, managers conduct a **cost analysis.** This involves identifying levels and types of costs and how they have changed over time. One way to increase profitability is to reduce costs. Cost reduction has been a major objective of U.S. firms in recent years to make them more competitive in the global market.

An increasing number of U.S. organizations—including Motorola, Harley-Davidson, Dell Computer, Coca-Cola Company, and the Internal Revenue Service—

cost analysis
The identification of levels and types of costs and how they have changed over time.

Give Feedback as a Customer

Feedback from customers is a valuable way to measure the performance of marketing activities. Give your own feedback as a customer to an organization from which you have purchased goods or services recently. In preparing to deliver the feedback, write down the things you especially liked and disliked about the product and service you received. If there is a hotline on the package of a product you have bought, call it. If there is an address for the customer service department of a catalog from which you bought an item, write a letter or send an e-mail. If you have received a survey in the mail or if someone calls you and asks you to participate in a phone survey, complete it. If there is an opportunity to give feedback to a healthcare professional, attorney, or hair-cutting salon, do it. Remember to use good communication skills as you present your feedback.

activity-based costing
The process of itemizing all costs associated with producing and marketing specific products in particular markets.

have adopted a fresh approach to analyzing costs. Called **activity-based costing,** this accounting approach itemizes all costs associated with producing and marketing specific products in particular markets. Activity-based costing can help managers see which products are profitable and can suggest areas where reducing costs can have the most impact. For example, consider a company that makes toothpaste and sells it to Wal-Mart and Kmart for $2.50 a tube. Suppose that Wal-Mart wants certain things done in terms of packaging and shipping that bring the manufacturer's total cost to $2.20, compared to only $1.60 for selling to Kmart.[32] The marketing manager can see how much more profitable it is to sell to Kmart and can check to see if it is profitable enough to sell to Wal-Mart.

Although relatively new in the United States, most Japanese corporations have been using a form of activity-based costing for decades. Japanese employees are made aware of their contribution to product costs, so they can try to keep their costs down. This approach fits well with the Japanese use of cross-functional teams, which work together to develop new products so that they can·be made and sold for a "target cost." In contrast, the typical American approach has been to design products, see how much they will cost, and proceed only if costs are low enough to generate acceptable profits.

Customer Satisfaction Analysis

At value-driven organizations, customer satisfaction is an important control measure. Marketing managers must determine how customers perceive products and the value of their exchanges (see "Put It into Practice: Give Feedback as a Customer").

While customer satisfaction is not the easiest outcome to measure, managers should continuously improve methods for receiving feedback from customers. For example, all employees could be trained to encourage, observe, and report feedback from customers.

One way to assess customer satisfaction is to develop systems to gather customer responses. For example, packaging may display a toll-free customer hotline. Publishers of computer software often include in their manuals a toll-free number for help. Marketers offer comment cards for customers to praise or complain about products and services in stores and inside packaged goods. Such methods are useful for identifying exceptionally good or poor performance, since they tend to generate feedback from customers who have strong feelings about product and services. Moreover, computerized information systems can collect and sort data about customer responses. At Yamaha Corporation of America, a telephone system linked to computers gathers data about who is calling, what product is involved, and how long the company takes to

The brand in the home furnishings trade that consumers value most is Rubbermaid, according to a recent survey published in their annual report. In the survey, consumers stated that "the one brand they know and trusted most was also the one they would buy." In the picture Japanese consumers provide product design feedback, a vital ingredient in customer satisfaction and basic for building brand value in Japan.

respond. Such data help Yamaha identify and resolve problems related to particular products or processes.[33]

To get a better perspective on customer satisfaction, marketers may conduct other research. A survey of current customers can provide information about their experience with the organization and its products and services. Surveys ask customers about buying and using products, as well as whether the customer intends to buy again or to recommend products to their friends. The New York public relations agency Makovsky & Company uses regular client surveys that include a question that gets right to the heart of customer value: "Are we giving you your money's worth?"[34] A survey that includes people who do not buy from the company can uncover past mistakes or problems with the company's image.

The organization may also measure customer satisfaction by checking the results of independent surveys. For example, some automobile companies and airlines use the results of customer satisfaction surveys by J. D. Power & Associates to compare their performance against that of competitors.

Marketers can use customer satisfaction information in two ways. First, they can use it to improve products and customer service. PR firm Makovsky & Company has improved client retention rates by holding monthly meetings in which teams and senior management discuss the results of client surveys. The teams decide how to resolve any problems they uncover, then report their progress three months later.[35]

Second, customer satisfaction information can be used to motivate employees. A company that is serious about creating value should have ways of rewarding employees who satisfy customers. For example, after years of losing money, Continental Airlines wanted to assure that air travelers would receive top-notch service. It began paying monthly bonuses each time the company ranked near the top of the Department of Transportation's ratings for on-time arrivals. Not only did employees soon move Continental's rating to first place, but business passengers who had deserted the airline began to return.[36]

Customer feedback about their satisfaction also provides an opportunity for the organization to communicate with its customers. For example, customers are more likely to be understanding about a delay or a price increase if someone from the organization explains the reason for it. In fact, if organizations take the initiative to keep customers informed, customers may actually be more satisfied with the organization than before, even if the news is bad. *Inc.* magazine's senior writer John Case forgave software publisher Intuit for putting him on hold, because the recorded message apologized and explained what the company was doing to correct the problem.[37]

The Marketing Audit

marketing audits
In-depth, systematic reviews of an organization's strategic business unit's environments, objectives, plans, strategies, activities, and personnel of concern to marketing.

To evaluate and control the marketing activities of an organization, **marketing audits** are conducted periodically. These are in-depth, systematic reviews of an organization's or strategic business unit's environments, objectives, plans, strategies, activities, and personnel of concern to marketing. Marketing audits are the most thorough approach to evaluating the marketing efforts of an organization. They may be conducted by outside consultants or by auditor teams composed of personnel from within organizations.

To begin, marketing auditors determine what kinds of information to gather and how to gather it. Table 20.3 lists some questions to start developing the required information. Overall, information should be collected to evaluate whether the right

T A B L E 20.3
Some Questions to Include in Marketing Audits

Products: The Reason for Existence
1. What is the overall demand for each product and how is it changing?
2. Is the product mix free from deadwood?
3. What is the life-cycle stage of various products?
4. How will user demands or trends affect products?
5. Is the company a leader in new product innovation?
6. Are inexpensive methods used to estimate new product potentials before considerable amounts are spent on R&D and market introduction?
7. Are there different quality levels for different markets?
8. Are packages/brochures effective tools for selling?
9. Are products in the most appealing colors (formats) for markets being served?
10. Are there additional product features or benefits to exploit?
11. Is the level of customer service adequate?
12. How are quality and reliability viewed by customers?
13. What is the mix of new and old products?

Markets: Where Products Are Sold
1. Have major markets been identified and measured?
2. Are small, potential market segments overlooked in trying to satisfy the majority?
3. Are markets for products expanding or declining?
4. Should different segments be developed; are there gaps in penetration?

Customer: User Profiles
1. Who are the current and potential customers?
2. Are there geographic influences on purchase and aspects of use: regional, rural, urban?
3. Why do people buy the product; what motivates their preferences?
4. Who makes buying decisions; when, where?
5. What are the frequency and quantity of purchases and use?

T A B L E   20.3
Continued

Competitors: Their Influence

1. Who are the principal competitors, how are they positioned, and where are they headed?
2. What are their market shares?
3. What features of competitors' products stand out?
4. Is the market easily entered or dominated?

Distribution Channels: Selling Paths

1. Does the distribution system offer the best access to target markets?
2. Do products require special handling?
3. What is the most profitable type of channel?
4. What are the trends in distribution methods?
5. Are intermediaries making sufficient profits from the line?

Sales Administration: Selling Efficiency

1. Are markets getting coverage in proportion to their potential?
2. Are sales costs planned and controlled?
3. Does the compensation plan provide enough incentive for its cost?
4. Is performance measured against potential?
5. Are selling expenses proportionate to results and potentials within markets or territories?
6. Are there deficiencies in recruitment, selection, training, motivation, supervision, performance, promotion, or compensation?
7. Are effective selling aids and sales tools provided?
8. Is personal selling integrated in the communication mix?

Pricing: Profitability Planning

1. What are the objectives of current pricing strategies: acquiring, defending, or expanding market share?
2. Are pricing strategies designed to produce volume or profit?
3. How do prices compare with competition with similar levels of quality?
4. Does cost information show profitability of each item?
5. What is the history of price deals, discounts, and promotions?

Advertising: Overall Program

1. What are the objectives of the advertising program?
2. Are advertising objectives and strategies linked to the marketing plan?
3. How is advertising effectiveness measured?
4. Is advertising integrated with personal selling, sales promotion, and publicity?
5. Is the ad agency's effectiveness periodically evaluated?
6. Are copy theme and content dictated to the agency?
7. Is advertising spending realistic?

Sales Promotion: Sales Inducement

1. Does sales promotion support marketing objectives?
2. Is it integrated with advertising, publicity, and personal selling?
3. How is sales promotion effectiveness measured?
4. Are slogans, trademarks, logos, and brands being used effectively?
5. Is point-of-sale material cost effective?

Source: Adapted from Hal W. Goetsch, "Conduct a Comprehensive Marketing Audit to Improve Marketing Planning," *Marketing News,* March 18, 1983, p. 14. Reprinted with permission of the American Marketing Association.

marketing activities are done and whether they are done right. Marketing audits also evaluate how well marketing activities are organized in the company.

In addition to collecting information from company records, auditors also interview marketing personnel, other executives, managers and employees, suppliers, channel members, and customers. Information collected from them includes both factual data and opinions about products, marketing strategies, and activities.

A complete marketing audit requires considerable time, effort, and resources so it is usually not part of the day-to-day control process. Rather, audits should be done periodically—say, every three to five years—to supplement normal control activities such as sales, profitability, and customer satisfaction analyses. Audits are useful for control purposes because they offer management an overall evaluation of marketing efforts and can spot problems and opportunities that are not apparent in less comprehensive evaluations.

Summary

Marketing activities should be structured to achieve the organization's objectives. Alternatives for organizing marketing activities within a company include functional, geographic, product and customer-based methods. Organizing marketing across companies in joint ventures include strategic alliances, networks, and virtual organizations.

Marketing managers implement plans and strategies by staffing positions, coordinating activities, communicating ideas and information, and motivating employees. Staffing decisions should take into account the opportunities provided by an increasingly diverse and global workforce. Coordination involves setting priorities, scheduling activities, building cooperation, and coordinating teamwork. Effective communi-

cation includes good speaking, writing, and listening skills, as well as the ability to send and receive nonverbal cues. Marketing managers need to motivate employees and teams, that is, inspire them to work in appropriate ways.

The process of measuring, evaluating and changing objectives, plans, and strategies as needed is called control. In the control process, marketing managers measure results, compare them with objectives, and take appropriate actions to align results with objectives. Financial results are evaluated by doing sales and profitability analyses, but customer satisfaction also should be assessed. To evaluate and control the overall marketing activities of an organization, marketing audits are conducted periodically.

Key Terms and Concepts

category manager (p. 534)
product manager (p. 534)
brand manager (p. 534)
strategic alliances (p. 535)
core competencies (p. 535)

network organizations (p. 536)
virtual corporation (p. 537)
Gantt chart (p. 538)
critical path method (CPM) (p. 538)
group incentive system (p. 543)

control (p. 543)
sales analysis (p. 546)
cost analysis (p. 549)
activity-based costing (p. 550)
marketing audits (p. 552)

Review and Discussion Questions

1. Which organization method would you choose for each of the following?
   a. a company that sells only fine jewelry to wealthy customers
   b. a manufacturer of appliances with operations in the United States, Europe, and China
   c. a large organization with many different brands of grocery products
2. What are the advantages of organizing by customer?
3. If you were hired as a marketing manager by a mid-sized

recording company that produced country music, folk, and pop vocals, as well as sheet music for some of its recordings, which method of marketing organization would you prefer? Why?
   a. In what ways might you use a diverse marketing staff to create value for channel members who are customers for your recording company?
   b. As you coordinate the marketing plan for one of your new artists at the recording company, how would you go about setting priorities, scheduling activities, and

building cooperation? Would you use the Gantt chart, critical path method, and/or computer software in your scheduling?

4. One list of good listening skills includes the following items (Samuel C. Certo, *Supervision* (Burr Ridge, Ill.: Austen Press, 1994), p. 160):

   a. Remove distractions, and give the speaker your full attention.
   b. Look at the speaker most of the time.
   c. When the speaker hesitates, give a sign of encouragement such as a smile or nod.
   d. Try to hear the main point and supporting points.
   e. Distinguish between opinions and facts.
   f. Control your emotions.
   g. Be patient; don't interrupt.
   h. Take notes.
   i. At appropriate times, ask questions to clarify your understanding.
   j. Restate what you think the speaker's point is, and ask if you heard it correctly.

   Use this list to assess your own listening skills. Which points are your strengths? Which are weaknesses? Be honest. What steps might you take to strengthen your listening skills?

5. A toy company makes inflatable balls with handles. Children play with the balls by sitting on them, holding the handle, and jumping up and down. The instruction sheet that comes with this product contains the following warning:

   > Warning: Do not over inflate. Service station line pressure varies. Over inflation and rapid deflation (explosion) can result. Do not exceed maximum shown above [in a table of acceptable pressures].

   a. What does this message mean?
   b. Is the wording of such information a proper area of concern for marketing managers? Why or why not?

6. Suppose you were assigned to manage a product development effort in a country whose culture valued group harmony over individual achievement. In this culture, being singled out for public praise is considered an embarrassment. How would you motivate this group of employees? In particular, how would you reward good performance?

7. If you found that the performance of a particular marketing effort fell significantly below the objectives of the marketing plan, how would you determine the cause(s) of the problem?

8. What is sales analysis? In what ways can marketers break sales down to get useful information?

9. What are marketing audits? Why should these be conducted periodically?

Chapter Project Measuring Customer Satisfaction

An important indication of the success of marketing activities is customer satisfaction, particularly at value-driven organizations.

Imagine that you are a marketing manager for a mail-order company that has recently launched a separate catalog for a new line of products. The products are designed to help people create storage space in apartments or small houses and include items like baskets, expandable shelves, recycling bins, cabinet and closet organizers, racks that hold bicycles and canoes, and so on. Create a plan for measuring customer satisfaction. Include methods for gathering information from consumers, detailing the questions you would ask. Include the ways employees should handle feedback from customers. Describe how you plan to use the feedback to create value for customers so they become loyal and increase the company's profitability.

Chapter Case Marmot Mountain

Marmot Mountain was founded in Colorado by Eric Reynolds, who, along with some mountain climbing friends, wanted nearly indestructible outerwear and sleeping bags for their expeditions. As they started production, they chose to emphasize quality. "We were fanatically dedicated to high performance and craftsmanship, and we found that there was a market for our single-minded zeal," recalls Reynolds. Each piece of each item was slowly, carefully crafted. Marmot's reputation as a company that produced only first-rate goods grew rapidly. "Marmot products were always considered the sine qua non of outdoor equipment," notes Peter Benjamin, a former executive with a competitor.

Producing only top-quality merchandise began to weigh Marmot down, however, and caused the company to fail to serve channel members. "Stories abound of the company's not delivering product because the highest-quality [goose]down couldn't be found, or of products being seconded because of two or three stitching errors," notes John Cooley, now vice president of marketing for the company. "The bottom line truly suffered." Communication between Marmot Mountain and retailers suffered as well, as there were no Marmot products in the stores. One year, Marmot delivered its fall line of outerwear—due before Labor Day—the following January. "We represented a serious financial incident for retailers," admitted Cooley.

Consumers did not give up on Marmot, which is what kept the company alive. "Having poor availability can be an advantage: it enhances the mystique that your product is hard to get," explains Steve Hitchcock, now vice president of sales. The mystique seemed to enhance the products' value.

Still, a turnaround was clearly necessary if the company was to survive. After Reynolds' departure and a series of buyouts, Steve Crisafulli took charge. He was horrified by the lack of efficiency in both production and marketing. "It was the single, least-efficient manufacturing facility I have seen in my life," he recalls. "The cost of labor and manufacturing of sleeping bags was higher than the selling price." So he began a series of major steps to turn Marmot Mountain around. He moved the company to California and addressed the problem of delivery head on. "Credibility in the outdoor industry turns on timely delivery," he explains. His strategy for improving delivery was simple: "The way to run a small business is to concentrate on one or two small things . . . Anything that negatively impacts delivery has to wait."

Deadlines were established. Managers were forced to communicate with one another as well as with channel members. Ten-minute meetings were conducted daily in which managers had to identify and head off conflicts that might affect scheduling. The daily meetings helped managers monitor progress on a continuous basis. Outside company headquarters, commissioned sales reps were forbidden to open new accounts for a year and a half until existing accounts could be serviced regularly. Advertising and promotion budgets were slimmed down and the money diverted to production.

Things improved so dramatically that Marmot began to deliver products to retailers early. Ironically, feedback from these customers told Marmot marketers that early delivery was nearly as much of a problem as late delivery. One shop owner wrote, "I've got my delivery schedule for good reason; I don't want stuff a month ahead of time!" So Marmot again took constructive action. As production and delivery problems were solved, the company spent more money on marketing, tripling the budget. New ads ran for nearly a year in half a dozen publications in an effort to increase brand awareness. Feedback from shop owners became much more positive. "Shipping has been good, product quality has been excellent as usual, and there's more recognition of the product than ever before," noted Bob Wade, owner of the Ute Mountaineer, a Colorado outfitter that had been a Marmot dealer for 20 years. "Overall, it's definitely a healthier situation." Retailers are satisfied and climbers are braving high winds and high altitudes in Marmot Mountain gear.

Questions

1. What method of organization would probably be best for Marmot Mountain? Why?

2. In addition to daily meetings, what other kinds of internal communication could help improve marketing at Marmot Mountain?

3. Using Table 20.3, outline the types of information that would be needed to perform a marketing audit of Marmot Mountain.

Source: David Goodman, "One Step at a Time," *Inc.*, August 1995, pp. 64–70.

Explore more at www.marmot.com

The result of strategic marketing planning is a marketing plan for a particular product or product line. In the case of a small business, the marketing plan may even cover the marketing activities of the entire firm. The following pages outline the information of a marketing plan should contain and present a sample marketing plan for a small business.

Components of a Marketing Plan

Although marketing plans need not follow identical structures, the following components constitute a complete marketing plan:

- Title page
- Executive summary
- Table of contents
- Introduction
- Environmental analysis

- Marketing planning
- Implementation and control
- Summary
- Appendix: Financial analysis
- References.

The sample marketing plan that follows contains the components in this list.

A neat title page gives the marketing plan a professional appearance and makes it easy to identify. The title page should contain the following information:

- The name of the product or brand that is the subject of the marketing plan.
- The time period covered by the plan.
- The name(s) and title(s) of those submitting the plan.
- The person(s), group, or agency to whom the plan is being submitted, for example, a higher-level manager or a lending institution.
- The date on which the plan is being submitted.

In preparing the title page, keep in mind that it is the basis for forming a first impression of the overall plan.

The executive summary sums up the contents of the marketing plan in a maximum of three pages. It is a useful source of information for managers who want to be familiar with the plan but do not need to approve its details. The executive summary should state the basic opportunity identified and the overall strategy for taking advantage of that opportunity. A budget summary also is helpful here.

The table of contents lists each section of the marketing plan and its page number. If the marketing plan contains numerous tables and figures, these may be listed after the table of contents. Preparing a table of contents helps marketers determine if the plan is complete and well organized.

The introduction provides the background necessary to understand the marketing plan. For a new product or strategic business unit, the introduction explains the product concept and the reasons it is expected to succeed. For an existing product or strategic business unit, the introduction summarizes the product's recent performance. The introduction can also tell the reader what the remainder of the marketing plan will cover.

The environmental analysis describes the relevant conditions affecting the likely success of the plan. In effect, it describes where the organization is now. This discussion generally includes an "industry analysis"— a section describing the competitive environment. The industry analysis covers such issues as who the competitors are, what market share each holds, what strengths and weaknesses each has, and whether new competitors are likely to enter the market.

Next, the marketing plan describes where the organization wants to go. The section on marketing planning covers the marketing objectives, target market(s), and marketing mix, and describes the rationale for each. The section on the marketing mix details the selected strategies for product, price, placement, and promotion. The marketing planning section can also include plans for or results of marketing research.

After the objectives and strategy comes a description of how the marketing plan will be implemented and controlled. This description should specify who will be responsible for the efforts and also provide a timetable. A marketing plan typically covers one year, though some plans cover a five-year time frame. The discussion of implementation and control also spells out how success or failure will be measured. Usually, this is determined by comparing the results of implementing the plan with the marketing objectives.

The summary section of the marketing plan is similar to the executive summary. However, it may be somewhat longer and more detailed.

A financial analysis of the marketing plan may appear in an appendix. This should contain a sales forecast and an estimate of the marketing costs involved in carrying out the plan so that profits can be estimated. Items to include in a cost estimate are advertising, marketing research, product development, package design, development of distribution channels, and training and compensation of the sales force, as well as variable costs.

Any sources of information used in compiling the marketing plan should be listed in a section titled "References." Sources may include books, journals, business periodicals, and company reports or memos.

Sample Marketing Plan: Little Learners Parent–Teacher Store

The following pages present a marketing plan for a small business, the Little Learners Parent–Teacher Store. While this plan is shorter and less detailed than an actual marketing plan, it illustrates the basic style of such a plan.

Marketing Plan
Little Learners Parent-Teacher Store
Fiscal Year 1998
Robin Lee, President

Submitted to:

Pat Johnson
Commercial Loan Officer
Commerce National Bank
June 1, 1997

CONTENTS

Executive Summary 3
Introduction 3
Situation Analysis 3
Competitive Analysis 4
Marketing Planning 5
    Marketing Objectives 5
    Target Markets 5
    Marketing Mix 5
Implementation and Control 6
Summary 6
Appendix: Financial Analysis 7
    Sales Forecast 7
    Budget 7
    Profitability 7
References 8

Executive Summary

Little Learners Parent–Teacher Store is an 1,100-square-foot retail store specializing in educational games and teaching aids. Its primary customers are elementary school teachers who want additional resources for the classroom and parents seeking educational resources to supplement their children's learning in school.

In 1998 the owners would like to expand in response to the opportunity presented by a retail vacancy next to the existing store. Expanding into the existing space will increase square footage by approximately 80 percent, to 2,000 square feet. Given the strong demand for the store's products in the first three years of its existence, it was expected that an expanded store could boost monthly sales by 38 percent over the previous year. The sales increase would more than offset the additional operating costs. These costs consist of a $1,500-per-month increase in rent and utilities, added annual marketing communication expenses of $5,000, and $16,000 for an additional salesperson. Setting up the new space would involve a one-time cost of $20,000.

The space from the expansion would be used to provide a much broader selection of educational toys and games, which should attract many more parents to the store. To reach the parents, the promotional strategy would emphasize more frequent advertising in the local newspaper, the *Palo Alto Times,* along with sponsorship of quarterly seminars for parents at the Palo Alto Public Library.

Introduction

Little Learners Parent–Teacher Store is an 1,100-square-foot retail store specializing in educational games and teaching aids. Its best-selling products include workbooks, science experiments, and classroom decorations such as posters and bulletin board art. The store has been in operation since 1995 in the downtown business district of Palo Alto, California. Its primary customers are elementary schoolteachers who want additional resources for the classroom and parents seeking educational resources to supplement their children's learning in school. The owners of Little Learners are two former teachers in the Palo Alto school system. All salespeople in the store have teaching experience, enabling them to better help shoppers evaluate the products for sale.

In each of the first three years of its operation, the store has exceeded its revenue projections. For fiscal year 1997, ending May 31, 1997, the business posted its first profit: $17,500 before taxes. Table A.1 summarizes income statements for three years and makes forecasts for the following year. To achieve its sales, the store has relied

T A B L E A.1
Comparative Income Statements: Fiscal Years 1995–1998

	FY 1995	FY 1996	FY 1997	FY 1998*
Sales revenue	$86,000	$177,000	$232,000	$321,000
Expenses:				
Costs of goods sold	44,000	94,000	119,000	165,000
Administrative costs	5,000	2,000	2,000	3,000
Salaries	50,000	66,000	68,000	84,000
Rent and utilities	20,000	21,000	22,000	40,000
Advertising and PR	1,500	1,500	2,000	7,000
Other expenses	1,000	1,500	1,500	2,000
Income before taxes	($35,000)	($9,000)	$17,500	$20,000

*Projected with expansion

primarily on recommendations among teachers and weekly advertisements in the local newspaper, the *Palo Alto Times*. Because the store has little direct competition, it has been able to maintain an average 48 percent gross margin, avoiding price reductions except to clear out seasonal items.

The retail space adjacent to Little Learners became vacant in February 1997, when the jewelry store occupying the space relocated. This vacancy presents an attractive opportunity given the strong sales Little Learners has experienced with minimal advertising. The remainder of this marketing plan details how the owners intend to take advantage of this expansion opportunity.

Situation Analysis

Palo Alto, California, is a middle- to upper-class community of mostly professionals. With Stanford University and many research-oriented employers nearby, the people of this community place high value on learning and education. Thus, a major environmental opportunity is that this area is a strong supporter of educational resources for parents and teachers, including the Little Learners store.

In fact, we believe that we have only begun to tap the demand for the types of products we sell. Our sales so far have been limited by a small budget for advertising and public relations, as well as space constraints that prevent us from stocking as broad a selection as would interest most parents. A telephone survey of 50 households within a five-mile radius found that only 24 percent were aware of the store, but 43 percent expressed interest in the categories of merchandise offered.

Population trends support the view that demand for a parent–teacher store will continue to grow. Over the last decade, the population of Palo Alto has grown by only 1 percent, but there was strong growth among households with children under 15. Furthermore, most of the population consists of professional people, a group that generally has high disposable income and values high-quality toys and educational opportunities for its children.

Competitive Analysis

Research into the stores located within a 20-mile radius uncovered only one store that directly competes with Little Learners. This store, called Educational Resources, has been operating for 10 years in Santa Clara, California. The location is somewhat less desirable, but the costs of operating there are lower. As the store is privately owned, no data are available on its sales volume. However, on a recent Saturday, a steady flow of customers was seen entering the store.

We do not expect major competition from new stores over the near term. Because Educational Resources has operated for 10 years without expanding or even, to all appearances, updating its interior, we believe that aggressive expansion is not in its owners' plans. Furthermore, because our own expansion into adjacent space is likely to attract less notice than opening new locations would, we expect that our expansion will attract few, if any, new competitors.

Thus, the major sources of competition for Little Learners are other types of retailers of educational products for children. Examples are toy stores, which sell some toys considered educational, bookstores, catalog retailers, and companies such as Discovery Toys, which sell quality products in the home. Despite these environmental threats, we believe that our major strengths—the year-round availability of the store's products and the expertise of the owners and sales staff—set Little Learners apart as an easy-to-use source of guidance in selecting toys, games, and other materials that enhance learning by children.

Marketing Planning

This section describes our growth objective and how we plan to achieve it.

Marketing Objectives   Our objectives are to achieve a 38 percent increase in sales by the end of fiscal year 1998 while keeping our profit margin over 6 percent. The increase is to be achieved by expanding the total square footage of the store to include the vacant space next door, for a total of 2,000 square feet (an increase of approximately 80 percent). The increase in sales is to be measured on a monthly basis in comparison to the previous year. We seek to achieve a pretax profit margin of 7.5 percent by the end of fiscal year 1999.

Target Markets   The target markets for the store have been teachers working within a 20-mile radius of the store and "active parents" living within a 10-mile radius. By "active parents," we mean parents who devote a relatively large amount of time and money to their children's growth and development—for example, signing them up for swimming lessons, sending them to the "best" preschools, selecting toys that purportedly have educational value, joining parents' groups, and visiting classrooms. We estimate there are 12,000 households that meet these criteria.

Active parents are the target market for the store's planned expansion. Not only are they interested in the kinds of products sold by Little Learners, they also are willing to spend heavily on such products. They tend to be less budget conscious than the teachers who shop at the store.

Marketing Mix   To attract the target market of "active parents," Little Learners will use most of the additional space to expand its offerings of educational toys and games. Compared to such materials as workbooks and posters, these are the items most often requested by the parents who shop at the store. The focus will be on top-quality, high-margin items that are hard to find at most toy stores. For example, there will be an extensive line of materials for science experiments, as well as top-quality arts and crafts supplies suitable for children. Top-quality, high-margin items support the store's image as a place to find materials superior to those available at a toy store. This focus appeals to parents who are willing to spend more if it means giving their children an edge.

The strategy to build revenues depends on increasing sales among parents who already visit the store and attracting more of the parents who live within a 10-mile radius. The primary means of increasing sales among current customers is the expanded product line. To attract new customers, we will rely on several types of communications. First, we will increase the frequency of advertisements the store runs in the *Palo Alto Times* from twice a month to once a week. To build awareness, each ad will feature a different product or product line available at the store, along with the slogan "The Store Dedicated to Joyful Learning."

In addition, Little Learners will sponsor quarterly lectures on topics of interest to parents. The store will arrange for child development experts to speak at the public library. Posters and press releases announcing these events will mention the store's sponsorship.

To supplement these regular communications activities, the store will seek to take advantage of other opportunities to receive publicity. These will include events at the store, such as a writing contest among elementary-school students.

Itemized costs for this strategy appear in the appendix to the marketing plan.

Implementation and Control

The owners of Little Learners Parent–Teacher Store will be responsible for implementing this marketing plan. As shown in Figure A.1, the timetable for implementing the plan involves occupying the new space by June 15, 1997, and opening for business there by August 15. We expect to achieve the 38 percent increase in sales by the end of the fiscal year (May 31, 1998). Success in carrying out this plan will be measured in terms of completing activities according to the schedule shown in Figure 1 and meeting the objectives of the plan.

If costs should be higher than projected, our contingency plan is to proceed as long as we can keep costs within 15 percent of the projected amount. This will delay our ability to profit from the expansion until fiscal year 1999. If the adjacent retail space should no longer be available, our contingency plan is to forgo expanding the size of the store and to reevaluate the mix of products offered in the current store. We may be able to increase sales and profits by replacing some current offerings with more of the kinds of products we are planning to sell in the additional space. However, in adjusting the product mix, we will avoid changing in ways that detract from fulfilling our mission of serving teachers as well as parents in their efforts to promote learning.

Summary

Little Learners Parent–Teacher Store is a store specializing in educational games and teaching aids. Its target markets are elementary school teachers who want additional resources for the classroom and "active parents"—those who devote a relatively great amount of time and money to their children's growth and development.

In response to the opportunity presented by a vacancy in the retail space next door, the store seeks to expand in fiscal year 1998. Expanding into the existing space will increase square footage by approximately 80 percent. Our marketing objective is to use this expansion as a means to increase sales by 38 percent, increasing total sales for fiscal year 1998 by $89,000. The increase in sales would more than offset the additional operating costs. The additional costs consist of a $1,500-per-month increase in rent and utilities, added annual communications expense of $5,000, and $16,000 for an additional salesperson. The cost to set up the new space would be a one-time expense of $20,000.

The space from the expansion would be used to provide a much broader selection of educational toys and games. This product mix is designed to generate more sales among "active parents." In addition, to draw more active parents into the store, Little Learners plans to increase its budget for marketing communications. The additional

FIGURE A.1

Schedule for Marketing Plan: Fiscal Year 1998

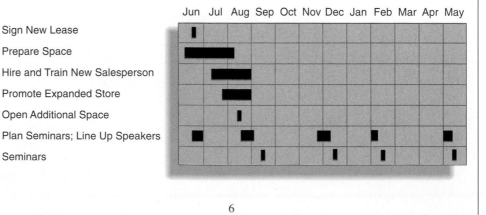

funds would be used to double the frequency of advertising in the *Palo Alto Times* and to sponsor public relations activities such as speakers at the public library.

The owners will be responsible for implementing this plan, which calls for opening the new space by August 15, 1997. Success will be measured in terms of meeting the schedule and achieving the sales and profit objectives.

Appendix: Financial Analysis

This appendix presents a sales forecast and budget in support of the marketing plan.

Sales Forecast   Little Learners Parent–Teacher Store sells to parents and teachers. By offering teachers a free subscription to a company-produced, two-page monthly newsletter, the store can identify which sales go to which category of buyers. Figure A.2 shows the pattern of sales to each category during the three years of the store's operation.

The marketing plan targets its expansion efforts at parents. Sales to teachers are expected to follow the historical trend of increasing at an average of 5 percent per year. The additional communications efforts should increase sales beyond historical patterns. A telephone survey of area households found that only about one-quarter were familiar with the store but that almost half were interested in the types of products sold. Therefore, we anticipate that more intensive communications will lead to approximately a 45 percent increase in sales to parents.

Budget   The budget for this marketing plan appears in Table A.2. The additional salesperson would cost about $16,000 per year, bringing the total cost for sales staff to $34,000. The additional communications expenses would be $5,000, bringing the total budget for promotion to $7,000. The total costs to expand into the new location are $20,000 to prepare the space, plus an additional $1,500 per month in rent and utilities.

FIGURE A.2
Sales History by Category

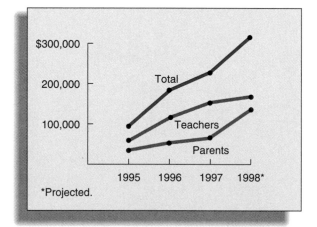

TABLE A.2
Marketing Budget:
Fiscal Year 1998

Marketing Expenses	
Sales staff	$34,000
Advertising, newspaper	6,300
Seminar speakers (4 @ $100)	400
Other, including posters, in-house PR	300
	$41,000
Costs for Additional Space	
Preparation of space	$20,000
Additional rent and utilities @ $1,500 per month	18,000
Total for additional space	$38,000

Profitability   In 1997 the store posted its first profit: $17,500 on sales of $232,000. With the expansion, profits for fiscal year 1998 are expected to rise to $20,000 on sales of $321,000, a profit margin of 6.2 percent. In 1999, when expenses will no longer include the cost of preparing the additional space, we project that the store's profit margin will be 7.5 percent.

References

Churchill, Gilbert A. Jr., and J. Paul Peter. *Marketing: Creating Value for Customers,* 2nd ed. Homewood, Ill.: Irwin, 1997.

Throughout this book, you've seen how a variety of people have achieved success in marketing: as entrepreneurs, as executives of large and small companies, as business-people in the United States and abroad. Both men and women have succeeded, including those from a variety of cultural and racial backgrounds. One thing these successful marketers have in common is a commitment to creating value for customers.

This appendix provides information to help you join these people in the challenging and important field of marketing. You'll learn some of the career opportunities that exist in marketing and how to begin your job search. But don't limit yourself to the ideas presented here; as a potential successful marketer, use your imagination!

Remember also, there is a *Marketing Interactive: Building Skills for Your Career* CD ROM. This exciting and unique CD ROM allows you to simulate the world of marketing and gives you the opportunity to apply the concepts you are learning in class. As you work through the different business situations, you will strengthen your critical thinking, decision making, and communication skills. You will learn how to use the Internet and other resources to solve real business problems, and you will learn the importance of building relationships in the business world. Marketing Interactive is organized around four career areas: Advertising, Marketing Research, Product Management, and Personal Selling/Sales Management. All four modules are infused with ethical, relationship, global and multicultural material. Each of these is referenced in the appropriate Part Opener in this text to remind you to explore the subject further.

Types of Career Opportunities in Marketing

You've studied chapters on conducting marketing research, managing new and existing products, pricing those products, managing distribution channels, and using marketing communications. You've read about businesses and nonprofit organizations. Maybe you already have a sense of what type of marketing opportunity you'd like to pursue, or perhaps you want to try to do them all and become an entrepreneur.

Major career opportunities exist for marketers not only in the United States, but in other countries as well. For instance, 3M employs marketing personnel in more than 50 countries.[1] Toys "R" Us, Inc. operates more than 120 stores in 10 countries, including Canada, Europe, the United Kingdom, Japan, and Malaysia.[2] Emily Morgan started her career path as a secretary in the advertising department of Levi Strauss & Company. As she learned the business, she became an assistant advertising manager, then held jobs in distribution, merchandising, and purchasing. Today, Morgan's title is Vice President for Customer Fulfillment, Asia. Based in Singapore, she oversees the Asian contractors for Levi's products, traveling to Korea, Malaysia, Pakistan, and other countries.[3]

Marketing Research

Marketing researchers are responsible for gathering and analyzing all kinds of information useful for planning, implementing, and controlling marketing plans and strategies. Marketing research is a popular field, employing tens of thousands of people.[4] Some marketing researchers work for the companies that produce and sell goods and services, some work for advertising agencies, and others work for or operate their own, independent marketing research firms.

Opportunities exist for marketing researchers both in the United States and abroad. The Dun & Bradstreet Corporation routinely conducts research on a global basis. According to the company's annual report, "Our divisions have unparalleled capabilities to provide comprehensive local, regional and global information services to customers throughout the world."[5] And Henkel KGaA, the German manufacturer of hair-care products, toiletries, and cleansers, works "closely with Nielsen to harmonize our marketing-research information across Europe."[6]

Marketing research can be an exciting entry into the world of marketing for recent graduates. Monitoring trends and identifying business opportunities, designing surveys, interviewing consumers, tabulating data, and writing reports are just a few of the tasks that researchers undertake.

Product Management

The process of managing new and existing products has undergone significant change with the establishment of cross-functional teams at many companies. Still other companies successfully use the traditional hierarchy in which the management of a product is overseen by a brand manager. Brand management or other types of marketing management are not entry-level positions, but support positions that are ideal for recent college graduates are available.

Distribution

A wide variety of opportunities—and positions—exist in the area of distribution. For instance, an operations manager supervises physical distribution functions such as warehousing. The traffic manager weighs the pros and cons of different types of transportation. People in inventory control forecast customer demand for goods and monitor levels of stock. Many organizations have a customer service department linked to distribution, designed to make sure the needs of customers are met promptly and effectively.

Retailing

Many people begin their careers in marketing through retailing. Nearly 20 million people work in retail trade in the United States,[7] and retailing is projected to be among the fastest-growing U.S. industries over the next decade.[8] People interested in a career in retailing can concentrate on either merchandise management (products themselves) or store management. Those who want to enter merchandise management generally do so as buyer trainees, then work their way up through assistant buyer and buyer to merchandise division manager. Those interested in store management start as management trainees, then move up through assistant department manager, department manager, and on to store manager. Many larger stores such as department store chains have their own training programs for both career paths.

Advertising

Many people view advertising as the glamour end of marketing. In a sense, they're right: Advertising gets the attention of consumers or organizational buyers. It can make or break a product; it can even make or break careers.

There are many types of advertising, and advertising is originated in different ways—by manufacturers, service providers, independent advertising agencies—through a variety of media. The career opportunities for those who are imaginative and persistent are good. Students who excel in writing may want to pursue careers in advertising copywriting or in writing promotional messages to use in direct marketing, while those who have artistic talent may be interested in the art department; still others may be interested in buying media space or time.

Entry-level jobs in advertising aren't easy to come by, and because of their popularity, the pay is often lower than in other marketing fields. If you want to pursue a career in advertising, you must be willing to start at the bottom of the hierarchy and work hard through its different levels—or, with at least some professional experience, strike out on your own.

Personal Selling

Entering the field of marketing via personal selling has two advantages. First, you may find that you're good at it, like it, and decide to make it a career. As a salesperson, you have the potential to earn a good income, somewhat set your own hours, engage in a certain amount of regional, sometimes national, or even international travel, and advance at a fairly rapid rate. Second, personal selling provides you with excellent training to move into other areas of marketing if you so choose.

As a recent graduate, you may land a job in order getting, order taking, or even missionary selling. You may be prospecting for customers and demonstrating products or answering questions and handling complaints from customers. You may attend trade shows, sales meetings, and motivational conferences. To be successful you must be self-disciplined and highly motivated, because a supervisor will not be with you all the time.

If you decide to pursue a career in sales, you may aspire to become a sales manager or director of sales, managing the organization's sales force. A sales manager's job generally entails a mixture of travel, including visiting salespeople in their territories as well as major customers, people management, and business responsibilities.

Nonprofit Organizations

Nonprofit organizations are engaging in increasingly sophisticated marketing efforts. Like businesses, they are competing for revenues, which may come through membership fees, donations, and the like. Nonprofit organizations as diverse as the Appalachian Mountain Club and Childreach International have employees engaged in marketing activities.

Many of these activities mirror those of businesses, such as conducting surveys, using direct-mail advertising, even merchandising. In addition, nonprofit organizations often engage in fundraising by approaching potential individual donors as well as corporations, or by applying for government grants or other public funds. Fundraising itself can be an exciting, challenging career that combines good writing skills and business sense with polished interpersonal skills.

Entrepreneurship

You think you've got good business sense and a great idea for a product, or the thought of owning a franchise appeals to you. You've got drive and self-discipline, and you want to control your own destiny; you want no limits on your career advancement or earning potential. In short, you think you want to be an entrepreneur.

Your aspirations are admirable, and there are opportunities in the marketplace for entrepreneurs. Entrepreneurship can generally be divided into two categories: franchise ownership and outright business ownership.

In a franchise agreement, the entrepreneur or franchisee enters into a business relationship with a franchiser, agreeing to certain terms such as the price at which a product will be sold and from whom supplies will be bought. In turn, the franchiser offers benefits to the entrepreneur such as the value of an established product name and chances to participate in widespread promotional campaigns. Success at franchising depends not only on hard work, but also on the ability to pick a franchiser that offers a solid track record, a growth industry, and a contract with desirable terms. Proceed with caution: Most franchise sales come from car dealers, gas stations, and soft-drink bottling, and most new franchises in the United States are in other, lower-income businesses.[9]

The entrepreneur who starts his or her own business takes all the risks but has the freedom and potential to gain more. We all hear stories about successful businesses that started in someone's living room or garage, with just a few dollars in capital, but most entrepreneurs must find some type of financial backing. When Erik Anderson and Jeff Sand decided to develop a step-in snowboard binding (the original snowboards required their users to sit down and undo plastic straps in order to get off), they raised $200,000 in loans from family and friends to start their new business, Switch Manufacturing.[10]

While there are examples of recent college graduates who instantly grab success as entrepreneurs, in many cases successful entrepreneurs have at least some professional experience. When Anderson and Sand launched Switch Manufacturing, they had 30 years' experience as designers, and they quickly hired a marketing director who had held a similar position with a marketer of skateboard equipment. A good job with a company that is already established can provide valuable training, contacts with people in the industry, and a chance to learn from your mistakes without losing your entire business. John Guardiola, owner of a Duraclean franchise, states in an ad for that company, "In my opinion, IBM is a superb organization. I wouldn't trade my 15 years there for anything. Yet, in spite of all the benefits a large, successful corporate structure can offer, I came to the conclusion it was time to go into business for myself." Guardiola made his decision to buy a franchise *after* having spent 15 years learning about business as an employee at IBM.

Of course, there are entrepreneurs who simply refuse to follow the traditional path, and you may be one of them. Sophia Collier and Connie Best, two such entrepreneurs, started an alternative soft-drink company when they were both in their early twenties. Soho Soda began because "there was no alternative beverage on the market," says Collier.[11] Her sum total of business experience was managing a food cooperative in Portland, Maine; Best had no real business experience at all. They encountered plenty of obstacles but pushed through to success. Two vital factors in their achievement were their persistence and the fact that they came up with the right product at the right time to create value.

Conducting Your Job Search

Once you have a sense of the kind of work you want to do, you are ready to conduct a job search. The best opportunity for you may be a traditional job, but observers of the business scene caution that in the future, other work arrangements may become as important as "jobs." A growing number of workers already are assigned to teams, rather than to particular jobs. Others tackle temporary assignments, moving from company to company, or from one department of an organization to another. At AT&T, for example, employees may be assigned to projects as the need arises, rather than holding a single job in a single department.[12]

These trends require marketers to apply their marketing skills to their own careers. Develop a marketing plan for yourself that focuses on your ability to create value. First, evaluate your own strengths and weaknesses, and identify the opportunities and threats in the area of the work environment that interests you. Then consider how you can create value for prospective employers and how you can continue to build your ability to create value.

Characteristics of a Good Marketer

What makes a good marketer? Certainly, marketers differ, just as marketing jobs differ. But successful marketers generally agree that the following traits are needed:

- Ability to work well with other people.
- Creative approach to solving problems.
- Self-motivation and self-confidence.
- Willingness to take appropriate risks.
- Ability to spot trends.
- Enjoyment of a fast-paced working environment.

As you begin your job search, ask yourself whether any or all of these characteristics apply to you.

Remember that not all marketing jobs require all these traits. For instance, a person interested in writing advertising copy may not need as strong a desire to spend time with other people as does someone who wants to begin a career in personal selling.

Further, some marketing fields require specialized skills and education. Thus, an advertising art director needs a background in commercial art. Someone who conducts cost analysis of physical distribution systems must be comfortable with math. An advertising account executive or director of marketing may be required to have an M.B.A. Learning what skills, education, and traits are expected of marketing professionals in different jobs will help you decide which job is best for you.

Researching Opportunities

After assessing your own skills and interests, explore the environment of employment opportunities. To do this, you will need to identify resources that can help you pinpoint which companies or nonprofit organizations have training programs or entry-level opportunities.

Career Placement Office   Frequent the career placement office at your college. Learn what information is available to you and how to obtain and use it. If possible, arrange an interview with someone in the office to help you focus your search. At some schools, recruiters from different companies visit to scout for good employment candidates. Even if you are unsure about particular jobs or companies, try to get interviews with recruiters. Interviews will give you valuable information that can help you identify areas where you can create value for employers, as well as practice in communicating with potential employers.

In addition to company listings, many colleges also have listings of alumni who are willing to speak with or correspond with graduating seniors about jobs. These can be valuable contacts, not only for specific jobs, but for current information about the marketing field.

Employment Agencies   Employment agencies, or "headhunters," can help you launch your career by helping you focus your search, providing you with an introduction to a company, and arranging interviews for you. An employment agency is paid a fee by the company that does the hiring and wants to place as many qualified job candidates as possible. Many agencies now specialize in certain fields, and some only accept candidates at certain levels, for example, middle management and above, so when you phone an agency to ask about employment opportunities, ask whether the agency handles recent graduates.

When you consider using an employment agency to help you find a full-time job, don't rule out contacting an agency that handles temporary assignments. A temporary agency's customers require qualified candidates only for a specified period of time— for instance, to handle a holiday rush or to replace a permanent employee who is temporarily disabled. A temporary assignment can be valuable in two ways: (1) it gives you immediate working experience in marketing; (2) it may lead to permanent employment later on.

Don't forget the state employment office, which lists job openings only in your state, and may have different job listings than those at employment agencies or the college career office.

Want Ads   The competition for jobs listed in the newspaper want ads is usually fierce, but don't hesitate to respond. Also, at the library, read sales and marketing trade publications such as *Marketing News,* as well as business magazines, which often contain job listings. These ads not only offer job opportunities, but also give you an idea of what types of entry-level positions are currently available, as well as what income you can expect to earn.

The Internet   A variety of job postings are available on the Internet. These include listings posted by businesses and the government. They may provide an up-to-date source of information, especially about technology leaders. IBM lists all of its job openings—over 20,000 a year—on the U.S. Labor Department's Internet job bank.

T A B L E B.1
Recruiting Sites on the World
Wide Web

Site	Address	Description
America's Job Bank	http://www.ajb.dni.us/	Operated by the U.S. Department of Labor; lists over 500,000 job openings from private companies and placement agencies
Career Mosaic	http://www.careermosaic.com/	Operated by Bernard Hodes Advertising; includes employer profiles, job listings, and an information center
E-Span Interactive Employment Network	http://www.espan.com/	Job postings for over 3,500 positions at over 1,500 companies, as well as salary guides and career job calendars
Job Web	http://www.jobweb.org/	Developed by the National Association of Colleges and Employers; offers career planning and job listings, as well as job search advice
Monster Board	http://www.monster.com/	Operated by Odion, Inc.; a career center with employer profiles, job listings, and human resource reference material
Online Career Center	http:/www.lquest.net/occ/ HomePage.html	Nonprofit board with job listings from over 250 sponsoring companies

Sources: Raymond A. Noe, John R. Hollenbeck, Barry Gerhart, and Patrick M. Wright, *Human Resource Management: Gaining a Competitive Advantage,* 2nd ed. (Burr Ridge: Irwin, 1997), p. 298; "Work Week," *The Wall Street Journal,* July 9, 1996, p. A1.

Table B.1 lists major sources of information about employment opportunities. Some of these, such as the Monster Board and the Online Career Center, also provide a place for job hunters to post their résumés and submit applications.

Another way to use the Internet to look for work opportunities is to visit the Web sites of organizations that interest you. Some Web sites provide valuable information about the organization's activities, history, and even its organizational culture. The information can help you decide which potential employers look like a good match for you. Also, a growing number of organizations are setting up systems that post job openings and receive electronic job applications or résumés over the Internet. Cisco Systems, based in Menlo Park, California, and the Staples chain of office products discount stores both post job openings on their Web sites as well as on Internet career services.[13]

Personal Contacts   Friends, relatives, and acquaintances may be your most valuable resources as you look for a job. A personal introduction to a recruiter by one of its employees helps distinguish you from other applicants. Don't be shy about contacting people you know, even if it's just to ask for information about a certain field in marketing. Most people who are established in their careers are happy to help students by answering questions and passing a résumé to the proper department, even if a specific job is not readily available. If you present yourself in a professional manner and convey your genuine interest in the person's field or organization, chances are you'll at least get a friendly reply; perhaps you'll even get an opportunity for an interview.

Writing Your Résumé

One of the most important aspects of your job search is writing your résumé. A résumé is a kind of marketing communications; it communicates to your potential employer what strengths you would bring to the organization and how you can create value.

Your résumé should present your qualifications clearly in a well-organized format. There are three résumé formats: (1) the chronological format, which presents your work experience and education in the sequence in which they occurred; (2) the functional format, which groups your experiences according to relevant skills; and (3) the targeted format, which emphasizes skills that apply to specific jobs. The chronological and functional formats are often most useful for recent graduates, who are still in the process of targeting their careers.

Whichever format you choose, your résumé should contain the following information:

- Full name, address, and telephone number. If you have a school address and home address where you can be reached, include both.
- Your highest and next-highest level of education, including relevant courses taken.
- Your work experience, including summer jobs and campus jobs, focusing on any experience related to aspects of marketing.
- Extracurricular activities and interests, including any awards or honors you have earned.
- A statement that personal and professional references will be available upon request.

As you write this information, evaluate your wording. A growing number of organizations enter the résumés they receive into a computer system that can retrieve them selectively according to key words. These words most likely would include job titles, industries, or references to specific skills desired by your prospective employer. Résumé-tracking systems favor applicants who use the right key words; other applicants' submissions will not be retrieved, even if the applicant is qualified or has used a creative résumé layout or clever phrases. This technology increases the importance of getting to know what constitutes value in the minds of prospective employers. When you know what they look for, you can mention those things in your résumé.

Another question facing today's job hunters is whether to use a paperless résumé. The answer is to use what your prospective employer finds most valuable. An organization that sets up a Web site to receive résumés via the Internet probably has a system in place to use this information efficiently. However, avoid using technology that only creates extra work for the recipient. A videotape is time-consuming to use and requires equipment to play, so unless it was requested, don't be surprised if the recipient doesn't watch it. If you send a diskette, be sure it is compatible with the employer's system.[14]

One final note about résumé writing: While your résumé should present your strengths and qualifications to their best advantage, it should not misrepresent them. In other words, don't claim experience you don't have, job titles you haven't earned, skills you haven't mastered, or courses you haven't taken. Doing so is not only unethical, it will catch up with you, perhaps costing you a job you wanted badly. Instead, emphasize your existing experience and your willingness to learn. No one expects recent college graduates to know everything about marketing.

Writing Your Cover Letter   When you submit a résumé, it should be accompanied by a cover letter, which introduces you to a potential employer. In your cover letter, state your purpose (inquiring about employment), list two or three of your main qualifications, and refer to the enclosed résumé. If you were referred to the organization by someone you know, mention the person's name and the nature of your relationship (friend, relative, etc.). Close the letter by politely requesting an interview and thanking the reader for his or her consideration.

Don't be tempted to be cute or outrageous in your cover letter in an effort to gain attention. Your effort will certainly attract attention, but it will probably land your letter and résumé in the wastebasket. Instead, adopt a professional, courteous tone, and keep the letter brief.

The Successful Job Interview

You may be granted an informational interview or an interview for a specific job. An informational interview is just what it sounds like—it provides you with a chance to learn more about the company and the types of positions that may be available. Although it is not an interview for a specific job opening, it is just as important, for it gives you the opportunity to create a favorable impression with a potential employer. So treat the informational interview and the specific job interview as equally important.

When you've been granted an interview, write down the date, time, address, and name of the person to whom you are to report. Ask for directions to the company if necessary. Some organizations conduct an initial selection interview over the phone, perhaps using a computer system to conduct that interview. Don't be intimidated; these systems can avoid some of the personal biases of screening candidates in person.[15] If your initial interview will be by phone, make sure you are clear about who will make the phone call. If you are to do so, write down the correct number and time to call.

Then do your homework. Find out as much about the organization in advance as possible. This indicates to the interviewer your genuine interest in the firm as well as your self-motivation. If you know someone who works at the company, call and ask about the company's best-selling goods or services, as well as qualities the company considers important in its employees. Ask the person to send you a copy of the firm's annual report or other pertinent written material, if possible. You can also request these from the personnel department. Search the Internet for information about the firm; perhaps the organization has its own Web site. Consult general publications such as *The Wall Street Journal* or trade publications for any news information about the company.

Next, prepare yourself for the interview. Review in your mind your strengths, weaknesses, and relevant experiences. Think through carefully and clearly why you would want to work for the organization, and why you would want a particular job. Ask yourself what you expect to learn from the job and what you think you can contribute. Ask yourself what your general and specific career goals are. Many interviewers will ask you these questions.

The day of the interview, arrive 10 to 15 minutes before the time scheduled for your appointment. Wear simple, appropriate business clothes. Pay attention to good grooming. During the interview, be alert but try to relax; most interviewers want to learn about you, not trip you up. Listen to the questions you are asked, and answer honestly, maintaining a positive attitude. Don't be afraid to ask questions of the interviewer, about the company, the position, the working environment, expectations of employees, and the like.

Even if the interview seems to go well, it's unlikely you will be offered the position after the initial interview. But if you are, be prepared to accept if you know you want the job. If you truly feel you need time to consider the offer, ask for a day or two. Regardless of how the interview went, thank the person as you leave. Within a day or so, follow up with a thank-you note to the interviewer and anyone else within the company with whom you had significant contact, such as someone who referred you to the firm. The thank-you note not only establishes you as someone who is professional and courteous, it marks you as someone who follows through to the end.

If you don't get the job, don't be discouraged. Most people experience some rejections during their job searches. Review what you learned from the job application process and use that knowledge to improve your job-hunting skills. Move on to the next application and interview with enthusiasm. If you persist, your job search will pay off. If you are offered a job, congratulations! You are on your way to a career in marketing.

In a business, the ultimate test of a marketing strategy is whether it satisfies customers and is profitable. Even nonprofit organizations need to ensure that marketing decisions are economically viable. Thus, marketers must be able to work with the financial numbers that help predict the success of plans and measure the success of operations. This appendix describes some techniques for doing so.

The Operating Statement

In general, as discussed in the chapters on pricing, a business's profit is the difference between its total revenues and its total expenses. But where do marketers actually get such numbers? Most often, accounting and financial personnel report revenue and expense figures in the form of an **operating statement**, often called an income statement or profit-and-loss (P&L) statement. The operating statement summarizes these performance figures for a specified period of time, typically a quarter or full year. Operating statements appear in the annual reports of publicly held companies. The organization also distributes this type of information to managers (and sometimes to all employees) to help them control their group's activities. For example, comparing operating statements over several periods shows whether some categories of expenses are growing too fast and whether profits are keeping pace with sales increases. Marketers who can interpret the information on an operating statement have the basic tools for evaluating their organization's profit performance.

Contents of the Operating Statement

Thanks to standards adopted by the U.S. accounting profession, operating statements in the United States all follow a similar format. Table C.1 provides an example, using Little Learners Parent–Teacher Store. Some people think operating statements are hard to understand. It may help to keep in mind that they are just a listing of how much money came in (revenues), how much went out (expenses), and the difference between those amounts.

As you review this sample, keep in mind that bigger organizations will have more complex and detailed operating statements. Furthermore, the specific items on the statement will vary somewhat from one industry to another. For example, a manufacturer's or a bank's operating statement may have about the same broad categories but will differ as to specifics.

Sales Revenue   The operating statement begins by reporting how much money the organization brought in from selling goods or services. *Gross sales* refers to the total amount paid by all customers during the accounting period. However, as any business owner knows, customers sometimes want to return merchandise. Therefore, accountants subtract an amount for **returns and allowances.** A return occurs when the customer brings or sends back the goods. An allowance occurs when the business responds to a dissatisfied customer by allowing the customer to keep the goods but not charging for them. The amount of sales revenue that remains after subtracting returns and allowances is called *net sales*. In Table C.1, the calculation is as follows:

Net Sales = Gross Sales − Returns and Allowances
= \$244,000 − \$12,000 = \$232,000

---

operating statement
Financial statement that summarizes revenues and expenses for a specified period of time; often called an income statement or profit-and-loss statement.

returns and allowances
An accounting adjustment to sales for items brought back by customers for a refund and items for which customers received a credit even though the items were not returned.

LITTLE LEARNERS PARENT–TEACHER STORE OPERATING STATEMENT FOR THE FISCAL YEAR ENDED MAY 31, 1997			
Sales Revenue:			
Gross sales		$244,000	
Less: Returns and allowances		12,000	
Net sales			$232,000
Cost of Goods Sold:			
Beginning inventory	$ 35,000		
Purchases	126,000		
Cost of goods available for sale		$161,000	
Less: Ending inventory		42,000	
Cost of goods sold			119,000
Gross margin			$113,000
Expenses:			
Selling expenses:			
Sales salaries	$ 45,000		
Other marketing	2,000		
Total selling expenses		$ 47,000	
Administrative expenses:			
Administrative salaries	$ 23,000		
Office supplies	1,500		
Other administrative expenses	500		
Total administrative expenses		25,000	
General expenses:			
Rent and utilities	$ 22,000		
Miscellaneous general expenses	1,500		
Total general expenses		23,500	
Total expenses			95,500
Net Profit (Loss) before Taxes			$ 17,500

cost of goods sold/
cost of sales
The total cost to produce or
acquire the products sold by an
organization during an
accounting period.

Cost of Goods or Goods Sold   Next, the operating statement shows the total cost to produce or acquire the products the organization sold during the accounting period. Depending on the nature of the product, this amount may be called the **cost of sales** or the **cost of goods sold.** A manufacturer would report the total cost to make the goods it sold. A service business uses the cost to perform the service. For an intermediary, cost of goods sold means the cost to acquire the inventory that the wholesaler or retailer sold to its customers.

How can the company's accountant keep track of this amount? The usual approach is to use some basic arithmetic. First, record the cost of the inventory on hand at the beginning of the accounting period, called *beginning inventory* in Table C.1. Then add the total amount spent to acquire more inventory throughout the accounting period, including any shipping charges. The sum of these two numbers is the *cost of goods available for sale* during the accounting period:

Beginning Inventory + Purchases = Cost of Goods Available for Sale
$35,000 + $126,000 = $161,000

But not all of the inventory that was purchased during the year was sold. Some goods are still on the store's shelves and in its storeroom. To find the cost of what was purchased, subtract what remains unsold:

$$\text{Cost of Goods Available for Sale} - \text{Ending Inventory} = \text{Cost of Goods Sold}$$
$$\$161{,}000 - \$42{,}000 = \$119{,}000$$

For a manufacturing business, the calculations will be similar. Instead of an inventory of goods to be resold, the manufacturer has an inventory of parts and materials. The manufacturer also has partly completed products (called *work-in-process inventory*) and finished goods in stock. As in the retailing example, the manufacturer finds the total cost of these items at the beginning of the accounting period, then adds the total spent during the year and subtracts what remains unsold. In addition, the manufacturer adds in the cost of the labor used to produce the goods, as well as the overhead costs of running the factory.

gross margin
The difference between net sales and the cost of goods sold.

Gross Margin   Unless an organization can make or buy products for less than the price it charges to sell them, it cannot hope to make a profit. Thus, the first measure of a business's profitability is its gross margin (or gross profit). **Gross margin** is the difference between net sales and the cost of goods sold. In Table C.1, the gross margin is computed as follows:

$$\text{Gross Margin} = \text{Net Sales} - \text{Cost of Goods Sold}$$
$$= \$232{,}000 - \$119{,}000 = \$113{,}000$$

To earn a profit, the store must keep its expenses less than the gross margin amount of $113,000.

Expenses   Accountants divide organizations' operating expenses into three major categories called *selling expenses, administrative expenses,* and *general expenses.* Selling expenses refer to the organization's marketing communications. For a store such as Little Learners, the major communications expense is for the salaries of its salespeople. In addition, Little Learners spent $2,000 in fiscal year 1997 on newspaper ads and public relations efforts.

Administrative expenses are the costs to manage a business. They include managers' salaries, office supplies, the wages of office help, and any other expenses in this area. For Little Learners Parent–Teacher Store, the major administrative expense is the owner's salary. The owner of this small business handles most administrative activities single-handedly. Other small-business owners use a part-time bookkeeper.

General expenses, as the name implies, cover any operating expenses not included in the other categories. The biggest general expense for Little Learners and many other businesses is rent and utilities. Other expenses that fall into this category include insurance, interest paid on loans, and maintenance of machinery and equipment.

Net Profit before Taxes   Subtracting total expenses from gross margin results in the "bottom line"—the company's net profit or loss before taxes. In fiscal year 1997, Little Learners Parent–Teacher Store earned a profit:

$$\text{Gross Margin} - \text{Total Expenses} = \text{Net Profit}$$
$$\$113{,}000 - \$95{,}500 = \$17{,}500$$

Some operating statements also show the amount of income taxes paid and the amount of profit remaining after taxes. The usual way to report a loss—that is, the difference when total expenses exceed the gross margin—is to place the amount of the loss in parentheses.

Operating Ratios

operating ratios
Ratios of operating statement items to net sales.

The most common way to evaluate the data in an operating statement is to use **operating ratios.** These are ratios of operating statement items to net sales. In other words, the person analyzing the operating statement thinks of the items on the statement as a percentage of net sales.

To find such an operating ratio, divide the item by the amount of net sales ($232,000 in the case of Table C.1). For example, selling expenses as a percentage of net sales at Little Learners Parent–Teacher Store would be computed as follows:

$$\text{Selling Expense Ratio} = \frac{\text{Total Selling Expenses}}{\text{Net Sales}}$$
$$= \$47,000/\$232,000 = .203 = 20.3\%$$

If Little Learners' owner wanted to evaluate whether the store was using its sales dollars effectively, she could look at the selling expense ratio over several years to see whether it was falling. (A falling operating ratio means the organization is getting more sales for its money in that area.) Or the owner could compare the selling expense ratios at other stores to see how Little Learners is performing relative to the competition.

Major Types of Ratios

gross margin ratio
The ratio of gross margin to net sales.

Three type of operating ratios provide a broad overview of a business's financial performance. These are the gross margin ratio, the net profit ratio, and the operating expense ratio. The **gross margin ratio** is the organization's gross margin divided by its net sales. For Little Learners, the computation would be as follows:

Gross Margin Ratio = Gross Margin/Net Sales
= $113,000/$232,000 = .487 = 48.7%

This figure is also called the gross profit ratio and the gross margin percent.

net profit ratio
The ratio of net profit (or loss) to net sales.

The **net profit ratio** is the organization's net profit or loss divided by net sales. Here is the net profit ratio for Little Learners:

Net Profit Ratio = Net Profit/Net Sales
= $17,500/$232,000 = .075 = 7.5%

operating expense ratio
The ratio of total expenses to net sales.

The **operating expense ratio** is the organization's total expenses divided by its net sales. Here is the computation for Little Learners:

Operating Expense Ratio = Total Expenses/Net Sales
= $95,500/$232,000 = .412 = 41.2%

The operating expense ratio is a quick check as to whether the organization is keeping its expenses under control. If this ratio seems high, or if the analyst is interested in a particular area of expenses, the analyst can compute operating ratios for specific types of expenses. An example is the selling expense ratio computed earlier.

Evaluating the Ratios   The way to evaluate any of these ratios is to make comparisons. The analyst can see whether the organization's performance is improving by looking at the same ratio over several accounting periods. To see whether an organization is performing better or worse than average, the analyst can compare the ratios for several organizations in the same industry. Sources of operating ratios for typical firms in various industries include trade associations, Robert Morris Associates, and Dun & Bradstreet. In general, high gross margin ratios and high net profit ratios are signs of good performance: the organization is turning a lot of its sales into profits. Conversely, low expense ratios are good because they suggest the organization is generating sales efficiently.

Other Performance Measures
Of course, the operating statement doesn't provide the whole picture of whether the organization's marketing and other efforts are a financial success. Some other widely used performance measures include return on investment or assets, inventory turnover, and market share.

Return on Investment or Assets

Do profits of $1 million a year mean a business has performed well? If you said, "It depends," you're on the right track. The corner gas station might be pleased to earn a million dollars, whereas that figure would be disappointing at Standard Oil. One way to get a context for a profit figure is to use the net profit ratio to see whether profits are a large share of sales dollars. Other ways to analyze profits include determining how much net profit was generated by the owners' investment in the company or by the company's assets.

return on investment (ROI)
Net profit from an enterprise divided by the amount invested to conduct that enterprise.

Return on Investment (ROI)   The figure that evaluates profits in terms of the owners' investment is called **return on investment (ROI).** ROI is the net profit from an enterprise divided by the amount invested to conduct that enterprise. In the case of Little Learners Parent–Teacher Store, assume the owner invested $200,000. The store's ROI would be computed as follows:

Return on Investment = Net Profit/Investment
$$= \$17,500/\$200,000 = .088 = 8.8\%$$

The owner can compare this figure with the earnings she could get from investing $200,000 in other ways.

From a purely economic standpoint, it makes sense to invest in enterprises that generate the highest ROI. When the ROI for an enterprise is not attractive, the owner can either look for ways to operate more profitably or find another use for the funds invested.

A marketer may be interested in the profitability of particular marketing activities, such as the launch of a new product. In that case, the "investment" part of the ROI formula would be the funds used to carry out those activities. For example, the expenses for launching a new product would include product design, marketing research, and marketing communications. To see how this works, assume that a bank spent $630,000 on planning and communications for a new type of credit line for consumers in its area. In the first year the bank offered this credit line, many consumers applied for and used the new service, generating $120,000 in profits from fees and interest payments. Here is the bank's return on investment:

ROI = Net Profit/Investment
$$= \$120,000/\$630,000 = .190 = 19.0\%$$

Similarly, a retailer might want to find the ROI of opening or operating particular stores.

return on assets (ROA)
Net profit from an enterprise divided by the total assets used to conduct that enterprise.

Return on Assets (ROA)   Another way to think of profits is in terms of the amount of assets used to generate those profits. Whereas the investment measure in ROI refers to what the owner has put into the enterprise, "assets" refers to what the business itself owns, such as its buildings, equipment, supplies, and cash. The way to measure profit in terms of assets is to find the **return on assets (ROA).** ROA is the net profit from an enterprise divided by the total assets used to conduct that enterprise. Total assets are reported on a financial statement known as a balance sheet.

In the case of Little Learners Parent–Teacher store, assume that its assets (mainly its inventory and some equipment) total $400,000. Its ROA would be as follows:

Return on Assets = Net Profit/Total Assets
$$= \$17,500/\$400,000 = .044 = 4.4\%$$

An increase in this ROA would signal that the store is using its resources more effectively.

Inventory Turnover

inventory turnover
The number of times an organization sells an average amount of inventory during a specified period of time; also called merchandise turnover rate or stockturn rate.

For marketers of goods, an important performance measure is **inventory turnover,** also called the merchandise turnover rate or the stockturn rate. Inventory turnover measures the number of times an organization turns over (sells) an average amount of inventory during a specified period of time. This measure shows whether goods are selling fast enough to keep inventory costs low. A high turnover rate also alerts marketers to items that may go out of stock at times, resulting in lost sales. In contrast, a falling rate of inventory turnover may signal that the target market is no longer as interested in the product.

To measure inventory turnover, the analyst may use two formulas. The first is based on the cost of the inventory:

$$\text{Inventory Turnover} = \frac{\text{Cost of Goods Sold}}{\text{Average Inventory at Cost}}$$

The simplest way to find the average inventory at cost is to take the average of the beginning and ending inventory figures on the operating statement. Using Table C.1 as an example, simply add together the beginning inventory and the ending inventory, then divide by 2:

$$\text{Average Inventory} = \frac{\text{Beginning Inventory} + \text{Ending Inventory}}{2}$$
$$= (\$35,000 + \$42,000)/2 = \$38,500$$

Then plug in the numbers to find the turnover for the fiscal year:

$$\text{Inventory Turnover} = \$119,000/\$38,500 = 3.09$$

In other words, by this measure, Little Learners turned over its inventory about three times in the year.

The second formula for inventory turnover measures inventory in terms of units sold:

$$\text{Inventory Turnover} = \frac{\text{Net Units Sold}}{\text{Average Inventory (in Units)}}$$

This makes sense in computing the turnover for a particular type of product. For example, suppose a maker of office supplies sells 650 cartons of yellow legal pads every month. Its average inventory of these pads is 800 cartons. Here is the turnover rate:

$$\text{Inventory Turnover} = 650 \text{ cartons}/800 \text{ cartons} = 0.8$$

Some of this manufacturer's money is being spent on carrying an inventory of yellow pads that doesn't sell out every month.

Market Share

market share
The sales of an organization's product as a percentage of all sales of such products.

Most marketers are concerned with the market share held by their products. **Market share** represents the sales of an organization's product as a percentage of all sales of such products. In other words, it tells what percentage of a market the company's product represents—how big its slice of the total pie is. For example, if Little Learners Parent–Teacher Store and its direct competitor, Educational Resources, both sell the same amount, they would each have half the "pie," or a 50 percent market share.

To compute market share, the analyst needs to know the sales for the total market and for the organization's own product. The analyst uses those figures in the following formula:

$$\text{Market Share} = \frac{\text{Sales of Organization's Product}}{\text{Total Sales for Product Type}}$$

Sales may be stated in terms of dollar volume or the number of units sold. Suppose an aircraft corporation sold 25 jumbo jets, out of industrywide total sales of 300. Its market share for jumbo jets would be as follows:

Market Share in Units: 25 units/300 units = .083 = 8.3%

Also suppose that these are state-of-the-art aircraft selling for $5 million apiece, compared to an industry average of $3 million. In terms of dollar volume, the company's market share is greater:

Market Share in Dollars = $125,000,000/$900,000,000
= .139 = 13.9%

A service provider sometimes cannot measure sales in terms of units. In that case, market share may be measured as the number of customers served relative to the size of the target market.

Marketers should interpret market share figures with caution. A large or growing market share suggests that an organization is providing the value customers are looking for. However, it does not indicate whether the organization is profiting or whether it could do even better with some other marketing strategy.

Wholesale and Retail Pricing

The pricing chapters introduced a variety of approaches to setting prices for goods and services. This appendix takes a closer look at the computations involved in two pricing tactics often used by wholesalers and retailers. These tactics are price markups and markdowns.

Markup

markup
The percentage by which channel members increase the price of a product when they sell it; may be stated as a percentage of cost or a percentage of selling price.

As a product moves through a distribution channel, each channel member charges the next a somewhat higher price. The channel members are said to "mark up" the price of the product. The percentage by which the price is increased is called, logically enough, a **markup.** Figure C.1 provides an example. There are two ways to state these markups as percentages—either as a percent of the cost or as a percent of the selling price.

Markup Based on Cost   The easiest types of markups to understand are those based on the product's cost—that is, the price the channel member paid to acquire the

FIGURE C.1
Example of Markups (in Dollars)

Manufacturer	Wholesaler	Retailer	Consumers
Cost to Make: $35	Cost to Buy: $50	Cost to Buy: $75	Cost to Buy: $125
Selling Price: $50	Selling Price: $75	Selling Price: $125	

Manufacturer's Markup = $15   Wholesaler's Markup = $25   Retailer's Markup = $50 product. To find the percentage of a markup based on cost, simply divide the amount of markup by the amount of cost:

$$\text{Markup Based on Cost} = \frac{\text{Markup in Dollars}}{\text{Cost in Dollars}}$$

This is the way many wholesalers and some small retailers express their markups.

In Figure C.1, for example, the wholesaler bought televisions from the manufacturer for $50 each. The wholesaler sells them to retail stores for $75, a markup (in dollars) of $25. The wholesaler's percentage markup is therefore $25/$50, or 50 percent.

Markup Based on Selling Price   Most retailers state markups as a percentage of the price at which they *sell* merchandise to their customers. This approach uses the following formula:

$$\text{Markup Based on Price} = \frac{\text{Markup in Dollars}}{\text{Selling Price in Dollars}}$$

Thus, in Figure C.1, when the wholesaler bought televisions at $50 and resold them at $75, the markup based on price would be $25/$75, or 33 percent.

Converting Markup Percentages   Sometimes the marketer knows the markup computed in one way but wants to convert it to the other type of markup. Some basic formulas are again useful. The following formula converts markup based on cost to markup based on price:

$$\text{Markup Based on Price} = \frac{\text{Markup Based on Cost}}{100\% + \text{Markup Based on Cost}}$$

Using the earlier example of the television wholesaler, the conversion is made as follows:

$$\text{Markup Based on Price} = \frac{50\%}{100\% + 50\%} = \frac{50\%}{150\%} = 33\%$$

The following formula converts markup based on price to markup based on cost:

$$\text{Markup Based on Cost} = \frac{\text{Markup Based on Price}}{100\% - \text{Markup Based on Price}}$$

Here is the computation for the example of the wholesaler:

$$\text{Markup Based on Cost} = \frac{33\%}{100\% - 33\%} = \frac{33\%}{67\%} = 50\%$$

Markdown

To stimulate more sales of a product, resellers may decide to reduce the price they are charging. Thus, a store might hold a clearance sale near the end of the summer, or a wholesaler might offer reduced prices on merchandise damaged in a flood. To arrive at the new price, wholesalers and retailers use markdowns. A **markdown** is the percentage by which a price is reduced. For example, CDs may go on sale at 20 percent off the full price.

markdown
The percentage by which the full price of an item is reduced in order to stimulate sales.

Finding the Markdown   The following formula computes the markdown percentage:

$$\text{Markdown} = \frac{\text{Markdown in Dollars}}{\text{Original Price}}$$

Suppose that a hotel wants to attract weekend visitors and offers rooms for $79, down from the usual price of $198. This markdown is $198 − $79 or $119, and $119/$198 equals .60, or 60 percent.

Finding the Markdown Ratio   When the seller uses markdowns, some units of the product are sold at full price and others at the reduced price. From a financial standpoint, the marketer wants to know more than the size of the markdown on a single unit. The marketer is interested in the overall effect of the markdown on earnings from the product. Therefore, the marketer computes the **markdown ratio,** which compares total markdowns for a group of products to total sales volume for those products. Here is the formula:

markdown ratio
The ratio of total markdowns (in dollars) for a group of products to total sales (in dollars) for those products.

$$\text{Markdown Ratio} = \frac{\text{Total Markdowns in Dollars}}{\text{Total Sales in Dollars}}$$

To see how this works, consider again the hotel offering a price discount on weekends. Suppose that in a month the hotel had booked 100 nights at the reduced rate ($79) and 200 nights at the full rate ($198). For that month, its total markdowns would be the amount of the markdown ($198 − $79) times the number of rooms booked at the reduced rate (100):

$$\text{Total Markdowns in Dollars} = 100(\$198 - \$79)$$
$$= 100 \times \$119 = \$11,900$$

The hotel's total sales would be as follows:

$$\text{Total Sales in Dollars} = 100(\$79) + 200(\$198) = \$47,500$$

With these numbers, you can find the markdown ratio:

$$\text{Markdown Ratio} = \$11,900/\$47,500 = .251 = 25.1\%$$

In other words, the special weekend rate resulted in an overall markdown ratio of 25.1 percent. Booking more rooms at full price would reduce this ratio.

Markdown ratios can help marketers control their pricing strategies. By analyzing markdown ratios, the marketer can determine whether discounts are taking too big a bite out of profits for a particular product or product line. For example, large retailers review markdown ratios for each department of the store.

Key Terms and Concepts

operating statement (p. 576)	gross margin ratio (p. 579)	inventory turnover (p. 581)
returns and allowances (p. 576)	net profit ratio (p. 579)	market share (p. 581)
cost of goods sold/cost of sales (p. 577)	operating expense ratio (p. 579)	markup (p. 582)
gross margin (p. 578)	return on investment (ROI) (p. 580)	markdown (p. 583)
operating ratios (p. 578)	return on assets (ROA) (p. 580)	markdown ratio (p. 584)

Review and Discussion Questions

Table C.2 shows an operating statement for Drafting on Demand, a temporary services agency that provides drafters to engineering departments that need extra help with projects. This business employs five drafters, all with experience in computer-aided design as well as in drawing blueprints. Use the operating statement in Table C.2 to answer questions 1 through 4.

1. Fill in the missing amounts (indicated by letters in parentheses).

2. Did the business have a profit or a loss for this reporting period?
3. Compute the following ratios:
    a. gross margin ratio
    b. net profit ratio
    c. operating expense ratio
4. To evaluate the financial performance of Drafting on Demand, what information would you want besides the ratios you computed in question 3? Explain.

T A B L E C.2
Sample Operating Statement for Review and Discussion Questions

DRAFTING ON DEMAND
OPERATING STATEMENT
FOR THE YEAR ENDED DECEMBER 31, 1997

Sales Revenue:		
Gross sales	$395,000	
Less: Allowances	1,000	
Net sales		$394,000
Cost of Sales:		
Direct labor	$140,000	
Overhead	70,000	
Cost of sales		210,000
Gross Margin		(a) _____
Expenses:		
Selling expenses:		
Sales salary	$60,000	
Advertising	5,000	
Total selling expenses	$ 65,000	
Administrative expenses:		
Administrative salaries	$85,000	
Office supplies	2,500	
Other administrative expenses	1,000	
Total administrative expenses	(b) _____	
General expenses:		
Rent	$ 9,000	
Utilities	2,500	
Interest	2,000	
Other general expenses	1,000	
Total general expenses	(c) _____	
Total expenses		(d) _____
Net Profit (Loss) before Taxes		(e) _____

5. A popular Thai restaurant decides to open a second location. The restaurant's owners forecast that setting up the restaurant will cost $430,000 and that in its first year it will earn a profit of $8,600.
   a. What is the expected return on investment for the new restaurant?
   b. Does this ROI look favorable? Can you suggest why this new restaurant might look like a good investment to its owners?
6. Can you compute inventory turnover from the operating statement in Table C.2? Explain.
7. According to the operating statement for Big Sound Audio Equipment, the company started the year with inventory of $600,000 and ended with inventory of $700,000. The cost of goods sold for the year was $7,800,000. What was the inventory turnover rate?
8. From an industry trade magazine, marketing manager Jon Bretts learns that European organizations bought $4 million worth of electric pencil sharpeners last year. They are expected to spend at least $4.2 million on the machines this year. Jon's company sold $800,000 worth of electric pencil sharpeners in Europe last year and is trying for a 10 percent increase in sales.
   a. What was the company's European market share last year?

   b. If Jon's company meets its sales goal for this year and total sales are as forecast, what will the company's market share be?
9. Solve the following problems using the data in Figure C.1.
   a. Find the retailer's markup percentage based on cost.
   b. Find the retailer's markup percentage based on selling price.
10. To make room for its spring clothes, Big Value Store reduced the price of $100 sweaters to $65 at its East Towne and West Towne locations. The East Towne store sold 50 sweaters at full price and 40 at the reduced price. The West Towne store sold 35 sweaters at full price and 100 at the reduced price.
    a. What was the markdown percentage for the sweaters?
    b. What was the markdown ratio for the East Towne store?
    c. What was the markdown ratio for the West Towne store?
    d. Compare the performances of the two store locations.

Appendix Project Analyzing Operating Statements

Obtain annual reports (for the same year) for two organizations in the same industry—say, two airlines or two manufacturers. You should be able to find annual reports in your school or local library, or you can request them by contacting the companies you're interested in.

Look up the operating statement in each annual report. Remember, it may be called by another name, such as income statement or profit-and-loss statement. Under whatever name, it will be the table that shows revenues, expenses, and profit or loss.

For each organization, find the gross margin ratio, net profit ratio, return on investment (or assets), and any other figures you think are important for this type of industry. Based on this information, at which of the two companies would you rather hold a marketing job? Why?

Notes

Chapter 1

1. Peter D. Bennett, ed., *Dictionary of Marketing Terms*, 2nd ed. (Chicago: American Marketing Association, 1995), p. 166.
2. Anne Murphy, "Entrepreneur of the Year," *Inc.*, December 1995, pp. 38–40+.
3. Anne Murphy, "Entrepreneur of the Year."
4. Anne Murphy, "Entrepreneur of the Year."
5. Walter R. Nord and J. Paul Peter, "A Behavior Modification Perspective on Marketing," *Journal of Marketing*, Spring 1980, pp. 36–47; Carl P. Zeithaml and Valarie A. Zeithaml, "Environmental Management: Revising the Marketing Perspective," *Journal of Marketing*, Spring 1984, pp. 46–53; Philip Kotler, "Megamarketing," *Harvard Business Review*, March–April 1986, pp. 117–124.
6. Of course, if customers believe that a product will not work well, that other people will criticize them, that they will feel bad about buying, owning and using it, or that using it will be unpleasant, these are not perceived benefits. However, we believe that these four dimensions are the types of benefits customers often seek in purchasing and using products and services.
7. Donna Fenn, "Leader of the Pack," *Inc.*, February 1996, pp. 31–32+.

Chapter 2

1. "A Little Advice for the New CEO," *Newsweek*, November 19, 1992, p. 57.
2. Brian O'Reilly, "First Blood in the Telecom Wars," *Fortune*, March 4, 1996, pp. 124–126+.
3. Patricia Saiki, "Rising Force," *Entrepreneur*, December 1992, p. 176.
4. Ravi S. Achrol, "Evolution of the Marketing Organization: New Forms for Turbulent Environments," *Journal of Marketing*, October 1991, pp. 77–93.
5. "Pervasive and Irreversible," *The Economist*, November 28, 1992, p. 18.
6. Cheryl Russell and Margaret Ambry, *The Official Guide to American Incomes* (Ithaca, NY: New Strategist Publications & Consulting, 1993), p. 217.
7. "Washed Up?" *The Economist*, March 9, 1996, pp. 23–25.
8. O'Reilly, "First Blood in the Telecom Wars," pp. 124, 126, 130.
9. Steven Pratt, "That Something Extra," *Chicago Tribune*, March 27, 1996, sec. 7, p. 3.
10. Peter Brimelow and Leslie Spencer, "Ralph Nader, Inc.," *Forbes*, September 17, 1990, pp. 117–121.
11. Paul M. Barrett, "Supreme Court Ruling Makes It Tougher for Workers to Win Job-Bias Lawsuits," *The Wall Street Journal*, June 28, 1993, p. A18.
12. Pratt, "That Something Extra."
13. "Minority Households Head for Big Gains in the 1990s," *Business Week*, December 7, 1992, p. 24.
14. *Statistical Abstract of the United States*, U.S. Department of Commerce, 1995, p. 63.
15. "It's Not Like Mr. Mom," *Newsweek*, December 14, 1992, p. 70.
16. Judith Waldrop, "Secrets of the Age Pyramids," *American Demographics*, August 1992, pp. 46–52.
17. John Chuang, "On Balance," *Inc.*, July 1995, pp. 25–26.
18. Ford S. Worthy, "A New Mass Market Emerges," *Fortune*, Fall 1990, pp. 51–55.
19. Worthy, "A New Mass Market Emerges."
20. Lynn Beresford, "Going My Way?" *Entrepreneur*, February 1996, p. 32.
21. Amy Miller, "Sundae School," *Inc.*, December 1995, pp. 29–30.
22. The Home Depot, "1992 Corporate Social Responsibility Report."
23. Michael Schroeder, "Charity Doesn't Begin at Home Anymore," *Time*, February 25, 1991, p. 91.
24. Pinchas Fleischman, "Honesty Is the Best Policy," *Selling Power*, March 1996, p. 92.
25. Sharon Begley, "The Great Imposters," *Newsweek*, March 18, 1996, p. 48.
26. Paul Lienert, "Recycling Becomes Parts and Parcel of Carmaking," *Chicago Tribune*, March 24, 1996, sec. 12, pp. 1, 6.
27. John E. Ettlie, "The Manufacturing Ecology Imperative," *Production*, February 1993, p. 28.
28. Allan J. Magrath, "The Marketin' of the Green," *Sales & Marketing Management*, October 1992, pp. 21–22.
29. Robert A. Mamis, "Waste Not," *Inc.*, May 1993, p. 48.
30. Michael P. Cronin, "Green Marketing Heats Up," *Inc.*, January 1993, p. 27.
31. Thomas McCarroll, "How IBM Was Left Behind," *Time*, December 28, 1992, pp. 26–28.
32. Samuel Greengard, "Getting Caught Up in the Web," *Home*, March 1996, pp. 30+; O. C. Ferrell and Geoffrey Hirt, *Business: A Changing World*, 2nd ed. (Burr Ridge, Ill.: Irwin, 1996), p. 418.
33. Greengard, "Getting Caught Up in the Web."
34. Bob Wehling, "The Future of Marketing," speech to the World Federation of Advertisers, Sydney, Australia, October 31, 1995.
35. Wehling, "The Future of Marketing."
36. "Promise and Peril as Scouts Turn to Internet in Cookie Sale," *The New York Times*, February 25, 1996, p. 11.
37. Rashi Glazer, "Marketing in an Information-Intensive Environment: Strategic Implications of Knowledge as an Asset," *Journal of Marketing*, October 1991, pp. 1–19.

38. Wehling, "The Future of Marketing."

39. Vladimir Edelman, "Primed for Crime on the Internet," *Inc. Technology,* September 12, 1995, p. 18.

40. Wehling, "The Future of Marketing."

41. "Pitney Bowes: Jumping Ahead by Going High Tech," *Fortune,* 126 (October 19, 1992), pp. 113–114.

42. Michael Porter, *Competitive Advantage* (New York: Free Press, 1985).

43. "Washed Up?" p. 24.

44. Leon Jaroff, "A Thirst for Competition," *Time,* June 1, 1992, p. 75.

45. Stewart Toy, "A Stronger Tailwind for Airbus?" *Business Week,* March 18, 1996, p. 51.

46. Michael E. Porter, *Competitive Strategy* (New York: The Free Press, 1980). Also see Porter, *Competitive Advantage*; and Michael E. Porter, *The Competitive Advantage of Nations* (New York: The Free Press, 1990).

47. "Why the Buses Don't Run on Time," *The Economist,* March 9, 1996, p. 66.

48. Bob Gatty, "Coping with Another Supermarket Threat," *Grocery Marketing,* January 1996, p. 5.

49. "Washed Up?" p. 23.

50. Joshua Hyatt and Jerry Useem, "The Defiant Ones," *Inc.,* April 1996, pp. 56–58+.

Chapter 3

1. *The Economist,* March 2, 1996, p. 63.

2. Peter D. Bennett, ed., *Dictionary of Marketing Terms* 2nd ed. (Chicago: American Marketing Association, 1995), p. 93.

3. "Going Global: Canada," *Inc.* advertising supplement, June 1993, p. 1.

4. Reginald Biddle and Toni Dick, "Selling Services to Canada," *Business America,* May 31, 1993, pp. 2–5.

5. Andrea Dabrowski, "Mexico, Si," *International Business,* March 1993, pp. 54–57.

6. Albert Warson, "Tapping Canadian Markets," *Inc.,* March 1993, pp. 90–91.

7. G. Pierre Goad, "Freer, but Not Free," *The Wall Street Journal,* September 24, 1992, p. R18.

8. "Profiles in Marketing: Frank Bracken," *Sales & Marketing Management,* April 1993, p. 10.

9. Dabrowski, "Mexico, Si."

10. "Going Global: Mexico," *Inc.* advertising supplement, September 1993, p. 1.

11. James L. Tyson, "NAFTA Fallout Irks Workers across America," *Christian Science Monitor,* January 3, 1996, pp. 1, 8.

12. Alexander F. Watson, "The Americas in the 21st Century: Defining U.S. Interests," *U.S. Department of State Dispatch,* January 1996, pp. 4–6.

13. Margot Hornblower, "No One Ever Said It Would Be Easy," *Time,* March 1, 1993, pp. 32, 41.

14. "All Strung Up," *The Economist,* April 17, 1993, p. 70.

15. Amy Borrus, "This Trade Gap Ain't What It Used to Be," *Business Week,* March 18, 1996, p. 50.

16. "Taking Aim," *The Economist,* April 24, 1993, p. 74.

17. "ASEAN Targets Trade Barriers," *The Wall Street Journal,* December 18, 1995, p. A11.

18. "Washed Up?" *The Economist,* March 9, 1996, pp. 23–25.

19. "China: The Titan Stirs," *The Economist,* November 28, 1992, pp. 3–6.

20. "The Faltering State," *The Economist,* November 28, 1992, pp. 8–9.

21. Timothy J. McNulty, "Market, Morals Split U.S. Policy," *Chicago Tribune,* February 19, 1996, sec. 1, pp. 1, 10.

22. Louis Kraar, "Asia's Hot New Growth Triangle," *Fortune,* October 6, 1992, pp. 136–138+.

23. Pete Engardio and Neil Gross, "Asia's High-Tech Quest," *Business Week,* December 7, 1992, pp. 126–130.

24. Robert C. Schmults, "The African Market: A Lion Awakes," *Insight,* August 9, 1993, pp. 18–21.

25. Schmults, "The African Market," p. 21.

26. Jeannette R. Scollard, "Road to Russia," *Entrepreneur,* March 1993, pp. 114–119.

27. Scollard, "Road to Russia."

28. Watson, "The Americas in the 21st Century," p. 5.

29. Laurie Goering, "Jobs Dearth Casts Pall in Latin America," *Chicago Tribune,* March 25, 1996, sec. 4, pp. 1, 4.

30. Gary Marx, " 'Bullish on Latin America': Foreign Money Pours in as Growth Takes Off," *Chicago Tribune,* June 20, 1993, sec. 7, pp. 1, 4.

31. Goering, "Jobs Dearth Casts Pall," p. 4.

32. "Calling China," *The Economist,* February 3, 1996, p. 58.

33. "Selling to the New Global Middle Class," *Business Week,* October 25, 1993, p. 152.

34. Valerie Reitman, "Enticed by Visions of Enormous Numbers, More Western Marketers Move into China," *The Wall Street Journal,* July 12, 1993, pp. B1, B6; Andrew Tanzer, "This Time It's for Real," *Forbes,* August 2, 1993, pp. 58–61.

35. "Going Global: Mexico," p. 5.

36. John Holusha, "Pushing Goodyear to Focus Abroad," *The New York Times,* March 3, 1996, sec. 3, p. 4.

37. Nathaniel C. Nash, "Europeans Agree on New Currency," *The New York Times,* December 16, 1995, pp. 1, 40; "A Dying Deadline?" *The Economist,* January 20, 1996, pp. 51–52.

38. Louis Kraar, "Indonesia on the Move," *Fortune,* September 20, 1993, pp. 112, 114, 116.

39. "Washed Up?" p. 24.

40. "Claiming Diversion of Grain, Farmers Sack Chicken Restaurant," *Chicago Tribune,* January 31, 1996, sec. 1, p. 10.

41. Jerry Flint, "Opportunities in Terrorism," *Forbes,* February 15, 1993, pp. 193–194.

42. Stephanie Anderson Forest, "Yankee Chicken, Go Home," *Business Week,* March 11, 1996, p. 36.

43. "Bans Spreading on British Beef," *Chicago Tribune,* March 23, 1996, sec. 2, p. 1.

44. Hal Plotkin, "In the China Shop," *Inc.,* September 1993, pp. 108–109.

45. Ronald E. Yates, "A Distress Call on Trade Barriers," *Chicago Tribune,* April 1, 1996, sec. 4, pp. 1, 4.

46. Joshua Hyatt and Jerry Useem, "The Defiant Ones," *Inc.,* April 1996, pp. 56–58+.

47. Susan Moffatt, "China's Crackdown on CD Counterfeiting: Too Little, Too Late?" *Fortune,* March 4, 1996, p. 32.

48. "False Friends," *The Economist,* January 13, 1996, p. 66.

49. Ronald E. Yates, "Espionage Fight Shifts to Corporate Battlefield," *Chicago Tribune,* March 24, 1996, sec. 5, p. 1.

50. Suman Dubey, "After 16-Year Dry Spell, Coca-Cola Co. Will Bring 'the Real Thing' Back to India," *The Wall Street Journal,* October 22, 1993, p. B7C.

51. Daniel Benjamin, "Germany Is Troubled by How Little Work Its Workers Are Doing," *The Wall Street Journal,* May 6, 1993, pp. A1, A7.

52. Jack Hayes, "No Bratwurst on Saturday: Big Macs Reign in Germany," *Nation's Restaurant News,* November 2, 1992, p. 18.

53. Susan Greco, "Will Your Product 'Travel' Overseas?" *Inc.,* July 1992, p. 118.

54. Andrew Tanzer, "Hot Wings Take Off," *Forbes,* January 18, 1993, p. 74.

55. Madeline E. Hutcheson, "When in Asia . . . ," *UPS International Update* (United Parcel Service), Spring 1993, p. 4.

56. Robert A. Mamis, "Not So Innocent Abroad," *Inc.,* September 1993, pp. 110–111.

57. June Fletcher, "A Global Economy Works for House Sales, Too," *The Wall Street Journal,* February 23, 1996, p. B8.

58. "Going Global: Mexico," *Inc.* advertising supplement, September 1993, p. 2.

59. Kevin Helliker, "They're Sore Because They Know the Irish Speak English the Best," *The Wall Street Journal*, July 13, 1993, p. B1.

60. "A Task for Two: Invent a Brand," *The Grocer*, September 12, 1992, pp. 48–49.

61. "Growing Your Business by Going Global," *Inc.*, September 1993, p. 107, citing Peter Schwartz, *The Art of the Long View*.

62. Andrew Tanzer, "China's Dolls," *Forbes*, December 21, 1992, pp. 250, 252.

63. "The Black Market," *The Economist*, February 10, 1996, p. 60.

64. "The Class of 1992," *The Economist*, September 5, 1992, pp. 62–64.

65. "Washed Up?" p. 25.

66. Brian Dumaine, "Exporting Jobs and Ethics," *Fortune*, October 5, 1992, p. 10.

67. Lynn Beresford, "Bad Rep," *Entrepreneur*, February 1996, p. 90.

68. Stan Sesser, "Opium War Redux," *The New Yorker*, September 13, 1993, pp. 78–89; Paula Dwyer, "Lots of Purring but Less Profit in New Markets Overseas," *Business Week*, May 3, 1993, p. 132.

69. Armin A. Brott, "How to Avoid Bear Traps," *Nation's Business*, September 1993, pp. 49–50.

70. "A Load of Rubbish," *The Economist*, January 13, 1996, p. 64.

71. Bruno Giussani, "Why Europe Lags on the Web," *Inc. Technology*, November 14, 1995, p. 23.

72. "Dinosaurs and Teenagers," *The Economist*, March 9, 1996, pp. 18–19.

73. "Spanish Customs," *The Economist*, February 3, 1996, p. 55.

74. Bob Wehling, "The Future of Marketing," speech to the World Federation of Advertisers, Sydney, Australia, October 31, 1995.

75. Jerry DeMuth, "Stop-and-Go Exports," *International Business*, July 1993, pp. 66, 68.

76. "Home Delivery Services: Convenience for Consumers," *International Business Newsletter*, June 1993, pp. 9–10.

77. Stephanie Losee, "New U.S. Export: Destressing Kids," *Fortune*, February 8, 1993, p. 10.

78. Dave Savona, "Global Go-Getters: Marvel Entertainment Group," *International Business*, September 1993, p. 20.

79. Donald L. Baron, "European Vocation," *Entrepreneur*, January 1993, pp. 117–122.

80. "Variety Is the Ice of Life," *Business Franchise* (Britain), July/August 1993, pp. 36–37.

81. "Fruits of Socialism," *Time*, January 11, 1993, p. 10.

82. Hal Plotkin, "In the China Shop," *Inc.*, September 1993, pp. 108–109.

83. "Motorola," *Fortune*, August 24, 1992, global business advertising section, pp. S-6– S-7.

84. Tim Smart, "Why Ignore 95% of the World's Market?" *Business Week*, Reinventing America 1992 special issue, p. 64.

85. Amy Borrus, "This Trade Gap Ain't What It Used to Be," *Business Week*, March 18, 1996, p. 50; Valerie Reitman, "Toyota to Export U.S.-Made Cars to South Korea," *The Wall Street Journal*, February 9, 1996, p. A8.

86. "Hyundai Goes It Alone," *The Economist*, March 2, 1996, p. 69.

Chapter 4

1. J. Paul Peter and James H. Donnelly, Jr., *A Preface to Marketing Management*, 7th ed. (Burr Ridge, Ill.: Irwin, 1997), p. 7.

2. Robert McGarvey, "Mad about Marketing," *Entrepreneur*, April 1996, pp. 133–137.

3. Rodale Press brochure.

4. Frederick E. Webster, Jr., "The Changing Role of Marketing in the Corporation," *Journal of Marketing* 56 (October 1992), pp. 1–17.

5. Richard Normann and Rafael Ramírez, "From Value Chain to Value Constellation: Designing Interactive Strategy," *Harvard Business Review*, July–August 1993, pp. 65–77.

6. "Rubbermaid: Breaking All the Molds," *Sales & Marketing Management*, August 1992, p. 42.

7. Jon Van, "Universal Access' Ameritech's Big Picture," *Chicago Tribune*, February 14, 1993, sec. 7, pp. 1, 4.

8. Van, "Universal Access."

9. Michael Barrier, "When 'Just-in-Time' Just Isn't Enough," *Nation's Business*, November 1992, pp. 30–31.

10. John R. Emshwiller, "Hang Ten International Rides Forward by Looking Back," *The Wall Street Journal*, December 30, 1992, p. B2.

11. Julie Tilsner, "Duracell Looks Abroad for More Juice," *Business Week*, December 21, 1992, pp. 52–56.

12. Leslie Brokaw, "Case in Point," *Inc.*, December 1995, pp. 88–90, 92.

13. Matt Murray, "GNC Makes Ginseng, Shark Pills Its Potion for Growth," *The Wall Street Journal*, March 15, 1996, pp. B1, B3.

14. George S. Day, "Marketing's Contribution to the Strategy Dialogue," University of Pennsylvania, n.d.

15. Sarah Schafer, "How Information Technology Is Leveling the Playing Field," *Inc. Technology*, November 14, 1995, pp. 92+.

16. Murray, "GNC Makes Ginseng, Shark Pills Its Potion for Growth."

17. Susan Greco, "Just Say No," *Inc.*, April 1996, pp. 50–51+.

18. Anne Murphy, "Entrepreneur of the Year," *Inc.*, December 1995, pp. 38–40+.

19. David Young, "Grainger Retools Strategy, Gets Faster, Busier, Bigger," *Chicago Tribune*, July 18, 1993, sec. 7, pp. 1, 6.

20. Boston Consulting Group, *The Product Portfolio* (Boston: BCG, 1970).

21. Robert Jacobson and David A. Aaker, "Is Market Share All That It's Cracked Up to Be?" *Journal of Marketing* (Fall 1985), pp. 11–22; Carolyn Y. Woo and Arnold C. Cooper, "The Surprising Case for Low Market Share," *Harvard Business Review*, November–December 1982, pp. 106–113; and Stephen J. Markell, Sue E. Neeley, and Thomas H. Strickland, "Explaining Profitability: Dispelling the Market Share Fog," *Journal of Business Research* 16 (1988), pp. 189–196.

22. Emshwiller, "Hang Ten Rides Forward."

23. Webster, "The Changing Role of Marketing," p. 11.

24. Amy Barrett, "Detergents, Aisle 2. Pizza Hut, Aisle 5," *Business Week*, June 7, 1993, pp. 82–83.

25. "Overrating Appraisals," *Total Quality Newsletter*, November 1992, p. 8.

26. Jeen-Su Lim and David A. Reid, "Vital Cross-Functional Linkages with Marketing," *Industrial Marketing Management* 21 (1992), pp. 159–165.

27. Ford S. Worthy, "Japan's Smart Secret Weapon," *Fortune*, August 12, 1991, pp. 72–75.

28. Frances Huffman, "Marketing Makeover," *Entrepreneur*, November 1992, pp. 129–133.

29. Huffman, "Marketing Makeover."

30. McGarvey, "Mad about Marketing," p. 133.

31. Dick Schaaf, "Complex Quality," *The Quality Imperative*, September 1992, pp. 16–18+.

32. Karen Lowry Miller, "Overhaul in Japan," *Business Week*, December 21, 1992, pp. 80–83, 86.

33. Peter D. Bennett, ed., *Dictionary of Marketing Terms*, 2nd ed. (Chicago: American Marketing Association, 1995), p. 79.

34. Gayle Sato Stodder, "Healthy Returns," *Entrepreneur,* February 1996, pp. 102, 106–107.

35. Joanne Cleaver, "Tech Firm Sees Window for Its Memory Product," *Crain's Chicago Business,* July 10, 1995, p. 26.

Chapter 5

1. Peter D. Bennett, ed., *Dictionary of Marketing Terms* 2nd ed. (Chicago: American Marketing Association, 1995), p. 169.

2. R. Douglas Shute, "Connecting to the Source," *Inc. Technology,* November 14, 1995, p. 27.

3. J. Paul Peter and James H. Donnelly, Jr., *A Preface to Marketing Management,* 7th ed. (Burr Ridge, Ill.: Irwin, 1997), pp. 39–40.

4. Bennett, *Dictionary of Marketing Terms,* p. 53.

5. Bruce W. Mainzer, "Consumer Research at United: The Only Good Research Is Research That's Available Now!" presentation at American Marketing Association's Attitude Research Conference, January 26–29, 1992.

6. Bradley Johnson, "Behind All the Hype Lies a Hidden, Crucial Asset," *Advertising Age,* October 2, 1995, pp. 30, 32.

7. William R. Pape, "Zeroing In on Data," *Inc. Technology,* March 19, 1996, pp. 23–24.

8. The Coca-Cola Company, Annual Report 1995, p. 31.

9. Casey Bukro, "Garbage Collection Goes On-Line," *Chicago Tribune,* March 17, 1993, sec. 3, pp. 1–2.

10. Edward O. Welles, "The Shape of Things to Come," *Inc.,* February 1992, pp. 66–69+.

11. Jerry E. Morton, "Information-Driven Retail Marketing," *Grocery Marketing,* January 1996, pp. 51–52.

12. Joanne Friedrick, "Getting to Know You," *Grocery Marketing,* October 1995, pp. 6–8+.

13. Malcolm Fleschner with Charles Lee Browne, "Value Sells," *Selling Power,* March 1996, pp. 48, 50, 52.

14. Bennett, *Dictionary of Marketing Terms,* p. 216.

15. Stephanie Gruner, "Capitalizing on Customer Data," *Inc.,* April 1996, p. 107.

16. Otis Port, "Quality: Small and Midsize Companies Seize the Challenge—Not a Moment Too Soon," *Business Week,* November 30, 1992, pp. 66–72.

17. Jeremy Main, "How to Steal the Best Ideas Around," *Fortune,* October 19, 1992, pp. 102–106.

18. Main, "How to Steal."

19. Bennett, *Dictionary of Marketing Terms,* p. 257.

20. Fleming Meeks, "And Then the Designer Left," *Forbes,* December 7, 1992, pp. 162+.

21. James Coates, "Low-Cost Software Brings Census Closer to Home," *Chicago Tribune,* May 2, 1993, sec. 7, p. 6.

22. William Bak, "Thoroughly Modern Marketing," *Entrepreneur,* May 1993, pp. 58, 60–61.

23. Joseph M. Juran, "Made in U.S.A.: A Renaissance of Quality," *Harvard Business Review,* July–August 1993, pp. 42–50.

24. Peter O. Keegan, "Operators Are All Ears with New 800 Numbers," *Nation's Restaurant News,* March 29, 1993, p. 15.

25. Michael J. McCarthy, "James Bond Hits the Supermarket: Stores Snoop on Shoppers' Habits to Boost Sales," *The Wall Street Journal,* August 25, 1993, pp. B1, B8.

26. Matthew D. Shank and Raymond LaGarce, "Study: Color Makes Any Message More Effective," *Marketing News,* August 6, 1990, p. 12.

27. Charlie Etmekjian, "Experiments: Their Changing Nature and Why They'll Still Be with Us During the 1990s," presentation at American Marketing Association's Behavioral Research Conference, January 24–27, 1990.

28. David Powers Cleary, "BirdsEye Frozen Foods," *Great American Brands: The Success Formulas That Made Them Famous* (New York: Fairchild Publications, 1981), pp. 7–12.

29. Udayan Gupta, "Costly Market Research Pays Off for Biotech Start-Up," *The Wall Street Journal,* August 2, 1993, p. B2.

30. "What's the Best Source of Market Research?" *Inc.,* June 1992, p. 108.

31. Hal Plotkin, "Dining à la Data," *Inc. Technology,* November 14, 1995, pp. 85–86.

32. "Gathering Intelligence Any Way You Can Get It," *The Office Advisor (Inc.* magazine newsletter), Spring 1993, p. 4.

33. Leah Haran, "PC-Meter Tracks Computer Users," *Advertising Age,* October 2, 1995, p. 36.

34. Walker Industry Image Study, 10th ed. (Indianapolis: Walker Research & Analysis, 1992).

35. "Data Drives Hospital System's 'Triage' Quality Improvement," *Total Quality Newsletter,* August 1993, pp. 5–6.

36. Walker Industry Image Study.

37. Annual Report of Procter & Gamble Company, 1993, p. 6.

38. Walker Industry Image Study.

39. Etmekjian, "Experiments," pp. 3–4.

40. Bickley Townsend, "Market Research That Matters," *American Demographics,* August 1992, pp. 58–60.

41. Eric Schine, "Computer Maps Pop Up All over the Map," *Business Week,* July 26, 1993, pp. 75–76.

42. Kazumi Tanaka, "Putting Your Business on the Map," *Inc. Technology,* June 18, 1996, pp. 94–99; "The 1996 Business Strategist's Software Directory," *Journal of Business Strategy,* January/February 1996, pp. 41–45.

43. Howard Schlossberg, "Shoppers Virtually Stroll through Store Aisles to Examine Packages," *Marketing News,* June 7, 1993, p. 2.

44. See Antonio S. Lauglaug, "Why Technical-Market Research?" *Journal of Business Strategy* (September/October 1992): 26–35.

45. Phil Guarscio, "How GM Targets 'Mature' Market Niche," *Advertising Age,* January 11, 1993, p. 26.

46. Lauglaug, "Why Technical-Market Research?"

47. Joanne Cleaver, "Online Espionage," *Crain's Small Business,* February 1995, p. 21.

48. Phaedra Hise, "Getting Smart On-Line," *Inc. Technology,* March 19, 1996, pp. 59–60+.

49. Gregg Cebrzynski, "TV Station Sued over Alleged Phony Survey," *Marketing News,* August 28, 1987, pp. 1, 42.

50. Martha Brannigan, "Pseudo Polls: More Surveys Draw Criticism for Motives and Methods," *The Wall Street Journal,* January 27, 1987, p. 27.

51. Gilbert A. Churchill, Jr., *Basic Marketing Research,* 3rd ed. (Fort Worth, Tex.: Dryden Press, 1996), pp. 63–64.

52. Walker Industry Image Study.

53. Cary Lu, "Look Who's Talking," *Inc. Technology,* March 19, 1996, pp. 29–30.

54. Friedrick, "Getting to Know You," pp. 7–8.

55. Laura Loro, "Downside for Public Is Privacy Issue," *Advertising Age,* October 2, 1995, p. 32.

56. "Inside Track," *Entrepreneur,* February 1996, pp. 86–87.

57. The examples in this paragraph are from Aimee Stern, "Do You Know What They Want?" *International Business,* March 1993, pp. 102–103.

58. Jennifer Cody, "They Hired Someone to Find Out if People Really Like Chocolate?" *The Wall Street Journal,* November 26, 1993, p. B1.

59. Valerie Reitman, "P&G Uses Skills It Has Honed at Home to Introduce Its Brands to the Russians," *The Wall Street Journal,* April 14, 1993, pp. B1, B10.

Chapter 6

1. Peter D. Bennett, ed., *Dictionary of Marketing Terms,* 2nd ed. (Chicago: American Marketing Association, 1995), p. 59.
2. Debra Phillips, "Head over Heels," *Entrepreneur,* February 1996, p. 23.
3. Pat Baldwin, "Ad Firm Links Brand Choice to Motivation," *Chicago Tribune,* August 9, 1992, sec. 7, p. 9.
4. Richard Phalon, "Walking Billboards," *Forbes,* December 7, 1992, pp. 84, 86.
5. "Keeping the Customer Satisfied," *Adweek,* August 24, 1992, pp. 40+.
6. Pat Sloan, "Getting a Tan, Family Style," *Advertising Age,* January 25, 1993, p. 12.
7. Jeremy Kahn, "Fresh as a . . . Beer?," *Newsweek,* July 15, 1996, p. 42.
8. Beth Healy, "For Banks, Lots of Clout," *Crain's Chicago Business,* February 26, 1996, p. 14.
9. Diane Crispell, "People Patterns: Students Picking College Bank on Reputation," *The Wall Street Journal,* May 12, 1993, p. B1.
10. Beth Healy, "Listen Up, Banks: Consumers Speak," *Crain's Chicago Business,* February 26, 1996, pp. 1, 13–14+.
11. "Sales of Prepared Frozen Vegetables Melt," *The Wall Street Journal,* December 15, 1992, p. B10.
12. Mike Dorning, "For Women, Shopping Is Not Just an Adventure, It's a Job," *Chicago Tribune,* January 20, 1993, sec. 3, pp. 1, 3.
13. Daniel McGinn, "Working to Beat the Rap," *Newsweek,* May 13, 1996, p. 49.
14. Linda Himelstein, "Levi's vs. the Dress Code," *Business Week,* April 1, 1996, pp. 57–58.
15. Bennett, *Dictionary of Marketing Terms,* p. 72.
16. Leon G. Schiffman and Leslie Lazar Kanuck, *Consumer Behavior,* 5th ed. (Englewood Cliffs, N.J.: Prentice-Hall, 1994), pp. 436–438.
17. Alecia Swasy, "Don't Sell Thick Diapers in Tokyo," *New York Times,* October 3, 1993, sec. 3, p. 9.
18. Margaret Ambry, *The Almanac of Consumer Markets* (Chicago: Probus Publishing, 1990); *Statistical Abstract of the United States,* 115th ed. (Washington, D.C.: U.S. Government Printing Office, 1995), p. 399.
19. Bennett, *Dictionary of Marketing Terms,* p. 276.
20. Cecelia Blalock, "The 21st Century Shopper," *Grocery Marketing,* October 1995, pp. 12, 14–15.
21. Joseph A. Kirby, "Betty Crocker Gets Multicultural Makeover," *Chicago Tribune,* March 20, 1996, sec. 1, p. 3.
22. William Dunn, "The Move toward Ethnic Marketing," *Nation's Business,* July 1992, pp. 39–41.
23. J. Paul Peter and Jerry C. Olson, *Consumer Behavior and Marketing Strategy,* 4th ed. (Homewood, Ill.: Irwin, 1996), p. 427.
24. James F. Engel, Robert D. Blackwell, and Paul Miniard, *Consumer Behavior,* 8th ed. (Hinsdale, Ill.: Dryden Press, 1995), p. 647.
25. Laura Bird, "Marketers Miss Out by Alienating Blacks," *The Wall Street Journal,* April 9, 1993, p. B8.
26. See Jerome D. Williams and William J. Qualls, "Middle-Class Black Consumers and Intensity of Ethnic Identification," *Psychology and Marketing,* Winter 1989, pp. 263–286; Engel, Blackwell, and Miniard, *Consumer Behavior,* p. 655.
27. Nancy Millman, "Blacks Put a Value on Accurate Portrayal in Ads," *Chicago Tribune,* April 25, 1993, sec. 7, pp. 1, 6.
28. *Ibid.*
29. Wilma Randle, "Closer Look at Black Spending," *Chicago Tribune,* August 25, 1993, sec. 3, pp. 1–2.
30. "'Black Pride' Plays Role in Buying Goods," *Marketing News,* February 19, 1990, p. 11.
31. Pamela Patrick Novotny, "Spirited Style," *Chicago Tribune,* August 15, 1993, sec. 6, p. 7; John Schmeltzer, "Ebony Good Fit at Spiegel," *Chicago Tribune,* July 26, 1993, sec. 4, pp. 1, 4.
32. Tim Bovee, "Hispanics Poised to Become Largest Minority in U.S.," *Wisconsin State Journal,* September 29, 1993, p. 1; Dunn, "The Move toward Ethnic Marketing."
33. Bovee, "Hispanics Poised."
34. Peter Brimelow, "The Fracturing of America," *Forbes,* March 30, 1992, pp. 74–75.
35. *Ibid.*
36. Dunn, "The Move toward Ethnic Marketing."
37. Bovee, "Hispanics Poised,"; Dunn, "The Move toward Ethnic Marketing."
38. Peter and Olson, *Consumer Behavior and Marketing Strategy,* p. 430.
39. *The Asian-American Market* (New York: FIND/SVP, 1990); Bryant Robey, "America's Asians," *American Demographics,* May 1985, pp. 22–29.
40. Donald W. Hendon, Emelda L. Williams, and Douglas E. Huffman, "Social Class System Revisited," *Journal of Business Research* 17 (1988): pp. 259–270.
41. Patricia Braus, "Selling Self-Help," *American Demographics,* March 1992, pp. 48–52.
42. Daniel McGinn, "Time to Shift to a Higher Gear," *Newsweek,* March 18, 1996, p. 46.
43. Faye Rice, "What Intelligent Consumers Want," *Fortune,* December 28, 1992, pp. 56–60.
44. William Grimes, "New! Original! Nonfat! Fat-Free! You Can Sell Anything if You Get the Label Right," *New York Times Magazine,* March 10, 1996, pp. 64–65.
45. "A Bicycle Built Precisely for Women," *Chicago Tribune,* June 24, 1996, sec. 4, p. 5.
46. Bob Wehling, "The Future of Marketing," speech to the World Federation of Advertisers, Sydney, Australia, October 31, 1995.
47. Russell W. Belk, "Situational Variables and Consumer Behavior," *Journal of Consumer Research,* December 1975, pp. 156–164. See also Jacob Hornik, "Situational Effects on the Consumption of Time," *Journal of Marketing,* Fall 1982, pp. 44–55; C. Whan Park, Easwar S. Iyer, and Daniel C. Smith, "The Effects of Situational Factors on In-Store Grocery Shopping Behavior: The Role of Store Environment and Time Available for Shopping," *Journal of Consumer Research,* March 1989, pp. 422–433.
48. Jerry Cole, "Supermarket Customers of the Future," *Food Industry News,* January 1996, p. 70.
49. Kimberly Lowe, "Hot Summer Sparked Cold Item Sales," *Grocery Marketing,* October 1995, p. 57.

Chapter 7

1. Roberta Maynard, "A Piece of the Action," *Nation's Business,* April 1996, pp. 69–74.
2. Gayle Sator Stodder, "Healthy Returns," *Entrepreneur,* February 1996, pp. 102, 106–107.
3. Bob Weinstein, "Head over Heels," *Entrepreneur,* May 1993, pp. 116-121.
4. "To Catch a Thief," *Grocery Marketing,* October 1995, pp. 14, 46–47.
5. U.S. Department of Commerce, *Statistical Abstract of the United States,* 115th ed. (Washington, D.C.: U.S. Government Printing Office, 1995), p. 297.
6. U.S. Department of Commerce, *Statistical Abstract of the United States,* p. 299.
7. See Clinton Crownover and Mark Henricks, "Patriot Games," *Entrepreneur,* September 1993, pp. 105–109.
8. Susan Greco, "Breaking Away," *Inc.,* October 1993, pp. 84, 86.
9. Harris Corporation Annual Report 1993, p. 14.
10. U.S. Department of Commerce, *Statistical Abstract of the United States,* p. 793.

11. Elizabeth Ehrlich, "The Quality Management Checkpoint," *International Business,* May 1993, pp. 56–58+.

12. Jaclyn H. Park, "Animal Logic," *GSB Chicago* (University of Chicago Graduate School of Business), Winter 1993, pp. 21–24.

13. "Schindler's Lift," *The Economist,* March 16, 1996, p. 71.

14. Nicholas K. Geranios, " 'Everyone Has the Fever' for Specialty Coffees," *Chicago Tribune,* December 6, 1992, sec. 7, p. 12.

15. Edward O. Welles, "Least Likely to Succeed," *Inc.,* December 1992, pp. 14+.

16. Dirk Dusharme, "News You Can Use," *Quality Digest,* May 1993, p. 8.

17. John Morris, "Customized Services Boost Competitiveness," *International Business,* November 1993, pp. 48ff.

18. Stanley F. Slater and John C. Narver, "Superior Customer Value and Business Performance: The Strong Evidence for a Market-Driven Culture," Report No. 92-125 (Cambridge, Mass.: Marketing Science Institute, 1992), p. 3.

19. "Employee Empowerment: It's an Interdependent Relationship," *FYI* (Harris Corporation), Spring 1993, pp. 6–7.

20. Michael Sullivan, "Translating the Voice of the International Customer," presentation at the American Marketing Association Business-to-Business Conference, March 28–30, 1993.

21. Brian McWilliams, "Re-engineering the Small Factory," *Inc. Technology,* March 19, 1996, pp. 44–47.

22. David Young, "Grainger Retools Strategy, Gets Faster, Busier, Bigger," *Chicago Tribune,* July 18, 1993, sec. 7, pp. 1, 6.

23. Mary Cobb Sullivan, "Groen President's Close Customer Contact Keeps Product Innovation Cooking," *GSB Chicago* (University of Chicago Graduate School of Business), Winter 1993, p. 35.

24. Evelyn Lauter, " 'We Have to Keep Coming Up with New Ideas and New Flavors,' " *Chicago Tribune Magazine,* January 31, 1993, p. 36.

25. Lauter, " 'We Have to Keep Coming Up with New Ideas.' "

26. Personal correspondence from Jerry Keller, AutoResearch Laboratories, Inc., December 23, 1993.

27. Maynard, "A Piece of the Action," p. 71.

28. David Young, "Illinois Tool Still Fastened to Keep-It-Simple Formula," *Chicago Tribune,* April 26, 1993, sec. 4, pp. 1, 4.

29. Steven Pratt, "At What Price Perfection?" *Chicago Tribune,* April 29, 1993, sec. 7, pp. 1, 6, 8.

30. Ehrlich, "The Quality Management Checkpoint," p. 58.

31. "To Catch a Thief."

32. Robin Yale Bergstrom, "Hanging a Vision on Quality," *Production,* July 1993, pp. 56–61.

33. Shawn Tully, "Why Drug Prices Will Go Lower," *Fortune,* May 3, 1993, pp. 56–58+.

34. J. Paul Peter and James H. Donnelly, Jr., *A Preface to Marketing Management,* 7th ed. (Burr Ridge, Ill.: Irwin, 1997), p. 77.

35. Brad Hirni, "A Fish Story," *Selling Power,* March 1996, p. 92.

36. Richard Watson, "Facing Up to Problems," *Business Franchise,* July/August 1993, pp. 39+.

37. Roger W. Brucker, "Merchandising: The Hit-and-Run of a Guerrilla Marketing Tactic," *Business Marketing,* April 1987, pp. 76+.

38. See Paul Sherlock, *Rethinking Business to Business Marketing* (New York: Free Press, 1991), pp. 22–23.

39. Sullivan, "Translating the Voice of the International Customer," p. 12.

40. Park, "Animal Logic," p. 23.

41. Robert Lee, "What Business Customers Have to Say: Listening to Our Leaders," presentation at the American Marketing Association's Business-to-Business Conference, March 28–30, 1993.

42. Example provided by Dr. S. J. Garner, Richmond, Kentucky.

43. John S. McClenahen, "Sound Thinking," *Industry Week,* May 3, 1993, pp. 24, 28.

44. Lee, "What Business Customers Have to Say," pp. 6–7.

45. Lawrence Surtees, "Northern Telecom: The Morning After," *Report on Business,* July 5, 1993, sec. B, pp. 1, 4.

46. Douglas F. Haley and Andrea Z. Morgan, "From Bean Counting to Marketing Intelligence: Transforming a Customer Service Scorecard into a Blueprint for Marketing Action," presentation at the American Marketing Association and American Society for Quality Control joint conference on Customer Satisfaction and Quality Measurement, April 7–9, 1991.

47. Peter and Donnelly, *A Preface to Marketing Management,* p. 80.

48. Personal correspondence from Jerry Keller, ALI, December 23, 1993.

49. Wesley L. Johnston and Thomas V. Bonoma, "The Buying Center: Structure and Interaction Patterns," *Journal of Marketing* (Summer 1981): 143–156.

50. Malcolm Fleschner with Charles Lee Browne, "Value Sells," *Selling Power,* March 1996, pp. 48, 50.

Chapter 8

1. Aimee Stern, "Land of the Rising Mail," *International Business,* November 1993, pp. 28, 30.

2. Adapted from Peter D. Bennett, ed., *Dictionary of Marketing Terms,* 2nd ed. (Chicago: American Marketing Association, 1995), p. 165.

3. Fisher-Price Annual Report 1992, p. 4.

4. Lynn Van Matre, "Celebrating a Golden Opportunity That Paid Off," *Chicago Tribune,* September 6, 1992, sec. 5, pp. 1, 4.

5. Jane Adler, "Hitting the Resale Shelf," *Crain's Chicago Business,* February 27, 1995, p. 27.

6. Brigid McMenamin, "Beverly Hillbilly," *Forbes,* March 29, 1993, p. 110.

7. Suzanne Alexander, "Firms Cater to African-Style Weddings," *The Wall Street Journal,* August 24, 1993, pp. B1–B2.

8. William Echikson, "The Trick to Selling in Europe," *Fortune,* September 20, 1993, p. 82.

9. Echikson, "The Trick to Selling in Europe."

10. Janet Izatt, "C-Change at Mercedes," *Marketing Week,* July 2, 1993, pp. 28–31.

11. Jolie Solomon, "Firms Moving to Keep It Simple for Consumers," *Chicago Tribune,* May 17, 1992, sec. 7, p. 7D.

12. Lisa Miller, "Ladies Floor," *The Wall Street Journal,* May 10, 1996, p. B8.

13. Kate Fitzgerald, "Small Appliances Big for 1992," *Advertising Age,* January 27, 1992, p. 12.

14. Susan B. Garland, "Those Aging Boomers," *Business Week,* May 20, 1991, pp. 106–112.

15. Alessandra Bianchi, "New Businesses: Mature Marketing," *Inc.,* May 1992, p. 26.

16. Laura Zinn, "Move Over Boomers," *Business Week,* December 14, 1992, pp. 74–79, 82.

17. Dawn Smith, "Exercising Those Little Grey Sells," *Marketing Week,* July 2, 1993, pp. 35–38.

18. Phil Guarascio, "How GM Targets 'Mature' Market Niche," *Advertising Age,* January 11, 1993, p. 26.

19. Jan Larson, "J. C. Penney Finds Profit in Africa," *American Demographics,* November 1992, p. 12.

20. Martha T. Moore, "Soul Searching: New KFC Menu Targets Blacks," *USA Today,* March 15, 1993, p. 5B.

21. Bradley Johnson, "Carnival Cruise Line Beckons Hispanics," *Advertising Age,* January 25, 1993, p. 46.

22. Leon E. Wynter, "Small Broadcasters Reach Asian-Americans," *The Wall Street Journal,* February 2, 1993, p. B1.

23. Jon Berry, "Marketers Reach Out to Blacks," *Chicago Tribune,* May 12, 1991, sec. 7, p. 9.

24. "Minority Leaders Blast J. C. Penney Plan to Target Blacks, Hispanics," *Marketing News,* October 11, 1993, pp. 1, 15.

25. Ryan Mathews, "The Changing Face of the American Consumer," *Grocery Marketing,* May 1993, pp. 31–32.

26. Bob Jones, "Big Money on Campus," *Entrepreneur,* September 1993, pp. 62+.

27. Charles Hayes, "Back at the Ranch," *Chicago Tribune,* May 2, 1992, sec. 4, pp. 1–2.

28. "Keeping Cool in China," *The Economist,* April 6, 1996, pp. 73–74.

29. Blayne Cutler, "North American Demographics," *American Demographics,* March 1992, pp. 38–42.

30. William Echikson, "Hey, Europe, Let's Do Munch!" *Fortune,* November 2, 1992, p. 18.

31. Joe Schwartz, "Climate-Controlled Customers," *American Demographics,* March 1992, pp. 24–26+.

32. Peter D. Bennett, ed., *Dictionary of Marketing Terms,* 2nd ed. (Chicago: American Marketing Association, 1995), p. 154.

33. James P. Gallagher, "Russia's New Wealthy Are Happy to Spend Their Money," *Chicago Tribune,* September 12, 1993, sec. 1, p. 16; James McGregor, "China's New Rich Seek the Good Life," *The Wall Street Journal,* January 13, 1993, p. A10.

34. "Frito-Lay Profiles Salty Snack Consumers," *Supermarket News,* March 18, 1996, p. 39.

35. Marilyn Silverman, "Developing Terrific Creative . . . Research Can Help," presentation at the American Marketing Association Marketing Research Conference, September 25–26, 1990.

36. Karen Lowry Miller, "You Just Can't Talk To These Kids," *Business Week,* April 19, 1993, pp. 104, 106.

37. "Winning in Foodservice Requires 'Convenient Quality,'" *Grocery Marketing,* November 1995, p. 16.

38. Lisa Anderson, "'Prudent' Shoppers True Blue," June 7, 1992, *Chicago Tribune,* sec. 7, pp. 1, 7B.

39. Bickley Townsend, "Market Research That Matters," *American Demographics,* August 1992, pp. 58–60.

40. This information was taken from Valerie Walsh and J. Paul Peter, "Claritas Inc.: Using Compass and Prizm," Working Paper, University of Wisconsin-Madison, 1996.

41. Flowers Industries Inc. Annual Report 1993.

42. Jon Bigness, "Car-Rental Companies Quietly Coddle Select Executives," *The Wall Street Journal,* May 10, 1996, pp. B1, B8.

43. Amdahl Annual Report 1992.

44. Judith Nemes, "Internet Buying Club Targets Businesses," *Crain's Chicago Business,* April 8, 1996, p. 18.

45. Loren Fox, "World Fuel Services' Business Takes Off by Supplying Needs of Smaller Airlines," *The Wall Street Journal,* May 10, 1996, p. B7D.

46. "The Writing Is on the Screen," *The Economist,* April 25, 1992, pp. 69–70.

47. American Public Radio, "Marketplace," October 25, 1993. Produced by USC Radio (Los Angeles: University of Southern California).

48. "Double Play," *Grocery Marketing,* October 1995, pp. 36, 38.

49. Gabriella Stern, "P&G's Calcium Pitch to Teens Sparks Criticism," *The Wall Street Journal,* August 18, 1993, pp. B1, B8.

50. Saul Hansell, "The Man Who Charged Up MasterCard," *New York Times,* March 7, 1993, pp. 1, 8.

51. Veronica Anderson, "Grooming a New Niche," *Crain's Chicago Business,* March 6, 1995, p. 41.

52. Silverman, "Developing Terrific Creative."

53. Schwartz, "Climate-Controlled Customers."

54. Peter Laundy, "Image Trouble," *Inc.,* September 1993, pp. 80–82, 84.

55. "How about a Nicotine Patch with a Micronite Filter?" *AdWeek,* August 24, 1992, p. 18.

56. Marcy Magiera, "Nike Eyes the Ladies," *Advertising Age,* October 14, 1991, p. 4.

57. "Wrinkled," *The Economist,* November 4, 1995, p. 69.

58. "Entry-Level Phone Service," *Time,* March 2, 1992, p. 43.

59. Dan Fost, "U.S. Hospitals Entice Mexicans," *American Demographics,* November 1992, p. 25.

60. Bryan Batson, "The Road Less Traveled," *Sales & Marketing Management,* December 1992, pp. 46–48+.

61. Stewart Toy, "The Big Squeeze on Carmakers," *Business Week,* March 11, 1996, p. 46.

62. Judie Lannon, "Brands across Borders: Do Advertising Ideas Travel?" presentation at the American Marketing Association Attitude Research Conference, January 20–23, 1991.

63. Joseph Weber, "Campbell: Now It's M-M-Global," *Business Week,* March 15, 1993, pp. 52–54.

64. Michael Sullivan, "Translating the Voice of the International Customer," presentation at the American Marketing Association Business-to-Business Conference, March 28–30, 1993, p. 2.

Chapter 9

1. Lesley Alderman, "Hot Stuff: Green Pens," *Money,* May 1992, p. 40.

2. Example contributed by William W. Sannwald, San Diego State University, San Diego, California.

3. Gretchen Morgenson, "The Foot's Friend," *Forbes,* April 13, 1992, pp. 60, 62.

4. Peter D. Bennett, ed., *Dictionary of Marketing Terms* 2nd ed. (Chicago: American Marketing Association, 1995), p. 140.

5. Tim Smart, "Kathleen Synnott: Shaping the Mailrooms of Tomorrow," *Business Week,* November 16, 1992, p. 66.

6. Bennett, ed., *Dictionary of Marketing Terms,* p. 2.

7. Jerry Flint, "These Are the Good Old Days," *Forbes,* January 4, 1993, pp. 60–61.

8. Bennett, ed., *Dictionary of Marketing Terms,* p. 279.

9. Flint, "These Are the Good Old Days."

10. Bennett, ed., *Dictionary of Marketing Terms,* p. 91.

11. Erick Schonfeld, "Next-Generation Phones," *Fortune,* April 1, 1996, p. 16.

12. James Coates, "Clearing a Path in Web's Clutter," *Chicago Tribune,* April 28, 1996, sec. 5, pp. 1–2; James Coates, "Believe It: A Web Library You Can Trust," *Chicago Tribune,* April 28, 1996, sec. 5, p. 5.

13. Ira Sager, "Downtime for the PC Biz," *Business Week,* April 1, 1996, pp. 82–83.

14. William M. Bulkeley, "More Teens Can't Live without Beepers," *The Wall Street Journal,* December 7, 1992, p. B4.

15. Andy Cohen, "Surviving in a Mature Market," *Sales & Marketing Management,* May 16, 1996, pp. 63–64, 66.

16. John Schmeltzer, "CDs Have Put the Turntable in a Tailspin," *Chicago Tribune.* September 7, 1993, sec. 3, pp. 1, 4.

17. Carl Quintanilla. "Unsold Seats Sully Concorde's Snooty Image," *The Wall Street Journal,* February 23, 1996, pp. B1, B6.

18. Schmeltzer, "CDs Have Put the Turntable in a Tailspin."

19. Joseph Pereira, "Footwear Fad Makes Nike, Reebok Run for Their Money," *The Wall Street Journal,* June 24, 1993, pp. B1, B5.

20. Kathleen Deveny, "Blame It on Dashed Hopes (and Oprah): Disillusioned

Dieters Shun Liquid Meals," *The Wall Street Journal*, October 13, 1992, p. B10.

21. Eric Morgenthaler, "That's No Spaceship, That's My Car: Neon Invades Expressways," *The Wall Street Journal*, August 23, 1993, pp. A1, A5.

22. Jon Van, "At Ingersoll, Flexibility, Change Are a Way of Life," *Chicago Tribune*, November 5, 1991, sec. 1, p. 12.

23. Bennett, ed., *Dictionary of Marketing Terms*, p. 27.

24. Shawn Tully, "Why Drug Prices Will Go Lower," *Fortune*, May 3, 1993, pp. 56–58+.

25. Bennett, ed., *Dictionary of Marketing Terms*, p. 29.

26. *Ibid.*, pp. 28–29.

27. Gary Strauss, "Extending a Bit Too Far?" *USA Today*, April 19, 1993, p. 7B.

28. Daniel C. Smith and C. Whan Park, "The Effects of Brand Extensions on Market Share and Advertising Efficiency," *Journal of Marketing Research*, August 1992, pp.1 296–313.

29. See, for example, Susan M. Broniarczyk and Joseph W. Alba, "The Importance of Brand in Brand Extension," *Journal of Marketing Research*, May 1994, pp. 214–228.

30. Pat Sloan, "Gillette Rolls New Series Line," *Advertising Age*, January 25, 1993, pp. 3, 41.

31. Ronald Alsop, "Brand Loyalty Is Rarely Blind Loyalty," *The Wall Street Journal*, October 19, 1989, pp. B1, B8.

32. Kathleen Deveny, "More Shoppers Bypass Big-Name Brands and Steer Carts to Private-Label Products," *The Wall Street Journal*, October 20, 1992, pp. B1, B8.

33. Betsy Morris, "The Brand's the Thing," *Fortune*, March 4, 1996, pp. 72–75+.

34. Deveny, "More Shoppers Bypass Big-Name Brands"; Patricia Sellers, "Brands: It's Thrive or Die," *Fortune*, August 23, 1993, pp. 52–56; Steve Weinstein, "The New Brand Loyalty," *Progressive Grocer*, July 1993, pp. 93–94+.

35. Morris, "The Brand's the Thing"; see also Bob Gatty, "Private Label vs. National Brands: Battle Royal and Retailer Opportunity," *Grocery Marketing*, November 1995, pp. 6, 12.

36. Patrick Oster, "The Eurosion of Brand Loyalty," *Business Week*, July 19, 1993, p. 22.

37. Yumiko Ono, "The Rising Sun Shines on Private Labels," *The Wall Street Journal*, April 26, 1993, pp. B1, B6.

38. Bennett, ed., *Dictionary of Marketing Terms*, p. 121.

39. Gatty, "Private Label vs. National Brands," p. 12.

40. Marc Levinson, "Stand by Your Brand," *Newsweek*, April 19, 1993, pp. 38–39.

41. Morris, "The Brand's the Thing," p. 72.

42. Weinstein, "The New Brand Loyalty," p. 94.

43. Tully, "Why Drug Prices Will Go Lower," p. 66.

44. Susan Greco, "Profits in Private Labels," *Inc.*, March 1993, p. 27.

45. Terance Shimp, *Promotion Management and Marketing Communications*, 3rd ed. (Hinsdale, Ill.: Dryden Press, 1993), p. 544–546.

46. Daniel L. Doden, "Selecting a Brand Name That Aids Marketing Objectives," *Advertising Age*, November 5, 1990, p. 34.

47. Larry Armstrong, "What's in a Name Change? A Classier Acura," *Business Week*, March 18, 1996, p. 117.

48. Nancy Ten Kate, "Words That Sell Keep Changing," *American Demographics*, August 1992, p. 18.

49. Alan L. Adler, "What's in a Name? Automakers' Time and Money," *Wisconsin State Journal*, April 26, 1993, p. 8B.

50. "A Task for Two: Invent a Brand," *The Grocer*, September 12, 1992, pp. 48–49.

51. Bob Coleman, "Knock It Off!" *Entrepreneur*, September 1993, pp. 121–126.

52. Cornelia Grumman, "Web of Internet Name Game Getting Tangled," *Chicago Tribune*, March 25, 1996, sec. 4, p. 1.

53. Steven C. Bahls and Jane Easter Bahls, "Fighting Fakes," *Entrepreneur*, February 1996, pp. 73–76.

54. David A. Aaker, *Managing Brand Equity* (New York: The Free Press, 1991).

55. Morris, "The Brand's the Thing," p. 82.

56. Morris, "The Brand's the Thing," pp. 82, 84.

57. Morris, "The Brand's the Thing," p. 72.

58. Bennett, ed., *Dictionary of Marketing Terms*, p. 223.

59. We wish to thank Gayle Fuguitt, Marketing Research Director, Big "G" Division, General Mills, for this example.

60. Laura Zinn, "Pepsi's Future Becomes Clearer," *Business Week*, February 1, 1993, pp. 74–75.

61. Gabriella Stern, "Kodak Unit Cuts Price for Large Bottles of Bayer," *The Wall Street Journal*, September 23, 1993, p. B8.

62. Richard Gibson, "Stirring Memories Gives Ovaltine a Lift," *The Wall Street Journal*, December 3, 1992, pp. B1, B10.

63. Example cited in C. Merle Crawford, *New Products Management*, 2d ed. (Homewood, Ill.: Richard D. Irwin, 1987), p. 44.

64. Richard J. Maturi, "Time for a Change?" *Entrepreneur*, September 1993, pp. 160, 162–163.

65. Gabriella Stern, "To Outpace Rivals, More Firms Step Up Spending on New-Product Development," *The Wall Street Journal*, October 28, 1992, pp. B1, B7.

66. Norm Alster, "Pass the Sugar," *Forbes*, April 13, 1992, p. 90.

67. Julie Liesse, "From Cereal to Snack to Cereal," *Advertising Age*, January 11, 1993, p. 20.

68. Jim Mateja, "VW Hatches a New Beetle," *Chicago Tribune*, January 6, 1994, sec. 1, pp. 1, 16.

69. Annetta Miller, "No Cheer for Procter & Gamble," *Newsweek*, July 26, 1993, p. 38; Zachary Schiller, "Procter & Gamble Hits Back," *Business Week*, July 19, 1993, pp. 20–22.

Chapter 10

1. Christopher Power, "Flops," *Business Week*, August 16, 1993, pp. 76–80, 82.

2. Betsy Morris, "The Brand's the Thing," *Fortune*, March 4, 1996, pp. 72–75+.

3. Peter D. Bennett, *Dictionary of Marketing Terms*, 2nd ed., (Chicago: American Marketing Association, 1995), pp. 73, 284.

4. C. Merle Crawford, *New Products Management*, 4th ed. (Burr Ridge, IL.: Irwin, 1994), p. 11.

5. "ConAgra's Healthy Choice: Getting to the Heart of the Matter," *Sales & Marketing Management*, August 1992, p. 43.

6. Leslie Brokaw, "Where Great Ideas Come From," *Inc.*, January 1993, pp. 72–74+.

7. "The Best New Products," *Business Week*, January 11, 1993, p. 111.

8. Kevin Goldman, "Scouring-Pad Rivals Face 3M Challenge," *The Wall Street Journal*, January 11, 1993, p. B4.

9. Andrew Hilton, "Mythology, Markets, and the Emerging Europe," *Harvard Business Review*, November–December 1992, pp. 50–54.

10. Nathalie Boschat, "Catering to Africa's Consumers," *World Press Review*, June 1993, p. 40.

11. John Carey, "Moving the Lab Closer to the Marketplace," *Business Week*, Reinventing America 1992 special issue, pp. 164–165+.

12. Joel Silverman, "The Next Thing in Running," *Outside*, January 1994, p. 49.

13. Procter & Gamble Annual Report 1993, p. 8.
14. Pete Engardio, "Motorola in China: A Great Leap Forward," *Business Week,* May 17, 1993, pp. 58–59.
15. Carey, "Moving the Lab," p. 168.
16. Gary Slutsker, "The Tortoise and the Hare," *Forbes,* February 1, 1993, pp. 66–69.
17. Eben Shapiro, "From Frozen Dinners to Styling Gels: Microwave Is Moving into New Areas," *The Wall Street Journal,* February 2, 1993, p. B8.
18. "Quick Insight: Pretest Your Product Strategy," *Journal of Business Strategy,* January/February 1996, p. 45.
19. "Tuned Out and Dropping Off," *The Economist,* November 4, 1995, pp. 65–66.
20. Betsy Spethmann, "Cereal-Makers Mount All-Day Campaign on the Snack Market," *Chicago Tribune,* May 9, 1993, sec. 7, p. 11.
21. "Tuned Out and Dropping Off," p. 66.
22. Goldman, "Scouring-Pad Rivals Face 3M Challenge."
23. Carey, "Moving the Lab," pp. 168–169.
24. Elizabeth Ehrlich, "The Quality Management Checkpoint," *International Business,* May 1993, pp. 56–58+.
25. James R. Healey, "Youthful Support May Steer Electric Vehicles," *USA Today,* March 9, 1993, p. 4B.
26. Jim Mateja, "Consumers to Test GM Electric Car," *Chicago Tribune,* October 14, 1993, sec. 3, pp. 1, 4.
27. "A Smart Card for New York," *Citibank World,* May 1996, pp. 1, 3.
28. Annetta Miller and Karen Springen, "Egg Rolls for Peoria," *Newsweek,* October 12, 1992, pp. 59–60.
29. Steve Lohr, "Test It in Tulsa—It'll Play in Peoria," *Chicago Tribune,* June 7, 1992, sec. 7, p. 3.
30. Alison Sprout, "Products to Watch: Thin Tortilla Chips," *Fortune,* October 19, 1992, p. 109.
31. Moira Madonia, "Baby Needs," *Supermarket Business,* September 1993, pp. 91, 151.
32. John Markoff, "Marketer's Dream, Engineer's Nightmare," *The New York Times,* December 12, 1993, sec. 3, pp. 1, 8.
33. Adapted from David A. Garvin, "Competing on the Eight Dimensions of Quality," *Harvard Business Review,* November–December 1987.
34. Harris Corporation Annual Report 1993, p. 23.
35. Harris Corporation Annual Report 1993, p. 23.
36. Alison Sprout, "Products to Watch," *Fortune,* September 21, 1992, p. 115.
37. Bennett, ed., *Dictionary of Marketing Terms,* p. 107.

38. Edward A. Robinson, "American Toolmakers Regain Their Cutting Edge," *Fortune,* June 10, 1996, 72C–72D+.
39. Kathleen Deveny, "Today's Toothbrushes: 'Improved' and Pricey," *The Wall Street Journal,* November 10, 1992, pp. B1, B10.
40. Randall Lane, "Does Orange Mean Cheap?" *Forbes,* December 23, 1991, pp. 144+.
41. Larry Armstrong, "Practical Honda Takes a Sporty Turn," *Business Week,* September 28, 1992, p. 136.
42. Alessandra Bianchi, "Well Said," *Inc.,* January 1993, pp. 98–99.
43. Bruce Nussbaum, "Hot Products," *Business Week,* June 7, 1993, pp. 54–57.
44. George C. Dorman, "Go with the Flow—Measuring Information Worker Quality," in *Total Quality Performance,* eds. Lawrence Schein and Melissa A. Berman, Research Report No. 909 (New York: The Conference Board, 1988), pp. 29–39.
45. Michael J. McCarthy, "Coca-Cola Introduces Marketing Gimmick: Its Famous Old Bottle," *The Wall Street Journal,* January 12, 1993, p. B4.
46. Sarah Schafer, "When It's Time for a Makeover," *Inc.,* December 1995, p. 118.
47. Raju Narisetti, "Plotting to Get Tissues into Living Rooms," *The Wall Street Journal,* May 3, 1996, pp. B1, B12.
48. Nancy Ryan, "Soft-Drink Refillables Fading Fast," *Chicago Tribune,* August 29, 1993, sec. 7, pp. 1, 8.
49. William Grimes, "New! Original! Nonfat! Fat-Free! You Can Sell Anything if You Get the Label Right," *The New York Times Magazine,* March 10, 1996, p. 64.
50. Grimes, "New! Original! Nonfat! Fat-Free!" p. 65.
51. "When in Rome . . . ," *Entrepreneur,* September 1992, pp. 133–137.
52. "When in Rome . . . ," p. 135.
53. "When in Rome . . . ," p. 135.
54. Valerie Reitman, "Enticed by Visions of Enormous Numbers, More Western Marketers Move into China," *The Wall Street Journal,* July 12, 1993, pp. B1, B6.
55. Catherine Vial, "Why EC Environmental Policy Will Affect American Business," *Business America,* March 8, 1993, pp. 24–27.
56. J. Paul Peter and James H. Donnelly, Jr., *A Preface to Marketing Management,* 7th ed. (Burr Ridge, Ill.: Irwin, 1996), p. 123.
57. Gerard Tellis and Peter Golder, "First to Market, First to Fail? Real Causes of Enduring Market Leadership," *Sloan Management Review* 37(2) (Winter 1996), pp. 65–75. See also "Why First

May Not Last," *The Economist,* March 16, 1996, p. 65; Roger Lowenstein, "Being There First Isn't Good Enough," *The Wall Street Journal,* May 16, 1996, p. B1.
58. "Why First May Not Last."
59. Lowenstein, "Being There First Isn't Good Enough."
60. Peter and Donnelly, *A Preface to Marketing Management,* p. 120.
61. Tara Parker-Pope, "Ad Agencies Are Stumbling in East Europe," *The Wall Street Journal,* May 10, 1996, pp. B1, B14.
62. Phaedra Hise, "From Notes to Market in No Time," *Inc.,* February 1996, p. 108.
63. Regis McKenna, "Marketing Is Everything," *Harvard Business Review,* January–February 1991, pp. 65–79.
64. Peter and Donnelly, *A Preface to Marketing Management,* p. 125.
65. Hideki Kaihatsu, "TQC in Japan," in *Making Total Quality Happen,* ed. Frank Caropreso, Research Report No. 937 (New York: The Conference Board, 1990), pp. 7–10.
66. Crawford, *New Products Management,* pp. 195–201.
67. Crawford, *New Products Management,* pp. 199–201. See also Brian Dumain, "Payoff from the New Management," *Fortune,* December 13, 1993, pp. 103–104.
68. Steve Blount, "It's Just a Matter of Time," *Sales & Marketing Management,* March 1992, pp. 32–33.
69. Blount, "It's Just a Matter of Time."
70. Blount, "It's Just a Matter of Time."
71. Hise, "From Notes to Market in No Time."
72. Joshua Macht, "Plastics Make Perfect," *Inc. Technology,* November 14, 1995, p. 106.
73. Elyse Tanouye, "Johnson & Johnson Stays Fit by Shuffling Its Mix of Businesses," *The Wall Street Journal,* December 22, 1992, pp. A1, A4.
74. McKenna, "Marketing Is Everything," pp. 67–68.
75. "Partnering for Products," *Inc.,* February 1996, p. 94, citing Coopers & Lybrand's "Trendsetter Barometer," New York, November 1995.
76. "Big Wheel," *Entrepreneur,* September 1993, p. 75.
77. Jon Lowden, "The Next Thing in Skating," *Outside,* January 1994, p. 51.

Chapter 11

1. Peter D. Bennett, ed., *Dictionary of Marketing Terms,* 2nd ed. (Chicago: American Marketing Association, 1995), p. 261.
2. U.S. Department of Commerce, *Statistical Abstract of the United States,*

115th ed. (Washington, D.C.: U.S. Government Printing Office, 1995), pp. 416, 451.

3. "Pick-Up Lines," *The Economist,* May 4, 1996, p. 70.

4. Michael R. Czinkota and Ilkka A. Ronkainen, *International Marketing,* 4th ed. (Harcourt Brace & Co., 1995), pp. 531–532.

5. Douglas Lavin and Krystal Miller, "Goodbye to Haggling: Savvy Consumers Are Buying Their Cars Like Refrigerators," *The Wall Street Journal,* August 20, 1993, p. B1.

6. "Andersen's Androids," *The Economist,* May 4, 1996, p. 72.

7. Lance Morrow, "The Temping of America," *Time,* March 29, 1993, pp. 40–41.

8. Janice Castor, "Disposable Workers," *Time,* March 29, 1993, pp. 43–47.

9. "Glasgow Has The Edge," *Management Today* (Britain), July 1993.

10. James Coates, "The New Hard Hats for a Software World," *Chicago Tribune,* February 25, 1996, sec. 5, pp. 1, 4.

11. Joshua Macht, "Together at Last," *Inc. Technology,* March 19, 1996, p. 74.

12. Rashi Glazer, "Marketing in an Information-Intensive Environment: Implications of Knowledge as an Asset," *Journal of Marketing* (October 1991): pp. 1–19.

13. "Marriott Scraps Front-Desk Check-In," *Chicago Tribune,* February 21, 1993, sec. 7, p. 4.

14. Leonard L. Berry, "Relationship Marketing," in *Emerging Perspectives on Services Marketing,* eds. Leonard L. Berry, L. G. Shostack, and Gregory D. Upah (Chicago: American Marketing Association, 1983), pp. 25–28.

15. Joanne Cleaver, "Brokers Stretching beyond Home Market," *Crain's Chicago Business,* November 13, 1995, p. SR10.

16. "Creature Comforts," *Entrepreneur,* 1996, p. 66.

17. Robert A. Mamis, "Can Your Bank Do This?" *Inc.,* March 1996, pp. 29–30+.

18. "Oiling the Wheels of Consumer Satisfaction," *Nation's Business,* April 1996, p. 12.

19. Paul Hofheinz, "Rising in Russia," *Fortune,* January 24, 1994.

20. *Ibid.*

21. "Another Bright Idea Helps Environment," *Crain's Small Business,* February 1996, p. 22.

22. Jennifer deJong, "Videoconferencing for the Rest of Us," *Inc. Technology,* November 14, 1995, pp. 74–75.

23. Howard Rothman, "Tapping the Great Outdoors," *Nation's Business,* April 1996, pp. 13–14.

24. Mark Henricks, "Right of Refusal," *Entrepreneur,* May 1993, pp. 122+.

25. Louis Kraar, "TV Is Exploding All over Asia," *Fortune.* January 24, 1994, pp. 99–101.

26. John Case, "Total Customer Service," *Inc.,* January 1994, pp. 52–58+.

27. "Service Shortfalls," *Total Quality Newsletter,* April 1993, p. 8.

28. Linda Cooper, "The Role of Research in Quality," presentation at American Marketing Association Marketing Research Conference, September 23–26, 1990.

29. Susan Greco, "The ABCs of Internal Guarantees," *Inc.,* March 1993, p. 29.

30. Phaedra Hise, "Getting Smart On-Line," *Inc. Technology,* March 19, 1996, pp. 59–60+.

31. Myron Magnet, "Goods News for the Service Economy," *Fortune,* May 3, 1993, pp. 46–50, 52.

32. Julie Schmit, "Ritz-Carlton: Room for Employees," *USA Today,* October 15, 1992, p. 6B.

33. Susan Greco, "Pricing Your Service for Profits," *Inc..* June 1992, p. 107.

34. Susan Greco, "Talking through Service Costs," *Inc.,* June 1993, p. 29.

35. Kent B. Monroe, "Buyers' Subjective Perceptions of Price," *Journal of Marketing Research* (February 1973): pp. 70–80; Jerry Olson, "Price as an Information Cue: Effects on Product Evaluation," in *Consumer and Industrial Buying Behavior,* eds. A. G. Woodside, J. N. Sheth, and P. D. Bennett (New York: Elsevier North-Holland, 1977), pp. 267–286; Donald R. Lichtenstein, Peter H. Bloch, and William C. Black, "Correlates of Price Acceptability," *Journal of Consumer Research* 15 (September 1988): 243–252.

36. John Schmeltzer, "Banks Slugging It Out among the Bananas," *Chicago Tribune,* April 21, 1996, sec. 5, pp. 1–2.

37. "More Banks Opening Internet Branches," *Crain's Chicago Business,* April 8, 1996, p. 17.

38. DeJong, "Videoconferencing for the Rest of Us."

39. Lori Bongiorno, "B-Schools Bitten by the Global Bug," *Business Week,* October 25, 1993.

40. Valerie Reitman, "Down-to-Earth Ads Are Aimed at Those Thinking of Heaven," *The Wall Street Journal,* August 13, 1993, pp. A1, A10.

41. Marcus W. Brauchli, "India Raises Capital by Reaching Out to Sell Mutual Funds to Rural Masses," *The Wall Street Journal,* June 17, 1993, p. A8.

42. "Elvis, Christmas Elves Sighted at Post Office," *The Wall Street Journal,* December 16, 1992, p. B1.

Chapter 12

1. "Madison Avenue Signs Judge Pao," *The Economist,* February 3, 1996, p. 54.

2. Richard Sookdeo, "How to Escape a Price War," *Fortune,* June 13, 1994, p. 83.

3. Larry Armstrong, "Altima's Secret: The Right Kind of Sticker Shock," *Business Week,* January 18, 1993, p. 37.

4. National Public Radio, "Morning Edition," July 10, 1996.

5. Lois Therrien, "Brands on the Run," *Business Week,* April 19, 1993, pp. 26–29.

6. "Chinese Grist to the Malthusian Mills," *The Economist,* May 4, 1996, pp. 33–34.

7. Alexandra Peers, "Forgery of a Painting by Botero, 'The Dancers,' Nearly Waltzes onto Auction Block at Christie's," *The Wall Street Journal,* May 6, 1993, pp. C1, C18.

8. J. Paul Peter and James H. Donnelly, Jr., *A Preface to Marketing Management,* 7th ed. (Burr Ridge, Ill.: Irwin, 1996), p. 203.

9. Shawn Tully, "Why Drug Prices Will Go Lower," *Fortune,* May 3, 1993, pp. 56–58+.

10. Peter and Donnelly, *A Preface to Marketing Management,* p. 204.

11. Tully, "Why Drug Prices Will Go Lower."

12. Peter D. Bennett, ed., *Dictionary of Marketing Terms,* 2nd ed. (Chicago: American Marketing Association, 1995), p. 215.

13. Susan Greco, "Smart Use of 'Special Offers,' " *Inc.,* February 1993, p. 23.

14. Stephanie Strom, "A Survivor for Seventh Avenue," *New York Times,* March 7, 1993, p. 12F.

15. Andrew Kupfer, "Who's Winning the PC Price Wars?" *Fortune,* September 21, 1992, pp. 80–82.

16. Michael D. Mondello, "Naming Your Price," *Inc.,* July 1992, pp. 80–83.

17. Richard Turner, "The Top Hits of Today and Tomorrow at Rhino Records Are from Yesteryear," *The Wall Street Journal,* October 2, 1992, pp. B1, B6.

18. National Public Radio, "Morning Edition," July 10, 1996.

19. Personal correspondence from Jerry Keller, AutoResearch Laboratories, Inc., Chicago, December 23, 1993.

20. Vladimir Edelman, "Sitting on Top of the World," *Inc. Technology,* March 19, 1996, p. 88.

21. Mondello, "Naming Your Price," p. 81.

22. Bennett, ed., *Dictionary of Marketing Terms,* p. 240.

23. Glenn Snyder, "Covering All the Bases for Better Video Rental," *Progressive Grocer,* July 1993, pp. 17+.

24. Bennett, *Dictionary of Marketing Terms*, p. 79.

25. David Kirkpatrick, "The Revolution at Compaq Computer," *Fortune*, December 14, 1992, pp. 82, 86.

26. Wendy Zellner, "Penney's Rediscovers Its Calling," *Business Week*, April 5, 1993, pp. 51–52.

27. "Read All about It," *The Economist*, April 6, 1996, pp. 69–70.

28. "Steelmakers Win Partial Victory in Trade Complaints," *Chicago Tribune*, July 28, 1993, sec. 3, pp. 1–2.

29. See Tom Peters, "Trade, Now More than Ever," *Quality Digest*, May 1993, pp. 16–17.

30. George M. C. Fisher, "Breaking into Japan," *Audacity*, Winter 1992, p. 2.

31. Bob Ortega, "Wal-Mart Bows to Pricing Reality by Changing 4 Letters," *The Wall Street Journal*, May 21, 1993, p. B1.

32. Patricia Sellers, "Companies That Serve You Best," *Fortune*, May 31, 1993, pp. 74–76+.

Chapter 13

1. Larry Armstrong, "What's in a Name Change? A Classier Acura," *Business Week*, March 18, 1996, p. 117.

2. Teri Agins, "Ralph Lauren Tries to Bring Polo to the Masses," *The Wall Street Journal*, April 24, 1996, pp. B1, B8.

3. Faye Brookman, "Going Upscale," *Supermarket Business*, Close-up: Private Label advertising supplement, May 1996, pp. 17–21.

4. Robert D. Buzzell and Frederick D. Wiersema, "Successful Share Building Strategies," *Harvard Business Review*, January–February 1981, pp. 135–144.

5. Greg Bowens, "A Demolition Derby for Hertz, Avis, and the Gang," *Business Week*, October 5, 1992, pp. 85–86.

6. Jim Mateja, "Escort Sticker Shock: One Price Sells 'Em All," *Chicago Tribune*, March 13, 1992, sec. 1, pp. 1, 6.

7. Brian O'Reilly, "Know When to Embrace Change," *Fortune*, February 22, 1993, p. 90.

8. Amy Barrett, "Something Shady at Sunkist?" *Business Week*, May 17, 1993, p. 40.

9. David Young, "Grainger Retools Strategy, Gets Faster, Busier, Bigger," *Chicago Tribune*, July 18, 1993, sec. 7, pp. 1, 6.

10. Procter & Gamble Annual Report 1992, p. 10.

11. Peter D. Bennett, ed., *Dictionary of Marketing Terms*, 2nd ed. (Chicago: American Marketing Association, 1995), p. 155.

12. Susan Greco, "Smart Use of 'Special Offers,' " *Inc.*, February 1993, pp. 23.

13. National Public Radio, "All Things Considered," August 18, 1993.

14. Paul Sherlock, *Rethinking Business to Business Marketing* (New York: Free Press, 1991), p. 64.

15. Jean Sherman Chatzky, "Changing the World," *Forbes*, March 2, 1992, pp. 83, 85.

16. Masayoshi Kanabayashi, "Japan's Top Soap Firm, Kao, Hopes to Clean Up Abroad," *The Wall Street Journal*, December 17, 1992, p. B4.

17. Meg Cox, "Audio-Book Makers Seek More Listeners," *The Wall Street Journal*, January 6, 1993, pp. B1, B8.

18. Kevin Helliker, "Bombay Co.'s Line of Furniture, Bric-a-Brac Fills a Void," *The Wall Street Journal*, October 28, 1992, p. B4.

19. Susan Greco, "Recession-Proof Pricing," *Inc.*, April 1993, p. 27.

20. Krystal Miller, "Honda Adopts Incentive Plan for Its Dealers," *The Wall Street Journal*, May 6, 1993, pp. A3, A5.

21. Michael V. Marn and Robert L. Rosiello, "Managing Price, Gaining Profit," *Harvard Business Review*, September–October 1992, pp. 84-94.

22. "Body Language," *Entrepreneur*, March 1993, p. 222.

23. Susan Greco, "Street-Smart Pricing," *Inc.*, May 1993, p. 25.

24. Wendy Zellner, "Not Everybody Loves Wal-Mart's Low Prices," *Business Week*, October 12, 1992, pp. 36, 38.

25. Amy Feldman, "Blue Jeans as Tuna Fish," *Forbes*, April 26, 1993, pp. 78–79.

26. Laura Bird, "Apparel Stores Seek to Cure Shoppers Addicted to Discounts," *The Wall Street Journal*, May 29, 1996, pp. A1, A10.

27. Jon Berry, "For Procter & Gamble's EDLP, a Sobering Report," *Adweek*, April 19, 1993, p. 9.

28. Gabriella Stern, "While Cost-Cutting Boosted P&G's Net in Fiscal Third Period, Sales Slid 2%," *The Wall Street Journal*, April 28, 1993, p. A4; Zachary Schiller, "A Nervous P&G Picks Up the Cost-Cutting Ax," *Business Week*, April 19, 1993, p. 28.

29. Berry, "For Procter & Gamble's EDLP, a Sobering Report,"

30. Laura Klepacki, "P&G Commits Its Heavy Guns," *Supermarket News*, April 12, 1993, pp. 1, 10–11.

31. Bird, "Apparel Stores Seek to Cure Shoppers," p. A1.

32. Melissa Campanelli, "What's in Store for EDLP?" *Sales & Marketing Management*, August 1993, pp. 56–59.

33. Campanelli, "What's in Store for EDLP?" p. 59.

34. Richard Gibson, "Broad Grocery Price Cuts May Not Pay," *The Wall Street Journal*, May 7, 1993.

35. Bird, "Apparel Stores Seek to Cure Shoppers," p. A1.

36. Bird, "Apparel Stores Seek to Cure Shoppers," p. A10.

37. "Upmarket Philosophy," *The Economist*, December 26, 1992, pp. 95–98.

38. Laura Zinn and Hiromi Uchida, "Who Said Diamonds Are Forever?" *Business Week*, November 2, 1992, pp. 128–129.

39. Robert C. Blattberg and Scott A. Neslin, *Sales Promotion: Concepts, Methods, and Strategies* (Englewood Cliffs, N.J.: Prentice-Hall, 1990), pp. 349–350; Robert M. Schindler and Alan R. Wiman, "Effects of Odd Pricing on Price Recall," *Journal of Business Research* (November 1989): pp. 165–178; and Kent B. Monroe, *Pricing: Making Profitable Decisions*, 2nd ed. (New York: McGraw-Hill, 1990).

40. Philip R. Cateora, *International Marketing*, 8th ed. (Homewood, Ill.: Irwin, 1993), p. 590.

41. Sally D. Goll, "Pepsi Looks for Pop from Asian Markets," *The Wall Street Journal*, June 25, 1993, p. A5C.

42. James R. Healey, "Celica Shows Hazards of Misreading Market," *USA Today*, December 10, 1993, p. 5B; "The Price Is High," *The Economist*, August 14, 1993, p. 63.

43. Valerie Reitman, "P&G Uses Skills It Has Honed at Home to Introduce Its Brands to the Russians," *The Wall Street Journal*, April 14, 1993, pp. B1, B10.

44. Neela Banerjee, "Russia Snickers after Mars Invades," *The Wall Street Journal*, July 13, 1993, pp. B1, B10.

45. Procter & Gamble Annual Report 1993, p. 10.

46. "Not at Any Price," *The Economist*, April 6, 1996, p. 70.

47. "Pillow Fight," *The Economist*, March 9, 1996, p. 66.

48. Procter & Gamble Report of Annual Meeting of Shareholders, October 12, 1993; Procter & Gamble Annual Report 1993, p. 11.

49. Rita Koselka, "Candy Wars," *Forbes*, August 17, 1992, pp. 76–77.

50. *Ibid.*

51. Greg Bowens, "Wiping the Mess from Gerber's Chin," *Business Week*, February 1, 1993, p. 32.

52. Agins, "Ralph Lauren Tries to Bring Polo to the Masses," p. B1.

53. Jim Mateja, "Japanese Decide to Cut Prices in a Move That's Long Overdue," *Chicago Tribune*, June 24, 1996, sec. 4, p. 5.

54. Larry Armstrong and Karen Lowry Miller, "Toyota's New Pickups: Oops,"

Business Week, February 15, 1993, p. 37; James R. Healey, "Big Price, Little Power Has T100 Sputtering," *USA Today,* May 23, 1993, p. 10B.

55. Bowens, "A Demolition Derby."

56. Michael D. Mondello, "Naming Your Price," *Inc.,* July 1992, pp. 80–83.

57. Mark Lewyn, "MCI Is Coming Through Loud and Clear," *Business Week,* January 25, 1993, pp. 84, 88.

Chapter 14

1. Peter D. Bennett, ed., *Dictionary of Marketing Terms,* 2nd ed. (Chicago: American Marketing Association, 1995), p. 44.

2. Laura Bird, "High-Tech Inventory System Coordinates Retailer's Clothes with Customers' Taste," *The Wall Street Journal,* June 12, 1996, pp. B1, B6.

3. Zachary Schiller and Wendy Zellner, "Clout! More and More Retail Giants Rule the Marketplace," *Business Week,* December 21, 1992, pp. 66–69+.

4. William Stern, "Mom and Dad Knew Every Name," *Forbes,* December 7, 1992, pp. 172, 174.

5. Frances Huffman, "Marketing Smarts: Innovative Ideas to Promote Your Business," *Entrepreneur,* May 1993, p. 140.

6. Paul Sherlock, *Rethinking Business to Business Marketing* (New York: Free Press, 1991), pp. 104–107.

7. Rashi Glazer, "Marketing in an Information-Intensive Environment: Strategic Implications of Knowledge as an Asset," *Journal of Marketing* (October 1991): pp. 1–19.

8. Meg Whittemore, "Extend Your Reach by Catalog Sales," *Nation's Business,* March 1992, pp. 33–34, 36.

9. The Quaker Oats Company, 1993 Annual Report, p. 12.

10. Steve Lohr, "Computers Greening with Times," *Chicago Tribune,* April 18, 1993, sec. 7, p. 3.

11. "The Green Scene: Plastic Surgery," *Entrepreneur,* May 1993, p. 20.

12. Wilma Randle and Michael A. Lev, "Saturn Seeking Happy Returns," *Chicago Tribune,* August 11, 1993, sec. 3, p. 1.

13. Ruth Miller Fitzgibbons, "Business Is Blooming," *Your Company,* Spring 1992, pp. 32–35.

14. *Ibid.,* p. 35.

22. Achrol, "Evolution of the Marketing Organization"; Walter Kiechel III, "How We Will Work in the Year 2000," *Fortune,* May 17, 1993, pp. 38–39.

15. Based on Bennett, ed., *Dictionary of Marketing Terms,* p. 114.

16. Roberta Maynard, "Prospecting for Gold," *Nation's Business,* June 1996, pp. 69–74.

17. Roberta Maynard, "A Piece of the Action," *Nation's Business,* June 1996, pp. 69–74.

18. Janean Chun, "Taking Charge," *Entrepreneur,* July 1996, pp. 204, 206.

19. Robert Frank and Jonathan Friedland, "How Pepsi's Charge into Brazil Fell Short of Its Ambitious Goals," *The Wall Street Journal,* August 30, 1996, pp. A1, A6.

20. Manjeet Kripalani and Tatiana Pouschine, "People Thought I Was Nuts," *Forbes,* June 8, 1992, pp. 120–121.

21. "Pills by Post," *The Economist,* February 6, 1993, pp. 70–71.

22. Susan Greco, "Riding on Big-Company Coattails," *Inc.,* April 1993, p. 28.

23. Gretchen Morgenson, "Greener Pastures?" *Forbes,* July 6, 1992, p. 48.

24. Steve Glain, "American Standard Succeeds in Korea by Outflanking Local Firms' Lock-Out," *The Wall Street Journal,* August 26, 1993, p. A6.

25. Larry Armstrong, "What's Wrong with Selling Used CDs?" *Business Week,* July 26, 1993, p. 38.

26. Stratford Sherman, "Are Strategic Alliances Working?" *Fortune,* September 21, 1992, pp. 77–78.

27. Glazer, "Marketing in an Information-Intensive Environment," p. 1.

28. Schiller and Zellner, "Clout!"

29. *Ibid.*

30. See George S. Day, "Marketing's Contribution to the Strategy Dialogue," unpublished paper (University of Pennsylvania, n.d.); Frederick E. Webster, Jr., "The Changing Role of Marketing in the Corporation," *Journal of Marketing* (October 1992): pp. 1–17.

31. Marty Jacknis and Steve Kratz, "The Channel Empowerment Solution," *Sales & Marketing Management,* March 1993, pp. 44–49.

32. Jerry G. Bowles, "Quality '92: Leading the World-Class Company," *Fortune* special advertising section, September 21, 1992, pp. 16, 18.

33. Nicholas W. Pilugin, "Wrigley Expanding Outlets in Russia," *Chicago Tribune,* August 4, 1992, sec. 3, pp. 1–2.

34. Michael Selz, "More Small Firms Are Turning to Trade Intermediaries," *The Wall Street Journal,* February 2, 1993, p. B2.

35. Robert A. Mamis, "Not So Innocent Abroad," *Inc.,* September 1993, pp. 110–111.

36. Jeanette R. Scollard, "Road to Russia," *Entrepreneur,* March 1993, pp. 114–119.

37. Gary Taylor, "Highway Robbery?" *International Business,* July 1993, pp. 33–34.

38. "A Close Look at Five Countries," *The Grocer* (Britain), September 12, 1992, p. 50.

39. Jeffrey A. Tannenbaum, "California Court's Royalties Ruling Chills Franchisers," *The Wall Street Journal,* May 28, 1996, p. A22.

40. Joseph Pereira and Bryan Bruley, "Toys 'R' Us Vows It Will Challenge Any Antitrust Charges Brought by FTC," *The Wall Street Journal,* May 22, 1996, pp. A3-A4; "Monopolists 'R' Us?" *Time,* June 3, 1996, p. 60.

41. Bennett, ed., *Dictionary of Marketing Terms,* p. 58.

42. Erika Kotite, "Food Fight," *Entrepreneur,* pp. 130–135.

43. *Ibid.*

Chapter 15

1. John H. Taylor, "Niche Guys Finish First," *Forbes,* October 26, 1992, pp. 128, 132.

2. Peter D. Bennett, ed., *Dictionary of Marketing Terms,* 2nd ed. (Chicago: American Marketing Association, 1995), p. 305.

3. U.S. Department of Commerce, *Statistical Abstract of the United States,* 115th ed. (Washington, D.C.: U.S. Government Printing Office, 1995), p. 550.

4. Julie Candler, "How to Choose a Distributor," *Nation's Business,* August 1993, pp. 45–46.

5. Erich Toll, "Get Smart," *International Business,* September 1993, pp. 29–30.

6. Glenn Snyder, "Covering All the Bases for Better Video Rentals," *Progressive Grocer,* July 1993, pp. 17–20+.

7. Rich Mendosa, "100 Fastest Growing Companies: Reef Brazil," *Hispanic Business,* August 1993, p. 44.

8. Candler, "How to Choose a Distributor."

9. Sarah Schafer, "Finding Overseas Agents," *Inc.,* May 1996, p. 108.

10. David Young, "Middlemen Caught in Evolving Market," *Chicago Tribune,* November 29, 1993, pp. ??

11. W. W. Grainger, Inc., 1992 Annual Report and Form 10-K, pp. 5, 7.

12. Young, "Middlemen Caught in Evolving Market."

13. Bennett, ed., *Dictionary of Marketing Terms,* p. 206-207.

14. Colby Coates, "Atlantic Transportation/ '93," *International Business* special advertising section.

15. "A Cutting Edge," *International Business,* March 1993, p. 68.

16. Gregory L. Miles, "Think Global, Go Intermodal," *International Business,* March 1993, pp. 60–61+.

17. "Freight Forwarders: A Prime Resource for the American Exporter,"

International Business, March 1993, p. 125.

18. Scott Williams, "An Inventory Control Solution for On-Site Warehousing," *Industrial Engineering,* September 1992, pp. 29–30.

19. The Quaker Oats Company, 4th Quarter 1993 Report, p. 7.

20. Nancy Ryan, "Targeting Checkout Speed Trap," *Chicago Tribune,* February 26, 1992, sec. 3, pp. 1, 4.

21. Susan Wels, "The Profitable Pursuit of Quality," *McKesson Today,* December 1992, pp. 1–5.

22. Sarah Schafer, "Quick Recovery," *Inc. Technology,* June 18, 1996, p. 84.

23. Personal communication, Lewis Hershey, Northeast Missouri State University.

24. Airborne Express, 1995 Annual Report, p. 9.

25. Airborne Express, 1995 Annual Report, p. 10.

26. Jennifer DeCoursey, "In the Nick of Time," *Sales & Marketing Management,* April 1996, p. 82.

27. Gordon Feller, "The Rough Road from Marx to Markets," *Journal of Business Strategy,* March/April 1996, pp. 47–51.

28. "Automating Procedures Increases Time for Customer Service," *McKesson Today,* December 1992, p. 4.

29. Bob Gatty, "The Big Truck Pile Up," *Grocery Marketing,* October 1995, pp. 16, 18.

30. Edward O. Welles, "Built on Speed," *Inc.,* October 1992, pp. 82–84, 88.

31. Gary McWilliams, "Putting a Shine on Shoe Operations," *Business Week,* June 14, 1993, p. 59.

32. Bennett, ed., *Dictionary of Marketing Terms,* p. 95.

33. Zachary Schiller and Wendy Zellner, "Clout! More and More Retail Giants Rule the Marketplace," *Business Week,* December 21, 1992, pp. 66–69+.

34. John Morris, "Customized Services Boost Competitiveness," *International Business,* November 1993, pp. 48+.

35. Joshua Macht, "Are You Ready for Electronic Partnering?" *Inc. Technology,* November 14, 1995, pp. 43–44+.

36. John Salak, "When Your Carrier Delivers the Goods," *International Business,* September 1993, pp. 30, 32.

37. Phaedra Hise, "How to Survive EDI," *Inc.,* December 1995, p. 131.

38. See Steve Biciocchi, "Every Business Should Want Superior Distribution," *Industrial Engineering,* September 1992, pp. 27–28.

Chapter 16

1. Peter D. Bennett, ed., *Dictionary of Marketing Terms,* 2nd ed. (Chicago:

American Marketing Association, 1995), p. 245.

2. Barbara Marsh, "Kiosks and Carts Can Often Serve as Mall Magnets," *The Wall Street Journal,* November 24, 1992, p. B1.

3. Frances Huffman, "Trade Secrets," *Entrepreneur,* February 1993, pp. 91–97.

4. Department of Commerce, *Statistical Abstract of the United States,* 115th ed. (Washington, D.C.: U.S. Government Printing Office, 1995), p. 417.

5. *Ibid.,* p. 779.

6. Lynn Beresford, "Marketing Smarts: Hands On," *Entrepreneur,* April 1996, p. 36.

7. Leah Ingram, "Wash 'N' Go," *Entrepreneur,* July 1993, p. 12.

8. Bob Gatty, "Cut-Throat Competition vs. the Independent," *Grocery Marketing,* April 1996, pp. 22, 24.

9. Frances Huffman, "If the Shoe Fits . . . ," *Entrepreneur,* April 1993, p. 161.

10. Christopher Power, "Flops," *Business Week,* August 16, 1993, pp. 76–80, 82.

11. Stephen Plauche II, "The Sales Force Will Need to Have the Best Team Spirit in the Nation," *The Wall Street Journal,* January 14, 1993, p. B1.

12. Wendy Zellner, "When Wal-Mart Starts a Food Fight, It's a Doozy," *Business Week,* June 14, 1993, pp. 92–93.

13. Sarah Schafer, "Street Cruising," *Inc. Technology,* June 18, 1996, p. 19; Debra Phillips, "Coffee, Tea or 'Net?'" *Entrepreneur,* February 1996, p. 23.

14. Jack G. Kaikati, "Don't Crack the Japanese Distribution System—Just Circumvent It," *Columbia Journal of World Business* (Summer 1993): pp. 34–45.

15. Charlotte Mulhern, "On the Level," *Entrepreneur,* February 1996, pp. 184, 186.

16. Katherine Ellison, "Avon Ladies Sell Hut to Hut in Brazil Wilds," *Chicago Tribune,* October 3, 1993, sec. 1, pp. 21, 26.

17. "Geerlings & Wade," *Inc.,* October 1992, p. 131.

18. Kaikati, "Don't Crack the Japanese Distribution System."

19. Laura Pedersen, "500 Pages of Merchandise, but Should I Invest?" *New York Times,* June 9, 1996, p. F4.

20. Janean Chun, "Going the Distance," *Entrepreneur,* February 1996, pp. 114–115+.

21. Pedersen, "500 Pages of Merchandise."

22. William M. Bulkeley, "Online Shopping Fails to Fulfill Promise," *The Wall Street Journal,* June 21, 1993, p. B5.

23. Ernan Roman, "More for Your Money," *Inc.,* September 1992, pp. 113–114, 116.

24. Amy Wu, "Urban Outfitter a Hip,

Affordable Alternative," *Chicago Tribune,* July 15, 1996, sec. 4, pp. 1–2.

25. John Schmeltzer, "Addition by Subtraction at Walgreens, Crate & Barrel," *Chicago Tribune,* October 24, 1992, sec. 2, p. 1.

26. Lisa Gubernick, "Secondhand Chic," *Forbes,* April 26, 1993, pp. 172–173.

27. Example from Lewis Hershey, Northeast Missouri State University.

28. Melissa Campanelli, "What's in Store for EDLP?" *Sales & Marketing Management,* August 1993, pp. 56–59; Nancy Ryan, "There's More to Retail Cuts than Low Prices," *Chicago Tribune,* September 5, 1993, sec. 7, pp. 1–2.

29. Julie Pitta, "The Crisco Factor," *Forbes,* July 20, 1992, pp. 306–307.

30. Peter Newcomb, "Endangered Species?" *Forbes,* July 20, 1992, pp. 52, 54, 58.

31. Milford Prewitt, "PepsiCo Kiosk Goes Underground in Moscow Subway," *Nation's Restaurant News,* June 21, 1993, p. 4.

32. Cheryl Jarvis, "A Novel Enterprise," *Nation's Business,* April 1996, p. 14.

33. Jane Adler, "For These Stores, Road Less Traveled Works," *Crain's Small Business,* May 1996, p. 6.

34. Adrienne Ward, "New Breed of Mall Knows: Everybody Loves a Bargain," *Advertising Age,* January 27, 1992, p. S5.

35. Mark Veverka, "Discount Stores Yield Value for Nordstrom," *Crain's Chicago Business,* May 27, 1996, p. 11.

36. Milford Prewitt, "Garfield's Operator Eyes Growth in Small-Town Malls," *Nation's Restaurant News,* May 10, 1993, pp. 14, 18.

37. J. Paul Peter and Jerry C. Olson, *Consumer Behavior and Marketing Strategy,* 4th ed. (Homewood, Ill.: Irwin, 1996), pp. 616.

38. Kate Fitzgerald, "Mega Malls: Built for the '90s, or the '80s?" *Advertising Age,* January 27, 1992, pp. S1, S8.

39. Meg Whittemore, "Shopping Malls Attract Small Firms," *Nation's Business,* December 1992, pp. 53–54, 56.

40. Russell Redman, "Selling the Image," *Supermarket News,* March 18, 1996, pp. 1, 9+.

41. Susan M. Keaveney, "Conceptualization and Operationalization of Retail Store Image: A Case of Rival Middle-Level Theories," *Journal of the Academy of Marketing Science* (Spring 1992): pp. 165–175.

42. Bennett, ed., *Dictionary of Marketing Terms,* p. 15.

43. "Luring Shoppers into the Bakery," *Grocery Marketing,* October 1995, pp. 32–33.

44. "For Retailers, Splitting Ears Can Lead to Open Wallets," *Chicago Tribune*, May 26, 1996, sec. 5, p. 7.
45. Ellen Neuborne, "Stores Say Remodeling Boosts Sales," *USA Today*, April 19, 1993, pp. 1B–2B.
46. Chun, "Going the Distance," p. 120.
47. Steven J. Johnson, "Retail Systems: No Longer Business as Usual," *Journal of Systems Management* (August 1992): pp. 8–10; Erika Kotite, "Rethinking Retail," *Entrepreneur*, December 1992, pp. 97–101.
48. Gretchen Morgenson, "Business as Usual," *Forbes*, February 3, 1992, pp. 80–81.
49. Zina Moukheiber, "Retailing," *Forbes*, January 4, 1993, pp. 172–175.
50. "Europe's Discount Dogfight," *The Economist*, May 8, 1993, pp. 69–70; "Japan Shops the Wal-Mart Way," *The Economist*, February 6, 1993, pp. 67-68; Cacilie Rohwedder, "Deep-Discount Fight Consumes Much of Europe," *The Wall Street Journal*, June 18, 1993, p. A5C; and Kevin Helliker, "U.S. Discount Retailers Are Targeting Europe and Its Fat Margins," *The Wall Street Journal*, September 20, 1993, pp. A1, A4.
51. Jennifer Steinhauer, "Fierce Foes Encroach on Superstores' Territory," *New York Times*, June 8, 1996, pp. 17–18.
52. Michael Garry, "Answering the Challenge," *Progressive Grocer*, July 1993, pp. 83–86.
53. Gretchen Morgenson, "Here Come the Cross-Shoppers," *Forbes*, December 7, 1992, pp. 90+.
54. Amy I. Stickel, "Emily's Charges into Meal Marketing Battle," *Supermarket News*, March 18, 1996, p. 35.
55. Pedersen, "500 Pages of Merchandise"; Chun, "Going the Distance," p. 114.
56. Pedersen, "500 Pages of Merchandise."
57. "How Much Catalogs Cost," *Inc.*, June 1996, p. 114.
58. See Johnson, "Retail Systems"; Thomas McCarroll, "Grocery-Cart Wars," *Time*, March 30, 1992, p. 49.
59. Kazumi Tanaka, "Putting Your Business on the Map," *Inc. Technology*, June 18, 1996, pp. 94–99.
60. Marc Millstein, "Roundy's Rounding Up Sales with Frequent Shopper Data," *Supermarket News*, April 22, 1996, pp. 25, 30.
61. W. Frank Dell, "Maximize Your Frequent Shopper Program," *Grocery Marketing*, April 1996, pp. 55, 57.
62. Alice LaPlante, "Shared Destinies: CEOs and CIOs—Kmart," *Forbes ASAP*, December 7, 1992, pp. 38, 40, 42.
63. Sarah Schafer, "How Information Technology Is Leveling the Playing Field," *Inc. Technology*, November 14, 1995, pp. 92+.
64. Bennett, ed., *Dictionary of Marketing Terms*, p. 235.
65. Millstein, "Roundy's Rounding Up Sales."
66. Michael Levy and Barton A. Weitz, *Retailing Management*, 2nd ed. (Chicago: Irwin, 1995), p. 81.
67. *Ibid.*, p. 83.
68. Pedersen, "500 Pages of Merchandise."
69. "Not at Any Price," *The Economist*, April 6, 1996, p. 70.
70. Levy and Weitz, *Retailing Management*, p. 87.
71. Mulhern, "On the Level."

Chapter 17

1. Robert Schwartz, " 'Net Gain," *Illinois Business*, 4th Quarter 1995, pp. 42–46.
2. "Five Marketing Missions, Five Sites That Sell," *FastCompany*, June–July 1996, p. 150.
3. Alan Salomon, "Memphis Distributes Word on Its Benefits," *Advertising Age*, October 2, 1995, p. 14.
4. Alessandra Bianchi, "The Ultimate Frequent Flyer," *Inc.*, May 1996, p. 125.
5. "Five Marketing Missions."
6. Ruth Hamel, "States of Mind," *American Demographics*, April 1992, p. 41.
7. "(Inter)netting Big Sales," *Selling Power*, March 1996, p. 44.
8. Peter D. Bennett, ed., *Dictionary of Marketing Terms*, 2nd ed. (Chicago: American Marketing Association, 1995), p. 6.
9. Based on Bennett, ed., *Dictionary of Marketing Terms*, p. 206.
10. Bennett, ed., *Dictionary of Marketing Terms*, p. 253.
11. Bennett, ed., *Dictionary of Marketing Terms*, p. 232.
12. Nancy Millman and Mike Dorning, "Making McSplash in News Media," *Chicago Tribune*, May 10, 1996, sec. 3, pp. 1, 3.
13. Bill Pietrucha, "A Tale of Three Web Sites," *Journal of Business Strategy*, January/February 1996, pp. 28–33.
14. See Don E. Schultz, "Integrated Marketing Communications: Maybe Definition Is in the Point of View," *Marketing News*, January 18, 1993, p. 17; Adrienne Ward Fawcett, "Integrated Marketing—Marketers Convinced: Its Time Has Arrived," *Advertising Age*, November 6, 1993, pp. S1–S2.
15. Betsy Morris, "The Brand's the Thing," *Fortune*, March 4, 1996, pp. 72–75+.
16. Pietrucha, "A Tale of Three Web Sites," p. 32.
17. Regis McKenna, "Marketing Is Everything," *Harvard Business Review*, January–February 1991, pp. 65–79.
18. McKenna, "Marketing Is Everything," p. 74.
19. "How to Advertise Abroad," *Sales & Marketing Management*, March 1992, p. 51.
20. Ed Nanas, "Computer Diskettes: A Big Little Marketing Tool Customers Can't Resist," *Your Company*, Spring 1993, pp. 8–9.
21. EBen Shapiro, "Tropicana Squeezes Out Minute Maid to Get Bigger Slice of Citrus Hill Fans," *The Wall Street Journal*, February 4, 1993, pp. B1, B5.
22. Shapiro, "Tropicana Squeezes Out Minute Maid."
23. Mark Gleason, "Time to Perform or Perish," *Advertising Age*, October 2, 1995, p. 32.
24. Pat Sloan, "Chesebrough Puts New Face on Its Brands," *Advertising Age*, January 27, 1992, p. 3.
25. Joanne Cleaver, "Go Ahead! You Can Talk about Yourself," *Crain's Small Business*, May 1996, p. 57.
26. James P. Miller, "Maytag U.K. Unit Finds a Promotion Is Too Successful," *The Wall Street Journal*, March 31, 1993, p. A9.
27. Sarah Schafer, "Informing Customers," *Inc.*, June 1996, p. 114.
28. "This Cookie Is Tops in Food Sales," *Fortune*, May 4, 1992, p. 100.
29. Murphy, "The Best Newsletters in America," p. 78.
30. Schwartz, " 'Net Gain," p. 46.
31. C. Merle Crawford, *New Products Management*, 2nd ed. (Burr Ridge, Ill.: Irwin, 1987), p. 44.
32. "Indicators of Market Size for 117 Countries," *Business International*, July 8, 1991, p. 225.
33. Jean-Pierre Jeanett and H. David Hennessey, *Global Marketing Strategies*, 3rd ed. (Boston: Houghton-Mifflin, 1995), p. 489.
34. Nathalie Boschat, "Catering to Africa's Consumers," *World Press Review*, June 1993, p. 40.
35. Schwartz, " 'Net Gain," p. 44.
36. Pietrucha, "A Tale of Three Web Sites," p. 33.
37. Melanie Wells, "McCann Awaits OK for New Coke Ads," *Advertising Age*, May 24, 1993, pp. 3, 46.
38. "Ad Director Finds Global Business Means Speaking in Tongues," *GSB Chicago* (The University of Chicago Graduate School of Business), Summer 1992, p. 40.
39. Normandy Madden, "Demo Gives Lift to Skoda," *Advertising Age*, October 2, 1995, p. 17.
40. Stephanie Gruner, "Telemarketing Dos and Don'ts," *Inc.*, February 1996, p. 94.

41. "How to Advertise Abroad," *Sales & Marketing Management,* March 1992, p. 51.

42. "Mixed Message," *Newsweek,* December 9, 1992, p. 8.

43. Kevin Goldman, "Hasbro, Turner Get Animated for Holidays," *The Wall Street Journal,* November 18, 1992, p. B1.

44. David Ellis, "Knowledge for Sale," *Time,* June 8, 1992, p. 69.

Chapter 18

1. Betsy Morris, "The Brand's the Thing," *Fortune,* March 4, 1996, pp. 72–75+.

2. "100 Leading National Advertisers" (table), *Advertising Age,* September 27, 1995.

3. "Business Beat: Top Billing," *Entrepreneur,* February 1996, p. 20.

4. Peter D. Bennett, ed., *Dictionary of Marketing Terms,* 2nd Edition, (Chicago: American Marketing Association, 1995), p. 140.

5. Bill Pietrucha, "A Tale of Three Web Sites," *Journal of Business Strategy,* January/February 1996, pp. 28–33.

6. Celestine Bohlen, "Crash Russian Course for Procter & Gamble," *New York Times,* December 19, 1993, p. 5.

7. "Virgin Atlantic Airways: The Iconoclastic Carrier," *Sales & Marketing Management,* August 1992, p. 45.

8. Bennett, ed., *Dictionary of Marketing Terms,* p. 51.

9. *Ibid.,* p. 9.

10. Tara Parker-Pope, "Ad Agencies Are Stumbling in East Europe," *The Wall Street Journal,* May 10, 1996, pp. B1, B14.

11. "The Enigma of Japanese Advertising," *The Economist,* August 14, 1993, pp. 59–60.

12. Pietrucha, "A Tale of Three Web Sites," p. 32.

13. *Ibid.,* p. 29.

14. Jan Gelman, "Build a Web Site? Don't Build a Web Site. Build One? Don't Build One," *Selling,* July/August 1996, pp. 34–39.

15. Bennett, ed., *Dictionary of Marketing Terms.*

16. *Ibid.,* p. 238.

17. *Ibid.,* p. 116.

18. Lynn Beresford, "Prime Time," *Entrepreneur,* February 1996, p. 32.

19. Theresa Howard, "McD Launches Infomercial to Promote 'Good Deeds,'" *Nation's Restaurant News,* July 26, 1993, p. 4.

20. R. David Thomas, *Dave's Way,* Berkeley Books, 1991, p. 164; David Lieberman, "Cable Threatens to Snatch Viewers—and Ad Money," *USA Today,* September 16, 1996, pp. 1B, 2B.

21. Bradley Johnson, "Computer Ads Switch on the TV," *Advertising Age,* October 2, 1995, pp. 1, 4.

22. "It Pays to Advertise—in Any Language," *Sales & Marketing Management,* January 1993, p. 13.

23. Jill Smolowe, "Read This!" *Time,* November 26, 1990, pp. 62–70.

24. Richard R. Szathmary, "The Great Outdoors," *Sales & Marketing Management,* March 1992, p. 76.

25. Jeff Borden, "Torco at Bat: There's Ad Joy in Mudville," *Crain's Chicago Business,* February 26, 1996, p. 4.

26. Szathmary, "The Great Outdoors."

27. Alessandra Bianchi, "On-Line Chic: A Web-Page Makeover," *Inc.,* July 1996, p. 99.

28. Debra Aho Williamson, "Score One for ESPN, Starwave," *Advertising Age,* October 2, 1995, p. 34.

29. Ginia Bellafante, "Cyberspace, 90210," *Time,* March 4, 1996, p. 65.

30. Zachary Schiller, "For More about Tide, Click Here," *Business Week,* June 3, 1996, p. 44.

31. National Public Radio, "Morning Edition," January 23, 1996.

32. Nancy Ten Kate, "Make It an Event," *American Demographics,* November 1992, pp. 40–44.

33. Mary Hayes, "Penney Taps Sunnyvale for New-Store Test," *The Business Journal,* September 14, 1992, pp. 1, 20.

34. Kuntz and Weber, "The New Hucksterism," p. 78.

35. Bennett, ed., *Dictionary of Marketing Terms,* p. 63.

36. *Ibid.,* p. 112.

37. *Ibid.,* p. 232.

38. *Ibid.,* p. 212.

39. Arsenio Oloroso, Jr., "So, You're on the Internet. Okay, Now What?" *Crain's Chicago Business,* July 10, 1995, pp. 3, 36.

40. Phaedra Hise, "Hits That Rate Attention," *Inc.,* September 1995, p. 115.

41. Morris, "The New Basics of Advertising."

42. Bennett, ed., *Dictionary of Marketing Terms,* p. 67.

43. Fred Danzig, "Sidebars," *Advertising Age,* October 2, 1995, p. 24.

44. Allison Lucas, "Law Comes to Tombstone," *Sales & Marketing Management,* April 1996, p. 83.

45. Bennett, ed., *Dictionary of Marketing Terms,* p. 253.

46. Morris, "The Brand's the Thing," p. 74.

47. *Consumer Promotion Report* (monograph) (New York: Dancer Fitzgerald Sample, 1982).

48. "The Coupon Turns 100," *Grocery Marketing,* October 1995, p. 23.

49. "Opening Up the World of Coupon Redemption," *Marketing,* June 3, 1993, p. 30.

50. Raju Narisetti, "P&G Ad Chief Plots Demise of the Coupon," *The Wall Street Journal,* April 17, 1996, pp. B1, B5C.

51. Narisetti, "P&G Ad Chief Plots Demise of the Coupon"; James Tenser, "P&G Plans to Test Sales without Coupons in N.Y.," *Supermarket News,* January 8, 1996, pp. 1, 8, 38.

52. Frances Huffman, "Redeeming Qualities," *Entrepreneur,* October 1992, pp. 168–169.

53. Huffman, "Redeeming Qualities."

54. Huffman, "Redeeming Qualities."

55. Millie Neal, "Quaker's Direct Hit," *Direct Marketing,* January 1991, pp. 52, 53, 70; Kathleen Deveny, "Segments of One: Marketers Take Aim at the Ultimate Narrow Target," *The Wall Street Journal,* March 22, 1991, p. B4.

56. Scott Hume, "Coupons: Are They Too Popular?" *Advertising Age,* February 15, 1993, p. 32.

57. Morris, "The New Basics of Advertising," p. 6.

58. Suzanne Alexander, "College 'Parties' Get High Marks as Sales Events,'" *The Wall Street Journal,* October 23, 1992, pp. B1, B8.

59. *Nation's Business,* April 1996, p. 50.

60. Roseanne Harper, "Consultant: Don't Let Sampling Taste Go to Waste," *Supermarket News,* April 22, 1996, p. 65.

61. Kathleen Deveny, "Displays Pay Off for Grocery Marketers," *The Wall Street Journal,* October 15, 1992, pp. B1, B5.

62. Edward A. Chapman, Jr., "Why Am I Here?" *Sales & Marketing Management,* February 1993, p. 30.

63. "Fuji Running 'Images' Contest," *Supermarket News,* April 22, 1996, p. 100.

64. Kuntz and Weber, "The New Hucksterism," p. 78.

65. "Video Stores Dislike This Promotional Dance," *The Wall Street Journal,* March 31, 1993, p. B1.

66. William Dunn, from "How to Sell the Story," *American Demographics,* April 1992, pp. 50–51.

67. "Brownie Points," *Entrepreneur,* May 1993, pp. 142–143.

68. Lee Berton, "Smelly Socks and Other Tricks from the Public-Relations Trade," *The Wall Street Journal,* November 30, 1993, p. B1.

69. "Standing Room Only," *Entrepreneur,* July 1996, p. 17.

70. Wendy Bounds, "Any Testimonials for the Product Will Have to Come on the Fly," *The Wall Street Journal,* August 23, 1993, p. B1.

71. Elizabeth Lesly and Laura Zinn, "The

Right Moves, Baby," *Business Week,* July 5, 1993, pp. 30–31; Stephen Power, "Lawrence Woman Charged in Pepsi Tampering Hoax," *Boston Globe,* July 1, 1993; Richard Turcski, "Pepsi Syringe Crisis Fizzles Out," *Supermarket News,* June 28, 1993, pp. 4, 45.

72. David Greising, "Managing Tragedy at ValuJet," *Business Week,* June 3, 1996, p. 40.

73. Robina A. Gangemi, "Planning Damage Control," *Inc.,* March 1996, p. 91.

Chapter 19

1. William Echikson, "The Trick to Selling in Europe," *Fortune,* September 2, 1993, p. 82.

2. Ronald E. Kutscher, "Outlook 2000: The Major Trends," *Occupational Outlook Quarterly,* Spring 1990, pp. 3–7.

3. *Chief Executive Officer* (Chicago: Heidrick and Struggles, 1987), p. 7.

4. Dennis Fox, "Ringing Up Prospects," *Sales & Marketing Management,* March 1993, pp. 75–77.

5. Linda Corman, "Look Who's Selling Now," *Selling,* July/August 1996, pp. 48–53.

6. Gerhard Gschwandtner, "How to Sell in France," *Personal Selling Power,* July–August 1991, pp. 54–60.

7. Mark H. McCormack, "The Hard Sell," *Entrepreneur,* April 1993, p. 41.

8. Robert McGarvey, "Think Big," *Entrepreneur,* August 1993, pp. 60+.

9. Patricia Sellers, "How to Remake Your Sales Force," *Fortune,* May 4, 1992, pp. 98–100+.

10. Francy Blackwood, "Seminars into Sales," *Selling,* July/August 1996, pp. 28–30.

11. Thomas N. Ingram, "Improving Sales Force Productivity: A Critical Examination of the Personal Selling Process," *Review of Business,* Summer 1990, p. 12.

12. Susan Greco, "The Art of Selling," *Inc.,* June 1993, p. 72.

13. Bob Alexander, "How to Succeed in a Changing World," *Selling Power,* March 1996, pp. 13–14+.

14. Jennifer Kingson Gloom, "A Sales Guide to Easy Street," *Boston Globe,* p. 1.

15. Jack G. Kaikati, "Don't Crack the Japanese Distribution System—Just Circumvent It," *Columbia Journal of World Business* (Summer 1993): pp. 34–35.

16. McCann, "Irate over Rates," p. 25.

17. Malcolm Fleschner, "Value Sells," *Selling Power,* March 1996, pp. 48, 50, 52.

18. Frances Huffman, "Speak Easy," *Entrepreneur,* December 1992, p. 156.

19. McCann, "Irate over Rates," p. 26.

20. Margaret Kaeter, "Building a Cyber Sales Force," *Training,* April 1996, pp. 37-40, 42.

21. Paul Sherlock, *Rethinking Business to Business Marketing* (New York: Free Press, 1991), p. 92.

22. Robert Fernandez, "Mail Order Is Part and Parcel of Firm's Success," *Chicago Tribune,* August 1, 1993, sec. 17, pp. 1, 7.

23. Sellers, "How to Remake Your Sales Force," p. 103.

24. Phaedra Hise, "What Telemarketers Must Know," *Inc.,* October 1993, p. 29.

25. McCann, "Irate over Rates," p. 26.

26. Gschwandtner, "How to Sell in France."

27. McGarvey, "Think Big," p. 72.

28. William A. O'Connell and William Keenan, Jr., "The Shape of Things to Come," *Sales & Marketing Management,* January 1990, pp. 36–41.

29. Gilbert A. Churchill, Jr., Neil M. Ford, and Orville C. Walker, Jr., *Sales Force Management,* 5th ed. (Chicago: Irwin, 1997), p. 183.

30. Greco, "The Art of Selling," p. 73.

31. E. A. Lennon, Procter & Gamble, written interview, December 9, 1992.

32. Guen Sublette, "Dream Team," *Entrepreneur,* August 1993, p. 78.

33. Parker Hannifin Corporation Annual Report, June 30, 1992.

34. Betsy Wiesendanger, "The Schmooze Factor," *Selling,* July/August 1996, p. 13.

35. Sublette, "Dream Team," p. 80.

36. Churchill, Ford, and Walker, *Sales Force Management,* pp. 372–373.

37. William Keenan, Jr., "Who Has the Right Stuff?" *Sales & Marketing Management,* August 1993, pp. 28–29.

38. *Ibid.*

39. Earl D. Honeycutt, Jr., Clyde E. Harris, Jr., and Stephen B. Castleberry, "Sales Training: A Status Report," *Training and Development Journal* (May 1987): pp. 42–47.

40. Martin Everett, "Your Job Is on the (Phone) Line," *Sales & Marketing Management,* May 1993, p. 66.

41. Sellers, "How to Remake Your Sales Force," p. 103.

42. Greco, "The Art of Selling," p. 75.

43. *Ibid.*

44. Everett, "Your Job Is on the (Phone) Line."

45. Jack Falvey, "A Fire Walk with the Sales Force," *Sales & Marketing Management,* August 1993, p. 14.

46. Peter D. Bennett, *Dictionary of Marketing Terms,* 2nd ed. (Chicago: American Marketing Association, 1995), p. 179.

47. Falvey, "A Fire Walk with the Sales Force."

48. Michele Marchetti, "Toasting Sales Support Staffers," *Sales & Marketing Management,* April 1996, pp. 33–34.

49. Ellyn E. Spragins, "Making Employees Accountable," *Inc.,* March 1993, p. 34.

50. Sublette, "Dream Team," p. 79.

51. Michele Marchetti, "Rewarding Team Players," *Sales & Marketing Management,* April 1996, pp. 35–36.

52. Alexander, 'How to Succeed in a Changing World," p. 20.

53. Churchill, Ford, and Walker, *Sales Force Management,* p. 216.

54. "Change Must Pass Culture Test Before It Lands on the Bottom Line," *Total Quality,* October 1992, p. 6.

55. Jerome A. Colletti and Linda J. Mahoney, "Should You Pay Your Sales Force for Customer Satisfaction?" *Perspectives in Total Compensation* 11 (Scottsdale, Ariz.: American Compensation Association, November 1991).

56. Churchill, Ford, and Walker, *Sales Force Management,* p. 664.

57. I. F. Trawick, J. E. Swan, W. McGee, and D. R. Rink, "Influence of Buyer Ethics and Salesperson Behavior on Intention to Choose a Supplier," *Journal of the Academy of Marketing Science* (Winter 1990): p. 10.

58. Alan Killingsworth, cited in Charles Futrell, *ABC's of Selling,* 4th ed. (Burr Ridge, Ill.: Irwin, 1994), p. 54.

59. Greg Steinmetz and Michael Siconolfi, "Partnership Problems at Prudential Embroil Insurance Business, Too," *The Wall Street Journal,* December 1, 1993, pp. A1, A8.

60. Jane Bryant Quinn, "Honesty Policy Should Apply to All 'Rogues,'" *Chicago Tribune,* May 19, 1996, sec. 5, p. 3.

Chapter 20

1. Part of this discussion is based on Peter D. Bennett, ed., *Dictionary of Marketing Terms,* 2nd ed. (Chicago: American Marketing Association, 1995), p. 40, 41, 222, 223.

2. Karen Lowry Miller, "The Man Who's Selling Japan on Jeeps," *Business Week,* July 19, 1993, pp. 56–57.

3. "Partnering for Products," *Inc.,* February 1996, p. 94, citing Coopers & Lybrand's "Trendsetter Barometer," New York City, November 1995.

4. Ravi S. Achrol, "Evolution of the Marketing Organization: New Forms for Turbulent Environments," *Journal of Marketing* (October 1991): pp. 77–93.

5. John A. Byrne, "The Virtual Corporation," *Business Week,* February 8, 1993, pp. 98–102.

6. Carla Kruytbosch, "Let's Make a Deal," *International Business,* March 1993, pp. 92–96.

7. Frederick E. Webster, Jr., "The Changing Role of Marketing in the Corporation," *Journal of Marketing* (October 1992): pp. 1–17; "The Network Organization: Managing in the 21st Century," *Supervisory Management,* March 1992, p. 2.

8. Byrne, "The Virtual Corporation"; Shawn Tully, "The Modular Corporation," *Fortune,* February 8, 1993, pp. 106–108.

9. Edward O. Welles, "Virtual Realities," *Inc.,* August 1993, pp. 50–57.

10. Roberta Maynard, "A Framework for Success," *Nation's Business,* July 1996, p. 16.

11. Sharon Nelton, "Winning with Diversity," *Nation's Business,* September 1992, pp. 18–24.

12. Edwin M. Reingold, "America's Hamburger Helper," *Time,* June 29, 1992, pp. 66–67.

13. *Ibid.,* p. 66.

14. Henry Fersko-Weiss, "Project Managers: A New Focus on Graphics and Resource Controls," *PC Magazine,* February 11, 1992, pp. 38–39.

15. Richard Dulude, "Quality and Market Share," in *Total Quality Performance,* eds. Lawrence Schein and Melissa A. Berman, Research Report No. 909 (Washington, D.C.: The Conference Board, 1988), pp. 22–25.

16. Dean Tjosvold, Valerie Dann, and Choy Wong, "Managing Conflict between Departments to Serve Customers," *Human Relations* 45 (1992): 1035–1053.

17. Matt Rothman, "Into the Black," *Inc.,* January 1993, pp. 59–65.

18. "Work Teams Have Their Work Cut Out for Them," *HRFocus,* January 1993, p. 24.

19. Richard Normann and Rafael Ramirez, "From Value Chain to Value Constellation: Designing Interactive Strategy," *Harvard Business Review,* July–August 1993, pp. 65–77.

20. Anne Field, "Precision Marketing," *Inc. Technology,* June 18, 1996, pp. 54–58.

21. Thomas V. Bonoma, "Making Your Marketing Strategy Work," *Harvard Business Review,* March–April 1984, pp. 69–76.

22. Mark Henricks, "All Together Now," *Entrepreneur,* April 1993, pp. 42, 45, 47.

23. John Schmeltzer, "Execs Unveil Road Map for a 'New Sears,'" *Chicago Tribune,* February 12, 1993, sec. 3, pp. 1–2.

24. Bennett, ed., *Dictionary of Marketing Terms,* p. 249.

25. Gregory A. Patterson, "Holiday Hopes of the Catalog Industry: Merrier Christmas, Happier New Year," *The Wall Street Journal,* December 2, 1992, pp. B1, B8.

26. Brent Bowers, "A Clothier Discovers a Sideline Can Dress Up Results," *The Wall Street Journal,* December 7, 1992, p. B2.

27. Kathleen Deveny, "Man Walked on the Moon but Man Can't Make Enough Devil's Food Cookie Cakes," *The Wall Street Journal,* September 2, 1993, p. B1.

28. Field, "Precision Marketing," p. 56.

29. Laurie Hays, "American Express Sizes Up Rivals, Turns Green," *The Wall Street Journal,* May 3, 1996, pp. B1–B2.

30. Rothman, "Into the Black."

31. Edward A. Robinson, "American Toolmakers Regain Their Cutting Edge," *Fortune,* June 10, 1996, pp. 72[C]–72[D]+.

32. Ronald E. Yates, "New ABCs for Pinpoint Accounting," *Chicago Tribune,* January 24, 1993, sec. 7, pp. 1, 4.

33. Neil Gross, "New Tricks for Help Lines," *Business Week.* April 29, 1996, pp. 97–98.

34. "Asking the Hard Questions," *Inc.,* June 1996, p. 114.

35. *Ibid.*

36. Scott McCartney, "Piloted by Bethune, Continental Air Lifts Its Workers' Morale," *The Wall Street Journal,* May 15, 1996, pp. A1, A8.

37. George Gendron, "FYI," *Inc.,* May 1993, p. 9.

Appendix B

1. 3M Corporation, Annual Report, 1991, p. 7.

2. Toys "R" Us and Kids "R" Us, Annual Report, February 1, 1992, inside front cover.

3. David Sheff, "Confessions of a Change Agent," *Fast Company,* June–July 1996, p. 73.

4. Judith George, "Market Researcher," *Business Week's Guide to Careers,* October 1987, p. 10.

5. Dun & Bradstreet Corporation, Annual Report, 1992, pp. 14, 16.

6. Dun & Bradstreet Corporation, 1992 Annual Report, citing Ludger Gigengack, Director of Quantitative Research, Henkel KGaA.

7. U.S. Department of Commerce, *Statistical Abstract of the United States,* 115th ed. (Washington, D.C.: U.S. Government Printing Office, 1995), p. 550.

8. Carol Kleiman, "A Look at What Jobs Are Hot—and Not—in the Next 10 Years," *Chicago Tribune,* June 23, 1996, sec. 6, p. 1.

9. Andrew E. Serwer, "Trouble in Franchise Nation," *Fortune,* March 6, 1995, pp. 115–116+.

10. Christopher Caggiano, "Kings of the Hill," *Inc.,* August 1996, pp. 47–53.

11. Bob Weinstein, "Liquid Assets," *Entrepreneur,* May 1993, pp. 92–93.

12. Barbara Ettorre and Donald J. McNerney, "Human Resources: Riding the New HR Wave," *Management Review,* June 1996, pp. 43–48.

13. Samuel Greengard, "Catch the Wave as HR Goes Online," *Personnel Journal,* July 1995, pp. 54–55+.

14. See "Paperless Résumés," *Training and Development,* March 1994, p. 14.

15. Raymond A. Noe, John R. Hollenbeck, Barry Gerhart, and Patrick M. Wright, *Human Resource Management: Gaining a Competitive Advantage,* 2nd ed. (Burr Ridge: Irwin, 1997), pp. 620–621.

Photo Credits

Chapter 1

P1-1, p.5: Courtesy of the Sears, Roebuck and Co. Archives, Hoffman Estates, Illinois.; P1-3A, p. 6: California Division of Tourism/Photo © 1996 Terry Huseby. P1-3B, p. 7: Robert Holmes.; P1-4, p. 8: Courtesy of National Wildlife Federation. Photography © James H. Carmichael. P1-5, p. 13: Courtesy of FCB/LK Advertising, New York.; P1-6, p. 14: Courtesy of CS First Boston.; P1-7, p. 20: Courtesy of The Lever Brothers Company.; P1-8, p. 20: Courtesy of American Express. Agency, Ogilvy & Mather. Photographer, Mark Seliger.; P1-10, p. 9: © American Suzuki Motor Corporation.

Chapter 2

P2-1, p. 27: © Jim Erickson/The Stock Market; P 2-2, 32: Courtesy of Oldsmobile. © GM Corp.; P2-3, p. 35: © 1996, Comstock; P2-4, p. 41: State Farm Insurance Company; P2-6, p. 44: © Ken Barboza; P2-7, p. 45: courtesy Philips Electronics; P2-8A & B, p. 47: courtesy Ford Motor Company; P2-9, p. 49: courtesy of MapQuest Publishing Group/GeoSystems Global Corporation; P2-10, p. 39: courtesy of Team Air Express owned by J. E. Brunson and B. J. Brunson. Ad created by R. C. Smith and LaWanda Ray.

Chapter 3

P3-1, p. 55: © Steven Peters/Tony Stone Images; P3-2, p. 58: courtesy of Ralson Purina Canada Inc.; P3-3, p. 60: photo courtesy of Motorola, Inc.; P3-4, p. 62: courtesy of Conservation Corporation Africa; P3-5, p. 63: reproduced or reprinted with the permission of The Coca-Cola Company; P3-6, p. 64: courtesy of Ford Motor Company; P3-7A & B, p. 66: copyright © REI 1996; P3-8, p. 70: courtesy of McDonald's Corporation; P3-9, p. 75: Sally Wiener Grotta/ The Stock Market; P3-11, p. 76: courtesy of Aenith Electronics Corporation; Giuseppe Molteni/Image Bank.

Chapter 4

P4-1, p. 83: © Andy Goodwin; P4-2, p. 85: reproduced by permission of Allied Domecq PLC; P4-3A, p. 89: MR. POTATO HEAD® is a trademark of Hasbro, Inc. © 1996 Hasbro, Inc.; P4-3B, p. 89: Minnesota Power Corporate Relations staff, 1996; P4-4, p. 91: courtesy of Equifax Inc.; P4-5, p. 95: courtesy of the Fleming Companies, Inc.; P4-6, p. 97: courtesy of Mayflower Transit. Mayflower and ship are trademarks of Mayflower Transit, Inc.; P4-7, p. 99: © 1996 Nation's Business/T. Michael Keza; P4-10, p. 86 © The Associated Press.

Chapter 5

P5-1, p. 111: Fresh Express Farms, Inc.; P5-2A & B, p. 114: courtesy of A. C. Nielson, Daniel Greenberg; P5-3, p. 118: © arl Shaneff—Mercury Pictures; P5-4, p. 122: courtesy of Continental Airlines and J,D. Power and Associates; P5-7, p. 128: courtesy of S2 Systems; P5-8, p. 130: TerrAlign is a registered trademark of Metron, Inc. Copyright © 1997 Metron, Inc. (800) 437-9601; P5-9, p. 131: courtesy of FMC Corporation; P5-10, p. 127: © Robert Holgren.

Chapter 6

P6-1, p. 141: © 1996, Comstock; P6-2, p. 144: courtesy of White Chantilly by DANA; P6-3, p. 146: courtesy of the United States Marine Corps; P6-5, p. 154: ITT Educational Services, Inc.; P6-6, p. 157: courtesy of Lisa Frank, Inc.; P6-7, p. 160: courtesy of Mars Incorporated; P6-8, p. 162: courtesy of Peapod/John Hollis; P6-9a & b, p. 164: courtesy of Chase Manhattan Bank; P6-10, p. 163: courtesy of The Park Bench Cafe.

Chapter 7

P7-1, p. 169: © Lonnie Duka/Tony Stone Images; P7-2, p. 171: courtesy of Wonderware; P7-3, p. 175: courtesy of The Boeing Company; P7-5, p. 179: © Ken Barboza; P7-6, p. 180: The Geon Company; P7-7, p. 181: courtesy of Cowley Associates, Inc., Syracuse, N.Y. 13152; P7-8, p. 185: courtesy of MountainGate. Ad design by Teri Gibson; P7-9, p. 184: © Nigel Marson; P7-10, p.178: courtesy of The Office Club.

Chapter 8

P8-1, p. 199: © Lara Jo Regan/SABA; P8-2, p. 200: courtesy of Moore Stickney Associates Advertising Agency; P8-3, p. 205: courtesy of Mitsubishi Motor Sales of America, Inc.; P8-4, p. 208: used with permission of Hallmark Cards, Inc.; P8-5, p. 209: © 1996 AT&T. Advertisement created by The Bravo Group. Photo: © WORLD COPYRIGHT ALLSPORT USA; P8-6, p. 211: courtesy of the Princess Hotels International, Inc.; P8-7, p. 217: courtesy of Platinum Technology; P8-8, p. 219: used with permission of Hartley Peavey and the insurers of the Chubb Group of Insurance Companies. Photo by Jim Salzano; P8-10, p. 223: © Paulo Fidman/ SYGMA; P8-11, p. 204: © Christopher Bissell/ Tony Stone Images.

Chapter 9

P9-1, p. 229: courtesy of PenWerks; P9-2, p. 231: courtesy of Balance Sports; P9-3, p. 232: courtesy of MBNA/The Martin Agency; P9-4, p. 234: courtesy of Ray-Ban® Sunglasses by Bausch & Lomb; P9-5, p. 236: courtesy of Starbucks Coffee Company; P9-6, p. 237: courtesy of Seiko Corporation of America; P9-7, p. 246: courtesy of Good Humor-Breyers Ice Cream; P9-8, p. 249: courtesy of BodyFX; P9-9, p. 250: courtesy of Interstate Brands Corporation; P9-10, p. 251: © AP Photo/San Jose Mercury News/Tom Van Dyke.

Chapter 10

P10-1, p. 257: courtesy Avis, Inc.; P10-2, p. 259: reprinted with permission of Progressive Grocer; P10-3, p. 265: courtesy of Zenith Electronics Corp.; P10-4, p. 268: The Sled Dogs Company, 1-800-SKATE-ON; P10-5, p. 269: courtesy of U.S. Robotics; P10-6, p. 270: courtesy of Weight

Watchers Gourmet Food Company, Inc.; P10-7, p. 271: courtesy of Pacific Handy Cutter, Inc.; P10-8, p. 292: courtesy of Dole Fresh Vegetable Co.; P10-9, p. 276: © 1994 Motorola, Inc.; P10-10, p. 279: © Jayne Wexcler.

Chapter 11

P11-1, p. 285: © Steve Dunwell/The Image Bank; P11-2, p. 287: reprinted with permission: Anderson Consulting; P11-3, p. 290: Transamerica Corporation; P11-4, p. 291: courtesy of the John G. Shedd Aquarium; P11-5, p. 294: printed with permission of IBM Corporation; P11-6, p. 298: © 1996 Nation's Business/T. Michael Keza; P11-7, p. 300: Mark Tatum, Marketing Communications Manager, Supercuts; P11-8, p. 302: courtesy of the Department of the Treasury, Bureau of the Public Debt; P11-9, p. 301: courtesy of the American News Service.

Chapter 12

P12-1, p. 309: courtesy of Nordstrom; P12-2, p. 311: courtesy of the National Cattlemen's Beef Association–1997; P12-3, p. 312: courtesy of Powerfood Inc.; P12-4, p. 318: courtesy of Monsoon; P12-5, p. 321: © Ilene Ehrlich; P12-6, p. 321: courtesy of Saatchi & Saatchi; P12-7, p. 324: photograph © Mark Laita; P12-8, p. 326: courtesy of Target Stores; P12-9, p. 323: © 1996 Nation's Business/T. Michael Keza.

Chapter 13

P13-1, p. 333: © David Joel/Tony Stone Images; P13-2, p. 336: © 1996 USPS; P13-3, p. 339: © Kevin O. Moosey; P13-4, p. 340: © 1996 James Schnepf; P13-5, p. 342: © Jon Riley/Tony Stone Images; P13-6, p. 347: Sofa Workshops—The custom-made sofa company; P13-7, p. 350: courtesy of Sprint Business; P13-8, p. 352: courtesy of Aspen Ski Tours; P13-9, p. 357: © AP/Wide World Photos; P13-10, p. 348: courtesy of Tech-Ceram Corporation.

Chapter 14

P14-1, p. 365: courtesy of Dan'Z Cookies; P14-2, p. 371: © AP/Wide World Photos/ Mark Fageol; P14-3, p. 369: used by permission of AMETEK, Inc.; P14-4, p. 373: courtesy of McDonald's Corporation; P14-5, p. 375: courtesy of the Southland Corporation; P14-6, p. 376: courtesy of Auto-By-Tel; P14-7, p. 379: courtesy of Lucky Brand Dungarees; P14-8, p. 384: photo provided by Rubbermaid Incorporated; P14-9, p. 384: Avery Denniston Corporation; P14-10, p. 378: © Eric Fultran.

Chapter 15

P15-1, p. 391: © Craig Preston/Black Star; P15-2, p. 393: courtesy of Baird & Warner, Inc., Chicago; P15-3, p. 396: Wittco Foodservice Equipment, Inc., Milwaukee, Wisconsin, USA; P15-4, p. 397: courtesy of Korean Air Cargo; P15-5, p. 402: © 1996 GE Information Services; P15-6, p. 404: courtesy of C.H. Robinson Co., 100 Mitchell Rd., Eden Prairie, MN 55347; P15-7, p. 405: © 1994, David Franzen; P15-8, p. 408: courtesy of Ryder System, Inc.© 1996 Reid Horn.

Chapter 16

P16-1, p. 413: © Ted Thai/Time Magazine; P16-2, p. 418: courtesy of Wells Fargo & Co.; P16-3, p. 420: BARBIE® doll image and Web page reprint © 1996 Mattel, Inc. All Rights Reserved. Used with permission; P16-4, p. 421: reprinted by permission of REI; P16-5, p. 424: reprinted with permission from Greenwood Trust Company; P16-6, p. 427: courtesy of Baskin-Robbins USA, Co.; P16-7, p. 432: courtesy of Sears, Roebuck and Co.; P16-8, p. 434: courtesy of Roundy's; P16-9, p. 436: courtesy of Cyrillus; P16-10, p. 430: courtesy of Bass Pro Shops.

Chapter 17

P17-1, p. 443: courtesy of HMV Direct Ltd.; P17-2, p. 445: reprinted with permission of Bayer Corporation; P17-3, p. 447: used with permission of Dreyer's Grand Ice Cream, Inc.; P17-4, p. 451: courtesy of Dep Corporation and Hamilton Projects. © Dep Corporation. MP & Design and Melrose Place are registered trademarks of Spelling Television, Inc. used under license. © 1996 Spelling Television, Inc. and Hamilton Projects; P17-5, p. 454: All rights reserved; courtesy of The Ericsson Corporation; P17-6, p. 455: courtesy of Pier 1; P17-7, p. 461: courtesy of Twin Dragons Software, Inc.; P17-8, p. 462: courtesy of the Dayton-Hudson Corporation; P17-9, p. 464: © James Wasserman.

Chapter 18

P18-1, p. 469: © Alan Levenson; P18-2A & B, p. 471: courtesy of StarKist Foods, Inc.; P18-3, p. 472: courtesy of the National Fluid Milk Processor Promotion Board; P18-4, p. 475: courtesy of Telstra; P18-5, p. 477: courtesy of Bozell Worldwide, Inc.; P18-6, p. 479: Edgar Degas, **Two Dancers** (detail), c. 1890. The Art Institute of Chicago. Amy McCormick Memorial Collection; P18-7, p. 481: courtesy of Embratur; P18-8, p. 486: reprinted with the permission of Men's Fitness Magazine, Inc.; P18-9, p. 491: American Pet Products Manufacturers Association; P18-10, p. 493: used with permission of Falk Associates Management Enterprises. Chicago *Tribune* photo by James F. Quinn; P18-11, p. 473: courtesy of Bronner Slosberg Humphrey.

Chapter 19

P19-1, p. 501: Photo courtesy of Avon Products, Inc.; P19-2, p. 503: © Jim Curley; P19-3, p. 505: courtesy of Amazon.com; P19-4, p. 506: Pioneer Hi-Bred International, Inc.; P19-5, p. 507: Walgreen Co. 1997 Annual Report; P19-6, p. 509: © Roark Johnson; P19-7, p. 519: courtesy of Xerox Corporation; P19-8, p. 523: The Raymond Corporation; P19-9, p. 508: © Al Tielmans.

Chapter 20

P20-1, p. 533: © Martin Chaffer/Tony Stone Images; P20-2, p. 536: © Scott Goldsmith; P20-3, p. 540: © Mojgan B. Azimi/Outline; P20-4, p. 542: © Michael Warren; P20-5, p. 542: courtesy of Wal-Mart Stores, Inc.; P20-6, p. 543: courtesy of Western Motivational Incentives Group; P20-7, p. 546: courtesy Caterpillar Inc.; P20-8, p. 547: courtesy of American Airlines; P20-9, p. 551: photo provided by Rubbermaid Incorporated; P20-10, p. 541: © Timothy Shonnard/Tony Stone Images.

Glossary

acceleration principle   A principle that holds that a small change in consumer demand for a product can result in a large change in the demand for organizational goods and services to produce the product.

accessory equipment   Portable factory equipment and tools that are used in the production process but which do not become part of the finished product.

activity-based costing   The process of itemizing all costs associated with producing and marketing specific products in particular marketing.

advertising   Any announcement or persuasive communication placed in the mass media in paid or donated time or space by an individual, company, or organization.

advertising agency   A firm devoted to planning and preparing advertising campaigns for other organizations.

advocacy advertising   Institutional advertising that supports particular positions, activities, or causes.

agent   A person or business unit that negotiates purchases, sales, or both but does not take title to the goods in which it deals.

agent (broker, manufacturer's representative)   A wholesaler that negotiates purchases, sales, or both but does not take title to the goods.

all-you-can-afford method   Spending all the organization can afford on communications.

approach   Initial formal contact with the qualified prospect.

Association of Southeast Asian Nations (ASEAN)   An agreement among Asian nations to eliminate tariffs and encourage trade among them.

atmospherics   Factors such as architecture, lighting, and layout that attract attention and stimulate sales.

attitude   The overall evaluation of an object, behavior, or concept.

average revenue   The average amount of money received from the sale of one unit of a product.

bait and switch   An illegal tactic by which customers are attracted to a store by an advertised low-priced product that is then reported to be out-of-stock or disparaged in order to sell a more expensive product.

basing point pricing   A type of uniform delivered pricing in which the seller charges the selling price plus the cost of delivering from one or more geographic points where the product is produced (basing points).

behavioral costs   The physical energy customers expend to buy products and services.

benchmarking   Identifying organizations that excel at carrying out a function and using their practices as a springboard for improvement.

benefit segmentation   The process of dividing the market on the basis of the benefits customers desire.

brand   A name, term, design, symbol, or any other feature that identifies one seller's good or service as distinct from other sellers.

brand equity   The value of a brand to an organization, including customer loyalty toward the brand, the brand's name awareness, perceived quality, and brand associations.

brand extension   The practice of using an existing brand name for a new product.

brand loyalty   The consistency with which customers continue to buy the same brand of a particular product or the commitment they show to it.

brand manager   The person responsible for marketing a particular brand of a product.

brand mark   That part of a brand that cannot be spoken.

brand name   That part of a brand that can be spoken.

breakeven analysis   A technique for determining the sales volume needed to cover all costs at a specific price.

breakeven point   The level of sales at which total revenues equal total costs.

bribery   Giving money, goods, or favors in exchange for purchases or influence.

bundle pricing   Offering several products as a package at a single price.

business cycle   The pattern of the level of business activity; moves from prosperity to recession to recovery.

business services   Services that support an organization's activities.

buying center   Members of an organization who have a role in selecting, purchasing, and using a product.

call report   A report summarizing the activities of a salesperson for a given time period.

canned presentation   A memorized, standard presentation given without variation to all prospects.

cash-and-carry wholesaler   A wholesaler that carries a limited selection of products and does not provide transportation for the products.

cash discount   A price reduction for payment in cash or for paying quickly.

category killer   Big, low-priced limited-line store featuring deep selection but also some breadth.

category manager   The person responsible for the marketing of several brands falling under a particular product category.

causal research Research that looks for cause-and-effect relationships.

cause-related marketing Marketing designed to promote a cause or an issue.

channel captain A channel member that is recognized by the other channel members as having decision-making power.

channel of distribution An organized network (system) of agencies and institutions that perform all the functions required to link producers with end users to accomplish the marketing task.

closing Asking for orders and getting prospects to commit to purchase.

coding Assigning numeric symbols to the data collected.

cognitive dissonance Post-decision doubts about whether the right alternative was chosen.

cold canvassing Locating leads and prospects from a phone book or other source and calling on them.

commercialization The stage in which management commits to introducing the new product into the marketplace.

commission Payment tied directly to the sales or profits from sales that a salesperson completes.

communication The transmission of a message from a sender to a receiver, such that both understand it the same way.

communication medium The mode that carries the message, such as television, radio, print, live speech, or music.

communications mix The blend of advertising, personal selling, sales promotion, and publicity that makes up a communications strategy.

comparative advertising Advertising that compares a brand with competitors' or with previous formulations.

competitive advantage An ability to outperform competitors in providing something that the market values.

competitive advertising Advertising that attempts to develop selective demand for particular brands of products.

competitive bidding Contract buying in which buyers invite potential suppliers to offer price and other terms of sale for a product meeting given specifications.

competitive environment All the organizations that could potentially

create value for the organization's customers.

component parts and materials Processed items that are made into finished products.

concept testing Having potential customers evaluate pictures, mockups, or written descriptions of the product.

concurrent engineering Linking product design with manufacturing engineering so that the tasks go on simultaneously.

consideration set The set of alternative brands that consumers identify and consider for purchase.

consolidated metropolitan statistical area (CMSA) A metropolitan area made up of two or more primary metropolitan statistical areas.

consolidators Intermediaries that make bulk purchases at a discount, then resell in smaller quantities to users or other channel members.

consumer behavior The thoughts, feelings, and actions of consumers and the influences on them that determine changes.

consumer products Goods and services sold to consumers.

consumer promotion Sales promotion directed toward consumers of a good or service.

consumerism A social force intended to protect consumers by exerting legal, moral, and economic pressures on the business community.

consumers People who purchase goods and services for their own use or for gifts to others.

control The process of evaluating performance against objectives, plans, and strategies and making changes when and where needed.

controlled test market The practice of offering a new product through a set of retailers who have been paid to set aside shelf space for the product in a desirable area of the store.

convenience store A retailer whose primary advantage is location.

convenience products Products that are purchased frequently and with minimal time and effort.

cooperative advertising payment Funds paid by manufacturers to get their products featured in local retail ads.

core competencies The things an organization does better than other firms.

core competencies The processes and activities that the organization does best and that are central to its success.

core values Values in a culture that are pervasive and enduring.

corrective advertising Advertising involving a company running new ads that correct a deceptive or unfair advertising message previously disseminated.

cost analysis The identification of levels and types of costs and how they have changed over time.

cost per thousand The cost of using a media vehicle to reach 1,000 persons or households.

critical path method (CPM) A method using a network of circles and arrows to chart the schedule of activities.

countertrade Bartering goods and services in foreign markets rather than selling them for money.

culture The complex of learned values and behaviors that are shared by a society and are designed to increase the probability of a society's survival.

customer value The difference between customer perceptions of the benefits and costs of purchasing and using products and services.

data Facts and statistics.

deceptive pricing An illegal pricing tactic that involves misleading customers about the relative goodness of an asking price.

decode The process of converting the group of symbols to the images or concepts contained in a message.

Delphi technique A sales forecasting technique that surveys experts' opinions and repeats the process until a consensus is reached.

demand The number of units sold in a market over a period of time.

demand-backward pricing A pricing approach that involves setting a price by starting with the estimated price consumers will pay and working backwards with retail and wholesale margins.

demand curve A graphical representation of the quantity of a product demanded at various prices.

demarketing A marketing strategy used to decrease the consumption of a product.

demographic segmentation The process of dividing the market on the basis of population characteristics.

demographics The study of the characteristics of a human population.

derived demand Demand for organizational goods that is dependent on the demand for consumer goods.

descriptive research Research that studies how often something occurs or what, if any, relationship exists between two variables.

developed countries Countries in which modern technology allows organizations to market a wide variety of products and services.

developing countries Countries that have not fully moved from agricultural to industrial economies.

differentiated marketing The strategy of operating in several market segments with marketing mixes tailored to each segment.

direct-action advertising Advertisements containing ordering information.

direct channel A distribution channel that has no intermediaries.

direct mail marketing Mailing of brochures, letters, and other materials that describe a product and solicit orders.

direct marketing Marketing efforts that use personal selling or various advertising media to solicit orders from consumers where they live or work.

direct ownership A mode of entry involving an organization setting up new facilities or acquiring a foreign firm in the same line of business.

direct relationships Relationships in which marketers know their customers by name and can communicate directly with them.

direct selling A personal explanation of a product by a sales representative with an opportunity to buy.

discount A reduction in price.

discretionary income The money an individual or household has left after paying taxes and living expenses.

disposable income The money an individual or household has left after paying taxes.

distributor A wholesale intermediary that serves industrial markets, offers a variety of services, and provides promotional support for a product.

diversification Strategies for growth by serving new customers through the delivery of new products.

diverting The practice of reselling products bought from a supplier at a reduced price in another part of the country where the supplier is not offering the same deal.

drop shipper A wholesaler that takes title to products but does not handle physical distribution.

dual distribution The use of two or more distribution channels to provide the same basic product to two or more of the organization's target markets.

dumping The practice of pricing a product below its costs or below the going rate in a market.

durable goods Products that are used over an extended period of time, typically three years or more.

early adopters Consumers and organizations who tend to emulate innovators.

early majority Consumers and organizations that tend to avoid risk and to make purchases carefully, typically after evaluating the experience of those who have previously purchased the product.

economic environment The overall economy, including business cycles, consumer income, and spending patterns.

economic infrastructure A country's internal facilities available for conducting business activities, especially communication, transportaton, distribution, and financial systems.

electronic data interchange A communication system that allows direct electronic transfer of information among companies.

encode The process of converting a message to a group of symbols that represent images or concepts.

environmental scanning The practice of tracking external changes that can affect markets, including demand for goods and services.

ethics The moral principles and values that govern the way an individual or group conducts its activities.

every-day low prices (EDLP) A strategy of setting prices consistently low rather than relying on occasional discounts on items.

exchange A voluntary transaction between an organization and a customer designed to benefit both of them.

exchange controls Laws that place a ceiling on the amount of money that may be exchanged for another currency.

exchange rates The price of a currency in terms of another currency.

exclusive dealing A restriction imposed by a supplier on a customer forbidding the customer from purchasing some type of product from any other supplier.

exclusive distribution A form of distribution in which a manufacturer sells through only one wholesaler or retailer in a trading area.

expense accounts The listing of a salesperson's work-related expenditures for a given time period.

experiment Research that involves manipulating one or more variables while keeping others constant, and measuring the results.

experiential benefits The sensory enjoyment customers get from products and services.

exploratory research Research that seeks to discover ideas and insights and to generate hypotheses.

exponential smoothing A form of time-series analysis that gives more weight to more recent data and less to older data.

exporting A mode of entry involving production of a product in one country and shipping it to another country for sale.

extensive decision making Decision making involving considerable search and purchasing effort.

European Union (EU) An agreement among 15 Western European countries to lower barriers to trade among them.

fads Products that experience an intense but brief period of popularity.

family brand The use of the same brand name for an entire product line.

family life cycle A set of stages families go through that influence needs and the ability to satisfy them.

fashion An accepted and popular product style.

feedback The receiver's response to a message.

fixed costs The costs that remain the same over a wide range of quantities produced.

fixed-sum-per-unit method Allocating a fixed sum to the communications budget for each unit to be sold or produced.

FOB origin pricing Geographic approach to pricing in which the seller's price is for the product at the point of shipment, where the title passes from seller to buyer.

FOB with freight allowed A type of uniform delivered pricing in which the seller allows the buyer to deduct shipping costs from the selling price of a product.

focus group interview A personal interview conducted simultaneously among a small number of individuals that relies on group discussion to open ended questions.

follow-up After-the-sale activities to make sure the customer is satisfied with the product purchased.

forecasting Predicting future revenues or costs.

formula selling presentation Sales presentation of product information in a thorough, lockstep format.

forward buying The practice of buying a big supply to take advantage of a reduced price from a supplier.

franchising A contractual distribution system in which a parent company (the franchisor) gives franchisees the right to operate the business according to the franchisor's marketing plan and to use its trademark.

freight forwarder A company that gathers small shipments from various organizations and hires a carrier to move them as larger lots.

frequency The average number of times a person, household, or member of a target audience is exposed to a media vehicle or an advertiser's media schedule within a given time period.

frequent-shopper programs Incentive programs offered by retailers to reward customers and encourage repeat business.

full-line forcing An arrangement in which an intermediary that wants to carry a particular product must buy the entire line.

full-service wholesaler A wholesaler that performs all distribution functions to some degree.

functional benefits The tangible benefits received from goods and services.

Gantt chart A chart that lists the activities to be performed and uses horizontal bars to graph the time allotted to each.

General Agreement on Tariffs and Trade (GATT) An international framework of rules and principles for opening up trade between member nations.

general merchandise wholesaler A wholesaler that carries a variety of goods in several distinct and unrelated product lines.

generic (brands) products Products that are named only by their generic class.

geodemography The linking of demographic data with geographic data, often at the local neighborhood level.

geographic information system The combining of various kinds of demographic data with geographic information on maps.

geographic pricing Pricing a good or service according to where it is delivered.

geographic segmentation The process of dividing the market on the basis of location or other geographic criteria such as population density or climate.

global marketing Using the same marketing strategy in all countries in which the company operates.

goods–services continuum A continuum for analyzing goods and services based on their degree of tangibility.

gray market The situation in which foreign distributors sell foreign versions of U.S. products in the United States.

green marketing Marketing efforts designed to minimize negative effects on the physical environment or to improve its quality.

group incentive system A compensation method based on paying a bonus to members of a group that achieves specified objectives.

gross income The total amount of money earned in one year by an individual or household.

gross national product (GNP) The total value of the goods and services produced in a particular country.

gross rating points (GRPs) A measure of the total advertising exposures produced by a specific media

vehicle or combination of them during a specified time.

guarantee An assurance that the product is as represented and will perform properly.

hard currency Currency backed by gold reserves and readily convertible into other currencies.

hedonic needs Needs related to the desire for pleasure and self-expression.

independent sales representatives Professional salespeople who act as independent contractors, paid on commission.

indirect relationships Relationships in which marketers do not know individual customers by name but marketers' products have meaning to customers.

indirect channel A distribution channel that has one or more intermediaries.

individual marketing The strategy of tailoring marketing mixes to individual customers.

industrial products Goods and services sold to organizations.

inflation A rise in the overall price level.

infomercial A television segment that blends information and advertising.

information Data presented in a useful way.

in-home interview A personal survey in which the interviewer goes door to door to visit subjects in their homes.

innovators Consumers and organizations who are venturesome and willing to take risks.

installations Nonportable industrial goods that are major, and that are bought, installed, and used to produce other goods or services.

institutional advertising Advertising that promotes the name, image, personnel, or reputation of a company, organization, or industry.

integrated direct marketing The combination of several types of direct marketing into a coordinated effort.

integrated marketing communications (IMC) The coordination of the elements of the communications mix into a consistent whole so as to provide greater clarity and marketing impact.

intensive distribution A form of distribution in which a manufacturer sells products through as many intermediaries in a trading area as possible.

intermediary (middleman)   An independent business specializing in linking sellers with consumers or organizational buyers.

intermediaries   Organizations that purchase goods to resell at a profit.

intermodal transportation   Transportation that combines several modes.

Internet   A linked, global network of computers at government agencies, universities, businesses, and Internet access providers.

joint venture   A business agreement in which two or more organizations share management of an enterprise.

jury of executive opinion   A sales forecasting technique that relies on estimates from company executives to predict sales.

just-in-time inventory   A system of replenishing parts or goods for resale just before they are needed.

just-in-time (JIT) inventory management   A system of holding little inventory and requiring suppliers to provide the exact quantity needed according to a precise schedule.

laggards   Consumers and organizations that are comfortable with traditional products and who buy new ones only when they become well-established alternatives.

late majority   Consumers and organizations that tend to avoid risks and who are cautious and skeptical about new ideas and products, only buying them when their ownership becomes commonplace.

licensing   An agreement in which an organization grants another organization the right to use a trademark, a patented product, or a process.

limited decision making   Decision making involving moderate search and purchasing effort.

limited-function wholesaler   A wholesaler that performs only some of the distribution functions.

line extension   A strategy of adding products to an existing line in the form of new flavors, models, sizes, and so forth.

list price   The selling price for an item before any discounts or reductions in price.

loss leader pricing   Setting prices near or below cost on selected items in order to attract customers to a store.

macromarketing   The study of marketing processes, activities, institutions, and results at a societal level.

mall intercept   A personal survey in which the interviewer stops people in a shopping center and asks them to participate.

major account management   The use of team selling to focus on major customers to establish long-term relationships.

manufacturer's brand   A brand that is owned and used by the producer of the product.

marginal analysis   A technique for finding the greatest profits by measuring the economic effect of producing and selling each additional unit of product.

marginal revenue   The change in total revenue that results from selling additional units of a product.

market   Individuals or organizations with the desire and ability to buy goods and services.

market development strategies   Strategies to grow by selling existing products to new customers.

market penetration strategies   Strategies to grow by selling more of the organization's existing products to its existing customers.

market potential   The expected total demand for a product in a particular market.

market potential   The total purchases that buyers in a segment will likely make during a specified period of time, given a specified level of marketing activity.

market price   The price actually paid by the customer.

market segmentation   The process of dividing a market into groups of potential buyers who have similar needs and wants, value perceptions, or purchasing behaviors.

market test   A sales forecasting technique that involves offering a product in a few test markets to estimate likely sales in the whole market.

marketing   The process of planning and executing the conception, pricing, promotion, and distribution of ideas, goods and services to create exchanges that satisfy individual and organizational goals.

marketing audits   In-depth, systematic reviews of an organization's strategic business unit's environments, objectives, plans, strategies, activities, and personnel of concern to marketing.

marketing decision support system   A coordinated collection of data, system tools, and techniques with supporting software and hardware by which an organization gathers and interprets relevant information and turns it into a basis for making management decisions.

marketing communications   The various ways marketers communicate with current and potential customers.

marketing concept   View that an organization should seek to meet its customers' needs and wants as it strives to achieve its own goals.

marketing ethics   The principles, values, and standards of conduct considered appropriate for marketers.

marketing management   The process of setting marketing goals for an organization and planning, implementing, and controlling strategies to meet them.

marketing mix   The strategic tools a firm uses to create value for customers and achieve organizational objectives.

marketing orientation   A business philosophy that focuses on understanding customer needs and wants and building products and services to satisfy them.

marketing plan   A document created by an organization to record the results and conclusions of environmental analysis and to detail the planned marketing strategy and its intended results.

marketing research   The function that links the consumer, customer, and public to the marketer through information.

markup pricing   A pricing approach that adds a percentage to the product's cost in order to arrive at a selling price.

mass (undifferentiated) marketing   The strategy of selling the same product to all customers with the same marketing mix.

mass merchandiser   A retailer offering a wide but somewhat shallow mix of products.

merchant wholesaler   A wholesaler that takes title to the products it sells.

metropolitan statistical area (MSA)   An urbanized area of at least 50,000 people that is encircled by nonmetropolitan counties and is neither socially nor economically dependent on another metropolitan area.

micromarketing The study of marketing processes and activities at organizational, product, or brand levels.

mission statement A statement of the organization's distinctive purpose.

missionary salespeople Support salespeople who work for manufacturers and call on channel members and end users.

mode of entry Ways in which organizations can enter foreign markets which include exporting, licensing, joint ventures, and direct ownership.

mode of transportation The class or type of carrier used.

modified rebuy A type of organizational purchase involving consideration of a number of alternatives before selection.

monetary costs The amount of money customers pay to receive products and services.

monopolistic competition A type of competition that occurs when there are many sellers of similar, but somewhat differentiated products, and each seller has a relatively small market share.

monopoly A situation in which only a single organization sells a product in a market area.

motivation The inner drive to fulfill needs

motivation The positive or negative needs, goals, desires, and forces that impel an individual toward or away from certain actions.

multidomestic marketing Using different marketing strategies in the different countries in which the company operates.

natural environment The natural resources available to or affected by the organization.

needs The goods or services consumers or organizational buyers require in order to survive.

need-satisfaction presentation Sales presentations that include asking questions and listening to customers' answers in order to identify their needs and desires.

network organization An organization of independent business units interacting with one another.

network (multilevel) selling The practice used by direct selling companies to have independent agents serve as

distributors and resell merchandise to other agents who eventually make sales to consumers.

new product A product that is new to the marketing organization in any way.

new task purchase A type of organizational purchase involving an extensive search for information and an extensive decision process.

niche marketing The strategy of concentrating on a single target market and tailoring the marketing mix to it.

noise Physical sounds, misunderstandings, or other distractions that cause a receiver to fail to decode a message properly.

nondurable goods Products that are used over a brief period of time, typically less than three years.

nonstore retailing A form of retailing in which consumer contact occurs outside the confines of a retail store.

North American Free Trade Agreement (NAFTA) An agreement among Canada, Mexico, and the United States to phase out tariffs and other trade barriers among them.

objections Prospects' reasons for not making purchases.

objective-and-task method Quantifying communication objectives, determining the communications mix required to meet those objectives, and budgeting the cost of that mix.

observation The collection of data by recording actions of customers or events in the marketplace.

odd-even pricing Setting prices a few dollars or cents below a round number.

off-peak pricing A strategy for pricing services that involves charging lower prices during slow demand times to stimulate sales.

oligopoly A type of competition that occurs when a few sellers of very similar products control most of the market.

on-line marketing Computer display of product information including how to order via modem.

operational planning The creation of objectives and strategies for individual operating units over a short time span.

order delivery The activities involved in getting products to customers and enabling them to be used.

order getting The process of developing business by seeking out potential customers, providing them with neces-

sary information about products, and persuading them to buy.

order taking The routine completion of transactions after customers have already decided to buy.

organizational buyers People who purchase goods and services for businesses, government agencies, and other institutions.

penetration pricing The strategy of setting a low price to attract the target market to a new product.

per capita income Income per person in a particular country.

percentage-of-sales method Establishing a communication budget based on a specified percentage of actual or estimated sales.

personal benefits The good feelings that customers get from purchasing, owning, and using products, or receiving services.

personal selling Selling that involves personal interaction with the customer.

physical distribution The process of handling orders and moving and storing goods to get them efficiently to customers.

piggyback service Intermodal transportation of truck trailers via train to a station near their ultimate destination.

pioneering advertising Advertising that attempts to develop primary demand for a category of product.

placement The channels of distribution used to get products and services to market.

political–legal environment The laws, regulations, and political pressures affecting marketers.

portfolio plan Decisions concerning the allocation of resources among an organization's SBUs.

positioning map A diagram showing how various brands are perceived relative to one another.

posttest Testing that evaluates the success or failure of an ad after it has run.

predatory pricing A pricing approach that involves setting very low prices in order to hurt competitors.

preparation Learning more about qualified prospects to create value for them.

prestige pricing Setting a high price to convey an image of high quality or exclusivity.

pretest Researching a test's audience reactions to an ad before launching the campaign.

price The amount of money, goods, or services that must be given up to acquire ownership or use of a product.

price discrimination The practice of charging different prices to buyers that do not reflect cost differences to the seller.

price elasticity A measure of the sensitivity of demand to changes in price.

price fixing Illegal agreements among competitors to set the price of a product.

price fixing Reaching an agreement with competitors about what price to charge.

price lining The strategy of offering merchandise at a number of specific but predetermined prices.

price war Repeated price reductions by competitors in an effort to undercut one another's prices.

primary data Data collected specifically for a particular investigation.

primary demand Demand for the product class as a whole.

primary metropolitan statistical area (PMSA) A metropolitan statistical area with at least one million people.

private brand A brand that is owned and used by a wholesaler or retailer.

probability sampling Selecting research subjects in such a way that each member of the population has a known chance of being selected because the subjects are selected randomly.

producers Businesses that buy goods and services to produce other goods and services for sale.

product Something offered by marketers to customers for exchange.

product advertising Advertising that attempts to create demand for goods, services, places, persons, or events.

product development strategies Strategies to grow by developing new products to serve existing customers.

product diffusion The process by which new products spread through a population.

product feature A fact or technical specification about the product.

product life cycle A model of the stages in a product's sales and profit history.

product line A group of products that shares common characteristics, channels, customers, or uses.

product manager The person responsible for marketing a particular product or product line.

product mix The full set of products offered for sale by an organization.

product position The perception of the product relative to competing products in the minds of potential buyers.

production orientation A business philosophy that emphasizes the manufacture and delivery of products.

profit The positive difference between total revenues and total costs.

promotion The personal and impersonal means used to inform, persuade, and remind customers about products and services.

promotional allowance A price reduction offered to resellers in exchange for the reseller performing certain promotional activities.

promotional discount A short-term price reduction designed to stimulate sales or to induce buyers to try a product.

prospecting The process of identifying potential customers.

psychographic (lifestyle) segmentation The process of dividing the market on the basis of how people conduct their lives, including their activities, interests, and opinions.

psychological costs The mental energy and stress involved in making purchases and accepting product risks.

psychological pricing Tactics designed to make a price look more appealing to buyers.

public warehouse A business that offers space and inventory support services for a rental fee.

publicity Nonpaid communication of information about the company or product, generally in some media form.

pull strategy Directing marketing communications to end users.

purchasing agents In organizational buying, employees or teams assigned buying duties.

pure competition A type of competition that occurs when there are many sellers of identical products and each seller has a relatively small market share.

push strategy Directing marketing communications to other members of the marketing channel.

qualifying Determining whether a prospect is in a position to buy a product.

quantity discount A reduction in the price per unit for purchasing a larger quantity.

quick-response inventory management A system in which channel members cooperate to reduce the lead time for receiving merchandise.

quota A limit on the amount of a product that may be brought into or taken from a country.

rate-of-return pricing A pricing approach that involves determining total costs and then adding a desired rate of return to them to determine the selling price.

rating The percentage of the total potential audience who are exposed to a particular media vehicle.

raw materials Unprocessed items that are made into component parts or finished products.

reach The number of different persons or households exposed to a particular advertising media vehicle or a media schedule during a period of time.

rebate A refund of part of the price of the product.

receiver The person or group for whom the message is intended.

reciprocity A relationship between two organizations in which they agree to purchase each other's products.

reference groups Groups of people that influence a consumer's thoughts, feelings, and behaviors.

reference price The price that buyers use to compare the offered price of a product or service.

regulations Rules written by government agencies that have the force of law.

relationship selling The development of long-term, mutually beneficial relationships between salespeople and their customers.

research design The plan for how to collect and analyze data.

retailer An intermediary that sells primarily to ultimate consumers.

reverse channel A distribution channel that moves goods from end user to producer.

routine decision making Decision making involving little search and purchasing effort.

salary A fixed payment made to an employee on a regular basis.

sales analysis Gathering, classifying, comparing, and studying company sales data.

sales force composite A sales forecasting technique that estimates sales by adding up salespeople's forecasts of expected sales in their territories.

sales forecast An estimate of likely future sales.

sales management The planning, directing, and controlling the personal selling activities of the organization.

sales orientation A business philosophy that focuses marketing activities on selling available products.

sales plan A formal statement of selling goals and strategies.

sales presentation Communication of the sales message to the customer.

sales promotion Media and nonmedia marketing pressure applied for a predetermined, limited period of time at the consumer, retailer, or wholesaler level in order to stimulate trial, increase consumer demand or improve product availability.

sales quota Sales goal used for managing selling efforts.

sales territories Groups of present and potential customers assigned to particular salespeople, branches, dealers, or distributors.

seasonal discount A price reduction offered during times of slow demand.

secondary data Data gathered for some purpose other than the immediate study at hand.

secondary demand Demand for a particular brand.

segment marketing The strategy of tailoring a marketing mix to a single target market or using separate marketing mixes to meet the needs of different target markets.

selective distribution A form of distribution in which a manufacturer sells products through more than one, but not all, of the intermediaries available in a trading area.

seminar selling An educational program designed to reach a group of people interested in a topic related to the organization's products or services.

service mark A brand for a service that has legal status by virtue of its being registered with the federal government.

service merchandiser (rack jobber) A wholesaler that performs many distribution functions in addition to providing and stocking racks for merchandise.

services Products, such as bank loans or home security, that are intangible or substantially so.

shopping products Products that are purchased after spending some effort comparing various alternatives.

single-source data A single database containing data on sales by product and brand, coupon usage, and exposure to television advertising.

simulated test market An experiment in which a sample of consumers has an opportunity to select products from mock grocery shelves.

site selection The decision of where to locate a retail store.

skimming pricing The strategy of setting a high, initial price to quickly recover the costs to develop a new product and then gradually lowering it.

slotting allowance A fee paid by a manufacturer for space in a retail store.

social benefits The positive responses customers get from others for purchasing and using particular products and services.

social class A national status hierarchy by which individuals and groups are classified in terms of esteem and prestige based on their wealth, skill, and power.

social environment The people in a society and their values, beliefs, and behaviors.

social responsibility Concern for the social consequences of a person's or institution's acts as they may affect the interests of others.

sole sourcing Purchasing all of a particular organizational product from a single source.

source The sender of a message.

source loyalty Stable, long-term business relationships between organizational buyers and suppliers.

specialty products Products that are unique in some way, purchased infrequently, and usually expensive.

specialty store A store that handles a deep selection in a limited number of product categories.

specialty wholesaler A wholesaler that carries a narrow range of products.

stakeholders Individuals and groups who are influenced and can influence marketing decisions.

Standard Industrial Classification (SIC) codes Codes developed by the U.S. government to classify types of businesses.

standard test market The practice of offering a new product through normal distribution channels in a limited area.

statistical inference The process of using data from a sample to draw conclusion about an entire population.

stimulus–response Sales presentation that provides a stimulus with the goal of influencing the customer to buy the product.

store image Everything consumers think about particular retail stores and chains.

straight rebuy A type of organizational purchase involving a routine order from the same supplier.

strategic alliances Long-term partnerships designed to accomplish the strategic goals of both parties.

strategic business unit (SBU) A part of an organization that has a distinct mission, has its own competitors, sells one product or a group of similar products, and can be planned for independent of other units in the organization.

strategic planning Activities that lead to the development of a clear organizational mission, organizational objectives, and the strategies that enable the organization to achieve its objectives.

strategic window The time period in which an organization's strengths match an opportunity.

subculture A segment within a culture that shares distinguishing values and patterns of behavior that differ from the overall culture.

supplies Industrial goods that are consumed in the process of producing other products, but which do not go into the products.

support salespeople Salespeople who help order getters and order takers in a variety of ways, but who do not conduct actual sales transactions.

survey   The collection of data through the use of a questionnaire.

survey of buyer intentions   A sales forecasting technique that relies on answers from customers regarding their expected consumption or purchases of the product.

SWOT analysis   The systematic evaluation of the organization's internal strengths and weaknesses and external opportunities and threats.

tabulating   Counting the number of cases that fall into each category or combination of categories of response.

tactical planning   The creation of objectives and strategies aimed at attaining goals for specific divisions or departments over a medium time frame.

target market   The particular market segment that an organization selects to serve.

tariff   A tax charged on imported or exported goods and services.

team selling   The use of a team of sales professionals who work together to sell and service an organization's major customers.

technical-market research   Research incorporating customers by demonstrating a product on a computer screen and asking customers to evaluate it.

technical specialists   Support salespeople who provide order getters with technical assistance.

technological environment   Scientific knowledge, innovations, and inventions that result from research.

telemarketing   The practice of telephoning prospects, describing the product, and seeking orders.

telemarketing   Conducting sales presentations over the phone.

temporal costs   The time spent purchasing products and services.

test marketing   A controlled experiment in a limited geographical area to test the impact of one or more proposed marketing actions.

time-series analysis   A sales forecasting technique that uses past data to predict future outcomes.

total revenue   The total amount of money received from the sale of all units of a product.

trade discount   A percentage reduction from the list price, offered to resellers.

trade name   The legal name under which a company operates.

trademark   A brand that has legal status by virtue of its being registered with the federal government.

trade promotion   Sales promotion directed to intermediaries to increase channel demand or support for manufacturers' products.

trade-in allowance   A price reduction for providing a good or a service, along with a monetary payment.

transaction (shopping) costs   The combination of temporal, psychological, and behavior costs.

trend analysis   A sales forecasting technique that relies on patterns in past sales to predict future sales.

truck jobbers   A wholesaler that operates a small warehouse and trucks that carry products to retailers.

tying contract   An agreement under which a marketer sells a particular product only if the buyer also purchases another, specified product.

uniform delivered pricing
Geographic approach to pricing in which the seller's price includes shipping and the title passes where the buyer receives the goods.

uniform pricing   The strategy of charging a single price for an entire product mix.

universal product code (UPC)   A code imprinted on a product or product package that identifies its type, manufacturer, and other characteristics such as its size or flavor.

unsought products   Products that consumers do not seek out and may not even be aware of.

usenet   The network of Internet addresses for electronic mail.

utilitarian needs   Needs related to basic functions and material benefits.

value analysis   A comparison of the costs and benefits of purchase.

value pricing   A pricing approach that involves setting prices so that the

exchange value is higher than the value of competing exchanges.

value-driven marketing   A business philosophy that focuses on developing and delivering superior value to customers as a way to achieve objectives.

variable costs   Costs that change along with changes in quantity produced.

vending machine   A machine that delivers a product when the buyer inserts payment.

vendor analysis   A procedure in which buyers rate each potential supplier on various performance measures.

venture team   A cross-functional team that is responsible for all the tasks involved in the development of a new product.

vertical marketing system (VMS)   A distribution channel that is centrally managed to achieve greater efficiency and marketing impact.

video selling system   A system that uses video screens located near checkouts or kiosks to advertise products and services.

virtual corporation   A network of alliances in which each member shares its expertise in a particular area.

wants   Specific goods and services that satisfy needs and additional goods and services that go beyond survival.

warehousing   The storing of products while they await sale or transfer.

warranty   The producer's statement of what it will do to compensate the buyer if the product is defective.

wheel of retailing   A theory of retail institutional change that explains how new forms of retailing will emerge and how others decline in popularity.

wholesaler (distributor)   A business that buys, takes title to, stores, and resells goods to retailers or to other organizations.

World Wide Web   A system that allows users to receive text, graphics, video, and sound by clicking on particular words and images.

World Trade Organization (WTO)   An organization designed to further negotiations and oversee resolution of disputes related to GATT.

Name Index

A&P, 436
A.C. Nielsen, 111, 114, 125, 131
A/E/C Systems International, 547
A.T. Kearney Inc., 138
Aaker, David A., 247, 589, 594
Achrol, Ravi S., 587, 602
Ackerman, Jerry, 285
Adams, Jane Meredith, 327
Addison-Wesley, 202
Adler, Alan L., 594
Adler, Jane, 207, 592, 599
Admiral Screw Company, 76
Advanced Hardware Architectures, 396
Advanced Recovery, 373
Advantage International, 9
Agins, Teri, 597
Agrawal, Neelu, 365
Aheam, Chris, 333
Airborne Express, 388, 389, 406
Airbus, 49
Alamo Rent A Car, 203
Alba, Joseph W., 594
Alberto-Culver, 347
Alcoa, 42
Alderman, Lesley, 593
Alexander, Bob, 508, 602
Alexander, Suzanne, 592, 601
Allen, Jay, 429
Alley, Carla, 513
Allied-Lyons, 85
Allied Van Lines, 236
Allott, Jeff, 537
Allred, Gloria, 327
Alsop, Ronald, 594
Alster, Norm, 594
Amazon.com Books, 505
Ambry, Margaret, 587, 591
Amdahl, 216
American Airlines, 350, 547
American Express, 20, 161, 209, 341, 548
American Home Products Corporation, 242
American News Service, 301
American Pet Products Manufacturers
      Association, Inc., 491
American Standard Inc., 88, 380
American Wilderness Experience, 295
Ametek Plymouth Products, 369
AMP, 100
Amp, Inc., 191
Amparts International, 66
Ampex, 276
Amster, Caryn, 541
Amtrak, 292
Andersen Consulting, 286, 287
Anderson, Eric, 131
Anderson, Erik, 570
Anderson, Lisa, 593
Anderson, Veronica, 593
Andersson, Hanna, 46
Anheuser-Busch, 35, 115, 144
Anthony, Barbara, 327
Anyone Can Whistle, 414
Apelbaum, Phyllis, 90
Apple Computer, 13, 86, 221, 268, 535
Approach Software, 314
Arens, William F., 474, 487
Argitis, John, 508
Armstrong, Larry, 594–598
Arndt, Michael, 242
Arnett, Alison, 533
Arrow Messenger Service, 90
Art Anderson Associates, 131
Aspen Health Services, 494
Aspen Ski Tours, 352
Associated Grocers of New England, 409
AT&T, 11, 33, 209, 263, 335, 571
Atkinson Research, 131
Au Bon Pain, 166

Auto-By-Tel, 376
AutoNation USA, 330
AutoResearch Laboratories Inc., 184, 194,
      320, 538
Avco Systems Division, 96
Averill, Barry, 199
Avery Dennison, 384
Avis Inc., 219, 257
Avon, 245, 501

B&B Technology, 178
Baby Superstore, Inc., 339, 431
Backer Spielvogel Bates, 211
Badavas, Robert P., 196, 197
Badenhausen, Kurt, 255
Bahls, Jane Easter, 594
Bahls, Steven C., 594
Baird & Warner, 396
Bak, William, 590
Baker's, 322, 393
Balance, 231
Baldwin, Pat, 591
Balentine & Company, 297
Bane, Melissa, 161
Banerjee, Neela, 597
Banino, Valerie, 462
Barbie Shoppe, 420
Barchetti, Katherine, 118
Barett, Paul M., 587
Barn Nursery & Landscape Center, 461
Baron, Donald L., 589
Baron, Laurie, 10, 11
Baron Messenger Service, 10, 11
Barrett, Amy, 589, 597
Barrier, Michael, 589
Barthmare, Jamie, 429
Bartusick, Mike, 163
Bashas' Supermarkets, 418
Baskin Robbins, 78, 85, 432
Bass, Charlie, 127
Bass Pro Shops, 430
Batson, Bryan, 593
Batts, Lana, 401
Bauer, Bob, 333
Bayer Corporation, 249, 445
BBDO Worldwide, 143
Beaudin, Kirk, 143
Beech-Nut, 357
Begley, Sharon, 587
Belk, Russell W., 591
Bellafante, Ginia, 601
Belle, Tom, 117
Belly Basics, 409
Ben & Jerry's, 41, 125, 355
Benerjee, Neela, 74
Benjamin, Daniel, 588
Benjamin, Peter, 556
Bennahum, David, 161
Bennett, Bob, 487, 488
Bennett, Peter D., 394, 587–590, 592–603
Beresford, Lynn, 355, 587, 589, 599, 601
Beretta, Franco, 204
Beretta, Pietro, 204
Beretta, Ugo Gussalli, 204
Bergstrom, Robin Yale, 592
Berman, Melissa A., 595, 603
Bernard Chaus Inc., 314
Bernoff, Josh, 279
Bernsohn, Terri, 251
Berry, Jon, 593, 597
Berry, Leonard L., 596
Bertini, Bob, 469
Berton, Lee, 601
Best, Connie, 571
Beveridge, Dirk, 518
Bianchi, Alessandra, 592, 595, 600, 601
Biciocchi, Steve, 599
Biddle, Reginald, 588

Big Island Candies, 118
Bigness, Jon, 593
Biosite Diagnostic, 123
Bird, Laura, 349, 591, 597, 598
Bird-X, 68
BirdsEye, 123
Birnbaum, Jesse, 330
Bisharat, Jaleh, 314
Bivens, Terry, 333
Black, William C., 596
Black & Decker, 368, 506
Black Diamond Equipment Ltd., 5
Black Entertainment Television (BET), 39
Blackwell, Robert D., 591
Blackwood, Francy, 602
Blalock, Cecelia, 591
Blattberg, Robert C., 597
Bloch, Peter H., 596
Blohm, David, 260
Bloomingdale's, 242
Blount, Steve, 595
BodyFx, 249
Boeing Company, The, 49, 175
Bohlen, Celestine, 601
Bombardier Inc., 292
Bombay Company, 343
Bongiorno, Lori, 596
Bonoma, Thomas V., 592, 603
Booklet Binding, 83
Borden, Jeff, 601
Bordenaro, Michael, 275
Borrus, Amy, 588, 589
Bosch, John, 185
Boschat, Nathalie, 594, 600
Bose Corporation, 408, 508, 515
Boston Athletic Association (BAA), 285
Boston Consulting Group (BCG), 92–94
Boston Markets, 50
Bounds, Wendy, 601
Bourne, Randall, 377
Bovee, Tim, 591
Bowens, Greg, 597, 598
Bowers, Brent, 603
Bowles, Jerry G., 598
Brackman, Jessica, 443
Bradlees Inc., 141
Braham, James, 275
Brallier, Jess M., 202
Brancatelli, Joe, 305
Brannigan, Martha, 590
Branzei, Sylvia, 202
Brauchli, Marcus W., 596
Braus, Patricia, 591
Braville, Magalie, 275
Braynin, Felix, 495
Breed, Allen, 91
Breed Technologies, 91
Bridges, Marialena, 146
Brimelow, Peter, 587, 591
British Airways, 290
British Knights, 494
Broderbund, 379
Brokaw, Leslie, 589, 594
Broniarczyk, Susan M., 594
Bronner, Michael, 473
Bronner Slosberg Humphrey Inc., 473
Brookman, Faye, 597
Brooks Brothers, 231
Brott, Armin A., 589
Brown, Rich, 39
Browne, Charles Lee, 195, 590, 592
Brucker, Roger W., 592
Bruckner, Bill, 507
Bruley, Bryan, 598
Brunckhorst Company, 245

Bryk, Bill, 178
Buchholz, Barbara B., 55
Buck, Genevieve, 429
Buckley, Steven, 53
Bukro, Casey, 333, 590
Bulkeley, William M., 593, 599
Burger King, 80, 166, 471
Buzzell, Robert D., 597
Byrne, John A., 602, 603

Cable News Network, 223
Cadillac, 96
CafeNet, 419
Caggiano, Christopher, 603
California Recycling Company, 373
Calvin Klein, 485
Campanelli, Melissa, 597, 599
Campbell Soup Company, 128, 129, 213, 223
Candler, Julie, 598
Cane & Able, 207
Carey, John, 594, 595
Carey, Max, 83
Caribe Hilton and Casino, 206
Carlson, Robert, 293
Carlton, Jim, 305
CarMax, 330
Carnegie Mellon Robotics Institute, 257
Carnival Cruise Lines, 208
Carter, Dennis, 247
Case, John, 552, 596
Cassidy, Tina, 24
Castleberry, Stephen B., 602
Castor, Janice, 596
Cateora, Philip R., 77, 597
Caterpillar, 546
CDnow, 450
CDW Computer Centers Inc., 378
Cebrzynski, Gregg, 590
Cedergren, Christopher W., 310
Centurione, Janene, 461
Cerulean Technology Inc., 196, 197
Chandler, Susan, 337
Chapman, Edward A., Jr., 601
Charles Schwab & Co., 466
Charney, Michael, 396
Chase Manhattan Bank, 164, 266
Chatzky, Jean Sherman, 597
Checkpoint Systems, 185
Chesebrough-Pond's, 458
Chevron Corporation, 406, 470, 475
Chew, Daniel M., 466
Chiaruttini, Giordano A., 135
Chin, Mary, 161
China Coast, 266
China Motor Bus, 17, 50
Chock Full o' Nuts, 52, 53
Chorbajian, Victoria, 507
Chouinard, Yvon, 5
Christopher, Doris, 321
Chrysler Corporation, 146, 265, 279, 330, 477, 535
Chuang, John, 587
Chubb Group of Insurance Companies, 219
Chun, Janean, 598–600
Churchill, Gilbert A., Jr., 3, 103, 113, 133, 520, 521, 524, 567
Churchill, Winston, 204
Citibank, 169, 266
CityBus, 17
Clambake Celebrations, 372
Claritas Inc., 214
Claritas/NPDC, 120
Clark, Don, 469
Clarke, Jim, 53
Clayton/Curtis/Cottrell, 133

ClearVue Products, Inc., 542
Cleary, David Powers, 590
Cleaver, Joanne, 199, 541, 590, 596, 600
Clede, Bill, 197
CMG Health, 298
Coates, Colby, 598
Coates, James, 590, 593, 596
Coca-Cola Company, 63, 69, 115, 243, 247, 272, 273, 347, 380, 398, 456, 457, 462
Coconuts Music and Video, 417
Cody, Jennifer, 590
Cohasset Colonials, 512
Cohen, Andy, 593
Cole, Jerry, 591
Cole, Kenneth, 173
Coleman, Bob, 594
Colletti, Jerome A., 602
Collier, Sophia, 571
Colonial Data Technologies, 235
Commuter Cleaners, 415
Compaq Computer Corporation, 193, 317, 323, 324, 356
Comverse Technology, 222
ConAgra, 7, 91, 260
Conservation Corporation Africa, 62
Continental Airlines, 122, 552
Conveyant Systems, 78
Cook Specialty Company, 181
Cooley, John, 556
Cooper, Arnold C., 589
Cooper, Helene, 74
Cooper, Linda, 596
Cooper Marketing Group, 213
Corbis Corp., 279
Corky's Bar-B-Q, 369
Corman, Linda, 528, 602
Corning, 261, 539
Corporate Express, 411
Corporate Resource Development, 83
County Fair Food Stores, 434
Cowan Financial Group, 507
Cox, Meg, 597
Crate & Barrell, 423
Crawford, C. Merle, 262, 277, 594, 595
Creative Professional Services, 296
Crilley, Joseph, 41
Crilley's Circle Tavern, 41
Crisafulli, Steve, 556
Crispell, Diane, 591
Cronin, Michael P., 587
Crown Books, 172
Crownover, Clinton, 591
CS First Boston, 13
CSX Intermodal, 179
Cub Foods, 173, 185
Cuneo, Alice Z., 467
Cutler, Blayne, 593
Cyrillus, 436
Czinkota, Michael R., 596

D'Agostino, Mercedes, 187
D'Alessandro, David F., 285
Dabrowski, Andrea, 588
Dale Carnegie & Associates, 508, 509, 522
Dan'Z Cookies, 365
Dana Perfumes Corporation, 144
Daniels, Kaye, 27
Danish Pharmaceutical Association, 543
Danko, George, 522
Dann, Valerie, 603
Danzig, Fred, 601
Dart Transit Company, 178
Darter Inc., 399
David, Steven N., 401
Davies, Lea P., 466

Davis, Pete, 540
Davoli, Robert, 197
Day, George S., 589. 598
Dayton Hudson Corporation, 349, 464
Deal, Norman, 275
Deborah Brightman Farone, 528
DeCoursey, Jennifer, 599
Deja Inc., 373
Dejay Corporation, 291
deJong, Jennifer, 596
Delahaye Group, 297
Dell, W. Frank, 600
Dell'Angela, Tracy, 251
Dellecave, Tom., Jr., 257
Demetrakakes, Pan, 275
DeMuth, Jerry, 589
Dep, 451
DeRose, Rodger L., 263
DesAcc, 462
Deveny, Kathleen, 593–595, 601, 603
Devlin, Barbara Hogan, 477
Devlin, Bob, 477
DHL, 77
Dick, Toni, 588
Digital Equipment Corporation, 262, 356
Dillon, William R., 117
Dinardo, Bill, 348
Dining a la Card, 533
Direct Tire Sales, 485, 489
Discover Card, 421
Disney, 141, 454
Disneyland Paris, 310, 320
Doden, Daniel L., 594
Dole Food Company, 272
Domino's Pizza, 124
Don Coleman & Associates, 209
Donnelley, R. R., 200
Donnelly, James H., Jr., 85, 206, 215, 252,
    287, 589, 592, 595, 596
Dorman, George C., 595
Dorning, Mike, 591, 600
Drane, Robert E., 109
Dresner, Richard, 495
Dreyer's, 453
Driver's Mart, 330
Du Bois, Paul Martin, 301
Du Pont, 179
Dubey, Suman, 588
Duffell, Ian, 413
Duggan, Mike, 301
Dulude, Richard, 603
Dumaine, Brian, 589
Dun & Bradstreet Corporation, 568
Dunkin' Donuts, 53
Dunlop Tire Corporation, 200
Dunn, William, 591, 601
Duracell, 16, 88, 472
Durham, Jim, 528
Dusharme, Dirk, 592
Dwyer, Paula, 589
Dyachenko, Tatiana, 495
Dyson, Esther, 180

Eagles, Elizabeth, 431
East-West Education Development
    Foundation, 373
Eateries Inc., 427
Echikson, William, 592, 593, 602
Eck, Thomas, 76
Edelman, Vladimir, 48, 588, 596
Edelman Public Relations Worldwide, 484
Edge, The, 288
Edutech, 344, 345
Eggleston, Thomas, 330
Ehrlich, Elizabeth, 592, 595

Eichorn, Julie A., 528
Eisenstein, Paul A., 330
Electric Library, 236
Electrolux, 203
Elliott, Dave, 389
Ellis, David, 601
Ellison, Katherine, 599
Elmes, Steven, 323
Elsner, Gary, 443
Embratur, 481
Emshwiller, John R., 589
Engardio, Pete, 588, 595
Engel, James F., 591
Enrich International, 544, 545
Enterprise, 360
Equifax Business Geo-Metrics, 95
Ericsson, 455
Ernst & Young, 169
Etmekjian, Charlie, 590
Ettlie, John E., 587
Ettorre, Barbara, 603
Etzel, Michael J., 71
Evans, Audrey, 414
Evans, Phil, 275
Eveready, 456
Everett, Martin, 602
Everex, 351
Expressions, 377
Exxon, 244

F.A.O. Schwartz, 251
Fadal Engineering, 270
Falvey, Jack, 519, 602
Farrar, Andrew, 383
Farrow, Paul, 537
Fawcett, Adrienne Ward, 600
Fedders, 210
Federal Express Corporation, 60, 77, 406, 445
Federal Insurance, 219
Federated Department Stores, 349, 409
Feibus, Michael, 161
Feldman, Amy, 597
Feller, Gordon, 599
Fenn, Donna, 587
Fernandez, Robert, 602
Ferrell, O. C., 587
Ferron, Jay, 330
Fersko-Weiss, Henry, 603
Fiat, 223
Field, Anne, 603
Fila Sports, 540
Fingerhut Cos., 337
First Chicago NBD, 138
First National Bank of Chicago, 296
Firtle, Neil H., 117
Fisher, George M. C., 597
Fisher-Price, 201
Fisk, Linda, 41
Fitzgerald, Kate, 592, 599
$5 Clothing Store, 343
Fizgibbons, Ruth Miller, 598
Flaherty, Deirdre, 350
Fleagle Foods, 415
Fleischman, Pinchas, 42, 587
Fleming Companies, Inc., 97, 428
Fleschner, Malcolm, 195, 590, 592, 602
Fletcher, June, 588
Flickinger, Burt, 333
Flint, Jerry, 588, 593
Florida Marlins, 217, 218
Flowers Industries, 215
FMC Corporation, 131
Foote, Cone & Belding, 462
Ford, Edward, 522
Ford, Henry, 200

Ford, Neil M., 103, 520, 521, 524, 602
Ford Motor Company, 45, 64, 170, 179, 214,
    337, 539
Forest, Stephanie Anderson, 74, 588
Fort Sanders Health System, 125
Fost, Dan, 593
Fostec, 181
Fox, Dennis, 602
Fox, Loren, 593
FPG International, 443
Frances Cerra Whittelsey, 327
Frank, John N., 337
Frank, Robert, 598
Fredrick, Joanne, 133
Freeman, Chris, 251
Freeman Cosmetic Corporation, 275
Fresh 1, The, 405
Fresh Express Farms, 111
Friddle, Don, 544
Friedland, Jonathan, 598
Friedrick, Joanne, 590
Friend, Michael, 293
Frito-Lay, 211, 267
Fritz Companies, Inc. (FCI), 406
Frothingham, Steve, 323
FTD, 393
Fuguitt, P. Gayle, 211, 227, 248
Fuji Photo, 491
Fuji Xerox, 277
Fujitsu, 382
Fuller, Samuel H., 262
Fuller Brush Company, 378
Fuller Medical, 90
Futrell, Charles, 602

G&F Industries, 408, 508, 515
G. Heileman Brewing Company, 245
G. S. Haly, 76
Gage Marketing Communications, 117
Gallagher, James P., 593
Galloway Lumber, 424
Gallup China Ltd., 136
Gangemi, Robina A., 602
Gangle, Paul, 142
Ganson, Art, 383
Gap, The, 422, 429
Garland, Susan B., 592
Garlick, Saul, 533
Garner, S. J., 592
Garry, Michael, 600
Garvin, David A., 595
Gates, Bill, 279, 469
Gateway 2000, 371
Gatty, Bob, 243, 401, 588, 594, 599
Gault, Stanley, 106
GE Supply, 403
Gediman's Appliance Store, 432
Geerlings & Wade, 420
Gelman, Jan, 601
Gendron, George, 135, 603
Genentech, 535
General Electric, 92–94, 186, 242, 522
General Mills Company, 152, 210, 227, 248,
    251, 266, 333
General Motors, 28, 32, 130, 158, 170, 200,
    208, 265
General Nutrition Centers (GNC), 89, 90, 102
Geon Company, 180
George, Brian, 547
George, Judith, 603
George, Tom, 9
GeoSystems Global Corporation, 47
Geranios, Nicholas K., 592
Gerber Products Company, 208, 357
Gerhart, Barry, 573, 603

German, Gene A., 318
Gessner, Susan, 501
Getman, Marvin, 24
Giant Step Productions, 288
Gibara, Samir, 106
Gibson, Richard, 531, 594, 597
Giddings & Lewis Measurement Systems Inc., 185
Gillette Company, 240, 258, 270
Gitano Group, 379
Giussani, Bruno, 589
Glain, Steve, 598
Glass, David, 383, 429
Glazer, Rashi, 587, 596, 598
Gleason, Mark, 600
Gloom, Jennifer Kingson, 602
Gloria, Thomas, 275
Goad, G. Pierre, 588
Gobeli, David H., 278
Goering, Laurie, 588
Goetsch, Hal W., 554
Gold Coast Dogs, 489
Goldberg, Whoopi, 39
Golden Wok, 124
Golder, Peter, 595
Goldman, Kevin, 594, 595, 601
Goll, Sally D., 597
Good Humor-Breyers Ice Cream Company, 246
Goodman, David, 556
Goody's Family Clothing, 347
Goodyear Tire & Rubber Company, 106, 130
Gorton, George, 495
Gotcha Covered Wholesale, 391
Graffin, Jill, 443
Grand Union Company, 184
Granoff, Peter, 438
Greco, Susan, 588, 589, 591, 594, 596–598, 602
Green Seal, Inc., 275
Greengard, Samuel, 587, 603
Greenspan, Sid, 187
Gregg, Michael W., 184
Greising, David, 602
Grimes, Suzanne, 522
Grimes, William, 591, 595
Grinyova, Ludmilla, 74
Groen, 182
Gronich, Amanda, 251
Gross, Neil, 588, 603
Grossman, John, 450
Groveland Trading Company, 276, 280
Grow Biz International Inc., 207
Grozbean, Brian, 326
Grumman, Cornelia, 594
Gruner, Stephanie, 590, 600
Gruzen, Tara, 81
Gschwandtner, Gerhard, 602
Gschwandtner, L. B., 430
GTE Mobilnet, 404
Guarascio, Phil, 590, 592
Guardiola, John, 571
Gubernick, Lisa, 599

H.J. Heinz, 357
Hägen-Dazs, 269
Haas Automation, 269, 270
Habitat for Humanity, 464
Hafner, Katie, 279
Haggar Apparel, 210
Haley, Douglas F., 592
Hallmark Cards, 208
Halssen & Lyon, 76
Hambridge, Sally, 463
Hamel, Ruth, 600

HandsOn Toys Inc., 383
Hang Ten International, 88, 93
Hansell, Saul, 593
Hapgood, Fred, 439
Haran, Leah, 590
Hardee's, 16
Harley-Davidson, 10, 340, 476
Harper, Charles M., 260
Harper, Roseanne, 601
Harris, Clyde E., 602
Harris Corporation, 174
Harris Semiconductor, 179
Harvad Bookstore, 282
Hasbro, Inc., 89
Hass, Robert W., 135
Hawkins, Deborah, 541
Hayes, Charles, 593
Hayes, Jack, 588
Hayes, Mary, 601
Hays, Laurie, 548, 603
Healey, James R., 595, 597, 598
Healy, Beth, 591
Heinbach, Henry, 106
Helliker, Kevin, 589, 597, 600
Hemingway, Ernest, 204
Hendon, Donald W., 155, 591
Henkel KGaA, 568
Hennessey, H. David, 600
Henricks, Mark, 591, 596, 603
Herndon, Kerry, 328
Hershey, Lewis, 599
Hershey Foods Corporation, 357
Hertz Corporation, 216, 219
Hewlett-Packard, 161, 321, 356
Hilsenrath, Jon E., 255
Hilton, Andrew, 594
Himelstein, Linda, 467, 591
Himmel Nutrition Inc., 250
Hirni, Brad, 188, 592
Hirt, Geoffrey, 587
Hise, Phaedra, 590, 595, 596, 599, 601, 602
Hitchcock, Steve, 556
Hites, Andras, 288
HMV, 446
Hoch, Stephen J., 350
Hochwald, Lambeth, 443
Hockett, David, 503
Hofheinz, Paul, 596
Hollenbeck, John R., 573, 603
Holmes, John, 510–512, 514
Holusha, John, 106, 588
Home Center, 380
Home Depot, 328, 369
Homepage, Peter, 3
Honda Motor Company, 156, 191, 240, 244, 270, 334, 343, 535
Honeycutt, Earl D., Jr., 602
Hoover Ltd., 460
Hornblower, Margot, 588
Hornik, Jacob, 591
Hoskins, Michele, 179
Hospital Home Health Care Agency, 27
Hough, Michael, 544, 547
Howard, Theresa, 601
Hua Chang Toy Company, 355
Hubka, E. Rachel, 509
Hudson, Richard L., 469
Huffman, Douglas E., 591
Huffman, Frances, 589, 598, 599, 601, 602
Huffy Corporation, 415
Hughes, Lyric, 55
Hughes, Tom, 497
Huizenga, H. Wayne, 330
Humana Health Plan, Inc., 199, 200
Hume, Scott, 601

Hurley, Jayne, 166
Hutcheson, Madeline E., 588
Hyatt, Joshua, 83, 588

I.B. Nuts & Fruit Too, 503
IBM, 13, 42, 46, 47, 221, 264, 294
IDG Books Worldwide, 225
IGA, 428
Igloo Products Corporation, 270
Ikawa, Allan, 118
Illingworth, J. Davis, 358
Illinois Tool Works, 184
Imperial Broom Company, 203
Incentive Partnerships, 543
Independent Fabrication, 323
Information Resources Inc., 116, 117, 490
Ingersoll Milling Machine Company, 239
Ingersoll-Rand Company, 270
Ingram, Leah, 599
Ingram, Thomas N., 602
Inland Steel, 288
Integrated Computer Solutions, 57
Intel, 327, 406
Interstate Brands Corporation, 250
Intuit Inc., 425
Invacare Corporation, 265
Iyer, Easwar S., 591
Izatt, Janet, 592

J.C. Penney, 208, 209, 324, 482
J.D. Power & Associates, 122, 552
Jacknis, Marty, 598
Jacobson, Robert, 589
Jakubik, Chris, 333
James, Julius, 466
Jarke, Joseph, 280
Jaroff, Leon, 588
Jarvis, Cheryl, 599
JavaStations, 393
Jeanett, Jean-Pierre, 600
Jenkins, Tanya, 142
Jewel Food Stores, 162
Jodoin, Ray, 348
John Deere Company, 261
John G. Sheed Aquarium, 291
John Hancock Mutual Life Insurance Co., 285
Johnson, Bradley, 590, 592, 601
Johnson, Jenny, 459
Johnson, Robert, 39
Johnson, Steve, 429
Johnson, Steven J., 600
Johnson & Johnson, 280
Johnson Publishing Company, 153
Johnson Wax, 263
Johnston, Wesley L., 592
Jones, Bob, 593
Jones, Christian, 323
Jordan, Michael, 242, 493
Joyner-Krsee, Jackie, 501
Juniper, Bob, 497
Jupiter Marketing & Advertising, 497
Juran, Joseph M., 590
Jurkowitz, Mark, 301

K. Barchetti Shops, 118
Kaeter, Margaret, 602
Kahn, Jeremy, 591
Kaihatsu, Hideki, 595
Kaikati, Jack G., 599, 602
Kaiser Permanente, 186
Kanuck, Leslie Lazar, 150, 591
Kao, Roger, 124
Kao Corporation, 342
Kaplan, Edward L., 189

Kaplan, Fred, 413
KARE-TV, 131
Karlicek, Frank G., 348
Karydas, Rita, 98–100
Kate, Nancy Ten, 594, 601
Kawasaki, Guy, 86
Kawasaki, 486
Keaveney, Susan M., 599
Keds, 143
Keenan, William, Jr., 602
Keller, Jerry, 592, 596
Kelley, Richard, 304
Kellogg Company, 251, 333
Kelly, Pamela, 125
Kennedy, John F., 36
Kenneth Cole Productions, 173
Kenney, Michael, 76
Kentucky Fried Chicken, 67, 70, 208, 376
Keough, Robert, 169, 348
Keyes Fibre, 431
Khrunichev Enterprise, 78
Kidsports International, 77
Kilcullen, John J., 225
Killingsworth, Alan, 524, 602
Kimberly-Clark Corporation, 273
Kinard, Bill, 517
King, Mark, 541
Kingston Technology Corporation, 407
Kinko's, 294
Kirby, Joseph A., 591
Kirkpatrick, David, 597
Kitchen Tune Up, 375
Klepacki, Laura, 597
Klöber GmbH, 322
Kloppenburg, Janet J., 467
Kmart, 13, 210, 236, 408, 433
Knowlton, Thomas, 333
Kodak, 11, 101
Korean Air Cargo, 402
Kosch, Dan, 511
Koselka, Rita, 597
Kosowski, John Z., 83
Kotite, Erika, 598, 600
Kotler, Philip, 587
Kraar, Louis, 588, 596
Kraft General Foods, 223, 310, 518
Kramer, Michael, 495
Kranz, Patricia, 74
Krasny, Michael P., 378
Kratz, Steve, 598
Kripalani, Manjeet, 598
Kruytbosch, Carla, 603
Kupfer, Andrew, 596
Kutscher, Ronald E., 602
Kyocera, 348

L.L. Bean, 119, 212, 423
LA Gear, 143
LaBadia, Beverly, 421
LaGarce, Raymond, 590
Landiak, Mark N., 83
Lands' End, 424
Lane, Randall, 595
Lanier, Judy, 512
Lanier Worldwide, 269
Lannon, Judie, 593
LaPlante, Alice, 600
Lapp, Frances Moore, 301
Larsen, Ralph S., 280
Larson, Erik W., 278
Larson, Jan, 592
Lau, Joanna, 88
Lau Technologies, 88
Lauglaug, Antonio S., 590
Laundy, Peter, 220, 593

Lauter, Evelyn, 592
Lavin, Douglas, 596
Law Firm Development Group, The, 503
Lawrence Bros., 335
Learners Parent-Teacher Store, 559
LearningSmith, 383
LeBoeuf, Michael, 514
Lee, Louise, 467
Lee, Robert, 592
Legg Mason, 255
Lennon, E. A., 602
Leo J. Shapiro & Associates Inc., 138
Lesly, Elizabeth, 601
Lev, Michael A., 598
Lever Brothers Company, 14
Levi Strauss & Co., 73, 149, 150, 207, 466
Levin, Steve, 225
Levine, Joshua, 242
Levine, Stuart, 508
Levinson, Marc, 275, 594
Levy, Michael, 426, 600
Lewison, Dale M., 433
Lewyn, Mark, 598
Library, Ltd., The, 426
Lichtenstein, Donald R., 596
Lieberman, David, 601
Liebling, James, 55
Lienert, Paul, 587
Liesse, Julie, 594
Ligon, Austin, 330
Lim, Jeen-Su, 589
Lindgren, Gary, 528
Lisa Frank, Inc., 157
Lockheed, 78, 322
Loftus, Sheila, 497
Lohr, Steve, 267, 595, 598
Longaberger Basket Company, 512
Lontos, Pam, 504
L'Oréal, 462
Loro, Laura, 590
Losee, Stephanie, 589
Lotus Light Enterprises, 396
Lovelock, Christopher H., 299
Lowden, Jon, 595
Lowe, Kimberly, 591
Lowenstein, Roger, 595
Lu, Cary, 590
Lube Stop, The, 291
Lucas, Allison, 601
Lucky Brand Dungarees, 379
Ludwig, Saul H., 106
Lutz, Robert, 330

M&M Mars, 275
M.J. Nursing Registry, 27
McBride, Anne, 159
McCabe, Kathy, 53, 323
McCann-Erickson Worldwide, 462
McCarroll, Thomas, 587, 600
McCarthy, Michael J., 590, 595
McCartney, Scott, 603
McClenahen, John S., 592
McConnon, Shaun, 169
McCormack, Mark H., 602
McCormick, Chris, 473
McCoy, Frank, 116
McCrabe, Kathy, 285
McDonald & Company Investments, 106
McDonald's, 70, 80, 166, 171, 201, 269, 373, 452, 478, 492, 531, 538
McGarvey, Robert, 86, 589, 602
McGee, W., 602
McGinn, Daniel, 591
McGladrey & Pullen, 528
Machalaba, Daniel, 292

Macht, Joshua, 595, 596, 599
McKee Foods, 368
McKendry, Martin, 127
McKenna, Regis, 595, 600
Mackenzie, Nanci, 395
McKesson Corporation, 172, 383
McKesson Drug, 404
McKesson Water Products Company, 407
McKinney, Webb, 161
McKinsey & Company, 93
McLeod, Harvey, 251
McMenamin, Brigid, 592
McNair, Loveda, 182
McNerney, Donald J., 603
McNulty, Timothy J., 588
MacTemps, 39
McWilliams, Brian, 592
McWilliams, Gary, 599
Madden, Normandy, 600
Madden, Thomas J., 117
Madonia, Moira, 595
Magic Cream, 98–100
Magiera, Marcy, 593
Magliozzi, Ray, 28
Magliozzi, Tom, 28
Magnet, Myron, 596
Magrath, Allan J., 106, 587
Mahoney, Linda J., 602
Main, Jeremy, 590
Mainzer, Bruce W., 590
Make-A-Wish Foundation, 493
Malovany, Dan, 365
Makovsky & Company, 552
Mamis, Robert A., 587, 588, 596, 598
Manpower Inc., 287
Marchetti, Michele, 522, 602
Marcial, Gene, 255
Margolev, Mikhail, 495
Maritz Motivation Company, 123
Markell, Stephen J., 589
Market Share Catalysts, 83
Marketing Coaches, 541
MarketWare Corporation, 130
Markoff, John, 595
Marlboro, 151
Marmot Mountain, 556
Marn, Michael V., 597
Marquez, Anthony, 301
Marriott Corporation, 288
Mars Inc., 357
Marsh Supermarkets, 122, 123
Marsh, Barbara, 599
Martin, Gary, 297
Martin, Michael H., 132
Martinair Holland, 402
Marx, Gary, 588
Maslow, Abraham, 143
MasterCard, 219, 266
Mateja, Jim, 594, 595, 597
Mather, Bill, 287
Mathews, Ryan, 593
MathSoft, 260
Matson Navigation Company, Inc., 408
Matthias, Rebecca, 368
Maturi, Richard J., 594
Maxis, 379
Mayer, Stephen, 494
Mayflower, 99
Maynard, Roberta, 591, 592, 598, 603
Mayor, Tracy, 337
Mazda Motor Corp., 101, 191
MCI, 353, 354, 358
Mead, William, 83
Medco Containment Services, 378
Meeks, Fleming, 590

Mellon Bank, 119
Men's Fitness, 486
Mendosa, Rich, 598
Mercedes-Benz, 203, 232
Merck, 244
Mercury Research, 161
Merdinger, Susan Greenfield, 70
Merlin Metalworks, 323
Merrill, Peter, 138
Merrill Lynch, 106
Messina, Marc, 389
Met-life, 24
Metcalf, Pete, 5
Meyers, Ken, 486
Michele Foods, 179
Micro Dental Laboratories, 288
Micro Warehouse, 406
Microsoft, 469
Middlemas, Bob, 309
Milbank, Dana, 469
Miles, Gregory L., 598
Miller, Amy, 587
Miller, Annetta, 594, 595
Miller, Herman, 45
Miller, James P., 600
Miller, Karen Lowry, 589, 593, 597, 602
Miller, Kim, 166
Miller, Krystal, 596, 597
Miller, Lisa, 592
Millington McCoy, 295
Millman, Nancy, 591, 600
Mills, Nancy, 206
Millstein, Alan, 422
Millstein, Marc, 600
Mine Safety Appliances, 522
Miniard, Paul, 591
Minnesota Power, 91
Minolta, 10, 11
Misale, Al, 178
Mitchell, Rob, 282
Mitsubishi Motor Sales of America, Inc., 205
Mitsuru Sato, 535
Miyaji, Makoto, 101
Moffatt, Susan, 588
Moncrief, William C., III, 504
Mondello, Michael D., 322, 596, 598
Monroe, Kent B., 596, 597
Monsoon, 318
Montgomery Securities, 169
Moore, Martha T., 592
Moore, Steven, 495
Morgan, Andrea Z., 592
Morgan, Emily, 568
Morgenson, Gretchen, 593, 600
Morgenthaler, Eric, 594
Morley, Chris, 27
Morris, Betsy, 594, 600, 601
Morris, John, 592, 599
Morris, John L., 430
Morrissey, Jim, 83
Morrow, Lance, 596
Morton, Jerry E., 590
Moseley, Ray, 81
Mosely, Frances, 285
Motel 6, 343
Mothers Work, 368
Motion Neon, 239
Motor Guide, 489
Motorola, 60, 78, 197, 276, 327
Moukheiber, Zina, 600
MountainGate, 185
Mr. Coffee, 251
Muckjian, Deran, 141
Mulhern, Charlotte, 599, 600
Murphy, Anne, 587, 589, 600

Murphy, Patrick E., 159
Murray, Matt, 102, 589
Music City Roadhouse, 494
My Favorite Mechanic, 298

Nabisco, 461, 549
Nader, Ralph, 36, 37
Nalco Chemical, 55
Nanas, Ed, 600
Narisetti, Raju, 106, 255, 595, 601
Narver, John C., 592
Nash, Nathaniel C., 588
Nathason, Mindy, 522
National Cheerleading Association (NCA), 416
National Fluid Milk Processor Promotion Board, 472
National Wildlife Federation, 8
Neal, Millie, 601
Neeley, Sue E., 589
Neiman Marcus, 90
Nelton, Sharon, 603
Nemes, Judith, 178, 593
Neoglyphics, 288
Neri, Astronauta Rodolfo, 154
Neslin, Scott A., 597
Nestlé, 261
Neuborne, Ellen, 600
New Pig Corp., 536
New York Road Runners Club Inc., 285
Newcomb, Peter, 599
Nicholas, Joy, 544
Nicole Miller, 481
Nigerian Breweries, 245
Nike, 143, 222, 389, 406
Niko, Augusto P., 62
NIR Systems, 175
Nissan Motor Company, 310, 357
Noe, Raymond A., 573, 603
Noodle Kidoodle, 431
Noodles of China, 182, 183
Nord, Walter R., 587
Nordica, 281
Nordstrom, Inc., 309, 424, 426
Norling, James A., 78
Normann, Richard, 589, 603
Northern Telecom, 191
Northstar-at-Tahoe, 447
NorthWord Press, 343
Novotny, Pamela Patrick, 591
Nussbaum, Bruce, 595
NutraMax, 244

O'Connell, Michael, 275
O'Connell, William A., 602
O'Gara-Hess & Esenhardt, 67
O'Kane, Brooks, 542
O'Keegan, Peter, 590
O'Reilly, Brian, 587, 597
O'Sullivan-Oshin, Louise E., 182
Offen, Bob, 469
Office Club, 178, 216
Office Essentials, 344
Olim, Jason and Matthew, 450
Oloroso, Arsenio, Jr., 601
Olson, Jerry C., 145, 152, 591, 596, 599
Olson, Robert, 438, 452, 474
Ono, Yumiko, 594
Ortega, Bob, 597
Oscar Mayer, 128
Outdoor World, 430
Owens, Vaughn, 497
Owens-Corning Fiberglas Corporation, 233
OXO International, 270

P&O Containers Ltd., 409
Pacher, Nancy, 289
Pacific Bell, 191
Pacific Handy Cutter Inc., 271
PaineWebber, 299
Pampered Chef, The, 321
Pampers, 223
Pampers Uni, 223
Panduit, 445, 462
Pantone Color Institute, 213
Panzarella, Tom, 181
Pape, William R., 590
Papp, Albert, Jr., 292
Park Bench Cafe, 163
Park, C. Whan, 594
Park, Jaclyn H., 592
Park, Whan, 591
Parke-Davis, 221
Parker Brothers, 141
Parker Hannifin Corporation, 517
Parker-Pope, Tara, 595, 601
Parsons, Guy, 323
Patagonia, 46
Patrevito, Tom, 83
Patterson, Gregory A., 603
Patti, Joe, 115
Pavel Bouska, 411
PC Flowers, 421
Peace Corps, 444
Peapod, 162, 434, 435
Peavey, Hartley, 219
Peavey Electronics, 219
Pedersen, Laura, 599, 600
Peers, Alexandra, 596
Pelissier, Gerry, 52, 53
Pelosi, Carol, 348
Pen Werks, 229
Penn Racquet Sports, 275
Pensak, David, 169
People's Daily, 55
Pepper, John, 3
Pepperidge Farm, 295
PepsiCo, Inc., 95, 129, 210, 223, 249, 259, 347, 355, 376, 380, 398, 425, 492, 494
Pereira, Joseph, 593, 598
Perez, Tony, 218
Pertman, Adam, 163
Peter, J. Paul, 85, 96, 145, 152, 206, 215, 252, 297, 567, 587, 589–593, 595, 596, 599
Peters, Tom, 597
Peterson, Thane, 279
Phalon, Richard, 591
Pham, Alex, 202
Phelps County Bank, 296
Philip Morris, 244
Philips Electronics Corporation, 44
Phillips, Debra, 591, 599
Pick 'n Save, 434, 435
Pickell, Orren, 242
Pier 1 Imports, 460
Pierce, Daniel, 443
Pietrucha, Bill, 600, 601
Pietrus, Carol, 541
Pillsbury, 476
Pilugin, Nicholas W., 598
Pioneer Hi-Bred International, 218, 506
Pitney Bowes, 48
Pitney Bowes's Mail Center 2000, 233
Pittia, Julie, 599
Pivot Corporation, 119
Pizza Hut, 129, 166
Planet Dexter, 202
PLATINUM Technology, 217
Plauche, Stephen, II, 599

Play It Again Sports, 207, 222
Playskool, 141
Pleasant Company, 282
Plotkin, Hal, 588–590
Polo/Ralph Lauren Corporation, 335, 357
Ponder Harrison, 494
Pope, David, 179
Port, Otis, 590
Porter, Michael E., 50, 588
Post, 333
Potekin, Barry, 489
Pouschine, Tatiana, 598
Powell's Books, 202
Power, Christopher, 594
Power, Stephen, 602
Powerfood, 312
Pratt, Steven, 587, 592
Premark, 255
Preobrezhenskaya, Elena, 74
Preston, Paul, 80
Prewitt, Milford, 599
Procter & Gamble, 3, 47, 48, 127, 136, 151,
    219, 223, 244, 252, 262, 267, 275, 276,
    339, 342, 349, 350, 355–357, 383, 401,
    407, 425, 457, 482, 487, 494, 516
Prodigy Services, 276
Prohaska, Julia, 282
Prudential-Bache, 525
Publishers Clearing House, 489
Punnett, Betty Jane, 56

Quaker Oats Company, 35, 333, 349, 372,
    374, 404, 488
Qualls, William J., 591
Quikava, 52, 53
Quinn, Jane Bryant, 602
Quintanilla, Carl, 593

Raccuglia, David, 219, 220
Racquet Workshop, 463
Raffetto, Fran, 501
Ragù, 445
Ralston Purina Comapny, 58, 240
Ramírez, Rafael, 589, 603
Randle, Wilma, 591, 598
Raptor Systems Inc., 169
Ray-Ban, 234
Raychem, 181, 189, 223
Raymond Corporation, 523
Readerman, David, 169
Recife, 230
Redman, Russell, 599
Reebok, 261
Reef Brazil, 396
REI, 66, 424
Reid, David A., 589
Reid, John, 287
Reidy, Chris, 141, 166, 383, 473
Reingold, Edwin M., 603
Reitman, Valerie, 588, 590, 595–597
Rensi, Edward H., 531, 538
Reynolds, Pamela, 501
Rhino Records, 319
Rhygin Racing Cycles, 323
Rice, Faye, 591
Rice, Mike, 257
Ricks, David A., 56
Rink, D. R., 602
Ritz-Carlton, 201, 297
Robbins Company, 402
Roberts, Barbara, 443
Roberts, Johnnie L., 39
Roberts, Michael, 275
Roberts, Ross, 337
Robinson, Edward A., 595, 603

Robinson Brick Co., 519
Rodale Press, 86
Rohwedder, Cacilie, 600
Rollerblade, 281
Roman, Ernan, 599
Rompel, Tom, 497
Ronkainen, Ilkka A., 596
Roses Southwest Papers, 171
Rosiello, Robert L., 597
Ross, Wilbur, 292
Roswell, Matthew, 255
Rothman, Howard, 596
Rothman, Matt, 603
Roundy's, 433
Rowan, Doug, 279
Rowland, Pleasant T., 282
Rubbermaid, 51, 86, 206, 255, 380, 384, 551
Rue de France, 125
Russell, Cheryl, 587
Ryan, Arthur, 197
Ryan, Nancy, 595, 599
Ryder, 409
Rysavy, Jirka, 411

Saban, Haim, 242
Sadd, Theodore, 275
Safeway, 242
Sager, Ira, 593
Saiki, Patricia, 587
Sainer, Elliot, 494
Saks Fifth Avenue, 242, 436
Salak, John, 599
Salomon, Alan, 600
Sample, John, 519
Sand, Jeff, 570
Santoro, Pete, 239
Sara Lee, 143
Saturday Audio Exchange Inc., 207
Saturn, 373
Savona, Dave, 589
Schaaf, Dick, 589
Schafer, Sarah, 589, 595, 598, 599, 600
Schein, Lawrence, 595, 603
Schiffman, Leon G., 150, 591
Schiller, Zachary, 106, 594, 597–599, 601
Schinc, Eric, 590
Schindler, Robert M., 597
Schlossberg, Howard, 590
Schmeltzer, John, 593, 596, 599, 603
Schmit, Julie, 596
Schmults, Robert C., 588
Schoifet, Mark, 24
Schonfeld, Erick, 593
Schrage, Michael, 363
Schroeder, Michael, 587
Schultz, Don E., 600
Schultz, Howard, 542
Schultz, Ray, 216
Schultze, Chris, 378
Schwarcz, Ronald, 68
Schwartz, Joe, 593
Schwartz, Larry, 10, 11
Schwartz, Peter, 589
Schwartz, Phyllis, 452
Schwartz, Robert, 600
Scientific Certification Systems, 275
Scollard, Jeanette R., 588, 598
Scott Paper Company, 431
Scott, Jim, 493
Scottsdale Princess Hotel, 211
Sea-Land Service, 297
Seals, Margie, 298
Sears, Roebuck and Co., 6, 242, 427, 545
Seattle's Best Coffee, 53
Seckinger-Lee, 272

Seiff, Kenneth, 119
Seiko, 237
Seinfeld, Jerry, 20
Sellers, Patricia, 594, 597, 602
Selz, Michael, 598
Serrano, Ron, 28
Serwer, Andrew E., 603
Sesser, Stan, 589
7-Eleven, 375
Shaich, Ron, 166
Shank, Matthew D., 590
Shapiro, Eben, 595, 600
Shapiro, Leo J., 138, 309
Shaw Industries, 338
Sheff, David, 603
Sherlock, Paul, 513, 592, 597, 598, 602
Sherman, Stratford, 598
Sheth, J. N., 596
Shiseido, 222
Shonka, Mark, 118
Shostack, L. G., 596
Shuman, Cheryl, 202, 203
Shumate, Joe, 495
Shute, R. Douglas, 590
Siconolfi, Michael, 602
Sidoine, Florence, 506
Siegel, Mo, 387
Sierra Medical Center, 222
Silverman, Joel, 594
Silverman, Marilyn, 593
Sinanoglu, Elif, 318
Skadberg, Dean, 401
Skinner, Steven J., 273
Skoda, 463
Skurdy, Stephanie, 478
Slater, Stanley F., 592
Sled Dogs Co., 268
Sloan, Alfred P., 200
Sloan, Pat, 591, 594, 600
Slosberg, Mike, 473
Slutsker, Gary, 595
Small-Weil, Susan, 203
Smart, Tim, 589, 593
Smart & Final, 392
Smart Card Forum, 544
Smith, Daniel C., 591, 594
Smith, Dawn, 592
Smith, Jane, 163
SmithKline Beecham, 270
Smolowe, Jill, 601
SnackWell, 547
Snyder, Glenn, 596, 598
Sofa Workshop, 347
Solo Point, 127
Solomon, Jolie, 592
Solomon, Stephen D., 411
Sony Corporation, 535
Sookdeo, Richard, 596
Southern New England Telephone Company,
    28, 33
Southwest Airlines, 341
Spartan Motors, 116
Spaulding, Mark, 275
Spencer, Leslie, 587
Spethmann, Betsy, 595
Spiegel, 153
Spoa, Christy and Nada, 415
Sportco Marketing, 370
Spragins, Ellyn E., 602
Springen, Karen, 595
Sprint, 350
Sprout, Alison, 595
SRI International, 211
Stackhouse, Jerry, 9
Stansell, Kimberly, 541

Stanton, William J., 71
Staples, William A., 159
Starbucks, 53, 236, 374, 542
StarKist Foods, 471
State Farm Insurance, 41
Steinhauer, Jennifer, 600
Steinkrauss, Robert, 169
Steinmetz, Greg, 602
Step Associates, 250
Stern, Aimee, 135, 592
Stern, Gabriella, 593, 594, 597
Stern, William, 598
Stewart, Jackie, 204
Stewart, Scott, 275
Stickel, Amy I., 600
Stinebaugh, Louis, 393
Stodder, Gayle Sato, 27, 590, 591
Stone-Geier, Joanne, 541
Stratus Computer, 222
Strauss, Gary, 594
Strawser, Mark, 528
Strickland, Thomas H., 589
Strom, Stephanie, 596
Stumpf, Mary Jane, 27
Suarez, Enrico, 142
Sub-Zero, 242
Subaru, 220
Sublette, Guen, 602
Subway, 204
Sucov, Jennifer, 279
Sudarkasa, Michael, 62
Suljic, Jasmine, 229
Sullivan, Mary Cobb, 592
Sullivan, Michael, 189, 223, 592, 593
Summit Racing Equipment, 513
Sun, David, 407
Supercuts, 300
Surtees, Lawrence, 592
Sutter Home Winery, 392
Suzuki, 20
Swan, J. E., 602
Swasy, Alecia, 591
Switch Manufacturing, 570
Szathmary, Richard R., 601

Taco Bell, 129, 166, 476
Talbots, 547
Tanaka, Kazumi, 590, 600
Tannenbaum, Jeffrey A., 598
Tanouye, Elyse, 595
Tanzer, Andrew, 588, 589
Target, 160, 324, 464
Taylor, Gary, 598
Taylor, John H., 598
Teach & Play Smart, 415
Team Air Express, 49
Tech-Ceram Corp., 348
Technautics, 174
Technicolor Entertainment Services, 389
Teerlink, Richard F., 340
Tellis, Gerard, 595
Telstra, 475
Templin, Neal, 161
Tenagra Corp., 463
Tender Care Doula Service, 27
Tenser, James, 601
Terry, Georgena, 160
Terry Precision Cycling for Women, 160
Therrien, Lois, 596
Thomas, Dan R. E., 293
Thomas, Dave, 220
Thomas, R. David, 601
Thompson, Stephanie, 111
Thor-Lo Inc., 231
Three-C Body Shop, 497

Thurow, Roger, 9
3M Corporation, 261, 264, 278, 279, 513
Tiffany's, 351
Tilsner, Julie, 589
Timberland, 408
Tjosvold, Dean, 603
TLI International Corp., 55
Toll, Erich, 598
Toshiba Corporation, 201, 264
Townsend, Bickley, 590, 593
Toy, Joseph, 304
Toy, Stewart, 588, 593
Toyota, 358
Toys 'R' Us, 243, 386, 422, 435
Transmedia, 533
Trawick, I. F., 602
Trinchero, Bob, 392
Tropicana, 457
TRW, 382
Tully, Shawn, 592, 594, 596, 603
Tupper, Earl, 254
Tupperware Corporation, 254, 380
Tureski, Richard, 602
Turner, Gene, 163
Turner, Richard, 596
TV Guide, 519, 522
Twin Dragons, 462
Tyson, James L., 588

Uchida, Hiromi, 597
Union Pacific Railroad, 513
Unit Trust of India, 302
United Airlines, 115
United Healthcare, 199, 200
United Parcel Service, 408
U.S. Department of the Treasury, 302
U.S. Equities, 289
U.S. Gas Transportation, 395
U.S. Postal Service, 336
U.S. Robotics, 269
United Way, 444
Universal Pictures, 448
University of North Carolina, 9
Upah, Gregory D., 596
Upton Tea Company, 76
Urban Outfitters, 422
Useem, Jerry, 588

Valley Expo Center, 24
Value Rent-A-Car, 360
Value Village, 424
ValuJet Airlines, 357, 494
Van den Bergh Foods, 482
Van Matre, Lynn, 592
Van, Jon, 589, 594
Varney, Bill and Sylvia, 374
Vena, Dan, 520
VeriFone, 115
Verlodt, Patricia, 270
Veverka, Mark, 309, 378, 599
VF Corporation, 384
Vial, Catherine, 595
Video Home Theater, 393
Video International, 495
Video Storyboard Tests, 484
Vijayan, Jaikumar, 161
Virgin Atlantic Airways, 471
Virgin Megastore, 413
Virtual Realty, 299
Virtual Vineyards, 438, 452, 456
Visa, 266
Vittoria, Joseph, 360
Volvo, 45

W.W. Grainger, Inc., 91, 339, 398, 399

Wabash National, 178
Wade, Bob, 556
Waggonerm, Kent, 389
Waitt, Theodore W., 371
Wal-Mart, 13, 51, 160, 161, 191, 242, 328,
    347, 349, 381, 408, 422, 429, 542
Walden Paddlers, 537
Waldrop, Judith, 587
Walgreens Drugstore, 507
Walker, Bruce J., 71
Walker, Kate, 467
Walker, Orville C., Jr., 103, 520, 521, 524,
    602
Walser, Nancy, 467
Walsh, Valerie, 593
Ward, Adrienne, 599
Warner-Lambert, 242
Warson, Albert, 588
Warwick Baker & Fiore, 203
Washington, Denzel, 39
Waste Management, 116
Waterjet Systems, Inc., 184
Watson, Alexander F., 588
Watson, Richard, 592
Waxler, Caroline, 39
Weber, Joseph, 593, 601
Webster, Frederick E., Jr., 536, 589, 598, 603
Wehling, Bob, 587–589, 591
Weight Watchers, 270
Weinstein, Bob, 591, 594
Weiss, Aaron, 463
Weitz, Barton A., 426, 600
Welles, Edward O., 590, 592, 599, 603
Wells, Melanie, 600
Wells Fargo & Co., 418
Wels, Susan, 599
Wendy's, 220
West, Don, 39
Western Motivational Incentives Group, 543
Western Publishing, 201
Westinghouse, 271
When International Jensen Inc. (IJI), 191
Whirlpool, 372
Whitford, David, 127
Whittaker, Shane, 503
Whittemore, Meg, 598, 599
Whittle Communications, 464
Wiersema, Frederick D., 597
Wiesendanger, Betsy, 602
Wiggins, Dave, 295
Wiley, Edwin M., 462
Williams, Emelda L., 591
Williams, Jerome D., 591
Williams, Scott, 599
Williamson, Debra Aho, 601
Wilson, Pete, 495
WilTel, 518
Wiman, Alan R., 597
Winchester, Oliver, 204
Windham Hill Records, 484
Winfrey, Oprah, 238
Wisch, Brent, 184
Wisner, Terry, 528
Wittco Foodservice Equipment, 397
Women's Workout World, 201
Wong, Choy, 603
Woo, Carolyn Y., 589
Woodside, A. G., 596
Woolworth PLC, 409
World Fuel Services, 216
Worthy, Ford S., 587, 589
Wright, Patrick M., 573, 603
Wu, Amy, 599
Wyland, Bill, 537
Wyland Galleries Hawaii, 537

Wynter, Leon E., 593

Xerox, 119, 121, 519

Yaleet Inc., 415
Yamaha Corporation of America, 552
Yates, Ronald E., 81, 588, 603
Yeltsin, Boris, 495
Young, Courtney and Dick, 391

Young, David, 589, 592, 597, 598

Zane, Chris, 18
Zane's Cycles, 18
Zavatsky, Sam, 207
Zebra Technologies Corporation, 177, 180, 189
Zeithaml, Carl P., 587
Zeithaml, Valarie A., 587

Zellner, Wendy, 597–599
Zenith Electronics Corporation, 265
Zexel USA Corporation, 257
Zimmerman, Andy, 207
Zimmerman, Dan, 365
Zimmerman, Denise, 544
Zinn, Laura, 592, 594, 597, 601
Zyuganov, Gennadi, 495

Subject Index

Acceleration principle, 177
Accessory equipment, 233
Activities and events, 493, 494
Activity-based costing, 550
Adaptive selling, 513
Addition strategy, 250–252
Additions to product lines, 259
Administered vertical marketing system, 374
Administrative expenses, 578
Advertising, 450, 453
    create messages, 476, 477
    direct mail, 480
    evaluate ad agencies, 472–474
    evaluate effectiveness, 483–485
    Internet, 481, 482
    legal/ethical issues, 485, 486
    logos on athlete's equipment, 482
    outdoor, 480, 481
    pretests, 482, 483
    print, 479, 480
    radio, 479
    review goals/budgets, 474, 475
    scheduling patterns, 482
    select media, 477–483
    television, 478
    types, 470–472
    videocassettes, 482
Advertising agency, 472
Advocacy advertising, 472
Africa, 62
African-American consumers, 153
Agent, 370, 394, 396, 397
AIDA model, 449
Aided recall, 483
Airline Deregulation Act, 33
All-you-can-afford method, 458–460
Allowance, 345–347
Antidumping laws, 68
Approach, 511
Asia/Pacific Rim, 61, 62
Asian-American consumers, 154
Aspiration group, 156
Association of Southeast Asian Nations
    (ASEAN), 61
Assumptive close, 514
Atmospherics, 428, 429
Attitude tests, 484
Attitude, 146
Automated Trade Locator Assistance System,
    135
Automatic merchandising, 418
Automobile Information Disclosure Act, 34
Average revenue, 315

Baby boom, 39
Bait-and-switch, 328
Balanced matrix, 277, 278
Banking, 138
Bar codes, 404
Basing point pricing, 354
BCG growth/share matrix, 92, 93
Beginning inventory, 577
Behavioral costs, 19
Benchmarking, 119
Benefit segmentation, 212
Bike design/manufacturing, 323
Billboards, 480, 481
Black market, 37
Body language, 71
Bonus packs, 489
Bootlegging, 37
Bottom-up planning, 95
Brand, 240
Brand equity, 246, 247
Brand extension, 240
Brand loyalty, 213
Brand manager, 534

Brand mark, 240
Brand name, 240
Breakeven analysis, 319
Breakeven point, 319
Bribery, 73, 525
British beef scare, 80
Broker, 394, 396, 397
Bundle pricing, 351, 352
Business classifications, 175, 176
Business cycle, 30, 31
Business portfolio analysis, 92–94
Business services, 233
Buyer's remorse, 147
Buyers, 192
Buying center, 192–195
Buying power, 65
Buying Power Index, 120

Call report, 526
Canada, 57
Canned presentation, 512
Car rental industry, 360
Career opportunities, 568–575
    assess skills/interests, 571, 572
    career placement office, 572
    cover letter, 574
    employment agencies, 572
    Internet, 572, 573
    job interview, 575
    personal contacts, 573
    résumé, 573, 574
    types, 568–571
    want ads, 572
Caribbean, 62
Case allowances, 491
Cases; see Chapter cases
Cash-and-carry wholesaler, 394, 395
Cash cows, 92
Cash discount, 345, 346
Catalog showrooms, 416
Catalogs, 420
Category killer, 416, 417
Category manager, 534
Causal research, 123
Cause-related marketing, 42
Census data, 120
Centrality, 194
Channel captain, 382
Channels of distribution, 364–389, 366
    building trust, 384
    channel captains, 382, 383
    channels for consumer goods, 369, 370
    channels for organizational goods, 370–
        372
    channels for services, 372
    conflicts, 381, 382
    distribution functions, 366–368
    ethical issues, 387
    global channels, 384, 385
    intermediaries and costs, 368
    leadership, 382, 383
    legal issues, 385, 386
    market coverage, 380, 381
    multiple distribution channels, 372
    political issues, 386, 387
    reverse channels, 373
    selecting channels, 376–381
    vertical marketing systems, 374–376
Chapter cases
    Airborne Express, 366
    banking, 138
    British beef scare, 80
    car rental industry, 360
    Cerulean Technology, Inc., 196
    Corporate Express, 411
    food, 166
    Goodyear Tire and Rubber Company, 106
    Hawaii's tourism industry, 304

Chapter cases—*Cont*
  IDG Books Worldwide, 225
  Levi Strauss & Co., 466
  malls, 24
  Marmot Mountains, 556
  Pleasant Company, 282
  Quikava, 52
  service professionals, 526
  Three-C Body Shop, 497
  Tupperware Corporation, 254
  used-car superstores, 330
  Virtual Vineyards, 438
Characteristics of good marketer, 571
Child Protection Act, 34
Children's TV Act, 34, 35
China, 61
ClariNews, 131
Clayton Act, 33, 34, 386
Closed sales territories, 386
Closing, 514
Coding, 128
Coercive power, 382
Cognitive dissonance, 147
Cold canvassing, 510
Cole's Directory, 509
Commercialization, 267, 268
Commission, 521
Communicating ideas/information, 540–542
Communication, 447
Communication medium, 447
Communication process, 447, 448
Communications budgeting, 457–459
Comparative advertising, 471
Competition-based method, 458, 460
Competition-based pricing, 320–322
Competitive advantage, 48
Competitive advertising, 471
Competitive bidding, 189
Competitive environment, 48–51
Competitive forces, 49–51
Component parts and materials, 233
Concentration, 367
Concept testing, 264
Concurrent engineering, 265
Connectedness, 194
Consideration set, 145
**Consolidated metropolitan statistical area
  (CMSA), 210**
Consolidators, 299
Consultative selling, 513
Consumer behavior, 140–166, **142**
  buying process, 142–147
  cultural values, and, 150, 151
  decision-making process, 147–149
  family, and, 157–159
  marketing influences, 159–161
  monetary conditions, and, 164
  physical surroundings, and, 162
  placement, and, 160
  pricing, and, 160
  product, and, 159, 160
  promotion, and, 161
  reference groups, and, 155, 156
  situational influences, 161–164
  social class, and, 154, 155
  social influences, 149–159
  social surroundings, and, 163
  subcultures, and, 151–154
  task, and, 164
  time, and, 163, 164
Consumer buying process, 142–147
Consumer decision-making process, 147–149
Consumer Goods Pricing Act, 34, 325
Consumer income, 31–33
Consumer interest groups, 36, 37

Consumer Product Safety Act, 33, 34
Consumer products, 230–232
Consumer promotions, 487–491
Consumerism, 36, 37
Consumers, 7
Contests, 489
Continuation strategy, 250
Continuity plans, 490
Continuous improvement, 297
Continuous media pattern, 482
Contract buying, 189
Contract manufacturing, 78
Contractual vertical marketing system, 375
Control, 543
Controlled test market, 266
Controlling marketing activities
  control process, 544–546
  customer satisfaction analysis, 550–552
  marketing audit, 552–554
  profitability analysis, 549, 550
  sales analysis, 546–549
Convenience products, 230, 232
Convenience store, 417, 418
Cooperative advertising payment, 491
Coordinating activities, 538–540
Core competencies, 90, 535
Core values, 150
Corporate vertical marketing system, 374
Corrective advertising, 485
Cost analysis, 549
Cost-based pricing, 317–320
Cost of goods available for sale, 577
Cost of goods sold, 577
Cost of sales, 577
Cost per thousand, 478
Cost-plus pricing, 317
Countertrade, 355
Coupons, 487, 488
Court actions, 37
Cover letter, 574
Critical path method (CPM), 539
Cross-functional teams, 96, 97
Cultural values, 150, 151
Culture, 150
Currencies, 66, 67
Customer benefits, 16, 17
Customer costs, 18
Customer roundtables, 461
Customer satisfaction analysis, 550–552
Customer value, 15

Data, 112
Database marketing, 204
Deals, 488, 489
Deceptive pricing, 326
Deciders, 192
Decode, 447, 448
Deletion strategy, 252
Delphi technique, 103, **104,** 262
Demand,101
Demand-backward pricing, 323
Demand curve, 310, 311
Demand estimation, 101–105
Demarketing, 44
Demographic segmentation, 205
Demographics, 38–40
Department stores, 416
Depository Institutions Deregulation and
  Monetary Control Act, 33
Deregulation, 33
Derived demand, 177
Description buying, 189
Descriptive research, 122
Developed countries, 65
Developing countries, 65

Developing new products; *see* New product
  development
Devil sticks, 251
Dietary Supplement Health and Education
  Act, 90
Differentiated marketing, 203
Diffusion process, 239
Direct-action advertising, 419, 421
Direct channel, 369
Direct exporting, 77
Direct mail, 480, 483
Direct mail marketing, 419–421, **420**
Direct marketing, 419, 420
Direct ownership, 77, 78
Direct relationships, 12
Direct selling, 419, 420
Discount, 344, 345
Discount stores, 417
Discretionary income, 32
Disposable income, 32
Dissociative group, 156
Distributor, 371, 392
Diversification, 88
Diverting, 425
Dogs, 92
Drop shipper, 394, 395
Dual distribution, 372
Dumping, 327
Dun's Business Locator, 120
Dun's Market Identifiers, 510, 511
Durable goods, 234

E Style, 153
Early adopters, 239
Early majority, 239
Eastern Europe, 62
Eco-label, 275
Economic environment, 30–33
Economic infrastructure, 57
EDLP strategy, 349, 350
Efficient customer response, 431
80/20 rule, 213
Elastic demand, 313
Electronic data interchange (EDI), 408,
  409
Emotional appeals, 476
Encode, 447
Environmental scanning, 28–30
Ethics, 42
  advertising, and, 485, 486
  channels of distribution, and, 387
  global marketing, and, 73
  international dimensions, 73
  marketing communications, and, 462–465
  marketing research, and, 131–135
  organizational buying, and, 191
  personal selling, and, 524–526
  pricing, and, 327, 328
  publicity, and, 494
  retailing, and, 436
  sales promotion, and, 492
European Union (EU), 37, 59
European-American consumers, 152
Every-day fair pricing, 349
Every-day low pricing (EDLP), 349, 350
Exchange, 7
Exchange controls, 68
Exchange rates, 66
Exclusive dealing, 386
Exclusive distribution, 381
Exclusive sales territories, 386
Expense account, 526
Experiential benefits, 18
Experiment, 123
Expert power, 382

Exploratory research, 122
Exponential smoothing, 103, **104**
Export agent, 77
Export Connection, The, 135
Exporter's Guide to Federal Resources for
     Small Business, The, 135
Exporting, 76, 77
Extensive decision making, 148, **149**
Extensivity, 194

Facilitating functions, 367, 368
Fads, 238
Fair Credit Reporting Act, 34
Fair Packaging and Labeling Act, 33, 34
Family brand, 240
Family decision making, 157
Family life cycle, 158
Fashion, 237
Fear appeal, 476
Federal Cigarette Labelling and Advertising
     Act, 34
Federal Trade Commission (FTC), 35, 463,
     485, 489
Federal Trade Commission Act, 33, 325
Feedback, 448
Finance allowance, 491
Fixed costs, 317
Fixed-sum-per-unit method, 458, 460
Flammable Fabrics Act, 34
Flighting pattern, 482
FOB origin pricing, 352, 353
FOB with freight allowed, 354
Focus group interview, 126
Follow-up, 515
Food, 166
Food and Drug Administration (FDA), 35
Forecasting, 101
Forecasting sales, 101–105
Foreign Corrupt Practices Act, 73
Formula selling presentation, 512
Forward buying, 425
Four P's, 22
Franchising, 78, 299, **375**
Free trials, 489
Freight forwarder, 403
Frequency, 478
Frequent-shopper programs, 433
Full-line forcing, 386
Full-service wholesaler, 394
Functional benefits, 17
Functional matrix, 277, 278
Functional organization, 277, 278

Gantt chart, 538, 539
Gatekeepers, 193
GE's industry attractiveness/business strength
     matrix, 93, 94
Gender Tax Repeal Act, 327
**General Agreement on Tariffs and Trade
     (GATT), 69**
General expenses, 578
General merchandise wholesaler, 395
Generation X, 207
Generic brands, 243
Generic products, 243
Geodemography, 214
Geographic information system (GIS), 129,
     433
Geographic pricing, 352–354
Geographic segmentation, 210
Global Market Surveys, 135
Global marketing, 54–81; *see also*
     International dimensions
     age, 72, 73
     Asia/Pacific Rim, 61, 62

Global marketing—*Cont*
     buying power, 65, 66
     competitive environment, 75, 76
     cultural factors, 70, 71
     currencies, 66, 67
     demographics/lifestyle, 71, 72
     Eastern Europe, 62
     economic environment, 63–67
     ethics, 73
     European Union, 59, 60
     GATT, 69, 70
     human rights, 74
     Japan, 60
     language, 71
     Latin America/Caribbean, 62
     laws limiting trade, 68
     laws of host nations, 68, 69
     modes of entry, 76–79
     natural environment, 74
     North America, 57–59
     political-legal environment, 67–70
     population, 71, 72
     social environment, 70–74
     technological environment, 74, 75
Global marketing, 223
Global marketing research, 135, 136
Glossary, 604-614
Goods-services continuum, 289, 290
Government organizations/agencies, 173, 174
Grading, 367
Graying of America, 207
Green label, 275
Green marketing, 44–46
Gross income, 31
Gross margin, 578
Gross margin ratio, 579
Gross national product (GNP), 65
Gross rating points (GRPs), 478
Gross sales, 576
Group incentive system, 543
Growth/share matrix, 92, 93
Growth strategies, 88
Guarantee, 269

Hard currency, 68
Hawaii's tourism industry, 304
Health claims about food, 37, 38
Hedonic needs, 144
Hispanic-American consumers, 153
Home shopping, 421, 478
Horizontal conflict, 382
Household panel members, 117
Humor appeals, 477
Hypermarkets, 417
Hypertext, 46

Implementation
     communicating ideas/information, 540–
     542
     coordinating activities, 538–540
     motivating employees, 542, 543
     staffing, 537, 538
Import restrictions, 68
In-home interview, 127
Independent sales representatives, 516
Indirect channel, 369
Indirect exporting, 77
Indirect relationships, 12
Individual marketing, 201, **203,** 204
Indonesia, 62
Industrial products, 230, 231–234
Industry attractiveness/business strength
     matrix, 93, 94
Inelastic demand, 313
Inflation, 30

Influencers, 192
Infomercial, 478
Information power, 382
Information technology, 46–48
Information, 113
Infoscan, 116, 117
Initiators, 192
Innovators, 239
Inquiry tests, 484
Inspection buying, 189
Installations, 233
Institutional advertising, 470
Integrated direct marketing, 419, **422**
**Integrated marketing communication
     (IMC), 452–454**
Intensive distribution, 381
Intermediaries, 172, 366–370
Intermodal transportation, 402
International dimensions; *see also* Global
     marketing
     channels of distribution, 384, 385
     market segmentation, 222, 223
     marketing communications, 461, 462
     marketing research, 135, 136
     organizational buying behavior, 176, 177
     pricing, 354–356
     retailing, 435
International trade agreements, 37
International trade fairs, 135
Internet, 46, 47; *see also* World Wide Web
     advertising, 481-483
     career opportunities, 572, 573
     marketing research, 131, 132
Inventory management, 403, 404
Inventory turnover, 581
IRI field personnel, 117

Japan, 60
Job interview, 575
Job searching; *see* Career opportunities
Joint ownership, 78
Joint venture, 77, **78**
Journalist, 131
Junk mail, 480
Jury of executive opinion, 103
Jury test, 482
Just-in-time inventory, 183
**Just-in-time (JIT) inventory management,
     407**

Knockoffs, 37

Labeling, 272, 273
Laggards, 239
Language, 71
Late majority, 239
Lateral involvement, 194
Latin America, 62
Leads, 509
Legal environment, 33–38
Legal issues
     advertising, 485, 486
     channels of distribution, 385, 386
     global marketing, 67–70
     marketing communications, 462–465
     pricing, 325–327
     retailing, 436, 437
     sales promotion, 492
     services marketing, 294
Legitimate power, 382
Licensing, 77
Lifestyle segmentation, 210
Limited decision making, 148
Limited-function wholesaler, 395
Limited-line stores, 416

Line extension, 249
List price, 340
Lobbyists, 36
Logistical functions, 367, 368
Loss leader pricing, 345, 347
Lower Americans, 155

Macromarketing, 8
Magazines, 479, 480
Magnuson-Moss Warranty FTC Improvement
  Act, 34
Mail surveys, 125
Major account management, 516
Malaysia, 62
Mall intercept, 126
Malls, 24
Management contracting, 78
Managing existing products; *see* Product
  management
Manufacturer's brand, 242
**Manufacturer's representative, 394, 396,
  397**
Marginal analysis, 315, 316
Marginal revenue, 315
Markdown, 583
Markdown ratio, 584
Market, 200
Market coverage, 380, 381
Market development strategies, 88
Market penetration strategies, 88
Market potential, 101, 221
Market price, 344
Market segmentation, 198–225, 201
  approaches to serving markets, 201–204
  consumer markets, 204–214; *see also*
    Segmenting consumer markets
  global implications, 222, 223
  organizational markets, 215–217
  steps, in process, 217–222
Market share, 548, 581, 582
Market test, 103, 104
Marketing, 6
  conflicts with other functional areas, 14,
    15
  regulation of, 35
  traditional orientations, 8, 10
  traditional role of, 95, 96
  types, 7, 8
Marketing analysis, 8, 10
Marketing audits, 552–554
Marketing communications, 442–467, 444
  AIDA model, 448, 449
  communication process, 447, 448
  communications budgeting, 457–459
  communications mix, 449–454
  global marketing, 461, 462
  goals, 444–447
  implementing/controlling communications
    strategy, 459–461
  legal/ethical issues, 462–465
  regulation of communications, 463, 464
  selecting communications mix, 455–457
  setting communications objectives, 454,
    455
  socially responsible communications, 465
Marketing concept, 12
**Marketing decision support system, 114,
  115**
Marketing ethics, 42
Marketing information, 113, 114
Marketing management, 21
Marketing mangers, 94, 97
Marketing mix, 22
Marketing orientation, 11
Marketing plan, 21, 98–100, 558–567

Marketing research, 110–138, 112
  analyze/interpret data, 127–129
  data collection, 124–127
  deceit/fraud, 134
  ethics, 131–135
  external sources of information, 116, 117
  GIS, 129
  global, 135, 136
  internal sources of information, 116
  Internet, 130, 131
  invasion of privacy, 134, 135
  MDSS, 114, 115
  primary/secondary data, 117–120
  questions which can be answered, 113
  research design, 121–124
  sources of information, 115–117
  steps, in process, 120–129
  virtual reality, 130, 131
Markup, 582, 583
Markup pricing, 317
Maslow's hierarchy of needs, 143
Mass marketing, 201
Mass merchandiser, 416–418, 417
Membership groups, 156
Merchandise allowances, 491
Merchandise assortment, 422
Merchant wholesaler, 394–396
Metropolitan statistical area (MSA), 210
Mexico, 57, 58
Micromarketing, 8
Middle class, 155
Middlemen, 366
Miller-Tydings Resale Price Maintenance Act,
  33, 34
Mission statement, 85, 86
Missionary salespeople, 506
Mode of entry, 76
Mode of transportation, 400
Modified rebuy, 183
Monetary costs, 19
Monopolistic competition, 49
Monopoly, 49
Moody's International Manual, 135
Moral appeal, 477
Motivating employees, 542, 543
Motivation, 143, 519
Motor Carrier Act and Staggers Rail Act, 34
MRI, 120
Multidomestic marketing, 223
Multilevel selling, 517
Multiple-zone pricing, 353

National Advertising Division (NAD), 485,
  486
National Traffic and Safety Act, 33
Natural environment, 44–46
Need recognition, 142–144
Need-satisfaction presentation, 512, 513
Needs, 7
Negative publicity, 494
Net profit ratio, 579
Net sales, 576
Network organization, 536
Network selling, 517
New category entries, 259
New product, 258
New product development, 256–283
  business analysis, 263, 264
  characteristics of new products, 268–271
  commercialization, 267, 268
  development process, 260–268
  failures, 276, 277
  idea generation, 260–262
  idea screening, 262, 263
  labeling, 272, 273

New product development—*Cont*
  organizational forms, 277
  packaging, 272–274
  pricing, 340, 341
  product design, 270, 271
  product features, 269, 270
  product safety, 271
  quality level, 268, 269
  shortening development time, 278–281
  test marketing, 265–267
  types of new products, 258, 259
New task purchase, 183, 184
New-to-the-world products, 258
News conferences, 493
News release, 492, 493
Newspapers, 479
Niche marketing, 202
Noise, 447, 448
Nondurable goods, 234
Nonpersonal selling, 449
Nonprofit marketing, 11
Nonprofit organizations, 300–302
Nonstore image, 429, 430
Nonstore retailing, 418–422
North America, 57–59
**North American Free Trade Agreement
  (NAFTA), 37, 58, 59**
Nutrition Labeling and Education Act, 34,
  274

Objections, 513, 514
Objective-and-task method, 459, 460
Observation, 124, 125
Odd-even pricing, 351
Off-peak pricing, 298
Oligopoly, 49
On-line marketing, 419, 421
Operating expense ratio, 579
Operating ratios, 578, 579
Operating statement, 576–579
Operation Amigo, 37
Operational planning, 84
Opportunities and threats, 90
Order delivery, 505
Order getting, 504
Order processing, 404, 405
Order taking, 505
Organizational buyer promotions, 490
Organizational buyers, 7
Organizational buying behavior, 168–197
  business classifications, 175, 176
  buyer-seller relations, 189–192
  buying approaches, 189
  buying center, 192–195
  buying criteria, 184, 185
  buying process, 182–189
  categories of buyers, 171–174
  characteristics of buyers, 187–189
  characteristics of organization, 187
  competition, and, 177–179
  demand, and, 177
  international considerations, 176, 177
  organization markets, 170, 171
  solving customer problems, 179
  technology, and, 179–182
  types of purchases, 182–184
  vendor analysis, 185–187
Organizational buying process, 182–189
Organizational markets, 170, 171
Organizing marketing activities
  network organizations, 536
  organizing by customers, 535
  organizing by product, 534, 535
  strategic alliances, 535
  virtual organizations, 537

Outdoor advertising, 480, 481, 483
Overseas Business Reports, 135

Packaging, 43, 272–2743
Penetration pricing, 340
Per capita income, 65
Percentage-of-sales method, 458, 460
Performance measures, 579–582
Personal benefits, 18
Personal selling, 451, 453, 502
    accuracy of reports, 526
    approaching qualified prospects, 511
    bribery, 525, 526
    building long-term relationships, 514, 515
    closing, 514
    ethical issues, 524–526
    manipulation of prospects, 525
    objections, 513
    order delivery, 505
    order getting, 504
    order taking, 505
    preparation, 510
    prospecting, 509, 510
    relationship selling, 507, 508
    role of, 503
    sales presentations, 513
    sales support, 506
    seminar selling, 507
    steps, in process, 508, 509
    team selling, 506, 507
    telemarketing, 513
Personal surveys, 126, 127
Phantom freight, 354
Physical distribution, 399
    cross-functional decision making, 407
    decision-making software, 409
    EDI, 408, 409
    freight forwarders, 403
    intermodal transpiration, 402
    inventory management, 403, 404
    JIT, 407
    order processing, 404, 405
    steps, in process, 399, 400
    transpiration, 400–402
    trends, 407–409
    value-driven, 406
    warehousing, 403
Physical surroundings, 162
Piggyback service, 402
Pioneering advertising, 470
Placement, 22; *see also* Channels of
    distribution
Planned obsolescence, 43
Planning styles, 95, 96
Point-of-purchase (POP) displays, 490
Political issues
    channels of distribution, 386, 387
    global marketing, 67–70
    services marketing, 294, 303
Political-legal environment, 33–38
Political marketing, 303
Population census, 120
Portfolio plan, 91, **92**
Portfolio test, 482
Positioning, 220, 221
Positioning map, 220
Post-purchase dissonance, 147
Posters, 480, 481
Postpurchase evaluation, 146, 147
Posttest, 483
Predatory pricing, 326
Premiums, 489
Preparation, 510
Press conferences, 493
Press release, 492, 493

Prestige pricing, 351
Pretest, 482
Price, 22, 310
Price discrimination, 358
Price discrimination, 326
Price elasticity, 313, 314
Price fixing, 43, 325
Price lining, 343
Price offs, 489
Price packs, 489
Price rollbacks, 31
Price war, 356
Pricing, 308–360
    breakeven analysis, 319, 320
    competition-based, 320–322
    competitive objectives, 336
    competitor responses, 356, 357
    cost-based, 317–320
    customer responses, 357, 358
    demand curves, 310–315
    discounts, 344–350
    economics of, 310–317
    ethics, 327, 328
    every-day low prices, 349, 350
    existing products, 341–343
    geographic, 352–344
    global marketing, 354–356
    government regulation, 325–327
    illegal activities, 325–327, 358
    marginal analysis, 315–317
    markdown, 583, 584
    markup, 582, 583
    new products, 340, 341
    price changes, 358
    price war, 356
    product lines, 343
    psychological, 350–352
    sales/profit objectives, 335, 336
    segmentation/positioning objectives, 335
    social responsibility objectives, 337
    steps, in process, 338–340
    survival objectives, 336
    value, 322–325
Primary data, 118
Primary demand, 235
**Primary metropolitan statistical area
    (PMSA), 210**
Primary reference groups, 156
Principal International Business, 135
Print advertising, 479, 480, 483
Private brand, 242
PRIZM, 214
Prizm database, 120
Probability sampling, 119
Problem, 121
Producers, 171
Product, 22
Product advertising, 470
Product classifications, 230–234
Product development strategies, 88
Product diffusion, 239
Product feature, 269
Product improvements, 259
Product life cycle, 234–239, **235**
Product line, 248
Product management, 228–255
    branding, 239–247
    branding equity, 246, 247
    product adoption/diffusion, 239
    product classifications, 230–234
    product life cycle, 234–239
    product mix/product lines, 248–252
    protecting the trademark, 245
    selecting a brand, 244, 245
Product manager, 534

Product mix, 248
Product modification strategy, 250
Product position, 219
Production orientation, 9, 10
Profit, 315, 316
Profitability analysis, 549, 550
Project matrix, 277, 278
Promotion, 23
Promotional allowance, 345, 347
Promotional discount, 345, 347
Prospecting, 509
Prospects, 509
Prosperity, 30
Psychographic segmentation, 210
Psychological costs, 19
Psychological pricing, 350–352
Public Health Cigarette Smoking Act, 34
Public services, 302
Public-warehouse, 403
Publicity, 452, 453
    ethical issues, 494
    negative, 494
    types, 492–494
Puffery, 525
Pull strategy, 457
Pulsing strategy, 482, 483
Purchase decision, 146
Purchasing agents, 190
Pure competition, 49
Pure Food and Drug Act, 34
Push strategy, 457
Pyramid selling scheme, 437

Qualified prospects, 509
Qualifying, 510
Qualitative forecasting techniques, 102–104
Quantitative forecasting techniques, 104
Quantity discount, 344, 345
Question marks, 92
**Quick-response inventory management,
    434**
Quota, 68

Rack jobber, 394, **395**
Radio advertising, 479, 483
Rate-of-return pricing, 318, 319
Rating, 478
Rational appeal, 476
Raw materials, 233
Reach, 478
Rebate, 344, 490
Recall test, 483
Receiver, 447, **448**
Recession, 31
Reciprocity, 192
Recovery, 31
Reference groups, 155, 156
Reference price, 322
Referent power, 382
Regional marketing, 39
Regulations, 35
Relationship selling, 507, 508
Repositionings, 259
Requests for bids, 189, 190
Resale price maintenance, 325
Research design, 121–124
Résumé, 573, 574
Retailer, 414
Retailer-sponsored cooperatives, 375
Retailing, 412–439
    creating value, 431, 432
    ethical issues, 436
    frequent-shopper programs, 433
    globalization, 435
    legal issues, 436, 437

Retailing—*Cont*
  mass merchandisers, 417, 418
  merchandise assortment, 422
  nonstore, 418–422
  nonstore image, 429, 430
  placement decisions, 425–427
  pricing decisions, 424, 425
  product decisions, 422–424
  promotion decisions, 427, 428
  role of, 414, 415
  service level, 423, 424
  specialty stores, 417
  store, 416–418
  store image/atmospherics, 428, 429
  store location, 425–427
  technological changes, 432–435
  types of retailers, 415–422
Return on assets (ROA), 580
Return on investment (ROI), 318, **580**
Returns and allowances, 576
Reverse channel, 373
Reward power, 382
Roadshow, 409
Robinson-Patman Act, 33, 34, 325, 344
Routine decision making, 148

Salary, 521
Sales analysis, 546–549
Sales engineers, 506
Sales force composite, 103
Sales forecast, 101–105
Sales management, 515
  evaluating/controlling salespeople, 522–
    524
  motivating/compensating salespeople,
    519–521
  organizing sales force, 515, 516
  performance recognition, 522
  recruiting salespeople, 516–518
  training/supervising salespeople, 518, 519
Sales orientation, 10, 11
Sales plan, 515
Sales presentation, 511
Sales promotion, 451–453, 486, 487
  consumer promotions, 487–491
  legal/ethical issues, 492
  organizational buyer promotions, 490
  trade promotions, 491
Sales quota, 522
Sales support, 506
Sales territories, 515
Sales tests, 484, 485
Samples, 489
Sampling, 118, 119
Sampling buying, 189
Scheduling, 538, 539
Sealed-bid pricing, 322
Search engines, 236
Seasonal discount, 345
Secondary data, 119
Secondary demand, 236
Secondary reference groups, 156
Segment marketing, 201–203, **202**
Segmenting consumer markets, 204, 205
  age, by, 206
  benefit segmentation, 210
  buyer thoughts/feelings, by, 206, 211–213
  family life style, by, 206
  family types, by, 206, 209
  gender, by, 205, 206
  geographic segmentation, 210
  income/education/occupation, by, 206, 209
  multiple bases for segmentation, 214
  psychographic segmentation, 206, 210, 211

Segmenting consumer markets—*Cont*
  purchase behavior, by, 206, 213, 214
  race/ethnicity, by, 206, 208, 209
Selective distribution, 381
Self-regulation, 35
Selling expenses, 578
Seminar selling, 507
Service mark, 240, 245
Service merchandiser, 394, **395**
Service professionals, 526
Services marketing, 284–305
  characteristics of services, 288–292
  classification of services, 293
  competitive environment, 295
  continuous improvement, 295
  distribution, 298, 299
  economic environment, 294
  government agencies, 302, 303
  growth of service sector, 286–288
  marketing mix, 295
  natural environment, 294
  nonprofit organizations, 300–302
  political groups, 303
  political-legal environment, 294
  pricing, 297, 298
  promotion, 299, 300
  relationship with customer, 289
  services quality, 295–297
  social environment, 294
  tailoring service to customer, 295
  technological environment, 294
Services, 286
Sex appeals, 476
Sherman Antitrust Act, 33, 34, 325
Shopping costs, 19
Shopping products, 230, 232
SIC codes, 175, 176
Simmons, 120
Simulated test marketing (STM), 266
Singapore, 62
Single-line stores, 416
Single-source data, 116
Single-zone pricing, 353
Site selection, 425
Skimming pricing, 341
Slogans, 476
Slotting allowance, 387, 491
Small business counselors, 541
Small Business Foundation of America, 135
Smart cards, 544
Social benefits, 17
Social class, 154, 155
Social environment, 38–43
Social responsibility, 40–42, **41**
Social surroundings, 163
Socially responsible communications, 465
Sole sourcing, 178
Sorting, 367
Source loyalty, 192
Source, 447
South Korea, 62
Special offers, 488
Special sales, 488
Specialty products, 230, 232
Specialty promotions/advertising, 490
Specialty store, 416, **417**
Specialty wholesaler, 395
Staffing, 537, 538
Stakeholders, 15
**Standard Industrial Classification (SIC)
    codes, 175,** 176
Standard test market, 266
Starch Readership Report, 483, 484
Stars, 92
Statistical analysis, 128

Statistical inference, 118
Stimulus-response presentation, 512
Store image, 428
Store location, 425–427
Store retailing, 416–418
Storing, 367
Straight rebuy, 182
Strategic alliances, 535
Strategic business unit (SBU), 92
Strategic marketing planning, 95
Strategic planning, 84
Strategic window, 91
Strengths and weaknesses, 89, 90
Subculture, 151, 152
Suggestive selling, 512
Superior customer value, 20, 21
Supermarkets, 416
Superstores, 416
Supplies, 233
Support salespeople, 506
Survey of buyer intentions, 103
Surveys, 124–127, **125**
Sweepstakes, 489
SWOT analysis, 89–91
Symptom, 121

Tabulating, 128
Tactical planning, 84
Target audience, 475
Target market, 201
Tariff, 68
Team selling, 506, 507, 521
Technical-market research, 130
Technical specialists, 506
Technological environment, 46–48
Technology
  global marketing, 74, 75
  organizational buying behavior, 179–182
  retailing, 432–435
  services marketing, 294
Telemarketing, 419, **421, 513**
Telephone Consumer Protection Act, 513
Telephone surveys, 126
Television, 35
Television advertising, 478, 483
Temporal costs, 19
TerrAlign, 130
Test marketing, 123, 265–267
Theater tests, 482
Thomas Register, 175, 176
Time, 163, 164
Time-series analysis, 104
Top-down planning, 95
Total revenue, 315
Trade allowances/discounts, 491
Trade discount, 345, **346**
Trade-in-allowance, 345, **346**
Trade name, 240
Trade promotion, 491
Trade publications, 479
Trademark, 240, 245
Trading company, 77
Transaction costs, 19
Transactional functions, 366, 367
Transportation, 400–402
Trend analysis, 103, **104**
Triage, 123
Trial close, 514
Truck jobbers, 394, **396**
Truck wholesalers, 396
Truth in Lending Act, 34
Tying agreements, 386

Unaided recall, 484
Undifferentiated marketing, 201

Uniform delivered pricing, 353
Uniform pricing, 343
United States, major trading partners, 57
Universal product code (UPC), 117, **274,**
    404
Unsought products, 230
Upper Americans, 155
Urgency close, 514
Usage rate, 213
Used articles/equipment, 207
Used-car superstores, 330
Usenet, 131
User status, 213
Users, 192
Utilitarian needs, 143

VALS 2, 211, 212
Value, 147, 166
Value analysis, 184
Value-driven marketing, **12**–17
Value equation, 16

Variable costs, 317
Variety retailers, 417
Vending machine, 418, 419
Vendor analysis, 185–187
Venture, 278
Venture team, 278
Vertical conflict, 381, 382
Vertical involvement, 194
Vertical marketing system (VMS), 374–376
Video selling system, 435
Virtual corporation, 537
Virtual reality, 130, 131
Visionary Shopper software, 130

Wants, 7
Warehouse stores, 417
Warehousing, 403
Warranty, 269
Wheel of retailing, 432
Wheeler-Lea Amendment, 34
Wholesaler, 392

Wholesaler-sponsored cooperatives, 375
Wholesaling
    agents and brokers, 396, 397
    merchant wholesalers, 394–396
    role of, 392, 393
    strategies to attract producers, 397, 398
    strategies to attract retailers, 398
    trends, 398, 399
    types of wholesalers, 394–397
Work-in-process inventory, 578
Workforce 2000, 537
Working class, 155
World Trade Organization (WTO), 70
World Wide Web, 46, 47, 481; *see also*
        Internet
World's ten largest cities, 72
World's ten largest countries, 72

Yellow Pages advertising, 480

Creating Value

Online Study Guide

The study guide to accompany **Marketing: Creating Value for Customers** is free and online. It includes Chapter Learning Objectives, the Chapter Summary, and Key Terms.

Online Chapter Quizzes

Each chapter offers an interactive online quiz that reviews the main concepts and topics discussed in that chapter. Simply enter your responses online and receive immediate feedback.

The Impact of Technology

Technology continues to make the marketing environment dynamic. Each chapter includes a current discussion of how technology impacts that chapter's subject area.

Irwin/McGraw-Hill

A Division of The McGraw-Hill Companies